Published by
STACKPOLE BOOKS
5067 Ritter Road
Mechanicsburg, PA 17055
www.stackpolebooks.com

Printed in the United States of America

10 9 8 7 6 5 4 3 2 1

FIRST EDITION

Library of Congress Cataloging-in-Publication Data

Beaudot, William J. K.
    The 24th Wisconsin Infantry in the Civil War : the biography of a regiment / by William J.K. Beaudot.
      p. cm.
    Includes bibliographical references (p.) and index.
    ISBN 0-8117-0894-2
    1. United States. Army. Wisconsin Infantry Regiment, 24th (1862–1865) 2. Wisconsin—History—Civil War, 1861–1865—Regimental histories. 3. United States—History—Civil War, 1861–1865—Regimental histories. I. Title.
    E537.5 24th .B48 2003
    973.7'475—dc21
                                                                    2002008086

Contents

Acknowledgments

Without so many good folks, the 24th Wisconsin would never have come alive again in these pages. My thanks to:

Eric Borgerding, whose ancestor, Henry Bichler, marched and fought with the 24th Wisconsin and lived to tell the story. Eric was always ready to renew my enthusiasm for the project.

Nancy Torphy, whose sharing of the letters from her ancestor, Amandus Silsby, actually began this entire project—and to all the descendants of 24th Wisconsin veterans.

Marc and Beth Storch, good Badger Black Hats, who provided images, invaluable information, and encouragement.

Skirmish comrades Bruce Miller, Robert C. Hubbard, Sr., the Old Sarge, and especially Joe Syler, who read the manuscript, providing informed criticisms and corrections; and to all the good friends of the 6th Wisconsin Volunteers, North-South Skirmish Association and American Civil War Skirmish Association.

John Chojnacki, my brother-in-law, for solid suggestions, and Dean Sarnowski.

Charles L. Foster, friend and expert on Civil War firearms and equipment, who was generous with invaluable information.

Maryanne Faeth Greketis, an authority on women's fashions of the Civil War era, who provided important details.

Mike Thorson, for his excellent painting of Arthur McArthur and the charge up Missionary Ridge that graces the cover.

Frankie B. Cole, whose creative camera work was always ready, and to Bob Jaburek of Electric Design for his invaluable assistance with illustrations.

Harry Anderson, former director of the Milwaukee County Historical Society and eminent city historian; and the marvelous mine of the history in that institution.

John Gurda, Milwaukee historian nonpareil, who provided numerous suggestions to improve the manuscript.

Frank Zeidler, former Milwaukee mayor, boundless reservoir of information, and friend.

Candis Kroll and Irene Weist for their unstinting assistance when technology threatened to get the upper hand.

Howard Madaus of Harrisburg, Pennsylvania, Alan Gaff, a true "Groundhog" historian, and Lance Herdegen at Carroll College.

Susan Ploetz, Milwaukee Public Library's Humanities division, for her tireless hunt through the arcana of U.S. government publications; and Jean Straub for finding those facts I always forgot.

Mary Suess, Milwaukee Public Library, for her patience while I spooled through years of microfilm. All the good folks at the Milwaukee Public Library Humanities and Periodical Departments, especially on Sundays when I requested the endless reels of newspaper microfilm.

The Milwaukee Public Library, my employer for over thirty-six years, whose staff and collections are invaluable.

Finally—but certainly not least—I am grateful to my lovely wife, Bev (truly, madly, deeply), and wonderful children, grandchildren, and in-law children—Michelle (and Traci and Lauren), Corinne (and Paul, Collin, Jarett, and Camden, and Mary Schroeder), Andre (and Maggie), and Renee (and Fonsy); and to Jean Litke and all the related clan. I love them all.

Introduction

This is part of the story of one Union regiment, the 24th Wisconsin Volunteer Infantry. Like tens of hundreds of other such units, its members went off to war for a variety of reasons. Some volunteered in anger over the Southern attempt to sunder the Union. Other men, while not philosophically opposed to slavery, felt that eradicating the peculiar institution would help defeat the rebellion. There were also those who enlisted to escape a prosaic life and find adventure, or to acquire the substantial monetary bonus offered; there were some who saw the war as an opportunity to gain glory, notoriety and the enhancement of political and other careers. Unlike the "Boys of '61"—volunteers who rushed to enlist in the first, febrile days of war—the men of the 24th and later regiments were a somewhat older and more mature lot; many were family men. Nearly all had jobs, businesses, and professions— men with "good situations," it was said.

Although many who marched in the ranks of the 24th were from rural counties and smaller towns, about two-thirds were from the largest city in Wisconsin, Milwaukee, and its proximate communities. An expanding and prospering community of some 40,000 on the shore of Lake Michigan, Milwaukee was, in the mid-nineteenth century, still a somewhat rough and coarse town, a city whose residents considered themselves Western. It was characterized by the Yankee–New Yorker economic and political foundations laid in the preceding decades coupled with a growing immigrant presence—predominantly from the Germanic states. Many of the latter fled after the abortive democratic upheavals in Europe of the 1840s; they arrived daily in great numbers. As a result, Milwaukee began to assume a particularly Teutonic flavor. Still, the overwhelming majority in the 24th Wisconsin bore the surnames of the British Isles.

Because the city and its proximate communities provided the great majority of volunteers, the unit became known as the Milwaukee Regiment; it was also occasionally known as the Chamber of Commerce Regiment. In its ranks were sons of some of the most prominent political and commercial families in the city. Judge Arthur McArthur, for example, watched his seventeen-year-old son leave the city in the 24th Wisconsin; in little more than a year, young Arthur gained a reputation as a gallant soldier and his act of bravery in Tennessee would ultimately gain him the Medal of Honor. (Young Arthur's son, Douglas, also earned the award during World War I, and won undying renown as a general in World War II and Korea.) Moreover, the plutocratic railroad and banking magnate Alexander Mitchell, perhaps the richest man in Wisconsin, saw his son, John, march off to war with the 24th Wisconsin. (John's son, Billy Mitchell, won great fame as a World War II aviator.) There were many other scions of wealth and prominence; some were considered "pets," and their actions and fates gained prominence in the city news sheets for much of the war.

The grand triumphs as well as ignominies of the Milwaukee Regiment were writ large for the entire city to read. Several volunteers served as soldier correspondents to daily news sheets, detailing the long marches and harrowing battles. In many instances, too, private letters were published in news. Fathers, ambitious for their soldier sons, often shared missives with news editors to further the reputations of their offspring.

"The 24th is composed so largely of young men, and is so exclusively a Milwaukee regiment, that a more than ordinary interest is felt in its welfare in the city that has not a member, a relative, or a friend in its ranks, and when it leaves our city it will carry with it the hopes, the tears, and the prayers of thousands of its citizens," wrote a news editor.[1]

When these soldiers returned after three years of fighting, their experiences, for a few decades at least, became woven into the city's cultural and historical fabric. They formed veteran organizations, and publicly told the tales of their youthful adventures. Newspapers printed their recollections. There was embellishment, of course, to turn good yarns into better ones; but the tellers, in print and orally, often laced their tales with realistic incident and graphic description—antidotes, perhaps, to the heroic and bloodless vision of the war growing among civilians. What was more, these veterans, as they grew into middle and later years, memorialized the sacrifices of comrades, men of Milwaukee who had fallen in battle in such distant places as Kentucky, Tennessee, and Georgia. They contributed money for the erection of monuments, tangible granite, marble, and bronze edifices that would outlast their mortality and attest to their story.

But as these men passed away, in the twilight of the old century and early years of the new, their deeds, briefly recalled in obituaries, faded from public view. The monuments became pocked, encrusted, and overlooked; cemetery markers, scoured by wind and rain, stood forgotten, unkempt and overgrown. Within a half century, only the scholar and amateur historian could cite the record of the Milwaukee Regiment.

What follows is not an objective history of the 24th Wisconsin and its battles. In large measure, only what the regiment's soldiers saw and recorded forms the basis of narrative. Nor are there attempts at presenting tactical and strategic analyses of these engagements. (Such has already been done admirably by contemporary historians.) There also is no assertion that the actions of the Milwaukee Regiment were pivotal in any battle or turned the course of war, albeit their charges at the battle of Missionary Ridge in 1863 and Franklin the following year were inarguably instrumental in attaining Federal victories. Moreover, the Milwaukee men took part in some of the bloodiest battles and campaigns of the war—in addition to Missionary Ridge and Franklin, they fought at Stones River, Chickamauga, and in the Atlanta campaign. In a detailed statistical analysis after the war, William F. Fox listed the 24th Wisconsin as among the 300 "Fighting Regiments" of the war. Over 10 percent of the unit were either killed in battle or died subsequently of wounds. It also sustained many hundreds of additional casualties.[2]

Not all of the narrative focuses upon campaigns and battles. Most of a soldier's life was spent in camp between battles. At one point, for example, nine months passed after the battle of Stones River before a new campaign was begun. For this reason, seemingly mundane matters dominated army life—food, clothing, shelter, comradeship, and the like. This was the stuff of a common soldier's life.

Native-born or immigrant, supporter of President Lincoln and the Republicans or Democrat who hoped for an early peace; farmer, tradesman, manufacturer, merchant, railroader, bookkeeper, or professional; wellborn and wealthy, or baseborn and common volunteer—these were the men, about a thousand in all, who volunteered in the summer of 1862, convinced, perhaps, that their deeds would defeat the attack against their nation. "It is no longer the boys who go to war, but the men in the middle of life, who go into the army with the determination to finish up this rebellion."[3]

In all of this, the men of the 24th Wisconsin were like hundreds of thousands of other men in blue who saw a duty to their nation, and determined to make personal sacrifice to fulfill it. If need be, they were prepared to suffer privation, maiming, and death in the bargain. This is their biography.

Prologue

"Your indomitable Regiment."

Arthur McArthur[1] stood before them once again. But now, a half century since he led them into battle as a youth during the great Civil War, he was in his autumn years, a general, lately retired after more than forty years in the U.S. Army. His hair, slightly flecked with gray, was closely cropped, unlike the thick cloud of black curls that had crowned his youthful head; and a full mustache bloomed where once the face had been smooth and childlike.

"Comrades," he began (the voice was no longer high-pitched as it was back then), "such occasions as these are appreciated only when they are over. We tonight can never realize what enjoyment the reminiscences of this meeting will bring." McArthur's gray eyes, once bright and undaunted, were framed behind the familiar pince-nez. At sixty-seven, his five-foot-ten-inch frame had filled out considerably, nearly doubling the spare one hundred pounds of youth. With a striking resemblance to Teddy Roosevelt, he stood erect, shoulders back. Perspiration must have beaded his brow, for the late summer night was uncommonly close; even the hoary men who listened intently, tight in their dark suits and hard-collared shirts, may have been affected by the humid atmosphere.[2]

McArthur and his old comrades had gathered in Milwaukee September 5, 1912, to mark the anniversary of that day when their regiment,

1

the 24th Wisconsin Volunteer Infantry, had marched off from Milwaukee to fight in the war against the Southern rebellion. Only days before in 1862, McArthur, less than three months past his seventeenth birthday, had strode before the thousand men of the new outfit, prepared to parade past the garrulous colonel, Charles Larrabee, and thousands of city folks who had come to see the Milwaukee Regiment. He wore a handsomely tailored lieutenant's blue coat and carried what appeared to be, because of his small size, a huge sword. His father, the judge, had given in after more than a year of the lad's incessant importunings to go off to war; the elder McArthur had used his Democratic Party influence with the governor to secure a commission for his son as adjutant in the regiment.

It had all been rather awkward and disastrous, this first experience of leading men in September 1862. The new volunteers, not yet fully schooled in army ways, had guffawed, and spectators laughed when he sputtered orders in that squeaking, quavering voice. Several companies were unable to hear him. He tripped over the sword scabbard. It had all been dreadful. But he vowed he would show these soldiers. After more than a score of bloody battles in Kentucky, Tennessee, and Georgia he proved he belonged with the Milwaukee Regiment, and gained undying fame and recognition for gallantry and bravery. At nineteen he became the "Boy Colonel of the West," the youngest man to hold such a rank in all the Union armies, it was said.

The war veterans remembered those days for the remainder of their lives. And as the old century waned, they put an unmistakable stamp upon the nation, keeping those recollections alive and all but dominating the political life of the nation. "Vote as you shot," was the watchword among these men who fought and bled to save the Union. Former soldiers were elected to office at every level, local, state, and national; several veterans were sent to the White House. Legislation favorable to veterans such as pensions was passed handily. They had formed a Grand Army of the Republic with thousands of local chapters chartered across the country. And they assembled by the tens of thousands in gatherings each year, twice coming to Milwaukee in the 1880s. Blue suits adorned with reunion badges and ribbons, and campaign hats perched on their graying heads, they marched through the streets, camped out in tents, and dined in open-air messes, attempting to recapture the great adventure of their youth.[3]

Several of the old army commanders, "Little" Phil Sheridan, the Milwaukee Regiment's beloved division commander, and "Old Cump" William Tecumseh Sherman, had come to the city after the great Civil

War, paying respects to friends and acquaintances in the 24th Wisconsin and other local units. In 1889, Nicholas Greusel, "Old Nick," the revered Illinois German who had led them in numerous bloody battles, had visited from Iowa where he settled after his war service; he was thin and frail then, and still bore the speech inflections of his native land. Too, one of their old corps commanders, Alex McCook, had traveled up from Ohio to join the old boys that year. A camera captured their presence.[4]

But all that was past now. These days, the hoary old veterans whose legs still carried them continued to gather, trading old stories about their youthful war experiences, burnishing and sometimes embroidering those tales, elevating dead heroes to great heights. But the ranks of the old soldiers were fast thinning. The nation, with the new century, was changing at a breathtaking pace, and seemed to weary of these white-haired, bearded men of a bygone time.

Milwaukee had, of course, been transformed too since 1862. Then it was still a somewhat rough and rude town of less than 50,000; now, in 1912, it had grown nearly tenfold. Where once men of Yankee and New York birth had dominated the day and Irish and Germanic immigrants waited for their turn, great waves of Poles and Italians now were daily enlarging the city's precincts. What had been a handful of wards had mushroomed to almost two dozen, and the cityscape expanded for miles to the north, west and south from the shores of the great blue Lake Michigan. Soldiers going off to war called Milwaukee, in the old century when the veterans were young, the "city of pale bricks and beer"; commercial structures now soared thirteen floors or more. The tall and massive new million-dollar city hall on the east bank of the Milwaukee River, of light sandstone and red brick, sent its lofty bell tower nearly 400 feet into the sky. West of the river, on the rise of Grand Avenue near the former Mitchell family Second Empire mansion (it was now owned by the Deutscher Club) stood the impressive monument to the city's Civil War soldiers. It was called "The Victorious Charge," and although the sculptor, John Conway, had not consciously set out to do so, the bronze memorial was thought by some to represent the Milwaukee Regiment whose ranks were nearly filled by the sons and husbands of the city. U.S. senator John Mitchell, himself a 24th Wisconsin veteran, had led an early effort to raise money for the monument.[5]

While the wintry old men gathered to look backward, Milwaukee, like the nation, rushed headlong toward modern times. The United States now numbered forty-eight, the final two stars of Arizona and

Fiftieth Reunion, 1912.
"Your indomitable regiment."
COURTESY OF THE MILWAUKEE COUNTY HISTORICAL SOCIETY.

New Mexico having been stitched onto the nation's banner that very year; there were now a dozen more states than in Civil War days. Motor cars barked and coughed choking gray smoke, frightening horses on Milwaukee city streets and bringing everything closer together. Nickelodeons flickered moving pictures in darkened theaters, and even then a man named D. W. Griffith was giving thought to a mighty celluloid Civil War epic. In April, the mightiest ship of the age, the *Titanic,* had sunk to the bottom of the Atlantic with 1,500 lives during its maiden voyage to America. And a Virginia Democrat named Woodrow Wilson was running for the presidency against the Republican William H. Taft and Teddy Roosevelt's rump Bull Moose Party. (Roosevelt, in October 1912, would be wounded in Milwaukee in an assassination attempt.)[6]

McArthur had not attended the entire day's festivities that September 5. He had been feeling unwell for several days. Events had begun early in the morning Thursday at the University building on Mason and Broadway streets in the central business district east of the Milwaukee River; one of the Grand Army posts met there regularly. The low-ceilinged room was expansive, dark wood trimming the walls. The gray old men sat at long dining tables, attentive in straight-backed chairs. Presiding over the grand reunion was likeable Ed Parsons, who had been a lieutenant (he later rose to captain) in the Milwaukee Regiment in 1862. His white hair bespoke seventy-six years, yet he still conducted business as a commercial merchant. He had been in the forefront of the local reunion organization, and had over the years written and spoken much about the war. When one of the war's great generals, Phil Sheridan, died in 1888, Parsons delivered a moving eulogy to him.[7]

A total of ninety veterans from many regiments gathered at the Grand Army post for the beginning of activities; few more than fifty, however, had marched and fought with the 24th Wisconsin. One of them was Tom Balding, the captain who had given encouragement to young McArthur early in the war; his speech still bore the traces of London birth and upbringing. Tom, whose deeply lined face still bore a kindly look, had won a battlefield promotion to major late in the war; now he worked for one of the big insurance companies, Northwestern Mutual, a rather prosaic existence compared with the great adventure of a half century past. Henry Drake signed the roll, too; he had earned lieutenant shoulder straps in 1863. Felled by typhoid fever that year, he had resigned and returned to the wholesale and retail drug trade, and his brother still retained a sheaf of letters Henry had written to him during the war, detailing grueling marches, cold camps, and bloody battles.[8]

Among others from the old Milwaukee Regiment anticipating McArthur's speech was Jim Bacon, who listed himself simply as a "commercial traveler." The story still circulated of his fear in the second summer of the Civil War that he would not be accepted into the 24th Regiment because he lacked teeth; the ability to "bite" musket cartridges was necessary to become a soldier. Tom Ford, the fiery-haired Irishman, was on hand, too; he had not made much of life after the war, and for a time had to satisfy himself as a common laborer. But he had become one of the chroniclers of the regiment, pulling together a series of articles late in the past century and publishing them in the *Evening Wisconsin* newspaper; laced with humorous episodes, his writings were also graphic. Gus Scheiding also inked his name into the registry; an immigrant from the Germanic states, he had volunteered from Oak Creek south of Milwaukee in 1862; but his service was cut short because of a disability discharge. Joseph Cramer, yet another immigrant (about one-third of the Milwaukee Regiment had been immigrants from the several Germanic states), had come down to Milwaukee to join, and served as a wagoner until the war ended; now he ran an art store and was said to love playing his violin.[9]

Yet another newcomer to America in 1862, Henry Bichler had then been the lone tailor in the Lake Michigan town of Port Washington; he shuttered his shop for more than three years to fight for his adopted country, only to be captured by the rebels in Tennessee. (Most of the soldiers, during the war and afterward, spelled the term "rebels" in all lower case.) He came to the reunion with his young son. Bichler was joined by a man who had much to say about his war service with the Milwaukee Regiment: Ed Blake, also from Port Washington, had carried the regiment's revered flag through scores of campaigns; he had even turned down a promotion to lieutenant because he would have had to leave the color company to do so. Blake may have felt some pique when McArthur was awarded the Medal of Honor for his actions at Missionary Ridge.[10]

McArthur had not felt well in the weeks before the grand reunion of the 24th Wisconsin: he had been stricken with what was said to be "acute indigestion." "Pinky" McArthur, his Virginia-born wife, had pleaded with him not to attend the gathering. But how could the old soldier say no to his comrades on this auspicious day, the fiftieth anniversary of the time they departed Milwaukee for almost three years of war. He had taken a carriage the few blocks from his Marshal Street home to the Grand Army hall at University building. The late-season heat and close air troubled him. There in the banquet room, they greeted their colonel.

The day had been long, with a sumptuous evening banquet capping the reunion. It was approaching ten o'clock before McArthur had been introduced to his appreciative comrades and friends. The general had planned to talk about the great campaign for Atlanta in 1864 led by frowning General Sherman. The boys of the Milwaukee Regiment had fought stoutly during the battles of May and June, and many a good soldier had fallen under the rain of rebel shot and shell. Resaca, Adairsville, Kennesaw Mountain, the Chattahoochee River, Peace Tree Creek, and Jonesboro—these were battles fought. Mere boys like Amandus Silsby, a student from Ohio who had joined the 24th Wisconsin while attending school at Prairie du Sac, had marched and fought with the Milwaukee Regiment and wrote to his abolitionist preacher-father; McArthur likely did not recall his name.

"He was speaking of the old days of the campaign, when they were all comrades in the joys and misery of that awful conflict, and extolling the valor of the old boys of the regiment which saw the hottest fighting of the great war," said James G. Flanders, a longtime friend who attended the banquet.

"Little did we imagine fifty years ago," McArthur continued, "that we should ever be allowed to gather in this way. Little did we think that on that march to Atlanta so many of us would be spared to see Wisconsin again. Your indomitable regiment . . ."

His voice trailed off. "He staggered slightly and grew pale," observed an old veteran. "He gripped his hands as though striving for strength to proceed."

"Comrades," McArthur gasped, "I can not go on. I am too weak. I must sit down."

Suddenly he stopped and put his hand to his heart. He made an effort to continue but his voice failed. He slumped into his chair and closed his gray eyes. His head fell forward. Every one of the old men in the audience rushed forward.

"Instantly the banquet room was in a turmoil of confusion as the members of the regiment rushed to the stricken comrade and gathered about him," Flanders told a news man. "Already his face had assumed the pallor of death and he lay back in his chair breathing easily. Tenderly we moved him to a couch and everyone stood at a respectful distance while the doctors worked busily." Dr. William J. Cronyn, a veteran, quickly pushed his way to the stricken general.

"In the room there was no more sound than death, as with staring eyes and bated breath we awaited the decision of the physicians. Not a sound was heard but the beating of our own hearts."

"Suddenly, Dr. Cronyn moved quickly, grasped the general's pulse, thrust his head to the dying man's breast—and straightened up. We knew the rest," Flanders said. A blood vessel had burst at the base of the brain, and death had been almost instantaneous.

"A sob escaped somewhere and then all was still," recalled an ashen-haired man.

"Then one of the old soldiers, in a voice broken with sobs, began to speak. At first the sound was indistinguishable, but presently we made out the first words of the Lord's prayer. Slowly, solemnly, the old soldiers gathered around the body of their great friend, and in voices heavy in grief, a last broken plea to the heavenly father was quavered out:

"Our father, which art in heaven . . ." Paul B. Jenkins, pastor of Immanuel Presbyterian Church, who had delivered the banquet invocation, led the rest of the prayer.

Another of the gray men took down the old battle flag of the 24th Wisconsin that had been brought over from the state capitol for the occasion. This was the badly tattered banner that young Arthur had grabbed up at the battle of Missionary Ridge in 1863; he had hoisted the flag into the air, shouting "On Wisconsin!" to his comrades. They fought their way to the summit, following the eighteen-year-old hero. It was said that the boy-soldier was the first to the ridge top, and afterward, when the rebels had retreated, General Sheridan had clutched the curly-headed youngster and said he would win a medal.

Now the silent men draped the flag over their comrade's body. "Sobbing like children, the men with whom he had fought during the bitterest years of the civil war left the room."

Ed Parsons, who presided over the grand reunion, was shocked to his core. Seeing his dead commander, he "staggered to his feet and burst into tears. 'We've been so long together,'" he murmured. A few minutes after McArthur was pronounced dead, Parsons was seen to be in serious distress. The shock of his friend's demise caused paralysis to his right side. Dr. Cronyn attended him, too. He suffered a stroke, was carried away insensate; the worst was feared.

Amid all the news coverage of the general's death a small story was printed only a few days before the tragedy: He had told some friends that when the time came for him to die, he hoped he could pass away surrounded by his old comrades; he would rather die that way than on the battlefield. Such, to some, was the stuff of nineteenth-century melodrama.

Another boyhood friend from the east side of Milwaukee, Charley King, carried the news of the general's death that Thursday evening. He, too, was an old army man. When he informed Mrs. McArthur of her husband's death, she was prostrated with grief and would not recover for several days.

Heavy dark columns rivered across the front pages of the daily newspapers the next day and after. Encomiums of all kinds were printed. Of his boyhood chum, King wrote: "He was our greatest soldier. He was by long odds the best read man in his profession as well as in political history in the United States army. He is looked upon far and wide throughout the army as the brainiest of our generals, and all Wisconsin soldiers know his gallantry in the field in the days when as a mere boy, barely 17 years old, he entered the service as adjutant of the 24th, and was in command of the regiment when only 18 years old."

"As boys we were next-door neighbors and intimate friends, and since our retirement from active service our friendship had only strengthened," he said. "I have no words in which to tell of how I mourn his loss."

King had also telegraphed the sad news to McArthur's sons, army captain Douglas and navy lieutenant commander Arthur. When Douglas received the cable, he was stunned: "My whole world changed that night. Never have I been able to heal the wound in my heart," he wrote years later in an autobiography.[11]

Chapter 1

The Great War Meeting

"What a trumpet sounds."

Road dust billowed toward the high, hot noonday sun from the throng of thousands surging along the main street in downtown Milwaukee. Horns blared and drums thudded from military bands. Colorful militia companies, long-barreled muskets locked at their sides, trod in uniform step. The roiling July 1862 congregation was prompted by President Lincoln's recent call to the states for 300,000 more volunteers this second summer of the Civil War. This conflict with the South, most were beginning to understand, would not be won easily, and many more thousands of men were needed to fill the ranks of Union armies depleted by over a year of fighting. A great War Meeting was under way.

Milwaukee, a city not yet twenty-five years old, boasted a population of some 45,000. It was a striking Western metropolis with many buildings of a distinctive pale brick that shimmered in the summer sunlight. The city—many called it Cream City because of those striking bricks—spread westward from bluffs overlooking the expansive blue of Lake Michigan, tumbled over the river from which its name derived, and fanned toward the horizon. The bustling city was in the midst of a population explosion that would, within a few years, see it eclipse 60,000.

Milwaukee's foundations were Yankee—migrants from New England, New York, and Eastern cities who were attracted to the rough-hewn settlement not far removed from its French fur-trading days.

Many migrants speculated, purchasing great swaths and parcels of land, subdividing, and selling them for great profit; they grew rich and powerful, controlling the city's politics in the bargain.

But in recent decades thousands of immigrants poured into the rising city. First came the Irish who settled in cramped wards between Lake Michigan and the Milwaukee River; the majority had become laborers and tradesmen. Then newcomers from the Germanic states, duchies, and baronies arrived; many were called "Acht und Vierzigers" (Forty-Eighters) who had fled Europe after the abortive democratic revolutions. They were seasoning the Western city's political, cultural, and commercial character with the distinctive Teutonic flavor. Thus, in 1850, 64 percent of Milwaukee's citizens were foreign-born; a decade later, the Germans alone would command an absolute majority in the city.

The business of the city was business, above all. While Chicago, ninety miles to the south, was rapidly out distancing Milwaukee in population and other ways, the Wisconsin town would soon become the West's largest exporter of grain and flour, millions of tons loaded aboard Lake Michigan schooners and steamers. Rail lines radiated toward the Mississippi River and to the north. Meat packers and brewers soon would mark Milwaukee. In the second year of the great Civil War, the city directory listed twenty-three breweries; most were small, but the portent of one of the city's future industries was apparent. The city's robust commercial heart pulsed with thriving banks, news offices, and mercantile enterprise; beer and music halls provided respite from enterprise.

Many of the streets in the central wards were graded, and curbing separated walkways from the thoroughfares; a nascent system of wooden sewers was begun. The rails of horse car lines ribboned toward the expanding city fringes. Elms shaded nearly all the prosperous neighborhoods north of the central business area. Most homes in the city bore the mark of settled permanence, albeit shacks still jumbled together in the poor Irish warrens south of the city's heart. Here and there opulent palaces clearly marked the residences of men of money and influence.

Summers in the lakeshore city were mostly mild although there were many days when temperatures soared and humid air weighed heavily. But in winter, the cold often crushed down from Canada in November, gripping the city in bone-numbing temperatures—some years until well past Easter. The dull light from the weak winter sun shown only briefly, or so it seemed in the depths of January and February each year. On most days, the slate gray skies foretold the onset of icy blasts that drifted deep snows high against buildings, structures, and fences, blanketing all in mounds of white stillness. Lake Michigan brooded.

Politically, the Western metropolis was stubbornly tied to the Democratic Party. It had failed to exhibit a friendly face for the Republican presidential candidate, Abraham Lincoln, in 1860, delivering nearly a thousand-vote majority to his opponent, Stephen A. Douglas. And four years later, the Lake Michigan city provided a two-thirds vote plurality to another Democrat, George B. McClellan, the former army general who hoped to succeed in politics where he had not in battle. War as an expedient to end sectional trauma was ill advised, the majority seemed to say with their ballots.

The Democratic Party drew much of its strength from the Germanic and Irish newcomers. They were leery of the new Republican Party with its taint of nativist Know Nothingism, and the uncompromising position on the abolition of slavery. Many laid blame for the inflamed sectional conflict at the party's doorstep.

There was recent evidence of how the rough frontier character of Milwaukee intensified the escalating antagonism between free and slave states. Less than a decade before the great War Meeting, a jailed fugitive slave had been freed by a mob before Federal marshals could lay hands on him. But then, more recently, in the summer of 1860, another mob just as readily lynched a black man suspected in the murder of an Irish immigrant.[1]

One of the young men who would volunteer for the new infantry regiment witnessed that awful deed in early September 1860. Gene Comstock, only seventeen, who had traveled to Milwaukee to take up the printing trade, wrote a graphic letter to his parents about the disturbing episode. He was attracted, he said, by the knelling of bells near midnight that aroused citizens to an ugly mob bent on mayhem. When the police chief attempted to quell the gathering crowd bent on stringing up the Negro named George Marshall, an assailant struck the constable insensible with a stone.

Marshall was marched down the street, the mob, numbering in Comstock's calculation, about 500, shouting "Hang him!", "Burn him!", "Tar and feather him!" Matches were occasionally struck and held to the Negro's face to insure the right man was still in hand during the march; at one point, the mob hit the prisoner with "stones and cudgels," the impressionable Comstock told his parents. "The clothes were torn off from him and he was a mass of blood!" Ultimately, the lawless band dragged their captive a few blocks to a construction site where a pile driver stood idly. A Third Ward Irish immigrant then struck Marshall with a stick of wood before the bloody man was hoisted up and a rope flung over the pile driver; he was hanged. In uncommonly graphic prose, Comstock wrote:

> He still struggled and while insensible put his hands up and loosened the rope so as it was even with his mouth when his strength failed him and he fell back with the rope in his mouth and was thus hung! In about a half an hour he was taken down and carried to the dead house.[2]

Almost coincident to this brutal incident was a tragedy that also brought the nation's sectional antagonisms to the streets of Milwaukee. Virtually an entire generation of immigrant Irish leaders was lost in a horrible Lake Michigan accident early in September 1860.

Wisconsin's firebrand Republican governor, Alexander Randall, pronounced that year that he would defy the infamous Fugitive Slave Law, refusing to hand over runaway slaves to Federal marshals for return to their owners. The captain of one of Milwaukee's militia companies, Garrett Barry, averred that his men, all Irish, would defy the governor, as it must, to support enforcement of the Federal law. Randall ordered the unit to turn over its state-issued muskets and equipment, and disband.

An effort was begun immediately to raise private funds to purchase new muskets and military impedimenta for Barry's company, the campaign to culminate in a trip to Chicago to hear the Democratic presidential candidate, Douglas. Four hundred Milwaukee citizens from the Irish wards chartered the handsome Lake Michigan side-wheeler, the *Lady Elgin,* September 6. On the return trip to Milwaukee on a foggy night a day later, a lumber schooner struck the twin-stacked, white steamer. The popular double-decked excursion vessel sank rapidly, and two-thirds of the revelers drowned. Bodies washed ashore south of the city for weeks afterward, and the tragedy touched nearly every Irish family in the city.[3]

In spring of the following year, when the sectional antagonisms burst into war, another young man, this one of Quaker parentage, struggled with his conscience about his role in the conflict. Howard Greene had migrated to Milwaukee from upstate New York in 1856 at the inducement of his brother, Thomas, a wholesale druggist; Tom offered his young brother a position in the firm. Welcome Greene, the father, seemed to favor Howard, the youngest of four sons, attesting to his "sweetness of disposition," his business acumen, and popularity. Beneath heavy eyelids, Howard Greene bore a sad countenance.

After the firing upon Fort Sumter, the twenty-one year old was having "very serious thoughts" about enlisting. "I dread and deprecate war, particularly civil war," he wrote his parents, "and I long and pray for peace." He was troubled that his feelings were far different from those generally held by the Friends—feelings that constrained him from volunteering only because it was contrary to his parents' wishes. He was clearly incensed that the U.S. flag had been "insulted," and the government "abused [and] imposed upon by Traitors it has been nursing in its bosom. . . . [M]y blood boils in my veins," he stressed, "and I think it is high time something should be done to put *a stop* to their traitorous designs, and I think a resort to arms *under the circumstances perfectly justifiable.*"

Just before Milwaukee's grand War Meeting in the summer of 1862, Howard Greene returned to Providence, New York, impelled by his sense of duty to the country. He wanted to volunteer. "I hope and pray that my parents will put no obstacle in *my path, but bless me and wish me God speed.*"[4]

In Milwaukee during that summer, two politicians, one with military experience and another with apparent higher political aspirations, jousted for command of a new regiment. Wisconsin's new governor, Edward Salomon, was an immigrant from Prussia who had bolted the Democratic Party to support Lincoln; he had been added to the so-called "Union" ticket as lieutenant governor in the 1860 election to attract the immigrant vote. The sectional trauma of the day had indirectly lifted Salomon to Wisconsin's highest office. The Republican governor, Louis Harvey, drowned in April 1862 while accompanying supplies for wounded Wisconsin soldiers in Tennessee; Salomon assumed the office.[5]

As governor, Salomon received supplications from many men who coveted high rank in the new regiments to be raised. The *Madison Journal* reported in mid-July that Maj. Charles Larrabee was granted a colonelcy of a unit to be organized in the second congressional district, which included Milwaukee. The forty-two-year-old former state congressman from the counties north of the city was the third-ranking officer in the 5th Wisconsin Infantry, then currently with Gen. George

McClellan's Army of the Potomac attempting to extricate itself from Virginia's Peninsula after an abortive campaign to capture Richmond.[6]

Meanwhile, a Milwaukee politician also cast his eye on command of an infantry regiment. Herman Page, one of the many New York-born men populating the city's politician landscape, had been sheriff and mayor for one term, and was currently chief of police. Portly, he had a receding hairline, but a chest-length gray beard flowed down from cheeks and chin. Governor Salomon accorded him the rank of lieutenant colonel. The forty-four-year-old Page, however, likely hoped to march at the head of a new regiment recruited from the streets of Milwaukee. Shoulder straps adorned with eagles could, after the rebellion was put down, lead to a more favorable political position in the city or the state. The daily *Milwaukee Sentinel* proclaimed Page as "a man possessed of all the requisite qualities of a good officer, and he has served that community so long and so well that we have no doubt of his capacity to serve the country at large."[7]

Page, although a Democrat, also made a good impression upon the men of money at the Chamber of Commerce. In an address a few days after his commission was granted, he opined that a full regiment would be raised in the streets of Milwaukee within thirty days—a prediction that was realized. Looking to larger issues, the police chief stridently struck the proper notes, casting aspersions upon the Democratic *Milwaukee Daily News* and its German-language kindred paper, the *See-Bote:* "I am sick and tired of the sympathy expressed for the rebels who are trying by every means to rend this Union." He drew an analogy: If the president confronted a highwayman, intent upon robbery, would he croak about sparing the robber's constitutional rights? Would Lincoln even stop to argue? "No!" said Page to thunderous applause, "give [the highwayman] the contents of your revolver. He has forfeited his constitutional rights to protection!"[8]

Politics, obviously, was part of daily affairs, and broadsides of printer's ink blasted across the front pages of rival news sheets. The Republican *Milwaukee Sentinel* lost no opportunity to lambaste its rival *Daily News,* while the latter often fulminated against alleged corruption in Lincoln's Washington and the trampling of the constitutional rights of Southern states by his government.

In such a charged climate, Milwaukee found itself on the final day of July 1862 with thousands gathering in the central business district at the Chamber of Commerce building to begin the parade to the great War Meeting. The city needed to induce new volunteers to join the fight. Enterprising news writers that day estimated those who had arrived from out of town Thursday, July 31 at 30,000; they had begun arriving the day before and joined more thousands of city residents who were taking part.[9]

Somewhere amid that seething throng was a slight youth little more than a month past his seventeenth birthday. He was the son of a prominent circuit court judge, Arthur McArthur, who strode in the forefront of the effort to raise funds and recruit men to the new infantry regiments. Arthur McArthur, Jr., carried not much more than ninety pounds on his slight five-foot-seven-inch frame. But he had already held an army commission. The youngster, with a ruddy complexion and somewhat narrow-lidded gray eyes, appeared even younger than he was; in his specially tailored coat, some may have taken him for a mere drummer boy but for the straps of an officer that perched on his narrow shoulders. His dark hair bore the same deep waves and curls of his father; he attempted to tame the thick mane with a part. The Scot heritage was evident. Bright and impetuous, the youngster had known a privileged and protected life, away from boys of lesser station. There had been tragedy and loss in his life, however.

His mother, a New England woman whom the elder McArthur had met when he came to America, had, in 1859, left husband and two sons in the rough-hewn Western city to return home to family in the settled Massachusetts environment; out of earshot of the McArthurs, it was whispered that she had suffered a breakdown of some sort.[10]

Young Arthur, whom his chums called "Mac," grew up among the families of prominence in the city's Seventh Ward—the near east side adjacent to the central business district and a short distance from the blue waters and soft summer breezes of Lake Michigan. One who chronicled those days from the remove of more than sixty years was Charley King. A year older than McArthur, King was the son of Rufus, Milwaukee's first school superintendent and early editor of the Republican *Milwaukee Sentinel.* Charley always told good soldier stories in those days late in the nineteenth century.

The boys who congregated in the leafy Yankee/Yorker enclave, King said, "met in force pretty much every pleasant evening in the spring, summer, and fall. . . . They were the merriest, jolliest gang of youngsters that this city of Milwaukee has ever turned out." King, who wrote and spoke of these days after the century's turn, also recalled that young McArthur "was no scholar in those days." He attended what was called Milwaukee University, something of a prep school. "He loved the [Lake

Arthur McArthur.
Age sixteen—he had to wait
a year. COURTESY OF GREG RUPNOW.

Michigan] shore, the woods, the camp fires along the Menom[i]nee [River]," said King. "He was ever ready for fun and adventure, but life was somewhat of a go-as-you-please affair to him in early 1861 [and] the opening of the great [war] was set him to thinking."[11]

Arthur was less than two months short of his sixteenth birthday when the rebellious South Carolinians fired upon Fort Sumter. Family legend has it that the "undersized boy" of barely seven stone desperately wanted to enlist. But Judge McArthur refused permission.

Another man who, in decades following the war turned considerable writing talents to spinning stories and telling tales about Milwaukee's Civil War soldiers, was Jerry Watrous. He had volunteered and served in the 6th Wisconsin Infantry, one of the famed Iron Brigade regiments; he had risen to officer ranks, and after the war edited a weekly society and soldiers newspaper, the *Milwaukee Sunday Telegraph*.[12]

As Watrous recalled it—and few could weave better soldier stories than he—after training at Camp Randall in Madison and being sworn into Federal service July 21, 1861, the 6th Wisconsin Infantry traveled through Milwaukee. Two of the unit's companies had been recruited from the city—the all-Germanic Citizens' Corps and the fully Irish Montgomery Guard. The city feted the new soldiers, who, afterward, stepped off smartly in natty state-issued gray uniforms and caps. When the regiment strode through the central business district toward the train station, youthful McArthur attempted to convince the captain of the Fond du Lac company (Watrous was a private in those ranks) to accept him. A politician of promise, Edward S. Bragg, himself of unimposing stature, responded to the youthful supplicant.

"No, my boy; you are not old enough for a soldier in my company."

"Then you will not take me?"

"No; you would not last a month."

At that, one wag in the company, a bulky Irisher named Harry Dunn, ever armed with wit, blurted, "Enlist him, Captain. Sure there is the making of a second Lieutenant-General Winfield Scott [the Federal army's commanding general of the day] in the lad." Dozens of soldiers in the ranks burst into laughter at Dunn's observation, and the ninety-pound youngster must have reddened in mortification; yet he importuned several other companies in the line. But the result was the same, and he retired from his effort in tears, wrote Watrous thirty-seven years after that day.[13]

Family legend and myth also burnished events, and sometimes failed to agree fully in details and chronology with sparse facts about the incidents of those times. At midpoint in the twentieth century, a family historian spun a tale of the sixteen-year-old stripling, as one writer described him, begging the stout judge. Arthur asked his father to use influence to gain an appointment to West Point. The senior McArthur's response was hardly encouraging:

"'Even if President Lincoln would agree with me in this,' said the judge, it would be "far wiser to stay at home for another year.' With his sensitive lips shut tight to keep them from trembling, young Arthur looked straight at the big man in Broadcloth, sitting at the far side of the mahogany table gleaming with crystal and silver. He could not trust his voice to answer." Here was a good family tale. "'The men will laugh at you.' The father's voice was growing impatient. 'Why, Arthur, don't you realize how your voice squeaks when under stress? Wait, at least, until you get over that falsetto.'" Color washed from the youngster's face—or so a writer of a later generation had it—but the boy would not promise. The judge warned that he would have a private detective watch his every move to prevent any impetuous action. Then in a gesture to placate the boy, he promised that his son might study at a military school in Illinois.[14]

Nearly a year passed, with Arthur dutifully attending military school. He posed for a likeness sometime during that period: Despite the pose in the long military coat, the handsome, light-eyed face appeared even younger than sixteen years. Then in May 1862, a month before his seventeenth birthday, the youth returned home, reiterating his wish for a military academy appointment. Certainly against his considered judgment, the elder McArthur wrote to the president. With a Wisconsin senator acting as intermediary, they gained an audience with the tall, gaunt Abraham Lincoln amid the crush of political and military supplicants. Lincoln explained that all ten appointments the president was authorized were already allotted. Arthur's boyhood chum, Charley King, in fact, would be in the Class of 1862. There was a real possibility, however, a spot might be found in the 1863 West Point class, if only the wavy-haired young man would wait that long. Arthur was likely crestfallen on the train back to Wisconsin, and upon his return he badgered his father incessantly.

Relenting, Judge McArthur used his influence as a member of the Union Democrats to wrangle a lieutenant's commission from Governor Salomon. His slight, underweight son, whose voice had not yet gained the timbre of manhood, was appointed adjutant of a new infantry regiment. A new uniform coat was made, and the straps of an officer sewn on its shoulders.[15]

Another youth, of modest background and means, who struggled amid the surge of bodies at the great War Meeting that hot Milwaukee afternoon, July 31, 1862, had a few things in common with McArthur. Amandus Silsby had traveled east from the Wisconsin River town of Prairie du Sac where he was attending school. There was little to distinguish him in the throng: Of average five-foot-seven-inch height, with brown hair and eyes, Silsby, the son of an abolitionist Presbyterian missionary, was caught in the tumult. The youth's light complexion must have flushed by a quickened pulse amid the myriad images and sensations.[16]

Silsby was born June 26, 1845, just days after McArthur, at College Hill in southern Ohio near Cincinnati. He and the Milwaukee youth also shared the loss of a mother, although such information was never exchanged between the two. He was the son of John and Amanda Whiteside Silsby, who had been married less than a year. Amanda had a difficult birth, and died within days of the infant's delivery; John named his son after his deceased wife. It must have been difficult for a man to raise an infant son, particularly since he was so deeply involved in his church's far-flung proselytizing efforts. Moreover, John Silsby remarried in April 1848, and between 1851 and 1862 sired five more children. Amandus was perhaps fourteen or fifteen when he was sent away to school; the youngster journeyed into the rough frontier state where he lived with a guardian, Andrew Benton, at Prairie du Sac, a community on the roiling Wisconsin River.

The seeds of his excitement had been sown even earlier than 1862. "A company has been forming here," Silsby had written to his grandmother in Illinois ten months before. "They are called the Buena Vista Flying Artillery [which became the 6th Wisconsin Battery]." The company's lieutenant was Samuel F. Clark, a former student and "a very daring fellow." Many of the privates were classmates, and Clark had marched his company to the school a few days before, Silsby wrote, "and while there the girls presented each member with a rosette." He observed: "The citizens of this place are going to give them a farewell dinner, and orators are appointed to deliver addresses [at their departure]." Admiring young girls, it seemed, provided a boost to recruitment.[17]

It must have all been very momentous for the impressionable young man, this martial ardor abroad in Wisconsin, penetrating every county and community. He had recently received a letter from another schoolmate who was a musician in the 6th Wisconsin Infantry "now in Virginia, on the 'sacred soil.'" Other friends were in the 5th and 2nd Wisconsin regiments in the East, and his uncle, William, had enlisted in an Iowa regiment. This war business was very exciting, and the men who joined were assured a measure of attention from the girls as well as the townies.[18]

It was somewhat understandable that when schoolboy Silsby learned of the great War Meeting gathering that next summer, he saw it as an opportunity for adventure—and perhaps more. All the state's railroads, in an effort to help raise volunteers, granted men eighteen years and older free round-trip passage to Milwaukee for the grand event. Silsby and two schoolmates determined to make the trip east; and despite the fact that none was older than seventeen, the station agent gave them tickets. The train left Wednesday, July 30 at 7 P.M., for an all-night trip. Since there was insufficient space in the regular coaches for all the potential recruits, they were consigned to drafty, dirty, uncomfortable freight cars. But upon reaching Spring Green, another Wisconsin River village some thirty-five rail miles west of the state capital, Silsby and his friends slipped into the regular fare cars and enjoyed the ride. In a letter to his grandmother describing the experience, the youngster wrote that every station "seemingly swarmed with heads . . . cheering for the Union." At Madison, the capital city, where the train stopped for supper, a band played "The Star-Spangled Banner." They arrived in Milwaukee at 4:30 A.M. Thursday, weary but still enthusiastic.[19]

Milwaukee men of money and influence, including Judge McArthur and several other fathers of men who would volunteer to fight, had stumped for the war effort; the Chamber of Commerce had raised thousands of dollars to pay bonuses to men who volunteered, thereby aiding families to be left behind. There was talk, after Lieutenant Colonel Page's assertion, that, indeed, city men might compose an entire Milwaukee regiment.

At sunrise Thursday, the final day of July, Milwaukee was awakened by a sixty-gun salute to begin the day's festive effort at recruiting more of the state's sons for war. At noon, another cannon boom announced the closing of businesses and the start of official ceremonies. Eight splendid bands, seven fire companies, and Capt. Elisha Hibbard's colorful militia Zouaves were among those who led the roiling procession up Wisconsin Street in the old Juneautown, as the east side of the river was once called, across the Milwaukee River to Spring Street, and west about a mile to Kneeland's Grove, an expansive, verdant picnicking ground where the patriotic pontification was focused.

Voice tinged with Prussian accent, Gov. Edward Salomon delivered the opening oration. "My heart expands as I look upon the multitude of patriotic men gathered together to assist in the work of putting down this rebellion," he began. "It shows me that the men of Wisconsin are not to be trodden down by the aristocracy which is striking at the life of our government." He railed against the "conspiracy of Slaveholders," and warned of the denigration of the nation into a "patchwork of feeble and discordant States" if the rebellion was not beaten. He concluded his lengthy delivery with a ringing appeal:

> Young men, you are best able to leave and can best be spared: what a trumpet call sounds in your ears! What a field of heroic struggle is offered to you! Your gallant comrades from the battle field, call upon you by name. Will you shrink? Will you turn your backs?

There were more appeals from other politicians, oratory soaring into the hot afternoon air. Then it was time for men to step forward, to apply signatures to rolls and pledge their lives to the defense of the Union. Amandus Silsby must have been moved by the ringing call to volunteer. But when he wrote to his grandmother just days later, he was fearful about telling her of his decision: Despite his tender years, the young man signed the roll of one volunteer company. Marching off to war within a few weeks, he would not gain the honor and fame of the other boy-soldier, Arthur McArthur, nor live to ripe maturity. But the two would, for the next few years, share the life of camp, the arduousness of march, and the deadliness of battle.[20]

Chapter 2

The Volunteers

—•— ≡◆≡ —•—

"Drums beat, fifes play, bands parade."

"Drums beat, fifes play, bands parade the streets in full blast, gathering crowds at every corner and literally blocking the streets and crossings." That was the way one news man described the atmosphere permeating Milwaukee during August 1862:

> The city is one complete hive of busy men and boys. . . . Playcards [*sic*] garnish every blank wall . . . , recruiting officers jostle you at every turn . . . , flaming handbills setting forth the advantages of enlisting in this or that company meet the eye at every turn. Little boys run after and hail you; men beckon to you across the streets and importune for an hours work in behalf of their company; men already enlisted swarm around public places urging old comrades to join them; and the ladies lend the sanction of their presence and efforts at every suitable opportunity.[1]

For nearly a month after the Great War Meeting of July 31, the city of Milwaukee feverishly turned to the task of recruiting men for new regiments. Flags; red, white, and blue bunting; and other patriotic adornments fluttered from nearly every building, post, and outcropping in the sweaty summer days. Businesses were urged to close at noon each day so the public would not be distracted from its duty. Some shopkeepers and tradesmen, however, chose profit over patriotism, failing to follow the dictum. To read the daily news sheets of the day, however, the task of raising recruits was taken up with near religious fervor.

More than a year had passed since other sons of Milwaukee had marched off to war in several of the nearly two dozen regiments recruited in Wisconsin. (The state ultimately organized fifty-two regiments of infantry and troops of cavalry and batteries of artillery.) But the men who volunteered in this second year of war were not the hot-blooded boys who charged forward to enlist after the attack upon Fort Sumter in 1861. Milwaukee had seen hundreds of these city lads march off in natty, state-issue gray uniforms. The war would be over in ninety days, just as soon as these Badger boys pitched in against the rebels— at least that was how the city viewed these matters in the first fiery breath of war.

But the grim reality was not long in becoming manifest: The state's initial unit, the proud 1st Wisconsin Infantry that included hundreds of Milwaukee men, was blooded in June at the battle of Falling Waters, Virginia. Howard Greene, the sensitive Quaker from New York, had seen them return to Milwaukee in August; they were "the hardest[,] dirtiest looking set of men I have ever seen." But after washing and shaving, they "looked like men again." Many, he predicted, would enlist again. "Brave for them." Greene still wrestled with his conscience about the war and his part in it.[2]

In July, the Federal army had suffered a disastrous defeat at Bull Run. Despite a tactical victory by the army under Gen. Ulysses S. Grant the following spring, heavy losses were reported at Shiloh, Tennessee. Then the vaunted march on Richmond by the Army of the Potomac had been stalled virtually at that city's gates; the new rebel general, Robert E. Lee, stopped the magnificent Federal army in a series of brilliant battles in June 1862, and the American Napoleon, Maj. Gen. George B. McClellan, was vanquished.

Thus, hundreds of Milwaukee soldiers had been killed or maimed in Virginia, Mississippi, and elsewhere. For those families who could afford the expense, corpses were sent home in tin boxes; fresh earthen mounds appeared in the city's cemeteries. For most mourners, however, the dead lay covered over by Southern soil; only the memories of the once vital young volunteers remained. Then, blue-coated men, disabled soldiers missing limbs or otherwise scarred, began to appear on city streets with increasing frequency. It was becoming awful, this war business.

The demands of this Civil War required yet more Milwaukee men to step forward and fill new ranks. It was calculated, and duly reported on the front page of one Milwaukee daily, that under President Lincoln's recent call for volunteers, 1,602 city men needed to sign the rolls while the remainder of the county's communities must add 609 more—a total of 2,211. Should state and local quotas for volunteers not be met, the onerous draft would be instituted. When that day came, dire reactions would cause violent eruptions in some Wisconsin communities.[3]

Using the whip of the impending draft and the carrot of generous bounties and other inducements that August of 1862, every city ward and precinct was scoured for able-bodied men willing to step forward to put down this damnable rebellion. A grand War Committee of prominent men, including Judge McArthur, had coordinated the effort for almost a month, presenting speeches and convincing the reluctant to enroll. Members of Milwaukee's Chamber of Commerce had offered considerable financial support for the recruiting effort from their own pockets as had citizens of great and modest means. Moreover, these moneyed men of Milwaukee also paid for the creation of a special flag to be awarded to the first regiment filled in the summer call for volunteers. Let that unit be composed entirely of Milwaukee men was the implication. Throughout that month, news sheets printed front page stories of gatherings and enlistments.[4]

Dozens of men established headquarters in the city's central business district east of the Milwaukee River in efforts to corral volunteers and raise companies. A captain's uniform shoulder straps would result if a hundred men could be coaxed to sign the company roll. Fifes twittered, drums pounded, and cannons boomed from nearly every intersection. Papers reported progress in nearly every four-page issue.

Although there were many young, fresh-faced lads who stepped forward to enlist, seventeen-year-old Amandus Silsby among them, the majority now beginning to answer the new call for volunteers represented an older and steadier set. The latter were men of the trades and professions who gave up what was said to be good situations to volunteer; many had wives and children. These were railroad men, farmers, clerks and merchants; bookkeepers, printers, and professional men—a practical lot, it was said. And, significantly, several were scions of wealthy and prominent families in Milwaukee, the offspring of men of position and power. Many of these new volunteers evinced breeding, background, education, refinement, and promise of bright futures. Several knew luxury and ease. In time, many would become the commercial

Charles Larrabee (post-war).
Milwaukee Regiment's colonel.
COURTESY OF THE WISCONSIN STATE HISTORICAL
SOCIETY (WHI(X3)22126).

leaders, lawyers, and bankers, the men who charted the city's destiny late in the century. If they wanted, the wealthy might have paid another man to serve in their stead.

Young, smooth-cheeked, and slender Arthur McArthur must have been excited. Not only did the embroidered bars of a lieutenant perch on the shoulders of his blue coat, but he would also be adjutant of a new infantry regiment, responsible for keeping the roll, and using his extensive knowledge of drill. He had, after all, spent long months studying military science, and was conversant with the army manuals of the day as well as treatises on tactics. Still, many older men, to be sure, snorted at the thought of such a tender, baby-faced, thin-bodied boy wearing an officer's straps. But after all, heads may have wagged, he was the judge's son.[5]

On the day after the great War Meeting, Charles Larrabee arrived in Milwaukee with a colonel's commission. At five foot eight inches, he looked the part in a neat new uniform; his dark hair, receded back on his forehead, and eyes and swarthy complexion revealed a French heritage. A heavy mustache drooped beneath his straight nose. He quickly made his obsequies to the prestigious Chamber of Commerce, whose membership of the moneyed and influential seemed to exert more control over city affairs than the mayor and his elected minions. Although the freshly minted colonel was not a Milwaukee man, many, especially Democrats, favored his appointment as regimental commander.

As major of the 5th Wisconsin, Larrabee had won commendations for his actions at the battle of Williamsburg during General McClellan's failed Peninsula campaign. But he was felled with a serious gastrointestinal disorder contracted in the Virginia swamps; he would never fully recover from the malady during his war service. Well regarded by many in his old regiment, he was "endeared to them by his bravery, and the uniform regard for the comfort of his men." Most of his fellow officers had, when he left Virginia July 26, signed a testimonial, expressing their "confidence and affection."[6]

The new colonel, however, had significant impediments. He was not a Milwaukee man, first of all. What ramifications this might have upon a new regiment whose soldiers, it was hoped, would be drawn largely from the city and adjacent communities may have been grist for idle speculation. Then there was the matter of Herman Page, Larrabee's junior in rank, who was apparently intent upon commanding a regiment of city men, perhaps earning political capital in the bargain.

In the colonel's first public utterance, he "expressed his determination to make [the new regiment] the best one in the state, and an honor to the city that had contributed so handsomely to its organization. The war is no holiday affair," he stressed. All well enough said for those concerned. But then Larrabee loosed remarks that set some teeth to clench, at least in the Democratic Party press of the day, revealing the division abroad in the city, about war aims. "The people of the south are united, and terribly in earnest," averred the colonel. "This is a war of utter subjugation, whatever men may think of it."[7]

Just days later, the Democratic daily had cause to clarify Larrabee's remarks. Although supportive of the war to preserve the Union of states, city Democrats still hoped for an early peace and a return to the nation as it was before Republican hot brands had inflamed the political climate with their abominable talk of abolition. Colonel Larrabee "did not advocate the 'subjugation' of the southern people in the sense in which the phrase is commonly employed," a front-page report stated. "He did urge[,] however, the necessity of conquering the military forces of the south and so far subjugating the Confederate States as to crush out the armed hostility to the government." The colonel believed only in the war for the Constitution, the return of the rebellious states to the Union with their constitutional rights unimpaired, said the daily. "There is no citizen of Wisconsin more patriotic at heart than Col. Larrabee and none with whom the brave soldiers of this state should prefer to enlist." The editors would have more to say on these matters.[8]

There was this related matter, too, this question of Negroes. At intervals during Milwaukee's rush to raise its regiment, the Democratic press cautioned the city about the "negro question." The war, said a news sheet, was not being prosecuted so "blacks are to be set free and made the equals of white men or remain in slavery, but it is whether we ourselves are to enjoy the blessings of a free government or not." Preservation of the government as it was before the secession crisis is the aim of the war, the Democratic press prescribed.[9]

This whole issue of slavery was a vexing one. Few writings left behind by men of the Milwaukee Regiment contained overt abolitionist sentiments. Even after the issuance of Lincoln's Emancipation Proclamation, freeing slaves in rebellious states, little more than ambivalence toward the Southern institution would be expressed. Implied in some soldier letters was a decided view of black inferiority; in others, a paternalistic stance was revealed. Although several companies, at least for brief periods, secured the services of freed blacks as cooks and wallopers, few soldier writers would dwell upon what they saw of slavery when they encountered its "legal" presence in Kentucky and Tennessee. It was all a rather troublesome matter.

That issue was not discussed when Larrabee planned to parlay his political connections in the counties north of Milwaukee, to call men to the banner of war. "Citizens are requested to make arrangements for the meetings," one Milwaukee daily proclaimed on its front page, "and the patriotic and loyal people are invited to rally their strength and give expression to their determination to uphold the constitution, the government and the execution of the laws against rebellion, treason and disunion." The sheet was staking a claim to a position on the war much stronger than that of its competitor, the *Daily News*.

With an entourage that included Judge McArthur and assorted politicians and luminaries, Larrabee boarded the steamer *Comet* in Milwaukee Harbor some few days later, traveling north to the Lake Michigan towns of Port Washington and Sheboygan; they also visited the inland farm communities of West Bend and Beaver Dam, stumping for men to volunteer.[10]

Leading the effort to raise a company in Port Washington was a man whose family name had been Americanized from Goltschmidt. Gus Goldsmith, born in one of the German states twenty-three years before, was a child when his family immigrated to Wisconsin; a railway engineer in Canada, he had enlisted in the three-month 1st Michigan Infantry, and fought in the first battle of Bull Run. Wounded and later imprisoned in Richmond's Libby Prison, he was exchanged by the rebels; family and friends had mourned him, as it was first reported he was killed. Returning home determined to return to the fight, Goldsmith established a recruiting station at the Union House Hotel in Port Washington.[11]

Goldsmith soon gathered over thirty men, many "sturdy and patriot German boys," like Charles Klein, the only son of immigrant parents who worked to support his aging parents. The twenty-six-year-old carpenter laid out the matter, it was said, asking them what was his "plain duty" as citizen in an adopted nation's hour of peril. "Go, if you think best," was said to be the reply. And so the farmer did, to be at his captain's side at a critical battle in Tennessee, and to return to his infirm parents after the war.[12]

Another of the immigrants who signed Goldsmith's roll was the only tailor in Port Washington. Henry Bichler, a twenty-nine-year-old immigrant from Luxembourg, who had been in America but six years, was determined, like Klein, to "stand by the Federal government." He signed Goldsmith's roll, closed up his shop, and left for war. Although he never gained promotion, he did his duty, marched, and fought; once captured and imprisoned by the rebels, he would return to the regiment after exchange, surviving the war and marching home with his fellow veterans in 1865.[13]

Among others in the company was Ed Blake, a nineteen-year-old Massachusetts-born lad who was having difficulty convincing his father "that his place was at the front in that glorious line of blue," as a latter day writer saw it, "for the protection of the old flag and the perpetuation of our great republic." Barnum Blake, the father, tried to induce his son with a generous sum of $10,000 to stay home. "Father, you cannot bribe me to desert my country!" was the reply. It was a good story chronicled more than thirty years later.[14]

The drive for volunteers in Milwaukee, meanwhile, continued in earnest. Erstwhile officers buttonholed men for units of all stripe. Within days nearly two dozen nascent companies attempted to gather signatures for the 100-man outfits. Many would not be successful. The recruiting effort was somewhat complicated since others were attempting to secure volunteers for a statewide Methodist regiment and one composed entirely of immigrants from the Germanic states and their sons. Agents for numerous other companies prowled the city and established recruiting offices at prominent locations in the central business district. Placards, banners, bands, barkers, and displays of all manner were set out to attract potential recruits. "Temperance companies, religious companies, mechanics' companies, clerks, rail road men, Methodists, farmers, boys, roughs, Germans, Irish, and almost every branch of business, occupation, class and nationalities are getting up companies," wrote a Milwaukee news man.[15]

By the first week in August, Wisconsin's largest city had enrolled many score volunteers, and it now seemed possible that sufficient men of Milwaukee might compose an entire 1,000-man regiment. It was a prospect that provided renewed impetus to recruiting activities during those humid summer days. In time, over three-quarters of all men—about 800 on the roster—would list Milwaukee or adjacent communities as their home. The unit was to become a veritable cross section of the community's trades and talents. Moreover, the volunteers reflected the basic constituencies of Milwaukee's population—Irish and German immigrants and their sons as well as offspring of New England and New York-born families. The predominant percentage of surnames was either English, Welsh, Scot, or Irish; immigrants and sons of Ireland alone composed about 12 percent of the total regiment's strength. Germanic surnames represented about one-third of the 24th Wisconsin.

For those who would survive the three-year ordeal, the stories of their great adventures would become part of the city's collective memory, the stuff of legend and lessons for the remainder of the century. Some men signing the roll of the new unit were friends and acquaintances who had grown to manhood in the city's streets. Still others were known to one another through associations and workplaces.

Howard Greene agonized about his decision to volunteer for over a year; he had turned twenty-two the March before. Although he likely had not informed his parents, he had in that time familiarized himself with military matters, perhaps scouring through army manuals and talking to friends about this business of war. He had decided, contrary to the dictates of his family's religious convictions, to volunteer. His motivation, he wrote his mother, was "from pure patriotism." What was more, he said, "I am confident that if God spare my life in the war, it will be of great benefit to my future health."

Then, there was another matter, an affair of the heart. The new soldier, who now cultivated a thick brown mustache, informed his parents about a young woman he had met on one of his business travels to St. Louis. He had discussed the decision to join the army with his "noble"

YOUNG MEN!
Look to Your Duty!

HEADQUARTERS
YOUNG MEN'S ASSO-
CIATION TIGERS!
No. 7 SPRING ST.

ALL YOUNG MEN OF THIS CITY
desirous of joining a good company, for the

Twenty-Fourth Regiment,

Are requested to meet at the HEAD QUARTERS
of the

"TIGERS!"

To-day, from 7 A. M. to 9 P. M. Fall in lively
young men, and do your duty.

YOUR COUNTRY CALLS

WM. H. ELDRED,
HOWARD GREENE,
aug11   Recruiting Officers.

Recruiting broadside.
Young Men's Association Tigers.

FROM: MILWAUKEE SENTINEL, 1862.

lady, Louise Webb, and she had reluctantly assented to his enlistment. "If you deem it your duty to go," Greene related she had said, "wait not a moment on my account, but go and God speed and if you are ever wounded or sick, let me know at once and I will immediately come to you." One day, she would have cause to regret her consent.[16]

In all probability, Greene belonged to the Young Men's Association, a prominent organization popular among the sons of the Yankee and New Yorker circles for fourteen years. Boasting a library, the association was also a focal point for social, cultural, and political affairs as well as a place for "coming men" to make important business contacts. The sad-eyed Greene was acquainted with the well-known lawyer, Ed Buttrick, and "Lish" Hibbard, the militia leader.

One Milwaukee daily printed a prominent, front-page advertisement announcing the formation of a company gathering under the auspices of the prestigious Young Men's Association. Although nearly $500 for bonuses was pledged by the membership, its advertisement made no note of it. A few days later, a fine band paraded the streets all day in a wagon festooned with banners to lure volunteers. The name of the company was to be the "Tigers." Howard Greene was one of the leading recruiters.

Greene and the other Tigers' recruiters established headquarters in the central business district, and their small cannon, the "Constitution," stood ready for action. Periodically, the gun was stoked with a blank charge and fired, the boom echoing from the cream-colored brick and brown frame buildings, gray smoke billowing over the business district.[17]

Although his service would not reach the heights of McArthur, there was another young man of wealth and position who cast his lot with Milwaukee volunteers. John Mitchell, two months short of his twentieth birthday, was the son of one of the wealthiest men in Wisconsin, the ponderous Scot immigrant, Alexander, a magnate of banking, railroads, and other endeavors. The Mitchells shared Sunday services with the McArthurs at St. James Episcopal on Spring Street west of the Milwaukee River.[18]

Mitchell was a man of culture and education. When sectional antipathies exploded into war, he had been studying in Europe; it was said that he immediately booked passage home, determined to do his duty and enlist. A youth of unimpressive stature, his height reached only five feet four. There was little physically to distinguish him: He had a typical light complexion and brown hair. His brown eyes, however, were weak and they would cause him difficulty in the army. With his father's virtually inexhaustible supply of money, John Mitchell had led a life of leisure, representing himself upon enlistment as a gentleman farmer.

He would serve as a lieutenant less than a year before physical difficulties and the rigors of army life caused him to resign. But he would publicly revere his war experience for the remainder of his years, and talk about it as he rose to become one of Wisconsin's most prominent politicians. He would help, with gentle wit and self-deprecating manner, to stitch the story of the Milwaukee Regiment into the city's fabric for the remainder of the nineteenth century. From the remove of twenty years, the matters of 1862 did not seem freighted with as much import as they once were. When writing about those August recruiting days two decades afterward, Mitchell remembered:

> There were a hundred or so recruiting commissions for the regiment we proposed to join. Every one, not troubled with diffidence, wished to become an officer. Consequently, there was a fierce struggle and some bargaining over the few unfortunates who were willing to enlist. We three [Fred Root, Robert Chivas, and Mitchell] had great difficulty. Our youth was against us. Grown men hung back, cautious parents preferred to confide their loved ones to a more mature leadership.[19]

Chivas, who spoke with the distinctive accent of one foreign-born, was actually Mitchell's cousin; wealthy and influential Alexander Mitchell likely aided him in his immigration to America three years before. His father had been an East India Company merchantman, and his mother had raised him—a fact that may have drawn him close to his aunt, Martha Mitchell. In Milwaukee, Chivas had established himself as a lumber merchant, and lived in the two-story Italianate Mitchell home on Spring Street. He also held a membership in St. James Church on Milwaukee's near west side. He was impressive, this twenty-year-old Scot, standing over six feet two inches tall and bearing the coloration of his native soil—auburn hair and light complexion set off with gray eyes. Already successful as a businessman, Chivas may have been looking for something more; perhaps in soldiering he would find it. He was not a U.S. citizen, so had no legal obligation to serve; yet he stepped forward "in the spirit of his God-fearing, liberty-loving ancestors," a later-day chronicler wrote. Along with fellow churchman Fred Root, Chivas scoured the ranks of retailers in the city for prospective recruits.

Root, a thirty-year-old merchant, was, at five feet five, like Mitchell, not impressive physically. He was a Virginian by birth who had migrated with his parents to Wisconsin some years earlier. He had become a devoted Sunday School teacher at St. James, and his pastor said he was "impulsive and warm-hearted." He would prove himself fearless in battle, almost reckless, Chivas later attested. Root would lead the company into battle until he was severely wounded a year later. Chivas would then step forward in his friend's stead, and in November 1863, the young Scot would charge up a steep, rebel-held hill in Tennessee alongside Arthur McArthur.[20]

As recruiters, the trio of friends stood in contrast: Chivas, well over six feet; Root measuring an unremarkable five feet five; and Mitchell barely reaching the minimum height for Federal service. They called their company the Merchants' Guards, and they employed novel techniques to attract prospective volunteers. "This crack company created quite a sensation" at their headquarters on one of the city's busy thoroughfares east of the Milwaukee River. The street was "illuminated in fine style. The muskets stacked gave . . . quite a military appearance," observed a newsman. In time, the new regiment would list 100 merchants, clerks, and bookkeepers. The company promised to exercise "a beneficial influence in the shape of powder and balls on the traitorous 'secesh,'" it was predicted. The going would not be so easy as the men who enlisted were soon to discover. Root, probably because he was oldest, became captain while Chivas and Mitchell were lieutenants. Chivas would regularly write letters to his "Aunty," detailing the long dull days in camp, the rigors of march, and the deadly earnestness of battle.[21]

Another of the many New York-born volunteers involved in the rush to raise a company was Ed Parsons, who would in decades to come speak and write regularly about his war experiences, lauding the exploits of young McArthur, Gen. Phil Sheridan, and others. He began button-holing volunteers for the Page Light Guard—with a nod toward the man named lieutenant colonel of the 24th Regiment. Educated at a local business school, the twenty-six-year-old, it was said, "gave up his situation as a bookkeeper at an extensive reaper manufactory." It was also reported that he made "great sacrifice of future prospects, and at certain present pecuniary loss." He was also reputed to possess "considerable military experience," having been a member of the state's premier militia company, the natty Milwaukee Light Guard. Just two years before, in fact, Parsons had won a handsome prize in the Guard's target excursion, taking third place. He was obviously familiar with the workings of the rifle musket, a skill that would prove valuable.

He would find himself under a cloud of recrimination in early 1863 when he accused some officers of the regiment with less than heroic conduct in battle. But he would later gain mention for his daring part in a charge up Missionary Ridge outside Chattanooga, Tennessee, alongside young MacArthur.[22]

Charley King, a well-known Milwaukee military man who would fight in two wars, wrote of these feverish days some thirty years later. When the city's recruiting effort for the new regiment pressed forward that summer of 1862, sixteen-year-old King served in Virginia, as an aide to his illustrious father, Rufus King. The general served as a division commander, and almost at that moment, near Gainesville, Virginia, in a prelude to the second battle of Bull Run, "Stonewall" Jackson's men would assail his unit.[23]

One of the older boys whom King also remembered was Elisha Hibbard—those who knew him well called him "Lish." The younger boys looked up to him because of his military bent. Why, he had led the colorful Milwaukee Light Guard Cadets—they called them "boy Zouaves"—a militia company of young men eighteen and under that was featured in nearly every city parade and ceremony.[24]

Yes, "Lish" cut a handsome swath on Milwaukee's East Side; wearing the company's tall bearskin hat stretched his modest five-foot-seven-inch height, and the natty gray uniform, scrubbed white belts, patent leather accoutrements, and brass and silver adornments enhanced his upright bearing. Married and a bookkeeper at an insurance firm, Hibbard, in 1861, had led many in that militia company to enlist in the 5th Wisconsin Infantry, a regiment that saw hard fighting in McClellan's Peninsula campaign. Now twenty-three years old, "Lish" used his experience, influence, and connections to complete a company with 100 men; he was the first to fill his roll, and the company would be designated A, the first of ten. He would win substantial promotion in the new regiment, and lead it in one of its bloodiest fights. Several soldiers in the regiment remembered him as a martinet, however, and applauded his eventual departure from the regiment in the new year.[25]

Charley King also noted men of more common stock, men who would fill the ranks, march long, and fight hard. One was Maine-born George Merrick, whom King recalled in a mixed metaphor as "a little red-headed terrier" and "quick as a cat." But hazel-eyed Merrick, a diminutive man whose stature just reached the Federal army minimum, was not quick enough to avoid being badly shot up the final day of 1862. To his veteran friends' amazement, Merrick, a nineteen-year-old store clerk when he joined, would be discharged and returned to Milwaukee "to live for many a year a wonder to his people" because he survived such grievous wounds.[26]

As the drums of recruiting reached a staccato beat, the good offices of Milwaukee's women were sought. They should, one news writer averred, lend their sanction to the recruiting effort. "Even the ladies can help to fill up the regiments. They must evince an interest in it, give the preference to the young men who serve their country, and throw no obstacles in the way of husbands, brothers, lovers volunteering." Affairs of the heart and matters of war, as schoolboy Amandus Silsby could attest, were to be coupled.[27]

Then there was this offer, no more than a nod toward feminine equality, at least as a temporary measure. A Congregational minister from a parish east of the river suggested permitting "young ladies" to take the places of all the clerks who enlisted. Magnanimously, he proposed that the female workers be paid half of the men's salaries while the war continued. Of course, the women would be expected to resign as soon as the soldiers returned. The churchman guaranteed twenty-five clerks for enlistment if the arrangement could be made. There was no later report if the effort was successful.[28]

The feverish activity and rush to raise companies by hopeful officers prompted one local daily to caution that not all should be motivated by the desire to gain commissions. The majority, it was proposed, must enlist as common soldiers, to bear muskets, and follow orders. The choices were several: In addition to the Merchants Guard were the Angus Smith Guards, the Chamber of Commerce Guards, Milwaukee Cadets, Milwaukee Zouaves, and more than a dozen others. Few of these units would succeed in signing the requisite 100 men.

Named in honor of one of the city's prominent meat packers, the Plankinton Rangers were being organized by Duncan Reed, better known as "Cam." A man of mature years who lived in old Walker's Point south of the Menomonee River, he had served for a time as deputy U.S. marshal. In later years, after his ignominious war service ended, he was listed as an engineer.[29]

John Plankinton, a wealthy meat packer, offered $5 to the first ten men to enlist in the company that bore his name. Meanwhile, another wealthy man of commerce paid $5 to the next twenty signing. Riverius Elmore, who bore his uncle's unusual given name, worked with Reed to gather the company. Elmore's father, Samuel, and uncle were prominent coal and brick merchants in the city who had migrated from Connecticut. Captain Reed and Lieutenant Elmore, although they formed Company E, would not serve with distinction during their brief service in the new regiment.[30]

The effort to raise a company called the Rough and Readys, meanwhile, was proceeding apace. David Horning, who hoped for leadership of the outfit, had also marched with the old 1st Wisconsin, the three-month regiment. With all the competition for volunteers, he was unable to muster 100, and would merge his men with those of the Plankinton Rangers to form Company E of the new regiment. Horning would serve ably, earning promotion to captain and leading the company through the entire war.[31]

In Horning's company were a score of men from the town of Granville, a rural community north of Milwaukee. And among these were two friends, Datus Worth and James Harvey, both twenty-three-year-old single farmers who lived with their parents. Worth, whom friends called Date, was a stocky man of average height with narrow and wide-set dark brown eyes and thick sandy hair; he would write home regularly in the months to come, signing many letters with the phrase "your erring son." He and Harvey would become closer during the trial and travail of army life, remaining together until the final battle.

Simultaneously, Henry Gunnison named his new company after the country's highest-ranking officer, Maj. Gen. Henry Halleck. Gunnison had standing in the Irish community, having served with the Union Guard militia company; he was also a survivor of the tragic *Lady Elgin* sinking of two years before. But despite Gunnison's energy and zeal, the Halleck Guard, too, would number about fifty by midmonth. He would merge with the Barry Guards, named after the militia captain who died in the 1860 tragedy, being raised by Courtland Larkin, son of Milwaukee sheriff Charles Larkin. Court was remembered as a young man of somewhat a delicate nature.[32]

At the same time, Sam Philbrook, for five years foreman in the Milwaukee & Mississippi Railroad's roundhouse in the city, pressed the call for volunteers upon his fellow employees as well as with railroad men on other lines. The New Hampshire-born husband and father who eschewed his given name, Alvah, was organizing an outfit called the Mississippi Roughs. Broad-shouldered, handsome, and pleasant-faced, his hair was receding and he wore a full dark beard; he had turned thirty-two just three months before. Philbrook had the look of command about him. Decades later, his epitaph would read: "He never took a backward step." When he left Milwaukee, he would carry a small bag of gold "wishing to keep it for the purpose of relieving his wants if he should ever be taken prisoner," his wife, Caddie, said, "or if returned, to keep as a relic." Also in his possession was a cased gold pen and pencil set; to these he would add a handsome gold-enameled Masonic emblem, a gift of his wife when he returned to Milwaukee on furlough in 1863. Philbrook's daughter, Carrie, an only child, was seven at the time; she would revere her father's memory well into the next century.[33]

The company "will probably embody more bone and sinew than any in the state," boasted an admiring writer. "Railroad operatives are proverbially hardy, hard working, free and easy, big-hearted fellows, always lovers of fair-play, always terribly in earnest and, in this case, will always be ready to give and take the heaviest blows wielded." In time, the broad-shouldered, dark-bearded, handsome Philbrook would raise a contingent of over 150 men, some of whom were added to other companies. He would become captain.[34]

Assisting in the collection of Philbrook's contingent was another veteran of an earlier regiment, the 6th Wisconsin. In the late spring of 1861, Christian Nix, an immigrant from one of the Germanic states, joined Capt. Wilhelm Lindwurm's all-Teutonic Citizens' Corps, and marched away to war. He was twenty-four, married and residing in the Ninth Ward on the city's south side. A machinist by profession, he had earned sergeant's stripes. But, taking the opportunity to gain a promotion in a new regiment, he returned to his adopted city. Nix, with blue eyes and blond hair, would serve well as second lieutenant.[35]

One of the volunteers attracted to the railroad company was thirty-five-year-old Sam Chase, a "rollicking whole-souled fellow," as he was remembered afterward, who piloted historic locomotives in the 1850s. When the New England-born volunteer was given a commission as the regiment's quartermaster, his fellow workers presented him with a handsome sword, sash, and brace of revolvers. He would leave behind for posterity, with those accoutrements, a series of letters to his sisters in New Hampshire filled with evocative observations and pronouncements.[36]

Still another of Philbrook's men was Ed Glenn, whom the boys predictably called "Sandy" because of his ruddy complexion, auburn hair, and Scot heritage. He was but eighteen, and had been a railroad telegraph operator in western Wisconsin. Standing the average height of five feet seven, Glenn would be a stalwart soldier until he received two ghastly wounds while aiding a fallen general during one of the bloodiest battles of the war.[37]

Bill Kennedy.
"Thorough-going soldier."
FROM: MEMOIRS OF MILWAUKEE COUNTY.

The handsome, dark-eyed municipal court clerk, Bill Kennedy, was mounting a call in the poor Irish wards for men to join him. Like Philbrook, he was thirty-two, and said to be a "thorough-going soldier and a fine man." A dark six-footer with a broad, brushy mustache, Kennedy also had militia experience in the Garrett Barry's Union Guards. A Vermonter by birth, he had come close to losing his life two years earlier in the *Lady Elgin* steamboat tragedy; he had been spared only because he and his new bride, Margaret, entrained east from Chicago on their honeymoon while his brother had been drowned during the tragic voyage back to Milwaukee. One news writer said of handsome Bill Kennedy that "many of his countrymen are anxious to serve under him."[38]

Henry Bridge, simultaneously, was attempting to induce more prosperous Irish brethren west of the Milwaukee River into the Allen Light Guards. Thanks to his backers, Bridge offered $25 extra for the first recruit from the Second Ward. His effort, like several others, fell short of 100 names, and he shortly coalesced his men with those of Kennedy's to form Company G. Bill Kennedy, the man who had nearly lost his life in a steamboat disaster, would rise to high office for gallant service. Bridge's future in the regiment would be clouded.[39]

Among the recruits who signed the roll of Kennedy and Bridge was an eighteen-year-old clerk named Frank Hale. Of average height, the blue-eyed, dark-haired youth "was just merging into manhood, and possessed all the noble traits of character that make the man," a comrade would write of him in early January. "I recollect the time his enlistment papers were made out how fearful he was that he could not gain the consent of his parents, and also the joy that lit up his manly countenance after the consent was given." Despite his youth, Hale's "manly bearing and gentlemanly deportment" quickly gained the attention of his officers, and he was named fourth corporal. He would march off to war with the "hope and pride of his parents," only to fall "another victim of this most accursed of rebellions."[40]

Not to be outdone, the call for men of Germanic background led by another veteran of the 5th Wisconsin, Carl Von Baumbach, was underway. An immigrant of aristocratic background (denoted by the appellation "von") from Hesse, the twenty-two-year-old drug clerk had arrived in Milwaukee with his family in 1847; his father, Ludwig, had been named imperial consul to the German states. Carl, who would later Americanize his given name to Charles, carried scars in his arm and leg from wounds sustained in the battle of Williamsburg during McClellan's campaign to take Richmond that spring. While on recuperative furlough, the stolid five-foot-eight-inch officer had been offered a commission. He had been among the distinguished gallery of military officers at the Great War Meeting in July, and his fellow Teutonic immigrants were perhaps attracted by his bearing and looks.[41]

Justus Lauterbach, one of Von Baumbach's volunteers, had a harrowing tale to tell. The twenty-six-year-old from Hesse, "tall, straight and well proportioned," had come to America in 1856 to seek his fortune. A tailor unsuccessful in finding work in Wisconsin, he traveled down the Mississippi River, leaving his new wife and parents. While working on a contract for gray uniforms in Arkansas after the firing upon Fort Sumter, he had been conscripted into the state's 1st Infantry. When the regiment was scheduled to depart for Tennessee, he hid in the basement of his shop, and later, with partial payment for the uniforms in hand, gained passage on a Mississippi River steamer bound for the North. Undeterred by the experience of a year before, Lauterbach volunteered for Captain Von Baumbach's company and was named sergeant. He later said that he became Gen. Phil Sheridan's tailor while the famed Federal commander led a division in Tennessee. Lauterbach lived to tell many stories.[42]

In time, the Milwaukee Regiment's roster would list over 30 percent of its roll with Germanic names, immigrants and their sons. These men were drawn from Milwaukee and elsewhere, and most would be listed among Captain Von Baumbach's Company C.[43]

Recruiting activities among the immigrants of the German states, however, occasionally butted heads with resistance; to many, anything with the taint of the Republican Party, even war, was to be resisted. A few weeks earlier, a recruiting officer strolled into Schwarting's & Sitting's saloon on East Water Street, the teeming commercial district adjacent to the Milwaukee River. Here the new burghers of the "Deutsche-Athen" quaffed their beer and "Rhinish wine." A man strolled into the saloon, and espying the recruiting officer's military uniform, "fell to using all the uprobious [sic] epithets he could find," reported the news man who recorded the scene. He called all recruiting officers rascals, and said they ought to be "hung," warning customers to have nothing to do with the man.

"The officer stood this as long as human nature was capable; he then got up and gave the fellow a straight-out thrashing, which he certainly deserved," cheered the Republican-oriented writer. The news man went a step further, suggesting that publications like the German-language *See-Bote* and kindred sheets (he meant the Democrat paper, the *Daily News,* of course) were conspiring to discourage volunteers from coming forward to do their duty. There was no report whether any men in the saloon subsequently volunteered.[44]

Then there was at least one blatant appeal to nativism printed by the Republican *Milwaukee Sentinel: "Ye Americans!!"* it admonished, "don't permit the foreign population to surpass you in patriotism. *Ye native-born citizens!!* leave not to foreign hands the duty you owe your native land. *Ye Yankees!!* your country calls." The appeal got results: In time that company would boast a predominance of English, Scot, and Welsh surnames. In all, the new regiment would list over half of its men with British backgrounds.[45]

Appeals were also made to the city for contributions to the War Fund, money that would be used to aid the families of those soldiers of common means while they went to war. Thousands of dollars were raised from the moneyed ranks, but even citizens of modest circumstances contributed what they could. A volunteer in the Irish Allen Guard, for example, a drayman by profession, said he would sell his horse and rig, and with the proceeds support his own family. A man named James Crummey immediately gathered 100 "subscribers" at $2 each to enter a drawing for the horse and vehicle. The winner was a prominent lawyer, James Mitchell (no relation to Lieutenant Mitchell);

and an impromptu deputation accompanied the animal and dray to his home, prepared for patriotic speechifying. Mitchell, however, waved it off, donating the animal and dray to the war fund.

At least once levity attended the fund-raising. In the Ninth Ward resided a group of Dutch immigrants, whom the news writer called "Hollanders." They had raised what was described as a handsome sum for the war fund. A poor neighbor, unable to donate money, offered his cow and calf. Led by lawyer John Rooney, the animals were herded to the main post office, and an auction began.

When Rooney coaxed bids to $10, he stopped proceedings and instructed a band to play "Yankee Doodle." Then the offers rose to $20 or $30. The musicians thereafter struck up "Hail Columbia!" The bids jumped to $40. Then Rooney announced that the winning bidder would have the cow and calf accompanied to his home by the band. A man immediately offered $50. Then it was related that the fellow lived in Sheboygan, some sixty miles north. So the animals were sold to a local resident for $42.[46]

"For the past three days Milwaukee seemed one vast camp," stated the Democratic daily near the middle of August, "in which nothing could be seen but knots and groups of men on corners and in the streets, and nothing heard but the shrill notes of the fife, and the heavy thud and thunder of bass and kettle drums."[47]

As the rolls of volunteers lengthened, it became apparent that Milwaukee's native and adopted sons might compose nearly all of the new regiment. But the vexing head of politics once again intruded—for politics was inextricably entwined with the day's military affairs. Why not, it was asked in some circles, insure that the police chief, Herman Page, become the unit's commander? He was a city man, after all, as were the majority of recruits, while Colonel Larrabee was from another part of the state entirely. Perhaps apprised of the rumblings from Milwaukee, Larrabee may have floated another idea. Rumor swept through the city, agreeable to many, that the colonel might lead another regiment, one recruited from the counties north of Milwaukee encompassing his former congressional district. That would leave the city's men for Page to command. Silver eagles perched on his shoulder straps, Page might yet win command, it was supposed.

Within a few days, however, Larrabee announced that he would remain colonel of the Milwaukee unit. He told the press that he was "proud of the officers and men. . . . He considers it as good material as any regiment." The recruiting efforts of the past few weeks had brought him to the city regularly, and "he counts himself a Milwaukeean, if not in residence at least in sympathy with the gallant men and patriotic citizens who are determined that Milwaukee shall contribute a Milwaukee regiment to the army of the Union."[48]

For a week tension over the leadership of the new regiment was almost palpable in Milwaukee political circles. Then the city stiffened a bit when Lieutenant Colonel Page resigned. "[I]t is unnecessary to state [the reasons], as they are well understood by the public. It is a serious loss to the community," one daily sputtered on its front page. "Mr. Page is universally regarded as possessed of as great sagacity and executive ability as almost any one in the State, while at the same time he would reflect dignity and character upon a body of troops of which he might have command. We hope to see him honored with the Colonelcy of some other regiment."[49]

A Republican daily noted that Page "had labored zealously, and we may add most effectively and successfully, to get up the regiment." The resignation was tendered to the governor "for reasons which to him [Page] were imperative. The public very generally will regret the complication of affairs that led Col. Page to this step." The Democratic daily presented no headline in the aftermath of Page's decision; only a small, three-line story noted that "Page of 'The Badger Regiment' sent his resignation to Madison Wednesday." The matter was closed. Page never sought military office again.[50]

Finally on August 18, it was proclaimed that about a thousand men had enlisted. The new regiment was designated the state's 24th Infantry.[51]

Within a week, shocking preliminary news filtered into Milwaukee of another military disaster for the Union army at Bull's Run; it was the second time that the rebel forces drove the Federals from that field. Soldier families steeled themselves for another wave of casualty lists. In time, the extent of the second Federal defeat in northern Virginia hung in heavy, black print on the front pages of the city dailies. There was renewed urgency to call the Milwaukee men into camp.

Chapter 3

Camp Sigel

⚊⚌⚎⚌⚊

"Undisciplined, undrilled and unseasoned."

The volunteers passed but a few weeks in the Milwaukee camp, and those days were hectic and event-filled. In a hurried fashion, the new officers with experience in the other regiments or the militia imparted their knowledge of drill, and attempted to introduce some rudiment of military discipline, largely without success. It was essential, in the Napoleonic dictates for warfare, that soldiers become practiced in long linear formations, moving from marching columns to a double-ranked battle line so musket fire could be delivered upon the enemy with devastating effect. There were formations and maneuvers for battalions, companies, and for the regiment. The raw volunteers needed to become acquainted with the many movements of the rifle-musket, the nearly four-foot-long, heavy gun that would soon become their most intimate companion. There would not be enough time, however, to complete the transformation from civilian to soldier.

Just about the time the new 24th Wisconsin was called into camp, startling news from the Minnesota frontier splashed across the dailies. "Sioux Indians Slaughtering Whites," blared a headline. "Indian Massacres." "Frontier Desolated." "Shocking Barbarities." Within days, lurid rumors of massacres swept from the North to the city. Hundreds of white settlers were murdered, it was said, and Wisconsin's native population was restless. Many white settlers fled from the state's northern

Camp Sigel.
"Invaded by the fair sex."
COURTESY OF THE MILWAUKEE COUNTY HISTORICAL SOCIETY.

fringes into cities and towns for protection. Why, the new Milwaukee soldiers might be sent north to fight Indians. But within several days, the situation was calmed and fears subsided.[1]

The 24th Wisconsin, unlike many of the early regiments, was not called to Madison, the state capital, into the sprawling training ground of Camp Randall. At first the regiment was to report to Camp Washburn, situated a considerable distance west of Milwaukee's business district on a site previously used as a trotting horse racetrack. "This selection is distasteful to most of the officers. It is too far away, too secluded, &c," caviled one news man.

Ultimately, the new regiment was ordered to assemble on the East Side of Milwaukee about a mile north of the central business district. Here was carved out several square acres for a training ground named after one of the war's early heroes, Franz Sigel, the Germanic immigrant general popular among Milwaukee's burghers. Camp Sigel was a short distance from the bluffs of Lake Michigan. "It lies on a high table land between the lake and the [Milwaukee] river. It is dry and healthy." To read the local press of the day, it was an almost idyllic spot. A dozen single-story wooden barracks bordered the hard-packed parade ground at the camp. A kitchen, guardhouse, and commanding officer's quarters also dotted the site.[2]

Men from beyond the city's environs who volunteered for the 24th Wisconsin began traveling to "the city of beer and pale bricks"—a description used by a young soldier in an earlier regiment. Within days, the thousand men were assembled into the ten companies. And officers who had not raised companies were assigned to new posts. An arrangement had been struck just days before between the sheriff's tender son, Court Larkin, and Henry Gunnison. They agreed to merge the former's Barry Guards into the Halleck Guards and form Company H. Gunnison, a thirty-six-year-old lawyer, became captain, and Larkin, the eighteen-year-old student son of the sheriff, gained a lieutenancy. Thirty-three men from the Lake Michigan town of Port Washington and nearby communities recruited by Gus Goldsmith were also merged into the ranks of the company; he was named lieutenant. Neither Gunnison nor Larkin, however, would serve long in the 24th Wisconsin. Goldsmith, the twenty-three-year-old immigrant machinist, would soon step forward to estimably lead the company.[3]

Also traveling to Milwaukee with the volunteers from Port Washington was a Catholic priest named Franz Fusseder, prepared to provide religious sustenance to the soldiers. The regimental chaplain was an immigrant from Austria, and the first graduate of the new Saint Francis Seminary on Milwaukee's southern fringe. The thirty-six-year-old blue-eyed clergyman became quite popular with the men as much for his card-playing as for his fractured way with the English language. Serving as chief surgeon was an immigrant from Saxony, Herman Hasse. He had arrived in Milwaukee as a youth seventeen years before, studied medicine in St. Louis, then returned to serve briefly in the all-German 9th Wisconsin Infantry. He would become a respected army surgeon who served until war's end, patching together numerous wounds, severing shattered limbs, and pronouncing many dead.[4]

The Milwaukee Regiment's new lieutenant colonel, replacing Herman Page, was Ed Buttrick, a prominent lawyer and friend of Howard Greene's who lived in the south side community of Oak Creek. At thirty-eight, he was among the older men in the regiment, and his appointment "is a general gratification to the friends of the regiment," said the city's Democratic daily. Buttrick would not long serve with the 24th Wisconsin as tension would soon develop between him and Colonel Larrabee. But the lieutenant colonel would be remembered for his attention to discipline and for his cordial manner as well.[5]

Meanwhile, imperious Lish Hibbard, as expected, was promoted to the rank of major in the regiment. He cut as fine a figure in his new uniform as he had before in the ostentatious militia outfit. With his experience and service in the 5th Wisconsin, he would be a leader in shaping the men into soldiers. Hibbard's former company, A, was now commanded by Richard Austin, a twenty-one-year-old bookkeeper who, like Chivas, stood over six feet tall. In addition to Colonel Larrabee and Major Hibbard, the new unit boasted several more men with prior military experience, most from the 5th Wisconsin. In all, more than a half-dozen officers had been blooded in battle before.

Among them was Tom Balding, a Milwaukee bookkeeper, who had, with Colonel Larrabee, seen action in the Peninsula campaign in McClellan's Army of the Potomac. A sergeant, he had been sent to Milwaukee during the summer on recruiting duty; offered a commission as lieutenant in a new regiment, the twenty-five-year-old became a member of the 24th. Thirty years later, Charley King, who remembered him as a "little cus of a Captain," would write about the time in Virginia when Balding, who immigrated from London in 1849, nearly "jammed a bayonet through me, confound him, the night the sudden orders came for our brigade to cross the Potomac, and I was rushing 'cross sentry post to beat the long roll and forgot the countersign. There was no fooling with him when he was sergeant of the guard." That kind of determination would be needed from Balding on bloody fields in Kentucky, Tennessee, and Georgia. He would serve ably in Company A, taking a gory wound at Missionary Ridge, winning commendation and rising to a captaincy. Balding, "Old Captain B" one old soldier would call him, also provided encouragement for the youthful adjutant of the regiment. Norm Burdick, a corporal in Balding's company, said that his captain "endeared himself to both officers and men, by his attention to the drill and discipline of the regiment;" he had a "ready smile" and always acknowledged salutes from subordinates.[6]

Burdick, a volunteer in the Young Men's Association Tigers, was a man of many parts. One of the many New York-born volunteers, he was twenty-six, and his narrow face was set off with spectacles; sometime during the next several months, he adorned his chin with a bushy vandyked beard. He had become a respected printer in Milwaukee since migrating to the city in 1852; it was a profession in which he would become well known after the war. A writer of accomplishment, Burdick would send dispatches to the Republican *Sentinel,* until a fateful final day in the year. He would also consume many hours writing to his sweetheart, the lawyer James Mitchell's daughter, Anna; they would be married in two years.[7]

The captain of Company K, Orlando Ellsworth was, at forty-nine, the oldest man in the new regiment. From the town of Lake south of the city, he had convinced sixty men from his community to sign the roll. The military career of the married farmer would be brief, however, end-

Jim Bacon (post-war).
Toothless private.
COURTESY OF THE MILWAUKEE COUNTY
HISTORICAL SOCIETY.

ing abruptly after a bloody battle in Tennessee on New Year's Eve. Then, steady Ed Parsons would be the company's anchor.[8]

On the roll in the all-Irish Company G raised by Henry Bridge, who was captain, and Bill Kennedy, its lieutenant, was a young man from Prairie du Chien, John Plummer. From a family of seven English-born sons, John had followed his brothers to Milwaukee, and clerked for a few years. All of the Plummer boys would serve in Wisconsin regiments; two of his older siblings had enlisted in the 6th Wisconsin, and were almost at that moment experiencing their first taste of battle in Virginia. John, twenty-one, had the willowy bearing of the family: Unmarried, as were most men in the 24th Wisconsin, he stood over six feet tall, and his face bore light coloration with blue eyes and fair hair; there were likely still traces of an English accent in his speech. He would in time become his company's captain, and, like nearly every officer in the regiment, sustain a grievous wound.[9]

Company G's roster listed a private, Jim Bacon, who had reason to fear he might not pass even the cursory physical examination. His mouth was bereft of teeth. Federal regulations required that any soldier needed to bite the end off paper cartridges to load his musket. A clerk by profession, twenty-one-year-old Bacon's five-foot-ten-inch height topped by auburn hair made him readily discernable in the ranks. But within a few days, he would be relieved: He was accepted into the regiment. The examining physician had failed to "put a finger in my mouth" to discern the dearth of his dentition. Many years later, Bacon, likely with a full set of store-bought teeth, would be active in the local veterans' organization; he would also amuse his middle-aged comrades about a confrontation he had with the colonel.

Private Bacon would also recall that he was not what was known as a thoroughgoing soldier, and his captain, Bridge, often became exasperated with his behavior. "I have known him to raise his sword over me," for some infraction, "and then put it back where it belonged, stainless. Now days we would call that kind of move a 'bluff.' He got mad at me for telling him the truth before he had been in service thirty days, and ever afterwards, as the old saying goes, I got it in the neck when he could give it to me." Bacon never revealed the exact cause of the dispute with his commanding officer. And Captain Bridge would not long lead the company.[10]

The Merchants Guards, those pillars of Anglican rectitude organized by Captain Root and Lieutenants Chivas and Mitchell, were sworn in and designated Company I. Each man received his $27 bounty. "This will prove no kid glove, silk stocking company, but one made up of bone and muscle and equal to the rough-and-tumble experiences of camp life," boasted one news man. "It was complimented by nearly all who noticed it, as being as good as any, if not the best company ever raised in the city. As an evidence, not a man was rejected of the whole number, and but one questioned concerning his age," observed a newspaperman.[11]

As expected, the officer who likely attracted the most attention was the smooth-cheeked adjutant of the regiment. He appeared more a drummer boy than a real soldier. Arthur McArthur's youthful good looks and slender frame evinced no portent of future glory. But the gray-eyed youth's neatly tailored uniform bespoke of money. He strutted about the camp above Lake Michigan, and if he was not careful, the scabbard to his saber dragged in the dirt behind him. There may have been back rank muttering about the political influence that had gained this boy lieutenant's straps. The colonel, too, was certainly not pleased.

Jerry Watrous, the 6th Wisconsin veteran whose life after the war was largely spent tending the flame of soldier lore, wrote much about the little soldier's life. Larrabee, "pompous" to Watrous's pen, declared Lieutenant McArthur too young. "I shall ask the Governor to give me a *man* for Adjutant . . . a qualified man, sir." A "hot telegram" was sent to Governor Salomon's office in Madison, and a two-word reply returned:

"Try him." Larrabee had no choice, but, by god, he would make it difficult for this stripling. Watrous's pen would always improve upon the
facts.[12]

There were other volunteers, too, common men who would march
and fight with the regiment for three years and into scores of bloody
battles. Forming in the ranks of Company B, the Young Men's Association Tigers, was Art Gilbert, a "military tenderfoot." A bookkeeper, he
was only seventeen, but the roster listed his age as eighteen. In his only
battle just a month ahead, the youth would fight in unusual footwear.
Also in Company B was Gene Comstock, the young man who had witnessed the hanging of a freed black man in Milwaukee two years
before. A nineteen-year-old printer now, he had, like many in the regiment, exhibited an interest in literature and drama.[13]

One of several pairs of brothers on the Company B roll was Mil-
waukee-born Harry and Charley Rogers. At five feet ten inches tall, both
were above average height and had the same gray eyes. Their father,
James Rogers, one of the earliest Easterners to settle in the city, was
now one of the wealthiest men in the state. The older brother, twenty-
one-year-old Harry, a farmer, had been made a corporal. Charley, a
nineteen-year-old bookkeeper, had enlisted in the 15th Wisconsin
Infantry, the unit raised largely among Wisconsin's Scandinavian immigrants in January; when the Milwaukee Regiment was announced that
summer, however, Charley gained a lieutenancy and joined his brother.
Neither Rogers was married, and they would earn commendations and
promotion through arduous service. What was more, Harry's ghastly
scars would mark him as a veteran long after the war.[14]

Meanwhile, in Company D, Sam Philbrook's railroaders, stood a
man of mature years who had traveled from the western Wisconsin
town of Lone Rock. Thirty-two-year-old Jim Hazell, a husband, father,
and railroad engineer, stood five feet ten inches tall. The gray-eyed private would be the regiment's first casualty, felled but a month later.[15]

If the regiment was to gain laureates, one was twenty-three-year-old
Tom Ford, the blue-eyed, copper-haired Irish immigrant and farmer
from Franklin, a community southwest of Milwaukee. With his brother
Dan, two years older, he enlisted in Captain Gunnison's Company H. A
third brother, meanwhile, marched in the 2nd Massachusetts, and the
father served in Bridges Battery of Illinois Artillery. Tom and Dan, both
of medium height, would march and fight for three years, and Tom, late
in his life, would publish a small collection of war stories; what he
lacked in grammar and syntax was more than compensated in the scores

of sometimes humorous episodes he described, one of which involved wearing a flaming red shirt in battle. But there would be a dark side to his writings, too, and many details were gruesome and caustic.[16]

One of the older privates in the ranks was Noel Brooks; known by his middle name, Byron, the boys in Company K called him "Elder." The gray-eyed, black-haired new soldier was said to be somewhat peculiar. Although reputed to be one of the best mechanics in Milwaukee, the thirty-four-year-old was an idiosyncratic bachelor. Before enlisting, it was rumored, he bought a coffin, "paid for it, and took a receipt." Of average height, the mature volunteer also procured a burial plot in a Milwaukee cemetery, and in his organized manner retained that receipt, too. "Thus he had prepared for himself a respectable internment." Within only a few months, those preparations would be needed.[17]

Impressionable Amandus Silsby, the schoolboy son of an itinerant preacher, meanwhile, had said good-byes to his guardians, the Bentons; school friends, and relatives with whom he lived in Prairie du Sac, some 100 miles west of Milwaukee. Likely, the seventeen-year-old's personal effects did not amount to more than a small gripsack. How he had explained it all to his father, this decision to join the rough and rude ranks of soldiers, and march off to war, is unknown. Afterward, the father would say it was for the cause of abolition. Now Silsby tramped about on the Lake Michigan bluff, trying to learn the ways of the army as a private in Capt. Richard Austin's Company A.

Also traveling to Milwaukee was a large group of men from western Wisconsin. Among them were George Cooley; his older brother, Homer; and a friend, Isaac Storey, called Milt, who lived near the Mississippi River. The Cooleys, both printers, were twenty-six and thirty respectively; Storey was a New York-born clerk. They were among about twenty men from that part of the state who volunteered; ultimately they composed one fifth of Company A. Only two months before, George Cooley's wife, Addy, died; "my darling left me to meet with the many loved ones who have gone before," he wrote. What part her death played in his motivation to enlist is unknown. The following year, Cooley would begin a diary of his war experiences, detailing miles marched and weather that affected the Wisconsin soldiers; he would sadly mark the anniversary of Addy's demise in those pages. Another of those who had come east was a thirty-nine-year-old Pennsylvania-born husband and father from Grant County in western Wisconsin. With a square jaw, intense gray eyes, and a sun-burnished dark complexion, William Gill came forward to collect the bonus offered to

William Gill.
An early death.
COURTESY OF THE NEVILLE
HISTORICAL MUSEUM.

volunteers. He soon posed for a likeness in his natty new uniform, and sent it home to his wife. He would not see battle, but despite his robust character, Gill would never return home again, becoming one of the regiment's early victims of disease.[18]

Henry Drake was another of the Walker's Point men in Captain Austin's company. The twenty-one-year-old soldier had immigrated from New York with his family eleven years before. With his brother, John, he had entered the retail drug trade in 1859. Single and of average height, he was soon named first sergeant; and before the new year was a month old, he would gain a lieutenancy. Drake would regularly write candid letters to his brother of his experiences with other young men from the Point. They would tent and mess together until death and wounds decimated their ranks.[19]

Camp Sigel quickly began taking on the trappings of a real training ground despite its location. It was not far north of the expanding residential neighborhood called Yankee Hill where many Easterners had constructed imposing mansions in the ornate architectural styles of the day. Judge McArthur's Second Empire home was even then under construction. The parents and families of these wellborn new soldiers as well as people of more common circumstance could readily observe the daily goings on. Conveniently, a horse-drawn street railway line coursed along the aptly named Prospect Avenue in front of the camp.

Spectators of low station easily visited the new soldiers, unimpeded by fences, gates, or guards with muskets. They crowded upon the wooden sidewalks to watch the military evolutions.

Local news writers were attentive to the "young men [who were] accustomed to the luxuries of good homes and their attachments to these luxuries cling to them wherever they go. They have relinquished good and lucrative situations in business where they were receiving" $10–$20 weekly.[20]

Sometime before August 27, military coats and trousers were distributed to the volunteers. Unlike the gray jackets, trousers, and caps issued by the state to the earlier regiments, the 24th found itself in standard blue Federal issue of the day. The outfit (many called it a "suit") consisted of a long, nearly knee-length, nine-button coat of dark wool with a stand-up collar, and light blue piping along collar and cuffs; to this was added full-cut blue wool trousers of a lighter shade. And the issue was topped with a jaunty little cap based upon a French design that later came to be called a kepi. The men were also given underdrawers, shirts, and stockings, and black, rough-leather infantry bootees whose tops reached the ankles. Finally, a long and heavy wool great- or overcoat of light blue was also issued.

The privates, corporals, and sergeants were also issued accoutrements that consisted of a black leather waist belt and oval brass buckle stamped with the letters "U.S." and a leather cartridge box or bullet pouch, complete with the same brass "U.S." emblem. The box or pouch was carried on the right hip, suspended from the left shoulder with a strap; this, too, featured a round brass emblem embossed with an eagle that perched at breast height. A small leather box attached to the waist belt carried percussion caps for the musket. The issue also included a tarred bag, the haversack, that hung from the shoulder on the soldier's left side, and a strapped, tin canteen covered in blue wool cloth. Finally, a square black knapsack was given to each man; strapped to the back, it carried extra clothing and personal articles. By degrees as these components were issued, the volunteers began to take on at least the outward appearance of soldiers, and many admired themselves. A once motley collection of individuals was being transformed into a largely undifferentiated aggregation. Although they looked the part to family and admirers, the Milwaukee men were not yet ready for battle.[21]

Later, the formality of that dress would succumb to field service. Shorter, four-button blouses were worn. In time, too, when the men became soldiers, the caps would give way to black felt, broad-brimmed hats that assumed the particular configuration determined by the wearer; these would become the attire of choice for the 24th Wisconsin and the armies of the West.

Slowly, or so it seemed to the men of the new regiment, matters were being pulled together. The clerks and merchants, farmers and railroad men, the well- and the baseborn, immigrant and native-born were pulled and pushed, shouted at and fussed over in the attempt to shape the companies and the regiment into some semblance of military organization.

Little written about these early days of the Milwaukee Regiment seems to have survived. Spare correspondence may have been penned, as the majority of the new soldiers lived in the city. Even the news sheets of the day printed no more than a few columns about the events at Camp Sigel. Most of the ink of those weeks was expended on the disturbing aftermath of another battle at Bull Run, Virginia—the casualty lists and official accounts of the latest Federal disaster. But twenty years later, a middle-aged veteran of the 24th Wisconsin, John Mitchell somewhat archly looked back on those days at Camp Sigel.

"A few times during our stay, the companies came together, through some tactical attraction of cohesion, for regimental drill," he said. "By dint of jerking the men out in front, and pushing them up in the rear, we managed to present a wavering line to the throng of admiring spectators. One gentleman told me that he had never met the Southerners in the field, but, to use his expression, 'he had encountered them in the "duello,"' and they were formidable fellows. I had a suspicion of that myself. To be forearmed, I bought a copy of 'Jomini on War' and a six-shooter. Both of them, by the way, peacefully reposed in my valise until my return [to Milwaukee]."[22]

The men of the Milwaukee Regiment had insufficient time to learn the "School of the Soldier," as it was called. *Hardee's Infantry Tactics* and *Casey's Tactics* were among the several prevailing military manuals of the day. They prescribed precise movements of men in columns and lines of battle. There were prescriptions for cadences such as "Common Time," "Quick Time," and "Double Time." It was all very confusing to most of these farmers, shopkeepers, railroad workers, and bookkeepers. While the late summer breezes off Lake Michigan wafted over Camp Sigel, the men sweated in their woolens and tried to "mind the step" commanded by their captains and lieutenants. They began to learn to march in the elbow-to-elbow manner described—a means to maintain alignment when marching in columns or in line of battle. But

Arthur McArthur.
Seventeen-year-old adjutant.
COURTESY OF THE MILWAUKEE PUBLIC LIBRARY.

most lessons of war would have to be learned on the deadly training ground of battle. Over all the activity, dark Colonel Larrabee glowered. And his waiflike adjutant scurried about compiling rosters and reports.

The Milwaukee Regiment's first dress parade was scheduled for Wednesday, August 27. Most of the ten companies were in uniform but they had no muskets; yet "it required but a brief survey to convince the least observant that it is a regiment of superb military material," trumpeted a news writer. These are not the Boys of '61, he wrote, "but the men in the middle of life, who go into the army with the determination to finish up this rebellion." They preferred tents, but unfortunately these were taken from the regiment to be sent to Minnesota where the army was attempting to quell the Indian uprising. "In warm weather[,] barracks are unpleasantly close," was the complaint. There was inequality in all of this since the officers who lived in the city were permitted to quit the noisome surroundings and journey home most evenings. Those from other locales and the men in the ranks had no choice but to eat the plate that was set, and hunker down in cramped quarters.[23]

Smooth-cheeked McArthur was to be put to his first public test. It was said that 15,000 Milwaukee citizens flocked to Camp Sigel that late summer afternoon to witness the grand event—a dress parade. The slight young man in his trim uniform stepped before the drawn-up ranks of a thousand new soldiers. Colonel Larrabee still fumed menacingly over the youngster's appointment as the Milwaukee Regiment's adjutant, and fussed still about his inability to convince the governor to remove him. The boy-soldier, not yet a hundred pounds, retained that irritating, squeaky voice of youth. Jerry Watrous, the old Iron Brigade veteran who always seemed to romance facts a bit, portrayed the scene at Camp Sigel that late summer day in 1862:

As adjutant, McArthur was responsible for bringing the ten companies to attention, and taking roll reports from the captains. A little cap perched atop his thick shock of dark curls and uniform hugging his spare frame, he turned on his heels.

"Attention, battalion!" his small voice quailed.

"Shoulder arms!" he shouted in his high, cracking voice. (On this detail, the latter-day chronicler was wrong: Muskets were not issued until days after the dress parade.) But only the three nearest companies heard the order, and obeyed; and only a few hundred men lurched forward, the remainder remained stock-still. There may have been a murmur from the crowd. It is likely that the portly father in a black suit, Judge McArthur, observed, disconcerted by his small son's detractors.

Then, Arthur, face probably flushed, completed the task of preparing the regiment for inspection. His ceremonial sword tucked into his right shoulder, he extended his legs into long, manly strides; the metal scabbard dragged in the dust behind. At the center of the double-ranked formation, the little lieutenant came to a halt, preparing to make a facing movement toward Colonel Larrabee. But his feet tangled with the scabbard. Laughter and guffaws erupted from the ranks and titters rippled through the spectators. News writers of the day, however, failed to report such details, satisfied to tell readers that the men "went through the evolutions with a surprising proficiency."[24]

More miscues followed during the march past the colonel and his staff. Larrabee was nearly scarlet with rage until, mercifully, the 24th was finally dismissed. It was all so embarrassing for the regiment. Colonel Larrabee let his officers know he would try again to shed the "white-faced, chicken-voiced boy" from the regiment's roll. That was how Watrous related it late in the century, and family legend passed it down fifty years later.[25]

That Larrabee was unsuccessful in his attempt to rid the unit of the little lieutenant would, ironically, augur well for the Milwaukee Regiment; in little more than a few months, the adjutant would begin to exhibit his almost fearless élan in battle; and in little more than a year, when Larrabee had long quit the regiment's ranks, young McArthur would earn undying fame. He would ultimately command the 24th Wisconsin, gaining the rank of lieutenant colonel. Only the depleted size of the regiment prevented him from sewing silver eagles on his shoulders—although to many he would become the "Boy Colonel of the West," the youngest man to hold such a rank in the Union armies, it was claimed.

But it was not the endless marching and drill that the men remembered from those days at Camp Sigel in 1862. The quality of the daily fare was a topic of recollection by some for almost thirty years. The men were critical of the army's culinary offerings; "the quality of the meat is neither healthy nor palatable," a daily news sheet caviled. "[T]heir officers will doubtless reform [the grousing about better fare]." Those complaints about what the army provided for its soldiers would never cease however.[26]

Bookkeeper Charley Swan—a comrade called him the "dilletani of Company B"—was a twenty-three-year-old sergeant at the time, and he quickly became disgusted with army bacon, "a specimen of which he attempted to cook without first tying it into the frying pan." The bacon absconded, said one camp wag, but Swan "at last secured [it] by strategy and led it to the colonel's headquarters to remonstrate." After listening to the complaint, Colonel Larrabee "cheered him by the remark that he would feel satisfied before he got through with the campaign if he didn't have to log-chain his ration to hold it from running away with a couple mules." Sergeant Swan, tall and straight, would fight in two battles before being wounded, captured, and imprisoned. He would be discharged because of disability.[27]

Thus, the 24th Wisconsin was hastily trained, and some semblance of military regimen imparted to the volunteers. Pursuing facts overlooked by local news men, a Kentucky writer a month later conducted a census of occupations in the Milwaukee Regiment, which "embraces in its ranks almost every known trade, profession, and employment." He counted:

Railroad employees, embracing machinists, engineers, conductors, car-builders, track-layers, brakemen, and superintendents 156, merchants, clerks and bookkeepers, 100, printers, 37, carpenters, joiners, and builders, 22, farmers, 196, tailors 20, laborers 47, shoemakers 29, blacksmiths 19, coopers 16, mechanics 5, bakers 3, tinsmiths 12, harness makers and saddlers, 5, watchmakers 2, painters 11, butchers 13, druggists 8, wagoners

22, masons 11, telegraph operators 2, gunsmiths 1, veterinary surgeon 1, lawyers 7, carriage makers 5, cooper smith 1. In addition . . . are tanners, bleachers, distillers, stone-cutters, bankers, upholsterers, calkers [*sic*], pump makers, plumbers, cabinet makers, confectioners, glove makers, brick makers, lithographers, musicians, school teachers, gas fitters, &c.

He said that the field and staff offices were "practical business men." Among them were "machinists, fresh from the workshops of Wisconsin, with capacity to command a company or build a locomotive."[28]

Finally, sometime after August 28 the shipment of rifle-muskets was trundled up Prospect Avenue above the lake into Camp Sigel. Sent by rail from the state armory in Madison, horses and drays transported the fifty rough-hewn crates, each packed with twenty muskets, from the depot to the training ground. Excitement mounted as five containers were carted to each company captain for issue to his men.

"The rifles are an excellent article, of Austrian manufacture," a news writer said. They were bulky, of .58 caliber, and were said to easily carry an ounce of lead a thousand yards. "They lack the exterior finish of the Springfield rifle, but are equally as well made otherwise," noted a local news man. These Austrian-made imports lacked the fine feel of good firearms: The stocks were of pale beech wood, and the fit of metal to wood did not suit men who were accustomed to well-made guns.

There was some grumbling, as the Massachusetts-made Springfield muskets or the fine British-manufactured Enfields were the guns of choice in the Federal armies. The foreign guns issued to the 24th, like the ones handed to some earlier Wisconsin regiments, were another matter. Measuring nearly fifty-four inches long and weighing nine and a half pounds, the guns featured a calibrated rear sight. The men of the 24th were also issued the companion triangular socket bayonet that clamped over the muzzle. Colonel Larrabee took pains to allay fears that the homely foreign muskets would not be adequate to the business of war. Such muskets had been carried by his old regiment, the 5th Wisconsin, he enjoined; and after a few engagements "secesh" prisoners had "paid these guns a high compliment, by saying they 'didn't know before that the Wisconsin Fifth was a regiment of sharp-shooters, or that their guns would kill at one thousand yards.'"[29]

Soon the soldiers began to learn the sometimes complicated process of hefting over four feet of rifle-musket. "Shoulder arms." "Right shoulder shift." "Present arms." These were commands that reverberated from

Camp Sigel's parade ground for days after the muskets were issued; it took uncounted and tedious hours to maneuver the guns in anything like required unison. No musket balls (technically, it was a conical-shaped bullet called the minié) or black powder were issued, however, and the practice of "Loading in nine counts" was yet to be learned. The procedure was vital for loading and firing the long, bulky gun to insure that massed fire could be delivered upon the enemy in a rapid manner.

On the final day of August, shortly before the Milwaukee Regiment was to leave the city for war, the soldier who used the sobriquet "Musket" provided the *Milwaukee Sentinel* with a description of the seemingly idyllic life at Camp Sigel. Corporal Burdick, the bespectacled printer, called his observations "Rough Notes of Camp Life":

> The camp experience had been very pleasant, and was rendered particularly so by the kind attention of our Milwaukee friends, who seem determined . . . to kill the boys of the 'Bully Twenty-Fourth' with kindness and sweetmeats, which go far to mitigate the fall from homes of ease and luxury to the rough fare of the soldier who fight for Uncle Sam, God and his country.

In the months ahead, Milwaukee readers quickly discerned the identity of "Musket" as he would fill columns about the experiences of his regiment in camp and in battle. Burdick of Company B would, with the war behind him, return to his printing trade, and help create the lore and legend of the Milwaukee Regiment.

Burdick's company, the Young Men's Association Tigers, drew particular attention from admiring citizens. In late August, he extended special thanks to James Heth, the confectioner, and his family for a "dinner of blackberry pie, cheese, &c." given to Company B. "Their memory will be cherished by us, as long as blackberries grow and cows continue to 'give down' the cheese-producing fluid." The colonel and his staff were given ice cream. The confectioner was, of course, taking care of his own: Two sons, twenty-nine-year-old Charles and twenty-year-old James, Jr., drilled in the ranks of the company. Both would survive the war and have many experiences to describe.

Only a day later a notice was published in the *Sentinel,* thanking the wife of Capt. Bill Eldred for the "very acceptable donation of soldier's needle books and pin cushions to every man in the Company." These were little packets of sewing needles and thread soldiers used to mend rent clothing and reattach buttons. "Nothing that we can think of at present could have come in better [use] than these little articles . . . for already were the seams of Uncle Sam's uniforms beginning to rip and the buttons to come off, and this timely present enabled some of the boys to take a 'stitch in time.'" From another quarter, it was proposed that a library of 100 to 200 books be gathered for the company. Here was a nod toward the literary interests of the Young Men's Association. "And there was the gift from Sam Spaulding, the local wholesale tobacconist who ran two shops in the central part of the city. He turned over a thousand choice 'segars.' "We will cherish his memory long after his segars have gone up in etherial [*sic*] clouds of smoke—incense offered to his praise," wrote "O.D.K." (The writer was possibly Cpl. Oswald Kissam of Milwaukee, who would die of disease in Nashville, Tennessee, just three months later.)

The admiring enlisted men of the company also presented their well-liked officers, Lts. Howard Greene and Charley Rogers, with handsome swords and sashes, testimonials of "esteem" and "confidence." Pvt. H. B. Furness, principal of the 7th ward high school, made the presentation speech. Despite his Quaker sensibilities, Greene was quickly gaining notice from fellow officers. "I never met an officer so well fitted for the army and so calculated to succeed," said Captain Root.[30]

"We have got the finest company of men, morally and intellectually that ever went out of this state," wrote Lieutenant Greene of his soldiers. Moreover, many had sacrificed much. Of the 100 on the roster, he said, nearly half "left responsible and profitable positions, to enlist as privates." Some gave up annual salaries of $1,000 for a monthly $13 as a private soldier. He himself had earned $2,000 annually working in his brother's firm, Greene & Button Wholesale Druggist, a thriving business in the teeming commercial warren along the river; now he was to be paid half that amount as an officer.

The "Tigers" bore the "reputation of being the best drilled and most orderly company in the Reg." boasted Lieutenant Greene. Yet, they were not "sufficiently posted in Military matters." Thus, the "Hossifers," as some called them, were required to "attend to that business."[31]

The men were ordered about in the process of learning the intricate evolutions of tactical manuals—the company, battalion, and regimental movements so vital to positioning troops on the battlefield. Daily the clerks and railroaders, farmers and professionals were engaged from morning until night in this business of becoming soldiers. As expected, the local press made more of the Milwaukee Regiment than there was. "[I]t is a matter of remark among those who have seen service, that the men are making greater proficiency in proportion to time since enlistment, than any regiment they ever saw." The whole affair was imperiously observed by Colonel Larrabee, astride his horse, "Bony," a name the press did not explain as referring either to Napoléon or the animal's anatomy. The while, hundreds of Milwaukee citizens observed approvingly.[32]

Wrote a news man:

Carriages fluttering with ribbons and laces dashed to and from the camp filled to overflowing with wives, mothers and sisters, and humbler wagons, omnibuses, and street cars were filled till it was found impossible for another passenger to cling on. Seats inside were an exception! More were stowed on top and on the platforms than could possibly be induced to accept a passage inside in ordinary seasons of transportation.

He described a "living flood" that poured to the camp until rain dampened the day. "Many went from idle curiosity, we suppose; but by far the largest number to see old friends, say goodbye to relatives, or to part with the dearest ones on earth."[33]

From two in the afternoon until sundown each day, "the street cars were crowded and literally overrun with passengers bound for the parade ground just outside the line of the camp, and scores if not hundreds of vehicles were dashing back and forth filled with 'the beauty and the chivalry' of Milwaukee." Here was civic pride and female affections compounded with martial ardor. One daily sheet also appealed to the unit's officers for a "Dress Parade at Moonlight" so those folks who were unable to witness the drills each day might see the "famous Milwaukee regiment" before it departed the city.[34]

Much to the delight of the young men, the camp was also invaded or rather almost overwhelmed by the fair sex. The women thronged everywhere. They were likely caparisoned in colorful warm-weather walking outfits of cotton or muslin, with bonnets trimmed in flowers and ribbons, delicate parasols shielding their pale complexions from the late summer sun. "There are so many handsome officers and privates to interest them that the ladies never tire looking at this really superb regiment. Every one expresses regret that they must soon leave us on the morrow." The hoopskirted ladies played a significant role, encouraging the new soldiers, fawning attention and partiality to those who had donned blue uniforms.[35]

But there were other women, of a baser sort, who attracted the attentions of the hundreds of soldiers who had all but flooded the city. In the warren of saloons and dance halls along the Milwaukee River and elsewhere, prostitutes brazenly worked their profession in all hours of the day. "There never was a time when the sinks of inequity [*sic*] plied so prosperous a trade," complained a news editor. "The inmates have apparently increased and flaunt themselves at all hours upon the street, and the revel and rout of the dissipated soldiers can be heard in all by-streets, where these orgesses [*sic*] lie to wait for bounty money."

Mayor Horace Chase took some action, issuing a proclamation against "houses of Ill-Fame" as well as public and private prostitutes within the city limits. In a move that infuriated sons of Teutonia who loved their beer gardens on Sunday, he also prohibited dancing and games on the Sabbath. The action was roundly criticized as useless since the women, after paying fines, simply returned to their trade.[36]

Perhaps in reaction to the growing iniquities abroad in the city and worried of even more wretchedness that faced their soldier sons during the war, something of a brief religious remonstration was evoked in the 24th Wisconsin camp. It was likely to go unheeded in the awful days of camp, march, and battle that followed, however. While some in the regiment would remain close to their pocket Testaments, many probably held religion in temporary abeyance. Pointed appeals against rascality were made. On the day before the regiment's departure, for example, Judge Hubbell visited Camp Sigel to ascertain the welfare of his son, Richard, the lawyer-turned-sergeant of Company I. He took the occasion to appeal for observance of temperate habits, particularly among the common soldiers. There were class distinctions, the men of money and position feeling that those in the ranks were more likely to succumb to temptation. But it would soon be obvious that even the scions of wealth and influence would become foragers nonpareil, card-players and imbibers along with those of supposed baser instincts. What the regiment's rotund chaplain, Father Fusseder, made of all this is not known.

The day before its departure, another veteran of the 5th Wisconsin, Ted West, visited his former comrades at Camp Sigel. The slender regimental adjutant had been sent from Virginia on a recruiting service to replenish the ranks of his badly depleted regiment. The narrow-eyed officer who lived in Waukesha, a town west of the city, cut a fine figure in his long blue coat. He likely passed pleasantries with old comrades Larrabee, Balding, Hibbard, and others. In the spring of 1863, West would join the 24th Wisconsin and become a respected lieutenant colonel, and command the regiment in some of its most desperate fights.[37]

Then, on a sweltering and wet Friday, September 5, 1862, the Milwaukee Regiment broke camp amid confusion. The time appointed for the soldiers to entrain was in doubt. A three-hour downpour from eleven o'clock that morning soaked men and equipment. Yet, Milwaukee citizens turned out on downtown streets early in the day to see the boys off; they waited, sodden and discomfited, until one o'clock before the regiment appeared. Then: "Cheer after cheer went up as they went down Main street," a newsman described, "and the Newhall [House] blossomed out with white handkerchiefs." But some of the young soldiers were having difficulties, another writer observed, burdened as they were in "woolen clothing, enveloped in a heavy overcoat, with a knapsack of fifty pounds . . . strapped to their back, and a heavy gun on the shoulder. . . . Several of the soldiers fell out . . . on this short march, and that more did not is good testimony to their endurance." The new 24th Wisconsin had covered little more than a mile and a half from Camp Sigel to the railroad station. When they later became part of Gen. Philip Sheridan's "foot cavalry," the Milwaukee soldiers would sometimes cover ten or more times that distance in a day.

Thirty years later, one old veteran, John Mitchell, would remember that day in less grand terms. The march to the station was "one of the toughest bits of work that the boys ever did." In addition to a heavy overcoat, the bulky Austrian muskets, and a knapsack, "crowded to its utmost capacity with extra socks, shirts, toilet articles, pictures, books, etc. (any old soldier can tell about the first knapsack load) they were carrying anywhere from forty to fifty pounds weight, with the temperature at nearly ninety degrees, and a muggy, close atmosphere." Many of the new soldiers were unused to such burdens, and a great many dropped from the marching ranks exhausted.[38]

Between five and seven thousand well-wishers crowded the muddy Union railway station near the Milwaukee River, and every available inch of the platform was taken up by enthusiastic friends, shaking hands and shouting "good words." The "scenes . . . between fathers and mothers with their sons, sisters with brothers and lovers, husbands with wives, friends with each other, were of a deeply affecting character," another news writer said. "Their loss will be felt here, and anxious hearts will continually follow them in their progress."

Another writer painted a moving word portrait:

> Every phase of human sympathy and affection was depicted on hundreds of countenances, and amongst the vast number present, dry eyes were the exception. In some instances, the grief of those left behind was unbearable and friends kindly forced them away and took them home. In others, wives rushed frantically through the crowd enquiring for the companies to which their husbands were attached, and when found, clung to them with desperate energy, and turned deaf ears to all hopes of the future.

Blue-eyed Lem Cochrane, an impressionable nineteen-year-old in Company B, was saying his good-byes. A horse trainer, the young man was said to possess a "kind disposition" and had many friends in Milwaukee. "Farewell mother, I must go; I will be a good boy. I hope we will meet again," he reportedly said. "He went away full of hope and ambition," related a comrade some months later. Another private in that company, Noah Griswold, was embracing his new wife before departure. Griswold was well known in Milwaukee, having managed the Gymnasium in Young's Block downtown, and was a former bookkeeper in a prominent boot and shoe store. In the new year, devastating news would prostrate Mrs. Griswold.[39]

Elsewhere in that throng must have been William Tucker, a south side produce dealer, and his wife; they were seeing another son, twenty-five-year-old George, march off to war. The Tuckers had already lost one son who was killed at Bull Run, Virginia, the year before, "one of the very first of Wisconsin's sacrifices to the cause of country," a newsman said. Another Tucker boy, Eugene, served in the 13th U.S. Cavalry. Soon, a fourth son, eighteen-year-old William, Jr., would join his brother in the 24th Wisconsin; and two years later, the last two of six sons, including the fifteen-year-old baby, John, would enlist in a Wisconsin regiment. "Such patriotism is worthy of all praise, and is in noble contrast with the cowardly croakings and fault-findings of copperheads and lukewarm friends of the country," noted the writer.[40]

After parting with her son, one aged mother walked a few rods then collapsed and was carried away. There were other instances of "distress," and "the heart must be hard indeed that could look unmoved," said a newspaper writer. Other partings were filled with patriotic hopes and wishes that the soldier would do his duty. Some farewells were filled with levity, and laughter intermingled with weeping.[41]

A few days before, Lieutenant Greene's sweetheart, Louise Webb, had traveled up the Mississippi from St. Louis to say good-bye to her love. They were intended now. The couple would see each other again, and he would write to her often; she was "one of the noblest, and best women God ever made," he told his parents.[42]

Ten large passenger coaches pulled by a steaming engine chuffed out of the station at four o'clock. One wing of the regiment crowded aboard. Shouts and cheers reverberated as the 500 men, many hanging out of windows, passed from view. Twenty minutes later, a similar group of rail cars carried the regiment's other wing from the platform. People waved as the cars grew smaller in the distance. Then "silence fell upon all present, and groups wended their way in every direction in sorrow and tears."[43]

"That Colonel Larrabee will give a good account of himself . . . does not seem to be doubted by any who saw the splendid body of men under his charge," a newspaper piece concluded patriotically. But the realities were quite another matter: "Undisciplined, undrilled and unseasoned to the life of the soldier, we were hurried forward to take part in a campaign full of hardship, long marches and severe fighting," Lieutenant Mitchell recalled.

The farewell was tearful "for there were many local pets in the regiment." They went with hope intact, expectant they would return.[44]

Mitchell, like Arthur McArthur, Bob Chivas and Fred Root, Ed Parsons, "Lish" Hibbard, and many others, were among those "pets" of Milwaukee marching off to war. But there were others, less well known in the city—impressionable Amandus Silsby, who would read his Testament faithfully, and Datus Worth, the "erring son" preparing to do his best in "Abe's service"—who faced unknown fates. Most of the volunteers would return in time, some whole, others maimed in body or mind. But many of these men would never see Milwaukee or their families or homes again. There would be little distinction, in the months ahead, between men of wealth and position and those of lesser means. We "go a band of Brothers," Howard Greene wrote.[45]

Chapter 4

Chaplin Hills–Perryville

—•—≡◆≡—•—

"I wished myself at home."

The month that followed the departure of the Milwaukee Regiment
from Wisconsin would be like none other that the volunteers had
ever experienced in their lives. From the time they reached the Ohio
River through the first week in October, they marched many miles and
fought in their first battle. Amandus Silsby, the young student; red-
headed Tom Ford; the fresh-faced seventeen-year-olds who shared a
given name, Art Gilbert and Arthur McArthur; the cousins, Lieutenants
Chivas and Mitchell; the sensitive Howard Greene, likely still aching
over the parting from his sweetheart, Louise; the Company A druggist,
Henry Drake; and the "pets" of Company B, among them Gene Comstock and Norm Burdick—nearly all would write in the days ahead of
the ordeal. But in all of the writing, there was much left unsaid.

Certainly, they anticipated march and battle, but the depth of pros-
tration and pain, weariness and deprivation could not be distilled into
mere words for home consumption. What they wrote at that time, and
from the perspective of twenty-five years or more, could not convey the
full force of what occurred. Nor could they guess it before. While the
part played by the 24th Wisconsin would not be pivotal or its losses
extensive, the coming days would change the lives of these men and
boys forever and begin the process of transforming them from civilians
to soldiers.

Afterward, one Milwaukee soldier would write that the 24th Wisconsin "has stood fire—passed through the trying ordeal—and now is on a par for fighting with the old troops." That assessment, however, would be premature. He also applauded the officers—Colonel Larrabee, Lieutenant Colonel Buttrick, Major Hibbard, the boy-adjutant, McArthur, and others for their conduct in battle.[1]

Some six weeks after departing from Milwaukee, eighteen-year-old Amandus Silsby finally wrote to his father, the Presbyterian missionary in Ohio. It was a long epistle detailing many weeks of army life. When it departed the city, the 24th Wisconsin had been given two days rations to carry in their haversacks, Silsby noted in his small, cursive hand, "but as is always the case, two days rations are only enough for one day." Before reaching Indianapolis, the new soldiers had nothing to eat and were forced to purchase "victuals." The young man used postage stamps as currency, and, thus, was unable to send letters home for several weeks, he said.[2]

After leaving Milwaukee on that solemn and sodden Friday, the 24th Wisconsin traveled by rail from Milwaukee to Chicago, changed to Lake Shore Rail Road cars to Michigan City, Indiana, shifted again at both Lafayette and Indianapolis, arriving at two the following afternoon. The Indianapolis & Jeffersonville line trundled the thousand men and boys through the southern half of the state to Jeffersonville, just across the Ohio River from Kentucky. The ride was grueling for the new soldiers.

Art Gilbert, Company B's tenderfoot, wrote of a series of incidents, which took place in the next few days, that were imprinted upon his memory for decades. First, there was "the swim in the Ohio Rapids." The eighteen-year-old bookkeeper also remembered "the Long Roll . . . our first call and only a drill—but it seemed real enough for a time." Then there was the harrowing episode involving an unidentified soldier in the 108th Illinois, another new regiment, who attempted suicide, for reasons unexplained, by cutting his throat. Caught by the surgeons, he was "sewn up—good as new," he wrote. He had not seen anything like that in his seventeen years.

Then within a few days, they were ordered to Cincinnati. "Here she goes,—there she goes—yesterday the 'little joker' was at Louisville—to-day, here," Gilbert said. "Our change was very sudden and very flattering to the 24th. We were the first regiment of the great army at Louisville to march to the succor of Cincinnati, and in forty minutes after the long roll sounded at camp Joe Holt, our tents were struck and packed and the regiment on the march." Actually, "without sleeping, with nothing to eat, and but very little water," the regiment was loaded on open cattle cars for the trip east.[3]

Cincinnati, whose precincts, like Milwaukee's, contained a distinct Germanic flavor, was rumored to be in great danger; the Rebel cavalry chief, Kirby Smith, and his men were galloping toward the southern Ohio city with hostile intent. The city's citizens greeted the new soldiers almost as heroes and "treated us very handsomely," Lieutenant Chivas wrote; and the good women turned out and "distributed . . . fruits, bread, cakes, pies and water &c., which was served as a lunch," the soldier-writer recalled. Later, the Milwaukee men were given another meal, a "tip top breakfast," one soldier called it, at the Fifth Street Market. "These hospitable persons not only insisted upon our taking our own time and eat plenty, but filled our haversacks with eatables and our canteens with coffee."[4]

From Cincinnati, the Milwaukee men clumped across army pontoon bridges to the south side of the Ohio, settling in a place near Covington, Kentucky, that they called Camp Hooker. "The regiment marched like veterans and elicited the highest praise from everybody," Private Gilbert noted. "It is indeed, a splendid regiment, and with a few more days drill I should not be afraid to risk it in battle. They are too well drilled now to be slaughtered, for in the simple movements of the battle-field they are now pretty well versed," he wrote. But, then, most chroniclers boasted of the prowess and polish of their regiments. Would that such preparation was the only thing necessary to insure the 24th's conduct in battle.

"Our camp life back of Covington was uneventful in the main, as I remember it," Gilbert wrote from a perspective of over three decades. But here, the regiment sustained its first casualty; ironically it was the ponderous First Assistant Surgeon, Charles Mueller, who succumbed to apoplexy, or stroke, at age thirty-seven. The Scot immigrant, Lieutenant Chivas of the Merchants Guards, wrote his aunt, Martha Mitchell, that the death was caused by stoutness "and partly I am told by a too liberal use of spirits." As sad as the episode was, Gilbert found humor in the telling of it. "Lucky thing the graveyard was handy, as a metallic coffin with this heavy weight in it about laid out those detailed as pall bearers." Gilbert's tent mate, Fred Child, was one of those ordered to handle the burden; "although exceptionally strong, he nearly lay down by the [deceased] surgeon at the grave to stay."[5]

After only three days, the regiment, marking its brief presence in Covington with a grave, was ordered back to Louisville. They were soon to learn that such sudden shifts were the way of the army. They boarded side-wheeled Ohio River steamboats to the accompaniment of the regiment's brass band puffing "some splendid airs very splendidly" and a steam calliope "tooting a few tunes"; the Milwaukee men watched as Cincinnati citizens waved handkerchiefs in farewell.

The "day was lovely and scenery beautiful. The party seemed more like one of pleasure than of war," mused one man. But problems soon arose. Piloted by a former Lake Michigan captain, the boats were stopped by a roiling fog several times; then one ran aground on a sand-bar. Soldiers were ordered to disembark to lighten the load so it could pass the shallows. But Colonel Larrabee's boat was stuck fast, and upon arrival at Louisville, much of the regiment had to spend two days aboard before the regiment's officers arrived.

The regiment disembarked at Louisville September 20. "The line of march was through a handsome portion of the city, and handsomely were we welcomed." Many of the Wisconsin soldiers may have recalled the admirers who thronged Camp Sigel back in Milwaukee only a few weeks before. "Handsome, lovely, beautiful girls threw the starry folds [of American flags] from their boudoirs and parlors, and threw kisses after them." It was all rather exciting for the Badger boys—they were heroes before they saw their first rebel. In their correspondence, the soldiers of Milwaukee, like hundreds of thousands of their comrades, almost universally spelled the word "rebel" without a capital; it was a means of denigrating the enemy, perhaps to show disdain for the armies that were attempting to sunder the glorious union of states. Moreover, very few used the term "Confederate."[6]

Louisville, Kentucky's largest city, was becoming a Federal army bastion, the gateway to the South at this point in the war. Numbering over 70,000 in population, it was nearly double the size of Milwaukee. The southern metropolis was an industrial center. At the head of the vital Louisville & Nashville Railroad, it was an important hub; moreover, situated at the falls of the Ohio River, the city was a vital river town.

The city was in a fortifying frenzy amid the rumors of attacks by rebel guerrillas. The cavalryman Kirby Smith, that ominous gray invader, with his 18,000-man army, occupied Lexington, Frankfort, and other Kentucky towns, menacing not only Louisville but Indianapolis and Cincinnati as well. Simultaneously gray riders led by Nathan Bedford Forrest and John Hunt Morgan were rampaging about middle Tennessee, threatening the entire state. Amid all the febrile rumor and churning activity, one local news writer took time to look over the new Badger regiment and was impressed. It "is considered the crack regiment of Wisconsin, and embraces in its ranks almost every known trade, profession, and employment."[7]

New units were rapidly assembling in Louisville, and regiments were hastily thrown together into brigades. The 24th began an association with Illinois units that was to continue for the next two and a half years, until the war ended. They were initially brigaded with two new Prairie State regiments, the 73rd and 88th, the latter a "crack" regiment raised in Chicago, along with the recently organized 21st Michigan. "Upon the whole we are glad to be here," remarked the soldier correspondent. The 73rd had an unusual composition: A dozen of its officers were Methodist ministers and many of its men were from prominent church families. They were, it was almost too obvious to note, known as the "Preacher Regiment."[8]

It is not known whether the new soldiers of Wisconsin heard the rumor about a woman in the ranks of the Michigan regiment. The story was not told until more than thirty years after the war, and then legend played a large part in the tale. Her name was said to be Miss Annie Lillybridge, a Detroit woman, and she fell in love with a lieutenant assigned to the 21st Michigan, then gathering in the counties near Grand Rapids and Ionia. She purchased male attire, it was said, and joined the new regiment, managing to keep the secret even from her sweetheart. Late in the century, it was written that the bluecoated woman passed through all the privations and dangers of camp life, sleeping on the cold ground "without a murmur." In the coming battle near Perryville, as the story would portray it, she behaved with "marked gallantry, and by her hand shot a rebel Captain who aimed at her lover."[9]

"In all directions [from the Louisville campground], excepting the front, as far as the eye can reach, on hill top and valley, in highways and byways, all is activity, bustle and preparation. Look which every way you may, portions of the grand army of the west may be seen." It was an impressive sight for the new soldiers of Milwaukee. All day long, from five in the morning until nine at night "martial music may be heard, and drilling is incessant in some direction. Forests are being felled to the right, left and front of us, in order to obstruct the advances of the enemy, and also to give a clear sweep for our guns."

Here a daily regimen was quickly established, despite the fact that the rains descended on the soldiers almost incessantly. "Col. Larrabee is indefatigable," the writer for the *Milwaukee Daily News* said. "He is justly proud of his regiment, and notwithstanding his rigid and strictly enforced rules, his orders are obeyed with alacrity, and the men are fast becoming convinced that his hard discipline is all for the best. We may now be said to be in active service," he wrote.[10]

All of this must have borne heavily on the Milwaukee Regiment's adjutant. Despite Colonel Larrabee's antipathy for Lieutenant McArthur, the gray-eyed lad likely busied himself with the innumerable written reports he needed to complete, and details required for the colonel. Company captains related roll calls, sick calls, and other matters to McArthur; these he dutifully turned over to the heavy-browed Larrabee. The young man, known to have retained a sheaf of letters during the war, was certainly a correspondent himself, penning descriptions of experiences and daily occurrences to his father, the judge. Only shards of this correspondence survived; what he wrote may only be inferred.

Reveille sounded at five o'clock. From then until breakfast, "we are engaged in bathing, washing, mending, &c. Our whole time seems to be required to keep things as they should be. Guns have to be cleaned every day, clothes mended, &c." Breakfast and surgeons' call were at 6:30 A.M. Guard mount followed at 7 A.M., noncommissioned officers' drill at 8 A.M., and company drill at 9:30. Dinner call was scheduled for noon, and squad drill from one to two in the afternoon, and battalion drill from three to four o'clock. Dress parade commenced at 5:30, with supper call at six. Tattoo sounded at 8:30 and taps at nine, a Milwaukee soldier described.

The 24th Wisconsin was frequently shuffled from one camp to another, much to the chagrin of the constantly uprooted privates. "We have been moving so much and so rapidly that frequently we have had no time to pitch tents, and have therefore slept in the open air. Our men got used to it, and many prefer it, especially when the weather is pleasant." He also wrote that Captain Von Baumbach, the immigrant who commanded Company C, had presented a fine revolver to each of his lieutenants.[11]

Joining the 24th when it arrived in Louisville was "sturdy" George Bleyer, who was made second lieutenant in Company A. He was one of several sons of Milwaukee's first Germanic immigrant, Henry Bleyer, who had come to the city in 1835. George, who had worked for a city daily, had become one of Wisconsin's fine compositors—they were called "typos" in that day. As well, the twenty-two-year-old was a man of much accomplishment, reading a great deal, studying language, and becoming a "most graphic and interesting writer," a comrade wrote later. He composed poetry, and many of his verses were printed in Eastern magazines. Even during his military service, it was later said, he was "constantly noting his poetic thoughts, and many vagrant couplets, quatrains and humorous verses circulated among his friends."

Bleyer had enlisted in the old 1st Wisconsin, and earned sergeant's stripes. When the regiment's three-month enlistment terminated, he had been offered a position as editor of the *Daily Wisconsin,* an important Republican Party newspaper. "After the war is over I will gladly come," Bleyer reputedly replied, "but now no consideration on earth can induce me to leave the army." He was so highly recommended that the governor accorded him a commission in the new 24th Wisconsin. He was assigned to Company A. During the coming months, he would write telling, biweekly dispatches under the nom de plume "Marion," describing in detail stories of camp, march, and battle.[12]

While his old regiment was in Alabama that summer, Bleyer had created a humorous piece about picket duty. As the sentry plied his post in the dead of night, fears sprang to life.

"Imagination fills my drowsy brain," the Milwaukee compositor wrote.

> With scenes of battles—fields of maimed and slain;
> The stumps and bushes into phantoms grow,
> The shadows shape themselves into the foe. . . .

Bleyer, apparently writing from firsthand experience, concluded the creation with the discovery that the phantom was only *"A soldier from a chicken forage tramp."*[13]

Within days of the 24th Wisconsin's arrival at Louisville, Maj. Gen. William Nelson, who commanded the garrison, had taken drastic steps to secure the city against the threats of rebel incursions. Called "Bull" because of his six-foot-five, 300-pound prominence, he commanded all Federal forces in Kentucky. Reputedly, news writers had it, he would save the state for the Union. He ordered all women and children to evacuate the city on September 22. Soon the Ohio River wharves were crowded with wagons, carts, buggies, and carriages trying to leave for the Indiana shore. The town was awash in blue soldiers whose wont was often to seek diversion. Then on the following day, the general ordered that all saloons and hotels that sold liquor to close. Rumor swept across the city that Confederate general Braxton Bragg was about to attack Louisville. The men of Wisconsin, so fresh from home and surrounded by inexperienced units such as their own, may have been fearful of the portent.

During those frenzied days, the Milwaukee Regiment experienced its "first real call," the ominous "Long Roll" of rattling snare drums that announced the approach of the enemy. Soldiers immediately donned leather accoutrements, grabbed up muskets, and stood in company line. Even twenty years later, it was still fresh in Art Gilbert's mind: "I well remember our standing in trenches already dug, waiting all night for their coming, but we had not the pleasure of a shot," he wrote. The Wisconsin soldiers, having only briefly fired their muskets, were subsequently ordered to dig more trenches.[14]

General Nelson then decreed the closure of all schools and businesses, and on September 24 he directed all healthy citizens aged nineteen to forty-five to report for military service in building defensive trenches around the city. The Wisconsin soldiers joined other new regiments in waiting for the attack. While news of the battle in Maryland fought September 17 began filtering into Louisville, there was little time to contemplate its import for the war. What effect the news of the bloody day had upon the new Badger soldiers was not recorded. Many, however, had friends in Wisconsin regiments who fought with the Army of the Potomac. Company D's lieutenant Christian Nix may have been more attentive than most to the news from the East, where many of his old comrades, the Germans of the 6th Wisconsin's Company F, had fought Lee near a creek called Antietam.

Most immediately for the Milwaukee Regiment, rations and accommodations continued to be a source of irritation, particularly for the wellborn in the 24th Wisconsin. "'Sow belly,' 'hard-tack,' and mother earth for a mattress were beginning to tell a sorrowful tale. The boys commenced to think they had got a long way from home," Lieutenant Mitchell remembered. It was fare with which one of his privileged background was clearly unaccustomed.[15]

One of the soldiers' unforgettable staples was hardtack, sometimes called army bread or crackers. It is a matter of amazement how a food so tasteless and compromising to good dentition could be so indelibly impressed on soldiers' memories. Measuring some three inches square and about an inch thick, the victual was often the consistency of concrete, "attributed to its great age, for there is a common belief among the boys that our hardtack had been baked long before the beginning of the Christian era," attested one common soldier. This conclusion was based upon the letters "B.C." printed on hardtack crates. As Company

G's Jim Bacon, he of the toothless mien, might have attested, even soldiers with a full set of strong teeth were seldom able to fracture the crackers. Yet on the march, the staple was often all the sustenance the soldiers might consume. Sometimes, a thin slice of raw fat pork with a spoonful of brown sugar was laid on a cracker, and crunched down as the men plodded along.

While camped, cooking crackers was another matter, and no small amount of "inventive genius" was required to prepare them palatably. "[W]e sometimes had fricasseed hardtack, prepared by toasting it before the hot coals, thus making it soft and spongy." If there was time for frying, the hardtack was dropped in fat and browned; seasoned with salt and pepper, it made "hellfire stew." At times, they were pounded into powder and mixed with whatever was handy. Most often, hardtack was merely something to fill the belly.[16]

Nearly as essential for the soldiers' well-being as water and food was mail; news from family and friends distracted minds from immediate soldier concerns, at least for a few minutes, and assured them that all was well back home. Letter after letter refrained about the importance of correspondence. The Granville farmer, Date Worth, for example, often closed his letters with a plea for his family to "write immediately" upon receipt of his missives; "don't allow yourself a moment to think your letters are not interresting [*sic*] to me." Similarly, in a report to the *Milwaukee Sentinel*, one 24th Wisconsin soldier identified only as "C.S." wrote that on September 28, the regiment received a large consignment of mail and newspapers. "[We] hope the citizens of Milwaukee will continue to favor us in that manner, as there is nothing that adds more to the enjoyment of the 'boys' than the reading of news from home." The term "boys" was applied to soldiers regardless of age, and would even be used to describe the old veterans after the war.[17]

In the Louisville camp, the Milwaukee Regiment sustained its first gunshot casualties. During one of the few occasions that the men of the 24th Wisconsin learned to load and fire their muskets with powder, bullets, and caps, two minor bloodletting incidents occurred. Few regiments conducted more than rudimentary training and practice with the bulky rifle-musket; the four-and-a-half-foot long gun was to be loaded, as the men remembered from their brief drills at Camp Sigel, in nine counts or movements.

The occasional firing of the cumbersome Austrian-made muskets took place at times such as these. A new soldier learned to tear open the paper cartridge with his teeth (Jim Bacon must have used other means), and clenching the half-inch-wide conical bullet in his mouth, poured sixty grains of black powder into the upright barrel. After seating the ounce of lead, the steel ramrod was withdrawn from its place beneath the beech-wood gun stock and the heavy lead ball pushed down. The nine-and-a-half-pound gun was then righted at the soldier's side, and a brass percussion cap fitted onto the firing cone, or nipple as it was called, under the hammer. The musket was then pulled to the shoulder, sighted, and the trigger pulled.

The musket kicked the shoulder, likely startling the unwary soldier; eyes flinched shut at the ignition of the powder and loud explosive crack. A cloud of gray smoke billowed from the musket, obscuring the target for a few seconds. If any of the Wisconsin men wondered how they might load and fire their guns effectively in the heat of battle, they did not write about it. Clearly, it would take some doing to fire at a charging enemy as it was very difficult to load the long muskets quickly in any position but standing. Corporal Comstock, the nineteen-year-old printer, would learn to take clear-eyed aim at an enemy the following year. Date Worth would later write of a similar experience.

The loading and firing practice occasionally produced near disastrous results for some soldiers. One man from Company F (some still called it the La Crosse Tigers) "blew off two fingers by the accidental discharge of his musket." And a man in Company H "put a bullet through his foot. Both [men] are doing well," noted soldier correspondent Lieutenant Bleyer who did not identify the casualties. Assistant Surgeon Moses Hoyt reported that it was necessary for him to amputate two fingers of one soldier's hand, and repair damage to the foot.[18]

In late September, more fresh regiments similar to the Milwaukee unit arrived daily from the Western states—Illinois, Wisconsin, and Michigan. In that month, the total Federal force in Louisville numbered between 36,000 to 37,000. Among the newer regiments trooping into Louisville that fall were several from Wisconsin. "There has been quite an intermingling . . . for the past few days,—friends and relatives in search of each other," wrote Lieutenant Bleyer. The 24th was "styled 'Milwaukee' by the boys and when they wish to go to the 'Cream City' [as the regiment's camp was called], they saunter into its lines and up and down its streets, meeting a friend or familiar face at every step, but not one sign of 'Lager Beer—2 [glasses] for 5 cents,'" he noted humorously.[19]

Then, from the Cumberland Plateau the forward elements of Maj. Gen. Don Carlos Buell's army began arriving September 26, Maj. Gen.

Alexander McCook's corps being the first to march into the city around three in the morning. There must have been relief among the new Milwaukee men at the sight of the battle-hardened veterans, but such was not recorded. The *Louisville Journal* headline was thick: "The Cloud is Lifting."[20]

For two days, the blue ranks trooped into the city, all happily welcomed by their new comrades. "Buell and his veterans . . . dusty, half-starved troops rested by the roadside, and lit up the sky with their camp fires—for they came by night—[and] the heart of the public beat slow again, and the nerves of the timid became settled and strong," observed a solider correspondent.[21]

Upon closer inspection, these were not soldiers who looked the part of saviors: They were dirty, ragged, and footsore men hobbling painfully with bare feet wrapped in rags. One Wisconsin volunteer wrote that many of the arriving soldiers had marched all the way from Alabama, some 1,200 to 1,500 miles. These were veterans of the fight for Island No. 10 on the Mississippi River, the battle of Corinth, and elsewhere. They had not known a bath for many months. Lieutenant Mitchell recalled years later that he ruminated about the portents of these unshod and threadbare legions. "Coming events cast their shadows before," he said. "These lank and tattered men were 'shadows.' In them, we saw ourselves, such as we were about to become."[22]

"Here we found the boys all barefooted, and no shoes to be had," recorded a Wisconsin drummer boy in one of those regiments. "My rags were worn out, and I had taken the pocket from my blouse and wrapped it around my feet; but as it was very thin stuff, I did not expect it would last over an hour or so."[23]

The ragged regiments camped all over the city and on islands in the Ohio River. Among the units that arrived was the vaunted Pea Ridge Brigade sent from Gen. U. S. Grant's army in Mississippi to bulk the Kentucky defenses. The unit, composed of the 36th and 44th Illinois and 2nd and 15th Missouri, bedded down near the city asylum for the blind on the Lexington Turnpike. For much of the long course of the war to come, the Prairie State veterans would be brigaded with the 24th Wisconsin, and a special bond would develop between the 36th and 24th, as the two regiments marched and fought together for the entire course of the war.

Although they did not understand it at this point, the officer who led the Pea Ridge Brigade into Louisville was to become one of the Milwaukee Regiment's favorite officers. There was not much that was impressive about Philip Sheridan. Like John Mitchell, Fred Root, George Merrick, and several others, he stood a mere five and a half feet tall; atop the compact, long-armed body was a large head that some described as bullet shaped. With deep vertical creases separating them, his dark piercing eyes were heavily lidded; cheekbones were high. The small man wore his hair close-cropped under a low-crowned plug hat cocked to the left. Perhaps to increase his modest stature, he sat atop a large black gelding called "Rienzi." At thirty-one, Sheridan bore a reputation as an aggressive colonel who had led some daring actions in Mississippi; many veterans attested that he was brusque and profane. When the man whom many soldiers would come to call "Little Phil" rode into Louisville September 14, he was preparing to sew a single brigadier's star to his shoulder straps. He was intent on even higher command.[24]

For some weeks, the Pea Ridge and other veterans were standoffish with all the new soldiers. Many, like the Milwaukee Regiment, were latecomers to the war, unlike the volunteers of 1861. There was suspicion among blooded soldiers that the recent volunteers signed the rolls only to receive monetary bonuses; the taint of mercenary hung about them. They would have to march many hundreds of miles and fight hard to prove themselves to the worn-down regiments. Those veterans who condescended to speak poked fun at the impressionable Wisconsin soldiers, and spun all manner of lies and improbable stories for those who gaped. "They tell of times that would appear incredulous to the uninitiated," said one 24th soldier. But the men of the Milwaukee Regiment did not much write about those gibes or jests. The experienced officers of the 24th likely offered antidotes to the more outlandish tales and dire predictions.[25]

Army commander Don Carlos Buell trotted into Louisville September 25, and the men soon got a look at their new leader. Forty-four-year-old Buell was somewhat portly, bearded with gray, thinning hair. A disciplinarian, he had little confidence in this freshly organized army of volunteers. "Buell is a rather bad *odor* with his men," Company A's Sergeant Drake told his brother. "I have heard his men call him Traitor, and in fact all sorts of names that language can express. They said that his army had Bragg tight three or four times but Buell would not let them fight. They say they have not seen him since they have been under him, and if they do they will shoot him." Strong views, indeed. The soldiers would muster little like of the old general in the weeks to come, and failed to lament when the War Department removed him from army command after the coming battle.[26]

Men of the Milwaukee Regiment soon learned from Buell's veterans about his lack of respect for volunteer soldiers. But that feeling cut both ways among the Western men. "Our leader don't want to end the war, and instead of the long roll beating and each man falling in . . . the order is to remain as we are and await orders," wrote a Milwaukee veteran caustically. When it was rumored that Buell was relieved in this early period, the Milwaukee men took a cue from the veterans, and "three times three hearty cheers went up from the whole western army." The rumor, like most, was false. "The whole army (I mean the men who do the fighting) not the reporters[,] not the officers who lie about the cities and towns, and fight great battles on paper, have become discouraged and unless some thing is done soon there will be another rebellion in these parts," warned the unidentified veteran soldier, probably from the old 1st Wisconsin, on the front page of a Milwaukee daily. It was all very unsettling to the untested men of the 24th Wisconsin.[27]

General Buell, given authority over the entire force, and his subordinates worked rapidly to reconstitute the command, grandiosely referring to it as the Army of the Ohio. Brigades were organized, usually combining new units such as the Milwaukee Regiment with veteran outfits like the Germans of the 36th Illinois. The short-lived relationship with the Methodist "Preachers" of the 73rd Illinois was severed when the Prairie Staters were shuffled into another brigade. The organization in the Union army that was the ideal assembled three 1,000-man regiments into a brigade, and three or more brigades into a division. Two or more divisions composed a corps, and two or more corps constituted an army. Buell commanded three corps.

The 24th Wisconsin was assigned to the new 37th Brigade along with the other "fresh fish" regiments, the 88th Illinois and 21st Michigan, both of which were organized in early September. The brigade's keystone was the veteran 36th Illinois, one of the stalwart Pea Ridgers. These swaggering soldiers from the counties west of Chicago had been in the war a year already, and they were quick to tell their new comrades about the hard marches and bloody fights they had seen, particularly the pitched battle at Pea Ridge, Arkansas, in March. They likely also exhibited considerable impatience in being separated from the other veteran regiments of that brigade, and forced to wet-nurse the new boys. But the association would last many months and withstand countless miles, wet and dreary camps, and grim campaigns. The Illinois soldiers, however, did "not look much like our Regiment," Sergeant Drake observed. "Their clothes and countenances bear testimony of the service they have done the country. I should think they had about 500 men in the ranks[,]

Nicholas Greusel.
The old Illinois colonel.
FROM: HISTORY OF THE THIRTY-SIXTH ILLINOIS.

less than half of our Regiment." The druggist, who had been made company orderly, could not then know how soon he and his Wisconsin comrades would resemble the Prairie Staters.[28]

The commander of the 37th Brigade was an avuncular colonel whom his men called "Old Nick." Already in his fifties and an immigrant from the Germanic states, whose accent was still thick, Nicholas Greusel, a short and slender man with a graying mane and beard, had seen service in the Mexican War. When the Civil War erupted, he joined the three-month 7th Illinois Infantry and quickly became major. A promotion to colonel when his service expired prompted him to lead a newly organized regiment, the 36th. He would affectionately call the 24th his "babies" during the coming battle.[29]

Colonel Greusel also had ties to the Badger State, where he had worked in the northern Wisconsin lumber trade before the war. For this reason, he may have developed a fondness toward the young Scot lumber merchant, Bob Chivas. Lt. John Mitchell would also develop a particularly close relationship with the old colonel, and introduce him to his father, Alexander, who would several times travel to Kentucky and Tennessee to visit; the banker and railroad man grew fond of the old Teutonic colonel. The colonel would quickly win the respect of the Milwaukee soldiers, and one Company G volunteer said he was like "his old and nearly worn out regiment, knows no fear, is generous, endures all hardships and pleasures of the camp with them."

Colonel Greusel's brigade was formed with two others to compose a division commanded by little Phil Sheridan, who now officially wore his general's star. But Milwaukee's Andrew Smith was not yet ready to say much more than that the ungainly looking officer was a "small, dressy, band-box general." He may have been speaking for many of his comrades when he said he would allow the new general time to prove himself. "[B]ut if he is a knowing and skillful general and adviser, his looks deceive him." Company G's Andrew Smith would, after the regiment's first battle a short time later, laud General Sheridan, however.[30]

The next six months would evince Sheridan's impetuosity and pugnacity, and his commanding sense of self-assurance. Through four major battles and hundreds of miles on the march, the men of Milwaukee would develop esteem for him. He would soon win fame and promotion for directing a brilliant fighting defense in Tennessee on New Year's Eve. Decades later, 24th Wisconsin lieutenant Ed Parsons of Company K personally welcomed the general to Milwaukee, and later orated a paean to his old division commander. Just now, General Sheridan, who had ambitiously maneuvered to attain a general's star, sat astride his big ebony horse, "Rienzi," which would in time become one of the war's most famous chargers. He scrutinized the three brigades and twelve regiments he would lead for the next several months.

General Buell constituted his Army of the Ohio into three corps commanded by Gens. Alexander McCook, Thomas Crittenden, and William Nelson. The 24th Wisconsin was assigned to the latter's command. But veterans and new soldiers in the corps were shocked when an affair of honor resulted in the death of their new commanding officer. Nelson was shot in Louisville's Galt House September 29 by his nemesis, Hoosier brigadier general Jefferson C. Davis (no relation to the Confederate president). The alarming turn of events created turmoil in the army's upper ranks, and within days, the story was headlined in Milwaukee newspapers. The city must have wondered at the portent of so dramatic an occurrence. None of the sordidness seeped into Wisconsin writings after the war and it was only briefly treated in Milwaukee soldier letters; yet it must have sent a shudder through the ranks.[31]

It did not augur well for the impending campaign in the fall of 1862. Maj. Gen. Charles Gilbert, at forty a fussy veteran of the Mexican War and the battle of Wilson's Creek in Missouri, was assigned in Nelson's stead, commanding the 22,000-man corps. The West Pointer would prove to be a martinet; and, like Buell, he would soon win disfavor with the volunteer officers and men alike. Several leading officers of the Milwaukee Regiment were to be subjected to his wrath. Gilbert's bearded mien was intent and unfriendly. This would be his final campaign.[32]

Maj. Gen. George H. Thomas, a forty-six-year-old Virginian who had remained loyal to the Union, was Buell's second in command. Solid, large-chested, he stood six feet and weighed well over 200 pounds; blue eyes flashed between a heavy gray beard and thick hair. He was said to be taciturn. The Mexican War veteran had been asked to lead the army, but had deferred to Buell. Thomas would prove his defensive mettle, preventing a defeat from becoming a disaster later that year. Through defeat and victory, the general would find few detractors among his soldiers. In all, the irascible Buell led some 81,000.[33]

Rumor was rampant in the camps of the new Army of the Ohio. On September 28, the unofficial correspondent to the *Milwaukee Sentinel,* "C.S.," wrote that the regiment would be uprooted from its "pleasant location" on the following day for "another tramp." He did not know the precise destination, but "it is strongly intimated that we go in the vicinity of Cincinnati, whither Bragg is reported to be going." Braxton Bragg, the men of Milwaukee knew, commanded the rebel forces that would soon confront them. That dark, glowering countenance with the heavily knit brows and salted, brushy beard would be their nemesis for the next year.

The men of the Milwaukee Regiment were "in excellent health and spirits," a soldier wrote, although some were hospitalized with various maladies. Among those left sick in Louisville was Date Worth, the twenty-three-year-old farmer. "The men have great confidence in the line and staff officers of the regiment, and are eager to be led into a battle under them, which, at the present writing, does not seem as if it would be long deferred, at least we hope not." The friendly environs of Cincinnati, however, would not be the destination.[34]

The 24th Wisconsin's initial campaign of the war was about to begin. Within a week, they would know firsthand the hardships talked about by veteran soldiers in their brigade. They would experience the hot and dusty marches, the thirst, and the deprivation. Milwaukee's "pets" would know what it was to be part of a faceless legion sent forward to do battle and save the Union.

On the final day of September, rumor had it that General Buell intended to move against the rebel army at Bardstown, about twenty-five miles south of Louisville. Although some dismissed the intelligence as mere camp talk, the rumor for once proved accurate. On Wednesday, October 1, 1862, the three corps, marching by different routes, left the friendly confines of Louisville. The soldiers were in high spirits, freshly supplied, and newly dressed. Martial music sent them on the roads south, and bayonets and sabers gleamed in the sunlight. Confidence was high.

Colonel Larrabee, in fact, predicted that the regiment would be back home before spring. "Mark my word on it," the colonel said. Sergeant Drake, who heard of the remark, was skeptical. *"Can't see it in that light,* can you?" he asked his brother. Despite his position as first sergeant in Company A, he was thus far not enamored with his soldier experience. "I think when I get home I shall appreciate the drug business more than ever. I certainly prefer it," he wrote.[35]

With 740 officers and men in its ranks, the 24th Wisconsin marched from Louisville, informed only that the regiment was bound for a "little picket duty." Thus, conical Sibley tents were left behind. "We . . . slept on the ground, rain or shine," Amandus Silsby of Company A wrote a few weeks later. But the new soldiers were burdened by all manner of civilized trappings—knapsacks, frying pans, coffee pots, boots, blankets, and the like. The veterans in the 36th Illinois probably hooted at all the impedimenta with which the Wisconsin soldiers were burdened; the men of Milwaukee would soon learn to trim their loads. "The heat was oppressive; the march almost beyond endurance," Lieutenant Mitchell remembered. Blankets, overcoats, and other immediately useless trappings were thrown away. The line of march was soon strewn with utensils and accoutrements as the men attempted to reduce their burdens. Thousands of tramping feet sent dust skyward into great billowing clouds. The blue uniforms quickly became brown with dust, and faces caked in powdery dirt.[36]

"We marched thirteen miles through as hot a sun as I've ever seen in Milwaukee in the middle of the summer," another Milwaukee soldier wrote home. "Along the road numerous niggers might be seen poking their ugly looking pates through the fences; and the best joke of the tramp was to see redheaded niggers. We had a good laugh at them." Such were the sensibilities of mid-nineteenth-century city men. But they would soon be exposed to the horrors of slavery, and many would change their views.

On Thursday, the men were roused in the darkness at four in the morning. Breakfast was prepared "extraordinarily quick; the process

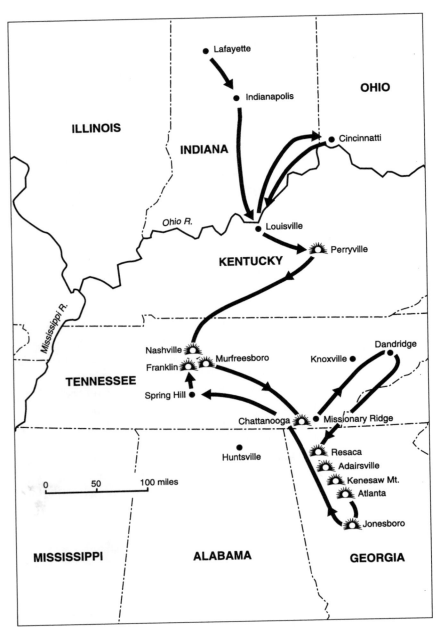

The Milwaukee Regiment's war.

COURTESY OF ELECTRIC DESIGN.

being simply, viz: to make a fire, get some unground coffee, brown it, pound it in my handkerchief with a stone, well mixed with sugar, and put it on the fire. Before it was half cooked, the drum beat to fall in, and the consequence was, that it was nothing but warm water sweetened— good enough for any 'dorg.'" The next morning, reveille was an hour earlier, and for breakfast, "we proposed to have as lucious one as possible, which consisted of a plate of fat bacon and crackers, and with a tinful of very impure water, we made a tolerably good breakfast, it being very palatable on account of our very ravenous appetite." Milwaukee wives and mothers were becoming discomfited by the less than hardy fare their men wrote about. The tainted water would soon take down scores of men.

The movement that day lasted until three o'clock—nine grueling, stifling, dusty hours. The line of march was filled with footsore stragglers. "Imagine for yourselves," Lieutenant Mitchell wrote, "when we arrived at the final place of encampment for that evening, some companies had only five men left. We had thirty-six men to stack arms out of fifty-six when we started on the march. They were strewed all along the road for four or five miles—men of robust constitutions—men whom you would have thought could stand any fatigue." They crossed the Salt River that day; some men removed their shoes, but others merely splashed across.[37]

Private Gilbert, meanwhile, was having more difficulties with footwear. Wading across a stream during the tramp (perhaps the Salt River), his rough leather infantry bootees became soaked; as he marched them dry, they stiffened so badly that they pinched his feet. He searched for new shoes among the regiment's supplies that night, but all he found was a pair of leather slippers. The quartermaster gave him the slippers with the agreement that when new shoes arrived for distribution, Gilbert would be given first choice. But he would march into his first and only battle shod in that uncommon footwear.[38]

Gene Comstock, too, was having some serious difficulty with his feet. "The first three days of the march my feet were skinned from heel to toe and so sore," he told his sister, Eliza. "I could have died then. I fell out by the roadside and was so downhearted that I could not help crying, but I got bravely over that. I was truly homesick, heartsick, and would have given thousands [of dollars] to have seen the face of any of you [his family]." He and others would in time become inured to the long absences from family and home; in many ways, the soldiers would find family with their daily comrades who shared the privations and horror of war. "Most every man in the regiment," Comstock wrote days later, "was foot sore[,] myself in particular. Some of the boys threw away their knapsacks with everything in them. I sold my second shirt to a teamster for $1.00 for which I paid $3.50. My woolen stockings I threw away and have now one shirt—on my back and no stockings."[39]

The load they carried seemed to grow heavier with each footfall. Loaded knapsacks weighed nearly fifty pounds, and the straps dug painfully into shoulders; the bulky Austrian muskets added nearly ten more pounds. "Our knapsacks are a great trouble to us," Silsby wrote. "I have stepped over a great many of them, also steel vests, & other heavy things." He also noted seeing a great many overcoats and blankets. "I lugged mine along with me 3 days when I was obliged to give up my blanket, as I could not carry '40 lbs & a musket,' 15 or more miles a day." Forty balls and powder packed in the cartridge boxes added more weight.[40]

Company G's tall toothless private, Jim Bacon, remembered that about a day out of Louisville "some kind of officer" ordered that the Wisconsin soldiers place their knapsacks in an ambulance wagon. But no sooner had the knapsacks been loaded than another officer ordered them to be thrown out. Here was military logic—or a ruse. The regiment marching in the rear of the Milwaukee soldiers was the veteran 36th Illinois, who "embraced the opportunity to replenish their wardrobes." Bacon lost his Bible in the bargain. But to his amazement the Testament, likely inscribed with his name, was returned to him some six months later.[41]

A soldier from the Old Northwest, perhaps a farmer with an eye for such things, was also taken by the dryness of the land. "The country was destitute of water. None was to be had except for pools and puddles along the road, which was very warm and putrid." A few days later, the same soldier noted in a diary entry that when men found a puddle they "dipped it up with a spoon and strained it through our dirty handkerchiefs." When a well was located, hundreds of soldiers waited for a chance to fill a canteen. Such was the paucity of vital water.[42]

General Gilbert, the corps commander, was not winning favor among the Wisconsin men. First, there was the matter regarding those burdensome knapsacks. Company G's Andrew Smith said the general was too "strict disciplinarian of the West Point School—too much so for Colonels, Majors, and Captains of volunteers. He frequently took off their shoulder straps." Colonel Larrabee, in an effort to help his weary men, had wagons brought up to carry the knapsacks of the "jaded men" during the grueling marches. Hearing of it, General Gilbert had Larrabee and Lieutenant Colonel Buttrick arrested and stripped of rank. Such actions were lightly regarded, and General Sheridan, impatient with such fussy generals as Gilbert, later returned the Wisconsin men's swords and even commended them.[43]

The 24th was one of the largest regiments in Sheridan's division, but when, on the third day of the march, they stacked their muskets, only about 300 men were present, "the rest had fallen out by the roadside and came straggling in all night and some were not seen till the next night," Corporal Comstock told his father.[44]

Over October 2 and 3, General Gilbert's corps marched some seventeen miles—a considerable distance to be sure, but far short of what the Milwaukee soldiers would cover as part of "Sheridan's cavalry." Little George Merrick, the five-foot-four-inch clerk in Company B, was likely struggling to keep pace. One man who impressed his comrades on the march was Sgt. George Allanson of Company B. A twenty-two-year-old newsdealer before his enlistment, the blue-eyed soldier was remembered for his "rheumatic legs [that] always *wobbled* on the march." But he kept up better than all of his company. Allanson would earn his shoulder straps early in the following year, catch rebel lead in two battles, and ultimately become captain of the Young Men's Association Tigers. Short-legged Lieutenant Mitchell, too, was striding along well: at least that was what he told his father. "Bob [Chivas] and myself have done the marching and sleeping out-doors very well," he wrote, "and we like the life very much."[45]

The corps snaked south along the Shepherdsville Road, gray-haired General Buell cantering along with General Gilbert's corps. Some soldiers made note of the fine looking country and the splendid residences interspersed with stands of timber. Yet there was no rain, and streams grew slack. Then, for a time, the weather grew dour, a wet drizzle compelling the men to don their heavy overcoats for protection; the wool became sodden: "if they kept us dry in one sense of the word, they kept us wet in another, for they almost sweat us to death. We camped that night . . . with weather as drizzly as ever, and enjoyed a sleep out doors as usual," described a Milwaukee volunteer. Even from the remove of thirty-five years, John Mitchell would recall the "nipping nights" when the men lacked sufficient covering, and rued the disposal of the good government issue.[46]

"The army in its onward march blocks up all the roads for a long ways, & resembles a sea of bayonets," Silsby observed. Kentucky, because it was a neutral state, was fair game for both Union and rebel alike; and the state was soon little more than "dust and mud." Rations, insufficient during the best of times, were again becoming a severe problem as the army marched farther from its base of supplies in Louisville. Lieutenant Mitchell assigned one of his Company I privates, a diminutive Irishman who "made a botch of every company maneuver," to be a "gobbler"; he was to sleep lightly in the morning, and "make a bee-line for the nearest rooster-crow" at dawn. The meaning was that he should pillage eggs and chickens from local farmers. Although Mitchell did not identify the Irish private to whom he assigned the task of securing breakfast, it may have been Milwaukeean James McCormick, who deserted the regiment in the aftermath of the Perryville battle. Silsby also admitted such "requisitions" to his father, the Presbyterian missionary. The boys seize everything they come across, the young soldier said, "geese, turkeys, sheep & pigs, & occasionally the 'fatted calf.'" Many, it appeared, had permitted Christian proscriptions to become early casualties of war. These were not tales John Mitchell would tell to his pastor at St. James Episcopal Church.[47]

The diligent army of foragers caused residents along the line of march to suffer great loss. The general issued orders against expropriation of private property by the soldiers. Such proscriptions, however, were ignored when growling stomachs encountered available provender. On one of the halts, some men of the 36th Illinois scaled a fence and filled their pockets with apples. The Wisconsin men likely learned of the episode at camp that night. General Gilbert caught some Prairie State soldiers in the "infamous act," and his fury rose to such heights that he ordered his escort to fire on the Illinois soldiers. "The men by the wayside all sprang to their feet, seized his [sic] musket," a regimental chronicler recalled after the war. It was becoming an ugly, almost mutinous incident.

"Ramming of cartridge and clicking of gunlocks was fearfully ominous and warned the escort to desist from putting the order into execution. The General saw the look of defiance and determination gleaming from the eyes of the men and did not repeat his heartless order." Gilbert angrily demanded to see the commanding officer. Capt. Silas Miller, commanding the Illinoisans, seated casually astride his horse, listened quietly to the general's invective before responding: "General, one word from me will call the boys out from that orchard a damn sight sooner than you can shoot them out, and should it come to that, I have the honor to assure you General that my boys never allow themselves to be outdone in a shooting business."

The defiant captain, whose exploit soon echoed through the ranks of the brigade, concluded pointedly: "[F]or the first flash of a carbine [from one of Gilbert's escorts] at one of them boys will be the death knell of every mothers son who had a hand in the business." Although none of the Milwaukee men wrote of the incident, it is certain such stories made the rounds while the brigade's every cook fire burned.[48]

General Gilbert was simply unable to understand these Western volunteers and give them a bit of leeway to fill their empty larders. On the evening of October 3, the corps camped at Cedar Creek, Kentucky. That day Gilbert had another confrontation, again with an officer of an Illinois regiment. The general stripped the colonel of the 86th Illinois, in another brigade, of his sword and placed him under arrest for watching some of his soldiers raid a persimmon tree. As he had earlier with Colonel Larrabee and Lieutenant Colonel Buttrick, General Gilbert took the subordinate's sword and put him under arrest. Although there was no record of any confrontation with Wisconsin soldiers, the reputation of General Gilbert among his men was tarnished beyond recall.

A young Milwaukee soldier in another regiment echoed what went on in the minds of his state comrades. "A soldier's life is no worse then I expected," he wrote to his parents, "but this management tries one's soul. We came to put down the rebellion, not to wear ourselves out by marching in the rear of the enemy. We ought to chase them faster; but now we let them escape!" The young man would soon rue those words when the horrors of the battle hit full force within a few days.[49]

On the afternoon of October 4, Gilbert's corps was ordered into Bardstown, evacuated by the rebels. The soldiers found a quiet, peaceful town with many residents on their way to Sunday morning services. The next day, General Gilbert was directed to push through Bardstown and march toward a Springfield rendezvous with General Crittenden's corps.

The area beyond Bardstown was browned by a summer-long drought, and with every dusty footfall the soldiers' thoughts turned toward water. "I never knew what it was to suffer for water before," Silsby wrote. "Now I am frequently glad to get any kind of water. I have drunk slimy standing water, that fairly smelt bad, & was glad to get it. I never saw a country so scarce for water before, as this is." The young soldier's experience was replicated in all of Buell's army. "The water is so thick and stagnant you can not see an inch into it," wrote a Wisconsin boy in another corps. "We drink from mud holes where swine are wallowing," and he noted a "deep sediment remains in the bottom of the cup." Waterborne disease would soon winnow the blue ranks.[50]

October 6 was warm and clear, and despite the parched throats and mouths, the men of the Army of the Ohio were in good spirits. "Country fine and splendid residences. Oak timber, rolling land," was a diary observation of a soldier in the 36th Illinois. The men were eager to confront the rebels and drive them from Kentucky.[51]

Skirmishing with elements of Confederate general Bragg's army increased between Bardstown and Springfield, as Gilbert's corps pressed upon the retreating enemy. As it approached the latter town that morning, the rebel cavalry waited. General Gilbert's lead elements of blue-coated horsemen thundered forward, and some infantry was deployed. The men in the 24th Wisconsin tensed in anticipation of a possible clash. But the expected collision did not occur that day, likely to the relief of the soldiers. In the aftermath, the Milwaukee men saw their first dead enemy soldier, tangible evidence of the price to be paid. When they marched through Springfield, they found a town "half deserted, dilapidated and odorous with bad whiskey and rebellion."[52]

Water grew scarcer each day. Squads were sent out to search for potable supplies. All came back discouraged: The men had found a well, but "there were hundreds there waiting for a chance to get at it." Beyond Springfield, a few fresh springs were located, but these were usually staked out for General Gilbert "who would send an aide in advance to select a romantic spot," wrote a caustic Illinois soldier, "where he pitched the General's Marquee and a detachment of body guards was sent to protect the sacred precincts as well as the spring from intrusion." There was no fairness in all of this in the eyes of Western volunteers.[53]

An hour before noon Tuesday, October 7, Gilbert's corps closed in toward Perryville along the Springfield Road. Perryville, south of Frankfort and southwest of Lexington and midway between the Ohio and Tennessee Rivers, was an unimposing town of only 500 residents. As the Wisconsin men would learn within a few days, the Boyle County community was set amid abrupt mounds of hills that rose and dipped like the furrows of a giant's brow. They were called Chaplin Hills, and for many the coming battle would bear that name.

General Sheridan's division, with General Buell riding near the front rank, moved forward to assess the situation. At two in the afternoon, an artillery battery, the 5th Wisconsin, opened fire on rebel cavalry. Buell's horse reared and threw the gray-haired general to the ground. He was painfully cut in the thigh. After the wound was stanched and bandaged, he was placed in an ambulance for the remainder of the day. The news rumbled down the blue columns of the corps, down to the last private in the rear rank of the 24th Wisconsin. By dusk that day, General Sheridan's division had pressed the rebel horsemen back through the defensive line surrounding Perryville.

General Gilbert's men inched forward, and about an hour before midnight the advance elements of the corps reached near Doctor's Creek. An Indiana regiment was sent forward to feel out the rebel position and seize the creek bed. When the Hoosiers collided with the gray-clad foe, they fell back. While the bulk of the corps was halted, General Sheridan's division was pressed forward at two in the morning. The 24th Wisconsin encamped on some heights to the right of the Springfield Road.

Gray-bearded Colonel Greusel made the rounds of his four regiments, and when he appeared before the Milwaukee men, his words may have quieted somewhat the apprehensions that probably crept into many a soldier's heart. On the morrow, when the battle broke, he would put his veteran 36th Illinois in the front rank.

"Men of the Badger state—you are drawn up here to be held in reserve, and are to support your brethren of the Prairie and Wolverine states." He offered encouragement to his "babies." "[I]f it should be necessary to withdraw the troops in front of you, and you should be ordered to take their places, I shall expect you to do it. From what I have seen of you, I know that you will do your duty."[54]

Lieutenant Greene had been detached sometime before as acting quartermaster, and that night, Tuesday, he found himself two miles from his company. Sergeant Hubbell, the student lawyer, remembered meeting him. Believing the battle would open the following morning, the Quaker officer asked Hubbell to relay a request to Lieutenant Colonel Buttrick that "if there was to be a fight not to fail to relieve *him,* as he *must* be there." Buttrick assented, and Lieutenant Greene returned to the Tigers of the Young Men's Association. "That shows the character of the man," Hubbell later attested.[55]

No fires were allowed that long night. The Milwaukee men lay on the ground, likely gripping their loaded Austrian muskets tightly, peering into the darkness, waiting for whatever came next. As did most of his comrades, Company G's toothless Jim Bacon had suffered terrible thirst in the hot and dusty march. But the twenty-one-year-old soldier determined to take matters in hand. He crept forward in the darkness, and stole inside rebel lines to a creek. While filling his canteen, the auburn-haired clerk was confronted by another Union soldier, a youngster in the 2nd Minnesota, who had taken the same chance for water. The incident was a small one, but a year and a half later when Bacon was out of the army and riding on a stage in Minnesota "comfortably filled with passengers," two army officers entertained the occupants with stories of the war. "One of the officers related his experience inside the enemy's line the night before the battle of Perryville," Bacon said. The tale had a familiar ring to the former Wisconsin soldier, and the teller "eyed me sharply and I was soon in embrace and hugged as I was never before or since by man." It was an incident that Bacon related to his veteran comrades twenty years later.[56]

The Milwaukee Regiment would later learn that Sheridan's 2nd Brigade under Brig. Gen. Dan McCook (brother of I Corps commander Alexander) was ordered to move forward and capture a prominence identified as Peter's Hill. In the predawn darkness of October 8, McCook deployed two regiments to fight for the prominence. The regiments descended the west side of Doctor's Creek, splashed across the water course, and made their way up the slope of Peter's Hill; on the forward side they exploded into the rebel line. Vivid orange tongues of powder licked at the gloom, and the bark of musket firing echoed back to Sheridan's other brigades. The rebels were driven off, and they retreated about one half mile away to another rise called Bottom Hill. Even though they were some distance back of the action that early morning, the Wisconsin men knew that the time to "see the elephant" was fast approaching.

When the sky pinked toward dawn around six, word filtered back that McCook's brigade had taken Peter's Hill. But he needed reinforcements. At daylight, the two other brigades of Sheridan's division were pressed forward, battle flags slapping the crisp Wednesday morning breeze. Another crescendo of musketry and cannons roared. Colonel Greusel's brigade was directed forward to take positions on either side of Peter's Hill. The 36th Illinois was positioned on the right of the Springfield Road, with its sister regiment, the 88th Illinois, on the left. Behind them were posted the 21st Michigan and 24th Wisconsin.

As it developed, the three columns of General Buell's army coalesced west of the town of Perryville, and their line ran south from the meandering Chaplin River. General Gilbert's corps was nearly due west of the town, and General Crittenden was positioned to its south. General Alexander McCook's command was positioned a good distance to the north opposite a wide loop in the Chaplin River.

As the new sun poked over the horizon to their front, the Milwaukee men surveyed the scene. Lieutenant Mitchell remembered it was a "mellow autumn day, the landscape was as pretty as a park; every prospect pleased, except the attitude of the enemy," he wrote decades afterward. Here was an idyllic calm before the storm.[57]

Company H's red-haired Irish corporal, Tom Ford, who enlisted from the farm community of Franklin south of Milwaukee, had not felt well since leaving Louisville a week before. That Wednesday morning he went to the regiment's surgeon, the immigrant Herman Hasse, for some palliative. All the doctor had was a five-gallon drum of castor oil. "Just set it on the top of that stump and take a swallow of it," Hasse prescribed. He also ordered Ford to place all his trappings in the surgeon's wagon. So the corporal marched forward to rejoin his company, wearing only a red shirt, pants, shoes, and a cap. Tom Ford would write of this with self-effacement more than three decades later.[58]

It was almost at this time, the Milwaukee soldiers would later learn, that the gray-clad enemy attempted to retake Peter's Hill only to be driven off by McCook's men in an hour-long artillery duel. Meantime, Sheridan ordered the two brigades to dig defensive rifle pits along the heavily wooded hillside. The soldiers loosened the hardened dry earth with bayonets and scooped the dirt with tin cups and plates and other ready implements, creating shallow trenches. It was shaping up to be a worrisome Wednesday.

Sheridan's first brigade, led by Col. Bernard Laiboldt, contained two St. Louis regiments of Germans, the 2nd and 15th Missouri (also former members of the Pea Ridge Brigade). Sent forward about 8:30 that sunny morning, they moved down the east slope of Peter's Hill; scattered shots from a woods 500 yards to their front scoured their ranks. Sheridan ordered forward two other regiments. The press of more Union soldiers caused the gray ranks to waver, and the attack was pushed successfully one-half mile until the blue line began clamoring up Bottom Hill. The cost was heavy casualties, however; blue-coated bodies scattered on either side of the roadway.

When the martinet general Gilbert arrived to assess the situation, he was shocked to learn that his diminutive subordinate, the new general of infantry, Sheridan, had pushed his division far forward, beyond the point he had ordained. He immediately ordered his subordinate to pull back to his original position on Peter's Hill, limiting his posture to the defensive unless ordered to attack. At eleven o'clock, Sheridan reluctantly complied; it was apparent he was impatient with his less than aggressive corps commander.[59]

For a time the Milwaukee soldiers were brought up and lay in reserve under the brow of a hill, "bullets and shells whistling and buzzing over our heads," Lieutenant Mitchell said. Then one man went limp, struck in the abdomen by a piece of shell. Gray-eyed Jim Hazell, the thirty-two-year-old railroad engineer who only weeks before joined Sam Philbrook's "Mississippi Roughs," was dead, the regiment's first battle casualty. Although his was the only fatality in the regiment, it would be a small comfort to a wife and two children left behind in Lone Rock, Wisconsin.[60]

Adjutant McArthur was there. Whether he was nervous or excited is not known. "[S]hot, shell and bullets made terrible music for a new regiment." The chronicler of the deed many years later wrote that Colonel Larrabee said he would give a horse to know what was heading toward his regiment from the other side of the hill. Without orders, the boy-lieutenant spurred his mount to the brow of the prominence, "coolly taking in the situation and drawing a furious fire" from the large body of rebels that was advancing.

The youngster whirled the horse and rode back. In a manner well beyond his tender seventeen years but indicative of one accustomed to having his way, McArthur suggested the 24th advance from the hollow, where they might be cut to pieces, to the hill to gain better advantage upon the advancing enemy. What thought passed through Larrabee's mind for that few seconds is unrecorded, but the regiment was advanced.[61]

The true test of that day lay yet ahead. Just now the Wisconsin soldiers had to be satisfied in watching the great event unfold. Sheridan's men were so situated that they could see Maj. Gen. Alexander McCook's corps moving into position about a mile to the north. On Peter's Hill, Sheridan was shocked as he watched elements of that corps stacking arms and ambling to Doctor's Creek to fill canteens with the brackish water. Little Phil could also see rebel divisions massing for an attack on McCook's unprepared position. He tried to signal that danger was imminent, but to no avail. The rebel waves smashed into the Federal left. The edgy Wisconsin soldiers observed in dismay as the gray lines surged triumphantly. They had friends there, in the 1st and 21st Wisconsin regiments who were being bludgeoned backward. "When [the] line was broken and the enemy's hosts were surging over the field, their advance line fringed with fire, every [field] glass was directed thitherward," recalled an Illinois soldier, "and when our lines went down before their irresistible charge, many a prayer went up to heaven. 'God help the boys now.'"[62]

Short-statured Lieutenant Mitchell, in an almost poetic flight, described the unsettling scene: "From this vantage ground, we surveyed the field of fight. Beneath the puffs of smoke that arose like incense to the god of battles, we could distinguish each move and counter-move of the contending armies."[63]

At noon that day, Colonel Greusel's brigade was advanced farther to the east. On the road, the Wisconsin men passed a grove of shade trees under which lay scores of wounded, "some with their legs off," the Company A youngster, Amandus Silsby, described, "and looking pale as a sheet, others wounded other ways. Nothing of which helped to steady our nerves. Next thing we met was a man led along with his face gashed up by a minie ball striking it side ways."[64]

That afternoon about three, Sheridan's artillery was trained upon the rebels attacking McCook's corps to the north. The 1st Missouri Battery elevated the muzzles of its brass-barreled guns, and thundered shot after shot obliquely, at enfilade in military terms; the projectiles burst into the crowded enemy ranks, rending formations. Rebel artillery, far fewer than their Federal counterparts, raised muzzles to return fire, but most of those shots fell far short of their marks.

It was sometime during these cacophonous minutes that another incident occurred that became indelibly marked on a soldier in the Milwaukee Regiment. Harry Rogers, at twenty-one the older of the Company B brothers, recalled from a vantage of two decades: "I can see just how that field looked—see it as well as I could in '62." A couple of officers rode up near where the regiment was lying, and Rogers, a sergeant at the time, took a couple of men to determine who they were. "The ginger-bread fixings on their arms [galloons] made me think they were rebels, and I asked them where they belonged." The gray-clad officers identified themselves as part of Gen. John Adams's brigade staff. "I told the boys to cover them with their pieces, and I climbed over the fence and demanded their arms." The major handed Rogers a dirk, "but the lieutenant said he never heard of an officer surrendering his sword to a non-commissioned officer."

The Milwaukee sergeant, who had carefully inked figures in a bookkeeper's ledger less than two months before, was adamant. "No matter what you have or have not heard of, hand me your arms and right away." The revolver was handed over, and the pair marched to Colonel Larrabee, who told Rogers to retain charge of the weapons. He stuffed the sidearm into his belt and buckled on the sword. "The captured arms and my Springfield rifle made me a well armed soldier." Either Rogers may have been hazy about details three decades later, as the Milwaukee Regiment carried Austrian muskets at the time of the Perryville battle; or he may have picked up a Springfield rifle-musket somewhere on the field. Moreover, Colonel Larrabee later claimed to have been among the men who captured the rebel officers.[65]

About 3:30 that afternoon, Sheridan became attentive to the movement in his front, just south of the Springfield Road. It appeared that the rebels were attempting to turn his left flank and capture the Federal battery that was savaging its ranks. Red battle flags snapped as the gray enemy marched in near parade-ground alignment. "They advanced most gallantly, marching in splendid order, not a man wavering or falling out of line," wrote an Illinois soldier. The attackers brushed through a cornfield in a long, sweeping line. Tension again mounted in the Wisconsin ranks, as it finally appeared that the onslaught would strike them directly. Breaking into a run, the rebels began their battle cry as they surged forward bent on a collision with the blue line. They yelled "like fiends broke loose from Pandemonium," wrote an Illinois man decades later. The blue batteries sighted on them and huge shotgun blasts of metal fragments cut bloody gaps in the surging ranks. After brief seconds to close alignment, the gray lines lunged forward again. The cannon shots cut down scores more, but still the rebels rushed forward, a wave cresting to break destructively. As they reached a rail fence, a hail of Union musketry savaged them.[66]

After about twenty minutes, Colonel Larrabee noted that the 24th Wisconsin was ordered forward to take the place of the 36th Illinois in the front rank. In thinking back on those desperate moments, some men found humor embedded in the deadly tableau. Ginger-headed Corporal Ford remembered a brigade orderly riding up to the colonel, directing him to march his regiment to the left of an artillery battery and "hold it at all hazards; the rebels are about to charge on it." Larrabee, Ford remembered, was somewhat hard of hearing and he cupped his hand to his ear, asking "What's that, sir?" Doubtless impatient, the orderly shouted the order again, and the Wisconsin colonel responded, "I will, by God, sir!" The colonel called the 24th to attention, and marched it to the left at double-quick time.

Cpl. Norm Burdick, who wrote much during his service, said the battle-hardened 36th Illinois "expected us to break and run like sheep." The spectacled printer still bore the red welts of bee stings, as only days before he had tried to confiscate a hive of honey. The angry insects "left tangible marks of their rebellious spirits upon his cheeks and nose," said a company comrade. But the 24th's "movement was rapidly and successfully accomplished under the fire of the enemy, who were in

position at a short range behind fences and in the edge of a cornfield."
Gene Comstock said that the Wisconsin men "came onto the ground in
double quick time yelling like fury."

"I was in the front rank in my company with no coat on and the
only red shirt visible in the regiment," Ford wrote three decades later.
He must have felt like a prime target; Dan, his younger brother, probably
watched his sibling in amazement.[67]

About that moment, the Germanic immigrant Lt. Christian Nix
arrived breathless with a fifty-man detachment of the 24th Wisconsin.
They had been assigned to guard supply trains, but after being relieved
had double-quicked two miles to join their comrades in battle. Some
weeks afterward, however, the story reached Milwaukee that Nix and
his men had straggled during the day's march. Nativistic sentiments
against new immigrants still died hard. Lt. George Bleyer later dis-
abused home folks of that spurious intelligence.[68]

When "the rebels [caught] sight of the new uniforms of our Regt,
. . . [they] immediately recognized the 'green hands' and turned their fire
on us," young Amandus Silsby wrote. The bullets hissed inches from his
head, or so it seemed. "[Y]ou may believe I wished myself at home."
Colonel Larrabee gave orders for the men to fire low and aim at the
rebels' knees. "One wounded man was worth 3 dead ones, as it took 2
more to carry him off."[69]

"I have heard a good deal about a person's feelings in the first battle," wrote the tall Scot in the Merchants Guards, Lieutenant Chivas.
"When first exposed to fire and when seeing the dead and wounded
falling around, for my part I will candidly say that I felt no peculiar sensation whatever." Here was a bit of youthful braggadocio from the
twenty-year-old immigrant.

Chivas's cousin, John Mitchell, recalled, "We were advanced to the
crest of a hill. The enemy stood below us in a corn-field. They saluted
us with a volley; the bullets, like a flight of bees, hummed harmlessly
overhead." This was their 'baptism of fire.'" He also boasted that the
Merchants Guard, his Company I boys, were "in the most dangerous
and consequently most honorable position, being in full view of the
enemy, which the other companies were not."[70]

"Old Nick" Greusel watched his Badger "babies" with pride. The
24th "went forward under cheers, soon engaged the enemy's right,
pouring in, and keeping up a cross fire on their [rebel] brigade, which
made havoc amongst them," he said. The colonel himself was winning

the admiration of his soldiers, personally placing regiments into line, "exposing himself with perfect *sang froid* to the bullets of the treacherous enemy," said a Chicago news writer.[71]

The Milwaukee Regiment was in the front line beside the 88th Illinois and the Preachers of the 73rd from the 1st Brigade. The Wisconsin men opened on the rebels behind the fence. The three units fired by regiments, as Private Silsby described: "[O]ne regiment would fire a volley and then the next Regt would fire &c. They fired so precisely that it sounded like the roar of cannon." The missionary's son ducked and dodged as the rebel lead hissed overhead. But after a while, he was able to "stand it better, & look around me. The cannon balls [made] such a screaming sound, and when they struck a log, it would tear into it and make the splinters fly. The shells had a kind of humming sound. Their bursting in the air I thought looked beautiful (providing they kept a proper distance)." He was becoming a soldier, as were many of his comrades. A Louisiana regiment, bayonets gleaming, charged, attempting to break the Union line. But two Federal regiments, concealed in a hollow, rose up in front of the Wisconsin soldiers and poured a "deadly volley" into the enemy. The gray lines broke and fled, leaving comrades crumpled behind.[72]

The Milwaukee Regiment was too far out front of the crest of Peter's Hill, and the order was given to fall back about twenty paces. Red-shirted Tom Ford "was so interested loading and firing at the rebels down in that cornfield" that he did not hear the order to withdraw. The regiment pulled back, re-formed and was ready to fire from its new position when men began shouting at Ford. Colonel Larrabee sent Adjutant McArthur galloping forward. "You, man with the red shirt, fall back," shouted the boyish officer. "I knew that meant me," Ford said. "Too quick did I about face and double-quick to my place in the front rank of my company." In Company B, blue-eyed Art Gilbert, still wearing unorthodox footgear, was pegging away as best he could. When he recalled that experience a quarter of a century later, he tried to turn an ironic phrase to describe himself as "a worthy comrade if only a kid in kid slippers."[73]

The scenes of battle also moved Lieutenant Bleyer of Company A, who had only weeks before gained his officer's bars. Late in the afternoon, the "rebels reached the edge of the corn field, within fifty yards of our lines, and poured a rapid fire" upon the blue regiments as they advanced. "The strait was a desperate one," he said. "The roll of musketry and the roar of cannon was deafening." An Ohio regiment, positioned under a brow of a hill in front of the Milwaukee Regiment, was driven back in disarray. The 24th poured a thunderous volley into the advancing foe. Brigade Commander Greusel took off his hat and twirled it in the air. His regiments responded with a resounding cheer and more lead.

Andrew Smith, in Company A, admitted his admiration of the rebel attackers. "Certainly no soldiers in the world ever went into a fight with more coolness and determination than they did. They would form a few hundred yards in our front four regiments deep, hoist their colors and charge with fury right up to the mouths of our guns, and when their ranks were thinned they would coolly close up from left and right."

The Federal battery "belched forth of grape and canister a perfect torrent, and the [36th] Illinois and 24th Wisconsin treated them as badly," Lieutenant Bleyer wrote. The attackers reached a rail fence, but there they wavered and stopped. Unable to stand up to the shredding storm of lead, the gray ranks turned heel to the Wisconsin men in a flight for safety. The ground behind them was seeded with dead and dying. "The day . . . was ours!" celebrated Bleyer the following day. "No more perfect victory was ever won."[74]

When the command to cease firing was given, Captain Root, only five feet five inches tall, took his life in his hands to stop his men from loosing more shots. "[W]ith a smile on his face, but with a heart that never feared to meet his God, he ran in front of his men, knocking their muskets up with his sword." He nearly lost his life in the action, a comrade said. Root would court more danger in the battles ahead.[75]

"Behind the fence and in the edge of the cornfield, where the enemy had so long and gallantly contended," wrote a 36th Illinois chronicler, "their dead and wounded lay in swaths. All through the field bodies attired in Confederate gray scattered among the long aisles of corn."

Along the Springfield Road, the situation quieted. The regiments were exhausted from the fighting and maneuvering. They fell with their muskets at their sides, too tired even to worry about food. They had not eaten since before dawn. The regimental historian of the 36th Illinois waxed almost poetic in postwar years about the battle's deadly tableau:

Despite the excitements of the day—despite the dead, sleeping their last long sleep, some laying within a few feet of living sleepers—exhausted nature exerted its sway, and the solemn reflections born of the hour could not keep them long awake, except the faithful sentinels, keeping watch over their companions, all were soon soundly sleeping. The chirping of crickets, or some new and unwanted sound, would cause those on guard

to hold their breath and listen intently for movements indicative
of a night attack. Occasionally their nerves were put in a quiver
of horror as they stumbled in the darkness over the cold body
of some dead brave.[76]

Red-shirted Cpl. Tom Ford slept uncomfortably with his brother
Dan and their Company H comrades that night, "laying on the ground
with nothing between me and the blue sky but my shirt, pants, shoes
and cap." At least he had had a good dose of castor oil.[77]

The hours past may have seemed horrific, but casualties in the 24th
Wisconsin were slight—Hazell, the railroad man and father of two, was
killed, and three wounded. Colonel Greusel's Brigade sustained 143
killed, wounded, or missing; the veteran Pea Ridgers numbered over
half of those casualties. When the regiment settled down for the
evening, it lay within a few rods of more horror of battle. Silsby,
impressed by the awful sight, described what he saw the next day in
uncommonly graphic detail:

I saw 130 dead men [rebels] in one place; one shell killed 5
men, a cannon ball had struck one man (who was laying
down), on the knee [and] ripped up the flesh the whole length
of the thigh, laying bare the bone, & ripping open his bowels
scattering them around him, &c. They turned green rapidly
(i.e.) the rebels bodies, on account of their drinking whiskey &
gunpowder, but I don't like to think of the sights I saw there.[78]

In a few days, men would quickly jot letters home to say they were
safe. Lieutenant Mitchell penciled a few lines on some greasy paper.
We "feel first rate," he boasted. "Our Regiment acquitted itself well
defending a battery, which was attacked by a rebel brigade." The slender old colonel, Greusel, "acted splendidly and is admired by the whole
Brigade."

Colonel Larrabee "gave his orders as cooly as on dress parade,"
Corporal Burdick wrote, "and it was probably owing a great degree, to
his coolness and nerve that the regiment acquitted themselves so well."
The printer was still likely nursing those bee stings.[79]

In several days, Division Commander Sheridan would officially
"praise . . . the good conduct of the officers and men of [his] whole
division. . . . The new troops vied with the old troops . . . in their coolness and steadiness." The fierce little general also complimented the

24th for "gallantry and good behavior," a Milwaukee soldier in Company B wrote home. "Tell my friends that the whole regiment is well, and that it fought 'bully' for a new one." Brigade Comdr. Nicholas Greusel also lauded the 24th's performance under fire. "Both officers and men behaved with coolness and deliberation, marching to the front with the steadiness of veterans, and firing very regularly, though under the heaviest musketry I ever experienced." And almost thirty years later, he would write about the Milwaukee Regiment "being only babies at Perryville, yet [they] stood shoulder to shoulder with my old veteran regiment [the 36th Illinois]."[80]

The heroics of the fresh-faced McArthur did not go unnoticed. It was reported that he "conducted himself bravely." After the century's turn, Jerry Watrous, the old Iron Brigade veteran who never tired of burnishing the lad's reputation, wrote: "Throughout the fight the boy adjutant was the only mounted officer the regiment saw or heard. He rode along the line, in front of the men, smiling like a schoolboy at a snow-balling, and at the right time and the right place his changing voice rang out with words that cheered the thousand youngsters."

At one point, Watrous wrote, McArthur galloped along the line of Wisconsin men and "with the same cracked voice that had so greatly amused them two months before" shouted, "They are coming, boys; hold your fire until they reach the brow of the hill, and then give them a volley." Here was a grand scene, indeed, created for readers on the eve of the war's fiftieth anniversary. After the battle, Watrous wrote, most praised the "squeaky-voiced adjutant," but "the colonel and his associates had nothing to say." The legend of Arthur McArthur was beginning to be writ large.[81]

Although the sights of the battle's aftermath—the dead and maimed men of gray and blue—were unsettling, the Wisconsin soldiers breathed with considerably more assurance after their first taste of battle. They had, indeed, been christened by shot and shell, death and destruction, and had stood the test. The 24th Wisconsin flag would soon bear a battle legend painted on one of its white stripes: CHAPLIN HILLS it would proclaim. In reflection, the fight near Perryville may have seemed relatively easy for Chivas, Mitchell, and others. But the war hereafter would require much more than youthful posturing. The months ahead would take a decidedly deadlier turn for the Milwaukee men. The days to come would be fraught with more exhausting marches, much boredom, and considerably more loss of Wisconsin life and limb. The volunteers were not quite veterans yet.

Chapter 5

Between Battles

❈

"On the eve of exciting times."

The first several days of October 1862 were anxious ones for many Milwaukee mothers, wives, and families. Since nearly half of the city had some connection with men in the 24th Wisconsin, anxiety spread widely in the community. Although indications of imminent battle in Kentucky grew more pronounced, the fate of loved ones and friends in the 24th Wisconsin was unknown for many days after the fight. On the other hand, news columns in late September and early October were filled with the sorrowful accounts of battles in the East—South Mountain and Antietam in Maryland—that had cost the Army of the Potomac heavy losses. Columns of Milwaukee names appeared on casualty lists printed in the four-page dailies.

Finally, in mid-October telegraphs clattered the news, and dark headlines proclaimed the story: "A DESPERATE BATTLE IN KENTUCKY!" Then, preliminary accounts were received that the Milwaukee Regiment had "behaved grandly, standing up to receive the fire like veteran soldiers." Only one man, the thirty-two-year-old husband and father from Lone Rock, Wisconsin, Jim Hazel, had been killed. Hundreds of Milwaukee homes were relieved and grateful. "Adjutant McArthur is reported to have conducted himself bravely, as well as all the other officers. The boys faced the whizzing bullets without flinching.

Tom Balding.
"Little cuss of a captain."
COURTESY OF MARC AND BETH STORCH.

The clothes and accoutrements of many of the men were perforated with bullets," related the Democratic daily.[1]

Lt. John Mitchell of the Merchants Guard, Company I, quickly jotted a terse letter to his father, assuring the influential Alexander of his safety: "We (our Reg.) no sooner began firing than the enemy took to its heels across the corn-field from which they had been firing. They left upwards of a hundred in the field." The Wisconsin men had captured a half-dozen prisoners, he wrote. To his mother, Martha, days later, Mitchell seemed to minimize the battle, echoing his cousin Chivas's views. "We have just passed through the crisis of a battle and find it is somewhat of a matter-of-fact operation after all." The next battle would not be so matter-of-fact.[2]

The boyish, gray-eyed adjutant, Lt. Arthur McArthur, was likely occupied with paperwork in the aftermath of the battle. He had to secure loss reports from the company captains, compile them in ledgers, and report to the colonel. It is probable that the lad communicated with his father, the judge, and younger brother during these days, detailing his experiences, and describing how he had stood up to his first battle. Since a spare handful of war letters survive, however, it is impossible to know for certain what he thought and felt, or how the din and blood affected the slender, wavy-haired young man.[3]

Had Colonel Larrabee, after Lieutenant McArthur's deportment at Chaplin Hills, softened his impression of the boy? Kindly captain Tom Balding of Company A was doing his best to gain favor for the lad. News writer and veteran Jerry Watrous, ever the guardian of reputations and battle lore late in the century, described a scene that took place the night after the battle.

When the gray brigade commander, the Illinois soldier, Colonel Greusel, thanked Larrabee that night for the 24th Wisconsin's good work, Balding, the Englishman, nudged the boy-adjutant and gently said, "I'll see that the General hears who it was that opened the way for the regiment to win praise. Keep on, my boy; you are on the up grade. The officers who sneered at you back in Wisconsin are already ashamed of themselves."[4]

But Colonel Larrabee failed to mention specifically McArthur's actions in his official report of October 10, 1862. In that account, duly printed on the front page of a Milwaukee daily, he praised the entire regiment: "I cannot commend too highly the conduct of both officers and men," he wrote. "They advanced under the fire of the enemy and formed in position with the coolness and celerity of veterans. I feel that you may depend upon them in the future." It was a splendid tribute that warmed many Milwaukee homes. Their sons, husbands, and friends had stood manfully to the first test of battle. The casualties had been mercifully light. Curiously, the colonel's report was never included in the official military records published two decades after the war. Reports after the Milwaukee Regiment's next battle would be far less sanguine.[5]

Maj. Gen. Don Carlos Buell's Army of the Ohio camped near the battlefield for two days, counting its losses, catching its breath, and reassembling itself into an ordered organization after the confusion of battle. Several of the Milwaukee men took time to view the effects of the recent confrontation with Bragg's army along the Chaplin River. Certainly, these nineteenth-century men were accustomed to death in their lives, but the utter magnitude of the slaughter here must have troubled them. Those who wrote were universal in their descriptions of the ghastliness.

Most immediate to hand was the effect of the Milwaukee Regiment's musket fire. Company B's corporal Gene Comstock, the blue-eyed, nineteen-year-old printer, wrote his mother that dead rebels lay about in front of the regiment's position "at every step" two days after the battle. "We were the only regiment firing in the corn field." He counted at least 300 dead bodies in gray. The soldier correspondent identified only as "C. S." said the "sight was horrible. The dead are lying all over the field, in numbers not to be counted. In one place in the woods five men and five horses were piled together, all killed probably by the same shell."[6]

Comstock's company comrade, Cpl. Norm Burdick, the other printer, the same day found: "Every house around here, within a circuit of eight or ten miles, is used as a hospital, and the yards around them are covered with the dead and wounded, both Union and rebel." He found 380 dead rebels in the cornfield in front of the 24th's position of Wednesday, "and such a sight I hope never to see again. They were shot by cannon balls, shell, grape, minie rifle balls, and every description of missile know[n] to the military art, and in every imaginable place. One man had half his thigh shot away and his bowels completely torn out by a shell; another had his head taken from his shoulders as clean as if done by a knife, and so on through the sickening chapter," he said. The line was littered with corpses and animal remains for eight miles where fighting raged that Wednesday.

Date Worth, the Granville farmer who returned to Company E the day after the battle, was also horrified by the grisly scenes. "The field of battle is awfull [*sic*] to look upon," he penciled in a neat, even hand. The "dead are cut and mangled in all conceivable shapes." Three days later many were still unburied, and "some begin to smell very bad." Here were cruel details for a family.[7]

Chivas, the rangy Scot lieutenant in Company I, was shaken as well. Although he had admitted an uncommon calmness during the battle, the carnage remaining after the fight was very troubling. "Every home for miles around was occupied as an hospital and was stuffed inside and out with the wounded and dying. Legs and arms might be seen lying around loose[;] poor wretches wounded in every conceivable place lay groaning on the ground. Dead men and horses were scattered all over the field," he penned graphically to his uncle. "There was one place in particular where the strife had been most terrific, the very ground seemed rent and torn, bullets, balls, and pieces of exploded shells lay on every foot. Federates and Confederates had been mixed up in the greatest confusion."[8]

The Milwaukee soldier "C. S." paid particular attention to the enemy's muskets in battle's aftermath, finding that Bragg's men, contrary to camp rumor, were as well armed as the blue soldiers; he had picked up bullets to prove it. "The cartridges they most used were the

Enfield ball cartridge, made in Birmingham, England, by E. & A. Ludlow. They had eight different and distinct kinds of balls," he wrote. "They [the enemy] had a great many of the Enfield rifles, and the Springfield musket also. The idea that they were poorly armed (especially in small arms) is all nonsense, as the arms they left behind sufficiently attest. The guns left behind were all as good as ours," he noted. Among the detritus of battle, he even found Austrian rifle-muskets similar to those carried by his own regiment.[9]

After two days, the glowering General Buell finally roused his army. Time enough had been spent licking wounds, and organizing regiments and brigades. In the weeks to follow many in the rank would grumble over their hastily kindled campfires each night about the incessant marching; and many would complain more bitterly about Buell's almost traitorous inability to follow up the victory and smash Bragg's rebel army.

Leaving the battlefield near Perryville, the former news worker, Lt. George Bleyer, described his impressions in almost elegiac prose: "The sun was setting, and from the high hill over which the Division was marching, I took a long last look at the field. In the far distance were hundreds of camp fires [the divisions of General McCook's nearly wrecked corps]." Lieutenant Bleyer, the son of immigrants, gazed for only a moment, before the 24th Wisconsin descended into a valley and was enveloped by the deep darkness of night. The route was northeast toward Harrodsburg where the regiment camped "on a bleak hill—not over comfortable quarters, as a 'stiff northern' blew all night long."[10]

"What [the 24th Wisconsin] suffered in the march . . . will never be known, because language is inadequate to describe the hardships of the march." So wrote Milwaukee sheriff Charles Larkin to the Democratic daily; he had traveled with the regiment for several of those days visiting his eighteen-year-old son, Company H's tender lieutenant Court Larkin; he was also soliciting votes for the impending November elections. "Without tents, they were driven with inadequate rations under the enormous burden of knapsacks, cartridges and guns," said the Democratic Party politician.[11]

In the weeks that followed, Buell's army was a marching host. Lieutenant Bleyer maintained an accurate record of the miles: Between October 1 and November 10, he would soon write, the Milwaukee Regiment slogged 400 miles. The longest daily trek measured twenty-three miles. And it would be on the road every day in those weeks except seven. Corporal Comstock and his comrades found it grueling.

"If I could write one half of what I think in the night when I am laying awake[,] I could make a long letter but it is impossible." He was too worn down to make his mind and pencil work properly.[12]

Yet there was some cause for optimism, at least expressed by Company I's second lieutenant, John Mitchell, a week after the battle. "Things at present seem to look bright for our side, brighter than ever before," he told his mother. "And we are rolling forward in high hope of a triumphant army to consummate what had been so well begun." Such optimism was quickly dashed, however.[13]

We "resumed chasing the enemy[,] catching from 50 to 100 shaggers every day till the 17th when we stopped no one knowing what for," Company B's Comstock wrote home. The regiment, he said, had been traveling without tents, and rumor bubbled through the camps that the army would march for Cincinnati, then be sent by cars to Washington. "As to the truth we can't tell, but hope it is so, for a more Godforsaken country than Kentucky never was heard of."[14]

Perhaps as much as the recent battle, the grueling marches and deprivations were changing the Milwaukee men: They were becoming hardened to army existence. Undoubtedly, muscles were growing tauter and bodies leaner. These mostly city men were being broken down, almost fundamentally transformed, as much by design as circumstance—even though they might not understand. The first indications were physical appearance. Gone were the days when a nicely tailored suit and a handsome cravat adorned these clerks and bookkeepers. Even bathing was an infrequent experience.

"I will describe myself as near as possible," the nineteen-year-old printer, Corporal Comstock, told his mother and sister: "I am as hard a looking chap as you generally see." Yet he felt fine physically: "I eat most everything that comes handy and am as healthy as ever I was in the whole course of my life, and am growing strong. Nothing bothers me but water and good water cannot be found in Kentucky." To his father weeks later he described himself: "The hat—all faded streaks with the front piece washed double with heat from standing over the fire and half torn off," he said. "The coat—the back all grease which was got on by a boy in Co K who stole it from me. My pants—inside of my boots and they are all grease got on by myself—and finish up with a half limp in my right leg the remains of my first three days march."[15]

Company A's Sergeant Drake, the druggist, experienced a similar toughening to soldier life: "You would hardly know me now, sunburnt, dirty . . . [and] besides quite a heavy beard and *mustache* which I now

John Mitchell.
"We have just passed through
the crisis of a battle."
COURTESY OF BOB BRUE.

support [on] my *phiz* wonderfully," he told his brother and business partner, John.[16]

Even Lieutenant Mitchell of the Merchants Guards, accustomed to a life of ease, luxury, and learning, discerned a difference. When he sent home likenesses of himself taken a few weeks later he told his father: "I was gay, I am now somewhat rough-looking; I was clean, I am now rather dirty." But there was a deeper change, and he would later create a darkly humorous ditty about himself.[17]

"[Y]ou have no idea what soldiering is," Corporal Comstock confided in his sister, Eliza, "neither did I." He went on to describe in fair detail what the men began to call their "traps":

My knapsack, filled with nothing but a blanket I took from a Secesh of the battle field, my overcoat, then comes my haversack filled with 3 days rations, knife, fork, plate, cup and spoon. Rations consist of eighteen crackers about the size of the soda crackers you have seen, a chunk of salt pork 3 inches wide and the same thick and 8 inches long, all fat, 36 ounces of sugar, and a half pint of coffee. That is what we have had every day since we left Louisville and nothing more. Next comes [a] cartridge box, belt and bayonet scabbard. In [the] cartridge box are 60 rounds of ammunition; and fetch up with a gun.

He had only the shirt on his back and no stockings; but he did have "an excellent pair of boots."[18]

As the Milwaukee men wearily tramped on, the Kentucky weather began to assume its fall mantle. Some days after marching from the battlefield, the regiment, halted at the roadside, encountered Maj. Gen. Alexander McCook's corps, among them several badly battered Wisconsin regiments, prostrated along the line of march. McCook's men had taken a bloody beating on the left at Perryville. There was the 1st Wisconsin Infantry, Lieutenant Bleyer's old regiment, now re-formed for three years service, "with its tattered flags redolent of a heavy engagement." The 24th gave them three rousing cheers that were returned in kind.

Then, the Milwaukeeans were passed by the badly cut up 21st, whose colonel, Ben Sweet, had been so terribly wounded that he would never return to the field, and whose major, Milwaukeean Fred Schumacher, the former city surveyor, lay in a shallow Kentucky grave. The immigrant Christian Nix had served with both of these men in the 6th Wisconsin.[19]

Milwaukee men cheered again to the 21st. "'Good old Wisconsin cheers' are very animating—there is an iron ring to them that tells that they come from hearts of the true metal," Lieutenant Bleyer penned. In a month and a half, the Milwaukee Regiment's mettle would indeed be tested in a bloody crucible on New Year's Eve in Tennessee.

They tramped on through country that was "very open . . . and rich and rolling." The army reached Harrodsburg on the Lexington Pike and camped again. "A heavy rain fell towards evening" and, as the regiment was again without its conical Sibley tents and poorly supplied with rations, suffering spread. "The boys will be pardoned if they detested soldiering in 'lively times,' and wished the war was over," Lieutenant Bleyer wrote to his Milwaukee readers.[20]

McArthur, like his fellow soldiers in the 24th, likely bore up as well as could be expected. Few chroniclers in those days mentioned the young, gray-eyed officer, but he must have been affected by the arduous marches and the cold camps. As the regiment's adjutant, he was kept busy tallying the roll of the ten companies and with other duties meted out to him by the colonel.

The Milwaukee Regiment now listed about 700 men in its ranks. In addition to the continued drain of men from the regiment's rolls caused by illness and assignments away from the unit, McArthur duly reported the steady loss of men who deserted. More than 30 had skedaddled already, and nearly every company was affected. No one complained of such matters, but there must have been disdain expressed toward these men. Many who stole away were what they called "bounty jumpers," men who joined only to receive the volunteer bonuses paid by the Chamber of Commerce and other organizations. After deserting, some of these miscreants signed the roll of other regiments, collected more bonus money, and swore the Federal oath. With greenbacks in hand, they simply slipped away from the new regiment again at an opportune moment. While the 24th Wisconsin camped and marched about northern Kentucky before the recent battle, a dozen quit the ranks. In battle's aftermath, too, in October and early November, nearly 20 more clandestinely packed their traps and were not seen again.[21]

What was more unsettling, on Monday, just five days after the battle, one man was drummed from the regiment. He was Ozias Brower from Perth, Canada, who had been recruited by Capt. Gus Goldsmith. The episode must have left an impression upon all the soldiers, but none described it in his writings. Whether Brower had exhibited cowardice in the recent battle, attempted to desert, or committed some other heinous crime was not recorded. But it was the practice for an entire regiment or even a brigade to be drawn up in a hollow square to witness the ceremony. As the young drummer boys rattled the "rogue's march" on their snares, Brower's brass eagle buttons may have been stripped from his coat. His head may have been shaved. A four-man guard carrying their Austrian muskets reversed may have preceded Brower while another file of men followed with bayonets at the charge. The miscreant was escorted beyond the camp's confines. He was no longer a member of the Milwaukee Regiment.[22]

That night, two rebel deserters slipped into the 24th Wisconsin's lines. One, surprisingly, identified himself as a Wisconsin lad from Manitowoc, the Lake Michigan port town far north of Milwaukee. He said his name was Michael Flynn, and described a circumstance strikingly similar to that of the tailor in Company C, Justus Lauterbach. While traveling in the South, Flynn claimed he had been forced into an Arkansas infantry regiment seventeen months before, and had been unable to escape until recently. "He says that Bragg's army is poorly fed, receiving a half-cup of flour and a half pound of bacon, and of little molasses for a day's rations." The other man said he was from Iowa, and while he worked in the South had been forced into a Louisiana outfit. "They are, however, well clothed." No note of their fate was made.[23]

With an air of Scots superiority, Lieutenant Mitchell carefully studied the rebel deserters who wandered into the Union army lines. He noted that they "appear to be of a very low grade of humanity, lean and cadaverous, ill-clad and dirty, disheveled and lousy; their countenances for the most part showing the predominance of bad passions." He would learn within a few weeks just how those "bad passions" served them in battle.[24]

Weather in the days that followed remained hospitable. "Indian summer, with its cool, translucent airs, and deep blue skies, is now the rage," Lieutenant Bleyer wrote. "The woods are shedding their russet-tinged garb, and grass is turning brown. Haze lies upon the valleys and creeps up the hills. It is the loveliest season of the year, and the army enjoys it largely. There can be no better marching weather." The former "typo's" poetic bent was apparent; he was probably also scribbling verse in a small notebook as he had done for many years.

Near Lancaster, Kentucky, just days later, two soldier correspondents to the Republican news sheet noted that the regiment had now tramped 150 miles since the first of the month. The route of march was at first one direction, than another, in seemingly aimless forward and retrograde movements. They passed Mountain, Washington, Bardstown, Shepherdsville, Springfield, Harrodsburg, Danville, and Lancaster. It all appeared as a bad game of chess with Buell and Bragg manipulating the dispensable soldier pieces.

Since the battle of the week past, the army had been nipping on Bragg's heels. On October 15, Federal artillery had driven the rebels from Lancaster, and took possession of the town; twenty miles southeast of Perryville, the place was "modest and retiring" in appearance. The inhabitants waved flags and exhibited strong Union feelings. "The town wore the aspect of a Northern Fourth of July," one soldier said. Lieutenant Bleyer wrote that the jubilant citizens "flung out the good 'old flag' from the court house, and from every door. The ladies and children wished us Godspeed."[25]

One writer related that a loyal citizen of Lancaster had informed him that people with Union sympathies had been subjected to insults and their stores taken by the rebels. One woman had been forced to bake three bushels of biscuits for Bragg's men. "The country is devastated for miles around—the corn wasted and the houses plundered of everything of any use," the Milwaukee man said. "The people living along the line of the road complain bitterly of the rebels. Everyone says they are heartily sick of rebel rulers, and welcome our army with shouts of joy."[26]

Forward movement soon commenced again, the line of march seeming to become more or less in the correct direction—southwest.

After more miles, still another halt was called Thursday, October 16, this time at Dicks River, some ninety-five miles southeast of Louisville. The army's general, camp critics had it, stopped again, apparently uncertain which way to turn his army. He seemed unaware of the location of his antagonist, Bragg. There was much grumbling from those in the back rank: "[H]ad we followed up briskly [we] might have annihilated the whole of the [rebel army] before they reached Danville, fifteen miles distant. The night was bright and we would have had no trouble in keeping close lines, but we withdrew, slept on our arms, and by daylight the next morning [October 9] Bragg had his whole army in Danville, and nearly all his wounded. It does seem an utter impossibility for our officers to out general the wary confederates," Company G's Andrew Smith fretted.[27]

Another Milwaukee soldier whose opinion found its way into the Republican news sheet groused that had Bragg been pursued with vigor "we could have bagged the majority, if not all his army, but it seemed as though we waited to give him a chance to get away . . . . There is no doubt in my mind that old Buell is either a d—d old traitor, or a muddle-headed old fool." Strong words, indeed.[28]

Cpl. Norm Burdick of Company B was equally caustic in his assessment: "Gen. Buell, probably seeing that we were pressing rather too closely upon the rear guard of his old friend, Bragg, halted the 'Army of the Ohio'. . . and gave it a rest of four days, at the expiration of which time, he faced about, and marched us, as if the rebels were after us, back to Lebanon, a distance of sixty miles, in three days time, where we had another rest of four days on the banks of the Rolling Forks."[29]

"The soldiers are tired and fretful with such continued marching, forward then backward, and all to no account," groused Company G's Andrew Smith. "They want to fight or go home. We think so much dilla-dallying disgraces the whole army in the eyes of our honest patriots at home." Confidence in the commanding general continued to erode among men in the Milwaukee ranks.[30]

The days of tramping and exhaustion felt as though they might never end. A footsore Sergeant Drake concluded that "10 days seems like a century to me." Soldiers attempted to find some diversion when they could. "Camp life is hard," Corporal Comstock said looking back on the days since the battle, "yet there is some fun in it. Gassing, smoking and telling stories while sitting around the fire at night, off in the woods in the distance getting nuts[,] some doing one thing some another. While we are on the march it is hard, for sometimes we lay down on the ground and go to sleep hungry rather than wait to build a fire and get things out to cook with." And having discharged the Company B cook—likely a "contraband" or freed Negro—he and his messmates had to do their own meal preparation.

"The utensils used are a tin cup the same one we drink out of—a tin plate the same one we eat off from. I have neither knife or fork and the ends of my fingers are nearly burnt off," Comstock described. "We sometimes fall short of rations when we get a plate that belongs to some of the boys that has been made into a sort of grater and some hard corn grate[d] about 3 ears of it to make corn meal and from that sort of gruel without any seasoning. Everything is cooked without seasoning."[31]

Sergeant Drake, the dark-eyed twenty-one-year-old who would soon wear officer's straps, had much the same experience. "We have had what most men would call *tough times.*" He said the men carried three days' rations, hardtack, and salted pork, in their haversacks while knapsacks were packed with blankets and overcoat; "at night sleep out in the open air without a tent to cover us, and when the dew falls as it does in this country, it will wet two thicknesses of woolen blanket completely through in one night. It is enough to dishearten any-one. But this state of things will not last long, I do not believe." He was wrong.

"One thing certain; if we keep on marching so[,] we will have not a well man in our Company (unless it be myself or the Boys from the Point who all stand the hardships well.)" He was speaking of the friends from the area south of Milwaukee called Walker's Point. "You know how I was troubled with a *lame back* before I left. Well I am happy to say that it has entirely left me. The only thing that troubles me is, sore feet which a great amount of *soaking & nursing* I expect to have all right in a day or two." But all of this strain and deprivation normally sapped the resolve of new soldiers. When feet were sore and bellies gnawed, the purpose of the war itself was questioned.[32]

In letters to his father and sister, Corporal Comstock stated he had changed his views on the war "and so with most every boy in the regt. We have come to the conclusion that bullets will never settle it," he wrote. "In conversation with the old soldiers [likely the 36th Illinois] I have come to the conclusion that this war can never be ended by bulletts [*sic*]. They say that when they enlisted [in 1861] they expected after about six month's service as the war would be ended. They have 'hoofed' it through Missouri, Arkansas, Tennessee, and Kentucky driving the rebels before them but that now they are back where they [rebels] were then and in greater numbers." Camp talk of a peace conference in

Washington gave rise to hope that, indeed, the hostilities might soon come to an end.[33]

When General Buell halted his army at Crab Orchard near Dicks River there was finally time, after more than a week, to write, and several Milwaukee men—the *Daily Wisconsin* printer, Norm Burdick, and Lieutenant Bleyer, the "typo"—composed lengthy recapitulations of the past few weeks; Lieutenants Mitchell and Chivas with the Merchant's Guards also wrote home as did Sgt. George Drake and several others. The matters were largely prosaic, but soldiers now took great pleasure in simple things such as a sunny sky or a starry night, bathing, washing clothes, and dining on food foraged from the rebel countryside.

"The boys took advantage of the rest, and cleansed themselves— the first time in sixteen days. The 'stacks' of arms were overhung with clean red shirts, and Dick's river was full of bathers. The weather was glorious, another day of Indian Summer." The regiment's camp in a wood was comfortable. "It is a pretty location." The Milwaukee men remained near the river for a few days, the respite seeming to improve their outlook after so many days of arduous tramping. The regiment was in "good spirits," Lieutenant Bleyer reported to his readers, although there was sickness in the ranks.[34]

There were some changes in officer ranks. Two officers, as a matter of fact, taken to Louisville sick, were the source of hostility that spilled onto the pages of Milwaukee's news sheets. The officers in question were the railroad freight agent, Capt. Henry Bridge, captain of Company G, and Peter Lusk, the thirty-five-year-old lieutenant in Company F; the former, in fact, went home to Milwaukee. Tenderfooted Art Gilbert, it was remembered, had early ran afoul of Bridge. What developed was a precursor to recriminations that arose following the next battle.

Andrew Smith and his comrades liked most officers, he said, but "we do not care if he [Bridge] stays there [in Milwaukee]. He is mean and cowardly." He charged that the news reports about the officer's wound by a shell fragment in the recent battle were a "barefaced lie." What was more, Smith wrote, Lieutenant Lusk reported injuries that he did not receive. "He was found[,] during the time the regiment was engaged[,] crawling under a haystack." Serious allegations, indeed. Severe enough in a private letter, but then, the recipient in Milwaukee turned over the missive to the editor of the Republican daily, the *Sentinel;* and the story was inked for the entire city to read.[35]

In Milwaukee, Bridge fumed, voicing his anger in the same daily. He wanted to vindicate Smith's charge "in full against a fearless and efficient officer." There was "no braver man" than Lusk, he wrote, "and as for hay stacks there was not one within a mile of the Regiment." As he and the beleaguered lieutenant lay in an ambulance some days after the battle, he overheard the lieutenant colonel, Ed Buttrick, say that "no officer had done better during the battle [of Perryville], or had proved more efficient than he (Lusk) had."

In his own defense, Bridge said he had sustained an injury to his left knee that subsequently proved of a "very serious character," from which a doctor said he might never fully recover. Questions about his conduct in the late battle, he said, should be directed to the regiment's leading officers—Colonel Larrabee, Lieutenant Colonel Buttrick, and Major Hibbard.

Also leaping to Captain Bridge's defense was the handsome court clerk, Bill Kennedy. "I never saw anything in his conduct that would lead me to the conclusion that he was either cowardly or mean." As to the captain's battle wound, "I have only to say I think Capt. Bridge a man of too much common sense to report anything of the kind." As to Lieutenant Lusk's conduct in the recent battle, Kennedy could offer no personal observation.[36]

What effect the public accusations had upon Smith as a rear rank private is unknown. Although he never gained promotion in the 24th Wisconsin, this son of a Milwaukee boilermaker later gained a captaincy as quartermaster of U.S. Volunteers in 1864. Neither Bridge nor Lusk would effectively return to the regiment, both resigning in December. Bill Kennedy was promoted to captain of Company G that month. There was another resignation, that of the captain of Company K, Orlando Ellsworth, who went home to the town of Lake south of Milwaukee. Filling his place at the head of the company was Ed Parsons, the twenty-six-year-old who had given up a "good situation" to enlist. Men of weak constitution unsuited for the harsh realities of war and those who exhibited the hint of cowardice were slowly leaving the ranks; officers of ability were being promoted. After the next battle, much more of this would occur. Meanwhile, Maj. "Lish" Hibbard, apparently because of his extensive military experience and maturity, was temporarily plucked from the regiment and assigned to General Sheridan's division staff as inspector general.[37]

At the same time, the matter of the so-called stay-at-homes, those "long range patriots," who talked much of war but failed to sign the roll and shoulder muskets, received a good share of camp criticism. Company B's correspondent, Cpl. Norm Burdick, who continued to write under the sobriquet "Musket" for his *Milwaukee Sentinel* audience, even went so far as to bring the matter to print, at least in a gently satiric way: In the six weeks since leaving the city: "We have camped, bunked in the open air; marched, skirmished, and been in one battle; and, now you folks at home, and your Representatives in Congress, and your big Generals can wind up the war as soon as possible. We are not disgusted with the service, by any means; but then you know home has its attractions, and $13 a month and glory will not balance the books for any very great length of time."[38]

Decades later, one of Burdick's comrades would lightheartedly recall that the spectacled printer was "forever writing to his girl when off duty, and pretending it was correspondence to the Sentinel." The romance with Anna Mitchell, the daughter of a Milwaukee lawyer, would ultimately blossom into marriage.[39]

Meanwhile camp rumor had it that Bragg was eyeing both the Kentucky town of Bowling Green and Nashville itself. General Buell countered with a march toward the Cumberland Gap. Leaving Crab Orchard on October 20, the 24th Wisconsin began three more days of hard tramping. The countryside, noted Lieutenant Bleyer, is "barren waste, and the boys did not like the idea of being starved and illy clothed." Yet the fall weather was "cool and bracing." One element that did plague the men was the infernal dust, which was "very thick, and for miles indicated the direction of the troops by the heavy clouds that ascended heavenward."

Weather turned colder the following day, Tuesday, and the roiling dust choked and blinded the weary soldiers. The countryside changed somewhat in the ensuing days, the landform beginning to roll while wooded spurs broke fenced farm fields that adjoined the road. Bleyer noted shocks of corn and stacks of hay; the wheat crop had been a good one, he noted, marked now by golden and brown stubble. The scores of Wisconsin farmers in the regiment like Date Worth must have observed these conditions, too. The road wound, ascended, and descended, and crossed creeks. The lieutenant took pleasure in the sheer physical nature of it all. "Such travelling is 'very good,' as it strengthens the chords [*sic*] of the legs, and exercises them in such a manner that men do not become tired as soon as they would on a level road," Bleyer wrote some days later. Many Milwaukee soldiers were becoming inured to such rigors.

On Wednesday, the newspaper worker related, the landscape became more pleasing to the eye. Woodlots grew more plentiful and the country became less open; belts of timber and poplar groves became frequent. Ravines were more acute, their sides knotted by underbrush and trees. With an artistic pen, the "typo" wrote: "As I looked upon some of the scenes . . . , I forgot the hardships of the march, and for hours marched on[,] lost in a flight 'to realms of Fancy's painting.' I wish that newspapers could transfer pencil sketches to their columns as well as they can the poor manuscripts of correspondents—and bless them with fewer errors—I would treat you to a few of Kentucky's landscape scenery."

Bleyer became rapt in the lovely pastoral settings, and went on to describe the beautiful sunset that evening and the camp ground on a branch of the Rolling Fork River, whose course was marked by cherry and burron trees, and copses of hazel and blackberry bushes. Trees were draped with leaves of vermilion, russet, brown, and deep green. The hilltops were golden, changing to crimson, deep red, saffron, and all against a hazy blue background of the sky, brushed with a few light clouds. "[T]wilight deepens into night: The stars appear . . . until the whole vault is dotted with them. A haze rests upon the valley, and from the woods lazily floats the smoke of the encampments. What can be more beautiful?" he concluded poetically.[40]

But there were others in the ranks who recalled only the difficulties. The youthful lawyer in his father's firm, whose once easy life in Milwaukee was now a distant memory, reflected upon the lot that had befallen him and his comrades. Sgt. Dick Hubbell noted:

[O]ur struggles have not been particularly sanguinary; the great effort has been to keep up on the march, and the young men whose lives have been idle, sedentary and even luxurious, have become so hardened to camp life that now they overcome obstacles once insurmountable, and endure fatigue and exposure enough to kill a city dray horse in a week. Up at twilight, with a hurried meal cooked by the smokiest fires; consisting of coffee boiled in a tin cup and hard crackers broken into it with a mouthful of pork, if there is time enough to cook that, and off for a day's hard march through dust thick enough to make white men the color of niggers and niggers resemble dead men in a state of decay, we plod along determined to tramp it out if it lead to the dusty side of eternity. We reach our destination at dusk only too happy to halt and 'conjure up' the same culinary phantoms that struck terror to our stomachs that morning. At

the command halt, &c., as soon as free, there is a general rush
pell mell, for rails to build bivouac fires, straw to make beds
and water for coffee. If these commodities (as is usual) are a
mile distant, the weary, footsore and dusty nondescript has only
one more straw on his Camel's-back and after eating his 'foreign element' stretched himself out to sleep until the order to
fall in at 3 o'clock the next morning, when fit or unfit, ready or
not ready, sick or well, he must go through the same routine of
the day before.

The twenty-three-year-old Company I soldier would soon take his
leave of such common hardships.[41]

The rapid marches were sapping the Milwaukee Regiment badly.
Sheriff Larkin, father of Court, likely conveyed the complaints of his
son that the once magnificent 24th, 1001 men strong when it departed
the city, was more than decimated. It numbered only 550. "When a halt
was called at night, instead of cooking their suppers, the men sank to
the earth for rest almost without breaking ranks, with no protection
from the heavy night dews except shoddy blankets. Thus in the morning[,] wet to the skin, stiff and cold, they were roused to the fatigues of
another day. Under these circumstances the wonder is not that so many
broke down upon the march, but that so large a number stood it." This
was a far different experience than the daily marching at Camp Sigel
only weeks before under the watchful eye of appreciative audiences.[42]

While the Milwaukee Regiment was encamped late in the month, it
learned of an extensive reorganization of the army. General Sheridan's
division was being transferred from the corps of imperious Gen.
Charles Gilbert, not an unhappy change, for the men in the ranks har-
bored a decided antipathy toward the martinet commander. "The boys
hail the change with expressions of joy, the [36th] Illinois is going into
ecstatic [sic] over it and the woods resound with their cheers," wrote
Corporal Burdick. Their new corps commander would be flamboyant
Maj. Gen. Alexander McCook. His command, which had taken the
brunt of the battle at Perryville, was demoralized and nearly ruined. But
the rotund thirty-one-year-old, another West Point graduate and veteran
of the Indian Wars, would soon raise some soldier hackles, and prove
only slightly better than his predecessor.[43]

Despite Lieutenant Bleyer's soaring prose flights about the landscape, the continued marches were grueling. The army's onward rush

left hundreds of stragglers in its wake, perhaps as many as 200 in the 24th, one soldier thought. General Buell issued a stringent order against men leaving the ranks, posting advance and rear guards on his columns to watch for stragglers. One man in the Milwaukee Regiment pitied a "poor, foot-sore fellow that could hardly crawl, much less walk at a common pace." If stragglers did not move along, they were prodded with bayonets.[44]

One private in the 21st Michigan, brigaded with the Milwaukee Regiment, died and a second man was on "death's door," Lieutenant Bleyer recalled. Sick, they had dropped by the roadside, but were "'pricked' up by the bayonet, by the rear guard." They straggled along to camp, but exhaustion overcame them. Both soldiers were hastily buried beside the road.[45]

It was but a few days later that the nearly idyllic fall weather that so pleased George Bleyer turned inhospitable. On the final Saturday of the month, a rough wind blew all day. Morning rain turned to snow, and when the Wisconsin men halted at noon, some three inches had fallen. Sheridan's Division paused over Sunday, a welcome respite, but conditions were decidedly "disagreeable." Here was an adjective common in several diaries of those days. Most men took shelter in sheds constructed of rail ties thatched with straw, and escaped the worst of the weather. The blue-eyed bookkeeper, Art Gilbert, recalled after the war several incidents that occurred in this period. The men of Company B, those "pets" of the city, "all worked together at building rail tents to shield us from the snow, and cutting the corn-stalks in the field that were covered with icy sleet." But the march and the weather would soon take their toll on the Milwaukee private.

Rations were low. On Wednesday, the division was awakened at four in the morning; but a delay caused the men to wait until the sun was high before moving. Their haversacks contained only three army crackers and no meat—Bleyer wrote with a hint of sarcasm—and that "made them very good natured [?]." Milwaukee sheriff Larkin also lamented in print: "The hard bread furnished the soldiers was like a rock. In vain, while eating dinner, I tried to soften it by soaking it in coffee."[46]

As the Milwaukee Regiment neared Bowling Green several days later, the devastation of war again became evident—a dramatic change from the pastoral views of former days that Lieutenant Bleyer had described. "[F]ireswept fields, missing fences and unoccupied and ruined houses; old camping grounds, staked and covered with straw, skeletons of mules and horses, and the other decaying refuse that tracks the course of an army. The country is ruined, and this generation will pass away before it will again be what it was before the rebellion."[47]

On the following day, Sunday, there was some cause for celebration in the Milwaukee Regiment as it reached the Louisville & Nashville rail line. Here the soldiers found the tents and other equipage not seen in a month. Looking back, disgruntled Corporal Burdick recapitulated that since October 1 "when starting out on our wild-goose chase after Mr. Bragg, having depended meanwhile upon the heavens and the Ruling Power there enthroned, for shelter and protection to our weary limbs, and not in vain; for twice or thrice during all that long and weary march, did our star-lit encampment go back on us, and show any signs of leaking, and then it was only to lay dust, and make out succeeding journey more endurable. Indeed we think that our worthy Chaplain, that 'God Almighty, he dakes care mit de Dwenty-Fort Regiment.'" The chaplain, Fr. Francis Fusseder, would take umbrage with Burdick's satiric representation of Teutonic-accented words.[48]

When the army camped near Bowling Green for the next few days, rumor had it that General Buell, who was unable to effectively fight his army of volunteers, had been removed from command. The cheering at such news that had weeks before been predicted by the old veterans of the 36th Illinois must have erupted in the Prairie State camp and been taken up by the Milwaukee soldiers.

At Bowling Green, Company B's seventeen-year-old Art Gilbert was finally felled by illness; "through the untiring care" of comrade John Ogden, who had also contracted some malady, and two slaves at the mayor's house, "I escaped dissolution," receiving a general's "autograph" on a pass, "and came back to Milwaukee a very sick lad, you bet." Gilbert and Ogden were out of the war, both soon to be discharged for disability December 18, 1862. The war would become but a memory.[49]

On the final day of the month, new army commander Maj. Gen. William S. Rosecrans arrived to assume leadership. Although the men had not yet seen the general, there was an unarticulated hope that finally a fighting commander was at hand to lead the army to victory. Not an unpopular change in the eyes of the Milwaukee soldiers, Corporal Burdick wrote, "it is but the truth to say that the news was hailed with joy by the entire army, as they had got tired of being pitted against an inferior foe, and then being choked off before they had an opportunity of giving him the drubbing that they were so well prepared and so eager to give." A sweeping pronunciamento from a young man not long removed from the life of ease who had seen only one battle. Lieutenant Mitchell at first spelled the general's name "Rosecranz," thinking perhaps he was of Teutonic heritage; the general's appointment, he said, "like most new ones, gives great satisfaction."[50]

Days later, Bob Chivas, the gray-eyed lumber dealer, enjoying the commodious accommodations, painted a pastoral prose scene of camp: "The tent entrance is thrown open and a large fire of brush is blazing before it. It is twelve o'clock at night and the Commissary Sergeant has just announced the welcome intelligence that we must draw rations and prepare to march to-morrow. John is lying at the tent-door half asleep with his overcoat wrapped around him and to finish this attempt at a picture the Capt. [Root] and myself are both writing our correspondence preparatory to marching. The nights are now becoming quite cold, ice of a considerable thickness being sometimes formed."

Chivas would also note humorously: "I have written this letter under great difficulties. Capt. [Fred] Root is snoring so abominably that the officer of the day ought to arrest him for creating a disturbance in Camp after taps. Whatever imperfections you may find in this letter attribute to Capt. Root's snoring." The arduous circumstances of a soldier's life seemed to cement the friendship born of family, work, and worship.[51]

The young officers, free to wax in private conversations and correspondence, shared concern about the physical condition of the regiment as well as the soldiers' declining attitudes toward fighting. "Long marches have [reduced?] the numbers in the Reg. largely, many are sick and broken down and have been left in the hospitals along the way," Mitchell wrote. "The men in this Reg. are mostly homesick and totally wanting in that spirit which makes a good and enduring soldier. In fact I do not wonder that we are beaten so frequently, in view of the spirit of the army."[52]

Chivas's view was darker: "The soldiers to tell the truth are heartily tired of the war, they want to go home and would if they had their way end the war on any terms. There is something of a similar sentiment tho not so strong throughout the whole North in my opinion and this together with other complications which will probably arise will render it actually imperative that the war be ended by next spring." Bleyer, in fact, said: "The boys will be pardoned if they detested soldiering in 'lively times,' and wished the war was over."[53]

Despite the trying conditions, Mitchell and his cousin fared well. "As for Bob and myself, we have campaigned without death, without wounds, without sickness, without foot soreness, without weariness and find after all that we never felt better in our lives." Somewhere between the penciled lines of those letters, however, was a question about how much longer they might bear up.

Mitchell, Chivas, and Root, who only months before were going about their lives largely unconcerned with war (that seemed so long ago, now), took time from the concerns of Company I to travel into Bowling Green for other diversions. Mitchell had two studio likenesses made. Despite his five-foot-four-inch stature, in one pose he wore his knee-length frock coat, dark trousers, and cap and jauntily leaned on his sword. In the second, he posed in a field uniform of a short, waist-length coat and light trousers. Short, slender, and narrow of shoulder, the well-educated twenty-year-old bore the look of youthful intensity; he attempted to add some maturity to his mien with a drooping mustache. The images would be printed in a book published early in the next century as a memorial for Mitchell's death.[54]

For the common soldier, time near Bowling Green was spent cleaning equipment. Some discussed the politics of the day, knots of men comparing this candidate or that. Sheriff Larkin, in addition to visiting his delicate son, Court, attempted to persuade soldiers to vote for Democratic candidates. It was something of a conflict of interest that Lieutenant Chivas criticized. Larkin "condescends to cultivate the acquaintance of the Privates and has generally something in a bottle for the officers, in this way he may become a general favorite throughout the Regiment." This was the way of Milwaukee Democrats, he seemed to imply.[55]

The Milwaukee men crossed the state line into Tennessee. There was scant note of the passage, and no premonition of the horrific whirlwind that lay ahead. As the Wisconsin men had trod through northern Tennessee, Company A's Amandus Silsby recorded the occurrences of the day. "The rebels are continually deserting and coming over to our side," wrote the eighteen-year-old student. "They say they were pressed into the service. We found one place where they had piled up their guns against the fence, for a long ways." The young man closed his letter, saying he was well "though not over fat, [and] can eat hearty . . . when I have a chance to." He also assured his father, the Methodist missionary, of his religious ritual. "I read my Bible regularly, 2 Chapters in the Old & 2 in the New Testament every day." He also wrote that he would continue to send $10 each month. Almost as a postscript, he noted that a felon, or inflammation, had been lanced from his right thumb, so his handwriting was somewhat illegible.[56]

The 24th Wisconsin arrived at an "outsquirt" of Nashville. Balloting for the fall election was conducted among the ten companies under the watchful eyes of Larkin and a deputy U.S. marshal. Silsby, Lieutenant McArthur, and many others, of course, were ineligible to vote because of their ages. With the balloting concluded, the officials left the regiment. Near the Tennessee capital, the Milwaukee Regiment busied itself cleaning Austrian muskets, "blacking" leather goods in preparation for brigade inspection, and in "'loosening' and 'limbering up' stiff joints and sore chords [*sic*]." Col. Nicholas Greusel, pale-eyed "Old Nick" of whom the boys grew fonder, inspected the 24th the next afternoon, complimenting it on appearance. On Monday, Maj. "Lish" Hibbard, inspector on Sheridan's staff, also looked over his old regiment, pronouncing that it was the best looking one that he had viewed so far. He may have been pardoned for the subjective view, of course.

"The regiment is encamped in a splendid grove of heavy timber and all that is lacking now to make it comfortable is 'green backs' and water—the latter is a good mile distant—the former is at Louisville," wrote Lieutenant Bleyer. He also reported that when his regiment had departed Louisville October 1, 858 men were fit for duty. A month and nine days later, the regiment counted 740 effectives. Of the 118 not answering the roll, 46 had been detached for other duties, and several others had deserted.[57]

The Milwaukee soldiers soon got a good look at the general who now led the army—a leader they soon affectionately called "Old Rosey." (Some men spelled the name "Rosy.") Forty-three-year-old General Rosecrans stood a burly six feet. Said to be short-tempered, his face, punctuated by the incessant cigar stub, featured a flattened nose, strong whiskered chin, and light eyes. His head was topped with blond hair, close cropped and combed forward to disguise incipient frontal baldness. Lieutenant Bleyer found the commanding general had a "dashing appearance 'on horse,'" being tall and heavy in person." Rosecrans possessed prominent features, he said—"nose of the Roman order—forehead heavy and arching—eye fine and piercing." But he was "unassuming in his dress." Lieutenant Mitchell found him "a man of pleasant appearance and generally popular."[58]

The general had an unmistakable air of dash and swagger about him; here was a fighter, camp wags offered. He had turned back rebels at Corinth, Mississippi. It was also rumored among the soldiers that Rosey loved his whiskey as well as his Roman Catholic faith. The 24th's chaplain, Father Fusseder, also likely appreciated the com-

General William Rosecrans.
Old Rosey.

mander's reticence about fighting on the Sabbath. When the general reviewed the units in another corps, a soldier recalled what he said: "Boys, when you drill, drill like thunder. It is not the number of bullets you shoot, but the accuracy of the aim that kills men in battle." In his General Orders No. 4, Rosecrans appealed to both officers and men of the army to aid him in "bringing it to a state of discipline at least equal to that of the rebels."[59]

The new commander soon reviewed Col. Nicholas Greusel's brigade, and complimented it on its appearance. Sergeant Hubbell, the twenty-three-year-old who was rapidly tiring of life in the infantry, found the whole affair "tedious, but the boys seemed pleased with their part."[60]

Although nothing in the recollections of 24th Wisconsin men suggested it, a profound sea change had occurred in the means to prosecute the war. In the aftermath of bloody Antietam in September, President Lincoln had issued a preliminary version of the Emancipation Proclamation to become effective January 1st of the new year: Slaves in the disloyal states would be freed. The document also urged the loyal states, Kentucky and Tennessee most notably, to adopt voluntary emancipation. "This 'peculiar institution' curses whatever it touches," wrote a

Bible-reading soldier in another Wisconsin regiment to his parents. "It is truly wonderful . . . to see the difference between free and slave territory," he observed; "the God of battles is on our side." The soldiers would not be certain for two and a half more years on whose side God really fought.

When he had traveled with the 24th Wisconsin, Sheriff Larkin, the Democrat, explicably saw things differently. He viewed the proclamation as actually aiding the rebels: They "were tired of the muss, as they called it, and were willing to quit and come back under the protection of the old flag." As he had been informed, recruiting for the rebel armies suffered. But the proclamation "produced an electric effect," and recruits "sprung up from every cross road, hamlet, and village."[61]

About this time, too, the soldiers of the Milwaukee Regiment were shocked with the news of the draft riots that had erupted in their state earlier in the month. The Wisconsin press labeled the events "War in Wisconsin," and related that the 28th Regiment had been dispatched north of the city to quell the riot. Eight-one prisoners were brought to Milwaukee for trial. They were marched to one of the city's training camps, where they "will undoubtedly be put into the army without any further chance of a draft," said a local news man. The men of the 24th, heads wagging in anger, certainly hoped that such men would never mar their company rolls.[62]

From his Nashville headquarters, Rosecrans continued reshaping the army, reorganizing and resupplying it with the vigor of a warrior general. He would call it his own, this army, renaming it the Army of the Cumberland, a bold stratagem to instill confidence among the soldiers. The army would soon cross the Cumberlands and crush the rebels, he seemed to imply. The composition of the 24th Wisconsin's brigade, now designated the 1st Brigade in General Sheridan's division, remained intact, with four rather slim regiments. Colonel Greusel retained command of the Wisconsin, Illinois, and Michigan men. But soon, the lack of promotion to brigadier began to trouble the old soldier.

Their proximity to Nashville just across the loop in the Cumberland River permitted many of the officers to obtain passes into the city. Common soldiers had to employ other means to leave their camps. Prior to the opening of hostilities, Nashville, on the south bank of a broad brown river, had been a bustling center of manufacture and commerce, and one of the two most important cities (with New Orleans) of the Confederacy west of the Appalachians. Called the "Athens of the South," it still boasted a population of some 20,000 white and about

5,000 slaves. Before the war, more than a hundred steamboats docked annually, and railroads north to Louisville and south to Decatur, Alabama, and southeast to Chattanooga and Atlanta were key arteries. It was the latter that would be the bloody pathway followed the Army of the Cumberland and the Milwaukee Regiment in the years ahead.

Now, after the Federal troops had occupied the city for nine months, different, less wholesome, businesses were in profusion. Soldiers outnumbered citizens two-to-one, and women of pleasure filled brothels along North Front Street. Rosecrans's provost guard once rounded up 1,500 sporting ladies and shipped them to Louisville, but the trade still flourished. As well, there was a boundless supply of liquor, and drunkenness was constantly in the news. Bleyer, Burdick, Comstock, and the other writers, however, did not touch upon such indelicate matters.[63]

"The entire city shows what war is in its true, melancholy light," Lieutenant Mitchell said. "Nothing but the all-pervasing [sic] soldier, with a sprinkling of sutler-individuals who pretend to be citizens. The finest stores, and there are some fine ones, are shut and everything has with it a desolate air. The magnificent capitol from its commanding situation has been chosen for and converted into a fortress, with stockades and a few pieces of cannon. The building is full of soldiers and their ever presence in the place remains one of the Goths in Rome." The military had transformed the city's streets into rough and filthy thoroughfares; cotton bales and parapets were used as barricades. There were few attractive aspects of the city. "The streets were very narrow," wrote another Wisconsin soldier. "The buildings are high, some seven stories, and well furnished; yet, as a whole, I did not like the appearance of the city." An Illinois veteran brigaded with the 24th Wisconsin took a dimmer view. "Its buildings are old, dirty & dilapidated. The streets are narrow, rough and decidedly filthy."[64]

The city's women, once openly scornful of Union officers, had become "gentle and courteous," and solicited favors "with grace and persuasiveness which nothing but stern sense of duty could resist." The unmarried Milwaukee officer who wrote under the nom de plume of "Marion" seemed to possess a ready rapport with the gentler set. "All gentlemen understand how difficult it is to resist the supplications of a beautiful woman, assisted as she is by the infirmities which belong to the best part of our manhood. When you realize the fact that Nashville is radiant with many of the most beautiful and brilliant women in our country, you may understand how it happens that our officers are apt to relent from stern duty, and grant to their bewitching appeals, favors to pass through our lines, when even the fate of an army might depend upon their consent or refusal," Lieutenant Bleyer said. Whether the officer was speaking from observation or from personal experience is unknown.[65]

"Nashville is a queer city," observed the lawyer, Sergeant Hubbell, "its streets no more than lanes and by-ways". He found some public buildings and residences "superb," however; the residences in the suburbs "princely," and in the Southern style, "surrounded by beautiful parks and artificial adornments, enough to make a poor soldier wish for home." The town was all but devoid of civilians. "Shoulder straps of every grade, and mule trains, fill every corner, highway and alley." The city was strongly fortified with siege guns and cotton bales. That feared Confederate horseman Kirby Smith, a constant thorn, and Bragg were said to be marching on the city with great force. But Hubbell discounted that as "humbug." The attacking force later turned out to be a band of bushwhackers and guerrillas "who skedaddled at the first big gun fired upon them." Hubbell must have been appalled by the realities of war, having just a few months ago lived in commodious comfort.

"We are all foot-balls, Mr. Editor, but I am happy to say we have become callused. We are encamped in a grove of lofty trees of immense height, and the sound of the axe and the crash of their mighty fall, can be heard all day long, as they are hewn down and cut up for firewood. Some will swear that such are the necessities of war. The rule is to 'gobble' (steal) everything useful and let old secesh suffer the consequences," the lawyer's son observed.[66]

Meanwhile, Adjutant McArthur still carried the names of Colonel Larrabee and Pvt. Jim Bacon of Company G on the rolls, but their days in the regiment were drawing to a close. The latter, still without teeth, would spin an amusing tale about a final encounter with his colonel. He related that because of his lack of dentition, he "had a hard time softening up some of the food furnished," particularly the granitelike hardtack. "Daily I hankered for soft food and got it whenever I could." He was acting as the colonel's orderly when the regimental cook came to Larrabee's tent with a plate of doughnuts. "They looked good and I timidly asked the cook for one or two before he entered the tent. He emphatically told me to go to that place opposite Heaven."

Bacon waited. Larrabee and his quartermaster, probably Giles Starkweather of Milwaukee, "were about as chuck up as they could be, and it did my heart good when I heard them find fault with the doughnuts."

The cook was ordered out of the tent. Bacon tried again. "So I braced up," and in the slurred speech of a toothless man asked for three or four of them, "but was told to go to the same place again." Undeterred, Bacon confronted the cook with a bayonet and musket. "I ordered him to set the plate of doughnuts on the ground and fall back two paces, which he did. I took them all, and told him if he ever squealed on me, the first time I met him he would have a through ticket to that place he told me to go to." The cook complied. Colonel Larrabee emerged from his tent, and spied Bacon seated on the camp stool gumming his doughnuts. He summarily dismissed the pushy private as his orderly.[67]

The camp of the 24th Wisconsin was taking on a winter aspect, "huge logs being piled up around the tents for firewood." Camp rumor, again inaccurate, predicted a move south on the following day. It was one of thousands of incorrect intelligences that wafted amid the smoke of many cook fires. "Our regiment . . . is the worse than an old maid's tea-party," groused hazel-eyed, spectacled Corporal Burdick, apparently unaware that the Milwaukee men were quite normal in the army way of things.[68]

With the approach of Thanksgiving, the upper- and middle-class character of the Milwaukee Regiment became manifest. Many wrote home from Nashville, requesting packages of goods. In making its appeal to the home folks, the *Milwaukee Sentinel* revealingly pointed out that many in the regiment were, indeed, the city's "pets." These "young men who have been accustomed to the luxuries of good homes, and their attachments to those luxuries cling to them wherever they go," said the news writer. The men relinquished "good and lucrative situations in business" with salaries of $10 to $20 a week—three or more times less than the $13 per month they were currently drawing from the government.

One of the Milwaukee soldiers wrote: "You don't know how much we hanker for the 'good' things of home, and how much pleasure it would give us to receive some cakes, jellies, canned fruits, pies, pickles, &c, &c. Don't forget to send a lot of biscuit cut open, with butter on them. I have not tasted any butter since the 25th of September."[69]

Company G's captain Henry Bridge, the man Andrew Smith and Art Gilbert so detested, returned from Milwaukee with a wagonload of "goodies" from the city. Was it a means of assuaging his less than brilliant leadership of Company G at the recent battle? Officers and common soldiers alike reveled in such treasures. One officer said that "each parcel, however small, or gift of minor value, telling to our hearts that we are not forgotten; that thoughts still linger around the fireside hearth at home, and the eye glistens and the heart swells as we look upon these tokens of remembrance." Among the gifts was a pair of mittens for every soldier in Company F made by a Mrs. MacDonald.

"The day was spent in examining and in an appropriate manner, the 'goodies,' and wound up by a dress parade at sunset," said an officer in Company F. "In the evening the band played many stirring strains in front of Col. Larrabee's tent, and Al. Brundage . . . the inimitable Al., made the [camp] ring with shouts of laughter at his 'old time' jokes and whimsicalities, and the good feeling was kept up much later than 'tattoo' or 'taps,' and when finally all was hushed and still, and morpheus claimed his own, sardines, stockings, envelopes, boots, sweet faces, ginger snaps, pretty babies, champagne bottles, cheese, mittens, Milwaukee ladies and other angels, were in visions interminably mixed, and every varying and floating before our slumbering senses. When shall we *ever* forget that day? Never."[70]

"Oh! How can I write!" exclaimed one of the Company B pets, Charles Ham. "I am so full, for yesterday P.M. I received your two welcome boxes of eatables, boots, mittens, &c. Five boys in our tent, besides myself, received packages." They opened the boxes with childlike delight. As one package after another was taken out and unrolled, it was held up to the view of all, and such exclamations as "Hurrah! Peaches! Isn't that gay?" abounded. And "ginger snaps!" and "nut cakes!" and "here is dried beef till you can't see!"

Ham received a can of peaches, two bottles of preserved chickens, bottles of catsup, cheese, tea, sugar, and "*monstrous* heavy" boots stuffed with goods. "In goes the hand and out comes, what? I can't tell by the feeling. It is unrolled, a general burst of laughter, a Bologna sausage! Again, sausage No. 2 and 3, and so on to the end of the chapter, or rather to the toes. Jelly and tea laugh at me from the corner and there a stately can of butter. 'Oh! come out here, you old villain.' It is immediately passed round and we taste, almost for the first time since leaving home, a mouthful of butter. It is an article that is almost impossible to procure. A dollar will seldom buy a pound." There was more: "splendid mittens," and beneath a paper in the box, "Pies, pies, home-made pies! That caps the climax!" Such simple pleasures now animated soldiers far beyond their intrinsic value.

The rest of the evening and early morning, the men busied themselves with a magnificent repast. They traded a large ham to a local farmer for sweet potatoes, and cooked up a kettle full, swathing them in

butter. They turned in, but within an hour awoke and roasted more pota-
toes. "That whetted our appetites for a piece of pie to go to bed upon."
Yet two more times, the soldiers awakened and disposed of the pie.
"And away in this wilderness, in a heathen land!"[71]

There were also visitors to lighten the holiday mood. "We have
almost daily arrivals of friends from Milwaukee, and it is impossible to
stick your head out of the tent without seeing some well known Milwaukeean, in citizens' dress, perambulating our 'broad and well-kept'
company streets."[72]

The portly Alexander Mitchell shared a camp with his son, John,
and nephew, Bob Chivas. And the millionaire James Rogers spent time
with his sons, Charles, the second lieutenant of Company B, and his
brother, Harry. Later, the confectioner James Heth, who had lavished
sweets upon Company B at Camp Sigel, traveled to Nashville to visit
with his sons, twenty-nine-year-old Charley and twenty-year-old
James. What the soldiers of common circumstances made of all this
fawning attention upon their sons by men of wealth and prominence is
unknown. Privates were normally deferential to the moneyed and powerful classes.

More than three decades later, one writer, perhaps Charley Rogers
who made much of his war service, recalled it was interesting to see the
older men "sitting on the ground like Turks and taking their meals from
a gum blanket spread on the ground." At one meal, the rotund Mitchell
allowed as how the coffee was, save for the lack of a little cream, the
best he had ever tasted. "At that time," the memoirist said, "the [24th]
had not advanced far enough in soldier experience to provide itself with
cows that gave cream."

The visitors, in fact, became camp favorites, and they were feted
not only by the regiment's colonel but also by the brigade and division
commanders. Good fellowship seemed to flow quickly between them,
and nascent friendships developed with Charles Larrabee, old Nick
Greusel, and even Little Phil. Whenever Sheridan visited Milwaukee in
the postwar years, he made it a point to spend time with Mitchell and
Rogers. Too, when the avuncular old Prairie State colonel, who would
not gain his general's star, arrived in Milwaukee for the 1889 Grand
Army reunion, he exchanged glowing recollections with John Mitchell,
then a U.S. senator.[73]

During his visit, James Heth told his soldier sons that stories had
circulated back home that the Milwaukee Regiment was "half starved
and used up." He did not identify the source of that information. "Many

boys expressed their indignation to him that such stories should be sent to their friends . . . and thus cause them unnecessary anxiety."[74]

Among others who traveled from Milwaukee were Caddie Philbrook and her daughter, Caroline. Wife and eight-year-old daughter spent a few days with their captain, the bearded and broad-shouldered commander of the Company D railroaders. They would long treasure those pleasant times.

The weeks before the repast were spent in constant drill. "Drills are had, in Sheridan's Division, five hours daily," reported Lieutenant Bleyer. "These drills are supervised by the Generals of brigades, and the commandants of regiments. Every commissioned company officer (unless excused by proper authority) is compelled to be present at such drills." Although Bleyer did not mention him, Adjutant McArthur was likely assisting the effort as well.

But onerous and taxing as they might be, the drills, soldiers had learned at Perryville, were vital to the regiment's survival in battle. They needed to become more proficient in movements that permitted the rapid maneuvering of many hundreds from a marching column to a double-ranked battle front. From this latter formation, hundreds of muskets could be brought to bear upon the enemy. With each man able to load and fire two or three shots a minute, a regiment of 700 could hurl 2,000 one-ounce leaden balls at advancing enemy ranks in that time. The Milwaukee men had witnessed the deadly effect of their fire into the cornfield at Perryville. A brigade line increased the volume of lead that could be thrown at the enemy to a virtual curtain of death.

Rosecrans watched as his new Army of the Cumberland practiced such drills and maneuvers, eager to insure that his soldiers would be ready for the confrontation with Bragg that was certain to come soon. "His quick eye discerned every fault, and a kind reprimand was instantly given," Lieutenant Bleyer noted. "He praised, wherever it was earned, and in a way that soldiers felt proud of what he said. Stopping before a company of beardless young men, who happened to be commanded by a lieutenant—also beardless—he spoke to the officer, about as follows: 'Have you youngsters ever been in a fight?' 'Yes, sir,' was the reply. 'What fight?' 'Chaplin Hills, sir.' 'It was quite hot, wasn't it?' 'Quite warm, General.'" And on he rode.

He asked a private of the 24th if his colonel did not give him "Hail Columbia." The private said that he sometimes did. "The General said that he supposed so, 'as the [24th] Regiment was the cleanest and best appearing regiment he has seen.'" Sergeant Drake later commented that the Milwaukee Regiment "is highly praised for its efficiency in drill and bravery."[75]

"Major-General Rosecrans is here and there, personally inspecting and supervising," a Kentucky correspondent wrote. "Yesterday he was in the saddle all day and until after dark. He infuses the same life into his staff and subordinates. Masses of ragged and unpaid, and poorly fed men, veterans of previous hard and fruitless campaigns, are being put in condition[,] and order daily emerges from these chaotic regions."[76]

Late in November, marching orders were sent down from Rose-crans's headquarters for a relocation, and the Milwaukee men pulled down tents, packed traps, and departed the old camp in the "outsquirt" of the city, and tramped seven miles south along the Chattanooga pike. Here a new site, named Camp Sheridan after their little division commander, was established. A short time later, an event occurred that consumed the attention of the 24th Wisconsin for days, and was widely remembered even late in the century.[77]

Lt. John Mitchell was having some difficulties with a new appointment. He had been plucked from the ranks of the Merchants Guards to brigade staff, to be aide-de-camp of old Colonel Greusel. He was uncertain whether the new position had something to do with his father's influence. "I have just asked the Col. the [cause?] of my change that I might tell you and he said, 'Tell your Father that it is based on personal observation since we left Louisville.' If such is the case, which I have no reason to doubt, it is highly complimentary." A horse was placed at the new aide's disposal.[78]

Mitchell's tall cousin, Chivas, remarked about "John's suddenly unexplained removal to Brigade Headquarters. John was very much pleased (as he had good reason to be) with his appointment. He at first feared that it was due to the influence of his friends, and more especially did that seem probable as Uncle was here at the time but he has since learned from Greusel himself that his appointment was owing solely to his (Greusel's) own personal observation. I think that John has got into the position he is best fitted for." Chivas left unstated the gradually deteriorating condition of his cousin's eyes. "John is now fully installed at the Headquarters. He always accompanies Col. Greusel on horse-back and I assure you he 'cuts a swell appearance.'"[79]

Colonel Larrabee, perhaps still bristling over the influential appointment of his youthful adjutant, was chagrinned with the Mitchell affair; he "expressed himself dissatisfied with the change and said he considered it a sarcasm that an acting Brigadier [Greusel] had me [as] aide de camp," Mitchell told his father. "Of course that was all non-sense as an acting Brigadier requires all the means that a positive Brigadier requires to handle his troops. For a lawyer he is very illogical. Col. Greusel being my friend, I think I shall stick by him and see what turns up."[80]

Meanwhile, in its camp outside Nashville, the Milwaukee Regiment, like all others, spent considerable time on the picket line. By army custom, bodies of men usually of company strength were sent forward of the main encampment by several miles. There, in shallow entrenchments and semipermanent fortifications, they remained on guard for a week or so.

Corporal Burdick took several news columns to describe the experience for his *Milwaukee Sentinel* readers: "Before enlisting, I had heard a great deal about the dangers of being 'on picket,' and had begun to think that it was indeed a 'post of danger' that I have heard so many young volunteers covet, when they should once get in the enemy's country." Being on picket, however, broke the monotony of camp life. The only negative aspect was the need to sleep "out in the cold at night;" but the regiment had become accustomed to that eventuality numerous times. "I think from present appearances it will be some time before our anxious friends will be obliged to record the death of any of our regiment from being 'shot on picket,' while in performance of that dangerous duty. But who can tell what a day may bring forth." Indeed, Burdick could not know that several good men would find death while performing that duty.[81]

Sergeant Drake, too, found that "there is some fun in it here for the enemy are right before us. For the last four or five days the enemy has fired on our pickets. Yesterday they attacked a foraging party of ours, capturing 100 wagons and four or five hundred mules with a number of prisoners, so our Colonel told us. At any rate there was heavy firing for two hours for I herd [sic] it. If we go out to-morrow morning we may have a taste of them," he told his brother.

The south side druggist, who would soon gain his lieutenant's straps in Company A, served as acting lieutenant on the picket line in mid-December. He did not carry his heavy Austrian musket, and worried about it. "[T]he Capt. undoubtedly thought I would be as *effective* with a Sword as [a] gun or he would not have given me one, but I must say that I feel a *little* more safe with a *gun* than with a *sword* for you have to stand up and be shot at without being able to return the compliment."[82]

From a perspective of over three decades, one soldier recalled some humor that attended the serious duty. Company B's David Merrill, who would in six months be discharged for disability, had a run-in with his second lieutenant, Charley Rogers. Many years after the war, he put a livelier turn to the story. One night, the private was on picket on the Nashville Pike; at two in the morning, Rogers, the officer in charge, inspected his sentinels. While with Merrill, who was lying beside the road, the officer spied someone walking toward them in the darkness. He ordered the private to fire on the intruder, but Merrill failed to pull the trigger. Lieutenant Rogers more forcefully repeated the command. Still the sentinel refused. "Give me that gun and I will fire," the officer demanded.

Merrill told his superior to lie down beside him and watch what occurred. A lone mule ambled out of the darkness past the Milwaukee men. When the animal moved farther toward the regular picket line, another sentinel fired. Then "the long roll sounded and one regiment came part way out of the lines." The writer failed to note whether the lop-eared animal survived the long roll.[83]

Rosecrans's and Bragg's soldiers were groping, closing upon one another. The antagonists were only spare miles apart, Bragg encamped at Murfreesboro thirty miles southeast. While blue-coated pickets inched their way south, the gray enemy probed north. There were bound to be encounters and confrontations, and Lieutenant Chivas boasted to his aunt Martha of a successful foray in early December.

Company I, posted a half mile farther than the Nolensville Pike "almost in the enemy's country," caught sight of gray uniforms. The good colonel, Greusel, visited Chivas and his men, and through his glass spotted enemy pickets moving in the woods. "We then determined to get up a little reconnaissance 'on our own hook.' With that view the Capt. [Root] with 3 or 4 men managed to [get?] to a position where the sesesh were plainly visible. In a short time a few shots were fired in that direction, and supposing that he might be in danger I started off with two men to his relief. We crawled along behind the fences and trees on our hands and feet until we discovered the party—all safe about 300 yards distant and within musket range of the rebel pickets." Captain Root had been watching the enemy pickets intently when five rebel cavalryman emerged from the woods. When they were within good range Root fired, scattering the enemy horsemen. But the firing alerted the enemy infantry to the Wisconsin presence, and the Company I soldiers had to be watchful. "We had just regained the pike when a rebel horseman rode up and exclaimed 'don't shoot,' when he observed us. We made him dismount, took possession of his arms and then questioned him. He stated he was a deserter, and gave us such information as we desired regarding the strength, position &c of the rebels in this vicinity." The prisoner was bundled off to General Sheridan's headquarters. "I suspect he is a spy as his manners were sometimes rather contradictory," Chivas wrote. "If he is, the General will sure to find out. At night we built a rail fence across the road as a barricade against the cavalry. A good many suspicious movements were carried out. Dogs barked, horses galloped on the road and lights were seen but no active demonstration was made on either side. The exploits of Co. I has made it famous for the time being. We have taken the first prisoner and fired the first shots at the enemy acting independently as a Company."[84]

Tension heightened along with seemingly continual alerts, and the Quaker lieutenant, Howard Greene, mentioned them: "Almost every day we get orders to rise at four o'clock, form Line of Battle and stand at Arms until Daylight, to be ready to march at a minute's notice, or some similar ones, until at least we begin to think there never will be an attack and that our Generals are crying 'Wolf, Wolf' for the fun of the thing. All I can say is that it may be fun to them, but it is rough on the Boys. Take it in a Cold Morning and stand in one place for two Hours holding a cold gun Barrel and it is anything but comfortable."[85]

Then General Rosecrans consolidated his army, pulling the Milwaukee Regiment and others back to within a mile of Nashville. "The object of this retrograde movement was, I understand, to concentrate our forces and enable the army to occupy a stronger position to resist the attacks from the enemy," opined Bob Chivas. "So instead of attacking the rebels as we believed was the intention of our General [Rosecrans] the rebels were then meditating an attack on us." Would the generals never use their army to good effect?[86]

With the move came a change in the 1st Brigade's command. As was promulgated some days earlier, Brig. Gen. Joshua W. Sill replaced Colonel Greusel. Old Nick once again returned to his Illinois regiment. Many felt the loss of the short Prairie State colonel, Greusel, and believed he had been passed over for promotion despite his courage and gallantry in battle. Even back rank privates appreciated Old Nick who "like his old nearly worn out regiment, knows no fear, is generous, endures all the hardships and pleasure of camp" with his men.[87]

Lieutenant Mitchell was especially troubled by Greusel's removal and his inability to gain higher rank. Greusel, like Mitchell, may have been a war Democrat; and the two men, whose ages were so disparate, shared other affinities. A comradeship, after so many miles of marching and hours spent together, had flowered; this was amplified by the friendship that developed between Greusel and Alexander Mitchell during the latter's visits to the army. "[A]ccording to the unanimous voice he is as worthy of a Brigadiership as any man in this army," Lieutenant Mitchell opined.

"The trouble with Greusel's appointment [to brigadier general] is that he has no political influence: he is simply a soldier." Could his father, the powerful and influential banker and railroad man, use his connections to help get the Illinois soldier his star? Such "influence in the matter . . . would not be misapplied." Greusel did confide in the Milwaukee lieutenant that should he gain higher command, he would retain Mitchell as his aide.[88]

Bob Chivas, Mitchell's cousin and tentmate, saw disappointment written on his friend's face. "When the announcement was first made of a change of Brigadiers, John thought of course he must return to his Co. and felt rather 'blue' in consequence. He was very agreeably surprised when General Sill offered him a position on his staff."[89]

Mitchell penned in self-effacement: I "find myself in the somewhat ludicrous position of Topographical Engineer . . . , in accordance with an order from Gen. Rosecrans." One topographical engineer was, under direction of General Rosecrans, assigned to each brigade, division, and corps staff, their assignment "to gather such information as [they] can on the configuration of the country and report thereupon."[90]

One of Mitchell's fellow officers, the gentle Howard Greene, found Mitchell's new position ludicrous. He felt that the short son of wealth had gained the appointment to General Sill's staff solely because of the influence of his father. "The Boys crack a good many jokes at John's expense for he was one of the poorest, if not the poorest Officer as far as Military knowledge is concerned . . . . He claims his Father had nothing to do with his promotion but that the General tells him he had often noticed his (John's) conduct on Drills and picked him out as a fair representative of the 24th." Some soldiers in the ranks caviled about the promotion. "I merely give you my private opinion of him as an Officer," Greene told his brother, "as a companion I find him very pleasant and sociable."[91]

Sill, sensitive to his predecessor's appointments, quickly became popular with his men. An Ohioan soon to celebrate his thirty-second birthday, he had been a division commander, but was given command of a somewhat small brigade. With intent dark eyes, hair at a moderate length, and whiskers sprouting from his chin and cheek, his soft features gave him a kindly look. The soldiers who served under him previously, Company B's corporal Burdick learned, "represented him as being a soldier and a gentleman, and any man who combined those qualities, is sure to win the respect and esteem of those who are fortunate enough to be placed under him." Sill would soon gallantly lead the Wisconsin, Illinois, and Michigan soldiers into one of their most ghastly battles.[92]

Late in the month, Corporal Burdick wrote from Nashville: The stay near the Tennessee capital was longer than anticipated but afforded time for "recuperating the health of the regiment . . . . The boys allow that they can get up and 'shake a musket' right lively, and they can 'take the rag off' any new regiment that shows in the vicinity of our division head-quarters." He meant, of course, that they now considered themselves veterans and would put any fresh-fish unit in its place.[93]

The Christmas holiday arrived on a Saturday, but the festivities were far less than the Milwaukee men had experienced the year before. Moreover, it was clear that corps commander General McCook had been wrong in his pronouncement of some weeks before: The soldiers were not in bed with their wives this day; they were still camped near Nashville with the enemy near and the prospect for some movement almost palpable.

"This is Christmas night and the [time?] of the day which everyone has vainly striven to make a merry one," Lieutenant Mitchell intoned to his mother. "Not that we are sad—not even the expectation of battle can make us that. But there is a feeling that we ought be revelling in mince pies, delving into preserves and dissecting turkies [*sic*], which is impossible." They already missed those packages of goodies that had been received in November.

Tomorrow the army would move at daybreak, he said, and Sill's brigade is "honored with the advance. That it will acquit itself well we have no doubt: the men are good and well-disciplined and the General is perfectly qualified for his position."

"Matters in the 24th have taken a sudden turn to-day," he wrote. Lieutenant Colonel Ed Buttrick had resigned his commission because of ill health and would return to Milwaukee. Not only did Buttrick and Colonel Larrabee have a troubled relationship, but the thirty-eight-year-old lawyer, one of the oldest men in the regiment, experienced physical difficulties. As a token of their esteem, all of the officers of the Milwaukee Regiment signed a testimonial to the Oak Creek lawyer. "You have gained [the regiment's] highest esteem and [the men] feel as badly over your departure from among them as we do . . . . [T]hey lose a warm friend and an efficient officer." Corporal Burdick heartily concurred: "His loss will be very much regretted, as he had endeared himself to both officers and men, by his attention to drill and discipline, and by a ready smile and word of recognition, with which he would answer a salute . . . ." Buttrick would return to his wife, but in the spring of 1864 be named colonel of the three-month 39th Wisconsin Volunteers.[94]

About that time, too, Colonel Larrabee, presumably because of diminished health that had not yet improved, was detached from the regiment for recruiting service back home; he would be accompanied by Company B's lieutenant Charley Rogers. Maj. "Lish" Hibbard rose to command the Milwaukee Regiment, while the stolid Teutonic whole-sale drug merchant from Company C, Carl Von Baumbach, became major.[95]

Some weeks before, the sheriff's son, Court Larkin, had remained behind sick in Bowling Green while the regiment marched away. The eighteen-year-old was now in Milwaukee, and in a candid burst, Lieutenant Mitchell offered his criticism. "Court Larkin, I suppose, has already presented himself. His falling-back in his [position?] was probably effected with the greatest possible [effort?]. Delicately-constituted young man! His ears were too finely organized for the loud sounds of war; his eyes too weak for the cruel sight of blood and his skin too thin to endanger itself before the leaden ball. And I may also add his head too thick to understand dishonor. How his presentation-sword will languish in its rusty sheath!" Larkin officially resigned December 14th. Like Buttrick, however, he later gained a commission as a twenty-year-old in the nine-month 38th Wisconsin Volunteers, serving until war's end.[96]

There was likely muttering and more than idle talk among the private soldiers over this course of affairs. Officers like Court Larkin, Peter Lusk, and others who somehow seemed to live life on an easier plain, could blithely quit the regiment simply because their natures might be too delicate or because they were afflicted with some minor malady; or they resigned because their reputations had been tarnished in battle. There were new strains, here, tensions between friends and acquaintances not manifest upon the streets of Milwaukee, and in the shops and churches before the war.

As the month waned, it became clearer each day that General Rose-crans would advance his army upon the enemy. The Milwaukee soldiers, like all the others, had hoped that active campaigning would cease and the relative inactivity of winter camp would prevail until spring. Affairs were not often to a soldier's liking. The *Chicago Tribune* in a mid-December edition had expressed the belief that the Cumberland army would soon bestir itself and move against the enemy at Murfreesboro—thirty miles south of Nashville. Scouts reported Bragg's numbers at 50,000. Some soldiers had heard that the rebel ranks were more like 65,000 or even 70,000. There was also the rumor of enemy divisions from Gen. Robert Lee's Virginia army being moved to support Bragg's drive against the Cumberland men. Exaggerating the size of the enemy force was just as readily done in a general's tent as over a common soldier's cook fire.[97]

Matters were evincing more urgency, with rebel cavalry probing Union picket lines, and blue-coated soldiers chasing the horsemen off with flurries of shots. Smoking his pipe, Company A's Sergeant Drake penned a lengthy letter to his brother, who took care of their business on Milwaukee's south side. "All men that are not able to march are to be left in Camp. They, those able to march, are to have five days ration in their haversacks, cooked, knapsacks to be packed, blankets and overcoats to be rolled up and ready to sling around the neck, at night sleep with our guns by our sides. That looks like business, don't you think so?" Two or three days past the pickets captured a spy and "he swore by all that was *great* and *holy* that the Rebs were bound to attack us to day, and annihiahlate [*sic*] us."

"It seems to be the opinion that we are to make an advance on Murfreesborough, where there is supposed to be 35,000 Rebels and more arriving every day, and you need not be surprised if you hear of a *big fight* in a few days, and the 24th is sure to be in it, for it is highly praised for its efficiency in drill and bravery." The army was once more to march without tents, Drake caviled. "[I]t is the general opinion that a big battle would be fought between here and Murfreesboro before long," he said, likely repeating camp rumor. "[W]e are on the eve of *exciting times*."[98]

Chapter 6

Stones River

—•—⚌◆⚌—•—

"The dread surroundings."

ᵎ

"**O**ur regiment has been through a campaign with which the one in Kentucky cannot be compared," the adjutant, Lieutenant McArthur, told his father. "But I am still alive, and never felt better in my life." The ordeal seemed not to dampen his youthful enthusiasm for war. Henry Drake wrote much the same thing. "Another large battle has been fought and your humble Serv[ant] is still in the land of the living, and still farther he escaped without a scratch of any kind," said the Company B sergeant. "The battle of Perryville was not a consequence to this one." The young man who had left the wholesale and retail drug business behind to enlist in the Milwaukee Regiment, however, was much shaken. In the letter to his brother, he concluded that "such an awful carnage, I never wish to witness again."

Sad-eyed Howard Greene in Company B was equally distressed by the ordeal. "Never before did I see such an incessant and determined fighting, and never was I among such a perfect storm of Bullets and Shells." Gene Comstock, the nineteen-year-old printer in the lieutenant's company also assured his family of his safety. "I am out of it as good as when I went in. I caught a cold but it is almost gone," he assured his parents.[1]

For these new soldiers, barely three months into the great Civil War, the battle northwest of Murfreesboro was the true baptism of fire,

The first regimental flag.
COURTESY OF H. MICHAEL MADAUS.

far more gruesome and galling than Perryville in October. The Milwaukee Regiment, only weeks before the battle in Tennessee, numbered more than a thousand; its ranks were now badly depleted. Coupled with the casualties from its first fight were hundreds of men sickened by disease or worn out from the march; moreover, scores had been assigned other duties and were not available for service in the regiment. Fewer than 600 answered the roll when the 24th Wisconsin marched south from Nashville. The mettle of men and officers was soon sorely tested, and many would be found to have skulked and skedaddled when rebel fire glowed white hot. For many, crossing Stones River as they did a few days after the battle, seemed like crossing the River Styx. Most of those who survived the carnage would be transformed into soldiers, and find their lives even more hellish.

Only a few weeks before the battle, matters were considerably brighter. The Army of the Cumberland, as the pugnacious Maj. Gen. William Rosecrans now called it, had been in the camps south of Nashville. The new commander had tirelessly brought new organization, cohesion, and discipline to his grand army. He had thrown off the old organization of his predecessor, Don Carlos Buell, and instituted an arrangement of wings (perhaps borrowing a plan instituted by Maj. Gen. Ambrose E. Burnside in the Army of the Potomac back East).

The Milwaukee Regiment was in the right wing, commanded by Maj. Gen. Alexander McCook, the bearded soldier whose double row of brass buttons strained to hold the army coat about his well-fed middle. He had not displayed a good grasp of the fighting at Perryville, and his corps had been badly mauled. In contrast was Little Phil Sheridan, the Milwaukee soldiers' popular division commander: Here was a wiry, restless, narrow-eyed general whose ungainly physical appearance belied tenacity in battle. His mettle would be badly needed on the final day of 1862.

Although the 24th Wisconsin's colonel Charles Larrabee still retained command, his time at the head of the regiment was coming to an end. The former politician was not only nursing an ulcerated throat but he was piqued, it seemed, because he had not been accorded brigade command. He was ordered to remain behind when his regiment marched off to do battle with Bragg's army, "a victim of circumstance and of his own proud and stubborn disposition," Bob Chivas said.[2]

Yet, in the final days near Nashville, the colonel's influence and discipline were evident. "The Regiment has, since its arrival in Nashville, improved greatly in drill," was the assessment of the news compositor turned soldier, George Bleyer. He continued his regular dispatches to one of the Milwaukee dailies, detailing events of camp and march for the city. "'Practice makes perfect,' and the [24th] in a short space of time and with little practice already vies with some of the older regiments. This is owning, the Brigade Commandant [the Illinois colonel, Old Nick Greusel] says, to the fact that 'the [24th] Regiment is a regiment of brains'". Brains alone, he would soon discover, were insufficient armaments for what lay ahead.[3]

The assiduous efforts of Colonel Larrabee and the major, the well-schooled Lish Hibbard, were reinforced by the seeming omnipresence of the army commander, Old Rosey, whom the soldiers, particularly those in the ranks, were beginning to appreciate. The "roots of the great evil in this army," as one news writer put it, were the officers, and Rosey made it clear that he would hold them responsible for the readiness of the men. On one of numerous reviews late in December, the general noticed a private's knapsack "very much awry." He pulled the man from the ranks and ordered his captain to step to the front.

"Captain, I am sorry to see you don't know how to strap a knapsack on a soldier's back."

"But I didn't do it, General," was the timorous reply.

"Oh, you didn't. Well, hereafter, you had better do it yourself or see that it is done correctly by the private. I have nothing more to say to him. I shall hold you responsible, sir, for the appearance of your men."

"But if I cannot make them attend to these matters?"

"Then," snorted the commanding general, "if you *can't* you had better leave the service. If you *don't,* I'll see that you do leave it."[4]

There was much here for the common soldiers to like about this brash army general with his broad face, stern chin, and light eyes who looked and acted as a true warrior.

As the month waned, the tug of imminent battle became readily apparent to the men. Scarce thirty miles separated Rosey's Army of the Cumberland from the rebels of Gen. Braxton Bragg, centered at Murfreesboro; enemy cavalry and infantry continually probed north toward Nashville. The Federal army was constantly alerted to the sound of the "Long Roll."[5]

Another Milwaukee soldier wrote: "Everything in and about camp indicates that we are on the eve of another great battle." Orders prescribed every man to carry forty musket cartridges, and no one was permitted to leave camp. "Therefore, taking it all in all, it looks as though there was stern work ahead." But he was confident: "The troops are all in fine spirits, and *if a fight should occur,* I do not doubt but that it will result in 'another great Federal victory.'"[6]

Talk about the campfires had it that Old Rosey had devised a grand strategy for the campaign against Braxton Bragg's army. He would send the three great wings of the Army of the Cumberland cascading down separate roads south of Nashville, aimed to converge at Murfreesboro where the rebel army waited. There, while two wings held rebels in check on the right, the third would splash across a river called Stones north of the town and crush in the enemy right flank; all of the army would finish the stratagem by springing upon Bragg's rear, sweeping him away. Perhaps the Army of the Cumberland would drive Bragg and his rebels out of Tennessee entire, hastening the end of the war. It was a grand prospect.

Strands of roads, like the lower half of a crooked web, radiated south and southeast of Nashville. These winding, macadamized, or rock-surfaced, thoroughfares, called turnpikes, were intersected with traverse ridges. Farmers had cleared patches, cultivating corn, cotton, and other crops; these intermingled with stands of woods and dense forests of heavy-barked cedar. Many of the evergreen brakes sprung up amid low limestone beds—jagged, fissured formations that were treacherous to man and animal. Here were excellent locations from which the enemy could strike and defend.

It was rumored that General Rosecrans, believing his army in fine trim, would order the move south from the Nashville camps on Christmas Day. A pall of gloom hung over the expansive sea of tents for a time; even the meager holiday celebration would be curtailed. But, then, word circulated that Old Rosey would not rouse his grand army until the next day.

Around six that Friday morning, December 26, the largest of the force, General McCook's wing with three divisions and thirty-seven infantry regiments plus assorted artillery and cavalry, marched south and slightly east by way of the McLensville Turnpike while the Army of the Cumberland's other two wings—those of the stolid and stern Maj. Gen. George Thomas, and Thomas Crittenden—pushed toward Murfreesboro by other but largely parallel routes. McCook's initial object was Nolensville and then Triune, Tennessee, some twenty-eight miles from Nashville.

The clear skies and soft breezes of the past two weeks gave way to gusts of chilling westerly winds; low gray clouds scudded. Then the clouds released sleet and rain. "It was one of the most drenching rains I have ever been out in," Lieutenant Greene described, "and the result was that we were soon wet through to the skin." The heavy blue wool overcoats and uniforms rapidly became sodden. General's Sheridan's division arduously slogged its way across farm fields through some of the heaviest mud some of the men had ever seen. "You have seen Milwaukee mud, so you can form a slight idea of what walking we have encountered," the pensive Greene wrote to his sweetheart, "only that in this instance it was just twice as bad. I slumped[?] in up to me ankles at every step, so that with the weight of Blankets on my back it was very laborious getting along."[7]

After a personal interview with army general Rosecrans, Colonel Larrabee was declared unfit for duty because of his ailing throat. He was to entrain for Milwaukee on a recruiting trip. But when the 24th

Wisconsin departed off from Nashville, Larrabee marched with it, hoping to change Rosey's mind. He slogged along in the drenching rain. "That night he slept not at all," a Milwaukee soldier said, "and his ulcerated throat grew rapidly worse. His voice was gone to all but a whisper." Regimental Surgeon Herman Hasse and other officers insisted he return to Nashville, which the colonel did. "The poignancy of Col. Larrabee's regret at not being with his 'boys' . . . was both felt and expressed." Maj. Lish Hibbard would command the Milwaukee Regiment.[8]

Lt. Ed Parsons, who led Company K, complained that "we crossed over cornfields and by-roads nearly to our knees in mud, our advance continually driving the enemy, and the booming of cannon continually ringing in our ears." Sheridan's division "thundered through" Nolensville, he said. Parsons, at twenty-seven, was one of the steadier men in the regiment; he would soon gain his captain's bars.[9]

Rebel cavalry and skirmishers were about, and occasional flurries of musket fire or the thud of distant artillery ahead of the long Federal column bespoke of heightening contact with the enemy. Apprehension mounted with each muddy footfall south. Lieutenant Mitchell, despite being on horse with General Sill's staff, lamented the lot of his comrades in the Milwaukee Regiment. "Many of the men had dropped by the way-side, and most of these who remained carried the seed of disease," he still remembered many years later.[10]

When General McCook ordered his men to halt and camp each evening, there was no respite for the chilled and muddy men. Since tents had been left behind in Nashville, there was no means to escape the suppurating conditions. Although rain abated sometime late in the day Friday, it was not for long. "We had hardly got our supper and a bed of corn stalks prepared, before the rain commenced on to come down again," pensive Lieutenant Greene said. He dried his clothing before the campfire, then decided to slip under his rubber blanket fully clothed, hoping to forestall another drenching. "So in I poked & lay there with my Rubber [blanket] over my head leaving only enough space for my pipe to protrude. My pipe finished I turned over and went to sleep." He had taken the precaution of placing his boots under some straw to keep them from getting wet; it was a new pair, but they were somewhat small for his feet.

Around midnight, Greene felt water gradually oozing through his clothes, the constant rain preventing any improvement in his situation should he arise. So there he lay, "merely turning over occasionally as one side got wet & cold, in order to try & keep my body in an even state of temperature." Under a still leaden overcast the next morning, Saturday, he shook himself out, badly chilled. Worse, the precaution he had taken with his boots proved ineffective. They were filled with water, and he could not force them on his feet. His friend, Dick Kasson, the first sergeant of Company G, loaned Greene his extra pair of boots; but these were a bit large and "minus soles." But scant protection was better than none. When his own small boots finally dried the next day, he forced them on his feet and would not be remove them for a week.

After marching only a few miles in a thick fog, McCook ordered another halt, and the 24th Wisconsin camped in a patch of woods near one of the "finest Plantations I have ever seen," Lieutenant Greene wrote. General Rosecrans, who made much of his Catholic piety, did not march or fight on Sunday, so his mighty Army of the Cumberland lay where it was December 28. It was a somewhat pleasant day. Many soldiers of Milwaukee likely observed the Sabbath; certainly Father Fusseder celebrated some service for those whose religion had not yet been held in abeyance. For others, the prosperous plantation owned by "wealthy Secessionists" was a tempting site. Its cellars, Lieutenant Greene said, "were stored with Bacons & other supplies." And since rations were short, as usual, "they waited for no invitations but walked in and helped themselves. In a short time he [the owner] was pretty well cleared out & the Boys lived well that day," Greene told Louise, the woman he would soon wed.[11]

Here were men, not much more than four months removed from the civil surroundings of Milwaukee; religion and righteousness had been integral to most of their lives. Yet, now, pushed by elemental needs for sustenance, they were no longer constrained by ordinary society's proscription against theft or expropriation. If the regiment's rotund chaplain knew of the depredations, there is no record of his reproach.

Lt. Bob Chivas was rightly caustic: "[W]e had to sleep in the rain without fires; but very frequently we had not even the privilege of sleeping." And more: "For one week my face and hands were innocent of water, except what came from above, and that was sufficiently plentiful to keep me clean." Like Lieutenant Greene, Chivas did not remove his boots for weeks. "Notwithstanding these hardships, we were always 'jolly.' In fact we felt pride in it, as 'Mark Tapley' did." Chivas used his usual sarcasm here, as Tapley, a Charles Dickens character in *Martin Chuzzelwit,* was perennially buoyant.[12]

It was Monday, marching day for General Rosecrans, and he ordered his three wings to press forward toward Murfreesboro. The day was pleasant enough, all in all, and the morning skies gave way to blue; some did not much mind the march. Yet, ahead, McCook's cavalry constantly skirmished with the rebels—a noisy reminder that battle lay just beyond the next turn in the roadway for the Milwaukee Regiment. Then, wrote one of its privates, they trod through a brooding cedar forest, "one of the most Godforsaken wilds I ever saw." After gaining another turnpike, the double columns of men moved nearer Murfreesboro and the assembled rebel army. Apprehensions can only have mounted.[13]

Off the turnpike in another cornfield, the Milwaukee Regiment camped. No fires were allowed as the enemy was close at hand. Then the cold, chilling rain came again, making for another sodden night. In the damp stillness that Monday evening, an incident proved a strange prelude to the awful clash of arms of coming days. Military bands of both Federal and rebel armies began to play their favorite tunes. Bluecoated drummers, fifers, and horns men struck up "Yankee Doodle," only to be countered by "Dixie" from across the way; and when "Bonnie Blue Flag" echoed over the fields, it was answered with "Hail, Columbia." But then the Federal band began the melancholy strains of the popular "Home, Sweet Home"; these were resonated by the grayclad musicians. A salubrious harmony must have caused the thoughts of many a 24th Wisconsin man to momentarily flee the field for home. None recorded those thoughts or the scene that evening, however.[14]

That night, Brig. Gen. Joshua Sill, the Milwaukee Regiment's brigade commander, seemed apprehensive about the morrow. The Ohioan with the intent gaze had only three weeks before celebrated his thirty-first birthday. He visited a hospital tent where one of his aides, wounded in the day's skirmishing, was being treated; for a time he looked upon the injured soldier. "Just before leaving [Sill] stood for a while leaning on his sword, rapt in deep thought," an aide from the 36th Illinois recalled, "and I imagined a shade of sadness on his fine face," as if a strange fatal premonition gripped him—"some sad present[i]ment of his fate was . . . silently passing through his mind." Later, it was said, he had dropped in on his diminutive division commander, Phil Sheridan, who had been his West Point classmate; upon leaving his superior's tent, he inadvertently picked up the general's uniform coat.[15]

Tuesday, December 30 dawned cold and dreary, almost as expected. Hoary whiteness coated the land, and a misty veil shrouded the rolling hills that ran down toward the river. After a hurried breakfast of boiled coffee and whatever the haversacks held, the soldiers gathered themselves. Major Hibbard, tall and stolid, briefly addressed the men, explaining what he expected of them and advising them, as had Colonel Larrabee, to aim their heavy Austrian muskets low; instead of sending lead harmlessly over the enemy's head, a low shot was almost certain to strike something.

He and Captain Von Baumbach, the stocky Teuton who was now second in command, arrayed the Milwaukee Regiment in a double-ranked line of battle, and pushed it forward. Fifty paces ahead in an open field strode the veterans of the 36th Illinois, the stalwart Pea Ridge boys. In a short time, the skirmishers out front encountered the enemy, and scampered back to the main battle line. "We . . . had gone about half way across when a masked Rebel Battery opened on us with shot and shell," Lieutenant Greene said. The projectiles "began to come so thick, that it was almost useless to cross in face of the fire, so we were ordered to halt and lie down."[16]

The Milwaukee Regiment found itself in the lee of a small hill out of line of sight of the rebel artillery. Cannon from both sides "played over our heads at a great rate," said Gene Comstock, the Company B corporal. To the regiment's right, the 8th Wisconsin Battery's rifled Parrott guns, breeches reinforced to sustain heavy powder charges, cracked deafeningly. For nearly five hours the men of Wisconsin lay, enduring the deadly play of artillery.

With suddenness, a "plug" (a sabot in military terms) from one of the heavy Badger artillery shells flew off and struck the well-liked Lieutenant Bleyer in the calf. The poet and correspondent had been given temporary command of Company F for the campaign. The wound gushed blood, but it did not appear serious. The accomplished poet whose evocative columns appeared above the pseudonym "Marion" was rushed from the field.

The regiment lay there only a short time before the right four companies, K among them, were called to attention, and ordered to support the 8th Wisconsin Artillery more closely. The Badger guns had been wheeled into position to return the rebel fire. Just as a soldier in Company K arose, "a Shell came crashing toward us striking a man about 20 pcs. [paces] from me in the forehead taking the top of his head completely off & scattering his Brains in all directions," wrote Lieutenant Greene in an uncommonly graphic description. It was Henry Pfaff, a twenty-three-year-old from the town of Oak Creek. His lieutenant, Ed Parsons, said the shot also "scattered the dirt and stones over me so that I thought at first I was struck." Several more cannon shells roared over

Parsons's head, so close, he said, that they ruffled the cape of his great coat. Another young man, Richard Jeffers in Company D, doubled over with a ball in his stomach. Three more men fell that morning.[17]

It was about three in the afternoon, Lieutenant McArthur remembered, that "our onward movement was ordered. We sprang to our feet with the happy anticipation of a fight fixed upon our minds," he said. The regiment marched through a cornfield, the Wisconsin battery "playing all the while." Here the seventeen-year-old nearly met his "untimely end" when another sabot from the 8th Wisconsin cannon, similar to the one that had felled Bleyer, flew out. "It struck six feet in the rear of my horse, which made me feel very uncomfortable." Here was understatement, perhaps borne on a feeling of youthful invincibility. The Milwaukee soldiers were halted in an open field when the Federal artillery battery "came rushing down," setting up its guns at the edge of a cedar woods. "Here occurred one of the most eventful artillery duels I every heard. The batteries, not [a] gun shot apart, firing at each other." As the 24th Wisconsin lay there, enemy guns were trained upon them, "and the way shot and shell did fly around our boys is amazing," McArthur told the judge. The letter was printed in a daily news sheet for the city to read.[18]

When darkness closed, the regiment was moved from its position, forming a reunified battle line on the edge of a brooding patch of cedar woods. Major Hibbard ordered Lieutenant Greene to move two companies of pickets forward to within 300 feet of the rebels; the Milwaukee men were "so near their [enemy] Camp Fires that we could hear them talking," Greene said. Occasionally, a nervous picket fired at a shadow or unusual movement, causing scores of Federal and rebel muskets to rattle into life, orange tongues of burning powder licking into the darkness. Men not on the picket line were obliged to sleep with their muskets at their side; no fires were again permitted, and there was little to hold the bitter cold night at bay.[19]

Lieutenant Parsons, who would soon win a promotion to captain of Company K, remembered that "our men were nearly benumbed with cold. I think I never passed a more cheerless night in my life." The major, Lish Hibbard, who had once imperiously marched at the head of the natty Boy Zouaves in Milwaukee parades before the war, had withdrawn into himself. "I went into the fight with a sad, foreboding heart," he told his father afterward, "yet I prayed hourly one prayer, 'O, God help me do my duty bravely and well.' You can not imagine my feelings the night before the worst fight and the responsibility of lives in my hands."[20]

During the night, General Rosecrans had directed McCook to deceive the enemy by igniting hundreds of bonfires beyond his line. Old Rosey hoped to trick his adversary into thinking the Federal right extended well beyond what it really did. The ruse, however, would prove to be the undoing of the Army of the Cumberland.

Little Phil Sheridan was fitful and busy. He awoke before dawn, inspecting the positions of his dozen infantry regiments and three artillery batteries. He conferred with his colonels, majors, and captains. General Sill, his trusted friend and 1st Brigade commander, was also concerned. A "fearless and able soldier" was how Sheridan remembered him; "he was modest, courageous and a solid military leader." In the cold gray before dawn, the Ohioan related that far off to the right of his line he heard uncommon sounds; the enemy, he said, had passed across the whole face of Sheridan's front toward the right of the division line, and might now be massing for an attack at dawn.

General Sill's four regiments—men of Wisconsin, Illinois, and Michigan—were arrayed on the far right of Sheridan's two other brigades—the Illinois and Missouri soldiers of Col. Frederick Schaefer, and the entire brigade of Prairie State troops under Col. George Roberts. The 24th Wisconsin was posted in the front of the brigade line, the hardened 36th Illinois to its left, and the 88th Illinois beyond that. Farther to the right, south of Sheridan, were arrayed the other two divisions of Gen. Alexander McCook's wing, soldiers of Gens. Jefferson C. Davis, who bore a somewhat embarrassing name, and Richard Johnson, who Sergeant Drake called a "rascal" for reasons he did not explain. Sheridan and Sill walked through the cedars behind their line, surveying the disposition of their men in the darkness; they paused briefly behind the Milwaukee Regiment and the 36th Illinois to confer.[21]

If Lieutenant Mitchell, the topographical engineer on Sill's staff, witnessed the meeting, he made no note of it. The two generals mounted and cantered to General McCook's headquarters, and awakened him to explain their fears that the enemy was massing for an attack beyond the right wing's flank. The rotund McCook dismissed the supposition out of hand. But when the division commander and his subordinate returned to their camp, as a precaution, two regiments from Colonel Schaefer's brigade, the 44th Illinois and 15th Missouri, were placed as a reserve behind Sill's line.

Before four o'clock that last morning of December 1862 Sheridan assembled his division. He "came along the line, on foot and unattended," it was said. "He called for the major and ordered him to rouse his men quietly, have breakfast and form a line of battle at once. He personally visited each of his twelve regiments and saw that his orders were executed." Dampness had seeped deeply into every soldier during night, and it was difficult to shake loose of the numbness. When blackness was giving way to gray over the hills to their front, they gazed at hoary cedar thickets and forlorn farm fields. The pastoral word portraits of George Bleyer and John Mitchell written some weeks past seemed not to apply to this landscape. Puffs of breath blossomed before every face as the Milwaukee soldiers quickly boiled coffee and gnawed at a few crumbs left to them. To most, it was evident that a deadly drama would be played out this day; but they could not imagine even in a bad dream how bloody and costly it would be.[22]

Company A's Sergeant Drake, the dark-eyed druggist who served as acting lieutenant, was "astonished" to hear bugle calls emanating from General Johnson's division off to the right; it was the signal for the artillerymen to take their horses for water; meanwhile, most of Johnson's infantry had not yet tumbled from their blankets. Now, not a thousand yards away, across a farm field and emerging from a cedar forest strode thousands of soldiers, shadowy at this hour, but discernable as dark rectangles of infantry. First, a distant cannon shot reverberated; the sounds of popping muskets quickly followed. The sounds of battle grew in earnest, and it soon became clear that the rebels were surging against General Johnson's division. The deadly symphony rapidly grew toward crescendo. Johnson's division was "taken by surprise," Sergeant Drake learned in the aftermath, "most of the men being asleep at the time, a great many of them not being able to get to their guns. They broke and ran lively, partly through Davis' division. Davis only stood for a short time[,] then he broke too." Another Milwaukee soldier was told that General Johnson had even been surprised in his tent.[23]

The soldiers of the 24th, many of whom had given up "good situations" and promising positions, knew that it was only a matter of time, now, before the screaming hordes of rebels would smash upon their line. Most probably, the men in the ranks clutched their bulky muskets tightly, pulling back hammers to insure a percussion cap was securely affixed on the firing nipple, squinting to the right and in front across the farm field toward the ominous, dark belt of cedar forest and rectangles of infantry that were moving forward.

"Stone's River was an unequal fight for our division," wrote a Milwaukee veteran years after the war. "The trouble began when it was discovered about daylight that the enemy had surprised our right flank and turned it and was in our rear." When it skirted the bonfires lighted as a ruse, Bragg's soldiers in fact lapped the entire Federal line. Of that day, Lieutenant McArthur concluded: "To tell the truth, I was perfectly appalled."[24]

It was just about seven that morning, dim light piercing through the mist, when a double line of rebels, stretching far beyond the Union right, stepped forward. Their ranks were close, the lines of men marching elbow-to-elbow in the accustomed formation specified in the military manuals of the day. Behind them strode five more columns, closely packed together. The enemy ranks were a motley color, a mixture of gray and butternut, tan and dun, and even some blue. "Their clothes at this season of the year, correspond[ed] exactly with Nature's garment and render[ed] them not easily to be seen," the lawyer, Dick Hubbell, wrote.

Blood red battle flags flapped slightly from their staffs in the heavy morning air. General Sheridan's batteries, poised and ready, had stoked their big guns—brass-barreled cannon that hurled 12-pound balls and Parrott rifles that belched out heavy projectiles a thousand yards. "Fire!" came the commands, and rope lanyards yanked to ignite the charges. But the artillerymen had not time to load more than a shot or two more. The rebel attackers stormed across the field at a trot, as shrieking yells, infernal screams many Federals would remember until their dying days, tore from their throats. "The rebel cheers make a noise similar to the cries of a company of school boys at play—not unlike an Indian pow-wow—sort of an undeveloped articulation," Hubbell said. Another Milwaukee soldier told his parents that "the rebels came yelling like mad devils."

"The enemy . . . continued to advance until they had reached nearly the edge of the timber" where the Wisconsin men were posted, General Sheridan wrote in his official report some days after the battle, "when they were opened upon by Sill's infantry, at a range of not over 50 yards. The destruction to the enemy's column, which was closed in mass, being several regiments in depth, was terrible."[25]

A solid column of six regiments deep drove in the Federal skirmishers "and the fighting began," Adjutant McArthur recalled. "The enemy, massed in overwhelming numbers, column closed upon column . . . bore down upon us with determined tread," wrote Lieutenant Mitchell. "The air was alive with whistling missiles." Somehow, in the confusion, he became separated from General Sill.[26]

"The spectacle was truly grand," said Mitchell's cousin, Lieutenant Chivas. "They rolled on in deep columns like an irresistible wave. The gaps made by our artillery which was playing upon them were immediately filled up. Their banners flying, and uttering a horrid yell, they advanced heeding neither shot, shell or bullet. Our men were firing and loading as quickly as possible, and picking them off very fast," wrote the twenty-year-old lieutenant. When the rebels came within a few rods of the Wisconsin line, the blue soldiers alternated companies, one firing, the next loading, and continued forward. "For a few minutes the shower of bullets and grape [shot] was like rain."[27]

Soon the enemy soldiers scampered up the stony hill, intent, it seemed, directly at the Milwaukee men. The rebel surge, a great gray and rusty-brown wave, broke upon Sill's men, who were positioned just at the edge of a forest of rough-barked cedars. "We had hardly time to bring our battery to bear upon them . . . before they were upon us," said one Wisconsin private. With Davis's division gone from their right, the Wisconsin men found their flank unprotected and exposed; snarling and determined rebels swarmed in front as well as on their flank.

Red-headed Tom Ford, the twenty-three-year-old Irish farmer in Company H, remembered his hands were so numbed from the cold and frost that morning he "had to place my finger on the trigger of the gun with my left hand before I could bring it up to aim. The rebels came down on us, colors flying and in solid column, shouting and hollering as if certain and sure of victory." But there was little time to aim. Triggers were quickly jerked, and the stock banged back on the right shoulder. Another cartridge was snatched from the box; teeth hurriedly tore open the paper and powder was hastily poured. Then the heavy lead bullet was pushed down the barrel with the steel ramrod, another cap snugged beneath the hammer, and the trigger pulled again. There was little time to actually sight the musket, or even to remember Major Hibbard's admonition to aim low.[28]

One of the first to fall in the rebel onslaught was young Frank Hale of Company G, a musket ball lodged between his shoulders. Not four months before he had feared his parents would withhold approval for his signing the roll of the Allen Guard. A comrade later recalled "the joy that lit up his manly countenance after that consent was gained." Because of Hale's "manly bearing and gentlemanly deportment," his captain, Henry Bridge, had made him fourth corporal. And just before the regiment departed from Nashville, Lt. Bill Kennedy had promoted him to first corporal.

"Frank was a young man just emerging into manhood," Lieutenant Kennedy wrote after the battle, "and possessed of all the noble traits of character that make a man. He was the hope and pride of his parents, but he had fallen another victim of this accursed of rebellions. He died an heroic death, nobly fighting in defense of the flag of his country. Still, it is hard that one so young, so promising, so beloved by all, should so soon be called from earth; but God willed it thus. His father and heart stricken mother have the sympathy of many friends in this their sudden bereavement." Blue-eyed and dark-haired Hale was only eighteen when he collapsed among the cedars.[29]

"The bullets seemed to be passing around my ears in perfect showers, something similar to a heavy hail storm. Then cannon shell, grape, cannister [sic] and sol[i]d shot began to fly," wrote the wavy-haired McArthur. "The Bullets came zip around me on all sides, over my head," Lieutenant Greene told his brother, "and now to look back on it, it seems to me a perfect miracle that I escaped without a scratch." A bullet cut through the tight boot, raking his ankle, but the wound was slight, merely a scratch. Cpl. Harry Rogers in Greene's company was also fortunate. A ball went through his cap, and another grazed his cheek drawing blood; still another bullet punctured Rogers's coat, and a fourth struck his musket "breaking it in his Hands," Greene said. "Hardly a man in our company but what had Bullet Holes in some part of his clothing, or else in his Blankets."[30]

It was about 8:30 that morning when a bullet struck George Cole, the first sergeant in Company B. He was quickly taken to a field hospital "just alive" where his wound was dressed. Some time later, the "rebels made a desperate charge, drove our forces back beyond the hospital," taking all of the wounded prisoners. Christian Nix was knocked from the ranks of Company D. The immigrant had worked for Hoyt's wholesale liquor store and was said to be a fine engineer. Jim Harvey, the twenty-three-year-old Granville friend of Date Worth, took a ghastly wound to the hand; he would recuperate for months before returning.[31]

In Ed Parson's Company K, men were falling under the perfect hail of enemy shot and shell. "The bullets were flying through our ranks, and laying many a brave man low," Parsons wrote. Among those struck was the thirty-four-year-old "inveterate bachelor," Byron Brooks, whom the boys called "Elder," one of the best mechanics in the city. Just before leaving Milwaukee, it would be remembered, the fastidious soldier had taken the precaution of purchasing a coffin and paying for a burial plot.[32]

Company E's officers were having a difficult time. The captain, the old politician Cam Reed, had become sick, probably vomiting behind a tree when the screeching rebels punched into the 24th's line; he soon disappeared from the field, and was presumed dead. The company's lieutenants, David Horning and young Riverius Elmore, it was later suggested, lost control of their men. Capt. Henry Gunnison was also ineffective with the men of Company H, it was alleged by some; Drake said he was "on a par with Reed"—cowardly. Similarly, the Milwaukee man who led Company C, Lt. Peter Strack of Milwaukee, and others acted like "cowards," Chivas would attest. This was the company of Germanic immigrants and their sons raised by the twenty-three-year-old druggist, Carl Von Baumbach; now acting as major, Von Baumbach had probably used influence to honor his old company with protecting the Regiment's flag—the color company. Even the flag bearer, who was not identified, "rolled up the colours tight and hid behind a tree," the tall Scot said. What was more, both Chivas and Drake would cast serious allegations against all the Teutonic officers. All "proved themselves cowards & a disgrace to the Regiment," said a disgusted Lieutenant Chivas. Severe ramifications would attend to the actions and indecisiveness of many of these soldiers.[33]

Lieutenant Greene was now effectively in command of Company B. "To tell the truth . . . Capt Eldred played the coward," he told his sister, forbidding her to "say a word to anyone about it." The captain, who weeks earlier had rebutted an allegation that he was malingering in Milwaukee, was frozen with fear. "When our men were standing up, facing the music, and I stood with them, encouraging them all I could with voice and action," Greene alleged, "Eldred hid behind a tree and uttered not a word, not a command." Greene would have more to say about his captain.[34]

Major Hibbard was frantic, and he sent the youthful adjutant, Arthur McArthur, galloping off to find General Sill, to tell him more regiments were needed immediately or the great enemy tide would engulf his men. Many Milwaukee soldiers had stood the rebel fire for fifteen or twenty minutes now. Men from Johnson's and Davis's shattered divisions fled in all directions except toward the enemy; many of them had flung away their muskets. Then what seemed like hordes of screaming butternuts were "all in my rear, pouring a horrid fire of musketry and grape into my regiment," said Major Hibbard. "After waiting for orders to fall back as long as I thought best, I brought off my men in ordinary shape. You cannot form any idea of how hard it was to make them stop." The phrase "ordinary shape" was freighted with many meanings.[35]

In the roar of cannon and the whiz and whine of bullets, amid shouts and screams, Major Hibbard's order to withdraw was not heard all along the line of Milwaukee companies. By that time, Lieutenant McArthur had returned from his futile gallop to tell General Sill of the crisis. The boyish lieutenant assisted Hibbard, conveying orders and dashing about the field. The companies on the left were the first to hear the order to retreat, and they began stepping backward, then turned and fled—"skedaddled" was how one Badger soldier put it.

"Two men on either side of me were shot down and at another time a man was shot down . . . who was touching my elbows," Lieutenant Chivas told his aunt. Those next minutes were chaotic and confused, and no one soldier was able to grasp the situation in its entirety. The Milwaukee Regiment's right flank was, indeed, exposed to the onrushing rebels, and one Louisiana regiment struck the Badgers like a sledgehammer. A contemporary historian dismissed the actions of the 24th Wisconsin during the next minutes with the observation that the "green regiment" simply "panicked," and after "firing only a few scattered shots, the regiment crumbled." Such assessment dismisses the situation too hastily. Although the Wisconsin men lacked cohesion, scores of soldiers fought determined defensive actions against the enemy; many good lives were lost and bodies maimed in the bargain.[36]

"It was not for a short time that we on the right discovered that the left wing was wanting, and then we followed," Lieutenant Chivas recalled. The companies remaining most likely included A, B, and I which sustained heaviest casualties. "A good deal of confusion existed for a few minutes in consequence of this break [in the ranks], but the regiment soon rallied, in good shape." The Scot lumber dealer did not blame Major Hibbard for the confusion. He "showed no fear, but did his duty and retained his presence of mind in the hottest of the fight." Gene Comstock, the nineteen-year-old printer, observed simply: "We stood and gave it to them till the regiment on our right [in General Davis's division] broke and ran when we followed suit." Companies A, led by Capt. Richard Austin, and I, Chivas's own, "were about the last to leave the field," the gray-eyed officer later wrote to his aunt, Martha Mitchell. Ironically, the two officers were among the tallest in the regiment.[37]

To other soldiers, the Milwaukee Regiment did not pull back in "ordinary shape." When the enemy charged across the open field a few minutes before, matters had been different. "There was a beautiful chance; we had them in full view, and we loaded and fired as quickly as possible," said Company B private Ed Douglas. But, then, without apparent orders, he took charge of himself. "I stood my ground as long as I thought it was expedient—until I was comparatively alone, and the bullets striking upon every tree around me." As he turned, a spent ball struck him in the heel; it "did no damage, but admonished me to quicken my pace, which I did, loading as I went." Where Douglas began, others rapidly followed.[38]

"We retreated into one of the open spaces" between the thick stands of cedars, Adjutant McArthur told his father, and "rallied behind a rail fence, with the intention of charging back into the woods." But General Sheridan, indefatigable that day, saw the remnant of the Milwaukee Regiment and called it back to the woods with the remainder of the brigade.

Many companies were torn apart as the rebel charges bludgeoned the blue lines from front and flank. Men became separated from their comrades. Young Amandus Silsby, the schoolboy from Ohio in Company A; the little immigrant tailor from Port Washington in Company H, Henry Bichler; and many others were missing. Lieutenant McArthur had never seen anything like this. "The firing by this time seemed to be on all sides. It seemed as though the enemy had entirely surrounded us. The shot and shell flew worse than at any time previous."[39]

During all of this, Company B's Captain Eldred still cowered, seemingly waiting for a chance to quit the field. "He did not give a single command, or speak one encouraging word to the boys during the whole of the Battle," the resourceful Lieutenant Greene said. "I took command of the company early in the day and kept it even when Eldred was present. I am sorry for him, for it will stick to him to his dying day." The swarthy twenty-two-year-old banker likely expected better of himself when he signed the roll in Milwaukee.[40]

Several Company B men fell with ghastly wounds. Lem Cochran, the florid-faced youth who said he was a horse trainer, was knocked from the ranks. Somewhat delicate, he had a difficult time on the march, and Colonel Larrabee earlier made him a wagoner because of his familiarity with animals. But now, Lem, back with his company, took a bullet to the forehead. Then little George Merrick, the nineteen-year-old store clerk, dropped to the ground, blood gushing from his groin. Minutes later, he regained his feet, and lurched at Norm Burdick, the printer and soldier correspondent.

"Oh, Norm, help me," the diminutive five-foot-four-inch soldier cried. With Charlie Heth, the older son of the Milwaukee confectioner, they carried their comrade to the safety of a nearby log house serving as a battlefield hospital. They did not believe Merrick would live long.

The three men passed "through the most terrific storm of shell, grape and ball that it is possible for the imagination to conceive. I consider it as nothing less than a miracle that I got off then, and while the Regiment was standing in line of battle, with my life. As it was, I did not receive a scratch," said the young printer.[41]

Almost at this time, another Company B man, Ed Douglas, and several others had knotted together as they fell back. Al Webber, the twenty-one-year-old clerk, "stood his ground like a hero," Douglas said. But he paid the price by taking a bullet in the neck, and slumped to the ground. "He didn't stagger, but dropped to the earth, like a column of water which has been held in its place and suddenly dissolved." Instantly, Al's younger brother William, a farmer everyone called Frank, rushed to his side. He was still alive, and he begged Douglas to help carry Webber from the field. "We dragged him . . . some distance, when he got upon his feet and walked with very little assistance from me." Looking back, they saw the entire regiment in "full retreat." "As the bullets whistled around us, Al begged us to leave him and make sure our own return, for we would certainly be killed." But they remained with the stricken soldier.

The trio filtered through the line of the 42nd Illinois, one of Schaefer's regiments that had been positioned in reserve; the Prairie State men lay on the ground, bayonets fixed preparing to rise up and charge the attackers. A short distance away, the three men found a log house belonging to a local farmer; it had been taken over by army surgeons as a hospital. "Deeming this a safe place," Douglas left his comrades, and pitched in with the Illinois boys "to have one more shot." The Webber boys were taken prisoner; although they were later paroled, they never returned to the regiment, being discharged in spring because of their wounds.

The feisty Douglas, a Milwaukee post office clerk well-known in the city, continued his personal battle. As the rebel attackers surged through the trees at the hill crest, pushing aside the remnants of the 24th Wisconsin, the 42nd Illinois "sprang up and charged furiously upon them," driving the enemy down the shallow slope and back across the open field," said Douglas. As blue and butternut flailed at one another, their lines surging back and forth across the field, Douglas was struck, "the ball passing through about four inches of flesh in the thigh." "I hobbled for some distance, but my leg becoming stiff, I was unable to proceed and lay down behind a low fence." The firing around him grew more intense with the rebels on one side peppering the Federals on the other. "Such a storm of bullets I never heard before coming from both ways. It wasn't whiz, whiz, whiz, but it was *whiz-z-z-z-z* steadily, dozens of them striking in the rail fence, which was not a foot and a half high." A bullet ploughed right through Douglas's writing portfolio. His harrowing experience was not yet at an end.

Then the Union artillery opened with canister shot, hundreds of small steel pellets spewing out like a huge shotgun; the muzzle was depressed too low and the "charge ploughed up the ground in every direction around me, covering me with dirt," the wounded private said. "I thought, 'another such shot, and I am gone,'" but no more were fired. Instead the cannon belched what Douglas described as "balls and bombs." "How they did screech through the air! I could see the bombs burst in the field before and behind me, and hear the pieces go humming by." The blue-eyed, light complexion twenty-one-year-old managed to crawl into a little sheltered spot among some fence rails, hoping the haven would protect him. "One bullet struck the rail directly opposite my head, [and] had it not been for the rail the balls would have gone through me lengthwise." Then a shell or cannonball struck the rail six inches from his head, driving a large splinter into his back. Douglas would live to tell the tale, but lost the leg to a surgeon's knife.[42]

Twenty-one-year-old Henry Drake was angry, "vexed" as he put it, because he felt the order to withdraw came too soon. But when the sooty-faced enemy, men of Alabama and Louisiana he later learned, snarled closer he had second thoughts, quickly concluding that "it would have been perfect folly for us to have remained any longer for the force was twenty times as large as our brigade that opposed them." Despite his rank, Drake disliked carrying an officer's sword; he kept his old Austrian musket instead. While the 24th Wisconsin rapidly pulled backward, men of the 15th Missouri, the second of Colonel Schaefer's regiments sent as reserve hours before, passed through them at the double quick, bayonets slanted and gleaming. Drake, like Ed Douglas, was gripped in a battle frenzy. "I was so excited," the dark-eyed soldier said, that he and a handful of Company A boys, including Charles Cookson, turned upon the enemy with the Missouri men. The Company B men fired, loaded, and fired again, sending about fifteen shots at the rebels "with considerable execution I thought," Drake told his brother. Then Cookson, a well-read young man who had been a clerk in a Milwaukee bookstore, was shot; the wound proved mortal.[43]

Somewhere amid the roiling melee of fleeing men and frenzied horses, General Sill gallantly gathered portions of his brigade, which was rapidly losing any semblance of cohesion, attempting to rally them. Separated from his staff, he pushed the band of men forward in a countercharge against the surging enemy attackers, driving the enemy from the cedars back to the open ground. But while shouting encouragement to his men, the bearded officer was struck in the face by a rebel ball. Spare minutes later, Lt. John Mitchell, the brigade's topographical engineer, reined in his lathered horse before the prostrate commander whose face and beard were awash in blood; the bullet had smashed into the general's mouth and punched through his brain, exiting the skull. There was no doubt that the wound was fatal. "He was still breathing and as the air bubbled through the stream of blood he seemed like a drowning man," the short-statured Milwaukee officer told his mother in an unusually gruesome passage. The brigade adjutant soon pounded up, and seeing the commander's fate, removed his sword and handed it to Mitchell for safekeeping. Then he mounted again, intent on informing Col. Nicholas Greusel, the Illinois officer, that he again commanded the 1st Brigade. When the general died, a Chicago battle correspondent wrote, "the sun broke through some cold-looking clouds, and flashed a clear bright light over the fields." A heroic tableau, indeed.

In the meantime, Mitchell, who made no note of the change in light when the general died, watched the enemy approaching; he feared if he did nothing, they would take possession of the dead general's body. "Collecting half a dozen stragglers I got them to take the body to the hospital in the rear." That was the last he saw of Gen. Joshua Sill. The short lieutenant galloped off to assist his friend, Old Nick Greusel.[44]

Just before General Sill attempted to rally his men, Sanford Williams, another soldier in Company B, the Young Men's Association Tigers, fell among the cedars with a badly smashed leg: "The bone was shot all to pieces, leaving the limb hanging by a portion of the calf." When the 24th withdrew, Williams, the twenty-seven-year-old, blue-eyed Wisconsin farmer, was unable to move back with them. Ironically, while in Nashville, Williams had become so sick that the surgeon offered him a discharge because of disability. But, it was remembered, he would not consider leaving his company "until he had done some fighting."

His immediate concern was to stanch the heavy flow of blood: He removed a cord from his heavy blue overcoat and cinched it as tightly as strength allowed; some of the flow was choked off. Then: "I crawled some forty rods," the soldier said, "the shot and shell striking thick as hail about me." But there was more. As he painfully made his way along the ground, he saw two men nearby helping another wounded soldier; a shell from a rebel cannon whooshed over Williams's head and ploughed into the ground; it exploded, "tearing the three men to pieces." As he painfully crawled on, a Federal battery of artillery hurtled down on him; he pulled himself from its path. In pursuit were three lines of rebel infantry, and all passed over him. Following General Sill's brief countercharge, the enemy lines reeled backward, again stumbling over Williams's prostrate form; then another blue line (probably the 42nd Illinois or 15th Missouri) sprinted over the wounded soldier, only to be pushed backward when Sill was killed. In all, eight battle lines churned past Sanford Williams within a short time.

Somehow, two comrades came to Williams's aid, carrying him to an old log shanty where the other wounded were gathering. Shortly after he found a spot on the earthen floor, a shell screeched through the door, knocking two legs from a piano. "A moment later another shell struck the wall a foot or two above him, covering him with plaster and bark." A soldier climbed to the building's roof, and erected a yellow flag to signify to both armies that this was a hospital.

Williams wanted to get a note to his parents that he was alive, and hurriedly jotted a few lines. At that, he saw his Company B comrade, Norm Burdick, who had carried little George Merrick to the log house. Williams asked him to wait a moment; Burdick, the hazel-eyed soldier who had lost his spectacles, waited apprehensively. But before Williams finished scribbling, the enemy burst inside and took Burdick prisoner. Whenever the men would meet in Milwaukee after the war, Burdick always claimed that he had been gobbled by the rebs because of his kindness for Williams; but the one-legged soldier countered that the loss of Burdick's spectacles was the cause, for "he could not see to get away from the enemy." The gray soldiers bundled off Burdick. Williams's ordeal was only beginning.[45]

Meanwhile, the regiment fell back forty rods, then "rallied again, fired several rounds, made a short charge, and then fell back about a half a mile," one Milwaukee private said. "The regiment did nobly," Company G's Ed Chamberlain said in retrospect. "It was first attacked, but stood its ground for fifteen or twenty minutes against a far superior force, when it retreated across a field, then rallied and fell back in good order." He was, of course, attempting to put a good light on a bad situation.[46]

Lieutenant Chivas would not use the words "nobly" or "good order" when he wrote about these confused minutes. He admitted that the regiment "broke and ran," but in the same letter to his aunt softened the assessment: "There will probably be a good deal said about the behavior of the 24th in this battle. The only unsoldierly thing we did was to run instead of retreat in good order, but we redeemed ourselves by rallying again in the field." The running he blamed upon the conduct of several officers. Both Chivas and his cousin, Lt. John Mitchell, however, attested that the major, Lish Hibbard, had conducted himself well.[47]

Major Hibbard explained that during this stage of the battle Wednesday morning he had been mounted, directing the regiment "until my horse was shot—the grape shot going through into the sole of my boot, and nearly throwing me from the saddle. The boys cried out, 'the Major is killed.' 'Not by a d—d sight,' said I," he wrote. He remembered that while about seventy-five men ran, perhaps 250 Milwaukee soldiers gathered around him in the open field beyond the evergreens. "When I rallied my men, and knew who would stand by me, I felt like whipping the whole South," he boasted. Just then the end of his sword was shot away. The Milwaukee bookkeeper, almost twenty-three then, detailed his actions to his prosperous father, William Hibbard, who took the liberty of having the letter published in a Milwaukee daily; the printing would cause some embarrassment for the major. Colonel Greusel attested that after about 100 yards, the 24th Wisconsin stopped and "stood right up to the rack" despite being "placed in a bad situation."[48]

Despite his diminutive stature, another officer who stood out was Chivas's friend and captain, Fred Root. The thirty-year-old merchant seemed indefatigable. "Through the rain and mud and fatigue . . . he had always the same cheerful, animated expression; the unbinding and undaunted pluck that must have brought the blush to him who came sneaking up after the battle and danger were over," wrote a comrade. Chivas was amazed at how his friend exposed himself to danger. "How he escapes . . . is akin to miraculous, and I suppose is," he told his pastor, the Reverend Ingraham.[49]

In all of this, Company B's Captain Eldred still made no effort to take charge of his men. "After the reg[iment] retreated, and the order was given to 'Rally,' he made no motion toward doing so, and I then stepped to the front, quickly rallied my men, and returning to him, told him his company was rallied," Lieutenant Greene told his sister, Lizzie. "He merely said 'all right,' and that was about all I heard from him, until Rockwell was shot." The city would soon learn of Eldred's behavior.[50]

Young George Rockwell, a New York lad who had traveled to Milwaukee before the war to work as a salesman for the Burchard Company, was knocked from the ranks by a cannonball. The twenty-two-year-old had volunteered for the Young Men's Association Tigers in August, and had been rapidly promoted to corporal and sergeant. "The Shot that struck poor . . . Rockwell would have cut me in two had I not dodged it," said Lieutenant Greene. "I heard it coming and dropped, letting it pass over me." Rockwell, not four feet from the lieutenant, attempted to escape from the bounding shell's path; "but unfortunately it had reached its destination and striking him, tore his right leg all to pieces." It was reported days later in the *Daily Wisconsin* that just before Rockwell gasped his final breath he murmured that he "had tried to do his duty." A writer eulogized: "We shall never look upon his noble face again. As we passed him day after day before we left, we little thought then that form would so soon be cold in death, but he died nobly defending his country's flag and her imperiled existence." After the battle, his body was sent by express in a tin box to his father in New York.[51]

Finally, Capt. Bill Eldred was energized—but apparently it was only his own safety that mattered. "[H]e started off for the ostensible purpose of getting a stretcher [for Rockwell] but instead of doing so, made the best of his way through the woods to the rear." Chivas noticed him spur his horse and dash off the field. In retrospect, Lieutenant Greene would write that since he had volunteered he had "watched human nature closely, and as a general rule I find that the greatest talkers (especially wherein their prowess is concerned) are in case of emergency or danger . . . the poorest actors. In the Battle of Murfreesboro, the greatest Braggarts, ran the quickest and farthest." By inference, Eldred, the dark married man, must have been loquacious.[52]

Major Hibbard, meanwhile, still struggled to control his regiment. We "would never have left that spot, if I had not received an order from General Sheridan to bring off my men" when the division commander saw the 24th's perilous situation. Stepping backward some distance farther, the Wisconsin soldiers stopped again; "we fixed bayonets and woe to the rebels if they had come against them," he boasted to his father. "I was afoot, and the way solid shot struck, was awful. Men [were] flying in all directions." There was naught but "smoke, noise and yells," he wrote days later.[53]

To several writers it seemed that the youngster, McArthur, was everywhere that morning, spurring his lathered horse with orders and directions from Major Hibbard. He must have been a sight, that dark cloud of curly hair beneath his cap, shouting in that high-pitched voice for this captain or that lieutenant to position his company here or align it there. "This young man, whose voice on dress parade could scarce be heard half a length of the line, could be heard on the battle-field amidst the roar of cannon, a quarter of a mile, as he issued commands, encouraged his friends, and threatened stragglers with instant death."

"At Stone River . . . the Adjutant proved to be a real hero, and inspiration to the men, and of great assistance to the officers of the [24th]." So wrote Jerry Watrous, the foremost of the nineteenth-century chroniclers of Wisconsin's war experience. "His bravery was so conspicuous that he attracted the attention of both brigade and division commanders. After the battle every soldier in the [24th] was the boy Adjutant's sworn friend, admirer and defender," he wrote when McArthur was an important regular army general.[54]

Hibbard also recalled the seventeen-year-old lieutenant during that desperate time, being ever ready to gallop across the field relaying orders to the company officers. "The Adjutant behaved like a young Ajax," the major told his father, Judge McArthur, "and I complimented him for his gallantry, and his father may be proud of him." The old judge must have glowed at the report of his slender son's actions. Here was another letter that the well-known jurist made certain was printed in a daily for all Milwaukee to read.

After dashing back through the woods into an open field, many men rallied with the major. "No regiment could have formed line more rapidly than they did after retreating. Surrounded on all sides, as they were, by confused masses of fugitives," the major wrote days later, the men behaved as well as could be expected. Even hardened veterans could not have resisted the fleeing hordes of Federal soldiers; "new recruits assuredly deserve praise for standing their ground," he said.

In a few minutes, the order was received to move the Milwaukee Regiment up to a fence where they joined the right of the 15th Missouri; but within a short time, the Missouri men were ordered to advance. The Badger soldiers marched forward with them to a second fence. Hibbard ordered his men to lie down. One of General Sheridan's orderlies then moved the 24th back into the woods where it joined the 88th Illinois; both regiments were then under the command of Colonel Greusel. At his direction, Hibbard marched the remnant of his men through a "cedar swamp [under] a terrific fire of artillery and infantry around us."[55]

Company B's Gene Comstock saw it this way: "We rallied in the cornfield and stood our ground for a few minutes when the order was given for a general retreat as the whole right flank was turned. We retreated through the woods," where the regiment had lain the day before, across another roadway, and into the dark gloom of a cedar forest. "Here the 24th got lost from the division," he said.[56]

"We fell back before them," remembered Tom Ford. "They crowded us into a . . . woods, where there was nothing but cedar trees and rocks, and it seemed as if all the birds and rabbits in that large field were looking for protection around our feet." Decades later the Irish farmer could still convey the impressions of those confused and chaotic minutes. "So thick and fast did the rebels send their shot and shell after us that you might think it impossible for a bird to escape them. The rebels had us surrounded for a while. You could see the rebel officers and orderlies galloping on their horses in the near distance, urging their men on to make a complete capture."

Despite the harrowing hours, Tom Ford, the copper-haired farmer, was still concerned about the money owed him by men in the Milwaukee Regiment for tobacco he had sold days before. As he muttered about it, a comrade, Jim Mangan, a schoolteacher from Franklin south of Milwaukee, chided: "Thomas, this is terrible. It seems impossible for any of us to escape being killed by those shells and bullets, if they continue this way much longer."

At that moment, Ford spotted one of the men, who owned him for tobacco, fall dead. "Yes," Ford responded to Mangan. "But what will I do now for the price of tobacco? Most of those are killed that I sold it to, and I will never be paid."

"To the devil with you and your tobacco," Mangan shouted, "if that is what you are thinking of now, in place of your soul." In the midst of wreckage of the army's right wing, he would remember that incongruous incident to the end of his days.[57]

Other Milwaukee men remembered the confusion of that late morning. "Nothing but the overruling care of Providence saved me then," Company K's Ed Parsons told his parents. "The tide of battle this time and several hours after, seemed against us. Our troops seemed to be moving in every direction, but the enemy was firing into us incessantly. The rattle of musketry and the booming of cannon and bursting of shells, was perfectly awful." The lieutenant likened the deadly scene of that December 31st morning to some paintings he viewed back home, portraying battles during the Mexican War. "On an open plain you see two opposing armies, the cannon belching forth death, horses flying in wild disorder, or falling to the earth in their death struggle, the dead and dying lying all around. . . . God grant I may never see such a sight again!" Parsons would witness more days such as this during the coming years.

Perhaps half of the Wisconsin, Illinois, and Michigan men were dead, bleeding, or missing in the belt of woods from where they fled and in the open farm field where they now found themselves. But the gray-haired Greusel was patching together some semblance of order here from the disparate pieces. He "had us out seemingly, through the only opening there was" amid the swarms of screaming rebel soldiers who pinched down on three sides of Sheridan's division, Lieutenant Parsons said. In the field, it "seemed as though we should be cut to pieces by the shells that were bursting around us. This was the first time I had ever seen a true picture of the battle field."[58]

Many men failed to stand up to the test, but many did. "John behaved himself like a hero," Bob Chivas told Martha Mitchell. "He was on horseback all day, riding in the thickest of the fight," his cousin said. His "conduct that day was the admiration of all who saw him. He was always cool and smiling—notwithstanding the responsibility and danger of his position." Chivas wrote much the same to a business associate a few days later. At least one fellow officer, the gentle Quaker, Howard Greene, did not share Chivas's assessment of Mitchell's demeanor.[59]

In the open field Lieutenant Mitchell was assisting avuncular Nick Greusel, the Illinois colonel, to gain some measure of control over the scattered regiments in the brigade. The weak-eyed lieutenant was the only aide available to the Illinois commander, and the immigrant never forgot it. The little officer "showed a good deal of Scotch nonchalance as his father," the tall, gray colonel said, "and evidently looked upon the exchange of metallic currency" as a "fair business transaction, even when the percent was heavily against us." By "metallic currency," of course, he meant shot and shell.[60]

Events among the men of the Milwaukee Regiment over the next few hours are uncertain. Tangled cedar glades, brooding and shadowy amid the pall of gray smoke, obscured precise movements of companies. Shouts and din reverberated through the evergreens, sound echoed and seemed to emanate from several directions, magnifying the menace. Official reports were vague and blurred. "The history of combat in

Phil Sheridan.
"Little Phil," the brigadier.

those dark cedar thickets will never be known," wrote a Milwaukee soldier. "No man could see even the whole of his own regiment, and no one will ever be able to tell who they were that fought bravest and they who proved recreant to their trust."

Few Milwaukee men provided any significant detail of those later morning hours; it was as if their regiment's tarnished conduct during the first hour or so had shocked writers into silence. But it was in this period of later morning December 31 that General Sheridan conducted the fighting defense that would win him fame and commendations. Little Phil maneuvered his brigades with brilliance, giving ground grudgingly, patching shattered units together here, shuffling remnants of regiments there, all the while maintaining his lines and punishing the attacking enemy. A mile and a half, two miles and more the blue lines were driven north. A news correspondent admitted that "faintness of heart came over me as the destruction of our army seemed to stare us in the face."[61]

Movement was continually on the regiment's heel—backward—the men pausing only seconds to load, take aim, and fire. "At length we arrived in the woods, and here was a general retreat, and I would not have given a snap of my fingers for the whole army," Lieutenant McArthur told his father. The men stumbled through a swamp where the firing seemed to reach a climax. Sounds were confusing in these cedar thickets. Finally, they reached the area where what seemed like hundreds of Federal artillery pieces were hub to hub, and "here my hopes began to revive," the seventeen-year-old youth said.[62]

By midmorning, Gen. Phil Sheridan—who would long be lauded for his presence and decisiveness that day—was at a flash point in the battle of Stones River. His disparate command became something of a hinge, a fulcrum upon which the entire Federal line that stretched north of the Nashville Turnpike, had begun to swing. Later historians would make much effort to describe how the great wings of General Rosecrans's army were forced together by Bragg's attack on General McCook's command. It was as a closing jackknife, some wrote. "It was left to Gen. Sheridan to stay the hitherto successful onset of the foe," a Chicago news correspondent wrote from the field that day. "Never did a man labor more faithfully than he to perform his task, and never was a leader seconded by more gallant soldiers." McCook's broken right wing reeled backwards in its flight from the "triumphant enemy who now swarmed upon its front and right flanks." The Army of the Cumberland was being forced to close back upon itself. One fourth of Sheridan's command would soon lie dead, bleeding, or missing. The little brigadier's two other brigade commanders, Colonels Schaefer and Roberts, met the same fate as General Sill. One of Little Phil's mounts, "Black Bess," was killed at Stones River.[63]

At the end of the four hours' fighting, Sheridan had successively pulled back to three lines of defense, the while under a brutal and sustained rebel fire from nine brigades. He lost about a thousand men, perhaps a fifth of his division strength, while punishing the enemy with two to three thousand losses. He may just have saved the Army of the Cumberland that day.[64]

"It was fight and retreat, then rally and make a stand until flanked[,] then retreat again, rally again and fight again," a Milwaukee soldier remembered after the war. "Seven times that day we formed line of battle under fire." An Illinois soldier also recalled: "In falling back we found the cedar woods so thick, and so filled with rocks and caverns and fallen trees, that it was almost impossible to get through it." The cedar thickets were brooding and shadowy places, cut by immense ravines and limestone fissures.[65]

"Finally when the ammunition was all used up and the ranks down to fragments, Little Phil ordered what there was left of the division back to the railroad entrenchments. Our remnant looked like the parts of a sail which a gale of wind leaves clinging to the spars when it strips a vessel of its canvas, just a fringe of men on each side of the flagstaff," said one who witnessed the scene.[66]

Defeat for the Army of the Cumberland was still a distinct possibility. The men of Milwaukee who coalesced around Sheridan—they may not have numbered 200—and the ill-organized assembly from several divisions that joined with them must have gripped their muskets tightly, rammed powder and bullets rapidly, and unleashed storms of lead at the mottled rebel lines that advanced upon them. Cartridge boxes were nearly empty of the sixty rounds of ammunition. Men pirated bullets from the dead and wounded. The heavy overcoats likely weighed upon their backs, but there was no time to unburden themselves. Desperation must have piled upon tension. "We were very nearly scooped," acting lieutenant Drake told his brother, "but our retreating army finally came to a stand still, and drove them back."[67]

The key to the battlefield was the highest point on an elevated space between the Nashville Turnpike and the railroad to Chattanooga. An immense train of wagons was parked there. "Such sounds as proceeded from that forest of pines and cedars, were enough to appall with terror the stoutest hearts. The roar of cannon, the crashing of shot through the trees, the whizzing and bursting of shells, the uninterrupted rattle of thirty-thousand muskets, all mingled in one prolonged and tremendous volume of sounds, as though all the thunders of Heaven had been rolled together and each individual burst of celestial artillery had been rendered perpetual, and above it all could be heard the wild cheers of the traitorous hosts, as body after body of our troops gave way, and were pushed back toward the turnpike. Nearer and nearer came the storm, louder and louder resounded the tumult of battle." The Chicago news writer seemed breathless.

"Suddenly the rout became visible, and crowds of ten thousand fugitives, presenting every possible phase of wild and uncontrollable disorder, burst from the cedar thickets and rushed into the open space between them and the turnpike," wrote a news man who observed from that rise. "Amongst them all, perhaps not a half dozen members of the same regiment could have been found together. Thick and fast the bullets of the enemy fell among them, and scores of them were shot down, but still the number constantly increased, by reason of the fresh crowds which burst every moment from the thickets."[68]

In murderous melee near the rail line, Fred Childs of Company B found himself. The eighteen-year-old Milwaukee clerk had been detailed some time before to a division ambulance corps parked north of the Wilkinson Turnpike. When the wild-eyed collection of rampaging Federal soldiers from Davis's and Johnson's divisions rushed in "one conglomerated mass" from the woods, they made a "general rush" toward the turnpike; "if Bull Run was any worse than what followed, it must have been terrific indeed—men, horses, wagons, all running into each other," Childs told his parents. He leaped into one of the wagons to avoid being crushed by the surging mass of fleeing men.

Just as the "disorganized mob of soldiers" reached the roadway, a troop of rebel horsemen, Texas Rangers, Childs thought, dashed toward General McCook's great supply train, firing at and killing teamsters and mules. Childs remained in the wagon until "bullets flew too lively to suit me," and then jumped clear. The gray cavalry demanded the blue coats surrender, and one turned to the Milwaukee soldier, demanding he give up his revolver. Childs said he had none. "He said I had, and got off to search me. He felt my pocket book . . . and took it." Inside was $14 in greenbacks and a $10 bank draft.

The enemy prodded about 200 soldiers and teamsters as prisoners, but the assembly had not traveled a quarter of a mile before the 4th Michigan Cavalry swooped out of the woods with whoops and rattling sabers; the blue horsemen ordered their comrades to get behind them when the rebels loosed a volley before spurring away with the Wolverine cavalry in pursuit. A few Federal soldiers near Childs tumbled to the ground with wounds.[69]

Meanwhile, a new defensive line was beginning to take shape in a position bent back to the north. The great mottled wave of rust and gray, however, was implacable. A second time, Sheridan was forced backwards to a new line in the cedars north of the Wilkinson Pike.

About eleven that December morning two key divisions and General Sheridan's "emaciated" command were established in the cedar forest west of the roadway. Maj. Gen. James Negley's division of General Thomas's center wing was linked at a right angle with Sheridan's left, and extended northwest toward the Nashville Pike. Colonel Greusel's brigade was on the left of Sheridan's line connected to Negley, while the two other brigades stretched to the right, connected to one of Thomas's divisions. The effect was to bend back the line, "refusing it to prevent rebel attackers from gaining any flank."[70]

Soon "the long lines of enemy emerged from the woods, rank behind rank, and with demoniac yell, intended to strike terror into the souls of the Yankees who stood before them, charged with fearful energy almost to the very muzzle of the cannon, whose dark mouths yawned upon them."

"A dazzling sheet of flame burst from the ranks of the Union forces. An awful roar shook the earth, a crash rent the atmosphere, and the foremost line of the rebel host [*sic*] were literally swept away from the field, and seemed to melt away like snow flakes before a flame, and then both armies were enveloped in a vast cloud of smoke, which hid everything from the eye. In the still visible ground between the pike and the railroad, the tumult redoubled," a Milwaukee correspondent wrote.

A heavy haze of gray powder smoke hung in the air, obscuring virtually everything beyond a few yards. Cannons thudded and roared. Grimy men, faces smeared with powder residue, feverishly pounded down charges and fired at uncertain targets. Bullets crashed through the pines and cedars. Dying men writhed in agony or lay silently clutching maimed torsos and limbs. Everywhere lay the detritus of battle—abandoned muskets, scattered leathers and accoutrements, discarded hats and caps, mounds of dead horses and mules, wrecked wagons and artillery caissons. Such scenes went unrecorded in the letters and diaries of Milwaukee soldiers.

"Under the great canopy of smoke that concealed the combatants, the flight of those in charge of wagons and ambulances became still more rapid and disordered," wrote the Chicago news man. "Thousands of fugitives from the broken right wing mingled with the teams, and frequently a mass of man, horses and wagons, would be crushed and ground together." For ten minutes, according to the correspondent, the "battle burst forth from the cloud." Finally, when the blue lines surged forward in a countermove, they found no rebels between the woods and the turnpike—"only the dead, dying, and disabled. There were hundreds of these, and their blood soaked the reddened ground."[71]

By noon, the entire Army of the Cumberland was in its final defensive position, a compressed semicircle. At the angle where Sheridan's hastily assembled line met that of General Negley's division of General Thomas's center wing, the battle was building toward a new crescendo. Decisive pressure was brought to bear upon Sheridan's men. But they gave no sign of faltering, the general wrote, only calling for more cartridges. All but two of his dozen regiments were reaching into empty bullet pouches. Once again, Sheridan had to pull back his regiments lest they be overrun.

What the men of Milwaukee saw and heard of Sheridan's masterful defensive fight rekindled their esteem. The "battle served to strengthen the feeling of admiration his command already had for him," Lieutenant Parsons said many years afterward.[72]

Days later when the exhausted men had time to talk of it, their admiration for Old Rosey grew as well. Wearing an old blue coat and chomping on a cigar, the pugnacious commander, "every inch a soldier," was seen galloping about the field. He met Little Phil in the open ground west of the railroad at one point. "His usually florid face had lost its ruddy color, and his anxious eyes told that the disasters of the morning were testing his powers to the verge of endurance, but he seemed fully to comprehend what had befallen us," recollected General Sheridan two decades after. "His firmly set lips and the calmness with which his instructions were delivered inspired confidence in all around him." When the army commander directed the placement of Sheridan's division, Rosecrans "renewed in us all the hope of final victory, though it must be admitted that at this phase of the battle the chances lay largely with the enemy."[73]

The pugnacious Rosecrans would later aver that Sheridan's division was "the hottest place I was in that day." In a dispatch printed in a Milwaukee daily, a writer observed: "It is their glory that their cartridges boxes and their guns were then empty." When Rosecrans pounded up to Sheridan's position, the diminutive fighter, "with most touching pathos," said: "Here is all that is left of us, General."

But Sheridan's men had not yet seen the end of battle on that final day of 1862. General Rosecrans ordered Sheridan to have his division replenish their ammunition. One at a time, the regiments were marched from the battle line, directed to the supply trains in the rear. Then, two of Sheridan's brigades were pushed into another part of the field by the commanding general.

"The desperate assailants withdrew at last. Their loss must have been fearful, as they call it the bloodiest struggle of the day." Finally there was a lull in the storm, and "scarcely a volley of musketry or a boom of cannon was heard for three quarters of an hour," the Chicago writer said. It was as though the two antagonists had, like their ammunition, expended all available energy as well. Indeed, Stones River would be one of the bloodiest battles of the entire war.

In the forty minutes since the first rebel rank strode forward against the hastily assembled Federal defensive position near the railroad and turnpike, all three lines of advancing sundry-hued ranks were dashed to pieces. "The battle was over. Until 4 o'clock the rebels continued to fire cannon from the direction of Murfreesboro, as though in angry protest against their repulse."[74]

"No other attacks were made on us to the east of the railroad for the rest of the afternoon," Sheridan said with relief. Just before dark, the remains of his division were withdrawn and moved about a mile northwest to the opposite side of the Nashville Turnpike, near the extreme left of the Federal line.[75]

The Badger soldiers were in all likelihood too exhausted to collect coherent thoughts about what transpired in the preceding hours. It had been harrowing and horrific, an experience beyond comprehension. It could not even be communicated, especially to folks back home. "[H]ow little the people back home know of the suffering of the soldiers," an Illinois man contemplated. As had occurred the night before, no campfires were permitted; the lines were too close. Some soldiers slipped beneath the cedars into the small rocky crevices and lighted little fires out of enemy sight. In those thickets and among the limestone fissures was a "dreadful field with its burden of mutilation and death."

In the dim winter twilight, a hush fell over the bloody field. Both sides were exhausted and badly mauled. The soldiers were relieved to see the fighting end. The ground was frozen and the wind blew strongly. Rain beat down against the fields, glades, woods, and men. There were no celebrations on the eve of the new year. Some of the wounded actually froze to the ground in their own blood. All night, both blue and gray men cried pitifully for help—water, food, a warm fire, even merciful death.

Little Phil's division was more than decimated. Early returns indicated a loss of nearly 1,700, of whom over 500 were still missing; many of these were prisoners or would within days filter back to their regiments. He had also lost his three brigade commanders and sixty-nine other officers. His men had only a week before numbered just about 6,500.

"Which fellow-man, can you most admire? The sublime devotion of these gallant braves, or the skill and coolness of the commander, who then offered the ragged remains his order, for renewed slaughter? Hearts of rock would melt in the presence of such touching tragedy." It was an *Iliad,* wrote the news man.[76]

Lieutenant Mitchell was busy that night, assisting old Colonel Greusel in compiling an accurate assessment of losses and strength. "Our brigade, weary from want of sleep, hungry and chilled to the mar-row, had fought valiantly. They were the first to repulse the enemy on that disastrous day," he said. Of 1,839 men present for duty before the battle commenced the day before, the brigade sustained 102 killed and 369 wounded, with 200 still missing—a total of 671 or perhaps a third of the Wisconsin, Illinois, and Michigan men.[77]

"But, say, that boy MacArthur [*sic*] was in his element and proved to be anything else than a kindergartner," Watrous celebrated thirty years later. "The regiment lost fully half of the four hundred and odd men carried into battle, and that day's bloody word made the beardless Adjutant a hero in the eyes of the whole brigade." The mantle of hero was being placed on the lad's narrow shoulders. "Our commander Major Hibbard, devoted a paragraph of his official report to the praise of little Arthur MacArthur."[78]

It was not quite a paragraph that Major Hibbard wrote: "To the Adjutant of the regiment, Arthur McArthur, Jr., I am more than indebted for his aide and effective service. Young and gallant, I bespeak for him an honorable career." The fresh-faced soldier would not only have an honorable career, but would one day win great renown. A private in Company A was more effusive about the boy adjutant. He "is the bravest of the brave, and last to leave a point of danger."[79]

Adjutant McArthur was likely sent about the Milwaukee Regiment to collect information on casualties. When the captains and lieutenants of the 24th Wisconsin's ten decimated companies looked about their ranks New Year's Eve, the result was shocking. They had certainly expected the worst after many hundreds of the Milwaukee Regiment had fled the fields and vanished in the woods. Expectantly, too, the rebels now held many captive. The losses at this early stage were astonishing. Company B's Lieutenant Greene reported he had marched from Nashville with forty-seven men; nearly half, including three confirmed dead, were gone. Second Lt. George Cole had been wounded, and taken prisoner. Sgt. George Rockwell, whose leg was torn off, was not expected to live; short-legged George Merrick, with a bad wound, was in enemy hands along with the florid horse trainer, Lem Cochran. Charlie Heth, older of the Milwaukee confectioner's sons, was missing. The rebels had even bundled off little drummer boy "Fritzie" Clisbie. Ed Parsons had counted fifty-two in Company K just a few days before; now eighteen remained. In addition to Henry Pfaff and Byron Brooks, James Gilbert and Gus Gage were dead. So was Lt. Christian Nix in Company D; he left a widow and his remains would lie forever in Tennessee. The company captain, Bill Kennedy, said fifty men had been reported ready for battle that morning; now only twenty-eight could be counted. In Company E, some were saying that Cam Reed had fallen. There were dead and mortally wounded in every other company, as well, and hundreds of prisoners. Young Amandus Silsby did not answer the Company A roll that night; nor did the immigrant tailor from Port Washington, Henry Bichler, when Company H counted its men.

The Milwaukee Regiment ultimately listed nineteen killed, fifty-seven wounded, and ninety-eight missing. Perhaps one-third of those who stood ready for battle the morning of December 31 were now casualties.[80]

That night, after his near escape from the rebel cavalryman near General McCook's supply wagons, Fred Childs rejoined his comrades. "They had been in the fight all day," he wrote, "and were pretty well cut up." He shared a cold and fitful sleep with his comrades.[81]

The regiment was withdrawn somewhat from the line to gain some respite. The first night of the new year was long and cold. The "groans of the wounded, which never ceased for a moment through all the sad and restless night," increased the discomfort. The men, aware that their commanders were deciding whether to attack or retreat, hardly experienced a restful slumber. Their fate on that first dawn of 1863 was not in their own hands. But the sun was not seen that Thursday, as gray wintry skies frowned on the battlefield. It was an ominous New Year's Day.[82]

Some of the soldiers were ordered on picket, and one Company B man said that many men "suffered severely. I was struck with a spent ball in the thigh, laming my leg very much," he told his parents. "I wish I could come and see you." Homesickness was amplified by such trying times.[83]

On New Year's morning "our boys drew rations, which they certainly needed, for all were quite hungry," a Company B soldier told his parents. "The ball opened again quite lively, and for two hours, I don't remember to have heard heavier artillery firing, in my life. The reports were so loud and rapid that the sound fairly deafened us and shook the earth."

Another Wisconsin soldier said later: "[F]rom Thursday until Sunday . . . much of the time we lay in the mud, the rain often pouring upon us. . . . Our rations were out, but a young horse was shot within ten feet of me, and we ate the noble fellow, [officers] and men all partaking, nor was it bad for a hungry soldier."[84]

Lieutenant Mitchell remembered a similar meal. That January 1 "we resumed our position in line with the other brigades of Sheridan's division. For the three remaining days of the battle, we were not actively engaged. We lay under arms in a state of suspense. During this time, we suffered from the inclement weather, and the almost total lack of provisions. Some of the men ate horse; less aristocratic palates, I was told, took mule." The son of wealth, however, could not bring himself to partake; he had been a gentleman farmer, after all, and would one day raise fine Percheron and other purebred horses. "I contented myself with parched corn," he said.[85]

The paucity of food also remained a vivid memory for red-haired Tom Ford, the farmer in Company H who always had an eye for such things. He described a large pile of forage corn stacked near General Rosecrans's headquarters that the Milwaukee men began pilfering. A heavy guard was soon posted with orders to hand out no more than one cob to each man. But some soldiers got two "by placing the first behind their back and thrusting forth the other empty hand. The pile of corn did not supply one-hundredth part of the vast numbers clustered around it. We ate our corn, and that was all we had to eat at that time."[86]

After a cold and troublesome night among the cedars, the Milwaukee men were roused and marched back into line. About dawn, rebel skirmishers crawled forward all along the Cumberland defensive position. Only half-hearted exchanges were made between the antagonists, however, and cannons muttered sporadically at one another. Sometime in those brooding hours, twenty-three-year-old Date Worth, likely still concerned about the fate of his friend, Jim Harvey, was captured by the rebels. He would soon find himself on a lengthy tour of "Rebeldom." His comrades lay in the line most of the day.[87]

"At last the New Year was ushered in, and what a New Year, not only to our poor wounded soldiers on that sodden field, whose sufferings language could not describe," said an Army of the Cumberland surgeon, " but to the thousands both north and south who mourned the loss of loved ones." All during that January 1, artillery grumbled bitterly about a mile and a half northeast from where the Milwaukee soldiers and Sheridan's division hunkered behind their hastily erected defensive works. Part of General Crittenden's left wing, the Wisconsin men would later learn, were gaining control of a prominence on the east bank of Stones River. The scrap between them and the rebels ceased at evening. The 24th was no doubt relieved they had no part of that fight.

"The field was covered with dead, whose faces became familiar to us in camp and on the march, and who but the day before were in the prime and vigor of young manhood," remembered an army surgeon. "We saw men living, whose broken and lacerated limbs were frozen to the ground upon which they lay. Many limbs were severed from bodies, not with the expectation of saving life, but to relieve the sufferer from an offensive mass and render his last hours more comfortable. Very few of our men who lay on the field during the night survived for any length of time."[88]

Friday, while his comrades hunkered down in their tight defense line the second day of the new year, the grueling experience continued for Private Williams of Company B, with his badly battered leg. January 2, he wrote, was clear and warm. He still lay in the log house behind enemy lines with hundreds of wounded. "The roar of the artillery makes the ground shake, and the moans of the wounded mix with the other sounds. It is awful, and they die fast. The bodies are carried out, and the wounded brought in to take their places. Hundreds lie outside and have no shelter."

And there was nothing to eat, he said. That Friday he penciled in his diary: "I suffer badly with my wound today." At noon, some partially cooked flour and water was provided; the meager gruel "tastes very good," he noted. All day he listened to the roar of battle in front.[89]

That day rebel cannons boomed again, followed around noon by a thunderous fight between contesting artillery and infantry. "It was then it seemed as though all the 'Powers of darkness' had been let loose," Lieutenant Parsons told his family. "With demoniac yells they rushed forward, but Rosecrans was too well prepared for them. He had his batteries all ready, and when he opened on them, the roar of cannon and rattle of musketry was perfectly awful. The whole earth seemed to quake. It was too much for the poor deluded Rebs; they were driven with great slaughter." But, again, the Milwaukee soldiers were spared from the fight.[90]

It was just before sundown, a Milwaukee soldier among the railroaders of Company D named "Henry" wrote, that "there was the most terrifying cannonading every heard." Captain Philbrook, his commander, timed the shots and calculated sixty-five were fired each minute, along with "a continual roar of musketry"[91]

On the following morning the wind and rain returned. Still, Sanford Williams and his wounded comrades had seen no surgeon; his leg grew ever worse. "[M]ust lay and bear it, though it is terrible," he confided in his diary January 3. "Wounded are dying fast. Can still hear the roar of battle, nearly all day, but can't learn how it is going. The Rebels say they are whipping us. The dead blood on the floor begins to smell bad. Horrid, indeed."[92]

Between eight and nine that morning, another frightful artillery engagement erupted, but there was more noise than damage. This was followed by a brief but determined rebel thrust by brigades east of Stones River, at General Crittenden's wing about a mile and a half from the Wisconsin entrenchments. Under a constant, heavy rain that day, rebel attackers threw the blue coats across the watercourse, but as daylight began to fade, momentum shifted and Crittenden's counterattack regained all the ground lost. Again, the men of Milwaukee could only listen to the thunderous shelling and crackling of thousands of muskets.

Sporadic firing growled throughout Sunday night, and into the next morning. Rain continued steadily. Sometime in those early morning hours, however, it was discovered that Confederate general Braxton Bragg had pulled his army from Murfreesboro after midnight, and was moving south. An exhausted Lieutenant Mitchell, who had experienced much during those bloody days, was deeply affected by the scenes of horror. His life of ease had not prepared him for this, and even twenty years later he would write that "the dread surroundings horrified me with war."[93]

Sam Chase, the Company D soldier who would become the regiment's quartermaster, had a sorrowful and gruesome duty befall him after the enemy had departed. "I was detailed after the evacuation to go over the battle field with fifty men to find the men of the 24th and bury the same in their blankets. The work lasted two days. Turning over the dead bodies of many that could not be recognized[,] certainly it was the most unpleasant two days I ever passed in my life . . ."[94]

The Irish captain of Company G, Bill Kennedy, and his lieutenant Ed Holton, walked back to the area of Wednesday's fight where they found the body of young Frank Hale. They wrapped the dead solider in a blanket and buried him; "a head-board was placed to mark the spot of internment," Kennedy wrote to Hale's parents. "The boys have gone to work to make a board coffin, which will be exchanged for a fine one as soon as Mr. Cochran reaches Nashville." The soldier named "Henry" later claimed: "I cut and engraved head-boards" for Hale and Rockwell.[95]

There were many burials in those days following the battle of Stones River, not only in the cold ground of central Tennessee but among the snowy grave yards near Lake Michigan as well. Milwaukee would be the scene of much mourning.

Chapter 7

A Long Winter Camp

—▸— ≡◆≡ —◂—

"Hope had to be left at the door."

Joseph Cochrane, the New York-born businessman who operated Milwaukee's street sprinkling wagons, left the city before New Year, traveling to Nashville to visit his oldest son in the 24th Wisconsin. He brought "lots of nice things with him, and expected to have a pleasant time." His nineteen-year-old son had been given the name Lemuel, but as was the way of such things, the boys of Company B called him Lem. He was something of a tender lad with a florid countenance, having grown up in a commodious home in the far western fringe of the city. He would not have had to be a soldier, yet he volunteered for the Young Men's Association Tigers. Lem said he was a horse trainer.

When the regiment departed Milwaukee in early September, the blue-eyed soldier told his mother he would be a good boy, and marched off "full of hope and ambition." A news writer said he possessed a "kind disposition, and had many friends in this city." Because Lem was unable to keep up on the march in Kentucky, the colonel made him a wagon driver; he was "determined to render his country every service in his power."[1]

The young man returned to his company sometime before the battle of Christmas week, only to be struck in the forehead on the second day of the fight when he and his comrades scattered under the weight of heavy rebel columns that bludgeoned them from front and flank. His wound was grievous, but the horse trainer lingered for a week in a field hospital before he died. After the battle, several of his company comrades wrapped the body in an army blanket, and lifted him into a grave on the field. A rude wooden headboard was shaped and the letters of the Cochrane name chiseled into its surface. The father did not learn of Lem's death until he reached Nashville.[2]

When Joseph Cochrane finally arrived in the camp of the 24th Wisconsin after January 3, his son's remains were disinterred and placed in a tin coffin for transport home. The grieving Cochrane also consented to escort the body of another Milwaukee soldier, Frank Hale, who also lost his life in the battle.

Eighteen-year-old Hale, his captain Bill Kennedy wrote to the clerk's parents, "was a young man that I can say, without fear of contradiction, none knew but to love him. In whatever position he was placed, or whatever the duty assigned him, he was always ready to obey without a murmur. And I am happy to say that I had the pleasure of making him first corporal of my company but a few days before the fight, as I considered it a reward of merit justly due him." Small comfort for a prostrated family, perhaps.[3]

In Milwaukee days later, arrangements were made for the funerals. Hale's body was placed in the vestibule of the Spring Street Congregational Church west of the Milwaukee River where it remained until the funeral Sunday, January 18. That same day, at St. James Episcopal Church on the city's west side, the Reverend Mr. Ingraham conducted Cochrane's funeral service. Against the cold whiteness of Wisconsin winter, the double cortege later united, and the crowd of dark-clad mourners accompanied their sad burdens to Forest Home Cemetery far south of the central business district.[4]

For the next several weeks, such scenes would be common in Milwaukee's gray winter light, as coffins bearing the bodies of men whose lives ended prematurely were lowered into the freshly turned earth. New gravestones would be erected in the frozen ground. "All along the [railroad] route, at different stations, coffins containing the bodies of soldiers can be seen, often in considerable numbers," a civilian observer said as he traveled from Tennessee to Wisconsin; they "afford to the thoughtful some sad thoughts as to the havoc and misery that follow the train of war." The roll of the dead would lengthen in Milwaukee.[5]

On Monday, January 5, the sad task of digging graves in Tennessee began. Buried in the cold ground near Murfreesboro was the thirty-four-year-old bachelor mechanic whom the boys called Elder. "Permit me to rescue from oblivion for a moment the name of Byron Brooks, an old friend, who never knew fear, who enlisted in the cause of his country. Before leaving Milwaukee he bought a grave and coffin. Peace to his ashes! I dropped a tear over his soldier grave at Stone River," said a man who visited the burial site. The body would ever remain far from the grave that was purchased back home.[6]

So, too, the corpse of the immigrant, Christian Nix, was interred near the battlefield. The light-eyed lieutenant, once employed in the wholesale spirits business, would never return to his adopted city. A makeshift wooden headboard was also carved for Charlie Cookson, who had been a Milwaukee bookkeeper. "You remember him," a comrade said, "a thin, light haired fellow." As well, the body of the first man to fall at Stones River, Henry Pfaff, and ten others would never again leave Tennessee. Their graves bore no epitaphs.[7]

On the final day of 1862, the editor of the *Daily Wisconsin,* William E. Cramer, expecting the news from Tennessee and elsewhere to be awful, had attempted to steel his readers with a front page editorial. "We have the faith that the events of 1862 are the darkest in the history of the war—and the opening of the New Year will gradually cast a brighter light on our national pathway, out of the tribulation, sorrow, and anguish through which the nation has been passing."[8]

The city was once again eager for news from central Tennessee, reports that their sons, husbands, and friends were safe. Many congregated at the imposing Chamber of Commerce Building east of the Milwaukee River the evening of January 4 where dispatches were to be read; the "rooms were crowded at an early hour to hear them. All the evening the crowd patiently waited for them, but none came along, and finally at eleven o'clock, it was announced that there had been a necessary failure in receiving the dispatches, where upon those waiting dispersed, many of them to pass a sleepless night of suspense over the fate of their children in the army."[9]

Then heavy dark news headlines carried the news: "TERRIBLE CARNAGE!" "OUR LOSS HAS BEEN SEVERE!" "TWENTY-FOURTH WISCONSIN LOSES [sic] TWO HUNDRED AND FIFTY MEN!" "LIEUT. BLEYER WOUNDED!" But details were spare.[10]

Shortly, a preliminary dispatch arrived from one of the 24th Wisconsin soldiers; he had sent the hurried wire from Nashville. Will Perrine in Company A directed it to the *Sentinel* on January 2, and the words clattered from the telegraph. Lieutenant Nix, the immigrant and mechanic for Hoyt's wholesale liquor business, Sgt. George Rockwell of Company B, and many others was dead, Perrine said; Dick Austin, captain of Company A, was also killed. Seen to fall was Lt. Bob Chivas, the young Scot immigrant and lumber dealer; he may have been killed. Capt. Bill Eldred of Company B was said to be missing but safe. The fate of Lt. Cam Reed, the long-time city resident and former state legislator, was uncertain.[11]

Colonel Larrabee's telegraph then arrived with equally distressing news. Remaining behind in Nashville because of an ulcerated throat and general physical debilitation, he had spoken with a soldier who "saw Chivas fall to the ground when the regiment retreated," he said. From others who had seen the disaster at Murfreesboro he learned that 300 in the Milwaukee Regiment had been killed, maimed, or were missing after two days of battle. On January 5, a somewhat revised count was printed, listing 262 of the 24th Wisconsin as casualties, some of the missing having wandered back to the regiment. Here was dire news, indeed, that made many a Milwaukee citizen fear for the fate of his loved ones.[12]

The *Sentinel*'s front page also carried a *Chicago Tribune* dispatch that Sheridan's division had "repulsed the enemy four times before it was driven. The [24th] must have seen hard and dangerous service. The testimony is it bore itself gallantly. We trust its losses are no greater than have been estimated," the newsman attested.[13]

There was some good news. Lieutenant Bleyer's wound, taken Tuesday on the first day of battle, was "not serious," Perrine reported. "I consider myself fortunate to be safe from this battle," the young son of a city physician said. Perrine would serve with the 24th until 1864 when he became a junior lieutenant in the 13th Wisconsin Artillery; after the war, he clerked for a bit then constructed "earth closets" or dirt cellars before leaving Milwaukee.[14]

Near Murfreesboro, during the time the first dispatches clattered into an anxious Milwaukee, Sanford Williams, the twenty-seven-year-old farmer in Company B, was in a bad way. He had lain in a fetid log house behind enemy lines on New Year's Day, his badly maimed leg untended. His comrade, Norm Burdick, had been taken prisoner, so the hurried note Williams had scribbled to his parents went south with the soldier correspondent.

Two days later, matters were no better. Finally on Sunday, January 4th, Williams noted that the rain had stopped and the sun came out. "The birds sang like June at home. No surgeons yet. I suffer a good deal today." But, then, at daylight the next day the rebel army skedaddled.

Sanford Williams (post-war).
An ordeal at Stones River.
COURTESY OF THE MILWAUKEE COUNTY
HISTORICAL SOCIETY.

"We see those glorious old Stars and Stripes again; we are once more, thank God, under its folds."[15]

The ordeal of Private Williams, a mature man who was yet to marry, was not at an end. On Wednesday, fully one week after the battle commenced and six days since he was wounded, he was finally loaded onto one of the sixty wagons that trundled north to Nashville. "Oh! Horror of horrors!" Williams wrote to his parents the next day. "Over the stone turnpike the ambulances rattle, jolt and bounce. No mercy. We suffered all that mortal could bear, got to the city at 11 p.m., and soon were put in comfortable quarters, with the attendance of nurses, doctors, and everything possible."

When the chief surgeon looked in on him, he said that because the injury had been so long untended, his foot would likely be amputated. He accepted the harsh prognosis fatalistically. "I thank God almighty that it is no worse. I can get a cork leg, but never hands, arms, eyes or mouth, which I see others lose," the private said. "One in our Company has part of his chin, both lips and front teeth cut away." The surgeon told Williams to finish his letter quickly as he would not be able to write for some time after the operation. He closed, saying he hoped "God will spare my life to see you all at no distant day." Williams's leg was hacked off, and he was later discharged. He would hobble about Milwaukee on crutches for decades, never having purchased that cork leg.[16]

As it had for Private Williams, the bloody crucible of Stones River would change the Milwaukee Regiment forever. Despite the fact that the 24th Wisconsin had already "seen the elephant," fighting its first battle at Perryville in October, it had not been prepared for the reality of war in its full fury. Soldiering before had been almost a lark. Certainly, there had been arduous marches, debilitating disease, and decided deprivation; but these were nothing when measured against that Christmas week near Murfreesboro. Now many good men and true were dead; scores more were left to bleed on that fetid field; and uncounted others were in the hands of the enemy, their fates unknown. Many of the prisoners and wounded would return to the regiment in time, but many more would never again answer the roll. Scores would be discharged and sent home to hobble and limp about Milwaukee like Sanford Williams. Along with the proliferating graves, they were all sad reminders for the city of the cost of this war to save the Union.

Of the period that followed the battle of Stones River, John Mitchell would long remember. "Here we encamped for six months. The troops lay idle, but disease kept busy. Dysentery followed diarrhea; then came the various fevers. I was taken down myself. An Ambulance stood ready to trundle me off to the hospital. It was only by resolute resistance that I saved myself from a place where hope had to be left at the door."[17]

Following the withdrawal of Confederate general Braxton Bragg's army from Murfreesboro January 3, General Rosecrans ordered the Army of the Cumberland to establish a new camp a few miles south of the town. Then there was time, after a week of marching and fighting, for the men, prostrated, exhausted, and dispirited, to draft letters and pencil a few lines in battered diaries. On Thursday, January 8, numerous soldiers wrote home; a few confided in their diaries. They took stock of themselves and their regiment. "We had a terrible loss[,] a slaughter whatever you are a mind to call it[;] men went down by the hundreds in a few minutes," one soldier said. "It seemed a sorry place to make so much ado about," Lieutenant Mitchell wrote laconically when he finally saw the town of Murfreesboro. The short-statured scion of Milwaukee wealth was haunted by what he saw at Stones River. "This battle is the one that tried men's souls," he recalled. "The old year went out amid carnage and strife (I don't blame him much: A good many others also went out of the carnage and strife as fast as their legs could carry them) and the new year came in with gloomy forebodings," the exhausted officer said, intimating that some had exhibited less than gallant behavior.[18]

The gentleman farmer wrote caustically to his mother, Martha: "Milwaukee is, or will soon be, flooded by military nondescripts with shoulder-straps and without any honor. They will be able to tell about everything here, making voluminous letter-writing unnecessary." And so it was that of the many hundreds of letters written home, scores found their way into Milwaukee's daily press. The war, for the Milwaukee Regiment, would also be fought in many of these letters and in news columns; some civilians would become ready combatants, prepared to enhance reputations or defend attackers.[19]

To the surprise of many in Milwaukee, the tall Scot, Bob Chivas, wrote, expressing amusement at the reports of his wounding and intimation of his possible demise, blaming such intelligence on men who not only skedaddled but ran thirty miles all the way back to Nashville. One of them was Will Perrine of Company A, he alleged, who had actually been sick in Nashville during the battle. Perrine, Chivas told Mrs. Mitchell, "derived his information altogether from stragglers from the battle-field, who thought that everybody was killed, wounded or taken prisoners but themselves." The report that he, Chivas, had been wounded, perhaps mortally, had, he said, "originated (as all false reports did) from one of the boys in our Co. who ran to Nashville and everybody he left on the field he supposed were killed or wounded because they did not run too." He, his cousin, John Mitchell, and Fred Root were all unmarked; "there were not even any holes in our clothes or bullet marks of any kind." The twenty-year-old lieutenant also told his aunt: "[We] almost miraculously escaped without even receiving a scratch, and I am happy to-day that our safety was not obtained at the expense of our honour." He alluded to the less than estimable behavior of some of his fellow officers.[20]

The news that "Cam" Reed had been killed was confirmed a day later. "He was a noble, manly fellow [who] had hosts of friends in this city and State," said editor Cramer. The former city and state legislator, who had climbed Pikes Peak, was one of the oldest settlers in Milwaukee, and "his death will be universally lamented." This intelligence was quickly followed by a terse dispatch from the officer's wife, who was in Nashville. With a bit of levity in such grave times, she said "he an't [*sic*] dead, and he knows it." Cam Reed would not have the last laugh, however.[21]

"I am sorry to say that *some of the officers of the regiment acted badly,* leaving the field. I will not mention names, but may at some future time," confided Lt. Ed Parsons, the twenty-seven-year-old clerk. "I have not seen Cam Reed since the battle, but understand he is unhurt." His family turned over the letter to a local news sheet, and it was published. Soon, the entire city began to learn of the less than valorous behavior of some of its soldiers.[22]

There was anger in the soldier letters, diaries, and news columns. The 24th Wisconsin had been so filled with confidence and expectation when it left Milwaukee four months past. Superior officers had lauded it for its drill, discipline, and appearance. It had stood the test at Perryville. The entire city had read the regular news columns and published letters about its exploits and achievements. And now—Stones River. At a critical juncture in the battle, many of its soldiers had not stood fast. Many had skulked and, worse, more had skedaddled—at least for a time. Fault had to be found. Blame had to be placed.

The major, imperious Lish Hibbard, also wrote a denunciation in a letter to his father: "Cowards ran to Nashville and reported every one killed. I fear these rumors will reach you, but I hope not. The people of Milwaukee may feel proud of the 24th, with the exception of some of the officers."[23]

In the days that followed, scorn was heaped upon the reputed miscreant officers, and the resultant controversy raged not only in the regiment but on the streets of Milwaukee as well. For many of the missives sent to family and friends were subsequently printed in the daily Milwaukee press, and the names of officers and accusations against them became common coin. Derision would give way to disgust, and the reputations of several officers were irrevocably tarnished. The politician Cam Reed, who had so ambitiously recruited for the Plankinton Guard that summer, was the first name on the lips of the accusers.

"Considerable resentment was created in camp when one read the obituary notice of Cam Reed," wrote Chivas. He referred, of course, to the January 2 dispatch of student Will Perrine that had appeared on the front page of the *Sentinel.* "Cam never had the most remote intentions of dying for his country. I shall never forget what Uncle said about him before leaving Milwaukee—that he would run, at the first battle. [Twas?] not necessary that he should die to be praised, and was not verified in this instance[,] for his resurrection has only brought him more ridicule. Poor Bill Eldred has also humiliated his military career rather ingloriously." Alexander Mitchell, wealthy and influential, would read the words with keen interest, and share the information with friends and acquaintances.[24]

Henry Drake, the twenty-one-year-old druggist who would soon win his permanent lieutenant's straps, was pointed and severe in his judgment. "Cam Reed showed the white feather," leaving his company; he "was found two or three days afterwards in a hospital. He had torn his shoulder straps off and tied a red rag around his arm. The Rebels thought him some drummer boy I hear and of no acct [account] and did not take the trouble to parole him." Reed had not returned yet to the regiment when Drake wrote of this matter. Lieutenant Mitchell was terse, saying that "above all, the doughty Reed deserves to be disgraced."[25]

Cam Reed, whose wife came east to be near him, remained in Nashville, and he attempted to resign his commission, "under pretence of sickness," it was said, "which subsequent action proved to be false," Lieutenant Greene told his sister Lizzie.[26]

In another letter, Chivas also accused several more officers in addition to Reed and Company B's captain, Bill Eldred. Among these were Capt. Henry Gunnison of Company H, and even the acting major, Carl Von Baumbach, the druggist who had come to Milwaukee with his parents from Hesse. They "disgraced the Regiment," Chivas charged, and "will probably all be dismissed or their resignations will be accepted which is the same thing."[27]

The damning specifics against Eldred, who helped raise the Tigers of the Young Men's Association, was not long in coming. During the battle, the good chaplain of the Milwaukee Regiment, the portly and fun-loving Fr. Francis Fusseder, had accompanied wagons of wounded trundling to Nashville during the battle. On an early return trip to Murfreesboro he encountered a 24th Wisconsin officer, likely Cam Reed. The "Captain crawled on his hands and knees to the hospital, was taken prisoner there, and with a red string around his arm, and was paroled as a hospital nurse." The same officer, Fusseder attested, had earlier urged Major Hibbard to "march the regiment to Nashville." Reed's brief military career came to an end ignominiously when he was cashiered from service for cowardice.

The good cleric also encountered Eldred on one of his trips back to Murfreesboro for wounded soldiers. The captain, it was said, had gotten himself out of harm's way, and was "sitting by the wayside when the Chaplain came riding along." Eldred hailed the priest, asking if he could carry any mail to Nashville. "The Chaplain replied that it was no time to talk upon such a subject, and that he ought to be ashamed of himself, and had better return to his regiment and fight for his country." During the cleric's denunciation, another regiment marched past, overhearing the two Wisconsin men. "They gave three cheers for the Chaplain, and three groans for the Captain." Eldred had not been identified by name in the letter; but when the missive appeared in the Republican daily, there was little doubt to whom it referred. Under such a cloud of accusations and aspersions, Bill Eldred was permitted to resign his commission, and leave the regiment. The effective date was January 17, 1863.[28]

But there was more: Lieutenant Chivas, who had been in the thick of the fight and escaped without even damage to his blue coat, and his cousin, Lieutenant Mitchell, accused Henry Gunnison, the hobbled captain of Company H. Lieutenant Drake also charged that Gunnison was a coward; "he came back to the reg two days after the big fight [he meant the action on December 31] supposing it was all over. He had not been there more than an hour before heavy firing commenced on the left. Gunnison immediately left his co. and I believe he has not been seen since."[29]

A writer who did not identify Gunnison by name said the officer "tried to get a horse and leave for Nashville, but did not succeed, nevertheless he left his company, and did not return until after the fight."[30]

The "case" against the thirty-six-year-old lawyer was not substantial, although the accusations likely hastened his departure from the Milwaukee Regiment. Gunnison always claimed in rebuttal that he had remained with Company H after the regiment had broken that Wednesday morning, and helped re-form it by raising his cap atop the cane, and twirling it about so his men could find the spot to rally. "*Rally*, Co. 'H', *rally!*" he shouted at the top of his lungs. "I have not been able to walk for two months, without the aid of a cane," he later attested, "and should not have left Nashville but for the certainty of battle. For over four weeks past, I have been completely disabled from service." He was ultimately, a daily news sheet said, "compelled to resign his commission on account of continued ill health." The official date of resignation was February 25. The enterprising immigrant from Port Washington, Gus Goldsmith, was named captain.[31]

The cloud of accusation and recrimination swirled about other officers, enveloping Carl Von Baumbach, the stout Teuton who had raised Company C and served as acting major during the late battle. Again, Lieutenant Chivas in an early letter said that the immigrant was among those who were "cowards and a disgrace to the Regiment." Mitchell, who shared views with his cousin, also looked with accusation at Von

Baumbach who, he said, "behaved badly." Neither man put forward any specifics, however. Even Corporal Comstock, the blue-eyed, nineteen-year-old printer in Company B, charged that Von Baumbach was "a coward of the worst kind. He ran before the battle commenced."[32]

Company A's freshly minted lieutenant, Henry Drake, said much the same about the major, and also alleged that Peter Strack, the lieutenant who led the largely immigrant Company C into battle, exhibited cowardice as well. Strack, a Milwaukee shoemaker, would also resign under the weight of allegations (whether voluntarily or under pressure is not known) in early February. He would in later years become a saloon keeper in the Germanic precincts.[33]

Lacking specifics, the allegations against Von Baumbach seemed to have no real merit; they may have been tainted with a bit of British and Yankee superiority. Antipathies against some immigrants were still pronounced. And it was possible the German in Company C may have been a bit clannish, conversing in their native tongue too much to suit English speakers. (Not long after, during the battle of Chancellorsville, for example, the largely Germanic regiments in the Army of the Potomac's XI Corps were reviled for breaking before Stonewall Jackson's attack upon the their flank.)

The twenty-three-year-old Von Baumbach had his defenders, not the least of whom was his influential father, Ludwig, the Imperial consul to one of the Germanic states. A war of words flared in Milwaukee's four-page news sheets. Although he himself was under a cloud of accusation, Capt. Henry Gunnison wrote of the acting major: "He appeared cool and attentive to his business as any officer in the regiment." Below a headline shouting "Justice for Capt. Von Baumbach," the *News* castigated its rival, the *Wisconsin,* for printing the whisperings against Von Baumbach, alleging that the acting major had "abandoned his regiment at the first fire at Murfreesboro." The elder Von Baumbach demanded to know the identity of those Milwaukee men who had spread such "malicious slander." The consul was livid. "As to those in this city who knowingly circulated these falsehoods and slanders against him, I must consider them unworthy of the name of soldiers and gentlemen," he fumed. The elder Von Baumbach also quickly communicated with his son, "requesting him to defend himself against those grave charges." There was more to all of this.

"My belief that those charges were malicious slanders and falsehoods . . . had been fully justified," said the Teutonic minister, "by the enclosed statement of his fellow officers, proving beyond contradiction, that he did not leave his regiment during the battle, but was with it during the whole of the battle." Appended to the story was an affidavit to that effect, signed by a dozen officers in the 24th Wisconsin. Contrary to the *Wisconsin's* claim, Carl Von Baumbach had been at his post during the entire battle at Stones River, they attested. Among the signatures, curiously, was that of Robert Chivas, the very officer who stated in at least two letters that the German druggist had acted cowardly and had, with other officers, "disgraced the regiment." Also signing the document were the youthful adjutant, Arthur McArthur; Capts. Fred Root and Bill Kennedy; Sam Philbrook the railroader; and Lt. Howard Greene. The matter, at least on the surface, was put to rest.[34]

Another of the men caught in the swirl of recriminations was Dick Hubbell, one of the lawyers in the regiment. He had written a long and revealing correspondence on January 15, describing the late battle from his perspective. For some of the boys, he had placed himself too much at the center of things. "The subscriber was present during the whole five days contest," Hubbell boasted, "at will to view any part of the field, and of necessity an observer of many things which others were unable to witness." He also, in some writing, seemed to imply that he had had a hand in rallying the regiment on the morning of New Year's Eve. Chivas, whose pen in those days was a ready rapier against those seeking acclaim, was amused. "You made a very good hit on Dick in your letter in regard to his rallying the Regt.," the Scot told his uncle. "The idea of a private rallying the Regt. and especially Dick is perfectly absurd. He was merely an on-looker at the fight, and a few balls had perhaps whistled near him, and it is likely his conceit had prompted him to attempt to rally the Regt. But he certainly was not exposed to the danger and cannot claim the glory which belongs to those who fought in the ranks." Hubbell became the "laughing stock" of the 24th Wisconsin, and he apparently returned to Milwaukee, his reputation compromised. He quit the regiment on the final day of January, and was accorded a commission as lieutenant in the 1st Wisconsin Artillery. Here may have been a safer place for the lawyer turned soldier determined to fight another day.[35]

The incessant columns written by soldiers for Milwaukee's dailies were, obviously, augmented by citizens eager to gain notoriety for their sons and relatives in the city's regiment. Family members and friends carried private letters to the press editors, and missives played across the pages of every sheet that winter. It would prove to be something of an embarrassment for Maj. Elisha Hibbard when personal doubts and boasts he expressed to his father in a private letter were published for all in the city to read.

"I cannot tell you how I behaved; my friends will do that. I did the best I could. I have not slept until last night for five days," he said. "I had no acting field officers, but was alone. God help me, how I brought off these men I cannot say. I fought on my own account, never having received an order until the one from Gen. Sheridan came. Such are the ways of conducting battles." The words were laden with emotion. "I trust the people of Milwaukee will think I did my duty to their sons and brothers." He also said that about seventy-five men from the 24th ran, "and have not yet stopped, I guess."[36]

Chivas was again ready to pounce with his pen. Just as he had reacted to the dispatches of Will Perrine and Dick Hubbell, Chivas found amusement. He assumed that Hibbard's letter was not intended for public exposure, but the prominent father, who owned a large insurance business, had other designs. "Wm. B. [Hibbard] immediately perceiving the vast renown the house of Hibbard would acquire by its being made public," Chivas said, "and I think can fancy him standing on a chair and reading it before the Board of Trade."[37]

Coupled with all of this was the matter of the effectiveness of Maj. Lish Hibbard, well known in the city for his years in the militia. Proof was the 24th's behavior in the late battle, some said. The Wisconsin soldiers had broken and, at least for some time, run in the face of a far superior force. The major had been less than fully effective at Stones River, it was whispered. Such antipathies may have festered since before the war. From his days in the Milwaukee militia, Hibbard probably gained a reputation as a martinet and disciplinarian. This did not now sit well with volunteers who had grown comfortable with Colonel Larrabee's leadership.

But Hibbard, too, had supporters. Col. Nick Greusel, the old brigade commander, wrote that the Milwaukee major had tried to get his regiment out in good order, but ultimately had to obey the orders of General Sheridan to retreat. In his official report written January 15, Greusel singled out Hibbard and his aide-de-camp, Lieutenant Mitchell, for special praise. "They behaved with coolness and presence of mind, ever ready to obey my command," he wrote. Chivas, though biased, told John's mother that her son "behaved like a hero. He was on horseback all day, riding in the thickest of the fight." He was always "cool and smiling" his cousin said, and his conduct that day "had the admiration of all who saw him."[38]

Although he may not have intended it as such, Colonel Larrabee also seemed to suggest that Hibbard had done the best that was possible under the circumstances. He was critical of reports, particularly one by Col. William Woodruff, commander of brigade to the right of the Milwaukee Regiment at Stones River, that the Wisconsin soldiers "gave away" immediately. Such intelligence was simply not to be believed, Larrabee wrote. "That it retreated a short distance in disorder is true, but so did nearly the whole right wing of the army"; the Milwaukee Regiment did not give way "until the whole right had given way leaving the regiment exposed to a fire on its right flank as well as its front." Such was the colonel's conclusion, after speaking with many soldiers in Murfreesboro and Nashville who had witnessed the battle. A member of the visiting Sanitary Commission who spoke of those events with officers and soldiers also concluded that the regiment had "rallied . . . within musket range of the enemy, and stood like old veterans. Major Hibbard is entitled to a great deal of the credit," he told the *Sentinel*.[39]

The accusations against officers were also tangled with the issue of the Milwaukee Regiment's fitness and readiness. The matter boiled up in soldier camps and on the streets of the city. It was a rare letter or news column about the 24th that did not touch upon these issues. And the virtual parade of delegations and visitors from the city spoke with the soldiers about these matters; many put their findings in writing for the city's dailies whose editors were only too happy to print them in their columns. The battle of words was also entwined with the contending political views of the day, each side pressing its position on the conduct of the war.

The Republican daily *Sentinel* carried a dispatch from another citizen who had traveled to Murfreesboro, alleging that "this regiment must soon be to some extent reorganized to save it from ruin and hopeless despondency. A new and active man must be placed at their head to lead them on."[40]

Within a week or ten days after the battle, representatives of the Milwaukee Sanitary Commission rushed to the camps south of Murfreesboro to visit the volunteers. Although their primary role was to insure that the condition of the Wisconsin men was good and care of the wounded was adequate, they also spoke with officers and men of other matters that were being bruited about the city. They arrived in Tennessee almost in the midst of the controversy surrounding the negligent behavior of officers, and the question of the regiment's leadership and the matter of what some came to regard as the demoralized state of the 24th Wisconsin. These men, as well as Alexander Mitchell and others who traveled east that winter, wrote and talked widely about such matters, contributing to the embroiled state of affairs.[41]

"You will probably see quite a number of commissioned officers home in a few days," reported one commissioner. "They chose the least of two evils and send in their resignations. I have learned since that some of the resignations were not accepted, but the officers dishonorably dismissed from the service." Actually, only Cam Reed had been cashiered; he was "dismissed after deserting under pretense of illness." For some, however, Reed's cowardly behavior seemed also to taint his lieutenant, Riverius Elmore, as well. The young man who bore the euphonious given name surprised everyone in both Milwaukee and the regiment when he submitted his resignation January 13. There had been not even the hint of impropriety on his part. A soldier in his company wrote that Elmore "acted bravely" as did the company's first lieutenant, David Horning, a young man from Wauwatosa, west of Milwaukee. He "is a man every inch of him, and we think more of him now, than we did before," the soldiers said. Elmore may merely have had his fill of the acrimonious climate in the regiment; he would later serve in another Wisconsin regiment. Horning would soon be promoted to captain of Company E.[42]

As a result of the battle of Stones River, nine officers left company ranks. The politician, Cam Reed, was cashiered from service. Three captains, two of whom had been accused of cowardly behavior—Eldred and Gunnison—resigned their commissions, as did a lieutenant. Although the departures were somewhat disruptive, the vacancies created opportunities for men of character to step forward. Howard Greene and Bill Kennedy gained captains' bars along with three others. Moreover, three sergeants, Henry Drake among them, were advanced to officer ranks. Much augured well for leadership in the Milwaukee Regiment—leadership that would be sorely tested later in the year.[43]

Part of the problem for the regiment's condition, as some saw it, rested with Col. Charles Larrabee, the nominal commander of the 24th, as well as a politician, who had not been with the regiment during the battle. Lieutenant Chivas, never one to shrink from controversy, lamented the long absence of the Milwaukee Regiment's forty-two-year-old commander. By inference, Chivas and others were critical of the acting commander, Maj. Elisha Hibbard. The colonel's "prolonged absence from the Regt. has been very unfortunate, both for him and for us," the tall, gray-eyed lumber dealer wrote in late January. The swarthy colonel had tried, against a surgeon's warning, to march with the 24th when it began the Christmas week campaign south from the city; but after a day's march in the drenching rain, the colonel's ulcerated throat worsened. Returning to Nashville, the officer had been treated with acids and alkalies, and steadily improved. Learning of the bloody battle at Stones River, he had feared for the fate of his regiment. When the wagons of Wisconsin wounded labored into the city, he had searched various hospitals for his men; he saw "most of them three or four times, sought out their wants, urged nurses to extra attention by promises of reward, and took [surgeons] to the cot of each one."[44]

The colonel traveled to Murfreesboro briefly, raising the hopes of his men. "We . . . are delighted at the prospect of again having Colonel Larrabee to command us," a private in Company I said. "We have had a trial of the man; we know him well." But, then, on February 18, Larrabee returned to Milwaukee, and rumors floated about the camps that he had been offered command of the brigade. "It is hoped that he will return soon," wrote another city soldier, "whether to take command of a Brigade or the Regiment, it makes no difference, only so we have him with us."[45]

The matter of Larrabee and the fitness of the regiment could not be put to rest; the colonel's detractors were busy in Milwaukee, sniping from long range. It was possible, of course, that the supporters of Major Hibbard, with his father spearheading the charge at home, hoped to gain ascendancy for their man; rumor and innuendo among the influential in Milwaukee may have been the tactic to gain that end.

"Rumors have been afloat prejudicial to the character of Col. Larrabee as an officer, and otherwise affecting the high reputation of the 24th regiment," wrote *News* editor George Paul. "We are aware that these are mere rumors, founded upon no distinct charge from any source." Moreover, one of the members of the Sanitary Commission who visited the 24th Wisconsin also addressed the city's readers about the rumored unpopularity of the colonel. "It is impossible for any man to be in Milwaukee and not hear of it. I do not know whence arose the complaints against him nor shall I enquire; it is enough for me now . . . to know that after the most careful enquiry [among men of the Milwaukee Regiment], I do not believe that Col. Larrabee could be supplanted by any living man, without producing a general dissatisfaction within the regiment."[46]

The absence of both Colonel Larrabee and former Lieutenant Colonel Buttrick had created leadership problems, it was said. Buttrick, the Milwaukee lawyer who had resigned in December, "was very popular with the men and officers of the regiment," wrote one soldier; "his departure before the Milwaukee men left Nashville had been detrimental." "As long as [Larrabee] held the reins, everything went well," said Lieutenant Chivas, "the 24th was second to none. He was sometimes eccentric and always obstinate but his discipline was firm and I think impartial." But when the colonel "relaxed his hold," the regiment gradually lost its former readiness and "at the same time I think Larrabee has lost his self-command. He has in fact become demoralized." Larrabee was the "victim of circumstance and of his own proud and stubborn disposition."[47]

Other writers expressed the resentment growing among the volunteers over the continued criticism leveled against the Milwaukee Regiment. "We, in the regiment, have heard from various sources, that the [24th] is spoken of with contempt in Milwaukee, and that we are considered demoralized and worthless, and that it is all owing to our commanding officers," one angry soldier wrote. "Allow me to dissent. If we are worthless (which I deny) it is not on account of our officers. No officer could have done more for his regiment individually and in a military point of view, than has Col. Larrabee. Had he been with us all the time, and able to command, we would have been better than the best. As it is, we are willing to stand the test with any of our 'comrades in arms,' either in drill, discipline, or courage. Possibly we might have done better than we did in the Stone River battle, but for what we did do in that memorable affair, we received the praise of our Division General."[48]

Again, *News* Editor George Paul fired a return salvo from his front page. Statements that the regiment was demoralized or neglected "are wilful untruths. It is the fullest regiment to day in the division. . . . It has more men for duty, and had had all the time, than any other old or new regiment that marched with it from Louisville. Whatever there is of despondency, is not exceptional, and is referable to general causes. The regiment has every time stood at the head of the list upon inspections and reviews."[49]

Many were troubled by all of the rumor, the gossip, and the unsettled atmosphere in the ranks. "A great deal of trouble arises from the letters written to the papers, for they are all colored with the likes and dislikes—grievances fancied or real—of writers," one private caviled. "A private who has been punished, or who had had some comrade made a corporal over his head, is very angry at his captain. Sergeants who expected to be lieutenants, but failed, are down on the colonel. Others who expected or wanted to be colonel, major or something else, raise a muss generally when they are disappointed. Subordinates sometimes intrigue to make their superiors unpopular in order to make vacancies. But these things are of course exceptions. One cunning, intriguing officer in a regiment is enough to set everybody by the ears." He had a warning. "So you must receive what you hear with a good many grains of allowance." Like so many others, the private letter, whose author was unidentified, was also published in a daily.[50]

Many discussed the behavior of the Milwaukee Regiment at Stones River. "The facts, disrobed of all the hyfaluten [sic] so common in the many letters after the battle are simply these," wrote another man in the Milwaukee Regiment. He seemed to get to the nut of the matter: "There was no very conspicuous acts of gallantry on the part of officers or men, simply, I suppose, because there was no opportunity for any. Some companies formed sooner than others, but all seemed inspired with a desire to do their duty. On a further retreat the same thing occurred again," he wrote to the Democratic daily.

"It made no charges upon the enemy, because it was not called upon to do so. It resisted no charges from the enemy, simply because the enemy did not chance to make any upon us. There were, therefore, no dashing acts of gallantry, no brilliant feats of heroism performed by a single newly developed Murat in the regiment. No young Napoleon cracked the shell of obscurity on the 31st of December, 1862, in the 24th Wisconsin . . . and stepped in full feather into military renown, so far as heard from. Officers, whose names have not been given to the public, did their duty faithfully, according to their respective ability, just as much so as those whose names have been set forth as specially entitled to praise."[51]

As anger rose higher, there was an attempt to deflect criticism. "Let those 'Copperheads' at home, who are not used to war's alarms, and who do but denounce those who have gone to fight in their country's cause, form themselves into a battalion, and come down here and go through what the [24th] has, and then see how much better they would do," a soldier wrote heatedly. "It needs only six month's experience in the field to convince any reasonable person that it is a great deal easier to say than to do, in military, and that every one tries to do his best."[52]

Finally in late March, the matter of the Milwaukee Regiment's readiness seemed to be put to rest. The imprimatur of the Republican Party's favored sheet, the *Sentinel,* whose correspondent had visited the Milwaukee Regiment in its Tennessee camp, appeared in a front page column. He pronounced: "[I] thoroughly canvassed the feelings of the Regiment in relation to its officers. I was induced to do so for many considerations, not the least of which was a feeling prevalent in Milwaukee amongst the friends of its soldiers that the regiment was now well officered,—that their sons, and brothers, and sweethearts and friends were in competent hands." It was "with pleasure as well as with surprise, that I am enabled to say *emphatically,*" that the 24th Wisconsin evinced "discipline, good order, and cheerfulness." Moreover, all of the regiment's officers were popular with the men, he reported.[53]

Through all the allegations and controversy, almost above the war of words, one name stood out in the Milwaukee Regiment—that of the boyish adjutant, McArthur. The plaudits emanated from several quarters. Colonel Greusel, in the final official report he would compose, mentioned the young lieutenant. Major Hibbard, too, praised the judge's son for "aid and efficient service." What was more, he wrote January 8 in his official report of the battle: "Young and gallant, I bespeak for him an honorable service." Lish also distributed plaudits to others as well: Captains Root, Austin, and Philbrook, and Lieutenants Elmore, Parsons, Kennedy, Greene, and several others including one of his critics, Bob Chivas. He mentioned, too, the dead immigrant lieutenant, Christian Nix; the regiment's surgeon, Herman Hasse; and the Port Washington priest, Father Fusseder, for his diligence in tending the wounded. To Welcome Greene, the major said that his lieutenant son, Howard, had "behaved splendidly."[54]

The adjutant's reputation was spreading in the army and among people of high and low station in Milwaukee. Will Perrine, whose column in the *Sentinel* had been criticized, said that Lt. McArthur "is the bravest of the brave, and last to leave a point of danger." When the delegation from the Sanitary Commission visited the camp of the 24th Wisconsin, one of its group was effusive about the youngster. The lieutenant rode into camp on horseback when the writer first saw him. "I looked at him as he approached, with some curiosity, for his fame had reached Nashville, and he was spoken of in the highest terms by the officers I had conversed with. As I gazed upon his boyish face, I thought of Norval on the Crampion hills," he said. Lt. Arthur McArthur, who was to celebrate his eighteenth birthday within a few months, was said to be a "coming man" in the regiment.[55]

During all of this, George Bleyer, the immigrant son of "sturdy Western stamp," was still off his feet in late January, nursing his leg wound in one of the many hospitals near Murfreesboro. It was an irony, this wound, caused by a Wisconsin cannon that first day of the Stones River fight. The twenty-two-year-old newspaper compositor and writer had displayed military promise, and just before departing Nashville he had been named to lead the boys of Company E. George Eddy of Company A said, "I can remember the expression of his countenance as he was struck." The gash had bled profusely, and he was quickly carried from the field. But all who saw and talked with Bleyer said the injury was not serious. "Of a genial and friendly disposition he was beloved by the officers and men of his Regiment," one friend said. The writer had, since the Milwaukee Regiment left the city, entertained comrades and city readers with detailed columns about march, camp, and battle under the pseudonym "Marion," his middle name. "Occasional gems of poetry still more spoke of the intellectual capacity within him."[56]

Late in January, Bleyer, who had been looking forward to returning to the regiment, took a bad turn. Lt. Tom Balding, the Englishman, related that the 24th's surgeon, Dr. Hasse, said that Balding had better see his comrade as soon as possible. On Sunday, January 25, Balding visited the compositor, "but the poor fellow was insensible. He breathed his last about two hours after I got there, without recognizing any one. I had a coffin made for him, and returned to camp, intending to take a detail over the next day, to bury him." But Balding was called out on picket duty, and he asked a sergeant to take six men and bury the gentle poet's body. The remains were "laid in a large rough pine box, with his clothes upon him," Balding said.

Bleyer's popular columns would never again appear in the Milwaukee news. One of the final stanzas of a poem he had written in the army now seemed appropriate:

> Dead lay the wounded boy,
> He was the soldier's pride,
> And many would have felt a joy
> Could they for him have died.[57]

Days after Bleyer's death, his brother, Louis, traveled to Murfreesboro to claim the corpse, and George's remains were disinterred from their battlefield grave. Louis Bleyer located a Union family who had become acquainted with his brother while in Nashville, and "the ladies . . . thoughtfully and humanely twined a wreath of evergreens and flowers, which was placed over the breast of the Lieutenant as he lay in the coffin." The coffin was "hermetically sealed" and placed in a larger box for shipment home.

Bleyer arrived in Milwaukee Tuesday, February 3, and the father, Henry, along with delegations from city newspapers and others, met George's body at the depot and accompanied it to the parent's home. "The coffin was there opened, and the body was found in an excellent state of preservation, it being an easy task to trace the resemblance between the cold, pallid face of him who lay in death before us, and the noble young man who was formerly a companion and a friend, whom none knew but to love and esteem, and who had died the death of a brave and true-hearted Christian patriot. May the sunlight of Heaven forever linger over his grave." After services, he was buried with many of his comrades at Forest Home Cemetery on the city's far south side.

"I suppose the *Wisconsin* people will miss poor 'Marion's' letters very much," said Tom Balding. Indeed, the city would miss the cultured George Bleyer very much, placing his name among its pantheon of dead heroes. Many more names would follow.[58]

Finally, after several weeks, the other soldier correspondent, "Musket," Cpl. Norm Burdick of Company B, again took up his pencil and reported in. The twenty-six-year-old printer apologized, "I have not been in a position to impart any very valuable information concerning the [24th]." His letter was written from Annapolis, Maryland, where the parole camp had been established for prisoner exchange. He had reached the safety of Federal lines about January 25, and "from that time until this I have been debarred from writing as full an account as I could wish, by reason of suffering from an awful cold caught in the purlieus of Libby Prison, at Richmond." He was in all likelihood still without his spectacles. Burdick, along with fifty or sixty of his Wisconsin comrades, had had an ordeal. He told *Sentinel* readers that his long silence had "one or two very good excuses."

He went on to describe his experiences on New Year's Eve of being marched into Murfreesboro by his rebel captors with about one hundred others, then packed into the town's courthouse square with a thousand other Federals from numerous regiments. There, in groups of a dozen or so, they "had the parole administered . . . by a bland looking old gentleman, in gold spectacles, who admonished us to go home and not fight any more. After signing the papers, a pert looking little rascal, about fourteen years old, with boots that came nearly up to his hips, and with his trowsers tucked inside, stepped up and with a voice and demeanor as important as a bull pup's exclaimed to each of us, 'Canteen, sir!' and would slip it off our necks with as much dexterity as if he had practiced highway robbery all his life; all rubber blankets were served the same way."

Norm Burdick (post-war).
Wrote dispatches as "Musket."
COURTESY OF THE MILWAUKEE COUNTY
HISTORICAL SOCIETY.

The first day of 1863 "dawned upon us half frozen and half starved.
. . . It was so cold that the prisoners had to keep up a continual 'double
quick' all night to keep the blood in circulation, and the warm rays of
'Old Sol' were never more heartily welcomed than by those prisoners in
the court house yard of Murfreesboro!" He then went on to detail the
long and arduous trail to Richmond's infamous prison. It was the last
dispatch written by Corporal Burdick, the printer who volunteered for
the Young Men's Association Tigers the summer—a lifetime—before.
He would soon be out of the war, discharged for disability on March 3.
But "Musket" would not long remain out of the army, as he enlisted as a
private in September 1864 in the 43rd Wisconsin Infantry. The unit
would fight against the rebel army of Maj. Gen. John B. Hood proximate to the 24th Wisconsin in 1864.[59]

Ed Douglas of Company B, who had been wounded December 31,
was also a prisoner in Murfreesboro on January 1. "It was the most
wearisome and lonely New Year's day *I* ever spent," Douglas wrote
weeks later from Annapolis, Maryland. Hunger was pronounced. "In
the afternoon, we were furnished with some flour, and I made up some
miserable pancakes, which I ate with a relish. We were kept in the
upper part of a store one night. The next we spent in the open air." Douglas, the twenty-one-year-old post office clerk, may not have been in

the same group as Burdick, since he wrote nothing about the parole being administered. And his trip south was quite circuitous—via Chattanooga, to Atlanta and West Point, Georgia, on to Montgomery and Mobile, Alabama, and finally to Richmond.

After his release from captivity, he wrote to his father from a steamer in the James River: "Thank God I again breathe the fresh air, and see the living sun-shine. Hurrah! I hope I am bound for home. Thank God I can once more see that happy place, the value of which I never knew before. Soldiering and a rebel prison have taught me a lesson that I will never forget. I am well and in good spirits." Douglas was discharged because of his wounds March 25.

Date Worth, the Granville farmer with the intent gaze, experienced similar circumstances after his capture, traveling to Chattanooga and Atlanta and ultimately to Richmond's Libby Prison. He, too, was exchanged at Annapolis, where he would spend many weeks recuperating from various ailments before being sent home. He would return to his regiment in spring.[60]

Among others, Andy Gallagher had been severely wounded by a fragment of a shell at Stones River, and was taken prisoner and conveyed with Burdick and others to Richmond. A volunteer in the largely Irish Allen Guard, he was later paroled and returned to Columbus, Ohio, where he was hospitalized. "The severity of the wound very much impaired his strength," and the examining physician suggested he remain at the hospital as a nurse. John Gallagher wrote to his son, recommending he retain that position. Gallagher was piqued by his father's suggestion: "If I were afraid to go to the battle field, I might, perhaps, seek a position [in the hospital], but I am not one of this kind." He enlisted in the 24th Wisconsin, he said, to do a "soldier's duty," not to be a nurse.

> You are alarmed at the dangers of the battle field. I admit that it is at times pretty rough, but it is the duty of every soldier, who is true to his country, to stand firm in the hour of danger, and not abandon like a coward, his trust. I enlisted with my comrades to give my services in crushing the rebellion, and now, while they are fighting, it would be far from honorably in me to seek safety as a nurse in a hospital. That I cannot do. I will go back to my regiment as soon as transportation can be furnished. Come well or woe, I will do nothing to disgrace myself. My ambition is to take a part in the pending conflicts. If I escape,

you will have reason to be proud of my conduct; if I fall, you will be comforted by the consciousness that I fell in the discharge of my duties.

Although he remained but a private in the ranks of Company G, nineteen-year-old Gallagher, a butcher by profession, was a good soldier who fought in all of the Milwaukee Regiment's remaining battles until he returned safely to the city.[61]

Back in Milwaukee, more funeral bells peeled in the thin winter air. "Yesterday was the occasion of another of those sad scenes now becoming so painfully frequent—burial of a fallen soldier." It was a bitterly cold day in Milwaukee; snows piled deeply and winds knifed icily from the north. Two more funerals were scheduled for Wednesday February 25 and the memories and lives of those 24th Wisconsin soldiers eulogized—George Cole at Plymouth Church on the city's east side, and George Cameron at Hanover Church on the west side.[62]

Cole, the tall first sergeant in Company B who served as acting lieutenant during the battle of Stones River, was another of those Milwaukee soldiers "as handsome and manly-looking a young man as there was in the regiment." Formerly a salesman at Wells, Simonds, & Company whose parents lived in a fine house on Prospect Avenue, the twenty-three-year-old had "enlisted from as pure motives of patriotism as ever animated the breast of a living being." Suffering from diarrhea before the battle, it was said, he was not truly fit for field duty; "but his pride and sense of duty would not permit him to remain behind." Cole had been grazed in the head by a rebel ball December 31 and, while falling back when the regiment retreated, was captured by the enemy, and bundled off to Richmond. He was partially robbed at the infamous Libby Prison. After being paroled by his captors, the fair-complexioned Cole, like Norm Burdick, caught a cold in his lungs on the trip north, and he was hospitalized at Annapolis, Maryland.

He had written confidently to his younger brother February 1, facetiously saying he had "undergone some changes in life." He was optimistic, he said, despite having arrived after parole "just alive." But he soon took a bad turn. Cole's mother and brother rushed to his bedside in mid-February, and "at the first of their visit[s] began to rally, but he was too much reduced to entirely recover, and although they ministered to his wants with all their tender solicitude and watchfulness of a mother and brother, yet he sank into his final rest a few days after their arrival at the hospital."

The grieving mother complained bitterly about some naval hospital staff. "The surgeon is an upstart, if not worse," she charged, who seemed to prescribe only whiskey and quinine for most of his patients. "No matter how many they were, that was his panacea." Again the news editor wrote: "He was a brave and noble young man, and had he lived and continued in the service, we fell [*sic*] a certainty that he would have won bright laurels." Ironically, Cole was posthumously promoted to second lieutenant. The death "was received with sorrow by the boys of his acquaintance in the Regiment," a comrade said; "there was no braver or truer soldier and gentleman in the army" than Company B's Cole. All the dead were now brave and true.

A few days after the funeral, the last letter written by George Cole was published in a Milwaukee daily. He was optimistic about the prospect for an end to the great Civil War. "There is one thing that is certain, and that is, the 'Rebs' are about 'played out.'" (He was one of the few who capitalized the word "Reb.") In talking with the enemy soldiers who had been conscripted into the army, he learned that "they never will shoot a Union soldier, without it is accidental, as long as they are in the service. Well, the next time I get into battle I hope we shall have nothing but conscripts to contend with, and I think they will be easily conquered."[63]

The fatherly captain of Company I, Fred Root, had been attentive to his men, George Cameron among them. The eighteen-year-old private, a dozen years Root's junior, had been felled by rebel lead during the retreat of December 31, but a surgeon had not considered the wound dangerous. "I had heard from him often, and each time he was getting better," Root said. "With all these statements before me I could not do otherwise than look for his speedy recovery, and expected he would join his company." Cameron died February 2 in Nashville. Little more than two weeks later, Root had the sad duty of writing to the young man's father. "George was as brave a soldier as ever shouldered a musket; always prompt to perform his duty, having the confidence of his officers, and the esteem of his fellow soldiers," Root penned. Prosperous Alexander Mitchell, who had concluded another visit with his son, John, and others, accompanied the body back to Milwaukee.[64]

Milwaukee's roll of dead expanded to include many soldiers felled by disease—typhoid, dysentery, and other maladies—that stalked the camps around Murfreesboro during the dreadfully wet Tennessee winter. Such deaths were no less mourned than those who fell in battle. Typical of them was Noah Griswold, a bookkeeper and clerk at a Milwaukee bootery and another of the Company B "pets." He departed Milwaukee that summer with the Young Men's Association Tigers, filled with "life, hope and happiness." It was written of the twenty-five-year-old, as it would be of so many others in the coming years, that he was "a young man of sterling merit . . . favorably spoken of by all who knew him." His wife had waved good-bye at the train station that rainy day in September. He had safely passed through the awful maelstrom of Stones River, but within days had been laid low with typhoid fever. He had rallied for some time, and the wife expected news of improvement. "But contrary to her eager hopes, the message came of his death, which was too much for the fragile woman's nature, and she fell into a swoon from which she doubtless feels that she could almost wish she had never recovered." In reporting Griswold's untimely demise, editor Cramer wrote. "The national tragedy of this country is now being written in the blood of thousands of brave soldiers, and amid the sighs from thousands of unhappy homes."[65]

The remains of yet another Milwaukee volunteer, Tom Spence of Company K, arrived in the city in early February. He was an old resident of Milwaukee, having migrated there in 1849. He had taken ill in Bowling Green several weeks before, and died there December 17. His body was exhumed from Kentucky, and returned home to the First Ward. With these words, he was laid to rest in Forest Home Cemetery:

> The day is past and gone,
> The evening shades appear,
> Oh, may we all remember well,
> The night of death draws near.[66]

Still another family was doubly devastated. Joshua Stark arrived in Nashville that winter to claim the body of his brother-in-law, Oswald Kissam. With his younger brother, Sam, the twenty-six-year-old bookkeeper had volunteered with the boys from the Young Men's Association, Company B. The older Kissam had been felled by disease in November. Then, Stark found that Sam, a nineteen-year-old printer, had taken sick as a consequence of "disease contracted from exposure and hardship of camp life"; he recovered briefly, only to suffer a relapse. He died February 11. Here was another young man of "much merit and highly esteemed by all who knew him." His employer said he was a "high-minded, promising young man, a favorite with his regiment." Such phrases were becoming worn, and likely failed to lift the damaged spirits of the family. The funeral for the two men was held February 20. These dead comrades, many bright and energetic friends in the days before the war, were the cost that mounted daily.[67]

In the winter camps of Murfreesboro, the issuance of President Lincoln's Emancipation Proclamation in January touched off controversy. Let North and South withdraw with honor, and return the nation to its state before the firing on Fort Sumter had brought war, some said. Let the Constitutional rights, including the one to own chattel, remain unimpaired. The Democratic *News* carried the view of a 24th Wisconsin soldier identified only as "R" who wrote: "The proclamation of emancipation is not, as a general thing, in favor with this army, and threatens dissatisfaction, which may be severe in its consequences, though it is to be hoped not." This view was widely held among soldiers in all armies. But within a month, a sea change of opinion would commence, and there would be no truck with talk about compromise with the rebellious states.[68]

A Milwaukee man who visited the 24th Wisconsin also broached the issue swirling about the proclamation; he wrote of strong opinions made by a Union man in Nashville. The "rebels were tired of the muss, as they called it, and were willing to quit and come back under the protection of the old flag." Confederate president Jefferson Davis, it was reported, faced difficulty recruiting men to his army's ranks. "[T]he moment the proclamation was issued it produced an electric effect through all the rebel[s] from every cross road, hamlet and village; and why? Because, as I understand it, the proclamation had reference to the slaves of those who, under the tremendous pressure of public opinion south, had remained true to the Union, as the emancipation of slaves of rebels had been provided for by the confiscation act of congress," the Unionist averred. A further deleterious effect was that the Union men of Kentucky and Tennessee were subsequently stigmatized as abolitionists by the secessionists, and their property was plundered by the rebel armies.[69]

Soldiers became caught up in the controversy, many feeling betrayed by their fellow citizens in the North. They were confused. Here they were, on the battlefield, risking all to preserve the great Union of States, while back home, in comfort and ease, citizens were sniping at them. Many Democrats and Southern sympathizers constantly fought in print and on the stump against the president's introduction of abolition as a war aim. Federal soldiers must not lose their lives to win freedom for slaves, many muttered.

In February, several officers from Ohio infantry regiments, both Republican and Democrat, gathered to "show the sentiment" that existed in the Army of the Cumberland and decry the "dishonorable compromises and incipient treason" arising in the North. When they addressed assembled regiments, great cheers thundered, which "would have sent a thrill of joy to the heart of every loyal man in the country." The story from an Ohio news sheet was printed prominently for Milwaukee readers.

The introspective Quaker, Capt. Howard Greene, whose family bore strong abolitionist sentiments, was confused by it all. "I am pretty well satisfied of one thing," he told his brother, "that is, we can never whip them into the Union. The Matter will eventually have to be settled by compromise, and therefore the sooner they can do so the better, for the sooner it is done, the fewer lives that may be sacrificed." He also expressed contradiction among those with whom he spoke: There seemed to be "unanimous opinion" that "if they would only leave the settlement of this Matter with the Armies opposing each other in the West, we would have peace in a very short time. The Rebels are tired of this War as we are, and are anxious to have it settled," he said. They might compromise so both sides might "get out of this scrape honorably."[70]

Ultimately, the soldiers' resolve about finishing the war grew, most closing ranks behind President Lincoln and the Federal government. In many ways, the volunteers in the West, who considered themselves distinct from their comrades in the East, were becoming a national army. They were, as Date Worth had it, Abe's soldiers. Having already invested such blood, limbs, and lives, the men were not ready to give up. They would have no sympathy for Copperhead pacifiers.

"All evils can be remedied at the ballot-box save the rebellion of men in arms," the Ohio soldier manifesto declared. "This can only be suppressed by bayonets." The rebellious South, it averred, would only "fling back in our faces all propositions for compromise and declare that nothing will suit them but the acknowledgement of their bastard nationality." They see kindred spirits in the North—peace advocates or Copperheads—as allies in the dastardly endeavor. Fellow Federal soldiers called upon comrades to resist such appeals. "[A]cknowledge the rebellion for what it is—traitorous," the draft stated for home folks. "If some miserable demagogues amongst you must vomit forth their treason, let them keep it at home. *We want none of their vile letters, speeches, or papers here.* We know for what we are engaged is an Abolition war. We have sunk all party considerations in devoted loyalty to our country, and whatever names unholy traitors may apply to us, we will, by every means that Providence puts in our hands, sustain the Union, so help us God," the men declared. "The army of the West is in terrible earnest. Earnest to conquer and destroy armed rebels. Earnest to meet force with force."[71]

In much the same sentiment, Francis Sherman, the colonel of the 88th Illinois brigaded with the Milwaukee Regiment, also made a ringing appeal to patriotism and the continued prosecution of the war to its fiery conclusion. A Douglas Democrat, Sherman promulgated a letter mainly to rebut Illinois and Indiana declarations decrying the continued persecution of the war. The soldiers in the Army of the Cumberland departed homes and fireside, Sherman stumped, and are "left here to contend against disease, death, and an ever vigilant foe, alone, whilst the fanatics of the North are giving aid and comfort to the rebels, and reviving their broken fortunes by these internal dissentions," he proposed.

"Let the disunionists of the North take heed. We do not propose quietly to allow them to trample on our rights, and help dig our graves." Men should not be allowed to "utter traitorous sentiments at our homes," he declared. "We, the soldiers of the United States, called forth to save the country, dropped our political differences when we entered the service, and took the oath that we would obey the 'orders of the President of the United States'—and we intend to do it." Sherman said that every officer and soldier to whom he spoke agreed with his declaration, and "will sustain to the death our Commander-in-Chief . . . in all measures and orders that he may issue for the crushing of rebellion." He called upon his fellow citizens to lay aside partisan feelings and "unite and come up with a steady front on the war question." He closed with a clarion pronouncement: *The soldiers are loyal,* and *will support the Government;* and they would *as soon war on traitors in Illinois* as in Tennessee." This was the view that gained ascendancy among most Milwaukee men.[72]

Many of the men of the Milwaukee Regiment grew confident, perhaps shaking off the torpor that followed the defeat at Stones River. Their pugnacious commander, Old Rosey, could claim some credit for the outlook. Howard Greene declared that had Burnside's Army of the Potomac at Fredericksburg and Grant's soldiers at Vicksburg been as successful as Rosecrans at Stones River, "we would have summoned this Rebellion to its Death to the tune of the Light Guard Quickstep," he told his sister. "Our whole Army have utmost confidence in Rosecrans

Henry Bichler.
The little German tailor.
COURTESY OF ERIC BORGERDING.

and think him the best General in the whole Army." Some called the general the "idol" of the army. Even news editors of the day, often critical of the army generals, favored General Rosecrans. "A master mind [Rosecrans] controls—one that knows when and how to move. The supplies have been brought forward and the battle losses supplied, etc. All which for a vast army like this takes time."[73]

The strength of the Milwaukee Regiment, however, had not been completely revived. Amandus Silsby, little Henry Bichler, Date Worth, and others had still not returned to the regiment in late January, and were reported missing. By that date it was thought these men were either dead and their bodies unfound, or they were in the hands of the rebels. Some who had been slightly wounded were returning to the ranks. Adjutant McArthur had collected the final toll of casualties from Stones River. Twenty-one had been killed and 8 more died of wounds; nearly 50 were so seriously wounded that they would all be discharged for disability within the coming months. In addition, 13 of the wounded were in rebel hands; 9 of those paroled would be so badly broken down as to be unfit for any duty, and they were discharged. In all, the Milwaukee Regiment sustained over 150 casualties—fully one-third of its strength.

The 24th presented the appearance of a "mournful skeleton of what it once was." In early February, it could barely muster 300 muskets. Five months previous, it had counted 1,000 good men; on December 6, it had counted 500—not including men detailed as clerks and other duties. The soldier correspondent "R" was cynical. "At this ratio of reduction from about 1,000 rank and file five months ago, where will it be in six months more? Also for the glories of glorious war! So cheap for those who stay home, so dear for those who take up arms!" Those who remained, he said, were "in fair condition as to drill and camp comforts" with convalescents returning to the regiment. Another soldier reported about that time that the Milwaukee Regiment's strength was 444 present for duty—"some coming up occasionally." In early February, Wisconsin agent G. Stamm related that the 24th counted 347 enlisted men.[74]

Early the next month, Jasper Vliet, the son of a prominent land developer, who was home on furlough, told a news writer that before he departed Murfreesboro the Milwaukee Regiment counted 400 fit for duty, "which was about as well as any [regiment] in the army," he said. "Picketing and foraging were the chief duties, and between the two, the boys had very little leisure on their hands. They were not exactly 'spoiling for a fight,' but were ready and willing to meet the enemy again which they expect to do as soon as the mud dries up sufficiently to enable the army to move."[75]

"An army in camp is not very prolific in exciting news items," another soldier wrote. "The ordinary routine of picket, foraging and fatigue duty is only occasionally relieved by skirmishing and such like deed of blood. The great anaconda is torpid and inert, after being gorged with such a feast of death as at Stone's River on the opening of the new year."[76]

Weather in January and February was inhospitable for the army still licking its considerable wounds: "[R]ains have been making frightful work with the roads, it being impossible to move the army over such bottomless mud," said one correspondent. "Mud has been so deep and so horrible—so dispiriting to man and beast, that it requires extraordinary courage to make up one's mind to move a rod out of a good macadamized road. The crossing of these, to pedestrians, was perilous!" wrote a news correspondent who visited the camps. A soldier who identified himself only as "S" also groused about the conditions. "For the last month it has rained, on an average, every other day," said the Milwaukee volunteer. The mud around the 24th Wisconsin camp was knee-deep and it was difficult to get around at all. Yet: "The trees are budding, and the grass growing, and it will not be a great while before everything in Tennessee will be clothed in the garb of spring."[77]

Old Rosey began to reorganize his battered army, disbanding his arrangement of "wings" and reinstituting the normal arrangement of corps. In mid-February, General McCook returned to resume command of his old XX Corps. "He looks the same jolly fellow he always was, and going on a forty day furlough to get 'spliced' [married] does not seem to have injured him in the least."

"No one can imagine, without personal knowledge, how much such a prolonged engagement and the physical exposure incident thereto, destroys the vitality of our army," pronounced one soldier, likely in reaction to the criticisms against the army's failure to move. "It is not alone the 'killed, wounded, and missing' schedule, which exhibits the diminution of strength that takes place, but thousands of others are for a long time rendered unfit for service by over fatigue and exposure, and very many pass from the field of battle without a scratch, to the crowded hospitals and thence to desolation [sic] of a soldier's grave unnumbered among the victims of the fight."[78]

Yet, optimism slowly returned; late in February, more reinforcements arrived in the Murfreesboro camps. "They are welcome, and we are very happy to see them, and will take the very earliest opportunity to introduce them to that 'fine old confederate gentleman,' Monsieur Bragg—think we can presume upon that liberty, having met the kind-hearted old man in two public balls—that given at Perryville and the one by the murmuring waters of gentle Stone river. (Oh, the old rascals!)" The 24th, however, received no new recruits; in fact, it would be another year before its ranks would be bulked again.[79]

It was during these winter weeks that the father of Tom Ford, the redhead who fought with Bridges's Battery of Illinois Artillery, visited the camps of the 24th Wisconsin; it was his intention to claim his sons, Tom and Dan, for the Prairie State artillery. He conferred with Colonel Larrabee, but the Wisconsin commander demurred, saying the Fords were good soldiers and were needed in the Milwaukee Regiment.

"But they are my boys," the elder Ford responded, "and I want them with me."

"They are not your boys, by God, sir," the irascible Larrabee shot back, "they are my boys, and I am going to keep them; you cannot have them."

Tom and his brother, farmers who volunteered from the town of Franklin in the southern part of Milwaukee County, would remember that terse exchange for decades. They would serve their terms in the 24th Wisconsin, mustering out with the regiment at war's end.[80]

Col. Charles Larrabee returned to the Milwaukee Regiment in early March. "He was received with three rousing cheers from the boys, and a serenade by the band—than which, there is none better in the business. The Col. made a speech to the boys after 'tattoo' last night, in which he said he was happy to meet them, but, that there was an appropriate occasion for everything, and drum having 'beat the men to quarters,' he would advise all to quietly retire, which they did, evidently, not expecting that kind of speech. It was natural to see him once more with us, and we all hope his health will permit him to remain. He certainly looked improved in every respect, and if he is as well as he looks, we have no fears." The forty-two-year-old politician's bent on discipline was still evident.[81]

There was another change that troubled many of the boys: Their avuncular, gray-haired brigade commander, old Nick Greusel, finally had had enough. Well into his fifties, he had been in the war since April 1861 and fought gallantly in several bloody battles. Not only was his tall, willowy body worn down, but he was frustrated by the absence of promotion to brigadier. He resigned in mid-February and returned home. Before the colonel departed from Murfreesboro, officers from all four of his regiments drafted a farewell testimonial to their popular commander. In part, they stated that in Greusel's resignation "the government has lost the service of a skillful, brave and competent officer. No words of ours can add to a reputation won at Pea Ridge, Perryville, and Stone River." The officers wrote that "we tender to him the strongest evidence of our regard and esteem," and closed with an appeal to the government to "honor itself and do justice to Col. Greusel by giving him a Brigadier General's commission." The Illinois officer, however, would never receive that star.[82]

Most of the Milwaukee soldiers would not see him again for more than two decades, when, as part of the great veterans' reunion in September 1889, Greusel came to the city to rekindle old army friendships and pose for a photograph with some of the men of the 24th Wisconsin. Temporarily taking his place at the head of the brigade was Col. Francis Sherman, the 88th Illinois officer who had authored the clarion manifesto during the Emancipation Proclamation controversy.[83]

Late in April, the Wisconsin, Illinois, and Michigan men received another brigade commander, permanently replacing dead General Sill. In his stead was named another Ohioan, Brig. Gen. William Lytle. Lieutenant Mitchell told his mother that the new brigadier was "well liked I understand." Another soldier was also impressed: "We like him as a commander, as he has the 'vim' in him, and knows his business." Cpl. George Cooley was also positive. "I like him as he is a fighting man." He had won his star at Perryville, and bore a solid reputation.[84]

The new brigadier, at thirty-six, was an author of renown. He had sad, dark eyes, under a high forehead, and a long, full, dark beard framed his chin and jaw. General Lytle was much famed as the creator of some of the most popular verse of the day, and his poem, "I Am Dying Egypt, Dying," could be recited by most schoolchildren. Had he lived, the literary lieutenant George Bleyer would have felt an affinity toward the gentle-looking general.[85]

The new commander also "instituted a new order of things with reference to drill," said another soldier, and the regiment was reduced from six hours daily to four. General Lytle regularly put the soldiers through their paces, and this caused Corporal Cooley to offer one caveat: "He has a very poor voice to command a brigade." The general's written poetic flights were more preferred.[86]

Meanwhile, the health of Lt. Col. Lish Hibbard had deteriorated; in fact, it "had not been very good for some time past." He would soon return to Milwaukee in an attempt to convalesce. Perhaps like Greusel, Hibbard also had enough, worn down by field service and the innuendo about his leadership and courage. Barely twenty-three, his official date of resignation was March 7. His imperious demeanor never did carry well with many of the Wisconsin soldiers, and some were elated with his departure. "On dress parade an order was read announcing Lt. Col. Hibbard's resignation, which was received with great satisfaction and joy in the whole regiment," wrote George Cooley. No one will mourn his loss, Jim Harvey wrote to his comrade, Worth, who was recuperating in Wisconsin.[87]

A handsome, slender soldier from Waukesha, Theodore West, took his place; in his mid- to late twenties, West had served well in the 5th Wisconsin Infantry. He had "the reputation of being a good military man," said *Sentinel* editor Tomkins Jermain, "and will doubtless be very popular with his command." Corporal Cooley guardedly agreed, confiding in his diary that while West was a fine looking man, "I shall like him as well upon a further acquaintance." By that he meant how he would perform in battle. Lt. John Mitchell, now a field officer in Company E, also concurred. "If he is to be [appointed] he is just what is wanted to make the 24th the nearest to perfection of any Reg. in this vicinity." Yet, there was one reservation: "Some of the officers of the 24th are rather adverse to the appointment of an outsider to the Lieut. Colonelcy and are circulating a paper of protestation, their panacea in such cases. As for me, I say all hail, Col. West, because I think taking all circumstances into account it is the most prudent thing that can be done."

West, with his experience, would complement Colonel Larrabee well, it was said. Since the commander's return to the regiment, Lieutenant Mitchell said, he "has managed the 24th splendidly and has raised the morale of the soldiers greatly. He is a great man for the executive, but is not so good a drill-master." Larrabee, however, would not again lead his regiment into battle.[88]

Within a month, West had proved himself to the men of Milwaukee and Wisconsin. The solider correspondent who identified himself only as "S" wrote he did not think "the people of Milwaukee know 'what for' an officer he is." "He has the compliment of being the best tactician in the division. His manner towards the boys is kind; he has made them fast friends to him. He is universally loved and respected by all, both in the regiment and brigade, and has shown himself to be both a soldier and a man, in every sense of the words. The parents at home may rest assured that their sons will not suffer in his hands, not as long as he has anything to do with us. He will see justice done in every case." Here was high praise for an officer, indeed.[89]

Perhaps almost as important as the changes was the issue of new rifle-muskets to the Milwaukee Regiment. They were handsome British-manufactured Enfields with dark wood and browned barrels. In mid-March, George Cooley wrote: "Today we changed our guns for Enfield rifles and I anticipate that the next time the 24th meets the rebels they will stand." Another correspondent was equally effusive. "Our old Austrian rifle has been exchanged for the Enfield, which, as our Colonel says, is 'very good!' The new guns are fine pieces of workmanship, and are much superior to our old worn-out, non-shooting arms." Many soldiers smarted over the reputation that their regiment still bore, and they needed to prove their worth in battle—to themselves and to family and friends. The English-imported rifled muskets might help.[90]

In addition, the twelve-man Sibley tents were taken from the regiment early in the month. As six of these tents filled one wagon, it was deemed logistically prudent to divest the army of such cumbersome lodgings and thereby shorten the supply trains considerably during active campaigning. In the Sibley's place was issued to each man a six-and-a-half by three-and-a-half-inch sheet of rubber-coated material, equipped with brass grommets or buttons. The men grumbled about the loss of their commodious havens and the substitution of what they called a "piece of rag," fit as it was only for dogs.

"This change of habitation is for the health of the men," the solider "S" wrote caustically. The army's medical department claimed that the new tents would improve the health of the army 50 percent. "How that may be I know not, but do know that the 'dogs' are not as comfortable as the Sibleys." They would soon learn the value of these seemingly insubstantial shelters. Officers, however, were still permitted to retain their more commodious wall tents, "as usual," he observed wryly.

On the march, the soldiers soon learned that they could erect their shelters quickly when a night's halt was ordered. Two men tied or buttoned halves together, staked down the corners, and propped up the little dwelling with makeshift poles. An observant news writer found "this operation is a wonderful sight, from the rapidity with which it is completed." Those men in the ranks who measured more than six feet found their extremities out in the elements. But no longer would the soldiers need to wait hours for the tents to arrive on wagons, or sleep largely unprotected if they failed to arrive. What was more, when the bugle for assembly sounded in the predawn hours, "the soldier whips up the pegs that secure his tent[,] divides it with his comrade, rolls up his blanket, enveloped that in the canvas to secure it from the rain, and slings the useful cylinder around his shoulder," a news man described. No more than ten minutes were required to break camp and resume the march.[91]

As spring opened verdantly, more changes occurred. Picketing had become "an occupation which it entered upon once a week. It has little else to do, though now and then a scout and drilling come in for their share," "S" said. After several months in a convalescent hospital and a furlough in Granville, Date Worth returned to his regiment and friend, Jim Harvey. "I am once again mixing in the throng of . . . camp arrayed once more with martial trappings & prepared for the fray." What he sometimes lacked in grammar and spelling, the twenty-three-year-old farmer compensated with irony and insight.

It was during one of their times on picket that the Rogers brothers of Company B—Harry, the bookkeeper who had turned twenty-two in April, and Lieutenant Charley, twenty—received a rude shock. A letter was handed them from their father, James, one of the wealthiest men in the state. The father had traveled with Alexander Mitchell to visit the boys before the last battle, and Rogers attempted to persuade his sons to return home.

"No, father," replied the younger Rogers, a lieutenant, "I came down here to stay until the war is over, or until I am killed or disabled." James Rogers proposed that if Harry must remain in the army, he should return home and gain a commission in another regiment. Thirty years later, when he related the story to his old veteran friends, Rogers recalled that he demurred, saying he had enlisted in the 24th; "I like the boys, and if I get promotion in this war it will be because I have earned it in battle, not because my father has influence with the governor."

Now, in the spring of 1863, they held a letter. Harry, who was given to premonitions, told his brother he feared the missive contained bad news. Indeed, the sixty-nine-year-old father had been taken gravely ill, and it was feared he would not survive. A postscript noted tersely: "Your father has breathed his last." James Rogers had died April 30. Through the intervention of General Sheridan, who had met the elder Rogers, a furlough was issued for the sons to return home.[92]

"The month of May has nearly passed over our heads, and still nothing of any importance outside the occasional scouts or the taking of a few prisoners, has occurred worthy of mention. We have during the month, in a general military point of view, been several times ordered to march, but never did." The soldier-writer identified only as "S" was attempting to fill the void left by the absence of dispatches from George Bleyer and Norm Burdick. "Our baggage has been cut down, and we are now allowed comparatively little clothing." The "general opinion" is that if Grant is successful in taking Vicksburg, the Army of the Cumberland will advance and attack Bragg. "'Rosy' is so close and strict that not even his staff can find out much with reference to their future intentions." After several failures to capture the strategic Mississippi River town, General U. S. Grant had initiated a new campaign against the bastion in April.

"It looks to us down here as though something was going to happen, but what it is no one knows. I think it is a fight. It looks to me as if 'Rosy' is trying to bring about a battle at this point." There were some 10,000 to 20,000 men on the go at all times, while others like the 24th were told "to be ready at a moment's notice to march. Should 'Rosy,' through his feints and forays, succeed in bringing on a general engagement here, woe unto the secesh. They could never whip us." Such strategy was just what General Rosecrans would use.[93]

"The whole army is in a healthy condition, and the men are resolute, determined, and repose unlimited confidence in Gen. Rosecrans."
The army was supplied by the railroad from Nashville to Murfreesboro,
a distance of thirty miles.[94]

A Milwaukee man who visited the 24th was struck by the change he
discerned in the faces of some of the young officers. Of Bob Chivas,
who had not yet reached his majority, he has observed: "As I looked . . .
in his face and scanned every feature, so changed in a few short
months—the boyish look all gone, exchanged for the ripened look of a
man and a soldier." Lt. Arthur McArthur celebrated his eighteenth birthday on June 2. Although he was still young, the beginnings of manhood
were also tracing upon the adjutant's face; and his voice was deepening.
What was more, shadows of war were discernible in his eyes.[95]

Observing the changes in these countenances, the writer may have
been speaking about most of the men of the Milwaukee Regiment. A
certain heaviness was beginning to cloud the eyes of these volunteers,
less than a year from home. They had already faced death and seen the
ghastliness of battle, and had lived in conditions undreamed of before
they became soldiers. These circumstances changed boys into men,
hardening them. As summer greened and blossomed, the Wisconsin
soldiers would experience new trials, more sickness and death, and
another defeat.

Chapter 8

Chickamauga

"My actions will tell all."

It is unlikely the Company B soldier had ever knowingly killed a man before. It is also improbable that he would ever do so again. "I have a pretty sure thing of laying out a 'reb,'" Gene Comstock admitted to his parents immediately after the battle. "One of my pardners fired at him and missed him. I took a quick sight, fired, and he droped [*sic*]." He needed to reiterate that grim fact. "I am sure that I hit him that I could almost swear that it was my bullet that dropped [him]." The Milwaukee printer was barely twenty years old.[1]

It was a rare display of cold candor, perhaps not so much braggadocio as surprise tinged with disgust. Nothing like this had occurred in the battles of the year before. Comstock had been a corporal until a month before when he was reduced in rank to private for some unspecified infraction. This, the dark-haired, blue-eyed young man had not mentioned in any of his weekly letters to his parents. His well-known father, Henry, carried on a fairly prosperous commission business north of Milwaukee's central commercial district.[2]

Accounts of actually killing a man in battle were uncommon, particularly in letters home. Although many soldiers wrote graphically about the bloodshed, maiming, death, and carnage, few spoke of the face-to-face killing of another man. In battle, few soldiers, because of fear, took careful sighting at individuals, firing instead at the massed ranks of enemy. Many, in fact, could not even bring themselves to shoot directly into enemy ranks, discharging their muskets above the foe. Christian precepts governed most soldiers. Most often, scant opportunity to take specific aim presented itself in battle because of the tumult and chaos. There was barely time to reload the long Enfield rifle-musket; even under ideal circumstances, soldiers could fire few more than two or three shots a minute.

Even news writers of the day witnessed entire regiments or brigades delivering fire and failing to wound a single on-rushing enemy. Such "random discharges, it seems . . . become a habit, and they become so excited at it that they would oftener miss a man at ten paces than they would hit him," the correspondent attested. Perhaps soldiers from rural communities were conversant with guns, accustomed to hunting or shooting. But most city men, such as dominated the ranks of the 24th Wisconsin, likely had little extensive knowledge of weapons. A few, certainly, had become familiar with muskets in militia drills before the war. And while training in the manual of the musket was common among volunteers, actual practice firing was infrequent; incredibly, reports of extensive marksmanship firing were left to such units as the U.S. Sharpshooters, specialized Federal regiments whose soldiers were required to be proficient in marksmanship. Random firing, complained the news correspondent, "besides wasting ammunition, does not intimidate the enemy at all; on the other hand, it makes them feel that there is little danger, consequently he is more bold, and delivers his fire more accurately." Comstock's sighting may not have been an accurate one, but he was certain the reb was dead.[3]

But all of that was months away as June 1863 arrived, and the Army of the Cumberland, after six months of relative idleness following the battle of Stones River, finally lurched into action. Indeed, grumbling back in Washington over the inactivity all of these months of Gen. William Rosecrans and his army was evident. The Army of the Potomac, although badly bloodied at Chancellorsville in April, was at least active under Gen. Joseph Hooker. And General U. S. Grant's army was choking Vicksburg into submission.

"The sarcasm on the inactivity of our Virginian army, that 'All Quiet on the Potomac' might with good reason be exchanged to suit us, for we have been 'all quiet at Murfreesboro' for six months," the young lumber merchant, Lt. Robert Chivas, told his uncle, wealthy and influential Alexander Mitchell. Still, he and most others expressed confidence in General Rosecrans, Old Rosey; he was as popular with the Cumberlands as Gen. George McClellan had formerly been with the men of the Army of the Potomac. He would not recklessly plunge south after General Bragg's rebel army without painstaking preparation, marshalling supplies, and insuring his soldiers were well ordered. Moreover, the geography confronting the Federal army was rife with difficulties—a massive mountain chain and broad rivers imperiling any movement of tens of thousands of men and material. No, Lieutenant Chivas concluded, the situation was not as easy as that confronting the other major blue armies. General U. S. Grant, for example, could anchor his army on the Mississippi River; and Hooker could "go out and fight the enemy at his door." The situation in Tennessee was different. "Our warfare is essentially of a rural character," the twenty-year-old Scot said. There was little to be seen in this part of the country save fences, fields, and woods; there was "no river or ocean to cling to as we march along." The Cumberlands must trod fifty miles before meeting the enemy, and then the gray antagonists "close up behind us like water," Chivas penciled.[4]

Finally, finally, June 23rd, the Army of the Cumberland was bestirred, "all in commotion, preparatory to a move," a Milwaukee soldier said. "All night the excitement was kept up, and the exodus from this land of sojourn was fairly commenced." Soon, leaden skies opened with a torrent of rain, as the Cumberlands lurched southward on the following morning, Wednesday. "We have been skirmishing with the enemy for the last three days," a Milwaukee soldier noted the following week. "You never saw such roads—mud knee deep," reported another man in the 24th Wisconsin. The rain would continue interminably.[5]

The Milwaukee Regiment's colonel, Charles Larrabee, had once again absented himself from the Milwaukee Regiment, and returned to Nashville. Although many men in the ranks liked the commander, he had not yet proved himself in battle. The swarthy officer from Horicon, Wisconsin, northwest of Milwaukee, still fussed over the army's failure to promote him to brigadier general. Larrabee, the politician, would finally end his fitful leadership of the 24th Wisconsin, resigning August 27. Some soldiers, George Cooley among them, were saddened by the departure. "I am very sorry to lose him as he has been a very good officer to his regiment but he has left us in very good hands."[6]

The "very good hands" were those of Lt.-Col. Theodore West, the handsome Waukesha officer who had seen hard service in the 5th Wisconsin during the first year of war. He carried a magnificent sword captured from a North Carolina officer at the battle of Williamsburg—a war prize he would soon have to relinquish. Popular with many men, he was called "Dore" by close comrades. Corporal Comstock acknowledged that narrow-shouldered but straight commander was "bunkum. Everybody likes him."[7]

The long ribbons of blue surged across the Cumberland Plateau toward the Tennessee River in late June, rapidly pushing the enemy free from key mountain gaps. In another letter home, Gene Comstock, two stripes still sewn on his sleeves, wished he might gain an officer's commission so that riding a horse could replace the grueling tramping. "Am getting sick of hoofing," he groused. Less prosaically, he wondered where the enemy would "give us a pitched battle." Perhaps Tullahoma or Chattanooga, Tennessee, where the Confederate general Braxton Bragg was headquartered, would be the place for the next deadly confrontation. The Milwaukee corporal also dismissed persistent camp rumor of enemy reinforcements coming from Virginia. "If we do have a battle I can only do one thing with honor and that every soldier does. *'Put your trust in God and keep your powder dry!'*" Comstock concluded. He would soon do just that. One of his comrades was more prescient: "I think if there is to be a fight it will be severe."[8]

On the final day of June, the advance of the Army of the Cumberland caught up with the rebel rear guard. On the following day, they pushed ahead to Tullahoma, reputed to be heavily defended by the rebels. The army camped within five miles of the "famously fortified city," and "all eyes were open" at the prospect of battle, recalled a Milwaukee officer a few days later. "All were anxious for the coming morrow." The continuous heavy rain added to the gloomy prospect. But the unidentified writer, probably on the division or brigade staff, overheard General Sheridan opine to Maj. Gen. Alexander McCook, commander of the XX Corps, that the rebels were likely pulling south of the Tennessee River. At three o'clock in the rainy darkness of Wednesday, July 1, "the troops stood at arms" ready for the assault on Tullahoma.[9]

But in what would soon be recognized as a brilliant piece of strategy, General Rosecrans had so disposed his three corps that heavy-browed Bragg felt compelled to withdraw from the town despite his stoutly constructed defenses. "What possessed the rebels to evacuate this place is more than I can tell," wrote a soldier who identified himself only as "S." The woods all around the place, exhibiting "a state of destitution hardly comprehensible," had been cleared for nearly a mile to create fields of fire for the defenders. "It would have been a sore job to have charged that mile, and the place could not have been taken without great slaughter."

Date Worth, who now began closing his letters as "your erring son," noted that Tullahoma's siege guns were left behind with burned carriages along with discarded military impedimenta. "Ghosts & rats now inhabit the place once the comfortable homes of fellow beings," he said. His close companion, Jim Harvey, had been made corporal.[10]

Passing quickly through Tullahoma with "flying colors," the men forded the waist-deep Elk River and marched to Winchester, Tennessee. Here, a Milwaukee officer made note of "a very sad affair." Nearing a house around which rebel sharpshooters were rumored to be hidden, a boy of perhaps ten burst from the door. Some soldiers of the 21st Michigan pulled muskets to their shoulders, sending several heavy lead balls into the small body, killing the lad instantly. General Lytle, the sensitive poet who led the brigade, went forward to comfort the weeping mother. Tears streaming, she told the general that she and her husband were staunch Unionists, and welcomed the blue army despite the death of her son. "[T]his is one of the daily misfortunes that happen in the army," concluded the Milwaukee officer.[11]

The town was "the only place we had been with those creatures called women in it," observed one soldier who wrote of more ephemeral matters. It was a shock to several Wisconsin men who confronted the women of these environs. "The ladies of the confederacy in this section . . . *chew* and *smoke tobacco.*" "At every house you pass, you will see the old women with pipes in their mouths, and the young ones with huge quids of tobacco stuck in their jaws. What would some of our Northern belles say to that? Here it is as fashionable to eat tobacco as it is at the North to eat ice cream and strawberries," he wrote with amusement.

A Company B soldier, Bill Maxfield from Milwaukee, was also taken aback. "As a civilization, it is the worst I ever saw." He wrote not only of the inhabitants' indulgence in tobacco but of their proclivity toward profane language. "The Lord knows it is an awful habit for men to fall into, but you would be surprised to hear some of the women down here belch out profanity." A woman had roundly cursed the soldier a few days before. He was also flushed by the forwardness of the girls who exhibited "no coyness about showing their ankles." With a hint of condescension, he concluded: "Men, women and children are all born, bred and brought up in this manner, and it grows upon them, I suppose." Yet he found the inhabitants "in the main as good hearted people as I ever saw."

All along the line of march now the soldiers, farm boys and city men of the 24th Wisconsin, commented at the sorry state of the land and crops in southern Tennessee, caused both by Federal and Confederate armies. Poverty was prevalent as thousands of bushels of grain, "harvested and stood in the shock," had been destroyed or plundered. Most houses were deserted save for women and children who professed in the strongest terms to harbor Union sentiments.[12]

"This is an awful hard campaign for mud and wet clothes but still it is not as bad as the campaign from Nashville to Murfreesboro," Corporal Comstock put in. Yet, General Sheridan's division was handling the situation well, its reputation growing. Even before Tullahoma, General Rosecrans had complimented the division for doing its duty "so well and faithfully. One thing is pretty sure that the rebs had as leave meet the 'devil' as Gen. Sheridan's division. We hardly ever see a rebel paper but what there is something about Sheridan's division. It is evident that they fear us more than any other division in this army."

During the long trek south, the army was forced to ford several rivers swollen by the incessant rains, and Comstock described the vexing process to his parents. "Take off the haversack, blanket, dog tent, rubber [blanket], and cartridge box, and tie them to the gun with pants and then get through as best [as] you can. The current is sometimes so swift as to take a fellows feet from in under him." The men lifted their Enfields high above their heads, and "all of us yelling like so many tigers, the band playing Yankee Doodle." He wrote a caustic comment about those artists like Edward Waud and others who sketched army scenes for tabloid news sheets. "Where was *Frank Leslie's artist*" now? he asked rhetorically.

Finally, two brigades of General Sheridan's division, including the 24th Wisconsin, encamped at Cowan Station on the Chattanooga & Nashville Railroad near the border with Alabama July 3. The area was almost entirely surrounded by a range of the lofty Cumberland Mountains. The Granville farmer, Worth, took time to view the magnificent vistas—mountains swathed in green "rising their lofty heads in solemn grandeur above the plane [*sic*]," and the streams tumbling clear, cool waters. The regiment was some 60 miles below Murfreesboro, but had traveled, according to Corporal Comstock's reckoning, about 125 miles since late June. "We have crossed and re-crossed from one pike to the other ever since we started. We were at all of the Gaps where the rebs tried to check our advance." The Wisconsin men were more than 40 miles from Chattanooga, the next great prize of war.[13]

By degrees, the first reports from the East and Mississippi filtered through the camps on July 4 when the XX Corps paused for a few days. The Army of the Potomac, under the recently named commander, Gen. George Meade, had beaten back the invasion of Gen. Robert E. Lee and his army near an unimposing Pennsylvania town called Gettysburg. And, after months of siege and maneuver, Gen. U. S. Grant had captured the Mississippi River fortress city of Vicksburg. When the extent of the victories was fully realized within the next several days, some in the Milwaukee Regiment grew restive. Lieutenant Chivas lamented to his aunt a fear "that the Rebellion will be crushed before we get another chance at it. All around us great victories are being gained & we are jealous that our reputations may suffer in contrast. Meade & Grant are already eclipsing 'Old Rosy.'" The officer, who likely echoed the sentiments of many comrades, concluded that the "chances for a fight are very remote under the present aspect of affairs" in the Army of the Cumberland. His power of prediction would be found wanting.

Still another Milwaukee soldier was disturbed by the "comparative standstill in this Department. The campaign may be considered ended," he wrote. Lt. Henry Drake of Company A, likewise, conjectured that movements had terminated for the present. "At least as long as Bragg's whereabouts are unknown. He can't be found by any of our scouts. I presume he is very near the Sea Coast by this time." Most of the men in his company talked of visiting Milwaukee in less than six months, he told his brother, the druggist.[14]

On July 4, Saturday, the nation's birthday, there was time for a brief celebration. A thirty-four-gun salute reverberated through the camps at noon. "The Fourth in this section has not amounted to much, and you would not recognize the day were it not for hearing the boys telling where they were a year ago this time." It seemed so long ago, now, when these men had not yet signed their names to the enlistment roll; it felt like a lifetime past, that summer of 1862. They had seen much as soldiers in that twelvemonth, and lost much. Their eyes had begun to take on the darker aspect of veterans.[15]

Despite the Independence Day event, eatables were "scarce," the men issued only half and quarter rations because of the growing length of supply lines. There was "not a potato, cabbage, beet, pea, bean, berry of any kind," caviled Corporal Comstock, or "pig, sheep or veal, within a mile of the place or of our picket lines." General Rosecrans had issued strict orders against foraging, but the hungry soldiers disregarded that proscription with impunity.[16]

Some of the men likely fired their Enfield rifle-muskets in celebration of the day, perhaps along with some careless horseplay. One man, Kenrick Day, from Oak Creek south of Milwaukee, who had enlisted with his brother, Edward, accidentally shot himself in the arm; the .58-caliber minié ball gouged the flesh between the wrist and elbow, and broke the large bone. But Day recovered in time; he would serve with the regiment until its final muster two years later.[17]

More seriously, the day was marred when a soldier in the 88th Illinois, one of the four regiments in the brigade, tried to commit suicide by the gruesome means of cutting his throat. "There is no reason for the act," a Milwaukee man said, "but it is thought it arose from mental depression, consequent to the fatigue and hardships of the last few days." The Illinois man, never identified, was said to have recovered, but his act had likely troubled several soldiers, including Date Worth, who wrote of it.[18]

Yet, there was much to cheer Lieutenant Chivas, as his closest companion, diminutive Capt. Fred Root, returned to take command of Company I. He had been gone for two months, nursing some camp ailment, likely caused by bad water or the poor sanitary conditions. He is "looking and feeling better than he did when he went away from us." The two had shared a pew with John Mitchell at St. James Episcopal Church on Spring Street before the war; Root, in fact, had taught Sunday school for Reverend Ingraham's congregation. "I have missed his society very much. He looked hearty and resumed army life like an old soldier." Chivas took great pleasure in Root's "very interesting account of Milwaukee, Milwaukeeans & other changes which have taken place during our absence." Chivas had not been back home since he left the city almost a year before. The six-foot Scot immigrant, his cousin, the short Mitchell, and the five-foot-five inch Root were a trio who had developed warm friendships in Milwaukee before the war; now they shared campfires, sparse rations, arduous marches, and battle, which brought them even closer. Chivas, his tongue thick with the brogue of his native land, often spoke candidly about his hope for a "nat little wound," a small badge of honor; he wanted nothing serious or debilitating, of course, merely a bit of blooding.

Now, Mitchell, his eyes strained and troublesome, had been accorded another staff assignment as a topographical engineer in a different corps. The friends met only occasionally, and at midmonth, Chivas would write to Mrs. Mitchell that her son was in "very good health & says his eyes are better than they have been for a long time."

Lieutenant Mitchell would be sent to Chattanooga when General Bragg evacuated the town; he would remain there while Chivas and Root shared more harrowing experiences in the weeks ahead.[19]

Root brought a new four-button blue fatigue coat for his friend. Chivas had begun the campaign from Murfreesboro with only a rubber blanket and extra shirt—"positively all of the baggage I got," he wrote. "Scarcely any of our officers have had a change of clothing since we left." But the new coat "together with a paper collar & a little blacking on my government shoes make me look quite stylish," he mused to his aunt.[20]

The next several days were easy on the men. Although they were issued only half rations since supply trains could not cross the wrecked bridges of the Elk River, the men fanned into the countryside to forage despite General Rosecrans's proscription. They virtually denuded the area of foodstuffs of all kinds, especially one of the soldiers' favorite delicacies, blackberries. Twenty-seven year-old Corporal Cooley, something of an impromptu baker, produced several delectable pies for his older brother, Homer, and close friend Milt Storey. The trio from western Wisconsin maintained a tight mess and shared such simple soldier pleasures as well as hardships and headache.[21]

When the Milwaukee Regiment departed from Tullahoma, 2nd Lt. Henry Drake had remained behind as did many others. He had been felled with the fevers; the typhus that had seized him in Nashville months past also flared anew, compounded by diarrhea. At one point he was unable to sit up for seven straight days, and told his brother that he was determined to resign; but he feared assignment to the Invalid Corps. "I am confident that I cannot stand the service, in fact I never have been well since my first attack of Typhoid Fever," he wrote. The twenty-two-year-old Milwaukee druggist was unwell when he left the Murfreesboro camps with his company, and the nearly unremitting rain had taken a toll. "There was over a week that I could not [wear?] a dry thread of clothing on my back." He contracted a severe cold, and Dr. Hasse, the regiment's surgeon, said he had barely escaped an attack of "Billious Fever." Drake was hospitalized, and when he returned to duty July 14, he wrote his brother, "I was looking rather thin and was censured by the Col. [West] for coming up so soon." But his health returned daily, he said, until "I now feel quite strong." But his well-being was not to last.[22]

Also attacked was the tender constitution of the young adjutant, McArthur. His father, the ever attentive judge, used his influence to secure an army pass, and he traveled from Milwaukee to Tullahoma to his son's bedside. Eighteen now, the slender lieutenant was desperately ill with typhoid, that waterborne scourge of soldier camps; permission was granted for a furlough home where complete bed rest and careful treatment by the family doctor might restore his constitution. Father and son left Tullahoma, and two days later, July 17, arrived back in the city. The young man would remain far from his regiment for over two months, missing the coming battle.[23]

In late July and through much of August, many men marked the first anniversary of their enlistments in the 24th Wisconsin. "During that year I have seen much suffering, privation, and want. I hope and trust that ere another year shall roll around[,] peace will reign triumphant and we all [will] be at home once more." It was a wish not to be realized. Cooley was appointed acting corporal August 1.[24]

Lieutenant Drake, undoubtedly dissipated and debilitated, had lain in Cowan Station for two weeks with persistent fevers and intestinal disorders; he located a resident who took him in. It was apparent his days as a soldier were coming to an end. About the time the 24th Wisconsin reached the Tennessee River, Drake was finally beginning to stand alone, and "for the last two days have had my pants on." He could manage to walk across the room only by bracing his legs in something of an inverted "V". "I am as lean as a *government draft mule*," he told his brother. "In fact I never was so thin in my life." He had been diagnosed with typhoid dysentery. Although the fever had been broken the "dysentery still runs," he stressed candidly. Many soldiers called them the "thin dirtys." Lieutenant Drake, his five-foot-seven-inch frame haggard and skin hanging loosely, finally went home to Milwaukee; his official resignation was August 21.[25]

On August 8, the 24th Wisconsin marched to Bridgeport, and camped at the corner of three states—Tennessee, Alabama, and Georgia. The Cooley brothers and Milt Storey went down to the broad water course to swim; the rebs were plainly seen on the island in the river. Corporal Comstock put it that the regiment was "now face to face, for the first time without shooting at each other, with the rebs." In only a few weeks, however, the Milwaukee soldier would be taking deadly aim at a gray antagonist.

The murky Tennessee River, about a quarter of a mile wide, its waters warm and its current swift, lay before them. For the Army of the Cumberland, this watercourse would be akin to the Rappahannock and Rapidan Rivers for the Army of the Potomac—one of the last barriers.

It would be another Rubicon. Again, a few days' respite was ordered. While General Rosecrans' three corps were separated, there was no apparent urgency in reuniting the Army of the Cumberland. The bridge from the river's north bank to the midstream island had been destroyed. "They have burnt a splendid bridge so that we cannot cross to get to them." The span featured nine large stone abutments each 200 feet apart, Comstock wrote. Only a few days later, the twenty-year-old printer was demoted to private. He made no note of this in letters to his parents, but he may have been punished for consorting or bartering goods with the enemy on the other side of the Tennessee.

"It is laughable to go down to the river and see the fun, the rebs in swimming on one side and the *'Yanks'* on the other." One 24th Wisconsin soldier swam halfway across the wide watercourse. A reb on the island pointed a musket at him, ordering him ashore. The Milwaukee man returned that night under a flag of truce. Corporal Comstock told his parents that the "boys lounge around the river talking to the rebs and it hardly looks like hostile armies so close." Occasionally, there were "sharp" exchanges, and at other times attempts were made to barter. Lt. George Allanson of Company B tried to coax one gray soldier to come over to the north bank for some coffee and supper. The reb replied that he had something better—herb tea. But the tall news dealer with the rheumatic legs soon got himself into a real fix.[26]

In the episode recalled over two decades later, Allanson ran into difficulty during a swim in the Tennessee and nearly lost his life. As another Milwaukee soldier stroked through the warm waters he heard "a panting, puffing sound" behind him; he discovered the twenty-three-year-old officer struggling to remain afloat. "If you do not catch hold of me, George, I will get you back to shore." But the moment the rescuer swam close, the panicked officer, who was much taller than his would-be savior, grabbed and held on to his enlisted comrade. The more experienced swimmer pretended to be pulled under, and Allanson released his grip.

"Now keep your hands off of me; if you catch hold of me again I will hit you right in the face. If you catch hold of me we shall both be drowned."

The floundering lieutenant swore he would not, and his comrade swam over, grabbed him by his fair curly hair and stroked toward shore with one hand. "It was hard work and we both got very tired." Within fifteen or twenty rods from the south bank, he shouted for someone to come out and help tow in the officer. "Well, both of us were as near

George Allanson.
Nearly drowned in the Tennessee
River. COURTESY OF THE MILWAUKEE COUNTY
HISTORICAL SOCIETY.

dead as alive. Allanson looked more like a drowned rat than anything else." After resting, the sodden comrades returned to camp.

The man who recollected the adventure, though unidentified, was Harry Rogers, at twenty-two the older of the Company B brothers; he served as orderly sergeant in the summer of 1863. He long afterward mused about the strange twist of fate that saving Allanson's life produced. "Don't you see that if I had allowed him to drown I would have got a commission?" Ironically, Sergeant Rogers would be accorded a 2nd lieutenant's bars that fall—a promotion he was unable to accept. "I never regretted having saved so good a man as . . . Allanson from a watery grave," Rogers proclaimed to his veteran friends three decades later.[27]

Brig. Gen. William Lytle, the renowned poet and brigade commander, inspected his soldiers at midmonth as they camped on the north bank of the Tennessee River. "The regt. never looked better than it does now," one soldier said. The 24th Wisconsin numbered perhaps 350, about one-third of the size it counted the summer before. The general "highly complimented" the regiment. Only weeks later, during a dress parade, the regiment again exhibited its prowess for the gentle Ohio general. "Every man keeping the step with the music as only old troops can," was how Comstock described it. The 24th Wisconsin, he said, was "hard to beat in the manual. When three hundred hands clasp as many muskets and only one sound arises[,] it's doing pretty well. Every move is like clock work." Such maneuvers and more would soon be sorely needed.

That night, as Friday passed to Saturday in the darkness of August 14, the rebs fired a railroad bridge leading from the island to the south bank of the Tennessee. It was a spectacle recorded by many Wisconsin soldiers. "There was considerable excitement," the twenty-year-old printer, Comstock, wrote. "There was no moon and the fire shone very bright, lighting up everything in the space of a mile." The rebs had apparently removed all of the iron work, and covered the wood with tar and pitch. "We could look straight across from our camp through an opening in the woods and see the whole thing." The sight was enjoyed "hugely." Cooley said: "It was a grand sight. . . . Our boys threw some shells into them while the bridge was burning."[28]

Amandus Silsby, the Company B private who had been finally paroled by his rebel captors some weeks before, was equally disposed to describe the bridge burning. In a letter to his abolitionist father he wrote: "Being previously tarred, it blazed up almost as soon as they set a match to it. The whole landscape brightened up, as if 'lit' by gas lights. Two of our batteries began to throw shells at the rebs. It looked splendid in the night time." Here was a diversion from concern about the impending clash of armies. "Finally came a tremendous crash & and all was over," the preacher's son told his father. Tom Chapman, a Company K man, told his mother: "We hold one side of the river and the rebs the other. We talk acrost evry day. They burned a bridge afew [*sic*] days ago and we shelled them but they did not leave."[29]

The almost idyllic days on the Tennessee River near Bridgeport, Alabama, were coming to an end. One evening, the straight and kindly colonel of the Milwaukee Regiment, "Dore" West, and several other officers regaled the men with some gentle harmonies. "They sang well and some of the songs were new," Private Cooley noted. Among the newer tunes was a particularly poignant one, "When This Cruel War is Over." Here was a wish shared by every man. Some cleaned their Enfield rifle-muskets, making certain everything was in working order. Although no overt orders were yet given, there was a growing sense among the men that another deadly dance was about to begin. "You talk of Uncle Sammy's *chickies* coming home next winter to spend Christmas & New Years," Comstock told his sister. "Don't place any dependence on that proposition. '*We'ens* don't intend to come home till we scatter the rebs *hither & yon.*" He concluded it would take the better part of two years to finish the job. The war had become a "job," sure enough, and most of the soldiers were prepared to finish it no matter the cost. When they first volunteered, many would have accepted a peace "at any price," he said; "but we can't see the point now."

Contact with the rebs across the river became far less frequent, enabling the engineers to lay temporary bridges across the Tennessee. Knapsacks and camp kettles were loaded on wagons and sent north in preparation for the new campaign.[30]

"ROSECRANS' ARMY MOVING FORWARD" proclaimed a headline to Milwaukee as the heat of summer sent its final sweaty salvos across the city. General Sheridan's division was moved from Cowan, Tennessee, the news columns proclaimed. Old Rosey was implementing another of his daring plans, sending his three corps like broad rivers along separate paths—the northern, the XXI, commanded by Maj. Gen. Thomas Crittenden, pushing due east toward Chattanooga; the middle, the XIV, led by stolid Maj. Gen. George Thomas, moving through the Cumberland Mountains and its attendant chains into northern Georgia; and the XX Corps, that of well-fed Gen. Alexander McCook, pushing across the Tennessee River in Alabama, snaking through the mountainous terrain to emerge at Alpine, Georgia.[31]

General Sheridan led his division forward with the XX Corps on the second day of the new month, Wednesday; the Milwaukee Regiment finally thumped across the broad Tennessee River on an undulating pontoon bridge. For the next several days, the march was continuous, each day a "hard tramp." Many roads wound "around the sides of a [*sic*] mountains," George Cooley said. His older brother, Homer, was sick and unable to keep up with the grueling march; he straggled along with many others, arriving at camp four hours after the regiment. Thigh and calf muscles strained at the almost steady upward grades. Then Cooley himself became sick in the heat and clouds of dust; a Company A comrade carried his Enfield. The men grew more weary with each footfall; one mile piled atop another until more than a score miles were marched that day.

Captain Howard Greene was having a difficult time of it. As had occurred the year before, it was his feet that caused the problem. During the hard marching of the past several weeks he had developed a painful abscess on his foot. Amandus Silsby, too, was hobbling from a "very sore boil on the instep" of his right foot. There may have been scores more limping.[32]

When the 24th Wisconsin stopped September 10 camp rumors were rife, one bit of information relating that Maj. Gen. Ambrose Burnside's army had captured Knoxville in eastern Tennessee. "Don't know whether to believe it or not," Cooley commented of this and other camp chatter. As to their own disposition, he was uncertain. "Where we are going is a matter of doubt and speculation." They would soon learn when General Crittenden poured over the Tennessee and pushed his XXI Corps east along the rail line from Nashville. The dour General Bragg had abandoned Chattanooga. Another of Old Rosey's grand strategic triumphs was at hand, and a splendid prize of the war won. First Nashville, then Tullahoma, and now Chattanooga were in Federal hands.[33]

For those who survived the impending battle of Chickamauga little more than a week later, it was one of the most momentous events of their lives. Even those who did not speak of it afterward probably recalled in some manner those harrowing and gory September days. Perhaps when sleep remained unattainable, the thunder of the guns reverberated through their minds; the tumult and blood of battle roiled through memory. "It seemed to me like a dream that I was permitted to stand on that same field, where . . . I listened to the roar of battle, the like of which was never exceeded on God's green earth, and the demoniac yells of an exultant foe," orated Ed Parsons more than three decades after that sanguine Sunday; "surely it was an experience of a life-time." Captain Root would reflect afterward: "We have fought one of the hardest battles of the war."[34]

For some, the titanic struggle on the banks of the Chickamauga Creek, over the dusty roadways and lanes, into the heavy timber wreathed in smoke, over the patches of farm lots scattered east of the Cumberland Mountains in northern Georgia, lasted three or four days. For most, particularly men of the XX Corps, the battle spanned only September 19 and 20. For the Milwaukee Regiment only that final day, a holy Sabbath, proved devastating. A writer of the time put it simply: It was "another dash at the game of *death*."[35]

The three corps of Rosey's army, "disjointed and unconcentrated" for so long, as General Sheridan later wrote, began to coalesce east of the precipitous mountain chain. For four days, Sheridan's division struggled up steep grades, artillery and wagons being dragged by hand, passing over the precipitous Lookout Mountain, then down its slopes into a broad valley that bore the nautical name of McLemore's Cove. The final day had been particularly grueling—without water, twenty miles of strain, sweat, and "insufferable" dust.

Harry Rogers (post-war).
"I'll be hit, sure." COURTESY OF THE
MILWAUKEE COUNTY HISTORICAL SOCIETY.

"As soon as we entered the cove," wrote an Illinois soldier in General Lytle's brigade, "the proximity of the enemy was evident and the troops were thrown into line of battle." Sleeping under arms that night, General Sheridan roused his division before daylight the next morning, and moved east, deeper into the valley. Just before dark, expecting to camp, the men built huge fires of railroad ties and fences for warmth and light; but then assembly was sounded and another forward movement begun. Exhausted, many of the men lay down on the roadside to sleep, and officers on horseback were in danger of falling from their mounts. But, lighted by the huge fires in an eerie tableau, the blue columns tramped wearily onward until three that Saturday morning, when they finally collapsed in camp for three hours. When they awoke, it was clear General Rosecrans had gathered his army, and as the morning advanced "a muttering sound as of distant thunder" rumbled ominously to the northeast; "every ear was turned, listening for it again," an Illinois soldier recalled. Before long, the ominous sound was repeated, beginning to roll down toward them from the northeast.[36]

The brutal march of the past several days had exacerbated the raw right foot of the sad-eyed Quaker, Captain Greene. One night during that tramp he and Sgt. Harry Rogers, now an acting lieutenant, had conversed, and the subject of the latter's premonition arose once again.

While recovering from illness early in the year, after Stones River, it had come to the twenty-two-year-old Rogers that he would be wounded in the next battle. "I never thought I would be killed," he recalled many years later, only wounded. When he first told his friend of the idea, Greene had laughed. But for the next eight months the troubling thought had stuck, and now a battle loomed. "Harry, how do you feel about that, now?" Rogers recalled Greene asking him. "Just the same. I'll be hit, sure, but you needn't worry about my staying with the boys. I'll be right along with them as long as I can stand up."

Captain Greene, however, had troubles of his own. His feet were rubbed so raw he could scarcely walk any longer. He had had similar difficulties on the march to Stones River, and the foot never had been right since. Rogers and others urged him to quit the company and take an ambulance. Finally, the kindly brigade commander, General Lytle, hearing of the captain's plight and his refusal to quit the march, directed that Greene should join his staff; a horse was provided.[37]

On that Saturday morning, September 19, while the XX Corps approached the meandering Chickamauga Creek, elements of General Bragg's army began the attack upon the corps of General Thomas several miles to the northeast. As the morning progressed the rumble of battle grew to a roar, as if a great menacing wave of sound was gathering its strength to plunge southwest. More of Bragg's divisions were piling in upon Thomas, pushing them backward through the timbered landscape and over the open farm lots between. As the morning and early afternoon progressed, two-thirds of McCook's corps was ordered to the northeast, into the swirling maelstrom of battle. Sheridan's division now stood alone near the Lee & Gordon's Mill—the far right of the entire Federal line. They had been in a similar situation before, at Stones River, and paid a heavy price for the dubious honor. Soon, two of Sheridan's brigades were sent into the voracious maw. The men of Wisconsin listened to the crescendo of "murderous shells" and mounting musketry; gray smoke wreathed the woods about a mile distant. "Glancing at the sun my very heart sank to see it still an hour and a-half high," worried an Illinois soldier. "The left [of the army] had already absorbed the centre, and the centre and right had absorbed every brigade in the army, except one holding a vital point," he wrote in retrospect. Lytle's brigade stood alone.

Then, as fall daylight began to fade around six that Saturday, battle began to ebb, here and there only a few straggling musket shots and thuds of artillery fire erupting before darkness. Although there was a brief flare-up after dark, the exhausted antagonists sank largely where they were. "The moon, which in a few nights had grown from the slenderest of silver sickles into a graceful, golden canoe, was far from its nightly voyage, shining faintly on two weary armies, bent on destroying each other, and waiting only for the line and gold of sunrise to renew the struggle." Here was a poetic hiatus of the lull in the battle, written by an Illinois soldier many years later.[38]

Sunday, the Sabbath, began to dawn. "Old Rosey," strict Catholic that he was, had long vowed never to do battle on the Lord's day. This day, however, he would have no choice. It was clear that the rebel attack would be renewed. As feared, leading elements of the corps of Maj. Gen. James Longstreet, Lee's "Old War Horse," were on the field, having entrained from Virginia; the remainder of the gray soldiers from the East would be rushed forward soon. General Sheridan remembered: "We were in a bad strait unquestionably."[39]

As a dense shroud of fog welcomed the morning light and obscured the battlefield, the right extreme of the Federal line was rearranged. This continual shuffle of regiments and brigades to the north was to be remembered by many. All of Sheridan's brigades were repositioned more tightly with the rest of the army, first near a farmhouse (the Widow Glenn place that had served as the commanding general's headquarters), then farther to the east and north. "Gradually the fog lifted and a warm and beautiful day greeted us; a day for praising and serving God, rather than destroying man," evoked an Illinois soldier. Around 9:30 that morning, the expected enemy assault began, again to the north against General Thomas's corps. The crescendo of thundering artillery and peppering musketry permeated the morning air. "Between nine and ten o'clock, the thickening sounds began to tell that the day's work was opening." Soldiers gripped rifle-muskets more tightly, hearts likely thundering in their chests above the growing din. The resolve to fight for the glorious Union was about to be tested anew.

General Lytle, the narrow-shouldered, bearded Ohioan and famed poet, sat his big sorrel horse "calm and dignified . . . to all appearance unmoved by the circumstances, though comprehending the gravity of the situation." Near at hand, also mounted, sat Captain Greene. Sheridan's men, in battle array, were positioned in the timber east of the Dry Valley Road. Now the battle heated to white intensity just before them. In the thickening billows of battle smoke, the three brigades of Sheridan's division were ordered farther north toward the expanding vortex of battle, and as they marched in column along the road, hordes of panicked blue soldiers—the remnants of the division of Brig. Gen. Jefferson C. Davis, which has been bludgeoned by Longstreet's men—churned into their ranks. The order to form line of battle was given almost instinctively.

Lytle's regiments were ordered forward to support the two other brigades. A half mile was covered at the double-quick, "amid a pall of dust that almost smothers the men," said one Milwaukee soldier who saw it. Soon they were in line at the foot of the hill. General Lytle, his tall mount prancing, rode before the ranks. "Stand firm, boys, stand like iron; never let the name of the 'Old First [Brigade]' be disgraced." So remembered the Milwaukee man of those pregnant moments. His words would soon be read by many in the city who scoured the news columns for information about their sons and husbands.[40]

"It seemed as though everyone was watching the 24th," Comstock told his father. Several generals, Sheridan, McCook, and Rosecrans himself, stood behind the regiment and "cheered us to 'Go it Badger boys' 'Go in Wisconsin' 'Give it too [*sic*] them 24th.'"[41]

"By company, into line," shouted General Lytle above the growing din, likely rising in his stirrups. Veterans that they were, the men executed the maneuver as if on parade, as they had hundreds of times before over the past thirteen months. In battle array, they strode east to the brow of a hill. The sight on the field was "appalling" to more than one man: "We were in an old field where the ground was covered with dry grass and old logs which the bursting shells had set on fire. A thick cloud of smoke had risen about as high as our heads and seemed hanging like a funeral pall in the air," wrote a soldier in the brigade. Not seventy-five yards away were the gray ranks of Longstreet, crouched and kneeling behind a low rail fence. "We set to work with a will, while the ranks of the enemy belched forth a stream of fire, and a battery of artillery on the right flank tore the ground with grape and shell." It was a vivid recollection from an Illinois soldier. Then, the nearly solid lines of gray attackers, shooting, wailing, grimacing, slammed into the men of Wisconsin, Illinois, and Michigan.[42]

The Milwaukee Regiment was in the forward brigade line, the 36th Illinois on its left and the 21st Michigan on its right. "We started off in a column of platoons, and went through the dust at double quick, for upwards of a mile," Lieutenant Chivas wrote of the moments before. "We then formed in line and advanced up a small hill with a loud cheer, the retreating columns of our men rushing through us." Reaching the hilltop, the Milwaukee men saw the enemy a few feet away advancing up the slope; "we drove their first line and maintained our position on the top, keeping up a steady and destructive fire on the enemy."[43]

Those harrowing minutes telescoped as the men of Wisconsin steeled themselves. The memories were vivid, days and even decades later. "Again the hoarse notes of the deep mouthed cannon, the roll of musketry, and the clangor of steel have swelled the tide of battle, and again almost the hundredth time, hundreds of Columbia's sons have fallen beneath the shock." So wrote one Milwaukee soldier. Lt. Charley Rogers, Harry's younger brother, put it more prosaically for his mother: "It was, I think, one of the most terrible battles that had been fought."[44]

Somewhere in that initial swirl of action the first Wisconsin man was struck down. "Poor Silas [Parsons], one of the bravest of the brave and much esteemed by the whole company and by all who knew him," his comrade, Bill Sherman, said. "Scarcely two musket lengths from the rebels, he was dealing out to them pills they did not much admire, when he received a shot square through the neck and fell without a word." As he lay there, the young man from Western Wisconsin stretched his hands toward his comrades, saying, "Come and take me away." Two soldiers carried Parsons to the rear of the Company A line, propped his head on a blanket, and set a canteen near his hands. "He appeared to be in no pain and bled but very little; was very calm and his right hand was fingering the gravel where he lay." Parsons's life was ebbing. "Seeing he was done for," Sherman asked him if he had any words. "No my actions will tell all," the dying soldier said.[45]

All was in confusion and chaos: The thunderous roar of artillery and musketry, the guttural shouts and final earthly screams of men, the acrid powder smoke seizing nostrils—all was a sensory jumble. Captain Parsons recalled hearing Colonel West shout the order for Company K to break into platoons. "Then away we go double quick into the jaws of death," Parsons wrote several days later, using present tense to heighten the effect, "down the road amidst clouds of dust for a half a mile; then to the right over the fields, but all the troops here have given way & are breaking in confusion through our ranks. Now the order 'Forward into line' & splendidly did the 24th come into line, forward with a yell & form our line just at the crest of a hill & within fifty feet of the enemy's line. Now we open on them & drive their first line but their solid columns are advancing from the Woods across the field. The two regiments on our right have given way. Now the regiment on our left goes, but still stands the gallant 24th."[46]

General William Lytle.
"I am dying, Egypt, dying."
COURTESY OF LANCE J. HERDEGEN.

When the Wisconsin soldiers first strode to the top of the rise, Jim Heth, the older of the Milwaukee confectioner's sons, and his "old *bum* comrade," Hank Passmore, were elbow to elbow in the Company B formation. They saw the rebs with "hats pulled down over their eye," Heth recalled. He and Passmore were probably acquainted from those now distant days before the war. The latter was a robust soldier, and on a hot day's march, "with his short bosom thrown open and the sweat pouring off from him, yelling to the boys that were tired out, 'brace up! Only two miles to camp!'" Always ready with a quip, Hank, seeing the blocks of gray regiments pressing up the hill toward them, shouted: "Get ready, Jim, and lay low for the sons of b———s!" Heth would remember that little episode for the rest of his life.[47]

"Gen. Lytle rode alone in front of the line, waving his hat and sword and cheering the men on. Oh! It was a glorious sight to see that line of men charge up the hill with a will and scatter the first line of rebels to the four winds," Company A's Bill Sherman described for his parents. "As we came up the hill[,] line after line of enemy could be seen advancing, yet the [24th] faltered not! There she stood, firm as a rock, and delivered, at short range, volley after volley into the ranks of the advancing foe. Still they came. The second line was scattered, and yet another made its appearance on our front, while others were moving on our flanks," he said. "A bursting shell tore our flag, already riddled with bullets from the staff but it was instantly picked up again. One rebel had the audacity to grasp at it, but his stooping position only made it easier for him to fall, for a bullet from the musket of the color guard, sent him to eternity, before he was aware of its presence." The color-bearer was forty-three-year-old John Borth, a laborer who was remembered as having a "sallow" complexion.[48]

The Cincinnati-born Lytle "bravely fronted his brigade." No thought of his popular poetry now, those immortal words, "I am dying, Egypt, dying" far from his lips. Captain Greene, at the general's side, said he "did not see a man flinch from his posts [sic]." The general cantered behind the ranks of the Milwaukee Regiment, shouting: "Brave, brave, brave boys." Lieutenant Chivas also remembered those words, "Brave Boys, Brave Boys, encouraging the men along the whole line." Then the slender brigade commander was struck by lead, perhaps shrapnel or a piece of buckshot, but he maintained his saddle and continued to lead the brigade, "cheering on the men right gallantly," Captain Greene said.[49]

When he described these turbulent minutes a week later, Dan Davis, the soldier correspondent behind the nom de plume "Nimrod," like Parsons, shifted verbs into the present tense to provide immediacy for Milwaukee readers. "One general volley assured them of our presence, which they had seemingly anticipated by the direction of our fire. Men begin to fall on every side and soon all firing was blended in one general roar. Thick and fast came bullets, shot and shell. Well were they returned, volley for volley and ball for ball—nobly did the brave fellows of the West stand to their work." The rebels massed their columns, ranks packed tightly. "Steadily their gray masses press on; as steadily death does his work. The conflict waxes fiercer. Sand, gravel, choking dust, balls and shells render objects almost indistinguishable. Almost half the men on our part of the line are killed or wounded, and still they are not swerved. The noble Lytle, surveying the scene, is said to have exclaimed, 'Brave boys. How long shall this continue?'" Yet another soldier recalled that the bearded general uttered the words, "Brave Wisconsin boys, I am proud of you!"[50]

His sword drawn, thirty-six-year-old General Lytle prepared to give his second line the order to charge when a bullet pierced his head. "He had just turned to give me an order when the ball struck him in the mouth, passing through his head and coming out near his eye." Howard

Greene provided gruesome detail for his sweetheart, Louise. The general had sustained a ghastly wound, and he fell head first to the ground. The Wisconsin captain quickly flew from his stirrups and caught the general "by the head and shoulders as he fell, his blood spurting all over me." Lytle's big sorrel galloped to the rear while Greene's mount, nicked by a bullet, also thundered away. The general's long, dark hair and chest-length beard were matted with blood. Although Captain Greene never wrote of it, one story circulated that the dying general begged that he be abandoned. "Not until the enemy had almost closed around him, did the aide obey his desire, and then the general was apparently dead." Two other brigade orderlies dismounted, and they tried to move the general to the rear. "We had gone but a few yards when one of them was killed and the other left," Greene said.

Captain Greene remained with his general as long as he could. Finally, Lytle "rolled his eyes, gave me a death grip around my legs, and his spirit passed from this world to a brighter and better one above." It is a sad and tragic end to so talented and revered a man. The 24th Wisconsin had lost its second brigade commander in as many battles. "The rebs by this time were on top of the hill a few yards to our rear and firing right down on us. I saw I could do the General no more good, so left and hobbled off the field." After the battle, when Greene's abscessed foot forced him to return home, he would travel to Cincinnati to visit Lytle's family, testifying to his gallantry and manliness, and describing those final few moments of the famed poet's life.[51]

Ironically, there was another story of Lytle's last moments written by the commander of the 21st Michigan, Col. William B. McCreery, who was leading his regiment in retreat. He said he happened upon the body of the dying Lytle. The general waved him to pass on, but McCreery called some of his men to assist him. Four men carried Lytle's body, but in only a few paces, muskets balls whistled past their heads, then a shell burst killed one of the Michigan soldiers. Another man lost a leg, and the captain was hit in the shoulder. He was taken prisoner.[52]

The Wisconsin soldier who carried Lytle's body, Ed Glenn, was struck in the leg. A railroad telegraph operator from Western Wisconsin whom the boys called "Sandy," he had enlisted at age eighteen in Captain Philbrook's company. "No braver boy went into that bloody fight of Sunday," his lieutenant, Tom Keith, attested. "When we commenced falling back borne down by swarms of the cursed rebels, 'Sandy' was struck by a bullet in the wrist of the right hand and as he was retreating he heard Colonel McCreery . . . calling for assistance to help him carry the body of General Lytle." Then the Michigan officer was struck down, and a bullet creased Glenn's side. The blue-eyed Wisconsin soldier "now found that if he staid [*sic*] longer he would be taken prisoner and he made an effort to escape, but was shot through the right leg below the knee shattering and tearing the bone all to pieces," Lieutenant Keith wrote to the Wisconsin soldier's parents some days later. Glenn, a New Yorker by birth, whose light complexion and russet hair bespoke of Scottish forebears, was actually wounded several times. In addition to the flesh wound in his left leg, another ball broke the bones of his right limb; and another gouged the young man's right wrist, severing the cords.[53]

Within a few yards of the Milwaukee Regiment, a rebel color-bearer stretched his hand as if to grasp the cannon of an Indiana battery that was "dealing destruction upon them," wrote "Nimrod" in almost breathless present tense. "No living thing can escape death on that ridge three minutes longer, and the order is given to retreat, when our line, single and unsupported [is] swept to the rear. Some stubbornly resist, but the murderous cross-fire which first caused the line to fall back soon caused the most determined to retire." Davis would in time be promoted to principal musician. "The men who knew the 'unwritten music' of Stone river, Perryville, &c., do not falter now; nearly every man unhurt is in his place," he wrote.[54]

"We kept the enemy in our front at bay, but the Regiments, and in fact the whole Division on our left [Gen. Thomas Wood's division of the XXI Corps] had given way," Lieutenant Chivas told his aunt, "and though the enemy had thrown themselves round our left flank and lapped it several hundred feet, still our men never thought of retiring, but faced round and directed their fire upon the foe advancing on our flank. The rebels were positively so close to us all this time that we could almost see the white of their eyes; they crawled up stealthily behind logs, trees and bushes. There was one rascal who had got a nice position behind a large tree only a few feet in front of our line, who had a miserable dirty yellow flag, with a cross on it, which he kept waving in our very faces." Meanwhile, Sergeant Borth and other men of the color guard stepped forward of the firing ranks, waving the standard, steeling the resolve and determination of the men.[55]

At that moment, the 36th Illinois gave way on the right, exposing the 24th's flank to the advancing enemy. Maj. Carl Von Baumbach, who would within minutes take command of the regiment, sent the acting adjutant, Tom Balding, to pull the left companies—Comstock identified them as Companies B, G, and K—backward into a position perpendicular to the regiment's line to deliver an enfilade into the enemy on that end of the line.[56]

"Now the regiments on our right & left are gone & the enemy are on both our flanks pouring in a terrible cross fire. Grape[,] Canister & Shells are cutting the branches & whizzing over[,] around & through us," Company K's Captain Parsons, the academically trained bookkeeper, recalled. "I looked around & saw a Regiment that had rallied a short distance on our rear coming up. 'Stand firm men,' I shouted, 'help is coming.'" Even though those moments were fleeting, it was nearly impossible to remain in place. "Now comes the order, 'About face.' We cannot hold the ground alone against such odds. Steady now, men, we will rally on the other side [of] this ravine." It was about noon.[57]

It was probably at this point that Gene Comstock, furiously loading and firing his Enfield into the "serried ranks of Longstreet" who lapped at the regiment's left side, shot at the Rebel soldier. Hearing the order to retreat, the Company B private, who would soon regain his two stripes, said that the last shot he fired was "at a reb not two rods from us." At a range of only five and a half yards, it was nearly impossible to miss. The ounce of deadly lead bit into the charging gray soldier and he slumped to the ground. That was the last Comstock saw before he turned on his heels and, with long strides, pulled free of the enemy attackers.[58]

As the determined enemy continued to lash at the Milwaukee Regiment's flanks, the order was given to "retire." Only a few of the Wisconsin soldiers used the onerous word "retreat." The 24th was the last regiment in that part of the field to step backward, most said. Color Sergeant Borth shook the regiment's flag at the advancing enemy, and more bullets shredded the stars, stripes, and battle legends. A shell then carried the silk fabric from the flagpole. But Borth grabbed the banner. General Sheridan later complimented the Port Washington soldier for his bravery. He would earn a lieutenant's straps the following year for gallant service.[59]

One of the "sturdy and patriot German boys" from Port Washington, Wisconsin, Charles Klein, who had turned twenty-seven in July, heard a bullet whistle past his head. He turned to the side to see his captain, Gus Goldsmith, who was steadying Company H for the rearward movement when the heavy lead ball struck him. The officer who had changed his name from Goltschmidt to sound American thudded to the ground at Klein's feet. Somehow in the deadly melee, Capt. Silas Miller, who assumed brigade command at the death of General Lytle, had the general's sorrel horse. He gathered up Goldsmith's body, flung it over the saddle, and bore him from the deadly maw. Milwaukee's John Tannatt took command of the Port Washington men.[60]

The Milwaukee soldiers did not so much face about as step backward, pausing alone or in small knots here and there to poke down another minié ball, push a cap on the Enfield nipple, bring the rifle-musket to shoulder, and jerk the trigger toward the thronging gray enemy. Within minutes, all semblance of order in the companies was shredded. Like pebbles under a crashing wave, Badger men scattered before the swarming enemy surge. Bullets and shrapnel sought them out. Jim Harvey, Date Worth's Granville comrade, was felled with a gory wound to the left shoulder. Worth feared it might be fatal.

Harry Rogers knew it would happen. Even before the Milwaukee Regiment was formed in line of battle, either a ball or piece of shrapnel hit him in the fleshy part of the right arm. He did not say a word, but kept to the line. Now, when the rebel hordes enveloped the regiment's flanks, and the retreat was begun, he and his brother, Charley, were separated. Harry was caught in a leaden maelstrom. When the brothers met again, Harry, the gray-eyed bookkeeper, held up his left hand, saying; "Charley look at that." The two middle fingers had been shot away. Not minutes later, before the regiment had rallied, the twenty-two-year old acting lieutenant was hit by buckshot in the same hand, severing the cords of his little finger. Then, he received a shot through the right wrist, the ball passing through the flesh but not breaking any bone. It seemed his five-foot-ten-inch frame was a target. Almost the next minute, another bullet "plowed through the top of his head gear, cutting off the hair of his head along it[s] track," the younger Rogers said. Still more lead chewed his right cheek to bone, and another shot hit his Enfield, glanced off, and bit into his lip. Still more reminders of "Confederate civilities" whizzed past him, but he paid no heed. Yet, with his "robust constitution," his brother assured their mother the following day, he could not fail to recover in two or three weeks. It would not be, however.[61]

Elsewhere, the auburn-haired Scot, Lt. Bob Chivas, may have smiled in his pain. He had finally received that "nat little wound" he had long craved; it was not serious—a "slight flesh wound in the leg," Captain Greene said. It was nearly miraculous that his six-and-a-half-foot frame had not attracted more lead. The determined soldier pressed on alongside his little friend, Capt. Fred Root, whom, he told his pastor, seemed to expose himself again with impunity that day.[62]

Ragged groups of Milwaukee and Wisconsin men knotted together, making a "desperate stand," it was reported. Col. "Dore" West "to rally the men, seized the flag staff"—the colors were missing, carried away by Sergeant Borth. The slender commander "rapped upon the staff with his sabre and rallied two or three companies for a moment; but seeing they would be 'gobbled up' by the rebel forces" on the flanks who were beginning to swing artillery pieces toward them, "he gave orders to his men to scatter as much as possible and 'rally on the reserve.'"

Within a few moments, no more, Colonel West found himself between the charging rebels and his own regiment. Then an artillery shell burst almost directly beneath him and his body was hurled headlong. When he attempted to regain his feet, he discovered shrapnel had struck his left hip; his bleeding leg was paralyzed. In minutes, the advancing gray enemy overtook him.

"He is a brave, brave man," one Milwaukee soldier wrote of his colonel. Like several others, the writer, unidentified, drafted a letter home the following day, assuring his family that he had escaped unscathed—at least physically. "I am all sound yet, but a little worse for wear." The battle of Chickamauga had eclipsed the awful fight at Stones River, which had impressed so many with its deadliness.[63]

"Everything was in confusion[;] I never saw such an awful sight in my life, men flying in all directions—horses without riders flying wildly over the field—officers and men urging others to halt and rally," twenty-year-old Lt. Charley Rogers wrote a day later. "Our regiment was broken up by others running through them, so that they got broken up considerably."[64]

When they rallied, the rebels were there, too, recalled the bleeding Harry Rogers. "Off to the left, and not far, we saw a cluster of rebels in a fence corner. Two or three of us raised our guns and fired amongst them, but they were there for business and a bullet ground off these two fingers and made another ugly wound in my hand. Then I had to quit." Captain Greene overtook Rogers, coming to his side. "What did I tell you, Cap?" Rogers said, perhaps with a wry smile. Rogers recalled those minutes for his veteran friends thirty years later, his hands and face still bearing the awful marks of that battle. His head spun and his legs grew weak, he said, and "I was very faint and wanted to sit down and rest. But they wouldn't allow me to do so, for that meant certain capture. But for a canteen of water by my side I would have fainted dead away and been gobbled. No, sir, when a man has a premonition I don't laugh at him." There was probably scant exaggeration in the telling.[65]

"It seems that our division was for a time entirely cut off, but General Sheridan soon got his division together & in very good shape," Captain Parsons boasted. Just before dark the Milwaukee Regiment was again ordered forward to support General Thomas's beleaguered remnant. "We marched out three miles to fill up a gap & help Thomas out. We then went back to the foot of the mountain & in a large open field was gathered a disorganized mass of all parts of the army, but every man was ready and willing to stake his place as soon as it was shown him."[66]

"Within two hours after the fight our Division was reformed and reported itself ready for service," wrote Lieutenant Chivas, giving emphasis to those detractors of his regiment's performance of the past December. "Considering that our numbers were reduced nearly one half, that the brigade commander was killed and another wounded [Silas Miller of the 36th Illinois], speaks well for the organization of our division."[67]

Major Von Baumbach, commanding the regiment after Colonel West fell, wrote that the 24th "retreated in some disorder but quickly reformed on a hill some 400 yards to our rear." Obeying orders from the new brigade commander, Colonel Miller, the 24th Wisconsin marched with the remains of the brigade down the Chattanooga and Lafayette Road.[68]

After General McCook's XX Corps and other units were battered and literally swept from the field, the remaining elements of the Army of the Cumberland, the Wisconsin men would soon learn, were pressed by the enemy onslaught that now concentrated against them. In what came to be regarded as one of the finest fighting defenses of the war, the brigades that had not retreated coalesced on the north end of the battlefield after midday. General Thomas brilliantly directed the remnants of his XIV Corps and the reserves led by Maj. Gen. Gordon Granger. Their names along with several others would be etched into the annals of war, and the defensive positions of Horseshoe Ridge and Snodgrass Hill became well-known locations on the maps of military historians. Whereas the stolid Thomas fought, ironically, Generals Rosecrans, McCook, and Crittenden quit the battle and galloped into Chattanooga.

For nearly five hours, the Federal defenders battled the increasing weight of the enemy that concentrated against them. Ultimately, however, the defense could not be sustained, and, as dusk began to shadow the woods and the gray attackers stormed over the breastworks, Thomas ordered a withdrawal. Although many units retreated in good order, others panicked and lost all semblance of cohesion. At nightfall, the battle had ended, and the Army of the Cumberland pulled back toward Chattanooga where, on Monday, defensive positions were established.

The large black type atop the Milwaukee news columns screamed: "GREAT BATTLE FOUGHT." "ROSECRANS BADLY WHIPPED!" "MCCOOK AND CRITTENDEN'S CORPS UTTERLY ROUTED." Once again, shocking stories were telegraphed from Tennessee. The city steeled itself for the casualty lists that would soon follow.[69]

As more information flowed from the East, there was renewed grumbling from some quarters in Milwaukee that the 24th Wisconsin had again failed to acquit itself with distinction. It seemed that the regiment's less than valorous behavior at Stones River had been repeated. Quickly, however, writers sprang to the defense. The Democratic daily also attempted to assure readers of the 24th Wisconsin's valiant conduct. "From the long list of killed and wounded in the 24th, we doubt not that this regiment displayed the utmost firmness and gallantry in the shock of battle." The soldiers, too, Lieutenant Rogers among them, weighed in: "Our old flag was torn from the staff by a shell and is completely riddled. Well may the people of Milwaukee be proud of the 24th; its record stands as clear to-day as any regiment from Wisconsin. Nor until every regiment on their flank had been scattered and were flying to the rear, and until we had been ordered to fall back twice, did a man offer to move, and when they did it was done reluctantly." The 24th Wisconsin was probably the last Federal regiment to quit the field on the right end of the entire Federal line, a point of distinction to which many of the soldiers would long point.[70]

"Our regiment did nobly, not a sneak or coward was to be seen—all did their duty. They received the highest praise from all who witnessed their conduct, full retrieving stigmas that may have been cast upon them by some," Lieutenant Chivas told his aunt the next day. This was certainly a change from the cowardly acts of some officers at Stones River. The Scot's close friend, Fred Root, told his pastor that the "dead, dying and wounded [were] falling like autumn leaves all around Chivas and myself." Yet the comrades "passed through a *storm* of lead, to which Stone River could not be compared."[71]

A Milwaukee physician, William Castleman, who visited the 24th Wisconsin in Chattanooga the following month, seemed to buttress the case of Chivas and others. "Gen. Sheridan said to me that if there ever was a spot on the fame of the [24th], it could not be found now by the finest microscope. Gen. Rosecrans publicly complimented it on the field as 'fighting splendidly.'"[72]

The roll of casualties was lengthy. Over 100 men from the Milwaukee Regiment fell or were taken prisoner that Sunday morning—nearly one-third of the number counted a few days before. Ten were killed, 8 more would die of wounds; of the more than 45 wounded, over half would never return to the ranks, speaking volumes of the desperate fight. Capt. Bill Kennedy, the six-foot, former municipal clerk who led the Irish of Company G, went into the fight with 29 men, and came out with 17. Company A, in which the Cooley brothers and Amandus Silsby fought, sustained the heaviest casualties, losing 19. "I am the only sergeant left with the company," noted Bill Sherman, "and there are only two corporals. Our company now numbers fifteen men for duty." Meanwhile, Capt. Sam Philbrook lost 18 of his Company D railroad men, including poor "Sandy" Glenn. Date Worth's company, H, was fortunate—only 5 wounded, including Corporal Harvey, and less than a half dozen missing.[73]

As he recovered from his small soldier's badge of battle, Lieutenant Chivas attempted to rationalize the overall result of the battle. "The object of the campaign has been fully accomplished," he told his portly uncle, Alexander Mitchell. "The enemy has been baffled and outwitted; he had gained no compensating advantage for the loss of Chattanooga in any way." As to the 24th, the regiment "covered itself in glory," he said. Chivas, who wrote from Chattanooga, also related that he had again met his cousin, John Mitchell, who lamented missing the battle. "I have the satisfaction of thinking that I am one ahead of him," the tall Scot gloated to Mitchell's mother.[74]

A Chicago correspondent wrote that after XX Corps commander General McCook "disappeared from the general history of the battle . . . extricating himself from his demoralized and routed corps, he headed for Chattanooga and [later] disappeared entirely from the field." The while, two of his divisions, those of Gens. Jefferson Davis and Phil Sheridan, "far behind their position, were assailed by immense squadrons of the enemy and fearfully battered." Although each commander had "but a handful left," those remnants "must have done gallant fighting or they would not have come off as well as they did. In fact, wherever Sheridan is, whether isolated or in company, and whether the odds against him are one or many, there is certain to be a fight."[75]

A Milwaukee newsman afterward related that the men of Sheridan's division "must have done gallant fighting or they would not have come off as well as they did." The ungainly little general was winning a wider reputation here in the West.[76]

In a field hospital that was overtaken by the rebel assault, Captain Goldsmith, the stolid Germanic immigrant, lay with numerous wounded comrades for seven days and nights, largely untreated, it was said; there was little care or nourishment. Under a flag of truce six days after the battle, 200 ambulances were sent within the enemy lines to retrieve the wounded, Captain Goldsmith and several other men of the 24th among them. He was sent at first to Chattanooga and then to Nashville for serious treatment. With the news of his brother's wounding, Bernard Goldsmith hurried from Wisconsin, intent upon nursing back his brother's strength. Also at Goldsmith's bedside was Charles Klein, one of the captain's sturdy, immigrant patriot boys. But the long exposure on the battlefield brought fever, and within three days, Goldsmith died. As with many soldier immigrants, he had given his life for his adopted country; "his spirit," a news man wrote three decades later, "went to join the legions of blue in the unknown camp beyond the grave." Bernard Goldsmith prepared the remains, and they were placed in a tin box, its lid sealed with solder. Within weeks, the body was laid near many of the captain's comrades in Forest Home Cemetery on Milwaukee's south side, near "the sound of old Michigan's moan, to sleep peacefully and in grateful remembrance." Many more bodies would follow to that rapidly expanding graveyard. To his pastor, the diminutive captain Fred Root offered an epitaph for Goldsmith: " . . . and so he falls, one more to swell the grand army beneath the sod."[77]

"Sandy" Glenn was also plucked from the battlefield September 26. "The rebels took him prisoner and paroled him there but left him where he fell for six days and seven nights, without dressing his wounds; what little he got to eat or drink was given him by a few humane rebels," Glenn's lieutenant, Tom Keith, told the wounded man's parents. "He asked a rebel captain to give him a drink of water and this is the answer he got from one of the *'Chivalry,'* who are looking for their rights. 'No I will not give you any, you damned Yankee Son of a B——; if I had poison I would put it in some water and give [it to] you.'"

Glenn's leg was sawed off three inches below the knee by a Federal surgeon, probably Dr. Herman Hasse. "I saw him today," Keith wrote October 7, "and he is getting along first rate, has good treatment and is in good spirits." Surgeon Hasse told the lieutenant that Glenn would be sent home in a month or six weeks. "He feels very anxious about how he is to get along in the future, but I assured him that he would be looked after and something done for him for he deserved it if any one of our noble soldiers ever did." One leg gone and his right hand useless, he was discharged after a long convalescence in November 1864 because of his disabling wound. After the war, "Sandy" Glenn, who had seen too much in his eighteen years, would also suffer the loss of his mental stability.[78]

Another wounded soldier who was recovered during the September 26 truce was Joe Lawrence, a man in Captain Root's Company I. He had taken a grievous wound in the thigh, which broke the bone. With blood oozing, pain began to throb after the initial shock of the injury abated. Like Goldsmith and Glenn, he lay untreated for five days and nights; he must have exhausted the contents of his canteen and the scraps of food in his haversack. Yet, after his comrades recovered him and he was taken to the division hospital in Chattanooga, he was "in good spirits, cool," Captain Root said of him. "Brave and manly, bearing his misfortune like a true soldier." The youth prayed to God "that he may soon recover to strike again the traitorous wretches." Brothers Joe and Job Lawrence, one a molder and the other a caulker, boarded together before the war; they had both enlisted in the Merchants Guard. Job, the twenty-two-year old, had deserted in November, but Joe, eighteen, remained faithful to the cause and soldiered on. The badly wounded young man, a spare five feet four inches tall, would never rise from his sickbed to strike the enemy, however; he succumbed December 10.[79]

Harry Rogers also lay abed in the corps hospital. But because his wounds were not considered as severe as the thousands of others, he waited three days before his injuries were even dressed. He was given a sixty-day recuperative furlough, and rode back to Milwaukee, "his arm resting on a pillow" during the lengthy rail trip. The leave was extended for thirty days when a city physician treated him. As he struggled to recuperate, Rogers was offered an officer's commission in the new 36th Wisconsin Infantry, but he had to decline. Given a lieutenant's bars in the Milwaukee Regiment, he was unable to accept and mustered from service in January. Lt. George Allanson, the man he saved from drowning in the Tennessee River, would soon rise to captain of Company B. Twenty-two-year-old Harry would also suffer partial paralysis of one hand along with the "ineffac[e]able brand of a brave soldier on his face." The puckered scars would be a reminder of his incredible ordeal until his death in the next century.[80]

Another man who returned to Milwaukee after the battle was the Quaker captain, Howard Greene, his foot still badly ulcerated. He had written to his intended, his "darling Louise," from Alabama some days before, calming her fears for his safety. "Everything is coming out all right one of these days 'When this cruel war was over,'" he said. It was the captain's first furlough home, and it would be brief. "We are gratified to see him here again," wrote a news man, "for he is one of those noble and faithful young men—brave, earnest and faithful young men—who adds to the good name of our city wherever he carried the American flag." Before returning to the regiment, he would be wedded to the fine, upstanding St. Louis woman.[81]

From Libby Prison in Richmond, Colonel West sent a letter to his brother, Sam, a book and stationery retailer in Milwaukee's central business district, saying he had arrived in the Confederate capital on the night of September 30. "My health is good and I am getting along finely," he said. "Remember me to all. Inform the regiment that I still live." In not many months, the Waukesha colonel would take part in a daring and successful escape from the Richmond prison.[82]

No matter how hard the men of Milwaukee attempted to rationalize their performance, the name Chickamauga became synonymous with another defeat. Nearly all the regiments on the right end of the Federal line were tarred with the brush of failure. The 24th Wisconsin had not covered itself in glory at Stones River. Now in another titanic battle, it had fought well and earned praise from General Sheridan and others, but there were still detractors—still doubt in the minds of the Wisconsin soldiers. Left unsaid was the need, finally, to secure unsullied triumph, to gain some retribution, to settle scores with the gray enemy and bring glory and honor to the Milwaukee Regiment. Wisconsin men likely seethed in anticipation of another battle in which redemption could be gained. They would not long have to wait.

Meanwhile, the young adjutant, Arthur McArthur, had recuperated sufficiently from his bout with typhoid to prepare for his departure from Milwaukee. He had likely read all of the preliminary battle reports in the local press, and it was clear the he must return to the regiment. Donning his frock coat and propping his cap atop that mass of thick, dark curls, he said good-byes to the judge, his father, and brother, and departed the city September 28. After an arduous journey by wagon from Bridgeport, Alabama, to Chattanooga, he arrived the first week of the new month. The eighteen-year-old soldier's brave deed and his rendezvous with legend would soon be at hand.[83]

Chapter 9

Missionary Ridge

◆━ ⚔ ━◆

"On, Wisconsin!"

As he crossed the broad Tennessee River into Chattanooga the first week of October 1863, the youth likely wore a new blue frock coat, lieutenant's straps perched on his narrow shoulders. He had been home in Milwaukee for over two months, trying, with the help of the best medical people his father, the judge, could provide, to loosen the grip of typhoid. Like many of his 24th Wisconsin comrades, the young man, just months past his eighteenth birthday, had contracted the disease in the Murfreesboro camps that summer. The malady would not fully quit his body for months to come.

Arthur McArthur, his face probably somewhat drawn and wan below the wavy tangle of dark hair, could not suspect that in less than two months he would win notice, promotion, and undying glory for his gallant action during an impetuous attack upon enemy positions. When he seized the striped and starred banner of the Milwaukee Regiment on the rocky, timbered slope of Missionary Ridge the day before Thanksgiving, leading the Badger soldiers to the summit, he did not surmise that for over a century his act would grow into the stuff of legend. That deed was almost endlessly embellished and augmented to storied proportion.

The youthful officer had departed from the Milwaukee Regiment in mid-July. His father, Judge McArthur, learning of his illness, had secured permission to travel to Tullahoma, Tennessee, where his son sweated in a hospital. He quickly bundled the emaciated young man onto a train, arriving in Milwaukee July 17. There, in the substantial Second Empire home amid the city's enclave of fortune and prominence, young Arthur received the best medical care. Slowly, as July turned to August, the dark-eyed lad regained some of the strength that disease and over a year of hard service had sapped.

But as weeks passed, Lieutenant McArthur must have grown concerned. By early September, news sheets of the day reported the movement of General Rosecrans and the Army of the Cumberland toward Chattanooga. "When he was constrained to leave for the North," a newsman noted, "there was not the remotest prospect of a battle."

Now soldier and civilian correspondents sent columns to an anxious Milwaukee as September progressed toward equinox. Then, dark heavy headlines blurted the news: "TITANIC BATTLE NEAR CHICKA-MAUGA CREEK." The forces of Bragg and Longstreet had battered the army of General Rosecrans. What was more, there were allegations that the pugnacious commander had quit the field; the Army of the Cumberland had been saved only through the tenacious defense of General Thomas, a rock, it was said, upon which waves of rebel attacks dashed unsuccessfully—at least long enough to stave off utter disaster. More Milwaukee soldiers, men with whom Arthur had marched and fought for a year, had been killed and wounded. The young adjutant determined he could no longer remain in the city. Perhaps against his father's protestations, the slight youth made ready to rejoin his regiment.[1]

The trip back, via Chicago, Louisville, Nashville, and Murfrees-boro had consumed only two days. But the rail connection beyond Bridgeport, Alabama, on the Tennessee River had been severed. With rebels hemming in the Union army, the only route open was a rocky and rutted old mountain track on the north side of the river by which supplies were being trundled to the Army of the Cumberland. The sixty-mile trek was arduous, and passage took four days. Although he did not write about such matters, Lieutenant McArthur likely saw the mounds of dead horses and mules piled along the entire road. The poor beasts, badly underfed, had starved; cut from their traces, they were left to bloat in fetid ghastliness. Broken wagons and discarded supplies also littered the roadway. To make matters worse, fall rains commenced about the time McArthur's mountain journey began, turning a craggy road into a muddy quagmire; many passes had washed out, and detours were the order of the day. Mud and dirt spattered the adjutant's new blue coat and trousers.[2]

Nearing Chattanooga, the brown Tennessee River bunched up in a series of broad undulations as it cut through the mountainous countryside. The Confederates commanded many of the heights along the watercourse, and their artillery played upon the infrequent Federal river traffic. Its back against the brown river, the Army of the Cumberland was besieged.

Chattanooga, this rail and manufacturing hub that had for months been the prize coveted by General Rosecrans, was all but surrounded by a series of daunting mountains and ridges thrusting hundreds of feet above the town. The city's rugged surroundings afforded a certain grandeur, but few soldiers paid heed to the natural aspect. Amandus Silsby, the preacher's son who bore his dead mother's name, had recently turned eighteen. He dutifully wrote to his father about the city. "Chattanooga was probably once a flourishing place, at least so the ruins of the mills, factories, & machine shops, would indicate." He also noted that the weather had turned rainy and cold. A correspondent for a Cincinnati news sheet also wrote of heavy rains and "this dreary region of unfathomable mud. The last [storm] was a cold, winter rain that appeared to come directly from the North pole." It served as a reminder, he said, "that this section has but very slight claims to the appellation of the sunny south."[3]

Virtually since the army had begun pouring into Chattanooga September 22, orders to construct heavy defensive fortifications and breastworks were carried out feverishly, lest Bragg's triumphant army renew its attack. For two weeks, the soldiers worked "unremittingly" on the fortifications.[4]

Tom Ford, the twenty-four-year-old red-haired farmer in Company H who spoke about these matters thirty years later, recalled a humorous incident in the first days of labor. The Milwaukee Regiment was assigned to construct a fortification called Fort Wood (after one of the division commanders, Thomas J. Wood). "We worked hard that day," he said. And when the "fatigue duty" was done, little Phil Sheridan, their popular division commander, promised a ration of whiskey. "We fell in, in two ranks, with our tin cups, in double-quick time," Ford recalled. The libation was passed around from buckets, each man receiving no more than a swallow. Ford's brother, Dan, two years older, stood in a rear rank; of an abstemious bent, he refused the whiskey. Tom, aghast as a good Irish man should be, quickly told his brother to

Tom Ford (post-war).
"Much pleased to get it."
FROM: WITH THE RANK AND FILE.

take the ration and pass it to him. "I was very much pleased to get it," the younger Ford said; one of the other Company H men muttered, "My God, I wish I had a brother in the army that didn't drink."

Ford and several others also long remembered the scantiness of the fare provided for the soldiers. With normal supply routes cut off or squeezed by Bragg's rebels, rations were severely curtailed. Sergeant Ford called it being "subjugated to quarter rations." As soon as the foodstuffs were issued, most soldiers consumed them; nothing was saved for the morrow. They would take their chances on "foraging or gobbling" something from among the Chattanooga precincts.

After running out of candles for their camps, some of Ford's comrades fabricated little lamps of tin cans of grease with rag wicks. When the grease ran out, the makeshift devices were discarded. But in only a few days, Ford's hunger drove him back to one of these little tins. "I found it with considerable grease in it, mixed with some [dead] flies. . . . I ate them all," he remembered three decades later, and "relished them very much"; it even dampened his appetite for the next quarter ration.[5]

Rations or the paucity of them was a constant refrain from soldier-letter writers and correspondents. With Bragg's virtual encirclement and the dreadful state of mountain roads, it was impossible to trundle in sufficient food for the army. "My health is good," began one Milwaukee man, "except that I am nearly starved to death." The letter, as were numerous others, was printed in a city daily. He said the "intolerable hunger" drove men to desperate measures, actually stealing corn from the already emaciated mules. "Last night, two crackers were issued to each man. I ate mine for supper last night, and so, today, have nothing. If they do not give us more to eat soon we shall all be under the sod." Yet another writer went on to complain bitterly about the meager fare. "The prospects are poor just now, for they are trying to starve us to death, and if they keep on a little while longer they will succeed. They pretend to give us half rations, but it is in reality only about half of that, which is poor fodder for hungry soldiers, and the work we have to do is very heavy." Another correspondent mentioned, too, that the soldiers were poorly clothed. Blue coats and trousers were threadbare, and shoes were battered and thin-soled.[6]

As Lieutenant McArthur soon discovered, matters grew worse. The Confederate general Braxton Bragg, after savaging the Cumberlands at Chickamauga two weeks before, had fortified the heights above Chattanooga; his men and artillery pointed down upon the town ominously. To vex his blue antagonists, he ordered guns situated on a massive prominence called Lookout Mountain that jammed into the loop of the Tennessee River southeast of the city, to let loose some artillery shells each day. But since the rebel cannons were of unimpressive caliber, none of the rounds created any damage. "Our troops have come to entertain a stolid indifference to all rebel cannonading," a Chicago news writer observed. "Their guns on Lookout and other important heights around our lines are evidently of small caliber, and wholly unable to inflict serious damage." Yet, the booming guns were disconcerting, serving as a constant reminder of the tenuous position of the Cumberlands. A Milwaukee soldier groused: "We wish the rebels would make the attack and be done with it."[7]

Unnerving to some was the fact that they could see their gray- and dun-uniformed opponents. "The rebel camp is in sight of ours, and we hear their bands play every evening," wrote a 24th Wisconsin soldier. "[T]heir pickets are only about 100 yards from ours." They were even able to see the headquarters of General Bragg on the long rise southeast of Chattanooga called Missionary Ridge. The "house is distinctly visible from many points within our lines," wrote another Milwaukee man, "standing just at the top of the ridge of hills with a road winding up to among the trees." Date Worth wrote of seeing Bragg himself riding along his lines and encouraging his men.[8]

A chilled, frost-laden October 8 marked the first anniversary of the 24th's battle baptism at Perryville, Kentucky. Only Gene Comstock made note of the occasion, however. Lt. Bob Chivas, the gray-eyed, auburn-haired Scot, was now in command of Company I. Fred Root was hospitalized with typhoid. And the third of the trio, John Mitchell, had resigned his lieutenancy several weeks before, and gone home; his deficient eyesight prevented him from further field service.

Chivas, who had recently turned twenty-one, said his men were scouring Chattanooga for rations. "The other day it took only about five minutes for our boys to effectively dispose of a beautiful garden," he unabashedly admitted to his aunt, Martha Mitchell, "filled with potatoes, radishes, squash, melons, etc.," Chivas said. Another soldier mentioned that his men took great relish in expropriating from the Southern locals.[9]

One correspondent complained that the nights were "most abominably cold; the wagons containing our few extra clothes and blankets were sent to the rear more than a week ago and we now begin to feel the want of them," wrote a Wisconsin man. The soldiers "lived like dogs," he said. At midmonth, the camps were filled with rumor. Old Rosey, their beloved general, was to be removed. That angered many.[10]

Like his counterpart General McClellan, who had led the Army of the Potomac, General Rosecrans was popular with the great majority of his men. As with Little Mac, who had been removed from command following the less than decisive battle of Antietam a year previous, Rosey, despite his pugnacious demeanor, was a conservator general, whose organization and supply of his army was paramount. Both Rosecrans and McClellen were of a similar mold—they were fearful of using their men hard in battle and possibly destroying the armies they had organized, outfitted, and trained.

The allegation abroad in some circles that Rosecrans had actually abandoned his army that Sunday at Chickamauga vexed many soldiers. "The reports in the papers about Rosecrans is pure *lies,*" stressed a "republican" officer whose letter was published in a Milwaukee paper. He wrote that he had seen the general when the 24th Wisconsin fell back; Rosecrans was "riding around trying to rally our men, and the bullets were flying around him like hail." As the Milwaukee officer passed, Rosecrans waved his hat, shouting above the din, "Halt, boys; rally and make one charge for me." If any man told the writer Rosey had quit the field, "I would whip him if he did not weigh over three hundred. Confound their lying faces; they out [ought] to be shot," he vituperated in print.

The 24th Wisconsin soldier, unsurprisingly, did not take much to General Thomas, despite his stout defense that saved the army at Chickamauga; he felt the large-chested general had been "puffed" in the papers. "I acknowledge he is a perfect bull-dog in a fight, but he isn't worth a cent to manage in such times as this." The Milwaukee man was obviously impatient with the deficiencies of supplies, as important a consideration for soldiers as the failure to advance upon the enemy. He was also impatient with Maj. Gen. Joe Hooker, whose army had assembled at Bridgeport and Stevenson, "yet doing nothing." As for Gen. U. S. Grant, the recently named commander and hero of Vicksburg, he "has got to do something very soon, or he goes up the spout." Soldiers were learning the way of such things after a year in the army; Grant, after all, was already the third army commander under whom they had served.[11]

But the new commanding general rapidly reshaped and reorganized the army. Regiments such as the 24th Wisconsin had sustained a substantial reduction in their ranks. Not only had they sustained hundreds of casualties during the awful fight at Chickamauga, but they also had left hundreds of officers and men, felled with typhoid, diarrhea, and other camp maladies, in hospitals all the way north to Nashville. Moreover, scores more were assigned to other duties or were away on furlough. Thus, many companies mustered 25 men or less, and the entire 24th Wisconsin, as a typical example, counted only about 300 ready for duty. Lieutenant Chivas, in a letter to his friend, Dick Hubbell, who now served with the 1st Wisconsin Heavy Artillery, lamented that Company I "was scarcely a squad of the gallant one hundred that left Milwaukee." The company, however, "had lost none of its untiring zeal and undaunted pluck."[12]

The old XX and XXI Corps were obliterated from the organization of the Army of the Cumberland, their regiments and brigades constituted into a new IV Corps. Ponderous General McCook was sent packing, his performance at Stones River and Chickamauga less than spectacular. Named new corps commander was Maj. Gen. Gordon Granger. The 24th Wisconsin became part of the newly bulked 1st Brigade in General Sheridan's division, containing nine regiments under the command of Col. Francis Sherman. This was the same Illinois officer who had recently promulgated a soldier manifesto against civilian peace efforts. The "depleted condition of my regiments . . . compelled the massing of a great number of regimental organizations into a division," recalled General Sheridan, "to give it weight and force."[13]

In addition to the 24th Wisconsin and the 36th and 88th Illinois were the 44th, 73rd, and 74th Illinois, the 2nd and 15th Missouri, and the 22nd Indiana. The 21st Michigan, which had marched and fought alongside the Milwaukee Regiment for over a year, was transferred to the army's engineer corps.[14]

The new commanding general, who arrived in Chattanooga October 23, also took action to ease the badly pinched supply problem that prevented the men from receiving a daily allowance of no more than a hard cracker or two. General Grant approved a daring maneuver involving men of the Army of the Cumberland in concert with soldiers from two other corps sent from the Army of the Potomac—the XI under Maj. Gen. Oliver O. Howard and the XII led by brash General Hooker. They were to drive off rebels and gain control of key access points along the Tennessee River. What became known as the "Cracker Line," a vital artery for supplies, was thus opened. Raising Bragg's siege of Chattanooga had commenced.

Meanwhile, for the soldiers hunkered down in the town, more dreary days passed; cold, fog, and rain were punctuated with arduous fatigue duty, picket, and occasional shelling from the rebel-occupied heights to the south and west of Chattanooga. Almost daily, the lugubrious "Dead March" of muffled drums thumped in the city's streets as ambulances slowly trundled past the camps bearing two or more coffins. A squad of soldiers, their muskets reversed, tramped behind en route to the expanding burial grounds. Disease was stalking the besieged army.[15]

There was yet another unnerving event. General Sheridan assembled his entire division to witness the execution of two soldiers from the 24th Wisconsin's brigade who had attempted to desert when the army streamed into Chattanooga following the debacle at Chickamauga. One of the men belonged to the 44th Illinois and another to the 88th; a third man was a Milwaukee soldier, but at the last minute he was ordered back to duty and "it is supposed he will be acquitted." The latter man was not identified. Sheridan remembered the incident. "To make the example effective I parade the whole division" for the execution. It was an unusually warm Friday afternoon, November 13, an unlucky day for some. The condemned men were marched behind their coffins, and as the band played a "plaintive tune," a file of twelve soldiers were drawn into line; half of the muskets were charged with blanks. Chaplains provided final words to the blindfolded soldiers seated on their coffins. The firing squad kneeled and on command, volleyed into the condemned.

With a groan, the bodies were flung back with the impact of the .58-caliber bullets. Jim Harvey had witnessed a similar execution months ago. "I never desire to see such a sight again," he had concluded.[16]

As the dates on the October calendar peeled away, an unusual quiet descended upon Chattanooga for several days. But then on the morning of November 2, rebel batteries on Lookout Mountain sent several shells into Chattanooga. It was a reminder of the precarious position in which the Army of the Cumberland found itself.[17]

"Heavy rains have fallen in the past week flooding the camps and raising the Tennessee river a foot or more," a news correspondent wrote November 3rd. Almost as suddenly, the inclement conditions changed. "The weather is pleasant and a settled calm reigns. Perhaps it is the ominous silence that precedes the coming storm," worried a New York newsman.[18]

The army is still "pressed for rations," complained "Euonia," in one of his weekly correspondences to Milwaukee's Republican daily. The writer was a new soldier-correspondent who would for many weeks attempt to fill the void left by Norm Burdick and George Bleyer. "For some time soldiers subsisted on a cracker or two." Yet they worked cheerfully on the fortifications and entrenchments. He was troubled by the sorry state of the 24th Wisconsin. Its ranks were less than 200. Having seen those "splendid lines before they left the State it [created] a feeling of sadness to see their thinned and depleted ranks now."[19]

Drums rattled the "Long Roll"—the ominous call to assemble that sounded through the camps Monday, November 23. The first serious forward movement was about to occur, it seemed. It was to be a reconnaissance—General Sheridan would later call it a "strong demonstration"—by a large force of his division in concert with that of General Wood, against Orchard Knob, a high mound that jutted between the Federal line and Missionary Ridge. The object was to move to ascertain the strength of the enemy and to occupy a series of knolls in front of the Army of the Cumberland, halfway between the fortified blue line and Missionary Ridge.[20]

Companies coalesced into regiments; rolls were called. Brigades formed into divisions. The soldiers moved out between one and two o'clock that afternoon, and remained in line for three-quarters of an hour, in full view of Bragg's defenders, some said. Then, the order to advance was carried to the various commands, and the blue ranks strode forward to within a mile and three-quarters of the rebel camps and artillery. The first Federal shot cracked at 2 P.M., and another advance was ordered. "Our troops advanced rapidly as on parade," a news writer described. After a few paces, "Crack! Crack! Whir! Whiz!" Within a half an hour, Sheridan's men moved through a forest, driving back the thin rebel line of pickets, and occupying their entrenchments. Enemy pickets fired one shot each, then "skedaddled, yelling out, 'the Yankees are coming,'" as one news writer described it. And, thus, the day passed.[21]

The next day opened quietly, the soldiers, bellies rumbling, munching on the brick-hard army crackers or soaking them in coffee. It was damp, clouds hanging low. The 24th Wisconsin was moved into a new position where it lay all day. Late that afternoon the "sharp crack of skirmishers" was heard on the west wide of Lookout Mountain, that massive and brooding eminence towering some 1,500 feet above Chattanooga. General Hooker's army was finally making headway, fighting its way up the precipitous slope. "It was a grand sight," a Milwaukee news writer said, "made doubly so by the excitement caused and enjoyed with the knowledge that we were driving them."[22]

"Euonia," the Milwaukee soldier, wrote that Tuesday dawned "hazy, foggy . . . a rain cloud settling around the summit of Lookout." At 11:30 that morning, musketry was heard on the western slope of the massive promontory. Joe Hooker was at them. The Milwaukee soldier trained an eyeglass on the craggy prominence, watching "men coming helter-skelter around the ridge." Then more blue soldiers appeared, advancing on the rebel positions. The stars and stripes snapped in the breeze up there, and "cheers rang out along our lines."

The fight was perhaps personified for many Wisconsin men by one of Hooker's soldiers, a daring color sergeant who waved the stars and stripes some fifty yards ahead of his regiment. "We watched him while we held our breath," wrote "Euonia" as he switched to the present tense to paint the scene for his Milwaukee readers. "Down he goes; alas! That such a brave man should fall. No, he is up again and he waves his standard to encourage those behind him. Again he goes down and rises but to wave the standard over his head. What a noble, gallant soldier." General Sheridan, too, wrote of that glorious event, remembering that a small knot of men finally reached the summit of Lookout Mountain and there planted the banner. "Just then a cloud settled down on the mountain, and a heavy bank of fog obscured its whole face."[23]

Finally, Hooker's men gained the rocky crest, driving the rebels before them. The summit was won. Within days, news writers would call Hooker's smashing success: "THE BATTLE ABOVE THE

Howard Greene
"Expected calamity."
COURTESY OF MARC AND BETH STORCH.

CLOUDS." It was a magnificent achievement that cheered the Milwaukee man watching below. Perhaps tomorrow, Chickamauga might be avenged.

Despite the glorious victory on Lookout Mountain and the prospects for success at arms on the following day, Howard Greene, the Quaker captain of Company B, was badly unsettled. He shared a campfire with his lieutenant, Charley Rogers, and the tall Milwaukee bookkeeper would remember their conversation for decades.

Greene, who had only days before returned from a leave home where he was married, was brooding. The sad-eyed twenty-two-year-old must have thought of his new wife, the lovely Louise. But, that Tuesday night, Rogers recalled, Greene "looked like one in the shadow of a great sorrow, expecting calamity." Later that evening, Greene tossed fitfully and moaned, and when Rogers spoke to him, his friend expressed dread at the morrow's battle. He asked Rogers to keep a close watch and be ready to take command of Company B.

"Howard, you must not talk that way; you will be all right."

"I hope so, but fear not," was the reply.

Rogers likely recalled his brother Harry's premonition at the last battle. His conversation with Greene and the events of the following day would haunt Charley Rogers for the rest of his life. He spoke about it to comrades and friends in his waning years.[24]

Wednesday, the camps came alive early, cook fires stirred, and trails of smoke spiraled into the misty morning light. It was the eve of Thanksgiving, so proclaimed by President Lincoln. Propitiously, after several days of gray and gloomy conditions, the sun returned. Once more, the "Long Roll" rattled. Soldiers doused fires and packed their traps; companies and regiments were assembled yet again, brigades aligned and divisions arrayed. Somewhat before noon, the boom of cannons reverberated from the left, from the direction where Maj. Gen. William Sherman's army would attempt to attack that end of the rebel line on Missionary Ridge. It was all part of General Grant's plan that also called for Hooker, from his position, to gain a foothold on Bragg's left.

The Wisconsin soldiers would later learn, much to their consternation, that the Cumberlands were to be something of a diversion, ordained only to occupy General Bragg's attention so he could not reinforce either flank against Sherman and Hooker. The commanding general wanted General Thomas's army to move only as far as the base of the ridge, driving out the thin rank of rebels from shallow earthen defenses and light fortifications. (Gen. U. S. Grant's relationship with his subordinate, Thomas, was much like the one he would later develop with the Army of the Potomac's Maj. Gen. George G. Meade—less than felicitous.)

The Wisconsin men waited, hunkered down within a mile or so of the precipitous prominence they knew as Missionary Ridge. Forenoon passed. Noon. Then the army was moved forward a quarter of a mile and paused once again. Another ninety minutes passed. They could see the ridge clearly, its lower half cut clean of timber; felled logs, tree limbs, and brush were strewn about the scarred slope. Rocks and boulders dotted the brown ridge side. Ravines and fissures cut this way and that all over the face of the prominence. Higher up a second line of rebel entrenchments had been excavated; beyond these trees, small oaks mostly, crowded toward the summit of the slope.[25]

During those pregnant minutes, quarter hours, and hours, each 24th Wisconsin soldier withdrew a wrapped cartridge packed in his leather cartridge box, tore open its paper between his teeth, poured powder, and tamped the conical .58-caliber lead bullet down the long brown barrel; snugging a brass percussion cap on the musket nipple, he brought the hammer to a safe half cock. He clicked a bayonet in place at the muzzle. The double-ranked battle line was formed, perhaps 200 standing in those diminished Wisconsin ranks. What thoughts raced through the mind of the youth, McArthur, and those of Lieutenant Chivas, Sergeant Ford, Private Silsby, and others were not recorded.

About this time, a man in the 2nd Missouri, Date Worth recalled later, was playing chuck-a-luck—"a great game . . . when the boys have money," he said—when a shell shrieked down, decapitating the soldier. The Granville farmer drew no inference from the gruesome episode.

The unsettling premonition may have played its dirge in the mind of Captain Greene. George Allanson found the Quaker captain at the rear of Company B "behind a log, I think, praying." Restiveness and concern must have been evident among some; among others there may have been grim determination to wreack revenge upon the rebels who had bloodied them, and killed and maimed their comrades two months before at Chickamauga.

Some recalled it was 3:30 or 3:45 that afternoon when six thunderous cannon shots from Fort Wood signaled for the Cumberlands to advance. Capt. Ed Parsons was precise: He said his watch registered exactly three o'clock. Two lines of battle stepped forward, left foot first. Other Federal batteries from other Chattanooga fortifications began their play upon the hill ahead, churning up the earth in great geysers of dirt and debris. Rapidly the enemy guns hurled shells in response, pummeling the earth before the advancing Federal line.[26]

"We had to go about a quarter of a mile through the woods, when we struck a broad field," wrote twenty-one-year-old Cpl. James Heth, the son of the well-known Milwaukee confectioner. The tall clerk was one of the city's "pet" Company B boys. The field, he told his father, "was as smooth as any front yard in town. It was intersected all over with ditches." About a half mile of this open ground lay ahead of the Wisconsin Regiment.[27]

"We had not advanced far before the double quick was sounded," eighteen-year-old McArthur later told his father, "and away we went toward the very jaws of death, as it then seemed." Shells screamed and exploded, musket fire from the rebel positions at the foot of Missionary Ridge peppered the ground. Rapidly, the once orderly battle lines dissolved into a surging mass of men—the Army of the Cumberland, a two-and-a-half mile swarm of blue-coated attackers. They sprinted and ran, muskets forward on their right sides, bayonet tips aimed at the enemy rifle pits where the valley floor met Missionary Ridge.[28]

When the two charging lines were halfway across the open field, Corporal Heth wrote, the first line began to show "some signs of disorder, and commenced to fall back." But the second line, in which the

24th Wisconsin ran, "kept steadily advancing." Soon, there was competition between the two ranks, each vying to be foremost. Companies and regiments rapidly merged and folded into one another. "We have had some pretty hard double-quicking since being in the service, but never do I remember of having such a hard one as we had going across that field," the confectioner's son remembered.[29]

Then the Cumberlands swarmed into the rebel rifle pits at the base of Missionary Ridge. Many of the enemy, eyes wide, threw down their muskets and surrendered; others turned their backs on the blue battalions and scampered up the slope.

From this point, contemporaneous and retrospective writings do not always agree. Most soldiers recalled that they gulped for breath in those lower entrenchments. It had been a pell-mell sprint, a heavy rifle-musket, laden cartridge box, and blanket bedroll burdening them. Many had not even fired a shot. Some likely stooped now, setting down the butts of their Enfields. Others slumped into the rifle pits, leaning against the earth. Mouths agape, they sucked in air as their hearts hammered, almost audible above the continued musketry and shelling from above. Minutes passed, perhaps five or more to some recollections. From above them, the rebel defenders fired. The Milwaukee men were in a precarious position; they could neither advance nor remain amid the onslaught of shell and bullet. Moments of unsettling indecision lengthened to minutes.

Did any now recall the gallant color sergeant in Hooker's army seen clambering up Lookout Mountain the day before? Had his action emboldened any of the Milwaukee soldiers? Could the Cumberlands do less than Hooker's men?

Ed Parsons, the twenty-seven-year-old New York-born captain leading Company K, looked around in those moments, and spotted General Sheridan, the bandy rooster of a division commander, with his staff. Astride his famed black horse, "Rienzi," he waved that peculiar low-crowned little hat of his. To Parsons, his general's intention was clear: "I want you to move up." Despite General Grant's plan, impetuous Phil Sheridan saw the prospect of winning glory here, perhaps to expiate the disaster of Chickamauga. In a letter to the Milwaukee officer after the war, Sheridan confirmed that Captain Parsons had interpreted his signal correctly. "I actually rode my horse into the trench of the enemy's pits to force our skulkers who were sheltering themselves there."[30]

A soldier in the 36th Illinois remembered that as the Cumberlands began their assault, General Sheridan dashed forward to the foot of the ridge. The ungainly commander dismounted, threw his cape to an orderly, and running forward with his men shouted, "Boys, we are going to take the ridge. Forward and help your comrades!" Worth, who had cultivated a set of chin whiskers, told his parents that the little general had shouted, "now boys up the hill & every man for himself."[31]

Captain Parsons, who only the year before had worked quietly as a cashier for a Milwaukee manufacturer, motioned the men to follow. Corporal Heth said, "the order came *forward.*" Quickly, knots of Wisconsin soldiers leaped from the enemy rifle pits and began the ascent. The disordered ranks lurched from the earthen pits. The 24th "as usual, was in a very hot place." The men of Milwaukee and the rest of Wisconsin were about to begin a "fiery ordeal" that would win them undying fame. Rebel cannons and muskets above rained down on the blue ranks. "There was one incessant storm of shell, shrapnel, grape and canister, and bullets," Sergeant Heth told his father. Because the muzzles of most enemy cannons could not be depressed low enough, many lead balls passed over the heads of the attackers; shotgunlike blasts of canister were another matter, however.[32]

The ridge was steep, cluttered with boulders, stones, and felled trees; fissures and depressions cut across its face. Men stumbled and fell, and picked themselves up to rush onward again. One Milwaukee soldier said no man could rush more than forty yards without stopping to gasp for breath. Cpl. George Cooley, the tall Milwaukee printer and usually terse diarist in Company A, said the men jumped from "ditch to stump and from stump to tree or log or brush heap." The Milwaukee men's line, like that of scores of other regiments, formed an inverted V shape with the red, white, and blue regimental flag at the apex. They rushed headlong to be the first at the summit. The soldiers, braving the peppering of musket balls and blasts of artillery canister, bent forward at the waist, as if battling a swirling storm. None wrote of firing their rifle-muskets or stopping to reload the Enfields, but many must have. Too, many discarded blanket rolls.

In twos, threes, and tens, in knots and bunches that now composed the 24th, Wisconsin worked its way about halfway up the 600-foot ascent, nearing the stands of small oaks. Company A's captain, Dick Austin, whom Amandus Silsby called a "shallow pated fop," fell, blood gushing from a wound to his left leg. A ball had penetrated just above the knee, passing through and grazing the bone. Lieutenant Chivas rushed to Austin's side, quickly tying a handkerchief above the gory injury to stanch the blood. He must have offered some words of comfort to his fellow officer.

Then the Scottish immigrant, in America for a few short years, moved upward again, leading the Merchants, Company I. The tall twenty-one-year-old waved his sword above his head, someone later remembered, shouting "brave words of encouragement." But in only a few rods, he fell, struck by a shell fragment or bullet. Chivas lay there struggling to free himself from the entanglement of his sword belt; in a thick brogue, he asked a comrade to loosen the leather strapping. He was left behind, and, presumably, his gray eyes closed for the last time on earth on that inhospitable mountainside. Bob Chivas, he of the "manly heart" and impressive stature, would soon enter the pantheon of 24th Wisconsin heroes.

Dick Austin, meanwhile, attempted to drag his badly blasted leg up the slope. It would soon be apparent that surgeons might need to saw off that limb. But Austin did not climb far before another rebel shot struck him in the neck, "the ball grazing just above the jugular vein." Captain Austin would one day consider himself fortunate.

"A frenzy to reach the top of the hill seemed to possess every one," wrote a Wisconsin soldier of that febrile time. "Our forces would have almost stormed the Region of Darkness itself. One and all determined to reach the top of the hill."

With Capt. John Horning in its lead, Company E was raked by the searing storm of enemy lead. More than one-third of its number was wounded in those desperate minutes; one of these died later while two others never returned to fight further.[33]

Captain Greene and Lieutenant Rogers, laboring for breath, paused briefly in the climb. "I told you you were all right, captain," Rogers said. "Not yet, Charlie," the Company B commander replied. "The words were scarcely said when—zip, ching! And as quickly as a flash of lightening Captain Greene crossed to the other shore." A bullet pierced his heart, and he was dead before his body slumped to the brown and bouldered slope. The premonition had been fulfilled on that precipitous climb, and his young Missouri wife, hundreds of miles away, became a widow.

Sometime later, Lieutenant Allanson went back to find his captain's body, and removed personal belongings and his sword; he sent the effects to Mrs. Greene in St. Louis. Milwaukee news writers, however, would make no mention of these matters, noting only that Greene was shot through the heart "while gallantly leading his men." Among the many sad ironies was this: Because Company B's ranks had been so badly reduced, Greene had been given the opportunity to leave the army honorably. But he had made a pact with the Rogers brothers "to stick by each other to the end—unless all could and should wish to leave together." Greene would be much mourned by his new wife, as well as his parents and siblings in the East along with numerous Milwaukee friends. His name, too, joined the growing legion of city heroes.[34]

Lt. Tom Balding, the Englishman in Company A whom Private Silsby said treated men as men, was knocked down, badly wounded with a piece of lead in the right lung. At first it was reported that "his is a doubtful case," but he would recover, and return to lead men in the regiment's final battles. Balding, who after the war would be successful in the commission business, may not have known that his captain, Austin, was also down. Company A now had no officers, and Sgt. Millard Coburn of Milwaukee was the highest-ranking man. Similar situations occurred elsewhere on that mountainside.[35]

John Borth, the sallow-complexioned color sergeant, who labored with the large striped and starred flag, was tiring. At forty-four, he was one of the oldest men in the regiment, and had listed himself as a laborer. The banner grew heavier with each step, with each leap over a boulder, and with each jump across a fallen tree. He stopped, breathing heavily amid the swirling smoke and the hellish roar of battle. Almost immediately, the slender adjutant was at his side; the smooth-cheeked lieutenant grabbed the flagstaff from the faltering and winded Borth. One latter-day writer would describe eighteen-year-old McArthur as he turned toward the summit—his face crusted in powder grime, uniform muddy.[36]

Corporal Cooley also recalled those roiling moments. Nearing the summit, he wrote of a sight that "made my heart sink": a regiment or part of one to the right of the 24th paused as if ready to break and run down slope. But then: "Some of the boys gave a cheer . . . ready to go on again." Then he noticed Lieutenant McArthur, ahead, the streaming 24th Wisconsin flag gripped firmly in his hands. There was only one man with him, probably Sergeant Borth. Cooley sprinted forward, and clasped McArthur's small hand. "He said he was glad to see me and wanted me to stand by him and if he fell, to take the colors and plant them on the ridge. I promised to do so," Cooley jotted later that day.[37]

Meanwhile, Corporal Heth struggled upward, taking advantage of any obstacles, depressions, and breaks in the rough and rocky slope. At intervals, he and other men pulled themselves forward by gripping branches with their left hands. "There was one incessant storm of shell, *schrapnel* [sic], grape, canister, and bullets, from the time we first commenced the climb [of] the hill until we got to the top," he said. Suddenly,

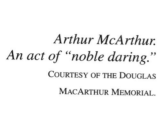

Arthur McArthur.
An act of "noble daring."
COURTESY OF THE DOUGLAS
MACARTHUR MEMORIAL.

a bullet gouged the dark wood of Heth's Enfield rifle-musket stock, skinning the knuckle of his right middle finger. Although only fourteen months had passed since he left home, the twenty-one-year-old was a lifetime removed from those days clerking in his father's Milwaukee confectionery.[38]

Elsewhere on that rock-strewn slope, tall and handsome Capt. Bill Kennedy caught up with Herman Allen, a lad of eighteen in his company, who was hobbling painfully. Kennedy, Milwaukee's court clerk just a year before, asked if the lad was wounded. The youngster said he was not. But the officer spotted blood oozing from both legs, and insisted Allen seek immediate medical attention. The youth whimpered, begging to be allowed to go on with his regiment. Only after Surgeon Hasse convinced him that he would be called when the 24th Wisconsin pursued the enemy beyond the summit did Allen relent. After recuperation, the young soldier would rejoin his Milwaukee comrades.[39]

The flag and its youthful bearer were the target for scores, perhaps hundreds of shots from the summit. But the slender form seemed almost miraculously to avoid the harvest of rebel lead aimed from above. "While I was carrying the flag a whole dose of canister went through it tearing it in a frightful manner," the daring McArthur told his father. "I only received one scratch and that was through the rim of my hat."[40]

Myth and legend about McArthur's great deed grew to monumental proportions in the years following the war. Douglas MacArthur, who listened to the tale of his father's heroics as a child, wrote that one color-bearer was shot, and when a corporal picked up the flag, a rebel bayoneted him. A shell took the head off another corporal. Then the youthful adjutant seized the flag. Suddenly, an enemy colonel thrust a sword at his throat; but as he lunged, a bullet cut him down, deflecting the blade. Only McArthur's shoulder strap was ripped.

The youth turned toward the Milwaukee men, waving the flag, the proud and boastful Douglas wrote with dramatic flare. "On, Wisconsin!" he shouted above the roar of artillery and the pocking of musket bullets. Men of the Badger state, who had faltered momentarily, charged forward again. But momentum was once again lost, Douglas visualized of those minutes near the summit. Then, on the crest, the flag waves, the proud son wrote in a dramatic present tense. "Silhouetted against the sky, the adjutant stands on the parapet waving the colors where the whole regiment can see him!" The scene must have been thrilling to the lad as he heard his proud grandfather's exaggerated telling.[41]

Several, including Major Von Baumbach, the portly Hessian, observed as the smooth-cheeked adjutant shouted at the Milwaukee soldiers, "cheering the men to follow him up to the summit of the ridge." Another said simply: "Brave little Adjutant McArthur took the flag and bore it to the summit." It was an act of "noble daring."

McArthur, Corporal Cooley, Sergeant Borth, and others swarmed to the top of the ridge line. The flag of the 24th Wisconsin, by all accounts, was either the first or second regimental banner to pierce the crest along the entire length of Missionary Ridge. Corporal Heth remembered the old flag looked "ragged and saucy." Soon scores of Wisconsin men reached the top near a small white house that many said had been occupied by Confederate general Bragg not long before. Hundreds of rebel soldiers threw down their muskets and were taken prisoner, along with scores of cannons that only minutes previous were savaging the ranks of the 24th Wisconsin. In desperation, hundreds of other rebels poured down the reverse slope of Missionary Ridge. All was euphoria in the Federal ranks. Cpl. Tom Ford remembered the Milwaukee men still had enough breath to snarl "Chickamauga! Chickamauga!" at the backs of the fleeing foe, words probably reinforced with shaking fists. "I never expect to see such grand sights again," wrote another Milwaukee soldier.[42]

Captain Parsons, who, it might be said, was most immediately responsible for the grand charge up Missionary Ridge, applauded the young adjutant. "Arthur was magnificent," he wrote to the youth's admiring father. "He seems to be afraid of nothing. He'd fight a pack of tigers in a jungle." Here was the stuff that puffed out the judge's ample chest, and the grist upon which to build a legend in later years.[43]

It had been perhaps an hour or ninety minutes since Phil Sheridan waved his jaunty hat at Parsons. At the regiment's back, the late afternoon sun dipped toward the wall of mountains to the west. The homely little general was among the Milwaukee men on the summit, sharing, reveling in their achievement and glory. "The boys crowded round him cheering and shaking hands with him," Corporal Cooley wrote. Ford, the henna-haired farmer, said the men shouted for rations and whiskey. Sheridan raised that low-crowned hat of his, shouting, "Boys, in two hours' time you will have all the hard-tack, all the sow-belly and all the beef you want; as for the whiskey I can't say yet for sure."[44]

Adjutant McArthur showed the regiment's tattered flag to General Sheridan, the dark-haired youth told his father. Much more would be made of this little episode in the years to come. Arthur's son Douglas likely retold the story of his father's gallantry many times, and wrote of it in his 1964 military memoir. He portrayed Sheridan embracing the slender eighteen-year-old lieutenant, writing in the present tense to give the scene immediacy: "And his [Sheridan's] deep voice seems to break a little as he says: 'Take care of him. He has just won the Medal of Honor.'" That dramatic scene and quotation found its way into several retellings of the story by later chroniclers.[45]

None of the contemporaneous accounts, however, seem corroborate the scene. General Sheridan, for example, failed even to mention Lieutenant McArthur's name in his official battle report despite the fact that the 24th Wisconsin commander, Major Von Baumbach, applauded the young adjutant. Furthermore, Sheridan did not include the episode in his memoirs; nor did Gen. U. S. Grant. Capt. Edwin Parsons, who became a loyal and admiring friend of Arthur McArthur, was also on that height; he did not write of the incident at that time or after the war. Corporal Heth, another of those at the summit when Sheridan arrived, observed that when the division commander arrived, "I thought the boys would pull him to pieces, shaking hands with him, &c." The soldier-correspondent "Euonia" did not include anything about the meeting of McArthur and Sheridan in his account of December 7, 1863. McArthur himself, writing three days after, said only: "After about two hours of steady climbing, we succeeded in reaching the top of the ridge." Thirty-six years later, a writer would note that the War Department's records of Arthur McArthur contained a notation: "Medal of Honor . . . for coolness and conspicuous bravery in action seizing the colors of his regiment at a critical moment and planting them on the captured works on the crest of Missionary Ridge . . . while serving as First Lieutenant and Adjutant, [24th] Wisconsin Infantry."[46]

What was more, Sgt. Tom Ford had an entirely different recollection when he spoke of the battle two decades later. He said that the flag bearer of Company C, a Milwaukee private named John Nelson, and he were the first of their brigade to reach the summit. Ford said nothing of the young adjutant at this point, concentrating, as was his penchant, on food. Driven by hunger, he was quick to jerk a haversack from a wounded rebel captain's neck; he rifled the contents and shared what he found with the knot of men around him. The foodstuffs were "saturated with the rebel captain's blood, but we ate it all the same."[47]

Finally, there was an account written sixty years later in which a young man, Ed Blake, who had been recruited by Gus Goldsmith in Port Washington, claimed that he was the first man to reach General Bragg's headquarters, and his comrade, Erastus Parr, also of that community north of Milwaukee, was the second man. "This is a matter worth making note of," wrote a historian in 1923 when Blake died, "because a number of generals and other officers have claimed that distinction." Blake would, the following year, gain great fame carrying the 24th Wisconsin banner.[48]

All of this does not obviate the meeting between McArthur and Sheridan atop Missionary Ridge. Details such as these are often unrecorded and forgotten; and a great number of letters and diaries that may have recorded the scene have probably been lost or are yet to be discovered. Another factor was that the Medal of Honor was accorded only to enlisted men early in the war; only later were officers included among the recipients. Finally, the recommendation for McArthur's prestigious award made to the U.S. Congress was introduced in 1890, as was customary in that era, by none other than the honoree himself; McArthur was at that time a Regular army officer. What cannot be denied is that the award was earned and justified.

But all of this was yet to come. As dark and relative quiet descended upon the battlefield of Chattanooga that Wednesday night, hundreds of cattle were driven onto Missionary Ridge to feed the exhausted soldiers.

"[I]n an hour's time," the folksy writer Ford noted, "they were in the frying pan." Men carried boxes of hard crackers to their campfires; many remained awake all night, consuming the eatables beside the flickering firelight. "Some died eating that night."

When it came time to bed down, Ford remembered that he, like many of his comrades, had discarded his blanket during the fight up Missionary Ridge. Under the bright moonlight, he scoured the vicinity and found a dead rebel colonel with a fine overcoat and cape trimmed with gold braid; he took the garment. But the theft from a dead man, who was "helpless to defend himself," troubled him so he could not sleep; he returned the overcoat, draping it over the dead officer. He would more than lose such compunctions in the following year. Ford later shared a blanket with one of his Company H comrades, sleeping with a full belly.[49]

The next day, a Milwaukee writer reflected on the grand spectacle of the charge up Missionary Ridge, and the exorcising of the defeat of Chickamauga. "It was worth ten years of civil life to see that long line, with its bayonets glistening in the sun, storming the enemy's works on the west slope of Missionary Ridge," wrote the man. Company H's Date Worth, now twenty-four, expressed amazement at the grand triumph, "never dreaming that we would have the audacity to plant our flag on the ridge."[50]

The Milwaukee Regiment's commander, Major Von Baumbach, penned plaudits to many of his subordinates two days later. He praised the gallantry of the dead and severely wounded officers, Greene, Chivas, Austin, and Balding. He heaped most credit upon the narrow shoulders of his adjutant for his daring and bravery. In due course, McArthur, along with John Borth, James Heth, and others, earned promotions for their actions.[51]

Captain Parsons wrote that the 24th Wisconsin lost thirty-nine killed and wounded. In addition to Greene and Chivas, one other man was killed—Dick Corgan, who had fought along with Amandus Silsby in Company A. But five of the wounded were so severe, they died within days; eight others would never return to the regiment, being discharged because of their wounds. Companies D, the railroad men of western Wisconsin, and E sustained the most casualties.[52]

Perhaps that night or the next day, Thanksgiving, Lt. Charley Rogers and others took up the sad duty of scouring Missionary Ridge for their dead and wounded comrades. The body of the likable young Scot, Bob Chivas, was found crumpled on the boulder-strewn slope, and was buried in a shallow temporary grave. Soon, Captain Greene's remains were laid next to him.

In the hospital in Chattanooga, little Fred Root still lay feverish. News of the battle had reached him over the past few days, of course. There must have been concern for his close friend, Chivas. He and the young lumber dealer, despite the ten years that separated their ages, had grown close. They were both relative newcomers to Milwaukee, the diminutive Root having been Virginia-born while Chivas found his way from Scotland. Both men became good soldiers and were respected officers. The immigrant had yearned only for a "nat little wound," but suffered more. Root, the thirty-one-year-old Sunday school teacher, had been, despite his diminutive stature, a fatherly figure to the boys of Company I and had been almost fearless in battle. Yet, he had written to his pastor after Chickamauga, "I hope never to be in another battle. God forbid it. But if duty leads me, then I shall go into it cheerfully, leaning on His almighty arm."[53]

Root had taken sick during the marches in Kentucky and Tennessee, and, as with Arthur McArthur and scores of others during the spring and early summer, typhoid had "laid its heavy, burning hand upon him, and carried him to the very door of death." Contrary to the direction of the regiment's surgeon, Dr. Hasse, Root had gone on picket duty with his men the past Friday. By Monday, Root was gripped by fevers and prostrated in the officers' hospital.[54]

When a 24th Wisconsin soldier, wounded in the charge up Missionary Ridge, was laid next to the diminutive captain, he blurted out that Chivas, who commanded Company I while Root was stricken, had been killed. Something inside the diminutive Sunday school teacher seized up, and he was overcome with a "fit of derangement." The former Milwaukee clerk ordered his servant to get his revolver. He placed the muzzle beneath his chin and pulled the trigger. That was how one news correspondent represented it.[55]

In the weeks to come, the fact that Root took his own life was suppressed by the Milwaukee news writers of the day. This was not the stuff to instill confidence in the hearts of the folks at home. "We are not advised precisely as to the disease, which terminated fatally, but believe it was a fever of some sort," observed one news sheet. Even "Euonia," the 24th Wisconsin soldier correspondent, reported that Root had died of typhoid fever, exacerbated by the news of his friend's death. "The shock was so great that he did not recover from its effects." It was another tragic demise. Root, too, would soon enter that hallowed hall of

Milwaukee's heroes. Little John Mitchell was now the only surviving member of those three friends who recruited the Merchants Guard in 1862.[56]

Finally, two months later, Dr. John Bartlett, a Milwaukee physician and friend of Root, revealed the true facts of the tragic demise. As Root lay in the hospital, his Negro servant, Sam, rushed in with the news of Chivas's death. Delirious with fever, he attempted to get up, muttering that "he must get to the head of his company." From his window, Root could see the crowds of Federal soldiers surging up Missionary Ridge. Raising himself, he seized his revolver. As he struggled to right himself, Bartlett explained, either his finger or the tangled bedclothes caused the revolver to discharge, and "the ball wounded his chin and throat, but not at all dangerously." Here was a more palatable explanation. He died of disease after all, so it was said.[57]

Elsewhere in Chattanooga, the soldiers of the 24th Wisconsin, officers and enlisted alike, were attempting to place their recent harrowing experiences in perspective. "It seems strange to me to be writing to the dear ones at home while the battle is raging without, yet so it is, and such are the varied fortunes of war. I poke up the fire and read the morning paper, while many a brave boy is sent to his long home, or, what is worse, left to languish away in some impure, unhealthy hospital, with no kind word or look to cheer his last moments," said a Milwaukee soldier. "God grant a settlement may come soon and speedily, either through the discouragement of the rebel leaders or a softening of their hitherto stony hearts. The end may be nearer than we think. Certainly their prospects never looked gloomier or their political sky more unpropitious."[58]

Somewhat later, "Euonia," the steady soldier-correspondent to the Republican news sheet, viewed the success at Missionary Ridge as nothing short of "miraculous." "It seems but yesterday that the rebel batteries . . . frowned upon us . . . and Missionary Ridge could be seen thickly dotted with rebel camps," he recalled. "By some magic art, the wave of some mysterious hand, the rebel cohorts have been hurled in confusion from their commanding position." He concluded that "this miraculous work has been done by the indomitable courage and bravery of our army."[59]

Major Von Baumbach, who would within a month give up his commission to return home, drafted his official report of the battle of Missionary Ridge. "Among the many acts of personal intrepidity on the memorable occasion, none are worthy of higher commendation than that of young McArthur," the Milwaukee druggist wrote, "who seizing the colors of his regiment at a critical moment, contributed materially to the general result. He was most distinguished in action on a field where many in the regiment displayed conspicuous gallantry, worthy of high praise."[60]

From that bold act would soon spring more great deeds. The determined officer with the schoolboy face would soon be granted a remarkable promotion. In time he would exhibit more daring and heroics, gain higher rank and renown, and become known as the "Boy Colonel."

Meanwhile, more mourning and grim funerals would exacerbate Milwaukee's bitter winter. The impending holiday season would be a sad one for the soldiers' families and friends.

Chapter 10

Another Woeful Winter

"The soldier's proudest epitaph."

"The elements could hardly have been more unpropitious." That Sunday morning in mid-December 1863 began with a sodden downpour in Milwaukee. As the day progressed, it turned to heavy, wet snow "accompanied by as strong a wind as we have had in a twelve-month," described one news writer. "In fact, it became a perfect gale, whose principle ingredients were hurricane, snow, and rain, and it was almost a foolhardy undertaking for one to venture out of doors." Another daily sheet added: "Seldom, indeed, even in this latitude, is a day encountered so very stormy and disagreeable."[1]

But there were many who would brave this day in the cold and snowy city on Lake Michigan. They were family and friends, mourners whose hearts, as icy as the streets and walkways, would not thaw. Two of Milwaukee's gentle sons, Bob Chivas and Fred Root, were being laid to rest. The younger of the two, the tall, sinewy lieutenant, had traveled to the city from Scotland at age twenty only a few years before; the other, in contrast, was a short captain a decade older, a son of Virginia who had migrated to Wisconsin as a youth. One had been slain among the boulders, brush, and oak logs as his regiment gloriously assaulted the precipitous Missionary Ridge; the other had, by some accounts, accidentally taken his own life while sick in the hospital.

The Sunday funeral was held at the bastion of Milwaukee's Episcopal community, St. James Church on Spring Street, the main thoroughfare on the west side of the city. Directly across that dirt roadway, now packed with dense and clinging snow, stood the two-story Italianate mansion of banker and railroad magnate Alexander Mitchell. The fiercely whiskered plutocrat and his wife, Martha, were among the mourners, as was their son, John, who only months before had marched with his two comrades. Chivas, the nephew of the Mitchells, had lived in that cream brick home before he, John, and Fred marched off to war. Now, only one of the trio of fast friends remained. John Mitchell, whose weak eyes had not permitted him to soldier on with his comrades, had been moved to write a mournful paean that would gain front-page prominence in one of the dailies. It began:

> Headed by a dreary drum,
> Slow, the mournful hearses come;
> And the troops, with solemn tread,
> Usher back the soldier-dead.[2]

The two coffins, borne by men in uniform and civilian garb, were placed before the pulpit. Rev. John Ingraham had difficulty conducting the service; he was married to Root's sister. Neither Root nor Chivas had ever married. His brother-in-law, said the pastor, possessed an "impulsive, warm-hearted nature," and he was zealous about church and Sunday school. Chivas and Root often talked about St. James, and the Scot had written to Pastor Ingraham from Tennessee that he would give anything to allow his friend the opportunity to be at church in Milwaukee. "Pure-minded, generous to a fault, and exceedingly nice in his ideas of justice and the dictations of conscience," said the lawyer, Dick Hubbell, who had signed Root's enlistment roll, "he created in his men an emulation of all that is good and noble in a manner they will never forget."

Of the lumber dealer, barely twenty-one, the reverend said he was characterized by "goodness of heart"; he was a scholar and a good Christian. It was also recalled that Chivas was not even a U.S. citizen, so had no obligation to volunteer; nonetheless, "he girded up his sword, and went forth to battle for the Union liberty, and right." Ed Parsons, who long remembered his old comrades, would eulogize many years later. "He came from a foreign land to water the tree of American liberty with his blood."[3]

Afterward many score followed the coffins back into the blowing gale of heavy snow. Large, wet flakes quickly plastered the somber clothing of the mourners, as the coffins were slid into the black hearses festooned with dark wreaths and flowers. A military band began its "melancholy music, the drums uttered their mournful and muffled notes." Soldiers from the 24th Wisconsin were there: Capt. Bill Kennedy and Dexter Kasson, both home on furlough; also paying respects were Attorney Ed Buttrick, the Milwaukee Regiment's old lieutenant colonel, and former Company A lieutenant Henry Drake, who had given up his commission in August. In addition, more than fifty members of the Milwaukee Light Infantry, a city militia company, and a company from the new 30th Wisconsin Infantry braved the brutal weather; from his headquarters in Minnesota, Maj. Gen. John Pope had sent a military escort. A deputation from the prestigious St. Andrew's Society, of which the two deceased and the Mitchells were members, also joined the cortege, as did numerous luminaries from the Chamber of Commerce.

"The terrible character of the day naturally helped to depress the feelings, but the fact that such a goodly number had defied the fury of the blast . . . afforded the strongest of evidence of how widely the deceased officers were respected, and how deep the hold they had upon the affections of the entire community," stated a news column the day after.[4]

Horses strained at sleighs, broughams, barouches, and other carriages as the long cortege began the slow trek to the burial ground. Forest Home Cemetery, the resting place of many significant figures in Milwaukee's history, was far to the south of Spring Street. The soldiers and band marched and the carriages trundled more than a mile west, then two and a half miles south, over the Menomonee River. The going was slow, and snow piled on the vehicles and whitened the soldiers' uniforms. In perhaps an hour, the cortege reached the sprawling cemetery. It was the "silent city of the dead," said Ed Parsons.

"Seldom has a more impressive event than this double funeral been witnessed in our midst," observed a news man. "The large gathering, in the face of the most severe and penetrating storms, was evidence alike of the estimation in which the deceased were personally held, and the cause for which they fell."[5]

Less than five days later, the flag-draped coffin of Capt. Howard Greene stood before another large assembly at the city's Unitarian Church of the Redeemer in the prosperous precincts east of the river. A Quaker whose family opposed their son's enlistment, Greene had for months struggled with his decision to volunteer. The sadness that marked his countenance was often reflected in the numerous letters to his family and his sweetheart. A man of sensitivity, the captain had also traveled to Cincinnati to visit the sisters of the dead general, William Lytle. He told them how their brother had died in his arms there on the bloody field at Chickamauga, and they gave him a carte de visite. Greene promised to send a likeness of himself; but he had not time to do so before the next battle. After her husband's death, Louise Greene mailed his image to Lytle's sisters. The captain's dark eyes bore a sad and weary cast, as if he had already seen too much in his twenty-three years; below his straight nose, a groomed mustache flowed above his full lips.

The grieving widow was likely, in the fashion of the day, adorned in heavy opaque black; a knee-length crepe veil shrouded her face completely. They had married only months before when he was last in Milwaukee on furlough. The dead captain's family, who had opposed his enlistment, had traveled from the East to attend the funeral.

Current and former 24th Wisconsin men Kennedy, Kasson, Buttrick, Drake, and others again took up the sad duty. The Reverend C. A. Staples delivered an eloquent eulogy to the gentle and brave hero. Then, as occurred before, a large train of carriages and sleighs, led by the Milwaukee Light Guard and a brass band playing the dirge, once again labored over the snow-packed streets to Forest Home Cemetery where another casket was eased into the frozen ground.[6]

The morning before Greene's funeral, one Milwaukee daily had printed John Mitchell's lugubrious poem on its front page. The deaths of his comrades had deeply affected him. The poem concluded:

> Drummers hush their death-march rattle,
> And the escort's trampings cease.
> Soldiers went they out to battle;
> Now they have returned in peace.[7]

Milwaukee's pantheon of fallen heroes enlarged steadily: Root, Chivas, and Greene joined men such as George Bleyer and others. Meanwhile, many others, like Christian Nix and Byron Brooks, both killed at Stones River, lay hundreds of miles southeast, sometimes in rude, poorly marked graves, in such places as Louisville, Nashville, and Murfreesboro or in the expansive new burial ground outside of

Chattanooga plotted by Army of the Cumberland commander Maj. Gen. George Thomas.

Eulogies and encomiums to the slain Milwaukee men arrived from every quarter. "To say that these three officers were perfect gentlemen, would only state what every one knows," wrote artillery lieutenant Hubbell from Kentucky; "but they were soldiers in every sense of that term. High-minded, unswerving, unequivocal Christians." Remembering his dead comrades from even before war, when they were young men of promise; he concluded:

> The young and the old—the gay and the gifted, are swept away in the harvest of battle, with scarce a sigh for their memory, or tear for their grave. But comrades, there are eyes that will weep for you; there are hearts that will be lonely. Though the sod may cover your clay, your friends, City, State and Country, will not forget you, as long as the name of Wisconsin continues to be the soldier's proudest epitaph, and her sons the Union's strongest arm.[8]

The same severe weather that brutalized Milwaukee, with temperatures plunging to thirty below zero, drove deeply into Tennessee in early January. The Wisconsin officer who called himself "Euonia" complained of the "extremely cold weather that has lately swept over the Northern States. Although we are in the 'Sunny South,' I think we have suffered more from the cold weather of the past two weeks than the people in the North." The change, he wrote, was sudden: a bright, clear fall-like day followed by a rainstorm, and then "a cold, biting frost, the thermometer falling rapidly to below zero." The soldiers, he said, still suffered from want of proper rations and insufficient clothing. "I don't know who is to blame."[9]

That month, the soldiers of the 24th Wisconsin all but foundered in East Tennessee. As part of a force that comprised the divisions of Generals Sheridan and Wood, they had departed Chattanooga within days after the glorious victory on Missionary Ridge, sent to Knoxville where the Confederate command of General Longstreet and his corps threatened that city. The force was woefully unprepared because of the shortage of rations and inadequacy of proper clothing. General Sheridan had gained possession of only a few overcoats before leaving Chattanooga and a small supply of "India-rubber ponchos." But there were no shoes.

As they slogged those scores of miles through the treacherous weather with frequent storms of snow and sleet, and over mountainous terrain, the soldiers fashioned whatever foot protection they were able, some wrapping their feet in blankets. Sheridan calculated at least 600 men in his division were poorly shod.[10]

Longstreet, who failed in his attempt to capture Knoxville, moved northeast, the Federal relief force in pursuit. Near Dandridge, the Confederates turned to harass the approaching Federals. From a piece of woods, one of the gray batteries was "causing us considerable annoyance," was how Ed Parsons told it twenty years later. Impetuous General Sheridan determined to charge the battery, and the 24th Wisconsin and its brigade were selected to effect the deed. The short division commander, who looked far better astride his horse than he did afoot, was in the van of his soldiers, giving orders for this regiment or that to position itself here or there.

Parsons, who commanded the regiment at that point, turned to the bugler, Dan Davis of Milwaukee, to sound the call to advance when the rebel guns belched a shot at the Wisconsin men. Just as Davis raised his left foot to step forward, an ugly cast-iron 12-pound ball whooshed between his legs, cutting a long strip from his heavy overcoat; the projectile then smashed the sword scabbard hanging from Parsons's right side before bounding over a hill behind the astonished soldiers. The 24th Wisconsin continued its charge, driving the rebel battery from the trees.

The next day Captain Parsons told Davis he thought the 12-pound ball might be located; after a brief search, the musician found the projectile, the strip of light blue wool it had cut from the bugler wound tightly about it. In his light-hearted retelling of the episode, Parsons said that had he been four inches to the right, he would not then be addressing the old veterans' gathering in 1883. And Davis, who had entered the piano-moving business in Milwaukee, told his comrades that he had carried the torn overcoat for the remainder of the war. Long discarded by the 1880s, the piano-mover said, "I'd give an even $100 for it this minute." It was another of those insubstantial episodes that printed themselves on a soldier's memory.[11]

For many weeks, the Wisconsin soldiers tramped about in eastern Tennessee, with seeming purposelessness, groused General Sheridan. He later wrote of "a general disgust [that] prevailed regarding our useless marches during the winter." Finally, after uncounted miles of cold, miserable marching, the Federal force entered winter camp near Loudon, Tennessee, southwest of Knoxville. Here the Milwaukee Regiment would remain for about two months near the formerly thriving town of 400 to 500, "now remarkable only for its desolate appearance and abandoned women."[12]

Like the brutal winter cold that blustered through Milwaukee before pummeling the border states in early January, the appointment of Arthur McArthur as major of the 24th Wisconsin set off a raging storm of controversy that was fought in newspapers throughout the state as well as in soldier correspondence. The young man's promotion, filling the vacancy created by the resignation of Carl Von Baumbach, was officially dated four days into the new year, on the final day of Gov. Edward Salomon's term. Salomon was a Democrat and political ally of Judge McArthur; several news editors accused the pair of colluding to gain the undeserved appointment at the eleventh hour of the governor's term.

The promotion, averred a Republican news sheet in Madison, the state capital, rode "recklessly over the claims and qualifications of hosts of others." The public, not surprised by the maneuver, was "exceedingly incensed." What was more, the editor claimed, the reports of Major McArthur's heroics during the assault up Missionary Ridge were but "well designed newspaper puffs." It was Sergeant Borth, the forty-four-year-old Port Washington man, who had carried the flag of the regiment to the summit, not McArthur. "It was simply a premeditated newspaper story, designed to serve the purpose which it did serve." The editor seemed to step back a bit when he stated that simply carrying a flag up a hill (he carefully minimized the height of Missionary Ridge) and planting it there, "even in the face of danger, neither entitles nor qualifies a man for command of a regiment." Finally, the *Wisconsin Daily Patriot* petulantly caviled at both the new major and his father. When the appointment was announced officially, Judge McArthur gave his son a new horse and buggy. Clearly, for some, this was the final straw in the tawdry business.[13]

Judge McArthur fumed over the allegations. He fired a return salvo from Milwaukee. The appointment, he stated, was made in strict accordance with the rule of promotion fixed by Governor Salomon. Further, Salomon, who had by this time left office, maintained that the "gallantry and soldierly ability of the Major is established by the concurrent testimony of his associate and superior officers." His son's age, finally, should be no impediment to promotion.[14]

Also taking up the defense was a 24th Wisconsin soldier who identified himself only as "Nimrod." He was Dan Davis, the young bugler in the Merchant's Guard who would one day be named the regiment's principal musician. It was merely a matter of "taste," he said, as to what qualities are requisite for the majority. "If age, stupidity, or imbecility are requisite, then there are those who are better qualified and better entitled to it." But Major McArthur at eighteen was charged only with the "crime of being a young man."

He stated that besides Major McArthur and Q.M. Sam Chase, the regiment had but eight commissioned officers. The normal complement of line officers alone was thirty. Furthermore, the 24th Wisconsin had been without a colonel since the battle of Chickamauga; in that time McArthur had "proved himself capable, and given general satisfaction" as adjutant. Davis castigated "those who have [not] been nearer than a thousand miles to the trial-ground." "Soldiers in the field are quite as good judges of who are, and who are not, qualified." His letter was printed in a Milwaukee daily for all to read.[15]

Although Maj. Arthur McArthur still appeared much younger than his fellow officers and most soldiers, the effects of more than a year of war, disease, deprivation, exposure, and military life were beginning to manifest themselves. In a likeness taken about this time, weariness seems to play about the eyes, and a few lines appeared on the youthful face. He still bore himself in an upright manner, and his thick, curly hair was worn full beneath a broad-brimmed campaign hat that he creased from front to back. The new silver oak leaves on his uniform straps seemed to weigh heavily upon his narrow shoulders.

Two officers mentioned as possible candidates for the majority before McArthur's elevation were Capt. Ed Parsons, commander of Company K for well over a year, who had turned twenty-eight in February; and the railroad man, Capt. Sam Philbrook, married, a father and in his thirties, who had led Company D since the 24th Wisconsin was formed. Although it was reported that those two officers "grumbled about political influence," eight others felt McArthur's precipitant promotion was earned. Despite his boyish looks and slender frame, McArthur had performed admirably as adjutant, insuring that daily rolls and reports were duly completed; he was conversant with the military manuals of the day, and regularly conducted drill; as a result, he knew the regiment perhaps better than any other officer. And he had proved his courage and daring at Perryville, Stones River, and Missionary Ridge. An informal vote among the men in the ranks revealed that they supported McArthur's promotion.[16]

In the end, the promotion augured well. That McArthur "should have lived through that storm of bullets, to receive his promotion, is one of the wonders of the battle," wrote a Milwaukee news man. "We hope the rule will be carried out in every instance, of promoting those whose bearing in battle inspire[s] regiments with enthusiasm and make them irresistible." The new major, still a half year short of his nineteenth birthday, would prove more than inspirational in 1864 as well.[17]

Another issue pressing upon several regiments in the 24th Wisconsin's brigade was the matter of their enlistments. Several were approaching the end of their three-year term, and there was concern about sufficient numbers signing the roll again. (The Milwaukee Regiment, of course, would not fulfill its enlistment for more than a year.) One Milwaukee soldier wrote that "many say they enlisted to *put down the rebellion,* and they do not want to quit the field till this is accomplished." There was also, for those less patriotically disposed, a sizeable cash bounty for veterans. And finally, the promise of a thirty-day furlough was a potent inducement.

Bonds of comradeship borne of battle and hardship had been cemented between soldiers; "friendship engendered by association in peril" was strong indeed, and many of these would last for the remainder of their years. Date Worth, who learned that his Granville comrade Jim Harvey's severe Chickamauga wound would not be fatal, personified such relationships, as did the Cooley brothers and Milt Storey and others. There were also purely practical issues, a soldier wrote, to favor experienced soldiers: "One veteran is worth at least three raw recruits. The sickly ones have been weeded out. Those that remain have learned to do efficient service in battle without unnecessary exposure, and also take care of themselves on the march and in camp."

An officer in the Milwaukee Regiment who wrote to his family touched upon related issues. Within a week after receiving the letter, the soldier's family provided a copy for a Republican daily, the *Milwaukee Sentinel;* the statement buttressed the news sheet's and party's position on the war.

He had received a suggestion from one family member that he resign since he had already passed through a great battle, Chickamauga. "I came because it was my duty to come," he said of his enlistment in 1862, "and because I could not bear the shame of remaining home. Now I feel it would be unmanly to resign, when the work is half done." He decried the "timidity" that underlay most officer resignations from the regiment. "I have put my hand to the plow and I do not wish to look back." He would not return home to kin or business "until the last vestige of armed opposition to the Government had disappeared."

Besides, he wrote, there was no good reason to leave the army. He was in good health as was his family, and he was untroubled by any business problems. He took pains to support the president's emancipation despite criticism from Democratic Party loyalists. "If the people at home will only all unite in favor of a vigorous war, nigger or no nigger, the war will be satisfactorily closed before next summer." The Milwaukee officer went on: "Should slavery perish I would not sorrow. Free negroism is better than slavery." His time in the South had shown him the evil of the institution. "Slavery corrupts the morals of the people," he said. "Women talk of breeding slaves more freely than a farmer's wife [in the] North would talk of breeding cattle. It's so, and I am no especial abolitionist."

Furthermore, he could not understand anyone in the North being a peace man. "There is no safe and honorable alternative to fighting," he said. He closed by issuing a clarion call for every young man to volunteer. Those who shirked their duty to the nation would be unable to hide from "derision and scorn of the people"; they must "vindicate their manhood and patriotism," he concluded.[18]

In early February the 24th Wisconsin was assigned to provost guard duty at General Sheridan's headquarters. The regiment's ranks were still badly depleted, only seven line officers and 230 men fit for duty in early March. "This may or may not be a good thing for the regiment; at present the duty is very heavy, more so than at any other time during the service," said the regimental musician, Dan Davis. It was probably during this period that the little general solidified his relationship with the Milwaukee men, especially Captain Parsons and Adjutant McArthur. When the latter was notified of his promotion to major during this time, the news was as likely well received by the general as the men of the 24th. The eighteen-year-old soldier now commanded the men of Milwaukee and Wisconsin, and he drilled the regiment to perfection. As General Sheridan's headquarters regiment, the 24th Wisconsin often entertained visitors with "well-performed dress parades." Said another soldier: "The Adjutant has proved himself as a good officer, is well liked, and deserves his promotion."[19]

For most soldiers, the winter weighed heavily. In a letter to his sister on Valentine's Day, Gene Comstock (he had overcome his recent demotion, and gained three stripes by this time), apparently a man of sensitivity and culture, commented about the passage of months. "It seems but yesterday that we used to congregate in the old Post Office (& Kings Bookstore) and look over the Valentines." Comstock's letter also detailed his ready knowledge of the drama and actors of the day. It would be useless, he said, to "try my hand at pen pictures" of soldier life; he was amused at the correspondence and stories appearing in the papers, most of which were *"botches."*

"This soldiering tells a fellow some queer things," he wrote. For example, men who were friends before the war, might, in the crucible of battle and camp, be enemies now, "although they associate together, for want of more acquaintances." And a man who was formerly slovenly might now be clean and tidy.

He concluded by describing for his sister a dance in the Wisconsin camp, "and you would have laughed to see the Ladies." The desperate times of war sometimes forced men to become dancing partners. The "Ladies" were adorned in an unusual style of dress he had not seen before, and they "chewed and spit on the floor like so many loafers on a street corner, but as a general thing were good looking."[20]

One day in March, Captain Parsons was called to Sheridan's headquarters. The general paid a "very high compliment to the regiment [and] was pleased to bestow on me a few words of commendation that I have always treasured up as one of the bright spots—an oasis in the desert—of those long and gloomy days of war," Parsons said decades later. Parsons, after all, had never been back to Milwaukee since marching off in September 1862.[21]

Although the ranks of the Milwaukee Regiment still remained desperately thin, at least two new men were added to the roll in mid-March. Company B's Lt. Charley Rogers, who after the war had a way of making a good war story better, was in charge of a detail at the guardhouse in which were incarcerated two rebel prisoners. They told Rogers they were Carolinians who had served in a Georgia regiment, but they now wanted to join the Federal army. The Milwaukee captain consulted with fellow officers, and it was agreed to have the two men swear allegiance to the Union and sign the roll of the company.

But caution must be taken, lest the two men actually be rebel spies. He told Jim Gallion and Bill Edmunds they would not be allowed to stand picket or guard, and Wisconsin soldiers would watch them carefully until they were "thoroughly tested." The "moment they showed the least sign of crookedness . . . their bodies would be as full of holes as a pepper-box," Rogers remembered.

"All right; jast [*sic*] try us," the pair replied.

They were sworn in, issued blue uniforms, Enfield rifle-muskets, cartridge boxes, belts, and brass trimmings. "They became favorites, and performed all of the duties of a soldier with the strictest fidelity," Rogers offered.[22]

Matters gained more urgency in early March, when it was announced that President Lincoln created the rank of lieutenant general for U. S. Grant, and accorded him command of all Federal armies. Changes percolated down the lines of command. Maj. Gen. William Sherman, old "Cump," was named commander of the new Military Department of Mississippi, composed of the three armies in the West— General Thomas's Army of the Cumberland, the Army of the Ohio under Maj. Gen. John Schofield, and Sherman's old Army of Tennessee, now commanded by brash Maj. Gen. James McPherson. George Cooley was not much impressed with dour and grizzled General Sherman. "He looks more like a Methodist minister than a general," he jotted in his diary. "Still," he concluded, "he is a fighting man as his acts indicate." Date Worth likewise thought that because of his sober demeanor and unassuming dress and style, the general could be taken for a preacher. Sherman stood some six feet tall, was sandy complexioned, and was a "little silvered with age."

The 1st Brigade, of which the 24th was part, now consisted of seven regiments under the leadership of Col. Francis Sherman, the Illinois officer who had incited the men against antiwar sentiment several months before. He would, however, not gain much favor with the Milwaukee men, and not long lead the brigade.[23]

Dramatically, Grant also wanted Little Phil Sheridan to come east, to command the Army of the Potomac's cavalry against Robert E. Lee's Army of Northern Virginia. In his place, a brigadier, John Newton, would assume command of the old 2nd Division. It would be a sad parting, felt equally by the soldiers of his old division as with the general himself.

A gala party was given for Sheridan March 22. Regimental bands played and officers danced with local ladies. But for the common soldiers, there was to be no formal departure ceremony. Twenty years later, when writing his memoirs, Sheridan still betrayed the feelings that prevented him from saying good-bye in a ceremony. "I could not do it," he said; "the bond existing between them and me had grown to such a depth of attachment that I feared to trust my emotions in any formal parting." When the train steamed from Loudon, Tennessee, for Chattanooga, Thursday, March 24, "the whole command was collected on the hill-sides to see me off." They had gathered spontaneously, and as the cars trundled noisily along the track, they waved and cheered.

None demonstrated more wildly than the 24th Wisconsin, one of Sheridan's favorites.[24]

Back in Wisconsin, Capt. Dick Austin was recovering from his "rough usage" in the charge up Missionary Ridge, and on January 23 arrived in Milwaukee from his father's home. Fortunately, he had avoided a disastrous amputation that the gruesome leg wound had at first promised, managing to recover without the operation. Austin said that "a couple of legs are vastly superior than one for locomotion." He had to labor on crutches, but anticipated returning to the Milwaukee Regiment soon.

Now a grateful city wanted to fete Austin, one of its heroes. Scores of friends gathered at the Newhall House, the splendid six-story hotel east of the Milwaukee River, in early February to present him with a "magnificent" sword with a gold-gilted scabbard and hilt, cord, and belts. The weapon, it was variously reported, was made in New York, and cost between $400 and $500, a princely sum.

Judge McArthur made the presentation speech. But when Austin was asked to say a few words, emotion of the moment overcame him and he "excused himself from making a speech." His former Company A comrade, the proud Lish Hibbard, offered appropriate comments in his stead.[25]

Within several weeks, "Dore" West, the lieutenant colonel who had led the 24th Wisconsin and was wounded and captured in the battle of Chickamauga, was also roundly feted in Milwaukee. He delivered a "thrilling" account of his wounding and capture in Tennessee in September, and the grueling trek to Richmond's infamous Libby Prison to a crowd of thousands at the Chamber of Commerce. He told of several escape attempts that failed, and ultimately of fifty-one days of tunneling, during which he was a leader, and the clandestine departure of over 100 officers. After six days and seven nights, 100 miles of secretive trekking in Virginia, and the assistance of slaves, West and his companions, including Wisconsin's colonel Harrison Hobart, arrived within the Union lines at Williamsburg.[26]

With his new commission as colonel of the 24th Wisconsin, West cut a handsome figure in his new uniform despite his obviously thinned flesh. Before he entrained for his regiment in late March, he was, like Captain Austin, feted at the splendid Newhall House, and presented with a an assortment of gifts including a sword, scabbard, and accoutrements—"a light and elegant weapon, of the finest steel, and beautifully ornamented"; the weapon was inscribed with the battles in which

West fought with the 5th and 24th Wisconsin regiments. The sword replaced the captured rebel weapon he had carried at Chickamauga. (It was ironic that the sword West had taken from an enemy in Virginia found its way back into Confederate hands in Tennessee.) Judge McArthur was again on hand, offering "remarks in his peculiar and inimitable vein of mingled eloquence and wit, which were responded to by frequent cheers and roars of laughter." West and Captain Parsons departed for Tennessee April 3.[27]

But elsewhere in the city, despite the pomp and proceedings, more sad stories were being written. Young Charley Webber, one of the Milwaukee Regiment's drummer boys, was lying desperately ill in his father's house. The lad, along with brothers Eugene and James, all sons of an immigrant from the German states, enlisted in Company G. Seventeen-year-old Charley rose to become chief drummer of the brigade. "He was a good soldier, and well liked by his comrades." But in October, he had been felled by the miasma of the Chattanooga camp, and was hospitalized with chronic diarrhea. In winter, his father, Wilhelm, brought him home to the Germanic precincts of the near west side, hoping to nurse him back to health. "Kindly care and good treatment were of no avail." The youth would die in June.

On April 17 the stirring among the Federal camps and commands that had been going on about Chattanooga stretched to Loudon, Tennessee. The 24th Wisconsin was ordered west to rejoin its comrades in the Army of the Cumberland. Colonel West; Captains Parsons and Philbrook, who would celebrate his thirty-fourth birthday April 30; and others who had been home on furlough rejoined the Milwaukee Regiment in Tennessee. With them were about forty new soldiers; companies C and G, whose ranks were badly depleted, received half of the volunteers. Other men, hospitalized in Chattanooga, were being released and sent back to their regiments. And a handsome new battle flag was brought from Milwaukee to replace the tatters of the old one. Painted in gold upon four white stripes were the battle legends: "CHAPLIN HILLS," "STONE RIVER," "CHICKAMAUGA," and "MISSION RIDGE." The price paid for those new honors had been high. That flag would see more hard service in the new year.

Elsewhere, veteran regiments, having reenlisted and fresh from thirty days furlough home, were returning to Chattanooga. Activity was shaking the army from its winter torpor; its strength was rebuilding. The Milwaukee Regiment was tightening its organization even to the point of ordering white gloves for a spring inspection. "I don't think the regiment will be pleased at so much style," George Cooley opined. "It is all the officer's doing." Yet, during the inspection, the first ever with white gloves, the Wisconsin men "looked gay." To many veterans, it was evident that a move against the rebels and possibly Atlanta would be commenced soon.[28]

The optimism that stirred anew seeped into newspaper columns. "May will, in all probability, witness battles of greater magnitude than have yet been known to the war," wrote one New York correspondent. "It is possible that even the very Waterloo of the struggle may then be fought." The men looked forward to spring when, surely, a new campaign would be launched. One Milwaukee soldier expressed supreme confidence, hoping the Army of the Cumberland would march "onward to Atlanta, and into the very gizzard of the rebellion."[29]

Chapter 11

Onward to Atlanta

⇥✦⇤

"The land is filled with such horrid scenes."

Before crumpling to the ground in exhaustion, Capt. Ed Parsons gazed at his image in a glass. The following morning, September 9, 1864, he drafted a lengthy letter to his parents, the first one in many weeks, describing his appearance after four months of almost steady campaigning from Chattanooga to Atlanta. The Milwaukee Regiment had marched nearly 150 miles and fought in a score of battles, large and small. Its ranks were desperately thin, numbering no more than a few score over a hundred. The day before Parsons penciled his letter, the 24th Wisconsin had strode through Atlanta, once the Confederacy's thriving manufacturing heart, now but a blasted, blackened, and devastated shell. The Company K captain wrote: "I think you would hardly recognize me in my present plight." He sat now, "sunburnt, unshaven . . . hat riddled with holes, in fact in a 'shocking bad' condition." His trousers were wet and in tatters, his knees peeking through the light blue wool; shoes were sodden, and mud plastered halfway to his waist. Even after a night's sleep, he was still weary, as much of mind as of body. "Mind, you, I do not complain of a soldier's life, only give you a faint idea of what some parts of it are."[1]

At the end of the campaign that summer, a news man would look over the exhausted Army of the Cumberland, and view its dramatically changed aspect. As he traveled among the various camps around Atlanta

Edwin Parsons (post-war).
"You would hardly recognize
me." COURTESY OF THE MILWAUKEE
COUNTY HISTORICAL SOCIETY.

"the sight of so many regiments that now parade scarce one hundred men, carried you back to the many bloody scenes of the past campaign," he wrote; it "brings to memory the deeds enacted by the many brave men, who were in the ranks in the spring, when the campaign was opened in all its fury." Those words accurately described the Milwaukee Regiment.[2]

When the 24th Wisconsin began the campaign toward the great Confederate citadel seventeen weeks before, it was a dramatically different regiment than it had been when it marched off from Milwaukee. Nearly two years of war had winnowed the ranks dramatically. Gone was the old colonel, Larrabee, along with two lieutenant colonels and Major Von Baumbach. Over half of the field officers who had strode away from Milwaukee in the late summer of 1862 were now gone— dead, discharged, or resigned. Such good and true men as Bob Chivas, Fred Root, and the sensitive Howard Greene were now buried, as was the splendid soldier-correspondent, George Bleyer; dead, too, were Capt. Gus Goldsmith and Lt. Christian Nix. Two of the "pets" of Company B, the old Young Men's Association Tigers, the Rogers brothers, were out of the army. Charley had resigned his commission and returned to Milwaukee in April; the older, Harry, scarred from his Chickamauga wounds, was medically discharged.

Many of the men who now led the companies had been or would soon be promoted from enlisted ranks—men such as "sallow" complexioned John Borth, who had carried the colors part way up Missionary Ridge, and Bill Sibley in Company I. Still remaining were steady old hands like Parsons, who turned twenty-eight in February 1864; the broad-shouldered railroad man, Capt. Sam Philbrook, just then scouring Wisconsin for more recruits; and Capt. Bill Kennedy. Sgt. John Plummer (his older brother, Philip, was, at that time, about to begin Grant's drive toward Richmond with the Army of the Potomac), from Prairie du Chien, remained in Company G; Tom Ford, the red-haired Irishman in Company H, and Gene Comstock, the Company B diarist, had avoided death and maiming. Elsewhere in those sinuous blue lines that marched south from Chattanooga in the spring of 1864 was the little Port Washington tailor, Henry Bichler, exchanged after being captured at Stones River, in Company H. Young Amandus Silsby, the Company A son of an abolitionist preacher, still read his Bible twice daily and looked forward to his twentieth birthday in July, and the three young men from the western Wisconsin town of Buffalo who had joined Company A—Milt Storey and brothers George and Homer Cooley—soldiered on. The younger Cooley, George, still jotted terse pencil notes in his pocket journal, and still mourned his dead wife, buried now these two years past. Date Worth, the "erring son" of Granville, still wrote home regularly; he learned that his friend, Jim Harvey, taken prisoner at Chickamauga, was now paroled and recuperating in Nashville from his shoulder wound.[3]

Despite being augmented by nearly 60 new men since January, including the two galvanized rebels who joined in Tennessee, the ranks of the Milwaukee Regiment barely numbered 250, one quarter of the size of two summers before. But after weeks of drill under the tutelage of the confident new major, McArthur, and almost incessant parading, the regiment was well honed. With Enfield rifles tucked on their right sides or propped on their shoulders, the men displayed an easy, confident marching gait. Like Ford, most wore so-called Kassuth, or black slouch, hats that were creased and shaped to the wearer's preference; the broad brims provided more protection from the high Southern sun than the little blue caps. The nearly knee-length dark frock coats had also given way to hip-length, four-button wool blouses. The marching men had pared away many pounds of excess impedimenta, and trappings now consisted of a blanket roll (wool blanket wrapped inside a gum covering or half of the dog tent) slung over their left shoulders; and a bulging haversack along with leather accoutrements, cartridges, bayonet, and canteen. Tin coffee cups, tied to haversacks, clanked as they strode. There was little extraneous on these lean, burnished veterans.

The regiment's new flag with its battle honors painted on the silken folds proclaimed the men as veterans; it snapped proudly in the Georgia sun as they tramped south. Although they would soon be entitled to many additional battle honors, these were never painted onto the silken stripes. Ed Blake, one of the first men to reach the summit of Missionary Ridge in November, had been promoted to color corporal and now strode in front of the regiment with the special squad of soldiers whose duty it was to protect the banner. Within the next seven months, the nineteen-year-old Port Washington man would earn another stripe and glory carrying those striped and starry folds.

From Cleveland, Tennessee, northeast of Chattanooga, the regiment marched in May. The weather was cool and pleasant as they assembled with the Army of the Cumberland, and moved confidently forward, marching fifteen miles to Red Clay, Georgia, that Tuesday.[4]

With some 98,000 men and more than 250 cannons, General Sherman aimed due south at the great industrial and communications heart of Atlanta. With his armies, he would avoid, if possible, a major battle with his adversary, the wily general Joe Johnston, who had replaced the cantankerous and unsuccessful Bragg as Army of Tennessee commander following the defeat at Missionary Ridge. Like General Grant and the Army of the Potomac in the East, Sherman's Military Division of the Mississippi would endeavor to outflank the Confederate army, to slip past it on the great push south. Like three great blue torrents of men, artillery, and wagons, irascible General Sherman directed his armies south, into the "very gizzard of the rebellion." Stolid General Thomas and the Army of the Cumberland; the Army of the Tennessee, Sherman's old command, led by Gen. James McPherson; and General Schofield's Army of the Ohio—this was the grand aggregation of men and material that had to negotiate a barrier of mountains before the generally flat and rolling landform leading to Atlanta. The 24th Wisconsin was now one of nine regiments—five from Illinois, two from Missouri, and one from Kentucky—in the brigade of Francis Sherman, the Illinois colonel. But he would, within the month, give way to Brig. Gen. Nathan Kimball, under whose leadership the unit would briefly become known as the "invincible brigade."

On May 5, the 24th Wisconsin reached a former pleasure resort for wealthy Southerners called Catoosa Springs. As General Thomas paused his army, Wisconsin men took the opportunity to visit the facility, situated in a beautiful valley that featured numerous sulfur springs, and a magnificent grove of cedars, pines, oaks, and maples providing shade from "the scorching rays of the southern sun." Some fifteen acres of the valley comprised a large resort hotel and numerous other buildings. Maj. Gen. Oliver O. Howard, the IV Corps commander, used the hotel for his headquarters.

A news writer who surveyed the idyllic scene used the opportunity to sling a little mud at the former barons of the South. He described Catoosa Springs as a place "where idle, worthless, but wealthy nabobs took refuge while under-going medical treatment for ills contracted during months of dissipation." Gamblers, pickpockets, and thieves, "young men in broadcloth," had been attracted to the site, seeking not only to fleece the moneyed men but also to "pluck the feathers" of genteel daughters as well.[5]

Several civilian correspondents remained proximate to the army, drafting regular and lengthy news columns. Although some writers castigated generals for often-deleterious movement, they tended to paint a favorable portrait of common soldiers. In some instances, the word portraits of the soldiers' lot were almost pastoral. One Milwaukee man described the daily regimen: At five o'clock reveille sounded, "just as the night is lifting her dark mantle from the earth and the glimmer of morning is seen in the east"; the soldier turned over, rubbed his eyes, and crawled from beneath his wool blanket. He was quickly on his feet, "blowing into life the smouldering [sic] embers," the remnant of the previous night's fire. Minutes later, he wrote in the present tense, "the fire jumps brightly, and coffee pots are filled from canteens; while the strong brew is warming, the men amble to a nearby creek to splash cold water into their faces and bring themselves fully awake." Here was a diverting scene, idyllic almost, that may have calmed anxious families at home.[6]

During a few days' respite, General Sherman planned the manner that two of his armies, including the Cumberlands, would proceed against a narrow and almost inaccessible wall of mountain called Rocky Face Ridge; the 500-foot escarpment blocked the morning sun until it was well in the sky. The immense prominence also provided the gap in the mountains that led to Dalton, where the Confederate army commander, General Johnston, had established a strong defense. The Milwaukee Regiment and the Federal armies would soon learn the defensive capabilities and tactical brilliance of the new enemy commander.

On May 8, General Howard's IV Corps made its initial movement toward the foot of ominous Rocky Face Ridge. "It was the steepest Mt. I ever saw," jotted Sergeant Comstock in his diary. "The sides are almost perpendicular." Captain Parsons told his parents that he was not optimistic about taking such a fortified spot. "Charging such a place seems like folly." On the next morning, Monday, the soldiers were aroused in the inky predawn darkness, and in three hours were marching to the top of Rocky Face; it was "a very difficult and steep ascent, being almost perpendicular in some places," Parsons wrote. The ascent "took the starch out," said George Cooley.

Another brigade in the division, Brig. Gen. Charles Harker's, drove out the enemy ahead of the Milwaukee men, pushing the mottled, ragged ranks along the line of the ridge for about a mile and a half to an equally ominous spot called Buzzard's Roost; here the rebels were "fortified and in a position from which I do not believe they could have been driven," the Company K captain, Parsons, noted. Between the contending forces was a ravine, and all along it was nothing but a ledge of rocks. No more than a company front could be arrayed in attack. Rebel sharpshooters were posted in trees and behind boulders and piles of rocks, ready to pick apart any rushes.

The Milwaukee men cobbled together a line of breastworks and lay all day. Far below them, to the east lay the Rebel defenses about Dalton, Georgia—clearly visible; there were four or five lines of rifle pits and every surrounding hill featured some kind of fortification. Even if the Federal army could clear Rocky Face Ridge and Buzzard's Roost of its defenders, the prospect of taking Dalton looked daunting and deadly.[7]

At dusk Harker's and Sherman's brigades, having failed in the attempt to dislodge the rebels from their rocky defiles, were pulled from the mountain. The descent was nearly as bad, and many Wisconsin men struggled down the precipitous, shale-strewn slope.[8]

The following day was nearly a repetition of Monday's experience, the regiment climbing on the north end of the ridge. It was again "awful work," exacerbated by a vexing all-day rain that, at night, blew into a virtual hurricane. But there was good news: General Grant and the Army of the Potomac had opened its drive south against General Lee and the Army of Northern Virginia, the armies clawing bloodily at one other in a place called the Wilderness. Optimism, despite their own precarious situation "halfway to the clouds, among rocks and stony gorges," burned slightly. Sergeant Comstock was certain: "The rebs catch it now every*where.*" But the fight would not be so easy, here in Georgia or in Virginia.[9]

Around uncomfortable campfires that night, a story may have passed among the huddled wet men of how rebel defenders on Buzzard's Roost had actually rolled boulders and large rocks upon the blue attackers. One bold Illinois corporal was said to have shouted at the antagonists that if they ceased their actions, he would read President Lincoln's proclamation of amnesty for surrendered Confederates, offering generous treatment. The gray and dun-colored men at first hooted in derision, but quieted occasionally as Lincoln's message was recited. When they heard sections with which they disagreed, the Southern soldiers set up a "fiendish yell," and hurled more rocks. But the Illinois man continued his recitation despite the "uncivil" reception. When he concluded, another outburst of shouts, laughter, and a new barrage of rocks were the response. No rebel surrendered, but it was an episode that long remained in soldiers' memories.[10]

For three more days, the game of cat and mouse continued between the Federal attackers and enemy defenders. "We are getting tired of this and want to see the back or belly of the enemy," groused Sergeant Comstock. He had lately taken up writing in a diary in lieu of the long letters home. One of those evenings, Captain Parsons and his youthful major, McArthur, lay on the ground listening to "the music of the bullets as they sang around" when a division staff officer dropped down beside the Milwaukee men. After a little "chaffing," likely prompted by the slender and smooth-cheeked eighteen-year-old regimental officer, the man asked, "Major, suppose the rebs down there [in Dalton] should make a charge and attempt to get up here, what would you do?" Here was a bait. Without hesitation, McArthur replied, "Fight like hell!" When Parsons recalled that incident to his veteran comrades nearly forty years later, he would remark that his companion was ever ready to fight like hell. It was another of those tales, told in war's aftermath, which burnished and enlarged McArthur's image. The months ahead, however, would indeed evince the mettle of the young man.[11]

During the sodden night of May 12–13, a wounded rebel between the lines called piteously to his comrades. "Oh, George, come and get me. Can't you come and take me away?" The gray soldiers were unable to assist. Soon after daylight, Friday, the 24th Wisconsin discovered that the rebel defenders had evacuated their rocky aerie and Dalton as well.[12]

With their bright new flag fluttering before them and the regimental band playing "Rally Round the Flag," the double column of Milwaukee men marched proudly through the town of Dalton, grateful that they had not been required to assault the stout defenses that Johnston's men had constructed.[13]

Whereas regular army rations of hardtack, sow belly, and coffee were plentiful at this early stage of the campaign, the soldiers missed no opportunity to supplement their fare with good meat, liberated from the southern plantations and farms. The country through which the Cumberlands marched was pleasant and beautiful. Halting to camp one evening, the Ford brothers, red-headed Tom and Dan of Company H, set off to forage. Soon they encountered other Milwaukee soldiers who carried chickens and hams, and asked directions to the farm where those goods had been gotten. The brothers shortly located a smoke-house, and they made a rush for the lone shoulder of meat hanging inside. But as they made to depart with the trophy, a woman confronted them at the door; she cried, saying she was a widow and that she and her children would starve without that last piece of ham. The Fords, chastened, gave up the meat. "We went to camp empty-handed," Tom, the elder, recalled many years later; "had plenty to eat of government rations and felt and slept better than if we had taken the meat from the widow." Ford could show such sensitivity yet seem almost callous to battle dead and dying in his writings.

The march to Resaca, Georgia, some fifteen miles, was over considerably more level land than before; yet it still took a toll. Camping one night, Sergeant Ford's feet were painfully blistered from the coarse government shoes. The rough leather footwear was issued without regard to left or right; only after miles of marching, sweating, and soaking did the shoes conform to a soldier's feet. Ford went to a nearby stream, removed his shoes with their thin soles and rough wool socks, rolled up his trouser legs, and plunged his aching feet into the cool stream. "Oh, but it did feel refreshing." One of those mundane little incidents that constitute the life of a soldier, it was recalled fondly from the remove of decades. Ford lay back, linked hands beneath his head, and fell asleep at the stream bank. He awoke as predawn grayness began to finger through the trees. To the sergeant's surprise, his feet were without pain and soreness.[14]

As they approached the town of Resaca on the afternoon of May 14, Colonel West, at the direction of his division commander, General Newton, sent forward a thin line of skirmishers. Some 235 Wisconsin men had been counted ready for duty that morning. Whereas the regiment's normal battle array consisted of a double line, each man's right shoulder tight to the elbow of his comrades, skirmishers were sent out front several yards apart. It was their disconcerting duty to move forward, Enfield rifle-muskets carried at the belt, loaded, and primed to fire, to encounter the advance elements of the enemy. The 24th skirmish line traded brisk exchanges of bullets with the rebel foe, then fell back to their comrades in the brigade's main battle line. Incessant rain had turned the ground to mud, and churning feet created a virtual red clay slush. Soon, enemy lead grew more insistent, while deadly pieces of cast iron screeched at the Milwaukee men. Colonel West and other officers dismounted from their horses. The trim Waukesha, Wisconsin, soldier strode forward, trotting toward a line of rebel rifle pits dug into the red earth. As he stepped upon a dirt mound, an enemy soldier nearby fired, and the bullet plowed into the colonel's left foot, lodging in the ankle. A Wisconsin soldier turned his rifle-musket on the assailant, and "paid the rebel off . . . by shooting his head before he had gone a dozen paces." Quickly, men gathered up their bleeding commander and carried him from the field. Colonel West's war would soon be over. Maj. Arthur McArthur, not yet nineteen, now led the Milwaukee Regiment. He would, indeed, "Fight like hell!"[15]

The regiment pressed forward, strides quickening into a lope, up a gentle rise toward the main line of rebel breastworks. The field over which they charged was thick with smoke and a sickening sulfurous smell, said Captain Parsons. "Surely to some this is the 'dark valley of the shadow of death.' Who will get across the field alive? There is no time to think who." Major McArthur shouted, "Now forward men, double quick." The 24th's bright new colors rippled in front; within a short time, the silken banner was pierced seven times. Rebels were eager to knock down the flag, as much because it was a prominent target as because it was the central point upon which all regimental alignment depended.[16]

It was "wonderful that half of the regiment were not mowed down. Most of the men behaved splendidly," said Colonel West. Major McArthur led the Milwaukee men onward "unflinchingly and gallantly" toward the enemy works bristling with cannons and rifles. That charge was conducted with no more than 215 men, as one company had been sent to other duty while another, for reasons unexplained, failed to make the charge. McArthur "is one of the bravest young men living," West would soon attest. "No one could have done better than he."

Men went down under the whining lead missiles and shrieking iron shrapnel. One of Captain Parsons's and the regiment's personal favorites, little Johnny Moore, was shot through the forehead, dead even before his body crumbled into the mud. The lad from Oak Creek, a farming community south of the city, had a countenance as youthful as McArthur's, and he had always done his duty without complaint; "his loss was much deplored," said a new soldier. "He was a noble little fellow and died like a hero in the thickest of the fight," Parsons said. His was another name added to the lengthening role of dead. There was little honor in such dying, of course, but these nineteenth-century men were raised on a romantic image of war. All the fallen were good soldiers who did their duty. In death all became heroes, martyrs even.[17]

Men fired, tore paper cartridges between their teeth, quickly poured powder, and thumbed the big lead bullets into the muzzles, jammed them down with a clank of metal ramrods, pushed brass percussion caps on the rifle-musket nipples, and fired again. All of these movements had become rote by now. Some soldiers undoubtedly stood behind trees, others kneeled or lay upon the ground. Careful aim was not always taken, anxious men being eager to fire as rapidly as possible; triggers were jerked. The air grew gray and murky in acrid smoke. Men's faces took on a coal dusty patina, and their mouths were begrimed with black powder residue. Twenty rounds were expended, each man loading and firing about two to three shots a minute. Men began to finger for additional ammunition. As George Cooley reached into his cartridge box, lifting the tin container for an additional twenty rounds, a bullet struck his dark Enfield gun stock and split in two; glancing from the wood, the ball slammed into his leg just above the knee. Although it did not inflict serious injury, Cooley was lamed for some time.[18]

Company G was in a particularly bad strait. Lt. George Allanson, the curly-haired six-foot Milwaukee news dealer with the rheumatic legs, who temporarily commanded the company, was struck, and went to the rear for medical care. His equally tall sergeant, John Plummer, whose English family resided in Prairie du Chien, was wounded in a finger on his left hand. It is unknown if he carried the news that his brother in the Army of the Potomac, Capt. Philip Plummer, had died during the battle of the Wilderness in Virginia nine days previously. Another sergeant, Henry Davis, was shot badly, a ball passing up the entire length of his arm and lodging in his body; it was a gory wound, and the former railroad conductor would die in ten days. He left a wife and three children to mourn his loss. Pvt. Bill Ormond of Oak Creek was fortunate: Hit only by a spent ball, he was put off his feet for a few hours. A corporal now commanded company G. One of the German immigrants in Company C, Sgt. Augustus Mueller, took a severe wound to the abdomen; there was little surgeons could do with such an injury, and the Milwaukee man died that day. In all a dozen men were killed and more than thirty wounded. The ranks of the Milwaukee Regiment were thinning rapidly.[19]

Irrepressible Sergeant Ford recalled that his company halted at a double cedar fence within sight of the rebel defenders behind their breastworks. It was ten rails high with a stake and rider; the farmer turned soldier surmised, in passing, that the two landowners likely disputed the boundary, each erecting his own fence. "We took advantage of that piece of contrariness . . . and soon pulled down both fences and piled them up into one," Ford recalled. He raised his head to fire a shot, when, suddenly, two bullets crashed into the top cedar rail inches from his head.

Sixty rounds of ammunition having been expended and unable to cling to its precarious situation, the 24th Wisconsin was ordered back from its forward position by Major McArthur. The Milwaukee soldiers, veterans that they were, with musket nipples plugged shut, likely poured water down the long barrels to loosen the caked residue of burned powder. Some may have learned to use vinegar to dissolve the black fouling that often clogged the barrel's grooves so thickly it was impossible to ram a bullet completely to the breech. Meanwhile, details of men brought forward from ammunition wagons for each comrade another six packets of cartridges, each containing ten paper-wrapped rounds. Packets were broken open; twenty loose rounds were stored on the top of the tin cartridge box liner with another ten in the bottom. The remaining cartridges were placed in haversacks or in trouser pockets. That night, the regiment moved forward again, but to the relief of the exhausted men was not engaged.

Tom Ford was so weary that night he callously used two dead men to provide a makeshift mattress; he propped another dying body as a pillow. "I slept very comfortably," he wrote decades later, "with the exception of being disturbed once in a while from a hiccough or movement of muscles or peculiar noises coming from my pillow." The man, in his death throes, apparently died during the night. Such were matters of war when a soldier seeks whatever comfort he can from the dead and dying.[20]

There was grumbling in the aftermath of the fight for Resaca about how brigade commander Col. Francis Sherman, the Illinoian, had used the Milwaukee Regiment. "In our charge . . . we all think [Sherman] made us run the gauntlet unnecessarily. . . . He took the rest of the brigade around through the woods," Cooley penciled, "but the old 24th is good for him yet and he knows it." Through it all, Major McArthur again comported himself as the "bravest of the brave, and although young in years, mature in military matters."[21]

Colonel West, meanwhile, was nearly delirious under the influence of chloroform. Part of the ball in his foot was extracted. In less than a week, he would be back in Milwaukee, out of the war. In time he would be placed in command of one of the city's army training camps. The 24th Wisconsin now clearly belonged to the major whose nineteenth birthday was still weeks ahead. He had traveled a long way from the day that squeaky-voiced boy had tripped over his sword scabbard at Camp Sigel.[22]

At daylight May 15, the Milwaukee soldiers were sent into the line again, the third time in twenty-four hours. For an hour and a half that Sunday, they were under heavy fire, trading shots with the enemy. "Each man in our regiment shot 120 rounds of ammunition," Lieutenant Allanson, who still nursed his wound, wrote his brother. "It is a very hot place." Still later, Major McArthur was directed to move his men to a rear line in support of an artillery battery that was "paying its respects to the rebs pretty freely," sending shell and solid shot into enemy lines. The cannons several times volleyed at the sound of a bugle, a dozen brass barrels belching at one time. "It was at short range and there were some splendid shots made," jotted Sergeant Comstock. He would later discover that sometime during the battle he lost his pipe, a serious enough occurrence that it deserved note in his diary.[23]

Before noon on the following day, it was discovered that the rebels had evacuated their works once again and fallen back. As the Milwaukee men pressed forward toward the vacant enemy positions, they discovered the bodies of men of their brigade. During the engagement of Sunday, shells had ignited the brush, and many of the dead were burned "almost to a crisp," Captain Parsons described to his parents. He also saw a scalp he was certain the enemy had removed from a Federal soldier. "These, you will say, are horrid scenes, but the land is full of just such scenes, and will be as long as this rebellion lasts." Parsons, Ford, and other Wisconsin men were growing ever more hardened, even inured to such horrors.[24]

"Two battles, two defeats and two retreats," was the way one news writer summed up the campaign south against General Johnston to that point. But there was scarce time to savor the success, or reflect upon its import. The march south was on again, the Army of the Cumberland pushing forward to nip at the heels of the retreating rebels. Several miles beyond Resaca, part of Johnston's army turned to delay the Federal advance near the town of Adairsville. It was not to be a large-scale battle, only a "demonstration," as the soldiers called it. Lives and limbs would be lost, nonetheless.[25]

While camped the evening before, Lts. Tom Keith and George Allanson, Major McArthur, and several officers were playing whist, when one of them asked, "Boys, how many of us will be here to-morrow night to play again?" It was a question that arose many times; it was posed partially in jest as a means to relieve apprehension before battle. Keith, exhibiting one of those fatalistic premonitions, said he felt this was the last time he would be with them. The young officer later that evening drafted a letter to his mother, saying he knew there would be hard fighting ahead; but he felt the coming campaign would be the final one against the rebels, resulting in a "glorious" victory.

"I shall do my duty," he wrote by a guttering candle, "and if I fall, I shall not be wholly unprepared." His faith that the "God of Battles" had thus far protected and cared for him was unshakable. But "if it should be my fate to go down . . . it will be His will, and therefore for the best." Although it may have provided little comfort to his mother, Keith was assured that *"I shall not have lived in vain, if I die for my country."* During that card game Monday evening, Allanson, the twenty-three-year-old officer who had been slightly wounded just days before at Resaca, said he "knew" he would be wounded again.[26]

About three that afternoon of May 17, Major McArthur, pursuant to orders, deployed three companies as skirmishers under the command of Lieutenant Keith. A force of rebels advanced toward the Milwaukee men from a distance of some 200 yards. Between the antagonists stood an unusual two-story brick, octagon-shaped residence, the mansion of a plantation owner named Sexton; the grounds also included a scattering of other buildings, including slave huts and a barn that housed a cotton gin. The mansion's walls had been constructed of cement, gravel, and lime to a thickness of several inches. As the men of Milwaukee would later discover, the octagonal house was opulently appointed with fine furniture, Brussels carpeting, lace and damask curtains, a piano, paintings, and a library.

Seeing the tactical importance of the house, both blue and butternut soldiers raced toward the structure. The rebels, men of the 1st Tennessee

Infantry, reached the house and buildings ahead of the Federals, and began firing through windows and doors, transforming the mansion into a virtual fortress. Federal artillery shells made small indentations in the thick walls, and only powerful shots from a Parrott rifle, an artillery piece with a reinforced breech and rifled barrel, penetrated the masonry. Among the first casualties were the plantation's fine grove of young oak trees, "which had doubtless yielded a grateful shade in the heat of summer"; they were shattered by the shower of artillery and musketry that rained unremittingly for two hours. "The Yankees cheered and charged," one Tennesseean said, "and our boys got happy." "At every discharge of our guns, we would hear a Yankee squall." Lieutenant Keith, leading his skirmishers, was the first to be killed; it was the work of sharpshooters, Corporal Cooley said. The sensitive young officer, who occasionally wrote poetry, had fulfilled his premonition. His mother likely reread a poem her son had fashioned four years before, memorializing the death of a friend. "God guide thy mother now, Her way is dark and drear." Those words were painfully appropriate for Mrs. Keith now.[27]

McArthur ordered his remaining companies forward along with another regiment in the brigade. Arraying his line smartly, the major shouted above the rising din, "By the left flank, charge." Just as his company changed direction, "a broadsider to the left jaw" knocked down Sergeant Ford. The bullet struck him in the lower angle of the jaw, breaking a bone before tearing down into the collarbone and lodging in his chest. As his company rushed forward, Surgeon Herman Hasse kneeled beside the bleeding Irishman, cut loose the leather straps holding his accoutrements and the string that bound his blanket roll. Spreading out the woolen blanket, he ministered to the wounded sergeant.

Elsewhere in that stand-up contest, one of Ford's company comrades, John Howard, a farmer from Franklin in southern Milwaukee County, was felled by a bullet that shattered his elbow. Days later, Dr. Hasse removed twenty-six pieces of bone, but still wanted to amputate. Howard refused, saying he would rather die than live with only one limb. But gangrene would seize the arm. It was severed three times in vain efforts to save his life, but "after a long season of suffering, [he] went to the other shore" July 10.[28]

For the next several hours, the two sides blasted at one another. "This was a regular 'Indian fight,'" wrote Captain Parsons; "we could not dislodge them." Sergeant Comstock disdained it as a "fearfully mixed up mess. . . . They [the enemy] fired from the windows and also had a cross fire on us, which made it very hot for our men." Lieutenant

Herman Hasse (post-war). Regimental surgeon.
COURTESY OF THE MILWAUKEE COUNTY HISTORICAL SOCIETY.

Allanson, as he had predicted, was struck in the right breast, his second wound in three days. Sergeant Comstock rushed to his side, helping the officer to a field hospital. Allanson would survive his wound, returning to the regiment just before the capture of Atlanta, and gain his captain's bars.[29]

The two galvanized South Carolinians in Company B, Jim Gallion and Bill Edmunds, "went in like young tigers—fought like young heroes." Gallion was fearfully wounded in the left hand; ironically, he was hit by rebels in whose army he had formerly marched. The wound was so severe, he would never return to the regiment. After the war, Gallion would travel to Milwaukee to find some opportunity, but "he did not like that kind of life," and returned home. One of the new men, Phil Smith, meanwhile, who had signed the roll of Company G only three months before, was felled with a severe wound to his right arm; the bone was shattered. The limb was later amputated, and the soldier returned to Madison for hospital care; Smith would die there in September.[30]

The wide-eyed farmer in Company E, Date Worth, told his parents that he became overheated while blazing away forty rounds during the skirmish. When he went back out of musket range to clean his musket and gather a new supply of .58-caliber ammunition, he had cooled down too rapidly and caught a cold. The ailment would settle in his chest and plague him for many weeks.

Finally, Colonel Sherman brought up the remainder of the brigade. But the added men were still unable to dislodge the enemy from the Sexton plantation. During the grueling hours of fighting, small groups of men were withdrawn to hastily pour cleansing water down their warm rifle-musket barrels and replenish ammunition before moving forward again into the fight. Sergeant Comstock remembered firing from behind a tree for an hour before being relieved. "[T]his is the hardest fighting I ever done," he wrote that night. At one point, Companies A, D, and F, the skirmishers, were cut off from the rest of the Milwaukee Regiment. The sergeant blamed Colonel Sherman for the confusion. Through all of this, "McArthur behaved well." At one point during the confused fight, the major turned to the Illinois colonel, saying he would give a thousand dollars to be able to extricate those three separated companies. It was not until darkness shrouded the scene that the companies were able to withdraw. Colonel Sherman would, within the week, be replaced by another brigade commander.

In the gathering gloom of twilight color Cpl. Ed Blake was directed to set fire to the plantation outbuilding that contained the cotton gin as well as the barn. Massachusetts-born, the young man, not yet twenty, had been studying in a local commercial college when war erupted. The structure was located between the contending forces, and the Port Washington soldier dodged and darted forward to fire the building. The conflagration "lit up the heavens with a lurid light," wrote a news man. Finally, night brought a desultory end to the sanguine contest about the plantation. When numbers were counted, the 24th had lost three killed and fifteen wounded. Under cover of darkness, the rebel force withdrew. The Wisconsin men went forward to retrieve the body of Lieutenant Keith that had lain between the contending lines all day. In Milwaukee, his name joined the legion of dead heroes. "He was an earnest, enthusiastic, brave and true soldier, and his loss will be felt in the regiment."

That night, too, blue soldiers, Milwaukee men likely among them (although none recorded the incident), ransacked the Sexton mansion, "rummaging among old trunks, and through pyramids of torn clothing and papers." After looting what they would, the soldiers piled bedding and old trunks together in two rooms, and struck matches. The fine mansion was soon a "pyre of flame." The soldiers were apparently fueled as much by greed as revenge; war, death, and maiming created conditions conducive to such behavior.[31]

Tom Ford was in a bad way. While he lay bleeding on his blanket during the remainder of the fight, four spent bullets plopped beside him.

He saw the number of maimed men around him increasing with the crescendo of firing. With his wound dressed, he moved toward the hospital with others who could walk. Near him was a Union captain. "He had his nose shot off, and all but part of the skin near his forehead, which was holding it from falling. It was swinging on his face like a pendulum of a clock." When a rebel cannonball pounded down the road near them, the captain shouted: "You rebel sons of guns [the word used was likely much stronger], I hope you will get your belly full before night," and at that instant the officer was struck in the abdomen by a minié ball.

In a field hospital Surgeon Hasse later probed Ford's ghastly wound for the lead bullet, but failed to locate it. The red-haired farmer was sent north to Chattanooga; as he was ambulatory, he was not loaded into an ambulance but trudged, with excruciating pain in his neck, face, and breast, with long unsteady lines of bloody and bandaged soldiers. At every stream, Ford dipped his slouch hat full of water to pour over his head. After six bone fragments were painfully removed from his lower jaw, he was out of the war. The cruel disfigurement was his ugly badge of battle for decades to come.[32]

Once again, the Confederate general Johnston "displayed his cultivated talents for retreat," yielding ground to avoid a full-scale battle; he "occasionally halted a corps or two to demolish our advance, and fighting it jauntily until our army was hastily thrown into position, when he 'folded his tents like an Arab and silently stole away.'" Another anticipated large-scale confrontation between the armies would have to wait. "Johnston conducted his retreat with great skill," wrote an admiring Northern news man.[33]

Sergeant Comstock was not happy with the state of affairs. The weather had turned intolerably hot, he wrote May 19 near Kingston, Georgia. "After a great deal of useless marching we went into camp in regular line of battle ready for a night attack." Capt. Ed Parsons, too, fumed that "the rebels literally contest our advance over every foot of ground." This was to be the pattern of their lives, with one notable exception, for the next several months. March, halt, pull together breastworks of trees, fences, brush, and earth, advance as skirmishers, fire artillery and musket bullets against the enemy behind their works, and wait for the tattered dun-colored army to withdraw in the night. The other armies in General Sherman's grand assembly or another corps then slid past and pushed south. In a few days, General Newton's IV Corps men took the lead again to either feint, or in the parlance of the army, "demonstrate," toward the enemy to cover a thrust by either General McPherson or Schofield, or to make a serious run upon the enemy.[34]

At times, the 24th Wisconsin was pulled back a short distance from the front to rest and recoup. Sergeant Comstock and others readily used available opportunities to bathe and wash clothes. The men foraged in the local countryside to supplement the wearisome army fare of sow-belly, hardtack, and coffee. As May waned, the Milwaukee men saw signs that another "hard campaign" would soon commence. Regimental baggage was reduced to only the amount that could be carried in one wagon. The men were directed to pack twenty days rations and an extra pair of shoes. They shoved as much hardtack and dried bacon into their trappings as possible.[35]

The Milwaukee men tramped across the Etowah River, forty miles south of Resaca, on May 23 on the wooden planking of the covered Gillum's Bridge. "Some doubt as to where we are going," Comstock wrote. It was often difficult for soldiers to learn much beyond their own regiment or brigade. The armies of General Sherman's grand aggregation were often widely separated. Then the rains began, soaking the rough wool uniforms, chilling the soldiers' bodies, and making the roadways a muddy morass. "We marched in every direction." For much of the time, the Cumberlands slogged off the roads, skirting the Allatoona Mountains, angling to the southwest. "This is an awful wild country," the twenty-year-old printer groused.[36]

The men knew but two changes of clothing now—on and off—the latter being only an occasional occurrence. As the rains continued almost unabated, the Milwaukee men often lay down at night in line of battle, and slept "without taking anything off," wrote Sergeant Comstock. The exhausted soldiers simply threw gum-coated black blankets over their sodden bodies. Many nights passed in ineffectual sleep, as the men were not permitted to remove even their cartridge boxes. When they reached the vicinity of Dallas, about thirty miles northwest of Atlanta, they erected dog tents, two men mating halves to form their low shelter. Although they were not engaged in pitched battles now, rebel fire still stalked them. About dusk one of these days, as Comstock jotted in his pocket diary, a lead musket ball glanced two feet from him, and punched through the shelter where his messmate, Tom Bate, sat. "It was a very close call," he noted tersely. Forward on the skirmish line, deadly lead missiles continued their steady work. Dolph Walter of Company E was seriously wounded one afternoon; the Milwaukee man contracted disease during his hospitalization, and died several weeks later.

A day later, May 27, a young Company A soldier, John Dewey, was wounded on the skirmish line and carried to the field hospital; he died the following day. "Poor boy, his troubles are over and he sleeps the sleep of death as a good soldier of his country," George Cooley noted. The words seemed to betray a hint of envy at Dewey's relief from this incessant harvesting by death. It was one thing to be killed in a mighty charge, and quite another to be felled in such inglorious circumstances. The slow winnowing of the Milwaukee Regiment continued when Company E's Peter Bernges was also killed by rebel sharpshooters as he filled canteens for his comrades. On the skirmish line, a man in the same company, Joe Singer, was severely wounded, a shot ripping away "a piece of skull from the crown of the head . . . exposing his brain." The soldier would almost miraculously survive the wound, but never return to the regiment's ranks. After the war, he was never the same.

Then one night, Billy Almey was detailed to relieve the 24th Wisconsin pickets. "He had not been out but a short time before the alarm was given on the left," and the private apparently hesitated to fire his rifle-musket. Only Almey's black slouch hat was found later, "and he has not been seen or heard of since." Almey was taken prisoner, but later exchanged. In a little skirmish on May 29, Company B's sergeant Ed Arnold was wounded; he would never return to the regiment, serving out his enlistment among the invalids of Veteran Reserve Corps in Washington.

Sherman's army now sprawled over an almost continuous front of miles, "in dense forests, over creeks, and hills and valleys, with only a few rugged and narrow parallel roads," described an Ohio news writer. With a touch of sarcasm lacing his words, the correspondent observed that "while skirmishing has been incessant, and, on two or three occasions, we have fingered the rebels, and on as many more we have been fingered in turn by them, and these mutual handlings have produced on both sides a good degree of caution and reserve."[37]

In the last days of May and in early June, several more Wisconsin men were wounded, either on the skirmish line or some yards behind where they trudged for rest. A Milwaukee Irishman, Jack Dunn of Company F, was nicked in the hand by a spent musket ball while he cooked breakfast; though not serious, it was his second wound of the war. And within the next few days, several more were wounded; none of these were serious, but they were continual vexations of an emerging kind of fighting. Bill George of Company F was also scathed in the hand, while another "chance shot" hit Jack Mahoney of Company A in the leg.

Lying behind the main line of fortifications the next day, a bullet struck Billy McAvoy in the cheek, then glanced and struck Dewey (Lewis) Martin on the shoulder blade; he was a young man from Eagle in southwest Wisconsin who had enlisted in Company A along with Amandus Silsby. Because the Federal breastworks had not been substantially built, enemy shots often penetrated the brush; Company B's Conrad Niederman, a German immigrant, was felled by a ball that ricocheted through the thicket. And Company H's lieutenant George Coote took a hit in the leg, and was carried to the hospital. Since the campaign had commenced, Date Worth told his parents, Company E had lost nine killed and wounded. Worth thought the 24th Wisconsin had sustained eighty casualties in the past few weeks.[38]

Major McArthur and four field officers were the only shoulder straps left; most of the companies were led by sergeants.

During these unnerving days of almost incessant fire between the Federal and rebel forces, Major McArthur's birthday occurred June 2. Now nineteen, he was sloughing off the boyish countenance and gaining a more mature mien. Like his men, the major's face was sun-browned almost to leather, creased, and wind-chaffed. Wavy dark locks, so long from a barber's scissors, were likely thick under the slouch hat that he creased front to back. His countenance, once as soft as a drummer boy's, was coarsening. Yet he was one of the youngest in the Army of the Cumberland, perhaps in all of Sherman's armies, to command a regiment. He had exhibited daring and presence of mind since he strode to the front of the 24th. In a short time, McArthur would gain another promotion, and become, it was said, the youngest man to hold such a rank in the army. His fame as the "Boy Colonel of the West" would soon spread.[39]

Another young man would not earn such renown. Amandus Silsby celebrated his nineteenth birthday just weeks after McArthur, on June 26. He marched, fought, and camped with his Company A comrades in near anonymity, doing the duties expected of him. As he had promised his father, he read his Testament twice each day, perhaps a verse or two, and, like his fellow soldiers, yearned for the war to end and the recovery of peace.

In Milwaukee, summer had finally arrived after tantalizing in April and teasing in May; sun spanked the creamy brick of many city buildings; trees had fully leafed and flowers finally bloomed; and the wintry gray of Lake Michigan had given way to balmy blue. There, direct news of the city's regiment had grown sparse in the pages of the dailies. The wonderful soldier correspondent, George Bleyer, "Marion," who produced detailed accounts biweekly, had been dead a year and a half now; "Musket," Norm Burdick, was home; the pseudonymous "Euonia" and others had also stopped writing about the 24th Wisconsin. Others were not disposed to compose long columns, perhaps dispirited by the drone of tramp and almost continual fighting. The men still sent letters home, but fewer of these missives were being reprinted in the city's dailies. Diarists like Comstock and Cooley satisfied themselves with terse jottings—weather, miles marched, and occasional camp chatterings.

In their place, readers were becoming accustomed to the broader brushstrokes of the war painted by correspondents from Cincinnati, Chicago, and New York papers and reprinted in the local news sheets. The writer for the Cincinnati paper generally followed the Army of the Cumberland during the campaign to Atlanta. He was often acerbic and biting, jabbing at the folly of the army, which made "as many false passes as the enemy, hits foul, goes down on all fours, and performs as many erratic gyrations and tumblings as would a brace of trained pugilists pitted against each other on a field as unequal as this." Such was the manner of war in Georgia as he saw it.[40]

Finally, news from the Army of the Potomac and its battles against Lee's army crowded onto the pages of the daily papers. Heavy headlines proclaiming the Wilderness, Spotsylvania Court House, and Cold Harbor darkened the daily columns in May and June. Many citizens, however, were becoming weary of the steady drumbeat of war that played in the news.

Meanwhile, a tangible artifact from the 24th Wisconsin was exhibited in Milwaukee. Judge McArthur received an express shipment in June from Colonel West—the "bullet-riddled remnant" of the regiment's first flag. The stars and stripes, a gift from the Chamber of Commerce a year and a half before, bore the painted names of the unit's first battles, "CHAPLIN HILLS" and "STONES RIVER." "I entrust its sacred folds to your keeping for the time being," the colonel had written to McArthur. "Exhibit it to the citizens of Milwaukee as a testimonial of the fiery ordeal through which the 24th had gone, and under whose folds so many brave heroes have fallen." Thus, before being transported to the state capital in Madison for permanent housing, the banner rested in the Chamber's rooms east of the Milwaukee River. Judge McArthur, always prominent in such matters, provided an oration.

As the men of money and power in the city gazed upon the "rent and battle-soiled fragments of their once beautiful colors," a Republi-

can editor reminded his business-oriented readers that they should realize how insignificant were their monetary sacrifices in the war effort
"compared with those of the heroes who have left home comforts, to
fall under the folds of this emblem of our nationality." Doubtless, John
Mitchell, peering through thick spectacles, the Rogers brothers, the
druggist Henry Drake, and others who had marched with the regiment
viewed the old banner, recalling the days when they were part of the
regiment's full ranks. Their comrades still fought on the fields of Georgia, and more would be wounded and die under the new flag.[41]

By the first week in June, matters had changed little for the Wisconsin soldiers in Georgia. Duty behind brushy breastworks, skirmishing with the clay-colored and gray enemy, snatching whatever respite
was available in camps, and scouring farther afield for eatables to supplement rations—these were the formal and informal orders of each
day. The heat of the lower South bore down on them like an anvil at
times; torrents of rain seldom brought relief. As was their want, some
soldiers from the brigade—with the continual shrinking of the ranks,
soldiers gathered friendships with men from Illinois, Ohio, Kentucky,
and Missouri in their brigade as well—wandered beyond the Federal
lines to bathe. In early June, while they splashed in the stream, a trio of
rebel cavalry suddenly dashed in on them; most of the blue soldiers ran,
either naked or in underwear, but two were snatched up by the gray riders. One of the prisoners, a canny man from the 88th Illinois Infantry,
under the guise of modesty, asked if he might don his uniform before
being marched away. Only one horseman tarried to wait for the captive
to dress. Suddenly, the Prairie State soldier leaped up, grabbed the
enemy by the throat, and pulled him from his horse; "and after a severe
tussle, he had him tight." The other Federal soldiers quickly returned
with their loaded muskets and turned the tables on the rebel.[42]

Lines of skirmishers were often quite close, and the opposing brush
and timber fortifications within eyesight. Veteran soldiers, however,
exhibited a "certain coolness and sang froid" when cannon shot
shrieked and musket balls whined. One hardened man walked to his
tent behind the lines with a plate of purloined flour with which he
hoped to produce something more palatable than the brick-hard government bread. A "wandering fragment" of shell shattered the plate and
scattered the flour. The soldier merely looked nonplussed at the crock-
ery fragments and dusting of flour on his hands, stating: "No more of
that on *my* plate, if you please." Still another soldier in a similar fashion
was loudly "saluted" by a rebel shell a few inches from his head. With-

out blinking, he turned in the direction that the projectile traveled, and nodded, "Good morning."[43]

Occasionally brigades and regiments were ordered to charge upon the enemy defenses, to push them back from such proximity to the blue entrenchments. In the aftermath, dead bodies lay sprawled and festering for days in the heat. Date Worth, like so many others, did not shrink from describing the gruesome details to his parents. Nothing remained of one "brave man but Uncle Sam's uniform[,] a few bones & the skull which had a hole in it the size of my hand," he said. "Another lay near by but the maggots had not quite devoured him."

Brigades, divisions, corps, and armies were shifted from time to time, as General Sherman leapfrogged armies to gain an advantage on his opponent, continually seeking to outflank General Johnston. Many movements were plagued: "Mud, mud and no end to it," Sergeant Comstock complained at midmonth. Emerson Opdycke, the colonel of the famed "Tigers" of the 125th Ohio, temporarily commanded the brigade, as General Kimball was sick. Ultimately, the fiery Ohioan would replace Kimball, and lead his men to grand glory and fame in the final months of 1864.[44]

It was near Dallas, Georgia, that the Milwaukee men were rolled from their night slumbers early June 15 to the sound of "skirmishers pecking away at one another." But by seven o'clock, matters quieted, and it was surmised the rebels had withdrawn once more. Orders were promulgated to prepare to charge the enemy fortifications, "leaving everything but . . . haversacks and canteens." Arrayed in double columns and three brigades deep, skirmishers in front, the Federal advance began to drive the enemy backward; the enemy was likely not eager to engage so formidable a force. Every time they had advanced before, one Milwaukee man thought, "Now it comes," the final assault, a major battle. But time after time, it did not come. A crucial confrontation, however, was less than a week away.

The division once again changed position, and two days later advanced to find the breastworks around Dallas vacant of rebels. "What a lucky thing we did not charge," wrote Sergeant Comstock, for the enemy fortifications around the town, like those at Dalton, were formidable to his eye. The Company A man also noted that a soldier from the 73rd Illinois had found his old pipe, lost a month before, and returned it to him. Tobacco was a close companion for many soldiers, a "necessary evil in the army," Worth wrote. "Some would trade the shirt on their back for a part of a plug."

The ranks of the Milwaukee Regiment were being steadily winnowed in the deadly harvest, and gaps in leadership opened. Several
new promotions and commissions had been formally made to men
who, for the most part, had risen from enlisted ranks to become line
officers. Among these was the former color-bearer, John Borth, who
now permanently wore lieutenant straps; nearly forty-five years old, he
had come a long way from his laboring days in Milwaukee. Blue-eyed,
curly-haired George Allanson, twice wounded in recent days, had
gained his captain's bars. Of the five promotions, all had volunteered as
private soldiers in the summer of 1862—now, a seeming lifetime past.[45]

During the campaign south, the veterans of the Milwaukee Regiment, like tens of thousands in the army, had learned one of the most
important lessons of soldiering—whenever a halt was called, they
immediately began constructing fortifications, called breastworks, of
material at hand. Farm fences were rapidly dismantled; small and
medium trees were chopped down; brush was cut or pulled loose; boulders and large stones rolled into place—all piled up to create a protective barrier. Using their bayonets or other implements, the men also dug
pits in the red Georgia earth. The "construction of rifle pits, abbattis
[*sic*] and barricades is as such a matter of course, as the preparation of
the vesper hard tack and bacon," wrote an Ohio news correspondent.
Between the present position and Chattanooga, the writer observed, the
landscape "displays a monument to [the soldiers'] energy and caution
which the next century cannot efface." Indeed, the wounds of war
scarred the land for scores of decades.[46]

The hot and often rainy days of June were passing. On the eighteenth, Pvt. George Cooley celebrated a sad anniversary—the death of
his wife in 1862. "It has seemed a long, long time since I last saw her
dear face and I pray that God may permit us to meet again in a better
and happier world," the twenty-eight-year-old printer from Buffalo,
Wisconsin, lamented in his diary. He would, within days, be visited
with more tragedy.[47]

General Sherman's path to Atlanta was now blocked by a massive
prominence called Kennesaw Mountain. The 500-foot high timbered
escarpment dominated the land for miles around. Its summit, sometimes called Bald Mountain, was rocky and bare of foliage. General
Johnston had heavily and almost impregnably fortified the mountain
with extensive earthen trench works and carefully positioned cannons.
The IV and other corps were moved into position June 19, as General
Sherman contemplated the next move. The work of the next few days

belonged largely to the artillery, which attempted to blast the Confederate army from its moorings on the frowning mountain. Rank and rank of cannons, at one point, "for near 3 miles along the line, poured forth volley after volley of shot and shell," wrote an Indiana soldier, "whole batteries firing at the same instant." Gray, acrid smoke billowed and gathered, expanding like a deadly wraith over the field. The Milwaukee men were ordered outside their breastworks without rifle-muskets to erect a new line of protective barricades. They inched their way toward the mountain.[48]

General Sherman, grizzled "Old Cump," and his counsels had finally decided upon assaulting the prominence head-on. It would prove to be a costly maneuver. In a preliminary move, various regiments and elements were directed to probe forward. On June 22, the 24th Wisconsin, on the mountain's south face, was ordered to assess the enemy's position and strength. The Milwaukee men, heads bent forward, stepped toward enemy rifle pits. But the enemy erupted from the earthen defenses, driving the attackers back. During the brief melee, a sergeant in Company D captured the sword of a gray officer. At three o'clock that afternoon, another Federal advance was ordered. "[W]e maintained our position under a dreadful fire lengthwise [enemy enfilade fire] with the line. It was terrible work. The right did not advance and so we got it thick on the flank," Sergeant Comstock noted later that day.[49]

Fred Kohler of Company A was badly wounded in the right arm; amputation might be the least of his worries. A ball also whined past George Cooley after it glanced from a tree. With his birthday only weeks away, Amandus Silsby was also knocked down by rebel lead that caught him in the arm and groin; the little Testament must have been tucked safely in his breast pocket or haversack.

While the 24th Wisconsin was being raked by fire from its left flank, a ball struck George Cooley's older brother, Homer, in the right breast; he slumped to the earth. Andrew Baxter of Company G was also killed. Seeing their opportunity, the rebels charged upon the exposed rank of the Milwaukee men, and the blue lines were thrown backward. "I was compelled to retire leaving 2 of my dead in the enemy's skirmish works," Major McArthur lamented.[50]

In a rare display of self-effacement, the nineteen-year-old major failed to note the fact that he was scathed in the right wrist, and nearly killed by another missile. As he had led his men forward up the mountain, a partially spent ball also struck him flush in the breast. It might have been a mortal blow, but the inside pocket of his uniform, near his heart, was stuffed with a pocket Bible, letters, and other papers. Legend later had it that among the other papers that blunted the blow was his commission to major dated January 2; the lead bullet scored a black mark on the document just over the name where it read: "To Arthur McArthur, greeting." Such were tales that fueled the old soldier reunions later in the century.[51]

George Cooley was distraught over his brother's fate. "He probably lies between the two lines. I greatly fear I never shall see him more," he confided in his journal. The heartfelt task of writing to his family about the tragedy confronted him. "Homer was a good boy and has always done his duty and stood at his post like a man and a soldier," he wrote. Such words would mark many a man's unwritten epitaph: He did his duty and stood at his post.

That Wednesday night, perhaps after dark, Cooley, his friend Milt Storey, Tom Tish, and another man searched the battlefield, and located the dead body of Homer "in a hollow covered with a piece of tent." Whether Homer had covered himself or some charitable Confederate had done so is unknown. "We put him in a safe place," the grieving brother penciled in his diary that night, "intending to get up at daylight and bury the body." The dead soldier, a once proud printer from Western Wisconsin, was thirty-two.

On Friday, a group of soldiers buried Homer Cooley beside Andy Baxter on a little knoll. Rough headboards were fashioned and names carved upon them. Later that day, Cooley wrote to his family while Milt Storey packed Homer's pipe, tobacco pouch, pocketbook, comb, pin cushion, and a lock of hair and sent it to the dead man's mother. Lettered on the outside of the parcel were the words: "The last effects of H. H. Cooley late of the 24th Wis. Vol. Infty." Another Wisconsin mother would soon grieve, as had thousands before her. The knowledge that her son did his duty and stood his post was small comfort, indeed.[52]

Then, Sergeant Comstock's tentmate, Tom Bate, took sick. It seemed that one day he was robust and ready for the march, and the next feverish, wan, and weary. The Milwaukee soldier died in Vining, Georgia August 10, almost two years after he signed the roll of Company A. "Poor boy," George Cooley would note in his diary again. "He was a good soldier and now rests in peace."[53]

It was perhaps the following day when Amandus Silsby, Fred Kohler, and a dozen more Wisconsin men were loaded onto wagons whose floorboards were without doubt blotted with blood. Most of the wounded were later transferred north by railroad to a Chattanooga

Amandus Silsby gravestone.
Chattanooga Chickamauga National Battlefield.
COURTESY OF NANCY TORPHY.

hospital. Kohler's arm was sawed off, but death could not be arrested, and he succumbed July 11. For a month, the brown-eyed Silsby also battled the inexorable creep of mortality, but finally it overtook him July 30 just after his nineteenth birthday. Ironically, his military grave-stone would later be dated incorrectly as August 31.

In war's aftermath, the man who would write Wisconsin's military history, William DeLoss Love, himself a preacher who was acquainted with Silsby's father, drafted an encomium. "His father gave him to the martial conflict because it meant freedom to the slave; the offering was accepted, and the son was taken." As a soldier, he kept a promise to the memory of his dead mother, remaining aloof from the vices of the army; and he was said to have followed a vow to his father that he would read his Bible twice each day. His father, the church missionary, could only mourn from afar. His son had dutifully sent him money, but there was not enough for a funeral. A simple white military headstone with his name, company, and regiment was later set among thousands of like markers in the cemetery at Chattanooga. Silsby's body would remain forever in Tennessee.[54]

The Sabbath day after the disaster at Kennesaw Mountain was not a contented one. The 24th Wisconsin, after losing more good men, had to close ranks even tighter. That night, they learned that General Sherman planned another grand assault for the Army of the Cumberland; after learning of the attack, the commanders of eleven regiments selected for part of the task, including the 24th Wisconsin, expressed concern. They feared the attack would be suicidal. Each of the eleven officers, it was said, wrote a farewell note to his family. Major McArthur may have tucked his missive inside the torn breast pocket of his blue coat.

"From the base to the top is about a mile and a quarter," a news correspondent wrote after the battle, "over rocks and logs up an ascent which is anything but agreeable." Another described: "Within twenty feet of the woods[,] bushes had been felled[,] the ends pointing toward the assaulting columns, carefully sharpened, so that an abbattis [*sic*] capable of perplexing and impeding our progress was encountered." Moreover, Johnston's men also had constructed what soldiers called "hay rakes" or *chevaux-de-frise,* created by cutting trees about six inches in diameter. Holes were bored into the wood at six-inch intervals into which were inserted tough pieces of wood. All ends were sharpened like the teeth of a farmer's hay rake. "To advance and charge over these things is simply an impossibility." Advancing soldiers would take much time in maneuvering through such obstacles, all the while being sought out by rebel shell, shot, and musket fire.[55]

Dark-eyed Lt. Tom Balding had returned to the 24th just two days before. The twenty-five-year-old former Milwaukee clerk still nursed the wound he had sustained at Missionary Ridge. "I do not think I will ever be able to stand as much hard service as I could before I was wounded," he wrote. The London native had seen hard service for several years, having began as an enlisted man in the 5th Wisconsin Infantry three summers before.

At 8:30 that Monday morning, June 27, the assaulting columns of General Kimball, three lines deep, were assembled, facing the west side of brooding Bald Mountain. For about fifteen minutes, all of the Federal artillery in the area blasted at the point of attack. Then, up the timbered sides the massed lines advanced, the slope gradually increasing. The air was close and hot. Cannons from both sides had commenced a bone-jarring duel. A news writer was apt in his description of such chaos:

> Whole brigades rush headlong through thick woods, where they cannot see ten lengths of a musket in advance, and come

suddenly on masked cannon, which are so close that to retreat is certain death, and only a part of them can hope to escape by falling flat on their faces. . . . While they lie there, many of them are discovered by the rebel sharpshooters, and die helpless. Others are slaughtered by a cross fire from other batteries. . . . [When they finally withdraw], so many of their comrades lie stiff and stark in their places, that they look as if still skirmishing with the enemy—a battle line of corpses.[56]

The assault was "badly repulsed," Lieutenant Balding said, after a struggle of several hours. Except for small gains here and there, the attack was "substantially a failure," concluded an Illinois soldier. Very soon after it commenced, in fact, "the ambulances began to pour their streams into the hospital." "Death and Mars held high carnival," a caustic news writer said. Casualties were fortunately few in the Milwaukee Regiment—only one officer, Adj. Horace Buchanan, and eight men were lost in the timbered maelstrom.[57]

"Owing to some misunderstanding, the line connecting with my left did not advance, thus exposing my left to a flank movement and my entire line to an enfilading fire." That was the manner in which Major McArthur assessed the debacle in his official report many weeks later. The terrible fire chopping at its flank caused him to order the Milwaukee Regiment to retire along with the other Federal columns. It was a retreat by any name.[58]

To the relief of the men in the ranks, the commanding general ordered no further assaults on the impregnable enemy lines about the mountain. The abortive attempt of June 27 had apparently convinced him that his opponent's lines, "stretching out over the vast Kinesaw [sic] Valley like the web of a spider," as one writer observed, were too formidable for direct attack. The 24th Wisconsin hunkered down in its own rifle pits, digging into the red muddy Georgia earth with practiced efficiency.

From June 28 to July 2, "there was unusual silence along the line." The blue and ragged, russet-garbed soldiers soon worked out a truce between them, "amicable relations," a news man called them. At any hour of the day, the opponents sat on the earthen lip of their works, "coolly" watching each other and occasionally indulging in a bit of bandying, and sharing patriotic songs. They often exchanged newspapers, and bartered coffee for tobacco and other goods. During those days, one soldier in the 44th Illinois, brigaded with the Milwaukee

Regiment, sauntered over to the rebel line with a sack of coffee in hand; a butternut customer was quickly found. Every Federal soldier, it was said, tried to extract as much of the "beloved weed" as possible, "cheating by every name laid down in the Yankee peddler's vocabulary." But a dispute arose as to the quantity of each commodity to be bartered. "Neither would come down an inch," the bemused news writer who heard the tale reported, and "they would have been wrangling yet, had not a third party happily suggested the idea of settling the dispute by wrestling, the best of three being the winner" who would get both coffee and tobacco.[59]

Both were solid men, and they readily agreed on the contest. The Illinois soldier bested the opponent "to the evident satisfaction of the lookers on (mostly gray-backs) who cheered lustily," and encouraged the blue combatant with such words as "Bully for the 44th Illinois." "Happy as a king, the hero of the tussle gathered up his treasures, and hurried homeward, whistling Yankee Doodle, leaving his discontented antagonist 'chewing the cud of discontent' behind him.'" Such occasional incidents lightened those summer days, if such was possible for soldiers daily near the door of death.[60]

Back in Milwaukee and in numerous other communities there was muttering about the snail's pace of Sherman's advance on Atlanta. "[W]eeks may roll by, months pass down into history, ere the objective point . . . is reached," a correspondent told his readers. Yet, Atlanta must fall and "repent of its sins in sackcloth and ashes" before Sherman's armies will end the summer campaign. The news man attempted to buoy his readers. "Patience, a few short weeks, and the old flag will once more float over Atlanta and its war-scourged people." But those short weeks would turn into long ones, and the soldiers suffered under the increasing heat of the Southern summer.[61]

General Sherman was frustrated, too, with the pace of advance, particularly on the part of the Army of the Cumberland under his stolid but deliberate subordinate, Maj. Gen. George Thomas. The armies had moved again, General Sherman quitting his line around Kennesaw Mountain, as he had so convincingly from defenses before, to slip past the enemy's flank. Looking ahead to the "Gate City," Atlanta, the commanding general did not intend to besiege this great Southern industrial bastion. He would cross the wide Chattahoochee River, and circle around Atlanta, breaking roads and rail lines as he went. Looking back, he wrote: "We have devoured the land and our animals eat up the wheat and corn fields close."[62]

For the soldiers on the march, little was known outside of the events occurring in their own regiments. Great secrecy attended army movements. Rumors, most untrue, rustled daily, and were as substantial as the smoke of cook fires. After General Johnston abandoned the town, the IV Corps marched through Marietta. Worth found it a beautiful place, with a military school he said General Sherman was rumored to have attended. Jim Harvey had finally rejoined Company E after nine months' hospitalization; two stripes had been sewn to his new blue coat. "I was really glad to see him again for he is my nearest & dearest friend in this business," the bewhiskered Date Worth noted. Capt. David Horning had been badly wounded a few days previously; like most others, the company was led by a sergeant. There were but fifteen or sixteen in the ranks. On the morning of July 6, the first Federal units began crossing the broad Chattahoochee. Atlanta lay only seven miles south, plainly seen through telescopes. But the capture of that grand war prize was nearly two months away.[63]

In thick forests south of Marietta, Georgia, the men of the IV Corps encountered enemy pickets, and drove them until the marching columns were a half mile below the town. "The country . . . through which we are now making a pilgrimage of blood, is more level and open than that encountered before," wrote a Milwaukee man. At dawn on July 3, the blue army was awakened from sleep by "the melodious notes of Old Hundred from one of the brigade bands"; the tune echoed against the green-capped hills. "Soldiers intently preparing the morning meal, stood still and listened to the melody and instinctively joined in it. It flew from regiment to regiment; brigade after brigade took it up, and ere the notes of the band ceased to reverberate, five thousand voices were raised in 'Praise God from whom all blessings flow.' A moment later all was still." The soldiers, many at least temporarily fortified by faith, quickly completed their breakfasts and silently packed up their trappings and fell into their line of march.[64]

In Milwaukee the following day, the city celebrated Independence Day with the usual picnics, parades, and speeches as well as musical flourishes, fanfare, and fireworks. In Georgia that clear and cloudless Monday, the soldiers spent the day musing about Wisconsin friends, wondering where, if back home, they might go on this day or, if there would be a dance or social that night. Around ten that morning, when picket fire was brisk and artillery boomed, the camps "were alive with joyous shouts, jumping, racing and games. Running a foot race for a purse made up of a few chews of tobacco, was the principal sport.

Instead of anvils and fire crackers, they had the stern realities of twenty-four pounders and rapid volleys of musketry," a Milwaukee correspondent observed pointedly. The day's orators "standing behind their well-digested manuscript, loaded to the muzzles with high-flown ideas and far-fetched metaphors, manned their Parrot[t]s and howitzers, sending greeting to their opposing audience sentences full of meaning, with import dreadful; and if periods were not always beautifully worded, they had the redeeming quality of being conical [*sic*]—a charming feature in the rhetoric of war."[65]

At noon, the holiday dinner consisted of "hard bread and bacon, with a cup of coffee to wash it down." That evening, a whiskey ration and a small supply of dried apples were distributed. A Chicago news writer commented that "we enjoyed and relished it full as well as the pleasure-hunters 'at home,' who sat down to their feasts of nick nacks, ice cream, confectionery, etc." Rebel lines were plainly in view across an open field, skirmishers on both sides keeping up a lively fire. "Our skirmishers thought they must do something, as it was the Fourth, and gradually advanced upon the enemy, despite a rain of bullet, shot and shell—capturing the rebels in their rifle-pits, in full view of the rebel army." During the sortie, one "poor fellow" in the 74th Illinois, in the same brigade as the 24th Wisconsin, was badly wounded. "He said he didn't mind the wound so much, but he had calculated so much, on accompanying us to Atlanta it seemed hard to go to the rear now." That evening, the "celebration" terminated with twelve rousing cheers for "our flag, Lincoln, Sherman and Grant." Then the men rolled into their blankets. On the following morning, Johnston's men had withdrawn south once again.[66]

The capture of Atlanta would soon be part of the war's great endgame. With the next advance, the Federals were in position to begin launching large artillery shells into the very streets of the Gate City. The men in the ranks could all but predict the final outcome based upon the scenes they saw. "The neglected corn-fields were ploughed by our shells as they had not been ploughed for weeks." Oak trees fifteen inches in diameter had been broken off twenty feet from the ground from the effect of four-inch shells. The soldiers were grateful, passing the former rebel works without loss, commiserating with the enemy who worked so hard in constructing them without being allowed to fire a single ball toward their enemy before abandoning the defenses.

In the IV Corps on July 7, artillery was rolled up behind "hastily erected but substantial works constructed by the 'Shovel Brigade.'"

Soon, a number of cast-iron "rebel demoralizers" were thrown into the enemy defenses. It was "the most tremendous cannonade of the campaign," wrote an Ohio news man. "Over 400 rounds were expended in half an hour. But there was no response. Musket fire was "quite spirited and harmless for an hour."

Two days later, the men of Wisconsin, with General Newton's division, splashed across the Chattahoochee River. It was a shallow stream about 400 feet wide at the point of fording. The banks were alive with beautiful fringes of willows and luxuriant with oaks, poplars, and beeches that grew to gigantic sizes. After a halt, the men took their ease in the muddy waters, attempting to find respite from the brutal heat of the day. "You can see at any time shoals of merry swimmers splashing in the clay colored stream, and sinking in its treacherous quick sands, from morning till night, and 'tattoo' and 'taps' scarcely prevail to bring them out of the waves. In another place men are seen patiently waiting for the small cat fish, which alone inhabit the river, to come by their way." Rations were plentiful, and beans, vinegar, desiccated vegetables, potatoes, and the "*delicacies* of the soldiers' allowance" appeared regularly. A young Wisconsin farm lad from Oak Creek in Captain Parsons's company, Thomas Chapman, said he was "well and fat." "The boys are all cheerful and go at it with a will. Our war cri [*sic*] is death to traiters [*sic*] at home and abroad." He complained only of not being paid in nine months. But the Company K private had found $10 "so that will help me some."[67]

Even uniforms were issued, "suits of new blue." Cast off gum-blankets, blouses, and such were "slung over the breastworks as far toward the rebels as possible, and it is a thousand pities the latter could not be allowed to appropriate them as a shield against the scorching visitations of the sun."

During the relative inactivity of those days, soldiers found diversions where they might. Berries were coming into season. With the blackberry fields near their camp denuded of the succulent fruit, the men sallied farther afield, rifle-muskets in hand, into the enemy's country. "Boldly striking out in skirmish line, with pails and guns, the boys proceeded half an mile ere they found a berry patch in which rebel cavalrymen were foraging. A few well-aimed shots scattered the rebels to the four winds, leaving the Yanks in possession of the field." George Cooley may have found time to concoct another of his delicacies.[68]

On Tuesday, July 19, General Howard ordered the 24th Wisconsin and two Illinois regiments on a reconnaissance toward Peach Tree

Creek, only three miles from Atlanta. Little opposition was encountered. Atlanta soon lay before them but two miles distant. The Wisconsin soldiers would shortly learn that the Confederate commander General Johnston had been removed. In his place was appointed the furious Texan, John Bell Hood, an impetuous, one-legged veteran of fighting in Virginia and in the West. He would for the remainder of the year lead an implacable force the Milwaukee Regiment confronted on several occasions; the results would be sanguine. On July 20, the rebel army leader, who had to be strapped to his horse, turned upon his assailants. At 3:40 in the afternoon, "with the clarity of lightning, the rebel host poured from their concealment, massed in enormous columns against Newton." Hood "made a sudden and desperate charge" upon the center of Sherman's long line.

General Kimball, whose brigade was arrayed on the right side of the division, had that morning directed Major McArthur and the 24th Wisconsin forward several hundred yards to ascertain the strength and position of the enemy. The regiment counted fewer than 200 men in its ranks. The thin line of Wisconsin skirmishers waited nervously in front. When enemy skirmishers confronted the Milwaukee men, the blue soldiers loosed a shot or two, then sprinted back, informing their commander. While he ordered the regiment back some 200 yards, the nineteen-year-old officer remained with a dozen men. When the main body had established a firm defensive line, McArthur and his men pulled back; the leapfrog maneuver was repeated until the 24th was again safely inside the Federal defenses.[69]

"We thought the fun was over," Moritz Tschoepe recalled of those moments, "when, all of a sudden, a tremendous noise broke loose in our rear and left." The Milwaukee German, who had not Americanized his family or given name, carried a wound from Stones River. General Kimball's adjutant rushed up and ordered the 24th back on its left flank. Only a small skirmish line protected the Federals from the bridges across the creek, and "here the rebels were determined to break through, cut us off from the bridge and our army, and give us fits. We double-quicked back through a regular hail of shot and shell and reenforced that thin line behind a fence. On the road behind us ambulances, wagons and stragglers hurried to the rear," the Company C soldier said.

Then Hood's men crashed upon the Federals. "They came without skirmishers and with yells whose volume exceeded any battle shout ever heard." It was that high yelping, keening screech from thousands of throats that likely fingered fear up many blue soldiers' spines. Newton's division had not fully completed erecting defensive breastworks, and they had barely enough time to grab rifle-muskets and fall into battle line before the attackers plunged upon them. Blood red flags snapped before them. "For the first few minutes everything hung trembling in the scale," wrote a news man.

Twenty years later those desperate minutes still exploded in memory. "On came the enemy again and again, and I could not help admiring their bravery," wrote Tschoepe, the Germanic wagonmaker from Milwaukee. General Newton ordered his artillery to open with canister, and the devastating shotgunlike blasts of thousands of small steel balls hacked apart the surging mass of attackers. The men of Wisconsin and their fellows loosed brutal volleys of bullets.

Tschoepe credited the artillery, Ohio soldiers of William Goodspeed's battery, with helping break the assault. The gun carriages thundered up at the gallop; after their horses were unhooked and brass barrels swung forward, the guns trained on the running rebels. The artillerymen threw off their jackets and rolled up their sleeves and "labored with a will over our heads. We repulsed every onslaught until the rest of our corps put in their appearance."

The attacking columns slackened their pace and began to waver. Alignments and formations were sundered. "They had come to a stand still in partial confusion, and tiring heavily and wildly. Color bearer after color bearer went down under the crash of our canister." Rebel officers vainly attempted to lash their men forward, flailing with swords and shouting at their men. But in twenty minutes, Hood's attack broke apart.

"The battle raged until nearly dark, the enemy fighting with great desperation." In front of Newton's division, the dead rebels were numerous. In the 24th Wisconsin, Sgt. John Barrett from the village of Wauwatosa, west of Milwaukee, was killed; three others were slightly wounded. The men would later learn that General Sherman's protégé and favorite, Gen. James McPherson, was also killed that day.[70]

A week later, one of the Milwaukee Regiment's favorite generals, the one-armed Oliver Howard, was promoted to command of the Army of the Tennessee in place of the dead McPherson. Corps commander General Hooker was so angered because he was not given army command (he had, after all, commanded the Army of the Potomac in 1863, achieved a glorious victory at Lookout Mountain, and led his corps estimably during the spring campaign) that he resigned and returned East.

That evening, July 22, was a "splendidly moonlight night, such as enables one almost to read," and a becalming silence fell across the lines and in camps about 2:30; it was a strange contrast "with the incessant rattle of musketry, which lured us to sleep." The enemy had once again withdrawn from the main line of fortifications about two and a half miles from the city, and had retired about a mile. For the next several days, the IV Corps was shuffled about, its men uncertain where the next confrontation with the implacable General Hood would occur.[71]

"Woke up this morning," George Cooley wrote August 2, "found that we could look right into Atlanta from our position." The men of Milwaukee had a "fine view of the city and all the rebel works [fortifications] surrounding it." The widower learned later that in Virginia General Grant and the Army of the Potomac had blown a gap in the Petersburg defenses. The Battle of the Crater, July 30, proved abortive, however, as the forces assigned to exploit the confusion caused by the gigantic blast were ineffectually led into slaughter.

For the next few days, the 24th Wisconsin was not heavily engaged; there was "more or less fighting on the right and demonstrating made on our part of the line, such as advancing the skirmishers . . . as if about to making an attack," Capt. Ed Parsons told his parents. One night during this time he was on picket, a safe place because Federal batteries opened a terrific fire on the Gate City in the evening and kept it up all night; rebel guns countered, raining shells on the blue camps, compelling the men to run for safety. "A number of our tents were torn by their shells and some men in our brigade hurt." The cannonading continued for more than a week.

The conditions were "particularly pestiferous," said a correspondent. Large-caliber enemy guns were aimed at the Federal defenses. When the solid balls screeched down on the fortifications, they threw up "head-logs" and other timber. As Captain Parsons attested to his parents, being in camp offered no safe haven. The soldiers camped in a dense woods, and the rebel gunners calculated that by smashing their shot through the dense timber, they would harass the blue antagonists with falling limbs and spiraling jagged splinters. It was "absolutely infernal," having to "pass a clear, moon-lit night in a tent near the line in woods through which these howling devils go thwacking among the trees, scattering limbs promiscuously, and, sometimes, sweeping low enough to rake through a whole row of tents," Parsons said.

"It seems very evident that we can not take Atlanta from the positions we are now in, as by charging their works we would only sacrifice a large number of men, with doubtful results," Parsons sought to assure his parents. Then late in the month, the IV Corps once again quietly withdrew from the lines and marched to the right, skirting west of Atlanta and shuttling past other corps. "This movement completely puzzled the rebels," he wrote. It was a deadly chess match with tens of thousands of weary and wary blue pawns.

"The daily record of this sort of fighting is tedious to make, and scarcely edifying to read," wrote an Ohio news man; "the history of one day, with a few blottings and interlineations, is the history of the next." Even news writers grew weary recording events during those final days before Atlanta.[72]

By the first of the new month, the Army of the Cumberland had marched to a point some twenty-five miles south of Atlanta, where the enemy was found in force. Once again, pugnacious one-legged General Hood turned upon his assailants; but the result was the same. The Ohioan, Colonel Opdycke, who formally took command of the brigade in August, was ordered to arrest the enemy at Peach Tree Creek, if possible; he arrayed his regiments in three lines near the Macon Railroad. At about five that Thursday, the 24th Wisconsin, in the first line of the battle, with the 44th Illinois on the left, strode forward 300 yards in front of the brigade; the sun was dropping at their backs. Through a dense thicket of pines the formations surged, and to the "astonishment and admiration" of the brigade commander, they emerged in "complete order" into a large field. Major McArthur evinced splendid control of his men. Those dreary hours of drill during the past winter were well spent, many might now agree. Across the open area grew another woods. There Hood's men bristled. Colonel Opdycke ordered his regiments forward.

Major McArthur shouted, "Charge!" and his double blue lines, eighteen inches of bayonet glinting at the end of musket muzzles, "drove them [the enemy] three-quarters of a mile, swinging completely on their rear." During the dash to the enemy position, Lt. Fred Schlenstedt of Company C fell, mortally wounded; the Milwaukee immigrant had been a steady officer, "liked by all," Date Worth said; he was one of those shoulder straps promoted from enlisted ranks. Three other soldiers were wounded. The 24th Wisconsin and 44th Illinois, wrote Opdycke, "responded gallantly, and soon were sole possessors of the position."

Orders passed through camp that night that another charge would be ordered in the morning, but at daybreak it was discovered, as had been so many times in the past four months, that the enemy had abandoned his defenses. Most of the rebel dead had been left to lay on the field. Stomachs were gruesomely bloated, and the stench of putrefaction permeated the air. "It was about as hard a sight as I ever saw," Parsons wrote with unsparing candor to his parents, describing the grisly scene. "Their [rifle] pits were literally a pool of blood and brains." The Federal fire from the flank had virtually chopped them to pieces.

That night, the Milwaukee Regiment was assigned another picket duty. "It was so dark we could not see an inch before us," the Milwaukee captain wrote. Some of the Wisconsin men had inadvertently been posted inside the enemy lines. "I had lain down and been asleep about an hour, when Captain Philbrook came around with a piece of candle in his hand and woke me up." The railroad man commanding Company D had actually been so close to the enemy defenses that he called out in the darkness, "supposing them to be our men." He quickly discovered his mistake. The Milwaukee men silently pulled back to their own line. "It was a wonder they did not gobble us all up." Colonel Opdycke reported that "about 13 of my skirmishers got detached from the line and were taken by the enemy."[73]

The enemy retreated again that night, and the blue lines pursued. Yet another Federal charge on September 2 proved unsuccessful in driving the gray and butternut army, but the defenders pulled away again. Only desultory firing between picket lines was heard for the next two days. The enemy was abandoning the Gate City. The commanding general, William Sherman, noted tersely: "So Atlanta is ours, & fairly won."[74]

Finally, on September 3, tall and black headlines bannered across the front pages of Milwaukee's daily press: "ATLANTA CAPTURED." The grueling and deadly four-month campaign from Chattanooga had finally ended. The relieved men of the Milwaukee Regiment were shuttled about, south of Atlanta, for the next several days. At one in the afternoon of the eighth, they marched through the city with "flying colors," observing the incredible devastation that Federal artillery had wreaked upon the once proud city. And, as devastating, Hood's men had exploded large stores of ammunition, adding to the destruction. George Cooley, whose brother had paid with his life in achieving the ultimate war prize, jotted that the city was littered with wrecked railroad cars and locomotives, blown up by the retreating rebel army; "shells, musket balls and old iron were strewn all over the ground." Once grand buildings had been reduced to barren and blackened chimneys. Ruin and desolation were at every hand.[75]

"I have much to be thankful for that I have been spared through this trying campaign," Captain Parsons wrote in camp that night. "You at home can little realize what a soldier's life is during a campaign." And so they could not.

The 24th Wisconsin, it was rumored, would be rested for a month now. Its tattered ranks were badly reduced by four months of campaigning and a score of battles and charges. Twenty-three had been killed in the long campaign, and seventy-six wounded—a casualty rate of striking proportion. Some of the wounded would return after their injuries were bound and partially healed, but many would not. The Milwaukee Regiment was not many more than a hundred now, one-tenth of its size when it departed Milwaukee two summers previous. Weeks before an observer had written to a city daily about the state of the regiment's condition. "I well remember what a fine appearance they made when they left Milwaukee nearly a thousand strong—Now they are a handful." The city writer tried to assure the families and friends, however: "The remnant is composed of good, true men, well disciplined." And of Major McArthur, fast growing older than his tender years, he noted: "This young officer is deserving of great credit for his fidelity to his country and to his regiment. He is always on hand ready to lead his men in every fight—wishing and seeking no opportunity or excuse to absent himself from his command." McArthur and the 24th Wisconsin would need all of that mettle and more in the months ahead.

Parsons heard rumors that the Milwaukee Regiment might now be transferred east to the Army of the Potomac, then digging deep siege lines to the south of Petersburg, Virginia, bottling up the great Confederate commander, General Lee. But, in Georgia, the army of Gen. John Bell Hood, the impetuous soldier some called the "Cockney General," had collected in the vicinity of Dallas, Georgia—north of the Milwaukee men. Here was an ominous portent for the coming months.[76]

Chapter 12

The Final Battles

━━ ⊫◆⊨ ━━

"He lies where he fell."

The battles of late 1864 remained fresh in memory when veterans of the Grand Army of the Republic gathered in Milwaukee in the summer of 1880; they were men of middle years, some prosperous and prominent, others of more common station. The fiery colonel, Emerson Opdycke, in whose brigade the 24th Wisconsin fought, declined a special invitation to attend from Ed Parsons. But in his reply the former brigade commander wrote: "The conspicuous heroism of the 24th Wisconsin is one of the most precious and fadeless recollections of my mind." He noted particularly the incredible charge at Franklin on the final day of November 1864. "I do not believe any troops ever made a more gallant charge. Without it all of our forces clear up to the Ohio river would have been swept away." It was a wonderful accolade by the tall Ohio colonel, and when the Milwaukee men read it that summer, their breasts must have swelled by inches, remembering the time when he led them.[1]

The heat of summer had drained from Tennessee by mid-October 1864, and daylight of those fall days faded quickly among the mountains of the Cumberland chain. The men of the Milwaukee Regiment found themselves back in Chattanooga, the scene of one of their glorious triumphs. With time lately weighing upon them, some of the soldiers may have trudged to the top of Missionary Ridge, to reclaim for memory those desperate but grand minutes of the year before. Several from the 24th Wisconsin, George Cooley and Gene Comstock among them, did make something of a pilgrimage to the top of "frowning" Lookout Mountain where Gen. "Fighting" Joe Hooker had won the famed "Battle above the Clouds."

Cooley, a corporal now, likely still felt the pangs of loss over the death of his brother, Homer, killed under the brow of another "frowning mountain" called Kennesaw. His diary entry was not particularly effusive about the trek up the precipitous Lookout. It was a "pleasant trip," he penciled. Sergeant Comstock, however, was much moved by the panoramic vista, although he was unable to find words enough to describe it. He did note that some enterprising photographer had set up a studio on that windswept summit; ready-made scenes were offered as well as images the entrepreneur posed of soldiers singly and in groups perched atop that craggy eminence. Numerous photographs from that location were later published.[2]

Those crisp autumn days in "battle-blasted" southern Tennessee were easy on the soldiers: Food was plentiful; knapsacks had been brought up from Georgia. "How my mind went back to the time when we all packed them," Company A's Corporal Cooley lamented; he referred to the time before Homer had been killed. "We are living high now," he jotted in his diary. Despite the proximity of the rebel army of the badly maimed Maj. Gen. John Bell Hood, there did not seem to be a true sense of urgency about it all. A "corps of Windjammers and sheep-skin pelters (in Yankee vernacular called a Band)" provided the soldiers with "some of the best music of the day." Since the mouths of the brass horns faced to the rear so troops marching behind could hear the music, concerts were presented with the players facing away from the audience. The 24th Wisconsin band was acknowledged as the best in the division, and they played many of the latest "takes," such as "Johnny Fill Up the Bowl," "Sally Come Up Quickstep," and "Mother, Is the Battle Over?" The close comrades, Date Worth and Jim Harvey, had, like most of their comrades, fixed up a "nice shebang," contented with "plenty to eat & no poor kin." Such were the diversions of the day. Indeed, the men yearned for an end to the war business—they had been at this now for over two years and were eager to return to Milwaukee, Wauwatosa, Granville, and numerous other towns and villages in Wisconsin. They had heard and seen enough of death and blood and shattered bodies; they had lost enough good comrades to last a lifetime. "I hope we will never go to the front again, and indeed I don't think we

Arthur McArthur.
The boy colonel, 1864.
COURTESY OF THE MILWAUKEE COUNTY
HISTORICAL SOCIETY.

will. Everything looks as though we were to be kept here," Sergeant Comstock optimistically told his sister. Still, there was the unspoken matter of Hood's motley-attired army lurking about western Tennessee.[3]

Major McArthur had returned to the regiment after a month in Massachusetts and Wisconsin. He had spent two weeks in the East visiting his infirm mother, the woman who had left him, his brother, and father in 1853 to return to her family; she had fallen ill and been institutionalized. He journeyed to Milwaukee for the second half of his furlough. But when he returned to the regiment, the youthful leader could not dwell on personal matters. When he received word of his mother's death on November 10, the young man must have been shaken; but that did not deter him long from the business of war. He would soon sew to his shoulder straps the gold oak leaves of a lieutenant colonel, gaining a brevet rank for his splendid leadership during the Atlanta campaign. The official date of his promotion was back on June 8. He ordered a dress parade on the very day of his return; the Milwaukee Regiment must be prepared for the final act. There would be more opportunity to "Give 'em hell!"[4]

There was even time to take part in the fall elections. The first focus was upon the race for the presidency between Abe Lincoln and George B. McClellan, the old commander of the Army of the Potomac. Soldiers in the East had affectionately called the general "Little Mac," for he took great care to see to their needs and not use them up in battle as did other army commanders. But the men of the West, the Army of the Cumberland and other armies, had never developed such a bond with McClellan. Besides, the soldiers were now Abe's men, for the president was the embodiment of the Union, and the Union was the reason why nearly all were still in this war.

The election commissioners set up balloting sites in the various camps around Chattanooga. McArthur's son would later retell the story of an incident, adding more than a little coloration to actual events. The lieutenant colonel, only nineteen, led his regiment to the appointed polling spot. "But to his amazement his vote was challenged because of his youth." The entire regiment was taken aback and "the situation grew tense." In a voice that probably had deepened in timbre from those days at Camp Sigel in Milwaukee, McArthur growled: "If the Colonel can't vote, nobody in the regiment can. So, Mr. Commissioners, get out of my camp." From a hundred throats a roar of approval erupted. The election officials stammered and expostulated. Then a bearded sergeant bellowed out, "Let's ride the rascals out on a rail." The commissioners hastily gathered their papers and departed.[5]

The romantic reshaping of the episode was apparent as it was later reported that the 24th Wisconsin gave Lincoln a majority of some sixty votes out of a hundred or so cast. It is unknown if the slender leader of the regiment was permitted to mark a ballot. Moreover, the Milwaukee Regiment gave Republican Party candidates for the U.S. Senate and governor healthy majorities. Ironically, the city of Milwaukee gave a plurality to McClellan, largely on the strength of the Germanic vote.[6]

The month before there had been another dress parade as the army of Maj. Gen. William Sherman lay near Atlanta after its capture. Major McArthur kept his men in trim, and the day after they had marched through the charred and blasted city, he had conducted an inspection and a dress parade. A news man would later describe that "from the thousand camps of this vast army, the stirring martial airs of countless drums and fifes, or the inspiring strains of cornet bands, call the soldiers to their . . . morning inspection." Officers and sergeants passed between the extended ranks to scrutinize their men. As a news man observed, "the bright bayonets and polished barrels of their Enfields glisten while the clear ring of ramrods, in their well cleaned gun-barrels, sound in the distance as the ring of the blacksmith's hammer on the anvil." Inspection was immediately followed by the parade. Behind the color sergeant and guard—"models of cleanliness and soldierly bearing"—who carried aloft flags "torn to threads by storms of bullets through which they have passed on many a battle-field," the soldiers tramped, raising great billows of dirt from the bare campground. Many of the regiments, the 24th Wisconsin among them, numbered barely 100.[7]

Within days, the remnant of the 24th Wisconsin was loaded aboard railroad cars bound north, up the rail line toward Chattanooga. The army of the one-armed, "lame Texan," General Hood, was on the move in Tennessee. He led, camp rumor had it, some 45,000, including the horsemen of the impetuous Nathan Bedford Forrest, the fierce cavalry leader whose name still churned fear in many Federal chests. Precisely what they were about was uncertain to the men in the ranks, but many may have speculated the rebels would go all the way to Nashville. "We hear no news but the usual camp rumors," Corporal Cooley wrote in early November. For a few days, portions of the Federal army had been shuttled to various points—Bridgeport, Lafayette, and Rossville, Tennessee. A IV Corps soldier groused that the "pursuit of Hood [had proceeded] over the hills and valleys of Georgia." At one point, the 24th Wisconsin marched forty miles in two days. Spirits were buoyed when they learned that General Sherman now led his army east toward Savannah, to the very "sea" of the Atlantic. "Would like to be with him," Cooley scribbled.[8]

On Thursday, November 24 "before we got a fire built, orders came to be ready to march in ten minutes," and before noon, the Milwaukee Regiment had tramped twenty miles. In Columbia, Tennessee just below the Duck River, they heard hard skirmishing and cannonading, thinking "it might lead to a general engagement but the day passed without any demonstrations." Hood was near, that was certain, and Forrest's daring horsemen were pressing upon the little army of General Schofield to which the Wisconsin men were attached.[9]

The Federal aggregation now moving north consisted of the XXIII Corps augmented by two divisions of the IV. In one division was the brigade of the impetuous Emerson Opdycke, still only a colonel despite his heralded actions at Shiloh, Chickamauga, Missionary Ridge, Rocky Face Ridge, and elsewhere. With penetrating pale blue eyes and a fair complexion that tended toward freckles, his countenance was topped with thinning light hair. The thirty-four-year-old Ohioan wore long sideburns, a mustache, and thin chin whiskers. "He looks like a hero," wrote one of the men of the 125th Ohio; the colonel stood six feet tall. His voice was "immense."[10]

Maj. Gen. George Thomas had sent the New Yorker, Schofield, with perhaps 22,000 men to find Hood while he assembled a more formidable force in Nashville to withstand whatever the brash Texan had in mind. New soldiers, largely draftees, poured into the great Tennessee city daily. On the twenty-eighth, the 24th Wisconsin and its sister regiments pulled back across the Duck River, and on the following day began a feverish march north. After days of cold and rainy weather, the sun returned that Tuesday, drying fields and roadways. The blue soldiers would soon learn that improved conditions permitted Forrest's riders full and fast range of movement.

The Milwaukee men practically trotted toward the next town of note on the turn pike to Nashville, a small village called Spring Hill, a dozen miles away. The IV Corps was sent to gain control before the enemy took possession of the town, and to protect the Federal retreat north. Within a mile of the town "we became aware of the enemy's presence in our front, the roar of cannon bespoke something serious and our officers expressed as much surprise as the men in the line," remembered one Ohio solider. "At the first sound we hastened our pace and the last half mile was made at the double-quick." Colonel Opdycke's men led the breathless line of soldiers, arriving at Spring Hill just in time to trade furious musket shots with the butternut- and dun-colored enemy. The 24th Wisconsin's lieutenant, Lewis Battel of Company D, was slightly scathed in this encounter.

An Illinois soldier, writing almost poetically from the remove of many years, remembered those feverish moments when the enemy "like waves angrily rolling upon a storm-washed beach . . . dashed across the fields, raising great clouds of dust, and charged impetuously." Colonel Opdycke's veterans, however, "were all inured to the turmoil of war, and to them this sudden dash of rebel fury had no terrors. A few rounds of musketry, poured with damaging effect into the rebel squadrons, checked the charge." Not a year before, these same soldiers recoiled in great fear of rebel cavalry, especially the horsemen of seemingly malevolent General Forrest; now the thin, scrawny ranks of the enemy were less cause for concern.[11]

Sgt. Tom Ford, who had recently returned to the regiment bearing the ugly pink scars of his face wound, pondered the effects of such a cavalry charge, worrying "how they could cut and slash and shoot us and trample us down with their horses." But after his experience that day, he changed his mind. The 24th Wisconsin was in front of the brigade, bayonets fixed and rifle-muskets slanted forward, when the enemy horsemen "came hollering like demons, carbines empty, sabers drawn over their heads ready to come down with a cut and slash." But every man stood firm, even though the riders kneed and spurred their mounts to break through the blue ranks. Horses, eyes wide in terror, reared and plunged before the porcupine of bayonets. When the enemy withdrew, the Federal batteries joined the infantry in showering them with lead and cast missiles.

Ford, who was often wont to exhibit a certain callousness in his postwar writing, described the result graphically. "You could see a rebel's head falling off his horse on one side and his body on the other, and the horse running and nickering and looking for its rider." Several horsemen were felled, but when their feet caught in stirrups, the horses dragged and trampled them, "dead and alive." Shot horses tumbled, catapulting their riders head over heels; other rebels were killed when the animals fell upon them. "Why, it is the greatest fun imaginable in time of war for a solid column of infantry prepared for the attack to have a cavalry charge." The red-haired farmer was one of the few Wisconsin men who fashioned recollections of these days.[12]

By dark the entire corps had been established behind defensive breastworks, and General Schofield's XXIII Corps slipped past Hood's army into the town. It was now necessary, however, to move the command north of the broad Harpeth River that looped about Franklin, Tennessee, before the rebels cut off further retreat and smashed the small Federal force—half the size of the Confederate army—before it found safety and reinforcements.[13]

General Schofield designated the brigade of Colonel Opdycke to protect the rear as the remainder of the army withdrew a handful of miles to Franklin. Division commander Maj. Gen. David Stanley informed the colonel that "our situation was critical, and the greatest efforts would be needed." The 24th Wisconsin and its longtime regimental comrades, the 36th, 73rd, 44th, and consolidated 74th and 88th Illinois, along with the colonel's own 125th Ohio, the Tigers, composed the brigade; all were small regiments, and the aggregate number was perhaps around 600 or so. There would be great glory to win in the day ahead. "Our brigade fell in at sunrise and was rearguard on the Columbia pike from Spring Hill to Franklin," wrote a Tiger soon after the war. Opdycke formed two lines of battle, and a section [four guns] of artillery. With the gray of morning just beginning to hint orange on the horizon, they moved off the line and began the retreat north. "We made several stands and thus materially delayed the enemy's advance."

The backward movement was much hindered, however, by stragglers from other commands who clogged the road. These were "mostly
new men with immense knapsacks. They were so worried as to seem
indifferent to capture." Colonel Opdycke, disgusted, determined to
bring these frightened, overburdened soldiers along. When one of these
fresh soldiers, looking all the world like "old time 'back-peddlars,'"
was encountered by the veterans of Wisconsin, Illinois, and Ohio, they
ran up behind him and "cut the man's straps"; prodding him with a foot
and a half of steel bayonet, the veterans compelled a faster gait. "I am
sure that we saved 500 men from capture by these measures," the
colonel noted in his official report a week later.[14]

"Our last halt was made at the hills two miles from Franklin. From
the summit of one of these we had a view of the entire rebel army following us," wrote an Ohio veteran after the war. "They were forming
for some purpose and surely were not going into camp with all their
banners flying. One of the boys suggested the Johnnies were inspecting
all those cast-off knapsacks." The sight of Hood's army so arrayed must
have been unnerving, even to veteran soldiers. "In their butternut, clay-
colored clothing they looked like the sands of the seashore—and full as
numerous." Many of the rebels now wore uniforms of a coarse fabric
that was not even dyed. Opdycke's men may have cast wary eyes
toward the "dense masses" of the enemy army advancing up the pike,
but they continued with measured, unhurried steps north.[15]

In Franklin, General Schofield's soldiers feverishly shored up
defensive fortifications from an earlier Federal occupation that arced
about the entire southern aspect of the town. Earth and timbers were
reinforced, and head logs placed atop the palisades. At the backs of the
assembling blue soldiers looped the Harpeth River. But Confederate
cavalry had destroyed the bridges across the watercourse, and the river
was cresting to flood level. Engineers were quickly directed to repair
those spans, one of which was a railroad bridge. A day would be
needed to ready the crossings for men, artillery, and supply wagons.
Meanwhile, more than three score cannons were situated to bring fire
upon the advancing ranks of Hood's minions. But a mile south of
Franklin where the Union line crossed the Columbia turnpike, a weak
spot occurred: A gap had been allowed to permit passage of cannons,
caissons, and wagons; a retrenched line was created seventy yards
behind the main fortifications just south of a farmstead owned by a Tennessee man named Carter. Situated some yards west of the road to
Nashville, the collection of buildings consisted of a red brick structure,

featuring a fifty-foot steep parapet wall topped with chimneys at each end. Slave quarters, a barn and brick smokehouse, and other structures were close at hand. The farmstead's slightly undulating fields to the south, containing a few more buildings and orchards, led to the main Federal line of defense.

About 2:30 that Wednesday afternoon the final day of November, the Milwaukee Regiment and its brigade reached the southern fringe of Franklin. Colonel Opdycke encountered his division commander, Brig. Gen. George Wagner; the superior directed the exhausted Wisconsin, Illinois, and Ohio soldiers to form a defensive front. The ruddy Opdycke "exploded," shouting that his men had guarded the army's retreat since before daylight; most had not rested in two days nor had they even had an opportunity to boil coffee. Moreover, the ground the general had selected was exposed and without any natural swale, or depression. A twentieth-century historian described the confrontation this way: "Opdycke, his blue eyes flashing and his lusty voice booming, would have no part of it." One of the colonel's Ohio soldiers wrote that his commander said, "I think we can be of more use in rear of the main line." His men would now be directed to eat and rest.

General Wagner must have been gap-mouthed at the insubordination. Nothing came of the incident, however, and neither general nor colonel mentioned it in their official reports. Later, the colonel was given instructions to use his discretion as to what position to place his brigade; but he must remain in close supporting position to act where and when the situation demanded. "I was familiar with the whole ground and knew that Carter's hill was the key to it all," boasted Colonel Opdycke in his official report a week later.[16]

The weary and hungry soldiers plodded past the main defense line, noting it was substantial—rails piled up where it crossed the roadway, and the whole line topped with large head logs. It varied in height between three and five feet, and blue soldiers manned the works, in some places three lines deep. They also passed a second, so-called retrenched line some seventy yards back, and these led into the scattering of Carter farm buildings. Finally, the Milwaukee men and their comrades stacked Enfield rifle-muskets by interlacing bayonets, pulled off their leathers, and dropped to the ground. Many may have removed the rough army shoes to gain relief from the footsore gallop of the past days. Hardtack and dried bacon was pulled from haversacks, and fires soon set alight; boards pulled from the farm buildings were used as fuel. The smell of coffee permeated the sunny afternoon air. Corporal

Cooley may have just then remembered: It was his birthday; he was twenty-nine now. The widower from Western Wisconsin was so distracted by the impending storm that he even failed to note the date in his diary.[17]

The battle of Franklin was to be "as fierce and bloody in proportion to the numbers engaged as any of the many fights that occurred during the war of the Rebellion" was how one Illinois soldier recalled it a dozen years after. It was "a terrible ordeal of fire and blood." "I have now been in 10 battles but I never saw more desperate fighting," Date Worth confided to his brother. A news correspondent wrote that "it will figure hereafter as one of the most remarkable struggles of the war." And in it several Wisconsin soldiers would win glory and fame. Others would find only death.[18]

During much of that Wednesday afternoon in Franklin, "Hood's entire army was in sight, blackening the summits of the hills, and apparently forming for an attack. At four o'clock a wall of marching men and glistening steel moved down the hillsides, "filling the valley and sweeping across the fields." At their approach, "the earth grew tremulous beneath the tread of many feet, and sounded like a low, hollow rumble of distant thunder. Fascinated by the sight, the men gazed in silence upon the advancing columns, now rapidly approaching the entrenchments behind which stood a thin, firm line of Federal soldiers, seemingly unconscious of danger."[19]

Cannons soon boomed from both attacker and defender, and the keening rebel screech cut across the late afternoon air. The men of Wisconsin, Illinois, and Ohio instinctively grabbed up their accoutrements and Enfields from the stacks. It was perhaps 4:00 or 4:30 on an otherwise sunny and lovely fall afternoon, "clear, cloudless and warm," one soldier remembered.

Hood's vast motley colored array—butternut and tan ranks sprinkled with gray and blue, punctuated with bright red and blue banners—swept toward the Federal defensive lines, roaring like a great wave. "Fierce sheets of flame burst forth along the works. The whiz of bullets was like the rush of a whirlwind. The exultant yells of triumph were changed to curses and cries of rage and shrieks of agony and dying groans," a Ohio news writer observed.[20]

As the attackers surged over the works "scores were spitted on Federal bayonets as they leaped over entrenchments." But the enemy, fighting with the fury imbued by their commander, pushed back the defenders. First small knots of men stepped backward from the barricades, then groups and crowds of blue soldiers pulled away as home-spun-cloaked hordes swarmed over the timber, brush, and rails. Colonel Opdycke assessed the situation immediately. "Up and at them, men," one soldier remembered the fair-haired leader shouting to his brigade.[21]

Capt. Ed Parsons remembered that he and Lieutenant Colonel McArthur were taking supper at that moment, "if you can call hardtack and coffee by so formal a name," with the men of Company A. The battle at the barricades grew in deadly crescendo, and suddenly blue soldiers were racing through them. Gray-eyed McArthur vaulted into his saddle, shouting "Up, Wisconsin!" There was no time to even form lines, and the men of Milwaukee rushed "pell mell to meet the enemy in desperate hand to hand melee." From the remove of years, Parsons, too, was not above giving a dramatic motif to the tale.[22]

"We simply blew the half-munched and half-moistened crumbs of hardtack from our mouths, dropped our coffee tins and seized our rifle," wrote a Wisconsin soldier many years later. Those moments were vivid and palpable, even when they were embellished three decades later. There was no time to think of food now; even the pounding in their chests was not discernible. Another Milwaukee soldier saw McArthur swing into his saddle, draw his sword, and spur his horse; and "that would have been order enough anyway," the soldier said. "We did hear the cry from a hundred throats, 'Let us go to the works! Let us go to the works! We started and aligned somewhat as we rush forward," he wrote.[23]

Sgt. Tom Ford, invariably concerned with food and sustenance, was angry. "Our coffee was just beginning to boil and our sowbelly and crackers frying, when the rebels charged . . . and drove our men out, and followed them up." The roiling melee ran past the Wisconsin men, knocking apart the stacked Enfields, upsetting coffee pots and frying pans. The rebels were right on their heels. "Every one of us was mad as he could be after losing his nearly cooked dinner, and we felt as if we could whip the whole rebel army." He heard the youthful colonel shout, "Fall in, Twenty-fourth; take arms. Charge." Then those words again: "Give um hell, boys. Give um hell, give um hell, Twenty-fourth." Ford said the Wisconsin men did, indeed, give them hell, driving the rebels back through the farmyard and over the breastworks from where they had started.[24]

"I saw the Colonel sabering his way toward the leading Confederate flag. His horse was shot from under him, a bullet ripped open his right shoulder, but on foot he fought his way forward trying to bring down those Stars and Bars," Ed Parsons recalled. A Confederate major now had the flag and shot the colonel through the breast. "I thought he was done for but he staggered up and drove his sword through the adversary's body, and even as the Confederate fell he shot our Colonel down for good with a bullet through the knee." A musket ball struck the wavy-haired commander in the left leg, just below the knee. When he crumpled to the ground, another bullet gouged into his shoulder. The men of Milwaukee had no time to determine the fate of their impetuous young leader, and battled on.[25]

"We can imagine no more thrilling episode, than when these devoted veterans, with heads bent to the storm and with bayonets lowered dashed through the spray of balls, and with cold steel charged home upon the multitudinous hosts swarming over and within the ramparts," wrote one soldier. Such were the desperate moments.

The hundred or so men of the Milwaukee Regiment rushed onward, reaching the main defensive works. They drove the attackers back over the piled logs, timber, and rails. The 24th and Opdycke's brigade thrust the deadly steel bayonets, reloaded, and fired their muskets in furious repetition. "Regular volleys could not be discerned," said an Illinois soldier. "It is an incessant crash of guns that was never silent for a moment." Some of the enemy shouted, "Don't shoot, Yanks. For God Almighty's sake, don't shoot," Sergeant Ford recalled. "Then some of them would get hit and cry out, 'Oh.'"[26]

At one point in those furious minutes, Color Sgt. Ed Blake, the young man from Port Washington, planted the regiment's tattered flag atop the breastworks "in the midst of the leaden hail." Rebel balls whined, shattering the flagstaff at several spots. Blake, who had turned twenty-two weeks before, stripped the shredded banner free, wrapped it about his body and buttoned his blue coat to prevent the enemy from seizing it. He then grabbed a musket, and began firing with his comrades. He would long recall that glory, and late in the century would display that bullet-ripped banner to a dead comrade's daughter. His heroic gesture would also become an integral part of his obituary. Elsewhere, Christian Bessenger, a twenty-six-year-old immigrant with a wife and two-year-old child in Wauwatosa west of Milwaukee, doubled over with a ghastly wound to the groin. A good soldier, the Company E corporal would be hospitalized and discharged in six months because of the injury.[27]

The rebel attackers reeled, and were bludgeoned back over the defensive barricade. The antagonists were so close, it was impossible to

Ed Blake with the second regimental flag.
He braved the storm at Franklin.
COURTESY OF THE WISCONSIN VETERAN'S MUSEUM.

reload the long rifle-muskets, and weapons were used as clubs, flailing at heads, legs, and torsos. "Men beat each other with the but [*sic*] of their muskets," Date Worth wrote, almost in disbelief at what he had experienced, "& the battle raged with unabated fury for about 4 hrs." Bayonets thrust and parried and stabbed. Blood ran freely, antagonists battling face-to- face, hand-to-hand amid a volcano of noise and chaos. But the russet- and clay-colored ranks could not sustain their momentum. They recoiled and were thrust back from the deadly pas de deux. A soldier in Colonel Opdycke's Ohio regiment recalled that perhaps an hour passed between the initial enemy assault and the second. Moritz Tschoepe, whose body still bore a scar from Stones River, was down with another wound. He would never return to the regiment.

It was likely during that hour interval that men of Wisconsin searched for their young lieutenant colonel, "our brave boy," Date Worth called him. "When we came to look for our boy leader we found him lying helpless, wounded, where we first struck the enemy." Here lay a hero, bleeding profusely from two wounds. He was quickly gathered up and carried to a field hospital. Arthur McArthur's war was over, but his renown would spread through the ranks of all the armies. The tale of him waving that national flag atop the summit at Missionary Ridge, and, sword slashing, thundering amid the swarm of rebels at Franklin would grow to large proportions. He would become the "Boy Colonel of the West."[28]

"When the first shots of the second enemy surge began," the Ohio writer noted, "the smoke settled down in a peculiar manner—a little higher than one's head. Underneath this canopy the light was a pale, sickly yellow." Such are the incredible details that burned into a soldier's memory, remaining vivid for decades.[29]

The earthworks were from three to five feet high, and atop them were large head logs. Between these and the earth was a space, something of an embrasure that allowed defenders to fire through. "Throughout the action large numbers of the enemy lay close under the entrenchments, so that the works which sheltered us also sheltered them." To retreat meant almost certain death or maiming from Federal fire. After dark, many rebels simply surrendered. But many others refused, fired back through the openings; and still others rolled over the top logs to grapple furiously with blue soldiers. "The crack of revolvers and other small arms . . . showed the temper of those so closely confronting each other."[30]

In one of the many enemy surges during the next several hours, Captain Philbrook noticed one of his Company D privates, an Irish immigrant with a thick brogue, dodging and ducking from the noise of rebel bullets whining past. "Mike," the 34-year-old broad-shouldered railroad man admonished, "quit dodging your head there. Stand up and take it like a man." As Sergeant Ford remembered, the final word had

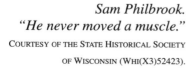

Sam Philbrook.
"He never moved a muscle."
COURTESY OF THE STATE HISTORICAL SOCIETY
OF WISCONSIN (WHI(X3)52423).

not left the captain's mouth when a bullet struck him in the middle of his forehead. He was dead before he fell. The unrepentant private growled, "Why the devil in hell don't you stand up and take it like a mon." And at that instant, a ball grazed his scalp near the forehead. "Holy Moses," he said, "there is nothing like the dodging after all. Every time I heard it before[,] I dodged it and it never hit me."[31]

If Ford, years later, described the incident correctly, the story told to Philbrook's wife and daughter was much different. The devastating blow to the widow was softened by one of her husband's comrades, likely Ed Parsons. It was at twilight, the friend told her, just as the new moon was rising. The battle at the barricades still raged. "He looked up and saw it, and turning to his regiment, he said, 'Boys, there is a new moon. Look over your shoulder, for it is a sign of good luck.'" The captain, who commanded the regiment after McArthur's wounding, knelt behind the breastworks during the furious battle. "As he spoke, a minnie ball struck him in the forehead, just above the nose. Falling to one side, he never moved a muscle." That was how Caddie Philbrook and her daughter, Carrie Alice, would remember the death of their hero. Another name was inscribed on Milwaukee's long roll of dead.[32]

"The air was still, and the smoke, caused by the burning of such a vast amount of powder, drifting lazily in the air, hung like a funeral pall over the fearful drama of death." When the sun went down over their right shoulders "the gathering darkness lent new horrors to the scene."

"The guns, foul and choked, launched a spitting fire into the darkness, for an instant lighting up the gloom, revealed the choked and powder-begrimmed faces of the men, who, haggard and wan, looked like hideous spectres evoked from the regions of despair." Here was a scene of ghastliness fit for the pen of Dante. By the recording of one soldier, each man fired some 300 bullets—"an amount far in excess of any other battle we fight in," wrote one of Opdycke's Ohio Tigers.

The sun slid down behind the high mountains and hills and yet for two hours or more, the raging fight continued. "[I]n this small space of ground the fallen seemed more numerous than the living; officers and soldiers, generals and privates fell side by side." The dead and wounded were "piled in heaps all along on both sides of our works," the Granville farmer, Date Worth, said. "The continuous roar of artillery & musketry is sublime and grand," he wrote, "but the fruits of a battle are terrible to behold." Weariness of war was evident in the words of a man who had seen too much in only two of his twenty-five years. Then darkness began to shroud the deadly field. It was perhaps six or seven o'clock. Still, sheets of fire lighted the gloom, and amid the shouts and curses could be heard the sound of thrusting bayonets lacing together. "Events of such thrilling interest for an instant struck the beholders dumb."[33]

Around eleven o'clock, by some recollections, when the firing finally ebbed and stilled, Opdycke's men were ordered to withdraw from the barricades. Within a short time they trudged over one of the hastily reconstructed bridges to the north bank of the Harpeth River; the wooden span was fired behind them. After floundering in the mud for more than an hour, the much wearied men of Wisconsin, Illinois, and Ohio marched the nineteen miles to Nashville, entering the environs of the Tennessee city around seven o'clock. "The limits of endurance" had been reached. Soldiers stacked their muskets and dropped to the ground, asleep in seconds.[34]

"I deeply regret we were obliged to leave his body in the hands of the enemy," wrote Captain Parsons a few days later, "a braver officer never lived." Caddie and Carrie Philbrook would never see their husband's or father's countenance again. He would have no stone or epitaph.[35]

Two weeks later an Ohio soldier returned to the scene of horror and spoke with a rebel who had remained in the hospital at Franklin. The number of killed greatly exceeded those of the wounded said the gray soldier, a rare occurrence in battle. "Our wounded were left where they fell," he said. "With each succeeding charge your bullets swept the entire field, and, like a winnowing of grain, over and over again this leaden storm sought the victims and crushed out what little life remained."[36]

Several days later, the stocky farmer, Date Worth, reflected upon his experience in the battle. "I can not explain to you how it is I am yet safe." Fatalism was evident when he concluded the letter to his brother, William: "I suppose the ball is yet in store for me if it had been molded."

Jim Harvey jotted a few lines of levity on a small scrap and slipped it in with Worth's letter. "Harvey says for himself that he slings a nasty musket & that he is kicking as yet [and] has an almighty appetite for sowbelly."

Camp talk the next day had it that the men of Opdycke's brigade performed brilliantly at Franklin. "The conduct of the first brigade, 2d division, IV corps is the subject of conversation in military circles," Corporal Cooley wrote. "It is universally conceeded [*sic*] that our brigade saved the day yesterday and but for our firmness the army wold have been driven into the river. Gen. Wagner speaks . . . in very high terms of praise." Sam Chase, the Milwaukee quartermaster, wrote that the 24th Wisconsin and 125th Ohio were soon called the "invincibles."[37]

There would be further commendations and accolades for Opdycke's brigade and the Milwaukee Regiment—small recompense for the dead and maimed. "It is rare in history that one can say a certain unit saved the day," wrote IV Corps commander General Stanley. "But in the case at Franklin when the 24th Wisconsin, with no orders from higher up, by its spontaneous action, repelled the enemy and rectified our lines." And he singled out the lieutenant colonel for special mention. "In this it was bravely led by its young Colonel, Arthur MacArthur." High praise, indeed, for someone not twenty.[38]

Colonel Opdycke years later wrote to Ed Parsons, praising "those dauntless men who with [Ed] Blake bearing the colors charged up the hill and into the whirlpool of battle. . . . I do not believe any troops ever made a more gallant charge. Without it all of our forces clear up to the Ohio river would have been swept away."[39]

"I will not say that the [24th] Wisconsin had all to do with the saving of the day at Franklin, but it had a large part in it and in this feat it was led by its gallant boy Colonel." The same Milwaukee soldier, who wrote long after when Arthur McArthur fought in another war, added: "Well they couldn't commission Arthur full Colonel because we didn't muster men enough, but they gave him a brevet rank" the following spring. And when he marched at the head of the 24th Wisconsin in Milwaukee that July, those silver eagle shoulder straps were plainly visible.[40]

In addition to Captain Philbrook, three were killed that final day of November, sixteen wounded, and three taken prisoner. Could the Milwaukee Regiment muster one hundred?[41]

"Metaphorically speaking, the battle of Nashville was fought at Franklin," was the assessment of an Ohio soldier. "Had the condition of Hood's army on the morning following the battle of November 30 been fully known to our side, there would have been no battle of Nashville to record."[42]

The command of General Schofield marched to Nashville, arriving there about the time the sun rose December 1. Although they knew that Hood was likely aiming his battered army at the great Tennessee city, the soldiers did not exhibit more than passing concern. The sprawling town was much changed since they had camped here two years before. It was now, to many an eye, a virtual Sodom and Gomorrah. "It is the most hopelessly filthy city on the continent," described a Milwaukee news man. Streets and pavements are awash in mire, alleyways were heaped and "purulent with offal. Over the whole pig-sty wretchedness, wallow vast and endless streams of bipedal and quadrapidal [sic] animals." Triple the throngs that surged along Milwaukee's Broadway Street, he suggested, and "you have an idea of Nashville today." Danger seemed to lurk at every corner. "Robbery and murder ran rampant on the streets at night." Perhaps three killings a night were registered. Even the year before, an Ohio news man was struck with the city's "apparently confused girdle of frowning earthworks and unmistakable military air."[43]

Some soldiers took time to visit. Corporal Cooley and others, nineteenth-century men who were literate and fairly well-read, found diversion, even attending theater performances a few evenings; they once saw "The Naiad Queen," a great operatic spectacle written in 1857 by J. S. Dalrymple. But on the return to camp, they were arrested and held at a local hotel appropriated for military incarcerations. Capt. Ed Parsons coincidentally happened along, and rescued the men. "We had fun all day," Cooley wrote. A new 24th Wisconsin chaplain arrived, the first man of the cloth on the regiment's roster since the departure of the rollicksome Francis Fusseder a year and a half before. Clergyman John Roe, a Methodist, came from the farming community of Muskego many miles southwest of Milwaukee. Corporal Cooley liked his looks. "He is a fine man and will no doubt be well liked." The new reverend would provide spiritual sustenance until the regiment mustered from Federal service.[44]

General Hood and his army, despite heavy losses at Franklin, soon closed in on Nashville. The rebel lines were plainly visible from Capitol Hill, where the ornate Tennessee statehouse stood. "They are drawn about the city in a semi-circle, and the men are engaged in digging trenches, and throwing up breastworks. Their lines are very thin, but the position they occupy is very strong" one news man wrote.[45]

"A good musket-shot is the average distance between the opposing breastworks," said another correspondent. "They seldom get nearer than five or six hundred yards." The enemy was poor in supply as well as manpower. "The rebels cannot afford to lose a single cartridge, so far as they have to transport it in wagons." Rebel prisoners boasted that their bold commander waited only for his ammunition wagons to come up before ordering an attack. "Hood's pig-headedness will scarcely drive him to the desperate hazard of assaulting this place," averred an Ohio writer in contradiction.[46]

Weather turned cold and grew severe as December wore on; sleet and snow made camp life miserable. The Federal batteries, many large-caliber cannons, boomed daily, reaching out toward General Hood's army south of the city. General Sherman, the soldiers learned, had reached to within forty miles of his goal—Savannah, the grand and genteel city on the Atlantic. General Grant and the Army of the Potomac, meanwhile, were extending lines to the south and west of Petersburg, Virginia, nearly bottling up General Lee. Optimism at the war's outcome grew among the Federal soldiers in Nashville.

In Milwaukee at midmonth, the fourth winter of the war seized the city. Citizens bundled against the rage of cruel wind that howled down from the north and west. The city slowed under its cold, white shroud. Christmas and New Year were only weeks away. There was cause for optimism. Not long before, one of the dailies printed a map below a heavy headline: "HOW THE WAR COMMENCED AND HOW NEAR IT IS ENDED." The map, in shades of gray, showed how the confederacy of seceded states had once controlled nearly all tracts of territory below the Ohio River. But now the dark gray had receded dramatically, encompassing only portions of Mississippi, Alabama, Georgia, the Carolinas, and southern Virginia as well as eastern Texas and a small portion of Louisiana and Arkansas. The Federal armies everywhere were successful; it was now only a matter of time.

Then, in mid-December, more headlines proclaimed that another battle was in progress in Nashville. "HOOD VIRTUALLY DEFEATED!" "The attention of the country, which for some time past had been mainly directed toward Sherman's operations, is now centered on the struggle between Thomas and Hood." There were no letters from Milwaukee soldiers published now; few wrote of the closing struggles. In Nashville, even Corporal Cooley jotted only token entries in his diary.[47]

Maj. Gen. George Thomas, the old Rock of Chickamauga, had taken his good time before venturing from his Nashville defenses to face his dun-colored nemesis. The War Department and his superior, General Grant, had grown restive with the lack of offensive movement in Tennessee. For two weeks, the tall and somewhat thick-bodied Virginian had reordered his ranks and prepared for an assault on General Hood's decimated lines. The gray general had a few days prior massed his army on the right, "thinking, perhaps, he could crush in our lines and carry the city." Finally, on December 15, stolid General Thomas ordered his men to push south.[48]

Corporal Cooley was terse in his description of that day: "This morning at daylight we moved out of our works and advanced upon the rebels. After a severe fight the rebels broke and ran. We kept up our pursuit and came up to them in their fourth line of works. We halted for the night." There was little beyond spare outlines of these affairs in most jottings. Capt. Charles Hartung, who wrote the 24th Wisconsin's official report in January, said that "we moved forward at double-quick, and the works were carried without opposition." It was an almost inglorious final battle.[49]

At daylight that uncommonly warm Thursday, a dense fog curtained the undulating landscape, and between the rolling ground and the gray billows, the Federal movement was obscured from the enemy. The 2nd Division of the IV Corps was in position on the right behind a cloud of skirmishers, almost to "point blank range of the enemy's first line."

"Great was the astonishment of the Confederates upon the clearing up of the fog, at seeing long blue lines of Federal troops drawn up in battle array and menacing them in front and flank." The skirmish line had advanced well to the front, close to the enemy defenses. "From logs, stumps and hillocks they poured in a galling fire," but received in return the "concentrated evidence of rebel wrath, in the form of grape-shot, canister, and musket balls."[50]

Red-haired Tom Ford made even less of it: "We marched out to them and made the attack. They held us back." He went on to explain that the 24th Wisconsin and the other regiments were relieved by a brigade of colored troops. The Milwaukee men had hunkered down to cook when the Negro soldiers charged the rebel lines, stalling at the phalanx of abatis and sharpened stakes the enemy had erected. "The rebels peppered them so thick and fast, they even stood up on their breastworks and took aim" at the attackers. The enemy ranks shot, shouted, and waved their hats "like so many demons."

Opdycke's brigade was marched out again at the double-quick, Ford wrote, advancing over the prostrate ranks of the black soldiers. As they advanced on the defensive lines, over the barriers, the rebel soldiers "ceased firing and had their arms stacked when we climbed their breastworks, took off their hats and surrendered, saying 'Hello, Jack; hello, Tom; hello, Jim. Say, Yanks, never send a black cloud to take our breastworks.'" The rebels explained that when they saw the colored brigade advancing, they fought with renewed vigor because they did not want to be captured by dark soldiers.[51]

Another soldier, in the skirmish line with the 36th Illinois, saw things differently, praising the African American soldiers' "ability to stand fire." Despite the determined Confederate defense, the colored regiments bore up well. The Negroes, he wrote, "were not outdone in gallantry and steadiness, and no body of regulars could have been under better discipline, or easier handled."

The IV Corps advance continued toward a prominence called Montgomery Hill. "During the formation of the assaulting columns, the summit was wreathed in smoke, and the deep booming of heavy guns waved defiance and poured down a continuous tempest of shot and shell." The Federal guns hurled back in response. The blue line advanced, and immediately the pace increased to the double-quick. "Cheer upon cheer swelled up from the ranks; the fatigues of last night's anxious watching; the strain upon the mind and muscle, incident to the excitement of the occasion was forgotten." The enemy's lines were rapidly overwhelmed with "scarcely a show of resistance," recalled an Illinois soldier. The "terror-stricken" rebel soldiers quickly panicked, throwing down muskets and other impediments and racing south. The fighting, if such it could be called by the veterans of more than a score of bloody battles, was over for the day.[52]

Only one man was killed during the charge, the last fatality in the 24th Wisconsin. The bullet, it seemed, had been molded that found its

Datus Worth.
"Your erring son."

COURTESY OF MARC AND BETH STORCH.

way to the Granville farmer, Date Worth. Within days, Jim Harvey undertook the "painful duty" to inform his friend's parents. "He never spoke a word after he was shot although he lived about a half an hour," he wrote in a very brief letter. "I pinned a slip of paper on his coat with his company & Reg. & then I was obliged to leave." Harvey, grieved, could write little more. The body of the "erring son" would lie in a military burial ground until spring.[53]

The next morning, they "skirmished till we came up to the fifth line of rebel works," Corporal Cooley noted. "A charge was made by our folks and the lines were broken again, the rebels flying for their lives. We pressured them till it was pitch dark when we went into camp." The corporal's estimate may have been inaccurate, but thousands of prisoners and numerous rebel artillery pieces were taken in those two days, he said.[54]

"The defeat of Hood was most signal and complete." The Federal army streamed south in pursuit. "Along the lines of retreat evidences of disaster marked the way. Small arms were thickly strewn along the road, [enemy] dead were left where they had fallen, and his wounded were uncared for." Hundreds of "careworn and dejected" prisoners were gathered up and marched away. Here and there, an assortment of a dozen Federal soldiers would not hesitate to charge upon a body of rebels ten times their number "readily capturing scores and more at a time."

That Friday night, the 24th Wisconsin camped on the north bank of the Harpeth River opposite Franklin. During the next few days, burial parties interred comrade and foe alike. It was, indeed, a "laborious sepulture," said an Illinois soldier.[55]

Several Wisconsin soldiers scoured the old battle field for the corpse of Captain Sam Philbrook during those days—but to no avail. After the battle of Franklin, the enemy stripped Federal bodies of uniforms and possessions. The railroad man's sack of gold coins, his watch, and the lovely gold medallion his wife had given when he left Milwaukee must have been looted. Bodies were left unburied; these, "defaced and swollen," were unrecognizable. Philbrook's widow, Caddie, could not bring herself to travel to Nashville, as so many widows and wives of wounded men had done during the past three years. "Everything was done to recover his remains," she told her mother-in-law.

"The most lovely ones of that regiment have been taken," Caddie Philbrook mourned. Many of them had been the city's "pets." Men like George Bleyer, a fine writer for the *Daily Milwaukee News;* the tall, entrepreneurial Scot, Phil Chivas; the gentle Quaker, Howard Greene; the "erring son," Date Worth; young Amandus Silsby, who read his Testament faithfully; and so many more. Of her own slain husband she could offer the simplest of soldier epitaphs: "He lies where he fell."[56]

Epilogue

"He sleeps upon the field of his glory."

The heavy drape that had shrouded the massive sculpture was pulled free, and a chorus of elation and applause rippled through the crowd of thousands. Four bronze figures, each larger than life, were fixed atop the twenty-foot granite base, facing the warm summer sun. On the right of the tableau strode a heavily mustachioed infantry captain brandishing a revolver primed and cocked; to his right, a common soldier, blanket roll over his left shoulder, advanced with bayonet fixed. Between the two lay a mortally wounded flag bearer clutching his breast, and above him a determined young soldier had just taken up the regimental colors from his fallen comrade.

Called "The Victorious Charge," the magnificent monument was unveiled in the summer of 1898. More than a dozen years before that date old Alexander Mitchell had agreed to finance a monument to Milwaukee's Civil War veterans, and had given the commission to a young man named John Conway. Upon his death some years later, his son, John, had taken up the cause. The younger Mitchell, of course, had marched with the old 24th Wisconsin Volunteer Infantry during the war, fighting in two battles before problems with his eyes had forced him to resign. Mitchell, now finishing a term in the U.S. Senate, had lost many friends during the war, including two close companions, Bob Chivas, his cousin, and Fred Root—one had been killed in battle and the other had died accidentally as a result of his friend's death.

The Victorious Charge.
Dedicated in 1898.

When Senator Mitchell was forced to withdraw his monetary support for the monument because of business reversals during the Financial Panic of 1893, the project had been taken up with enthusiasm by Lydia Ely Hewitt, who worked tirelessly, organizing bazaars and securing public subscriptions. She had raised $30,000 in the next five years.

The unveiling and dedication was set for the week of Milwaukee's popular celebration for the semicentennial of Wisconsin's statehood. More companies of city volunteers had gone to an international war, fighting in Cuba. Almost at that moment, the last week of June 1898, one of the community's most renowned soldier sons, Arthur McArthur, was leading American troops against the forces of Spain in the Philippines. The army general, who recently turned fifty-three, had spent some time in Milwaukee the year before while he was stationed in Minnesota, and he would return permanently in the new century.

Some 30,000 people flocked into Milwaukee for the weeklong festivities that included a Grand Carnival, cycle races and an illuminated parade, concerts, a ball and fireworks. The highlight of the celebration for many, however, was the unveiling and dedication of the Civil War monument. An early morning rain threatened to dampen the event that Tuesday, but by early afternoon, clouds scudded out over Lake Michigan and the sun spread its warming rays. At 2:30, the parade stepped off from east of the Milwaukee River with bands, flags, military units, and carriages. A large contingent of old veterans, some in blue army coats, marched manfully, still minding the step as they had as young men decades before; the rheumatic or crippled legs, or weak hearts of some old soldiers required them to ride, however.

Ultimately, the colorful assembly marched to the west side of the city, to the magnificent stretch of Grand Avenue that widened into a boulevard between the mansions of the prosperous, including the former palatial estate of the Mitchell family with its four-story, mansard tower, expansive grounds, and ornate gazebo: The home had been expanded to grand Second Empire proportions in 1870 from its simpler Italianate origin; three years before, in 1895, however, it had been sold. Here, among other civic monuments and statues, Conway's magnificent new sculpture took its place between the divided road way at Tenth Street in what was called the Court of Honor.

There were several speakers, including Gov. Edward Schofield, himself a Civil War veteran, who extolled the work of Lydia Hewitt and others in raising the necessary subscriptions for the work. "It is true that a nation's loyal heart enshrines its heroes in memory's existence more lasting then bronze," the bearded governor orated, "it is also true that such outward tokens of the memory's existence are worthy exhibitions of civic pride and national honor."

No record was retained of which old veterans were on hand to view "The Victorious Charge" for the first time. Several who attended were likely stooped and wizened; others were supported by canes. Hair and beards had gone gray or white, and many pates were wispy. In their midfifties or older, these men came to ponder the massive figures and, perhaps, to think back on those days, over three decades flown, when the Milwaukee Regiment had ended its days as a volunteer regiment.[1]

Nearly thirty-three years had passed since December 1864, when the Milwaukee Regiment once again found itself in Franklin, Tennessee—the third time it had reached that town during the war. It was in pursuit of the battered and threadbare homespun remnants of Maj. Gen. John B. Hood's army. The day after Christmas—again there was no time to mark the holiday—Maj. Gen. George Thomas's army reached Lexington, Tennessee. Two days later, it learned that the rebels had escaped south of the Tennessee River, and "further pursuit was abandoned." The IV Corps was ordered to Huntsville and Athens, Alabama. "The defeat of Hood had dashed to the ground the last hope of the rebels, of succeeding in establishing their independence," opined an Ohio soldier, "and they rightly ask: 'Why persevere in a course that will inevitable lead to destruction?'"[2]

Eighteen-sixty five was marked Monday night and Tuesday morning with "the boys . . . shooting the old year out and welcoming the new year." Many were festive, but most "couldn't see it," George Cooley penciled in his pocket diary.[3]

The soldiers, confident and cocksure, shortly thereafter strode through Huntsville, determined to tolerate little from the Southern citizens. As the companies marched, their double ranks filled the street and sergeants walked along the sidewalks at the side. The band played "Away Down South in Dixie." War-scarred Tom Ford remembered an incident clearly. A woman sat at her door, holding a pan of potatoes she had just peeled; Ford, the farmer, noted the vegetables were of an unfamiliar variety. "Please madam, what do you call those potatoes," he asked. The woman shot back: "I don't call them at all; they come without calling."

Sgt. Charley Powell, an "able" man two inches taller than six feet who was behind Ford, did not appreciate the sarcasm. As he passed the woman, he raised his right foot and "never losing a step to the music, hit the pan a kick, and pan and potatoes flew out on the street on the top of the regiment." The woman was stunned to silence. "Now, damn you, see if they'll come without calling," Powell shouted. "The regiment charged on the potatoes and came to shoulder arms again with a potato on top of the bayonets, and not one potato was lost."[4]

When the 24th Wisconsin settled into the northern suburbs of Huntsville, the war for the Milwaukee soldiers was nearly over. The IV Corps and indeed the Army of the Cumberland were no longer at the focus of the fighting. General Sherman and his sprawling armies were spreading east toward Savannah and the sea; Generals Grant and Meade and the Army of the Potomac had taken an unsuccessful thrust at the Confederates in Virginia as the year ended. There was continual rumor, too, that the regiment might be shipped east to Virginia or elsewhere to help in the fight against General Lee or Johnston.

In December, Ed Parsons, the senior captain who had led the Milwaukee Regiment after Lieutenant Colonel McArthur was wounded at Franklin, went home on furlough. While there, he met a vivacious, dark-eyed woman, Abbie Fay, the daughter of a businessman in Oconomowoc, a town many miles west of Milwaukee. A whirlwind courtship ensued, and the couple was married on New Year's Eve. One of Abbie Parsons's favorite tunes, one she sang for years, was entitled "The Captain with the Whiskers Took a Shy Glance at Me." Parsons, who had cultivated a brushy muttonchop growth on his cheeks, returned to the regiment two days after his marriage, but would resign his commission in March.[5]

In Alabama, the 24th settled into winter camp. The enterprising veterans added fireplaces to their large Sibley tents, building chimneys of mud and sticks. At the end of January, regular mail and packages began arriving. Corporal Cooley made note of an assortment he received from western Wisconsin—pie, cake, pickles, preserves, apples, tobacco, clothing, and reading matter. He also read avidly of the rumors that peace was at hand. His diary entries grew terser, but he did jot that he liked "first rate" the skirmish drill the regiment practiced. The final note was made on February 2. Four Company A comrades were leaving for home on furlough, and he asked them to express his two journals to his brother when they arrived. "I am on guard duty and am snatching a few minutes to do the diaries and some relics and curiosities up so as to be ready for him tomorrow."[6]

Within a few days, Lieutenant Colonel McArthur returned to the Milwaukee Regiment after the long recuperative leave for his Franklin wound. While home, he posed for a handsome image: His newly tailored frock coat, adored with the gold oak leaves of a lieutenant colonel, hugged his still slender frame, and a saber scabbard hung only inches from the floor. He carried a few pounds more than one hundred, now, and his long face was fleshier, his cheeks darkened a bit with incipient growth; his eyes suggested he had seen too much in his nineteen and a half years. The dark-haired McArthur would within a short time after his return to Tennessee adorn his shoulder straps with silver eagles, having been accorded a brevet, or meritorious rank, of full colonel.[7]

News from General Sherman's army heightened optimism in those winter months. He had turned north after taking Savannah, and on February 21 captured Columbia, South Carolina. The volunteer soldiers did not lament the city's burning.

Sergeant Comstock, meanwhile, found time to write a letter home nearly every day in February and March. He read a lot, and consumed a novel by a writer named Reynolds, whom he called the "Prince of Authors." Still, the days weighed heavily, and the routines grew dull. Occasionally, however, there was spirited activity. On March 20, the brigade formed a regular line of battle with two ranks of skirmishers in advance. "We had a grand charge through a thick underbrush. Many pants and blouses badly wounded, none killed," he penciled.[8]

On the ides of March, the IV Corps had been uprooted from Huntsville, and the soldiers entrained for East Tennessee, perhaps to bulk General Grant's army for the final surge against Lee's Army of Northern Virginia. En route, however, a dispatch was received that "Babylon" had fallen—General Lee had surrendered at Appomattox and Richmond was won. "The cruel war was over and the world had a brighter look," wrote an Ohio soldier. "Our rejoicing found vent in the firing of muskets which no orders could stop. Our pickets changed sides of trees and stumps to dodge the bullets coming from camp." Within a week, the devastating news of President Lincoln's assassination shocked the soldiers. "Voices of grief mingled with indignation."[9]

By early May, the Milwaukee Regiment had returned to Nashville, and on the eighth, a Grand Review of the old IV Corps was held in the city. The event was staged in conjunction with similar parades by the Army of the Potomac and General Sherman's armies in Washington. On June 10, 1865, the 24th Wisconsin was mustered from Federal service, and was on its way home.

The day before the regiment's arrival, a Milwaukee news sheet printed a poem, appropriately titled "Our Boys Are Coming Home." It read in part:

> The vacant fireside places
>   Have waited for them long;
> The love light lacks their faces,
>   The chorus waits their song;
> A shadowy fear has haunted
>   The long deserted room;
> But now our prayers are granted
>   Our boys are coming home![10]

On Thursday, June 15, a little after 4 A.M., cannons announced the arrival of the train carrying the 24th Wisconsin into Milwaukee. "[W]e welcomed home the remnant of that gallant band of heroes, less than one third the number who left us so recently." Three hundred and twenty-five were counted in the ranks; just three years before, over a thousand had left the city. The delighted veterans arrived at Union Station on Water Street on the west side of the Milwaukee River. As the locomotive chuffed toward the platform, a flurry of waving flags and handkerchiefs enthusiastically greeted it while the band struck up "Home Sweet Home."

"Each soldier as he emerged from the car was seized upon and clasped in loving arms," observed a news writer. "The confusion and disorder were complete, and for a few moments it seemed as through the boys would never get into line again." Another gave his impression of the bittersweet scene: "[T]ears of joy and tears of sorrow and disappointment alike were shed. Wives were there to receive their husbands, parents were there to receive their sons, children to receive their long absent fathers, sisters to receive brothers, and every one extended a hearty welcome to the scarred and bronzed veterans—whose cup of happiness seemed full to overflowing," he said. The writer lamented, too, for those "who wait, alas, in vain, for the return of those so near and dear to them—hundreds who went out upon that day, stalwart men, in the hey-day of life can never return." Many soldier bodies had returned to Milwaukee in sealed tin boxes. "Some sleep in their graves in the far off South, or rest in their graves at home, and will never hear the voice of father or mother, or brother or sister, or wife or child again."

The regiment marched north along Water Street to Huron, trumped across the bridge to the east side of the river, then turned north again. Crowds filled the sidewalks and leaned from nearly every window in the central business district. The blue ranks reached the Great Fair Building, a sprawling, multifaceted frame edifice erected earlier that year to help raise funds for a permanent home for disabled soldiers. "Galleries, side-rooms, beams, timbers, every place and every thing was occupied. Crowds, too, as many as 5,000 was one estimate, surrounded the building, striving to look in at the windows and get a glimpse of the veterans, or waiting patiently for the soldiers to come out." Bands played "When Johnny Comes Marching Home Again."

Here the regiment was "regaled with the substantial collation spread by the ladies of the Home," a repast that included strawberries and cream. "The immense hall was literally crammed, both on the lower floor and in the galleries," described a news writer. "It is a small instalment [*sic*] of what we owe them," described another writer.

The mayor was on hand, and speeches of welcome offered. "Your good Uncle Samuel is a bigger man than when you left here—he had grown several inches in the last four years!" orated the politician. "[Y]ou return with thinned ranks and aching voids. Where are Chivas, Root and Green [*sic*], and the martyred host of heroes that went forth from us to return no more?" was a rhetorical question. "The joy we experience this day is not unmingled with sorrow. Those that return not had also their mothers, their sisters, their wives and their little ones. Seeing you to-day, the fountains of grief are opened afresh. As you passed up our streets the mother looked in vain upon your thinned ranks, and with tearful eyes sobbed—, Where is he? And the young wife, parting from him around whom were thrown all the cords that bound her to earth—parted with him at the call of his country."

Colonel McArthur—he had passed his twentieth birthday only days before—thanked the city. The Milwaukee Regiment, he said, had been "engaged in fifteen closely contested battles, marching over more than six thousand miles of the confederate territory, and leaving fifty percent of the original organization dead in the south. . . . [W]e return to you, feeling that we have done our duty." He ordered three cheers for the "generous and noble citizens of Milwaukee."

One writer observed that scarcely any of the officers who departed the city three years before returned came back again. "The bodies of others lie with their soldier comrades of the line, buried on battle fields, which attest to their valor." Although the 24th Wisconsin would soon cease to exist, a news man said, "the record of its valorous deeds will always remain fresh in the memory of the people of Milwaukee." The "officers are now virtually citizens. They are to return to the private walks of life, and are to be respected only according to their deserts. We have no privileged classes among us. The war is ended and the distinctions which war created should cease."[11]

Thus ended the "eventful career" of the Milwaukee Regiment. The discharged men, like hundreds of thousands of other former Federal soldiers, soon packed away war memories with their old blue coats and other military trappings, and merged back into civil society. Most returned to their former professions and labors. Family life was rekindled after three years of absence, and those unmarried soon wed and began raising families. Although many from the Milwaukee Regiment remained proximate to the city, a good number, perhaps as many as one-third, traveled west for opportunity. The Dakotas, Nebraska, and other states and territories of the Great Plains beckoned; others pushed to the Pacific, taking up pursuits in California or the Pacific Northwest. A few went South.

Many soldiers had returned to Milwaukee before war's end, of course, shot up and maimed of body or mind. Among them was little George Merrick, grievously wounded in the stomach at Stones River; he came home after discharge in early 1863 with a one-quarter government disability pension in his pocket. That the five-foot-four-inch veteran of Company B, twenty-two at war's end, was able to function with his body so brutalized was a "wonder to his people," it was said. He returned to his former profession, clerking for several years at the law firm of Levi and Fred Riebrock, then spent some time in Little Rock, Arkansas, before coming back up north to Chicago for many years. Ultimately, with his wife Kitty and four children in tow, he removed to Minnesota. Invited to attend an 1889 reunion of Company B, he declined. "Am getting old and think I must be childish, for tears spring to my eyes when I think of the old times and my brave comrades." Merrick lived a good, long life, dying of a stroke in 1920; he was about seventy-seven years old.[12]

Similarly, Sanford Williams hobbled home to the city in 1863, a leg sawn off on the Stones River battlefield. His older brother, James, had been discharged because of disease that summer, and died in September. Receiving a disability pension, Williams, the former post office clerk, worked at various positions until 1881 when he was named an assessor in the city Water Department for the final years of his life. He lived on the south side of the city on Kinnickkinnic Avenue. Another Company B veteran, Williams died in 1889, about age fifty-four, leaving his wife Annie to collect a widow's government stipend.[13]

There would be many other stories over the ensuing years, of men carrying scars unseen, who had witnessed and suffered too much for their constitutions to bear. Among them was Joe Singer, who came back to his home town bearing a disability. "In the hour of its need, Joe answered the call to duty, and did the work with the musket" in Company E. While on the skirmish line at Dallas, Georgia, years before his return, a piece of his skull was shot away from the crown of the head, exposing his brain about one by one and a half inches. The twenty-three-year-old never recovered sufficiently to return to his regiment. Like the majority of veterans, Singer never attained great monetary success in life. For the final years of the 1870s, he lived in the city's Germanic precincts and was listed as a driver or expressman, likely delivering goods and services. Receiving a disability pension, Singer was "very quiet in his natural condition," wrote editor Jerry Watrous.

On November 4, 1881, Singer, then forty, was discovered missing from his home. Six weeks later, Watrous wrote of his disappearance, "and not a clue is left of any kind as to his fate. He was sober, industrious and faithful in all his duties," the editor said. "With the lapse of time his wound troubled him more and more, and at times his mind seemed to be affected by it." He complained during the past few months of "much more pressure and pain," and determined to quit the delivery business at the end of November. His family relations and finances were good. A day or two before disappearing, he received $250 in the settlement of an estate; he customarily gave money to his wife. "[D]id he commit suicide in one of his despondent moods, which were frequent of late, or has he wondered off, rendered insane by his wounds?" Watrous asked. His wife inclined to believe the latter. There were two children, aged five years and seventeen months. Singer was never seen again.[14]

Two decades after the 24th Wisconsin was mustered from service, Harry Rogers, his hands war-scarred and missing digits, said it best. He was forty-three then, engaged in a real estate business with his younger brother, Charley, the captain who had led the "pets" of Company B after Howard Greene's death on Missionary Ridge. The Rogers brothers, who took up their father's prosperous business, soon become active in veterans' affairs. For a dozen or so years after the war, Rogers said, the old soldiers seemed to "shun" talking about the war. "Their three or four years of hard service, in a terrible war, was more than they anticipated, and it proved a well rounded up load, mentally and physically." But now with families grown and careers established, "they look back to those stirring times from '61 to '65, and recall the experiences and incidents with the keenest of pleasure." The ties of friendship and affection among the old soldiers were powerful; no fraternity or secret society compared with them. All who fought in that great war, Rogers observed, were "more proud of that service than anything they have done in the whole course of their lives."[15]

The seeds of what became the great veterans' movement of the Gilded Age began germinating in Milwaukee in 1879, something of a watershed year for the Civil War soldiers. The veterans of the 24th Wisconsin formed a reunion organization, and gathered that winter to renew friendships, tell stories of camp, march, and battle, and remember dead comrades. Phil Sheridan visited Milwaukee for the event, and a deputation including Ed Parsons, Bill Kennedy, Charley Rogers, and Surgeon Hasse met the graying little general at the train station, escorting him to the opulent Plankinton House where the veterans assembled. Sheridan said he remembered the 24th Wisconsin and its "conspicuous heroism"; no better regiment served in his command, he applauded. The general recalled as clearly as though it were yesterday the occasion upon which he took leave of the regiment, away back in "those agonizing slavery days," wrote Ed Parsons. The old veterans enjoyed the general's visit as well as the festivities and repartee of the reunion "in a perfect glow of enthusiasm." General Sheridan returned to Milwaukee once more before he died in 1888.[16]

In 1879, too, Jerry Watrous, the Iron Brigade soldier and journalist, also served as a catalyst for Wisconsin veterans when he bought a weekly society or feature newspaper in the city, soon transforming it into a largely soldier paper. He solicited the whereabouts of veterans who no longer lived in southeastern Wisconsin, attempting to rekindle old friendships and associations. For the next twenty years, while the nation experienced the rise of the politically and culturally powerful Grand Army of the Republic (GAR) veterans' organization, Watrous's *Milwaukee Sunday Telegraph* would serve as a conduit among many former comrades. He printed hundreds of recollections and vignettes about the war years penned by the old veterans.

Many comrades were located, at least briefly. Ed Buttrick, the 24th Wisconsin lieutenant colonel who had resigned late in 1862 and later served as colonel of the 39th Infantry, married Nancy Sawyer after returning to the city. He briefly engaged in mining before relocating to Parkersburg, West Virginia, where he stood for Congress as a Republican in 1883; despite the ascendancy of the party in the postwar years, he apparently lost the election, however.[17]

Fr. Franz Fusseder, the rollicking priest who had been the regiment's chaplain for several years, was the pastor of the Catholic church in Beaver Dam northwest of Milwaukee; his belated replacement, John Roe, lived in Omaha, Nebraska. John Plummer, one of the Prairie du Chien brothers who served in several Wisconsin regiments, married a southern woman, Sue Gilbert, then settled near Wilmington, North Carolina, purchasing a large plantation and building a town he called Plummerville.[18]

Richard Austin, the officer whom Amandus Silsby regarded as something of a martinet, also relocated from Milwaukee to Chicago after the war. Henry Gunnison, the Company H captain whose reputation was somewhat tarnished at Stones River, returned to Milwaukee after his resignation in March 1863; he, too, later made Chicago his home.[19]

Even officers whose military reputations were besmirched by the debacle at Stones River remained in the city for a time after the war. Cam Reed, who had been cashiered from the 24th Wisconsin because of cowardice, became inspector of Lake Michigan steam vessels, and resided in Milwaukee for several years. Riverius Elmore, the tender Company E lad who resigned somewhat in disgust of the officer turmoil in the Milwaukee Regiment following Stones River, clerked in Milwaukee for a time after the war before moving to Rock Falls, Iowa.[20]

Peter Lusk, who also resigned his lieutenancy under a cloud of criticism after Stones River, relocated to Elgin, Illinois, and was not heard from again. Similarly, Bill Eldred, the Company B captain who resigned in January 1863 in the aftermath of his cowardly behavior during that battle, returned to the city to sell real estate until 1870, when he moved to Indianapolis; sometime in the following decade he relocated to Minnesota. Court Larkin, the young man who gave up his officer's straps following Stones River, later during the war became major of the 38th Wisconsin Infantry, gaining some measure of respect. He subsequently returned to Milwaukee, and became an attorney in his father's firm on Water Street from 1866 to 1879 before leaving the city; at his death in 1920, his body was returned to the family plot at Forest Home Cemetery. Finally, Peter Strack, one of the Germanic officers who resigned after Stones River, became a saloon keeper in Milwaukee for several years before residing in the rural community of Germantown northwest of the city. He would die there a relatively young man in 1876.[21]

In addition to the 1879 reunion of the 24th Wisconsin, veterans' gatherings occurred many times in Milwaukee during the 1870s, 1880s, and 1890s. Parades featuring graying men in blue coats adorned with reunion ribbons, tenting grounds, barbecues, and campfires were common in those decades. The Grand Army of the Republic and Army of the Cumberland came to the city, as did state veterans' organizations. News men printed scores of war stories from the middle-aged soldiers.

In 1889, during encampment week, John Mitchell, then a successful banker like his father, opened the opulent and sprawling family mansion on Grand Avenue to his old comrades. On his lawn in front of the Second Empire home, he erected a spacious pavilion tent furnished with tables, chairs, ice water tanks, and other refreshments.

Old Nick Greusel, thin, grizzled, and probably in his eighties by then, traveled from Iowa to attend; he wore an old army uniform and brocaded naval hat for the event, and posed for a likeness with several others. Maj. Francis Sherman, who also served for a time as brigade commander in Tennessee, entrained in Illinois. Even former general Alexander McCook was on hand. Carrie Philbrook, the oldest daughter of Captain Sam, traveled down from Minnesota; she was married now to a Northwestern Railway superintendent, Joseph McCabe. Her presence always brightened the old boys. On Thursday morning, Mitchell, a light frock coat adorning his abundant middle, assembled nearly 200 men in the central business district, and formed them by companies; preceded by a drum corps, they marched to the Mitchell mansion for summer libations.[22]

There were absences, of course, of men dying before their time. Handsome Bill Kennedy, the well-liked captain of Company G who rose to major, was elected county treasurer after the war, earning plaudits and praise for his services; he also won election to the county board of supervisors in 1876. In 1874, he married a woman from Spring Prairie, Wisconsin. His health had already begun to decline when in 1881 members of the Milwaukee Regiment presented him with a "handsome escutcheon. It was a surprise to the gallant soldier, and while speaking of it, with his eyes full of tears, said 'it was more highly prized than anything he ever before possessed.'" He and his wife then removed to the Dakota Territory where he purchased a "considerable" tract of land. Soon, however, a long and painful illness ensued; Kennedy died in the spring of 1883 on one of his visits to Milwaukee; he was only fifty.

Reunion of 1889.
John L. Mitchell (standing l.), Alexander McCook (seated l.),
Nicholas Greusel (seated r.)
COURTESY OF THE MILWAUKEE COUNTY HISTORICAL SOCIETY.

"His death causes deep grief among all citizens who knew him," eulogized editor Watrous. "So they pass away. Twenty-five years will whip past with lightning speed and then we shall almost look in vain for a comrade of the late war."[23]

An untimely end befell the regiment's acerbic colonel, Charles Larrabee. He migrated to the Pacific Northwest after the war, considered running for the U.S. Senate, then located to Los Angeles, California. Sometime during this period, he posed for a formal oil portrait: He had apparently regained his health, for the stern face was fleshy behind the drooping mustache; his hair had receded further, revealing a broad forehead; and the artist captured those dark eyes that once glowered upon young Lieutenant McArthur.

The former regimental commander long bore the disappointment of not having won promotion to brigadier. Moreover, a taint always seemed to hang over his war service. In 1867, General Rosecrans, who lived in California, was disposed to write Larrabee. "I am annoyed to hear that calumny had had the audacity to whisper that you left the Army of the Cumberland in some kind of disgrace," Old Rosey said. "No officer of his grade stood higher in my estimation for ability, courage or patriotism, than you did; when I became satisfied that the condition of your health, and other personal circumstances made known to me, imposed on me the duty of accepting your resignation. You are at liberty to use this letter as you please."

Larrabee was killed in California, having "met with a sad fate in the wreck of the southern overland train at Tehachipi" en route from San Francisco to Los Angeles, Sunday, January 20, 1883. Here was one of the sad fates that befell many 24th Wisconsin men.[24]

The regiment's second colonel, "Dore" West of Waukesha, became a wholesale merchant in Philadelphia. Tragically, he died as a result of blows received in a Washington disturbance in the mid 1890s. Lish Hibbard, the imperious major, became a general insurance agent after resigning his commission in the spring of 1863. Ultimately, however, he would remove to Chicago while still conducting the business with a partner.

Carl Von Baumbach, the immigrant whose father was imperial consul to the German states during the war, engaged in a wholesale drug business upon his return to Milwaukee in 1864. He had served ably as the regiment's major until his resignation late in 1863. In 1867, he married Clara Rosenthal, and six children were born to the couple—three boys, all of whom died of childhood illnesses save Ludwig, who was tragically killed in a hunting accident. He removed to St. Cloud, Minnesota, engaging briefly in fur trading with the Indians, but in 1885 returned to his former occupation in Milwaukee, incorporating under the more Americanized given name of Charles Von Baumbach Company. Within five years the prosperous firm boasted thirty clerks and an annual gross of $800,000. Active in Grand Army affairs, the stout and bushy-bearded Von Baumbach died in 1901 at age sixty-one.[25]

Dr. Herman Hasse, the estimable regimental surgeon who had patched scores of men together, sawed off uncounted limbs, and watched hundreds die of wounds and fevers, returned to his Milwaukee practice. Distinguished in his gray beard and thick hair, he was involved in veteran activities until 1884, when he migrated to California. In 1915 he retired in Santa Monica, studying botany, his favorite pastime.[26]

The old century was passing and a new one loomed. Many veterans grew rheumatic and rheumy-eyed—normal infirmities often exacerbated by three years of hard war service. Few, it seemed, made note of the end of Federal military occupation in the South, and the rapid ascendancy of many former Confederate soldiers into state governments there as well as the U.S. Congress. The weariness of age appeared to distract veterans from mounting concerted outrage when the freed black men were once again enslaved by laws, policies, and terror. The Gilded Age was coming to an end, a new international war was being fueled in the press, and the era of the Civil War was fading.

When the old boys, as they called themselves, of Company B slated a reunion in February 1889, many of the old unit who could not attend responded with written vignettes and recollections. Art Gilbert, who wrote from Brooklyn, New York, recalled how he fought in his first battle wearing only slippers; the seventeen-year-old was discharged for disability in late 1862. Ed Douglas, who was so badly shot up and captured at Stones River, wrote from Hot Springs, Arkansas; he said that despite some great adventures, including a trip nearly to the Arctic Circle, he still remembered fondly his brief service with the Milwaukee Regiment. Fred Childs was in Greenwich, Connecticut. Another of the old Company B veterans croaked that he was now but "a gray-haired, toothless rheumatic old indolent." Others drafted missives, too, among them Gens. Arthur McArthur, posted at Fort Leavenworth, Kansas, at the time, William Rosecrans, Alexander McCook, and "Cump" Sherman.[27]

Gene Comstock, the Ohio-born printer who enlisted in Company B and wrote copiously during the war, married, and the couple had two children. They lived for a time in Chicago, then removed to Texas where Comstock died in the spring of 1888 of tuberculosis; he was only forty-five years old.[28]

Another of the company's printers, Norm Burdick, became one of the pillars of Milwaukee society. Using the sobriquet "Musket," it was often recalled, he wrote long detailed dispatches to the news during the war; he was captured helping a comrade at Stones River. In 1866, Burdick married and established a fine printing firm with a 24th Wisconsin comrade, John Armitage, who rose from enlisted to officer ranks. Slender and distinguished by a gray beard flowing from the chin and upper lip of his narrow face, Burdick wore a pince-nez in lieu of his Civil War spectacles. His business on Michigan Street grew to become one of the most respected in the city, and the company often printed books and pamphlets for the old veterans. Norm Burdick lived modestly on the west side of the city, and died in the spring of 1910 at age seventy.[29]

George Cooley, a printer and former Company A corporal, came to Milwaukee from western Wisconsin after the war, likely seeking better opportunities. He had enlisted after the death of his wife in 1862 and maintained a fine diary during the war. He remarried in 1869, and two children were born to the new couple—a daughter and a son. He again took up his old profession, at one time becoming a newspaper compositor. Cooley died in 1884 at age forty-eight; whether the three years of hard war service had contributed to his untimely demise is unknown. Mary Cooley remained in the city for many years, residing modestly near the central business district and collecting a widow's pension.[30]

George Allanson was remembered as the tall lieutenant who was saved from drowning in the murky Tennessee River by Harry Rogers. He still bore the scar of his Adairsville, Georgia, wound, and his fair curly hair had grayed and thinned considerably since those days in Tennessee and Georgia. He sold newspapers and tobacco at the Union Depot, and lived at Twenty-Fifth and Grand Avenue near Burdick. He died in 1901.[31]

Harry and Charley Rogers lived in Milwaukee the remainder of their lives. The disfigured older brother, a sergeant during the war years, had predicted his wounds before Chickamauga. He lived into his late sixties, dying in 1908; Charley, the younger, survived ten years longer, passing away in 1918 when he was seventy-five.

Henry Drake, who wrote regularly during the war and earned a lieutenancy, returned to the wholesale and retail drug business with his brother after recovering his health following his resignation in 1863. The firm had two locations several blocks apart near the bank of the Milwaukee River. He lived on the south side of the city, and died in 1913.[32]

James Heth, whose father had provided the "pets" of Company B with tasty sweet morsels and tobacco at Camp Sigel, went back to the confectionery business with his brother, Charley. But by the late 1870s, the business had been closed or was sold and renamed. In the late 1880s, he sought opportunity in Minnesota.[33]

As the new century loomed, a new conflict involving young soldiers was being fought on foreign soil, eclipsing somewhat the Civil War.

With increasing acceleration, old soldiers in blue were dying, and the strength and zeal of their veterans' movement was beginning to wane. Still, many stiff and gray-haired veterans limped toward the new century, bearing with them the "garrulity of old age," as Ed Furness put it.

For those who lived in Milwaukee, the approach of the new century brought a myriad changes. The city's population reached toward a third of a million, and three-quarters of those bore Germanic surnames. Milwaukee had overcome the disastrous Third Ward fire that left 2,000 homeless in 1892, and the financial panic the following year when five banks were shuttered. Eye-appealing new architecture included a soaring city hall, and the thirteen-story Pabst Building, the city's tallest building. The brewing industry led by Pabst, Schlitz, Blatz, and Miller was a leading employer; so, too, were machining, iron and steel manufacturing, and leather tanning. Although the city was said to be a working-class town, there was much of culture. The new Pabst Theatre, a magnificent music hall, had opened, as did a striking public library across the street from the old Mitchell mansion, now the Deutscher Club, on Grand Avenue. Somewhat earlier, a school of panorama painters, nearly all Germans, produced numerous colossal canvases depicting historical and Biblical scenes. These precursors of cinema included several Civil War battles, including the battles of Missionary Ridge and Atlanta, which were of particular interest to the veterans of the 24th Wisconsin. Such were changes that men like Tom Ford, Tom Balding, and others witnessed.[34]

In 1898, when the "Victorious Charge" monument was unveiled in Milwaukee, Ford, his ugly facial scar from the Adairsville, Georgia, wound still evident, lived in Milwaukee, working as a laborer. He served as secretary of the 24th Wisconsin Reunion Association for a time, and in the next decades published a series of war vignettes in the *Evening Wisconsin* newspaper; he also spoke much about the need to improve common education. When a pastiche of Ford's humorous and sometimes graphic reminiscences called *With the Rank and File* was published in 1898, the frontispiece photo of him was retouched to obscure the war scars disfiguring the right side of his face. He married twice, both Irish women, and ended his days living in the old Irish ward south of the central business district. He died at the advanced age of eighty-one in 1920.[35]

Veteran of both the 5th and 24th Wisconsin, the Englishman Tom Balding, who, like Kennedy, won a brevet to major late in the war, became a "leading citizen" and member of a big commission firm. The short, dark-haired veteran, Watrous wrote, was the first man to befriend the youthful Lieutenant McArthur at Camp Sigel when his squeaky voice amused everyone. A Londoner, he later gained employment with one of the largest insurance firms in the city, Northwestern Mutual Life, ultimately rising to the company's executive board. He and his wife and son lived in a fine residence on Lake Drive overlooking Lake Michigan. He lived a good, long life, succumbing to a heart attack only weeks before his eighty-fourth birthday in 1920.[36]

Red-haired Jim Bacon, whose lack of teeth nearly doomed his enlistment in the summer of 1862, remained in Milwaukee for many years. He died in 1919, nearly an octogenarian, just after World War I came to a close.

Ed Blake, the gallant color-bearer who ultimately won commendations and shoulder straps for his gallantry, returned to Port Washington after the war, engaging in an extensive "mercantile business." He also served in the state assembly and senate for Ozaukee and Washington Counties in the 1880s. In 1897, he was found "peacefully floating down the stream of time." Twice married, in 1894 he moved to Chicago, where he died in 1923. "He gave the full measure of his youth and strength to his country and his state," his obituary read, "and in our hearts must his memory ever be treasured."[37]

Short-legged Henry Bichler reopened his tailoring business in a town north of Milwaukee, and prospered in Ozaukee County. Born in Luxembourg in 1833, he had shuttered his shop in 1862 to join William Goldsmith's company. He was "one of the unassuming boys of Company H," who had been captured in the whirlwind of Stones River. Near the century's turn, a news writer found him with the "frosts of the autumn of life silvering his once dark hair, his step is not as buoyant and agile as it need be, and certain twinges of pain come more frequently to remind him of these never-to-be-forgotten days when he . . . used his energies so freely in behalf of freedom and humanity." At the fiftieth reunion of the 24th Wisconsin in 1912, he came with his son to hear his old colonel, McArthur, speak. Bichler died just days before his eighty-third birthday in 1916, as a world war raged.[38]

Joe Cramer, the twenty-one-year-old Company E veteran, returned to Grafton, Wisconsin, not far from Bichler, after mustering out in 1865, becoming a daguerreotypist. Near the end of the century, he opened a photo business in Milwaukee, retiring in 1902. Fond of music, it was said of him that he played his violin daily. Cramer celebrated his golden wedding anniversary in 1916, and died a year later; he was nearly seventy-four.[39]

The years following the war were typical but tragic for Christian Bessinger, the Company E corporal. The Germanic immigrant was badly wounded at the battle of Franklin about the same time as Colonel McArthur, but he survived the war. Married before he volunteered, his wife ultimately bore him eight children. The blue-eyed, sandy-haired veteran worked in a limestone quarry in the rural community of Richland, Wisconsin, but was badly injured in an explosion that took his sight. In 1880—Bessinger was in his early fifties—the family moved to Missouri where, in 1911 at age seventy-three, the blind veteran died. His tombstone bears no inscription about his war service.[40]

Two of the most prominent veterans of the Milwaukee Regiment were John Mitchell, the scion of wealth whose weak eyes forced him out of the war in 1863, and Arthur McArthur, who remained in the army and rose to prominence in its ranks. Mitchell was a young man of twenty-one when he returned to the city; impaired eyesight prevented him from pursuing a career in law, so he followed his father into banking and other business interests. Mitchell also resumed an avocation he loved—farming and raising fine horses—and purchased 400 acres southwest of the Milwaukee; the short-statured veteran soon developed one of the finest farms in the state. During the financial panic of 1873, his Wisconsin Marine & Fire Insurance Company Bank failed; he turned over the six million dollars in securities owned by the institution and all assets except his homestead as collateral to creditors. Within nine months, the bank's financial condition was righted. "His was the very soul of integrity and honor."

Much involved in veterans' affairs, Mitchell immeasurably aided the National Home for Disabled Volunteer Soldiers that was established west of the city. During the GAR reunion in 1889, Mitchell made available to his old comrades the grounds of the palatial family estate on Grand Avenue. The city's splendid monument to its Civil War veterans, "The Victorious Charge," was erected on the street within eyesight of the entrance to the magnificent Second Empire mansion.

John Mitchell entered politics at age thirty, serving in the state senate in two non-consecutive terms as a Democrat in 1872 and 1876; fourteen years later, he won election to the U.S. Congress in 1890 and 1892, resigning when he was elected to the Senate by the Wisconsin legislature. The former lieutenant married Harriet Danforth in 1878, and seven children were born to them; the eldest, Willie, would become a famed flying ace in another war. Gaining the rotundity of middle age, Mitchell sprouted a long, shaggy, untrimmed beard; thick spectacles were another familiar aspect. After leaving public office, Mitchell, ever the scholar, studied linguistics at the university in Grenoble, France, earning a degree at age sixty. He returned to Milwaukee in 1902 and died in 1904 after an illness of several weeks. He was buried with full military honors at Forest Home Cemetery with his cousin, Bob Chivas, and friend, Fred Root, and so many of his old 24th Wisconsin comrades. One of the pallbearers was Lt. Howard Greene, whose uncle and namesake had marched and fought with Mitchell and died charging up Missionary Ridge.[41]

As the old century waned, the other famed veteran of the 24th Wisconsin returned briefly to Milwaukee when, in 1897, McArthur was stationed in Minnesota. He, his wife Pinky, and two sons established a temporary residence on the city's near east side. In one of the last issues of the *Milwaukee Sunday Telegraph,* Watrous printed an etched likeness of young Arthur McArthur, age seventeen, "when a mere stripling, not robust in health, with a voice not yet fully changed." Watrous seemed never to tire of telling, printing, and embellishing stories of the youthful McArthur. "His voice was so weak it could scarcely be heard while performing his duties on dress parade, and that fact brought him ridicule and consequent chagrin. Though a boy, weak-voiced, not strong, he was a young tiger when the real work of the regiment began—when it went into battles. There were no braver men, no more heroic officers, than the young adjutant."

When the McArthurs returned to Milwaukee in 1897, Watrous wrote: "The survivors of . . . MacAthur's old regiment have vied with each another in honoring their former leader; have spared no pains to make his stay in the city pleasant. His companions of the Loyal Legion held a special meeting to welcome him to his old home. Col. MacArthur is still a young man: one would hardly suspect that he has served through the war. There are no gray hairs, his eyes are bright as ever, and his cheeks and forehead are without wrinkles. He is a soldier, a thorough soldier, an honor to the old army, one of the glorious men of the volunteer forces, a citizen to be proud of, a Wisconsin man who has added much to the state's good name."[42]

The colonel proudly wore the Medal of Honor that had been awarded for his heroism at Missionary Ridge, an award that he himself had instigated. While assigned to army headquarters in Washington in

1890, he had the duty to review officer records. He discovered that Congress had permitted the Medal of Honor, initially designated only for enlisted men and noncommissioned officers, to be accorded officers in 1863. This change had been ignored, however, and not one officer received the honor. More than a decade after, however, three officers did receive the medal. McArthur, long piqued that his Civil War service had not been recognized by the army, submitted an application, buttressing it with documentation and affidavits from such men as Carl Von Baumbach, the major in command at Missionary Ridge, Ed Parsons, and George Allanson, as well as Gens. Emerson Opdycke, Nathan Kimball, and others. On June 30, 1890, a military board awarded McArthur with the Medal of Honor.[43]

After his war career ended, McArthur and his wife returned to Milwaukee in 1907, establishing apartments on Marshal Street near the old Yankee/Yorker precincts of his boyhood home north of the central business district. He told a news man that he was "glad to be back home. I shall stay in Milwaukee for the rest of my days and renew old friendships just as fast as I can. In all the experiences of a long life spent moving about the world, no city has appealed to me as much as does Milwaukee." McArthur, whose son had changed the spelling of the family name to MacArthur, was buried at Forest Home in 1912. Disinterred in 1926, likely at the instigation of his son, McArthur's body was reburied at Arlington.[44]

One of the keepers of memory's flame for the 24th Wisconsin was Ed Parsons. A New Yorker by birth but Westerner by propensity, Parsons served as the ranking captain during most of the war. He commanded the regiment after Lieutenant Colonel McArthur's wounding at Franklin, and resigned in March 1865, returning to his new wife, Abbie. The couple raised a son and two daughters. Parsons cleared his round cheeks of the muttonchop whiskers cultivated during the war, trimming the growth to the Vandyke that would characterize him for the remainder of his life. Parsons, whose residence was on the near west side, became a successful commission merchant in Milwaukee, and was much involved in veterans organizations, often speaking about his old regiment. In 1895, he returned to Chickamauga to speak at the dedication of the Wisconsin monument. Somewhat later, a striking granite memorial to the 24th Wisconsin, replete with a handsome soldier in a slouch hat and blouse, was erected.

The seventy-six-year-old Parsons suffered a stroke when Arthur McArthur died while addressing the fiftieth reunion of the 24th Wisconsin; his death appeared imminent. But the little soldier recovered, albeit in a diminished state that caused him to close his business. He celebrated his golden wedding anniversary within two years, but Abbie died just three years later. The old captain, several of whose war letters were published in the city's press, was stricken by what would become a long illness. Perhaps it was a broken heart over the loss of his beloved wife in 1915 that took the old captain down. Parsons, who always welcomed friends and old comrades to his home, died in 1920 at age eighty-four. One of the last soldiers of the 24th Wisconsin, Parsons was buried with full military honors at Forest Home Cemetery. Nearly seventy years later, a descendant, Michelle Boehlen, placed a new headstone at the captain's grave.[45]

Before his death, Parsons often recollected the names of his dead comrades, and frequently visited that "silent city of the dead, our beautiful Forest Home." The burial ground on the far southwest side of the city had grown from 72 acres in 1850 to 200 at the century's turn. Parsons became one of the keepers of the regiment's flame. "It will not be long ere the bugle sounds for our columns to *halt,* and we will say, 'Let us pass over the River and rest with you under the shade of the trees,'" he once said late in the old century.[46]

"His dust sleeps" in Forest Home Cemetery, Parsons said of another hero, Bob Chivas. The tall Scot's imposing grave monument, likely erected by old Alexander Mitchell, bore the names of his battles: Perryville, Stones River, Chickamauga, Mission Ridge, as well as the national emblems of Scotland and America—the thistle and eagle. Upon the folds of a granite flag were chiseled "the sword and cap of the Union soldier." To memorialize him, the veterans named one of Milwaukee's Grand Army posts in his honor.[47]

The name of the pensive Howard Greene was remembered, too. His father, Welcome Arnold Greene, wrote a brief encomium to the beloved son who died near Chivas on the rocky slope of Missionary Ridge. "The Recollections of Howard Greene" recounted the soldier's "sweetness of disposition," his Quaker forebears, his upbringing, and events of his youth; it told of the sad-eyed and earnest young man's migration to Milwaukee to join his brother in business, and of his Civil War service. Decades later, the words were recast into an eight-page typescript by Greene's nephew, who was born in 1864 and given his uncle's name; that young man, a soldier, served as a pallbearer at John Mitchell's funeral in 1904. Finally, Welcome Greene's recollections were turned over to a third Howard Greene, who also joined the military and served as "an extremely raw junior officer" in World War II.

The deeds and lives of many others may not have been long recollected, however. Who recalled eighteen-year-old Frank Hale, the regiment's first battle death? Was the name of Homer Cooley, killed at Kennesaw Mountain, on many lips? Where were written the names of Byron Brooks, the old bachelor whose Milwaukee grave site was never used; or of Christian Nix, the immigrant officer killed and buried at Stones River?

The remains of Datus Worth, the last man killed in the Milwaukee Regiment, had been exhumed in March 1865 by his brother, William. He paid $5 to a Nashville undertaker for unearthing and embalming the body, $25 for a stainless case, and $10 for express shipping back to Wisconsin. The "erring son" was laid to final rest in Granville just before spring.[48]

Amandus Silsby, the God-fearing private solider who died and was buried in distant Tennessee, was also not much remembered. His father, John, the Methodist missionary then living in Selma, Alabama, applied for a pension in 1887 based upon his son's service. As evidence, he sent to the U.S. Pension Office a letter written by Amandus in 1862, indicating the dutiful young soldier regularly sent $10 to support his father. The letter was also a reminder that the young lad, as he had promised, perused his Testament every day. Before the pension application was finalized, however, John Silsby, age seventy-one, died.[49]

Sam Philbrook, the dark-haired captain killed in one of the last battles of the regiment, was memorialized for a time when his pretty daughter, Carrie Alice, was named "Daughter of the Regiment" at the first gathering of 24th Wisconsin veterans in 1866. Carrie later married and moved to Minnesota with her husband, Joseph McCabe, who worked for the railroad; she died prematurely at age thirty-six, leaving a daughter, Olive. Caddie Philbrook, the widow, returned to the East, living in Boston until her death in 1910, devastated, of course, by the loss of her daughter. Caddie Philbrook's body was returned to Milwaukee where it was interred next to her daughter's and proximate to so many veterans of her husband's regiment—at Forest Home Cemetery. A light brown obelisk marked the family plot.

Captain Philbrook, the handsome, broad-shouldered husband and father, stood among the tallest in the Milwaukee Regiment's pantheon. His body rested rudely, an unknown under the field of Franklin,

Tennessee, until along with others it was relocated to either the Stones River or Chickamauga military cemetery. Years later an epitaph was chiseled into the stone obelisk of his father's grave in Ossipee, New Hampshire; it read: "He never took a backward step." In many ways, he personified the 24th Wisconsin. Whatever his motivation for volunteering, he had turned away from wife, family, a good situation, and given his life—all there was to give. Ironically, only intangible and fleeting memory remained of him as the Civil War receded. "The acacia does not bloom at the head of his grave, nor does stone or lettered monument designate his final resting place," wrote a news man. In time, even the memory of the dark, bearded captain, along with the faces and names of his comrades, faded. The sacrifices of those who were killed or felled by disease, and those who survived to tell the regiment's tale, were forgotten. As it was written of Sam Philbrook, so could it be said of others: "He sleeps upon the field of his glory."[50]

Notes

INTRODUCTION

1. *Milwaukee Daily News,* August 29, 1862.
2. William F. Fox, *Regimental Losses in the American Civil War, 1861–1865* (Albany, N.Y.: Albany, 1889).
3. *Daily Wisconsin,* August 28, 1862.

PROLOGUE

1. McArthur's son, Douglas, changed the spelling of the name to MacArthur. The former spelling is used throughout this book.
2. *Milwaukee Journal,* September 6, 1912.
3. Stuart McConnell, *Glorious Contentment: The Grand Army of the Republic, 1865–1900* (Chapel Hill: University of North Carolina Press, 1992).
4. [Frank A. Flower], *History of Milwaukee, Wisconsin* (Chicago: Western Historical Society, 1881), 783.
5. Bayrd Still, *Milwaukee: The History of a City* (Madison: State Historical Society of Wisconsin, 1948), 279–320; H. Russell Austin, *The Milwaukee Story: The Making of an American City* (Milwaukee: *Milwaukee Journal,* [1946]), 161–68; Diane Buck, *Outdoor Sculpture in Milwaukee: A Cultural and Historical Guidebook* (Madison: State Historical Society of Wisconsin, 1995), 59–61.
6. Austin, *Milwaukee,* pp. 154–69.
7. [Flower], *Milwaukee,* 803; Edwin B. Parsons, "Sheridan," In: Military Order of the Loyal Legion of the United States, Wisconsin Commandery, *War Papers,* vol. 1 (Milwaukee: Burdick, Armitage, & B. Allen, 1891), 275–84 (hereafter cited as MOLLUS).
8. [Flower], *Milwaukee,* 804, 1041; Milwaukee City Directory, 1912.
9. Milwaukee City Directory, 1912; John Scheiding, manuscript; Krista Jautz, manuscript.
10. *Port Washington (Wisc.) Star,* June 5 and May 22, 1897.
11. *Milwaukee Journal,* September 6, 1912; *Milwaukee Sentinel,* September 6, 1912; *Milwaukee Free Press,* September 6, 1912; Douglas MacArthur, *Reminiscences* (New York: McGraw-Hill, 1964), 36; William R. Manchester, *American Caesar: Douglas MacArthur, 1880–1964* (New York: Little, Brown, 1978), 38; Kenneth Ray Young, *The General's General: The Life and Times of Arthur MacArthur* (Boulder, Colo.: Westview, 1994), 338–40; *Milwaukee Sunday Telegraph,* February 4 and April 15, 1883; *Dictionary of Wisconsin Biography* (Madison: State Historical Society of Wisconsin, 1960), 251; U.S. Pension Office file, George Merrick file.

CHAPTER 1

1. Still, *Milwaukee*, 39–41, 151.
2. Eugene Comstock, letter, September 8, 1860, State Historical Society of Wisconsin.
3. Still, *Milwaukee*, 153; John G. Gregory, *History of Milwaukee, Wisconsin*, (Chicago: S. J. Clark, 1931), 3:762–66; *Milwaukee Sentinel*, September 8, 9, 10, 1862; *Milwaukee Daily News*, September 8, 9, 10, 1862. Some writers later argued that the vacuum caused by the deaths of so many Irish leaders opened opportunities for immigrants from Germanic states to begin political ascendancy in Milwaukee.
4. Welcome A. Greene, "Recollections of Howard Greene," State Historical Society of Wisconsin; Howard Greene, letter, May 13, 1861.
5. Salomon, a sympathizer of the democratic revolutions in the German baronies, duchies, and principalities, fled Prussia in 1849 and immigrated to Wisconsin. He became a schoolteacher, a surveyor, and a court clerk, then moved to Milwaukee in 1852, becoming a lawyer. Salomon, whose two brothers became Wisconsin soldiers during the Civil War, was the state's first Germanic-born governor. He was vigorous in raising fourteen new regiments and refilling the ranks of older ones. He also instituted the infamous draft, quashing an antidraft riot in several communities north of Milwaukee. He evoked sufficient antagonism from politicians to prevent his renomination in 1863. After leaving office, he returned to his Milwaukee law practice. He died in Frankfurt am Main, Germany, in 1909, having returning to his native land. *Dictionary of Wisconsin Biography*, 313–14.
6. Of French ancestry and a New Yorker by birth, Charles Larrabee had a peripatetic existence during his formative years before settling in a small community northwest of Milwaukee, and rising to prominence in the politics of the new state. Elected as a delegate to the Territory's second constitutional convention, Larrabee later gained prominence as a circuit court judge, and was elected to Congress in 1848 as a Stephen Douglas Democrat. During his one term in Congress he had urged conciliation between the North and South—a position that did not endear him to Republicans. He was defeated for reelection in 1860. On April 17, 1861, he enlisted as a private in the Horicon Guards, which became a company in the 5th Wisconsin Infantry; he was elected second lieutenant and ultimately became the regiment's major, earning a reputation as a good officer. He would command the Milwaukee Regiment a year before his illness and antipathy over failure to gain higher rank prompted his resignation. See *Milwaukee Daily News*, July 31, 1862; *Dictionary of American Biography* (New York: Charles Scribner's Sons, 1933), 11:506; *Dictionary of Wisconsin Biography*, 222; *Biographical Directory of the United States Congress, 1774–1989* (Washington, D.C.: U.S. Government Printing Office, 1989), 1345; Lyman C. Draper, "Sketch of Charles H. Larrabee," in *Collections of the State Historical Society of Wisconsin* (Madison: State Historical Society of Wisconsin, 1909), 9:366–88.
7. Page, New York-born in 1818, migrated to Milwaukee in 1844, and established a successful dry goods company. He was later appointed to the city sheriff's department, and in 1853 was elected sheriff. He served one term as Milwaukee mayor, 1859–60, and increased the efficiency of the sheriff's department during that time. He died in Dresden, Germany, in 1873 while traveling in Europe. See *Milwaukee Sentinel*, July 20, 1862; [Flower], *Milwaukee*, 717–18, 803, 1573; Howard L.

Conard, *History of Milwaukee County from Its First Settlement to the Year 1895* (Chicago: American Biographical, [1895]), 2:116–17; Still, *Milwaukee,* 149, 358 n; Gregory, *History of Milwaukee,* 2:1102–3; *Daily Wisconsin,* August 9, 1862.

8. *Milwaukee Sentinel,* July 24, 1862.

9. Ibid., August 1, 1862.

10. The elder McArthur, born in Glasgow in 1815, migrated to America as a youth. He attended Massachusetts schools, studied law, and practiced in New York before moving to Milwaukee in 1849. Active in Democratic Party politics, he became city attorney and in 1855 was elected lieutenant governor on a ticket with William Barstow. The Republican opponent, Coles Bashford, charged fraud in balloting, and contested the election. Governor Barstow resigned shortly after taking office, March 21, 1856, and McArthur succeeded him. Then the state supreme court upheld Bashford's claim. Governor McArthur at first determined to hold onto his office come what may, but veiled threats of possible violence by Bashford supporters convinced him to relinquish the governor's office after only four days as chief executive. He resumed his position as lieutenant governor until January 1858. Elected circuit court judge, he served from 1858 to 1869. A Union, or War, Democrat, he later joined the Republican Party, and in 1870 was appointed associate justice of the District of Columbia Supreme Court by Pres. U. S. Grant; he served until 1888. McArthur died in 1896. *Dictionary of Wisconsin Biography,* 243–245.

11. Charles King, speeches delivered in 1903 and 1910, and reprinted in *The MacArthurs of Milwaukee* (Milwaukee: Milwaukee County Historical Society, 1979), 17, 18; MacArthur, *Reminiscences,* 6; Clayton D. James, *The Years of MacArthur* (Boston: Houghton Mifflin, 1970), 1:12. Born June 2, 1845, in Massachusetts, McArthur was four when his family migrated to Milwaukee in 1849. See also *Dictionary of American Biography,* 21:521; *Dictionary of Wisconsin Biography,* 244; National Guard, Adjutant General's Office, Regimental Descriptive Rolls and Regimental Muster and Descriptive Rolls, 24th Infantry, State Historical Society of Wisconsin, Madison.

12. Born in New York, Jerome Watrous worked on a newspaper in Fond du Lac north of Milwaukee before the war. At the outbreak of hostilities, he enlisted as a private in Bragg's Rifles and served with distinction with the 6th Wisconsin Infantry, ultimately rising to adjutant of the fabled Iron Brigade. At war's conclusion, he removed to Milwaukee to start a newspaper, the *Milwaukee Sunday Telegraph* (later the *Milwaukee Telegraph*), a society and feature weekly. He filled numerous columns in the 1880's and 1890's with recollections of Civil War veterans from many Wisconsin regiments. His writings and speeches did much to keep alive the memory of his own regiment as well as others. Despite his years, Watrous also served briefly during the Spanish-American War; he was in the Philippines at the same time as General McArthur. Married three times, he died June 5, 1922. See also William H. Washburn, *The Life and Writings of Jerome A. Watrous: Soldier-Reporter, Adjutant of the Iron Brigade* (N.p.: William H. Washburn, 1992); *Dictionary of Wisconsin Biography,* 367.

13. Jerome Watrous, "How the Boy Won: General MacArthur's First Victory," *Saturday Evening Post,* February 24, 1899, 770.

14. Mary Gates Muggah and Paul H. Raihle, *The MacArthur Story* (Chippewa Falls, Wisc.: Chippewa Falls Book Agency, 1945), 16.

15. Watrous, "How the Boy Won," 770.
16. This and all physical descriptions of soldiers as well as details on promotions, wounds, etc., are taken from National Guard, Regimental Descriptive Rolls, 24th Infantry.
17. *Roster of Wisconsin Volunteers: War of the Rebellion, 1861–1865, Arranged Alphabetically* (Madison: Democrat, 1866), 2:223.
18. Amandus Silsby, letter, September 21, 1861, Nancy Torphy Collection, and Chattanooga and Chickamauga National Military Park. The 2nd, 5th, 6th, and 7th Wisconsin Infantry Regiments were briefly brigaded together in 1861. Wisconsin's governor Randall had hoped for an all-Wisconsin brigade, but that plan was thwarted when the 5th Wisconsin was removed from the brigade. Soon, the new all-Western brigade consisted of three Wisconsin regiments plus the 19th Indiana. With the later addition of the 24th Michigan Infantry, the unit won undying fame on battlefields in Virginia, Maryland, and Pennsylvania, earning the name Iron Brigade, and paying a heavy toll of thousands of casualties. Alan T. Nolan, *The Iron Brigade* (New York: Macmillan, 1961).
19. Silsby, letter, August 4, 1862.
20. *Milwaukee Sentinel,* August 1, 1862; *Daily Wisconsin,* August 1, 1862; *Milwaukee Daily News,* August 2, 1862; [Flower], *Milwaukee,* 717–18; Conard, *Milwaukee,* 116–17; Silsby, letter, August 4, 1862. After the governor's speech, the gathering separated into three throngs, each centered on a speaker's platform. Fiery Illinois congressman Owen Lovejoy, along with Wisconsin's U.S. senator James R. Doolittle, State Attorney General James H. Howe, and other speakers bombarded their assemblies with patriotic appeals.

CHAPTER 2

1. *Milwaukee Daily News,* August 15, 1862.
2. Greene, letter, August 18, 1861.
3. *Milwaukee Daily News,* August 12, 1862.
4. *Milwaukee Sentinel,* July 19, 1862.
5. *Milwaukee Daily News,* August 7, 1862.
6. Ibid., August 8, 1862; *Milwaukee Sunday Telegraph,* May 2, 1883.
7. *Milwaukee Daily News,* August 3, 1862.
8. Ibid., August 6, 1862.
9. Ibid., August 16, 1862.
10. *Milwaukee Sentinel,* August 4, 1862.
11. *Port Washington (Wisc.) Star,* May 22, 1897.
12. Ibid., June 19, 1897.
13. Ibid., May 27, 1916.
14. Ibid., June 5, 1897.
15. *Daily Wisconsin,* August 13, 1862. Many of the foreign-born of Germanic ancestry and their sons who enlisted formed part of the 26th Wisconsin, regarded as an ethnic regiment by some scholars. Its reputation was tarnished at the battle of Chancellorsville in 1862 when it earned the sobriquet the "flying Dutchmen." With unsuspecting fury, the Confederate general Thomas "Stonewall" Jackson slammed into the XI Corps, to which the 26th was assigned, and sent the Federals flying in retreat. Although subsequent reports indicated the Milwaukee unit had rallied and held its ground against the overwhelming gray horde, other regiments, nearly all

of which were immigrant units in the corps, tainted their reputation. In later service in the Western campaigns of the war, and with Sherman, it won praise, however. The 26th was ultimately listed among the foremost "Fighting Regiments" of the war. E[dwin] B. Quiner, *The Military History of Wisconsin* (Chicago: Clark, 1866), 540–47; William L. Burton, *Melting Pot Soldiers: The Union's Ethnic Regiments* (Ames: Iowa State University Press, 1988), 109; Fox, *Regimental Losses,* 399, 513.

16. Greene, letter, September 1, 1862.
17. *Milwaukee Daily News,* August 12 and 15, 1862.
18. Alexander Mitchell was born in 1817 in Aberdeenshire, Scotland; he immigrated to Milwaukee in 1839 to become secretary of the Wisconsin Marine and Fire Insurance Company. The firm soon began operating a banking component despite the fact that it was technically illegal. In 1853, a compromise was worked out, and the bank was officially chartered. The robust, bewhiskered capitalist ventured into railroad building, becoming president of the Milwaukee & St. Paul Railway Company, which absorbed other lines and evolved into the Chicago, Milwaukee, & St. Paul Railroad, operating over 5,000 miles of track. A War Democrat, Mitchell was also active in state and national politics, particularly during the Civil War. He was elected to Congress in 1870 and 1872, and became one of the most powerful men in the Old Northwest. John L. Mitchell was born in Milwaukee October 19, 1842. He graduated from the Hampton, Connecticut, Military Academy and studied in several European schools. See also *Dictionary of American Biography,* 13:39–40; *Dictionary of Wisconsin Biography,* 256–57; *Biographical Directory of the United States Congress,* 1513–14, 1517.
19. *Milwaukee Sunday Telegraph,* December 16, 1883.
20. J[ohn] Ingraham, *A Sermon in Memory of Captain F. A. Root and Lieutenant R. J. Chivas . . .* (Milwaukee: Presses of Star and Son, 1864), 10; William DeLoss Love, *Wisconsin in the War of the Rebellion,* (Chicago: Church & Goodman, 1866), 696.
21. Charles King, "Boys of the Loyal Legion," speech read December 7, 1892, in MOLLUS, Wisconsin Commandery, *War Papers,* (Milwaukee: Burdick, Armitage, & Allen, 1896), 2:205; *Milwaukee Daily News,* August 15, 1862; *Daily Wisconsin,* August 13, 15, 1862; *Roster,* 2:276.
22. Edwin Parsons was born February 16, 1836, in Lockport, New York. He migrated to Milwaukee with his family as a lad of ten. Educated in Milwaukee schools, he graduated from a local business college. Parsons, a bookkeeper and cashier at the firm of Kirby, Langworthy, and Company when the 24th Wisconsin was recruited, joined. The Milwaukee Light Guard, formed in 1857, was Wisconsin's premier militia company for several years. Its light gray jackets faced in black; patent leather cartridge boxes and knapsacks, gleaming white cross belts with a tiger's head brass breastplate; and tall bearskin hats were readily evident in the city's parades, celebrations, and events. The unit, which ultimately consisted of two companies and a band, also went on encampments to other cities, and once made a grand swing through upstate New York and Canada. At the war's outset, the members tendered their services in the three-month 1st Wisconsin Infantry. See [Flower], *Milwaukee,* 803; Herbert C. Damon, *History of the Milwaukee Light Guard* (Milwaukee: Sentinel, 1875), 137.
23. Another New Yorker by birth, Rufus King graduated from West Point in 1833. As a thirty-one-year-old, he migrated to Milwaukee to assume the editorship of the

Milwaukee Sentinel, the Whig and later Republican daily. He rose as well in Republican Party politics. The first president of the city's board of school commissioners, he was also active in militia affairs. He accepted a ministerial post to the Vatican offered by President Lincoln, but at the war's outbreak gained a commission of brigadier general of volunteers. He served as commander of the all-Western brigade mentioned previously before being promoted to division command. Ill health forced his resignation, and he was once again named minister to the Papal States; King spent his final years in New York before dying in 1876. His son, Charles, was also a noted military man. Born in Albany in 1844, he served on his father's staff during the Civil War until his appointment to West Point from which he graduated in 1866. Fighting in the Indian Wars, he served in the military until 1879 when he became an instructor of military tactics, then colonel of the Wisconsin National Guard regiment. During the Spanish-American War, he was recalled to active duty, and served in the Philippines as brigadier general of volunteers from 1898 to 1899. He ended his public life as an instructor at a Wisconsin military academy, and died in 1933. See *Dictionary of American Biography,* 5:400–401; ibid., 10:400; *Dictionary of Wisconsin Biography,* 206–7. The battle of Gainesville, a prelude to the second battle of Bull Run, was fought late in the afternoon of August 27, 1862. See also Alan Gaff, *Brave Men's Tears: The Iron Brigade at Brawner Farm* (Dayton: Morningside House, 1985).

24. The Cadets, part of the Milwaukee Light Guard, were organized in 1858 as a junior company. It was intended that its members would learn their military lessons, and after reaching majority, join the older company. Hibbard was elected first sergeant of the unit in January 1858. (Damon, *Milwaukee Light Guard,* 77, 88).

25. Born in Troy, Wisconsin, in 1839, Hibbard gained employment in Milwaukee at an early age as a bookkeeper; after the war he entered the commission business. ([Flower], *Milwaukee,* 1159).

26. King, "Boys," 2:201–6; *Daily Wisconsin,* January 29, 1863; Gregory, *History of Milwaukee,* 1:272.

27. *Milwaukee Sentinel,* July 26, 1862.

28. *Milwaukee Daily News,* August 16, 1862.

29. Ibid., August 13, 1862; Milwaukee City Directories, 1857–1858, 1858–1859, 1860–1861, 1863, 1865.

30. *Milwaukee Daily News,* August 13, 1862; Milwaukee City Directory, 1862; *Roster,* 2:267; Conard, *Milwaukee County,* 2:187–88; [Flower], *Milwaukee,* 1316.

31. *Milwaukee Daily News,* August 13, 1862; *Roster,* 2:267.

32. *Milwaukee Daily News,* August 16, 1862; *Roster,* 2:274.

33. *Milwaukee Daily News,* August 13, 1862; Caroline Philbrook, letter, January 20, 1865, Alvah S. Philbrook Papers.

34. *Milwaukee Daily News,* August 13, 1862; *Milwaukee Sentinel,* August 14, 1862.

35. Little is known of Nix prior to the war; see also *Roster,* 2:265.

36. Chase, born in January 1827 in south central New Hampshire, migrated to Milwaukee in 1854. He lived for a time in a small community northwest of Milwaukee, and worked for the LaCrosse & Milwaukee Railroad before taking a position with the Milwaukee & Prairie du Chien line (renamed the Milwaukee & Mississippi). See also Harry H. Anderson, "The Civil War Letters of Lieutenant Samuel B. Chase," *Milwaukee History,* 14, no. 2 (summer 1991): 38–39.

37. *Roster,* 2:266.

38. *Daily Wisconsin,* August 13, 1862.

39. Ibid. August 13, 1862; *Milwaukee Daily News,* August 13, 1862.

40. *Daily Wisconsin,* January 13, 1863.

41. *Milwaukee Daily News,* August 13, 1862. Von Baumbach was born in Kirchheim, Hesse, June 18, 1840; his father, Ludwig, had served in the armies of Europe. An "Acht und vierziger," Ludwig was a member of parliament agitating for a democratic constitution; the effort failed, and he was compelled to leave his native Hesse. He immigrated to America, settling first in Ohio before his move to Milwaukee in 1847. See Andrew J. Aikens and Lewis A. Proctor, eds., *Men of Progress: Wisconsin* (Milwaukee: Evening Wisconsin, 1897), 334–35.

42. *Port Washington (Wisc.) Star,* June 12, 1897.

43. *Roster,* 2:262–64.

44. *Milwaukee Sentinel,* July 26, 1862.

45. Ibid., August 14, 1862; *Roster,* 2:276–78.

46. *Milwaukee Sentinel,* August 16, 1862.

47. *Milwaukee Daily News,* August 13, 1862.

48. *Daily Wisconsin,* August 14, 15, 1862.

49. Ibid., August 21, 1862.

50. *Milwaukee Sentinel,* August 21, 1862; *Milwaukee Daily News,* August 22, 1862.

51. *Milwaukee Sentinel,* August 18, 1862.

CHAPTER 3

1. *Daily Wisconsin,* August 22, 23, 26, 1862. The incident triggered August 17, 1862, was the result of festering dissatisfaction among native populations. Sioux chief Little Crow began a series of forays and raids at New Ulm, Minnesota. For seven days, parties killed nearly 750 whites in southern Minnesota. The frontier was aflame with news of an Indian uprising; Wisconsin settlers feared similar depredations from local tribes. As rumors of massacres swept the state, settlements were deserted in days, with many settlers traveling to large cities for protection. Ultimately, the U.S. War Department dispatched Gen. John Pope, the commander badly defeated at second Bull Run in July 1861, to quell the disturbance. The Sioux were defeated in a series of battles. See Frank L. Klement, *Wisconsin and the Civil War* (Madison: State Historical Society of Wisconsin, 1963), 38–42.

2. *Milwaukee Sentinel,* August 21, 1862; *Daily Wisconsin,* September 3, 1862; Gregory, *History of Milwaukee,* 2:825–26. Camp Randall, near the state's capital, was Wisconsin's Agricultural Fair Grounds, hastily converted to a training ground. All but a few infantry regiments trained there. Carolyn J. Mattern, *Soldiers When They Go: The Story of Camp Randall, 1861–1865* (Madison: State Historical Society of Wisconsin, 1981).

3. *Milwaukee Daily News,* August 21, 1862; *Roster,* 2:274–76.

4. *Roster,* 2:256; Louis F. Frank, *The Medical History of Milwaukee, 1834–1914* (Milwaukee: Germanic, 1915), 39.

5. *Milwaukee Daily News,* August 24, 1862; Milwaukee City Directory, 1862.

6. King, "Boys," 2:204–5; [Flower], *Milwaukee,* 804; Norman Burdick, letter, December 21, 1862, in *Milwaukee Sentinel,* December 29, 1862.

7. Aikens and Proctor, eds., *Men of Progress,* 328–29; *Evening Wisconsin,* March 25, 1910.

8. *Roster,* 2:278–80.
9. Tom and Philip Plummer would serve with distinction in the Iron Brigade regiment; the latter would die in the harrowing battle of the Wilderness in May of the following year. See also *Roster,* 1:505; U.S. Census, Wisconsin, 1860; Milwaukee City Directories, 1859, 1860–61, 1862.
10. James B. Bacon, "With the 24th Wisconsin," *Milwaukee History* 14, no. 2 (summer 1991), 67.
11. *Milwaukee Daily News,* August 22, 1862.
12. Watrous, "How the Boy Won," 770.
13. *Roster,* 2:261.
14. [Flower], *Milwaukee,* 804, 807; Jerome A. Watrous, *Memoirs of Milwaukee County* (Madison: Western Historical Association, 1909), 2:394–95.
15. *Roster,* 2:266.
16. Ibid., 275.
17. *Daily Wisconsin,* January 16, 1863.
18. George A. Cooley, diary, June 18, 1863, State Historical Society of Wisconsin; Alan D. Gaff, *Our Boys: A Civil War Photograph Album* (Mount Vernon, Ind.: Windmill, 1996), 44–45.
19. [Flower], *Milwaukee,* 1041; William J. Anderson, *Milwaukee's Great Industries: A Compilation of Facts Concerning Milwaukee's Commercial and Manufacturing Enterprise, Its Trade and Commerce, and the Advantage It Offers to Manufacturers Seeking Desirable Locations for New or Established Industries* (Milwaukee: Association for the Advancement of Milwaukee, 1892), 179. George H. Walker, a ponderous Virginian who came to Milwaukee in 1833, founded Walker's Point south of the Menominee River. He acquired a government patent for 160 acres in 1849, served in the territorial legislature, and was Milwaukee mayor in 1851 and 1853. See also *Dictionary of Wisconsin Biography,* 364.
20. *Milwaukee Sentinel,* November 26, 1862.
21. Frederick P. Todd, *American Military Equipage, 1851–1872,* (Providence, R.I.: Company of Military Historians, 1974), 1:185–226.
22. *Milwaukee Sunday Telegraph,* December 16, 1883.
23. *Daily Wisconsin,* August 28, 1862.
24. Watrous, "How the Boy Won"; *Milwaukee Sentinel,* August 28, 1862.
25. Watrous, "How the Boy Won"; Muggah and Raihle, *The MacArthur Story,* 17.
26. *Daily Wisconsin,* August 28, 1862.
27. *Third Reunion of Co. "B." 24th Wis. Volunteers* (Milwaukee: Burdick, Armitage, & Allen, 1889), 25; *Roster,* 2:262.
28. *Louisville Journal,* October 9, 1862.
29. The terms musket and rifle-musket, although technically correct, were not generally used by soldier-writers of the time; the word gun was more common. A musket featured a smooth bore, whereas a rifle-musket had, as implied, a grooved barrel that increased range and accuracy. See also *Milwaukee Daily News,* August 29, 1862; Todd, *American Military Equipage,* 1:131–35; William B. Edwards, *Civil War Guns* (Harrisburg, Pa.: Stackpole, 1962), 256–60. Information about arms and equipage used by the 24th Wisconsin was also gleaned from conversations with well-known Civil War firearms collector and dealer Charles L. Foster.
30. *Milwaukee Sentinel,* August 30, 1862, September 2, 4, 1862; *Daily Wisconsin,* September 3, 1862, December 14, 1863.

31. Greene, letter, September 1, 1862; Milwaukee City Directory, 1862.
32. *Milwaukee Daily News,* August 29, 1862.
33. Ibid., September 6, 1862.
34. Ibid., August 29, 1862, September 3, 1862.
35. Ibid., September 3, 1862; *Daily Wisconsin,* September 4, 1862. Information on the women's couture of the day is from Maryanne Faeth Greketis, an authority on fashion of the Civil War.
36. *Milwaukee Sentinel,* August 22, 1862.
37. *Daily Wisconsin,* September 8, 1862.
38. *Milwaukee Sunday Telegraph,* March 3, 1893.
39. *Daily Wisconsin,* January 9, 1863; *Milwaukee Sentinel,* September 6, 1862.
40. *Daily Wisconsin,* June 15, 1864; Milwaukee City Directory, 1862; *Roster,* 2:259, 658, 667; 1028.
41. *Daily Wisconsin,* September 6, 1862.
42. Greene, letter, September 1, 1862.
43. *Milwaukee Daily News,* September 6, 1862.
44. *Milwaukee Sentinel,* September 6, 26, 1862; *Daily Wisconsin,* September 6, 1862, January 9, 1863; *Milwaukee Daily News,* September 6, 1862; *Milwaukee Sunday Telegraph,* March 3, 1893.
45. Greene, letter, September 1, 1862.

CHAPTER 4

1. George Bleyer, letter, October 10, 1862, in *Daily Wisconsin,* October 20, 1862. The newspaper misdated the letter as September 10, 1862.
2. Silsby, letter, October 16, 1862.
3. Arthur Gilbert, letter, February 25, 1889, in *Third Reunion,* 9–10; Gilbert, letter, September 11, 1862, in *Milwaukee Daily News,* September 16, 1862.
4. Robert Chivas, letter, September 12, 1862, Alexander Mitchell Papers. State Historical Society of Wisconsin. "Milwaukee," letter, September 17, 1862, in *Milwaukee Daily News,* September 25, 1862.
5. Gilbert, letter, September 11, 1862, in *Milwaukee Daily News,* September 16, 1862; Chivas, letter, September 12, 1862.
6. Bleyer, letter, September 22, 1862, in *Daily Wisconsin,* September 30, 1862; Comstock, letter, September 20, 1862.
7. *Louisville Journal,* October 9, 1862.
8. The 21st Michigan mustered into Federal service at nearly the same time as the Milwaukee Regiment, September 6, 1862. It was part of the Army of the Cumberland, and brigaded with the 24th Wisconsin until November 1863, at which time it became part of the army's Engineer Brigade. It mustered from service in June 1865. The 73rd and 88th Illinois were mustered into service in August and September respectively, and both would serve with the 24th Wisconsin until 1865. (See Frederick H. Dyer, *A Compendium of the War of the Rebellion* (1908; reprint, Des Moines: Thomas Yoseloff, 1959), 1077, 1083–84, 1290.
9. Annie Lillybridge became a "universal favorite in the regiment, and the colonel frequently assigned her as a regimental clerk, a position that brought her proximate to her lover who then was adjutant. While on picket duty, she was disabled by a shot to the arm; her wound grew worse daily. She was sent to a Louisville

hospital where she remained for several months." Ultimately, Annie was discharged for disability. Frazar Kirkland, *The Pictorial Book of Anecdotes of the Rebellion* . . . . (St. Louis: J. J. Mason, 1889), 621.

10. "Milwaukee," letter, September 17, 1862, in *Daily Milwaukee News,* September 25, 1862.

11. Ibid.

12. [Flower], *Milwaukee,* 803, 804; King, "Boys," 2:201–6; *Daily Wisconsin,* January 29, 1863; Gregory, *History of Milwaukee,* 1:272. After its three-month service, the 1st Wisconsin was reorganized as a three-year regiment. It was assigned to the Armies of the Ohio and the Cumberland, and fought in close proximity to the 24th Wisconsin. *Annual Reports of the Adjutant General of the State of Wisconsin, 1861–1865* (Madison: Democrat, 1912, 32–46.)

13. Bleyer, "On Picket," in *Milwaukee Sentinel,* May 5, 1863.

14. Gilbert, letter, February 25, 1889, in *Third Reunion,* 12.

15. Mitchell, *Milwaukee Sunday Telegraph,* December 16, 1883.

16. William A. Bircher, *A Drummer-Boy's Diary: Comprising Four Years of Service with the Second Regiment Minnesota Veteran Volunteers, 1861 to 1865* (1889; reprint, St. Cloud, Minn.: North Star, 1995), 79–80; Bell I. Wiley, *The Life of Billy Yank: The Common Soldier of the Union* (Indianapolis: Bobbs-Merrill, 1952), 237–39.

17. Datus I. Worth, letter, April 1, 1864, Mark and Beth Storch Collection, DeForest, Wisconsin; "C. S.," letter, in *Milwaukee Sentinel,* September 28, 1862.

18. Bleyer, letter, September 22, 1862, in *Daily Wisconsin,* September 30, 1862; Moses Hoyt, letter, October 2, 1862, in *Milwaukee Sentinel,* October 7, 1862.

19. Bleyer, letter, September 22, 1862, in *Daily Wisconsin,* September 30, 1862; "C," letter, September 18, 1862, in *Daily Wisconsin,* October 7, 1862.

20. Alexander McDowell McCook was from a family known as the "fighting McCooks" of Ohio. His father and seven brothers, and five first cousins and their father, all served in the Union armies. Alexander, born in 1831, graduated from West Point in 1852. At war's outbreak, he was commissioned colonel of the 1st Ohio Volunteers, who saw action at first Bull Run. Thereafter, McCook commanded a brigade in Kentucky and rose to corps command. He would be blamed for the disastrous results at Stones River and relieved of command. Although exonerated, he was thereafter assigned garrison and other duties. His second wife was Annie Colt of Milwaukee, whom he married there in 1885. He died in 1903. One brother, Daniel, commanded a brigade in Sheridan's division at Perryville while another sibling, Edward M. McCook, was promoted for gallantry at the same battle. And his first cousin, Anson G. McCook, a colonel of an Ohio regiment, also fought at Perryville, Stones River, Chattanooga, Lookout Mountain, Missionary Ridge, and elsewhere. See *Dictionary of American Biography,* 11:600–4; Ezra J. Warner, *Generals in Blue: Lives of Union Commanders* (Baton Rouge: Louisiana State University Press, 1964), 294–95.

21. "C," letter, September 28, 1862, in *Daily Wisconsin,* October 7, 1862.

22. Mead Holmes, Jr., *A Soldier of the Cumberland: Memoir of Mead Holmes, Jr* . . . (Boston: American Tract Society, 1864), 87; Mitchell, *Milwaukee Sunday Telegraph,* March 3, 1897.

23. Bircher, *Drummer-Boy's Diary,* 25.

24. The son of Irish immigrant parents, Sheridan was born March 6, 1831. Graduating West Point near the bottom of his 1853 class, he served on the West Coast as a quartermaster lieutenant. At war's outbreak, he gained a post in Missouri and was later given command of a cavalry regiment in Mississippi. See *Dictionary of American Biography,* 9:78–81; Warner, *Generals in Blue,* 437–39.
25. *Daily Wisconsin,* October 7, 1862.
26. Henry Drake, letter, September 28, 1862. Born in Ohio in March 1818, Don Carlos Buell was a West Point graduate and veteran of the Seminole and Mexican Wars, winning promotion for gallantry on three occasions. In the adjutant general's office at war's outbreak, he was appointed brigadier general of volunteers in May 1861, and was ordered to train Federal forces in Kentucky. Assuming command of the Army of the Ohio in November, he was directed to invade and liberate east Tennessee, an area of Union sentiment. Under a cloud with the War Department because of his recommendation to abandon east Tennessee, his 50,000–man army reached Nashville in February 1862. By propping up the faltering Union forces at Shiloh he restored his sinking fortunes somewhat, as his April 7 attack drove the Confederates from the field. By September 1862, Buell had concentrated his force at Murfreesboro, Tennessee, to counter the thrusts of the Confederacy's Kirby Smith and Braxton Bragg. Relieved of command after Perryville, he was all but kept out of the remainder of the war, on leave or awaiting orders. Buell resigned in 1864. After the war, he settled in Kentucky, engaging in mining. He died at age seventy-one, November 19, 1889. See *Dictionary of American Biography,* 3:24–25; Warner, *Generals in Blue,* 51–52.
27. *Daily Wisconsin,* October 11, 1862.
28. Drake, letter, September 13, 1862. The 36th Illinois was recruited from the Aurora, Illinois, vicinity west of Chicago, largely Kendall, Kane, and McHenry Counties, and mustered into Federal service September 23, 1861. It saw action and duty in Missouri, Arkansas, and Mississippi before being assigned to the Army of the Ohio and, later, Army of the Cumberland. It fought in every major battle from Perryville to Franklin, and was mustered from service in October 1865. From its initial roster of over a thousand men, its losses were eleven officers and 193 enlisted men killed and mortally wounded, and one officer and 127 enlisted dead of disease. The 88th Illinois, known as the second Board of Trade regiment, was organized in Chicago, fought from Perryville to Nashville, and mustered out in June 1865, having sustained losses of 103 killed or mortally wounded. The 21st Michigan, from Grand Rapids, brigaded with the 24th Wisconsin through the Chickamauga campaign, served until war's end and was mustered from service in June 1865. See Dyer, *Compendium,* 124, 163–64, 1061–62, 1083–1084.
29. *Annual Report of the Adjutant General of the State of Illinois, 1861–1862, 1864* (Springfield: Baker & Phillips, 1863, 1865), 24, 54, 60, 66, 86, 94, 152; Victor Hicken, *Illinois in the Civil War* (Urbana: University of Illinois Press, 1991), 301–2.
30. Andrew P. Smith, letter, October 26, 1862, in *Milwaukee Sentinel,* November 7, 1862. The 24th Wisconsin roster listed both Andrew P. Smith, Company G, who was promoted to captain in the U.S. quartermaster service in April 1864; and an Andrew Smith, Company F, who served as a private until mustering out in June 1865. Both wrote letters. *Roster,* 2:273, 271.

31. A Kentuckian by birth, William Nelson was the division commander sent to Nashville in July 1862 to protect General Buell's line of communication. When Rebels Bragg and Smith invaded Kentucky, Nelson was sent to organize troops and placed in command of Louisville. An imperious and profane soldier, he had occasion to reprimand Brig. Gen. Jefferson C. Davis, an Indianan, for alleged negligence. A few days later, Davis, returning with Gov. Oliver Morton in tow, encountered Nelson in the lobby of the Galt House. During the ensuing altercation, Davis shot Nelson, who died within a half an hour. Davis was never charged with the crime. See *Dictionary of American Biography,* 13:426; Warner, *Generals in Blue,* 343–44.

32. *Milwaukee Sentinel,* September 30, October 3, 1862.

33. *Dictionary of American Biography,* 9:432–35; Warner, *Generals in Blue,* 500–2.

34. "C. S.," letter, in *Milwaukee Sentinel,* October 3, 1862.

35. Henry T. Drake, letter, October 1, 1862, State Historical Society of Wisconsin.

36. Silsby, letter, October 16, 1862; Mitchell, letter, October 16, 1862, Alexander Mitchell Papers. State Historical Society of Wisconsin. The 250 or so who were not with the regiment included many who had been hospitalized for various maladies such as dysentery; others had been assigned sundry duties as provost guards or hostlers. Moreover, between the time the 24th departed from Milwaukee and the battle, 17 had deserted, many to return to Wisconsin or elsewhere to volunteer again in some other regiment and collect bonuses. Finally, 22 more would desert the ranks before the year ended. *Roster,* 2:256–81.

37. *Milwaukee Daily News,* November 7, 1862; Mitchell, letter, October 16, 1862; Drake, letter, October 7, 1862.

38. Gilbert, letter, in *Third Reunion,* 12.

39. Comstock, letters, October 16, 18, 1862.

40. Silsby, letter, October 16, 1862.

41. Bacon, "With the 24th Wisconsin," 68.

42. Bircher, *Drummer-Boy's Diary,* 26, 27.

43. *Milwaukee Daily News,* October 16, 1862; Andrew P. Smith, letter, October 26, 1862, in *Milwaukee Sentinel,* November 7, 1862.

44. Comstock, letter, October 18, 1862.

45. *Third Reunion,* 25; *Roster,* 2:260; Mitchell, letter, October 7, 1862.

46. Gilbert, letter, in *Third Reunion,* 12; *Milwaukee Daily News,* November 7, 1862.

47. Silsby, letter, October 16, 1862; Mitchell, *Milwaukee Sunday Telegraph,* March 3, 1897; *Roster,* 2:277.

48. L[yman] G. Bennett and W[illiam] M. Haigh, *History of the Thirty-Sixth Regiment Illinois Volunteers: During the War of the Rebellion* (Aurora, Ill.: Knickerbacker and Hodder, 1876), 240–41.

49. Holmes, *Soldier,* 91.

50. Silsby, letter, October 16, 1862; Holmes, *Soldier,* 92.

51. Wallace P. Benson, *A Soldier's Diary,* (n.p.:) Printed by His Sons, 1919, 29; Bennett and Haigh, *Thirty-Sixth Regiment,* 243.

52. Bennett and Haigh, *Thirty-Sixth Regiment,* 240–41.

53. Bircher, *Drummer-Boy's Diary,* 27; Bennett and Haigh, *Thirty-Sixth Regiment,* 240–41.

54. Eugene Burdick, letter, October 9, 1862, in *Milwaukee Sentinel,* October 17, 1862.

55. Richard Hubbell, *Daily Wisconsin,* December 14, 1863.

56. Bacon, "With the 24th Wisconsin," 69.

57. Mitchell, *Milwaukee Sunday Telegraph,* March 3, 1897.

58. Thomas J. Ford, *With the Rank and File* . . . (Milwaukee: Press of the Evening Wisconsin, 1898), 6.

59. Bennett and Haigh, *Thirty-Sixth Regiment,* 252–55.

60. Mitchell, *Milwaukee Sunday Telegraph,* March 3, 1897; *Roster*, 2:266.

61. Watrous, "How the Boy Won," 770.

62. Bennett and Haigh, *Thirty-Sixth Regiment,* 259.

63. Mitchell, *Milwaukee Sunday Telegraph,* March 3, 1897.

64. Silsby, letter, October 16, 1862.

65. *Milwaukee Sunday Telegraph,* October 14, 1883; *Milwaukee Daily News,* October 25, 1862.

66. Bennett and Haigh, *Thirty-Sixth Regiment,* 264.

67. Ford, *Rank and File,* 7; *Milwaukee Daily News*, October 25, 1862; "Musket," *Milwaukee Sentinel,* October 17, 1862; Henry B. Furness, letter, February 24, 1889, in *Third Reunion,* 25; Comstock, letter, October 10, 1862.

68. Bleyer, letter, November 10, 1862, in *Daily Wisconsin,* November 18, 1862.

69. Silsby, letter, October 16, 1862.

70. Chivas, letter, October 16, 1862; Mitchell, letter, October 16, 1862.

71. *Milwaukee Daily News,* October 25, 1862; *Milwaukee Sentinel,* October 16, 1862.

72. Silsby, letter, October 16, 1862.

73. Ford, *Rank and File,* 7–8; Gilbert, letter, in *Third Reunion,* 12.

74. Bleyer, letter, October 9, 1862, in *Daily Wisconsin,* October 17, 1862; Andrew P. Smith, *Milwaukee Sentinel,* November 7, 1862.

75. Hubbell, *Daily Wisconsin,* December 14, 1863.

76. Bennett and Haigh, *Thirty-Sixth Regiment,* 268–74.

77. Ford, *Rank and File,* 8.

78. *War of the Rebellion: A Compilation of the Official Records of the Union and Confederate Armies, 1861–1865* (Washington, D.C.: U.S. Government Printing Office, 1880–1902), pt. 1, vol. 16, 1036 (hereafter cited as *O.R.*); Silsby, letter, October 16, 1862.

79. Mitchell, letter, October 10, 1862; Burdick, letter, October 9, 1862, in *Milwaukee Sentinel,* October 17, 1862.

80. *Daily Wisconsin,* October 16, 1862; *Milwaukee Daily News,* October 25, 1862; *Third Reunion,* 8.

81. *Milwaukee Daily News;* Jerome A. Watrous, "The Boy Adjutant," *Putnam's Monthly,* December 1906, 375.

CHAPTER 5

1. *Milwaukee Daily News,* October 11, 12, 14, 16, 1862.

2. Mitchell, letters, October 10, 16, 1862.

3. It is speculated by archivists at the Douglas MacArthur collection in Norfolk, Virginia, as well as some historians, that Arthur McArthur's personal papers were somehow lost in the Philippines while he was there during the War with Spain. No more than a few letters of his war writings remain.

4. Watrous, "How the Boy Won."

5. *Milwaukee Daily News,* October 25, 1862.

6. Comstock, letter, October 19, 1862; "C. S.," letter, October 10, 1862, in *Milwaukee Sentinel,* October 17, 1862.

7. Burdick, letter, October 10, 1862, in *Milwaukee Sentinel,* October 17, 1862; Worth, letter, October 10, 1862.

8. Chivas, letter, October 16, 1862.

9. "C. S.," letter, October 10, 1862, in *Milwaukee Sentinel,* October 17, 1862. Agents for both Federal and Confederate governments scoured Europe's arms makers, purchasing large quantities of muskets from England, Austria, the German states, and elsewhere.

10. Bleyer, letter, October 18, 1862, in *Daily Wisconsin,* October 29, 1862.

11. *Milwaukee Daily News,* January 15, 1863.

12. Bleyer, letter, October 18, 1862, in *Daily Wisconsin,* October 29, 1862; Comstock, letter, October 18, 1862.

13. Mitchell, letter, October 16, 1862.

14. Comstock, letter, October 18, 1862.

15. Comstock, letters, September 17, 20, October 18, 1862.

16. Drake, letter, September 26, 1862.

17. Mitchell, letter, November 5, 1862.

18. Comstock, letters, October 16, 18, 1862.

19. Bleyer, letter, October 18, 1862, in *Daily Wisconsin,* October 29, 1862. Schumacher's remains would later be disinterred from the battlefield and transported back to Milwaukee. On the final day of October, the much-respected soldier was accorded a solemn military burial at Forest Home Cemetery. Sweet went on to command the Confederate prison at Camp Douglas, Illinois. See *Milwaukee Sentinel,* November 1, 1862.

20. Bleyer, letter, October 18, 1862, in *Daily Wisconsin,* October 29, 1862.

21. *Roster,* 2:256–81.

22. Bleyer, letter, October 18, 1862, in *Daily Wisconsin,* October 29, 1862; *Roster,* 2:274; Wiley, *Billy Yank,* 205.

23. "C. S.," letter, October 16, 1862, in *Milwaukee Sentinel,* October 30, 1862.

24. Mitchell, letter, October 16, 1862.

25. "C. S.," letter, October 16, 1862, in *Milwaukee Sentinel,* October 30, 1862; Bleyer, letter, October 18, 1862, in *Daily Wisconsin,* October 29, 1862.

26. "C. S.," letter, October 16, 1862, in *Milwaukee Sentinel,* October 30, 1862.

27. Andrew Smith, letter, October 26, 1862, in *Milwaukee Sentinel,* November 7, 1862.

28. Letter, October 14, 1862, in *Milwaukee Sentinel,* November 5, 1862.

29. Burdick, letter, October 18, 1862, in *Milwaukee Sentinel,* October 28, 1862.

30. Andrew Smith, letter, October 26, 1862, in *Milwaukee Sentinel,* November 7, 1862.

31. Drake, letter, October 16, 1862; Comstock, letter, October 18, 1862.

32. Drake, letter, October 16, 1862.

33. Comstock, letters, October 16, 18, 1862.

34. Bleyer, letter, October 18, 1862, in *Daily Wisconsin,* October 29, 1862.

35. Andrew Smith, letter, October 26, 1862, in *Milwaukee Sentinel,* November 7, 1862.

36. *Milwaukee Sentinel,* November 11, 22, 1862.

37. Bleyer, letter, October 18, 1862, in *Daily Wisconsin,* October 29, 1862; *Roster,* 2:270, 272, 273.
38. Burdick, letter, October 18, 1862, in *Milwaukee Sentinel,* October 28, 1862.
39. E. B. [Henry B.] Furness, in *Third Reunion,* 25.
40. Bleyer, letter, October 23, 1862, in *Daily Wisconsin,* November 1, 1862.
41. Hubbell, letter, November 12, 1862, in *Daily Wisconsin,* November 20, 1862.
42. *Daily Milwaukee News,* January 15, 1863.
43. Burdick, letter, November 20, 1862, in *Milwaukee Sentinel,* November 29, 1862; Bleyer, letter, October 23, 1862, in *Daily Wisconsin,* November 1, 1862.
44. "S", letter, *Milwaukee Sentinel,* November 6, 1862.
45. Bleyer, letter, October 23, 1862, in *Daily Wisconsin,* November 1, 1862.
46. Gilbert, letter, in *Third Reunion,* 12; Bleyer, letter, October 30, 1862, in *Daily Wisconsin,* November 8, 1862; *Milwaukee Daily News,* January 15, 1863.
47. Bleyer, letter, November 10, 1862, in *Daily Wisconsin,* November 18, 1862.
48. Burdick, letter, November 20, 1862, in *Milwaukee Sentinel,* November 29, 1862.
49. Gilbert, letter, in *Third Reunion,* 13; *Roster,* 2:261.
50. Burdick, letter, November 20, 1862, in *Milwaukee Sentinel,* November 29, 1862; Mitchell, letter, November 2, 1862.
51. Chivas, letters, November 2, December 8, 1862.
52. Mitchell, letter, November 2, 1862.
53. Chivas, letter, November 2, 1862; Bleyer, letter, October 18, 1862, in *Daily Wisconsin,* October 29, 1862.
54. Mitchell, letter, November 2, 1862. When the images were published decades later in a memorial booklet, they were mistakenly identified as having been made in Nashville.
55. Chivas, letter, November 2, 1862.
56. Silsby, letter, October 16, 1862.
57. Bleyer, letter, November 10, 1862, in *Daily Wisconsin,* November 18, 1862.
58. Bleyer, letter, November 18, 1862, in *Daily Wisconsin,* November 26, 1862; Mitchell, letter, November 13, 1862. An Ohioan, Rosecrans was born in 1819, and graduated from West Point in 1842, just one year after Buell. He served only briefly in the army, and engaged in coal mining and other pursuits until the war's outbreak. Named to Maj. Gen. George B. McClellan's staff, Rosecrans later commanded the left wing of Maj. Gen. John Pope's Army of the Mississippi near Corinth. As commander of the Army of the Cumberland, he fought the Confederates inconclusively at Stones River. He had a less than positive relationship with the War Department, which caused him trouble. He was a brilliant tactician, and maneuvered the Confederates under Braxton Bragg from Chattanooga. But after a near disaster at Chickamauga in September 1863, he became besieged in Chattanooga. Gen. Ulysses S. Grant relieved Rosecrans as commander in October, and he remained in an unassigned status until he left the army in 1867. In his final years, he engaged in mining operations, and served in the U.S. Congress from California. He died March 11, 1898. See *Dictionary of American Biography,* 7:163–64; Warner, *Generals in Blue,* 410–11.
59. Quoted in James Lee McDonough, *Stones River: Bloody Winter in Tennessee* (Knoxville: University of Tennessee Press, 1980), 41.
60. Hubbell, letter, November 12, 1862, in *Daily Wisconsin,* November 20, 1862.

61. Holmes, *Soldier,* 126–27; *Milwaukee Daily News,* January 15, 1863.

62. Klement, *Wisconsin in the Civil War,* 30–31.

63. McDonough, *Stones River,* 56–61.

64. Mitchell, letter, November 13, 1862; Holmes, *Soldier,* 119–20; Bennett and Haigh, *Thirty-Sixth Regiment,* 305.

65. *Daily Wisconsin,* December 2, 1862.

66. Hubbell, letter, November 12, 1862, in *Daily Wisconsin,* November 20, 1862.

67. Bacon, "With the 24th Wisconsin," 68.

68. Burdick, letter, November 20, 1862, in *Milwaukee Sentinel,* November 28, 1862.

69. *Milwaukee Sentinel,* November 26, 1862.

70. John W. Clark, letter, November 25, 1862, in *Milwaukee Sentinel,* December 5, 1862.

71. Letter, November 25, 1862, in *Milwaukee Sentinel,* December 2, 1862.

72. Burdick, letter December 21, 1862, in *Milwaukee Sentinel,* December 29, 1862.

73. *Milwaukee Sunday Telegraph,* August 18, 1894.

74. *Milwaukee Sentinel,* December 3, 1862.

75. Information from descendant, Robert Philbrook; Bleyer, letter, November 18, 1862, in *Daily Wisconsin,* November 26, 1862; Drake, letter, December 8, 1862.

76. *Louisville Journal,* November 6, 1862.

77. Clark, letter, November 25, 1862, in *Milwaukee Sentinel,* December 5, 1862.

78. Mitchell, letter, December 12, 1862.

79. Chivas, letter, December 5, 1862.

80. Mitchell, letter, December 12, 1862.

81. Burdick, letter, December 21, 1862, in *Milwaukee Sentinel,* December 29, 1862.

82. Drake, letters, December 1, 18, 1862.

83. David L. Merrill, letter, February 24, 1889, in *Third Reunion,* 15.

84. Chivas, letter, December 5, 1862.

85. Greene, letter, December 16, 1862.

86. Chivas, letter, December 15, 1862.

87. Andrew Smith, letter, October 26, 1862, in *Milwaukee Sentinel,* November 7, 1862.

88. Mitchell, letter, December 15, 1862.

89. Chivas, letter, December 15, 1862.

90. Mitchell, letter, December 15, 1862.

91. Greene, letter, December 16, 1863.

92. Burdick, letter, December 21, 1862, in *Milwaukee Sentinel,* December 29, 1862. Sill, born in 1839, was an 1853 West Point graduate, sitting in the same class as Philip Sheridan, James McPherson, John Schofield, and several other prominent Civil War generals. He became colonel of the 33rd Ohio Infantry. By November 1861, Sill was commanding a brigade in Buell's Department of the Ohio. In April 1862, he took part in the celebrated great locomotive chase into Georgia, and gained the rank of brigadier general of volunteers. Although he commanded the 2nd Division of Alexander McCook's I Corps, he missed the battle of Perryville. See Warner, *Generals in Blue,* 448–49.

93. Burdick, letter, December 21, 1862, in *Milwaukee Sentinel,* December 29, 1862.

94. *Milwaukee Sentinel,* January 14, 1863; Burdick, letter, December 21, 1862, in *Milwaukee Sentinel,* December 29, 1862; *Roster,* 2:256, 656.

95. *Roster,* 2:256.

96. Mitchell, letter, December 25, 1862; *Roster,* 2:274, 632; *Milwaukee Sentinel,* March 21, 1864.

97. *Chicago Tribune,* in *Milwaukee Sentinel,* December 12, 1862; Drake, letter, December 18, 1862.

98. Drake, letter, December 8, 1862.

CHAPTER 6

1. McArthur, letter, in *Milwaukee Daily News,* January 28, 1863; Drake, letter, January 8, 1863; Greene, letter, January 17, 1863; Comstock, letter, January 8, 1863.

2. Chivas, letter, January 19, 1863.

3. Bleyer, letter, December 8, 1862, in *Milwaukee Daily News,* December 10, 1862.

4. *Daily Wisconsin,* December 30, 1862.

5. Greene, letter, December 16, 1862.

6. "Soldier," letter, December 9, 1862, in *Daily Wisconsin,* December 17, 1862.

7. Greene, letter, January 11, 1863.

8. *Milwaukee Daily News,* February 8, 1863.

9. Parsons, letter, January 8, 1863, in *Daily Wisconsin,* January 21, 1863.

10. Mitchell, *Milwaukee Sunday Telegraph,* December 16, 1883.

11. Greene, letter, January 11, 1863.

12. Chivas, letter, January 9, 1863, in *Milwaukee Sentinel,* January 22, 1863. Mark Tapley was a character in Charles Dickens's 1843–44 novel, *Martin Chuzzlewit.* He "possessed unquenchable good spirits and optimism," and felt life's challenge was to remain jolly in the most depressing circumstances. Rosemary Goring, ed., *Larousse Dictionary of Literary Characters* (New York: Larousse, 1994), 703.

13. Comstock, letter, January 8, 1863.

14. McDonough, *Stones River,* 78.

15. Bennett and Haigh, *Thirty-Sixth Regiment,* 322; Warner, *Generals in Blue,* 449.

16. Greene, letter, January 11, 1863.

17. Greene, letters, January 11, 17, 1863; Comstock, letter, January 8, 1863; Edward Douglas, letter, February 2, 1863, in *Milwaukee Sentinel,* February 9, 1863; Edward Chamberlain, letter, January 4, 1863, in *Milwaukee Sentinel,* January 13, 1863; *Daily Wisconsin,* January 13, 1863. A sabot was a piece of soft metal attached to a projectile to take the grooves of rifling in the artillery barrel.

18. McArthur, letter, in *Milwaukee Daily News,* January 28, 1863.

19. Greene, letter, January 11, 1863; *O.R.,* pt. 1, vol. 20, 363.

20. Parsons, letter, January 8, 1863, in *Daily Wisconsin,* January 21, 1863; Elisha Hibbard, letter, January 5, 1863, in *Daily Wisconsin,* January 20, 1863.

21. Philip H. Sheridan, *Personal Memoirs* (New York: Charles L. Webster, 1888), 1:220–21.

22. Richard O'Connor, *Sheridan the Inevitable* (Indianapolis: Bobbs-Merrill, 1953), 90.

23. Drake, letter, January 8, 1863; "Henry," letter, January 8, 1863, in *Milwaukee Sentinel,* January 17, 1863.

24. "Wisconsin's Boy Soldier Who is Now a General," typescript, 1899, Douglas MacArthur Memorial Collection, Norfolk, Virginia; McArthur, letter, in *Milwaukee Daily News,* January 28, 1863. The battle, known as Murfreesboro or Murfreesborough, in Confederate sources, is variously identified by Federal writers as Stone, Stone's, or Stones River; the last-named is the most commonly used.

25. Mitchell, letter, January 8, 1863; *O.R.,* pt. 1, vol. 20, 348; Hubbell, letter, in *Daily Wisconsin,* January 24, 1863; Sanford Williams, letter, January 8, 1863, in *Milwaukee Sentinel,* January 14, 1863. By this period in the war, particularly in the West, the predominant uniform coloration of the Confederate soldiers was no longer gray. A growing number of coats and trousers were of a coarse material, homespun some called it, of a light rust or butternut color. Moreover, the poorly attired Confederates also wore blue uniforms that were taken from Federal soldiers.

26. McArthur, letter, in *Milwaukee Daily News,* January 28, 1863; Mitchell, letter, January 8, 1863.

27. Chivas, letter, January 5, 1863.

28. Ford, *Rank and File,* 9.

29. William Kennedy, letter, January 7, 1863, in *Daily Wisconsin,* January 16, 1863; *Daily Wisconsin,* January 13, 1863.

30. McArthur, letter, in *Milwaukee Daily News,* January 28, 1863; Greene, letter, January 17, 1863.

31. George Cole, letter, February 1, 1863, in *Daily Wisconsin,* February 24, 1863; *Daily Wisconsin,* January 5, 1863.

32. Parsons, letter, January 8, 1863, in *Daily Wisconsin,* January 21, 1863; *Daily Wisconsin,* January 16, 1863.

33. Chivas, letter, January 8, 1863; Drake, letter, January 8, 1863.

34. Greene, letter, January 31, 1863.

35. Hibbard, letter, January 5, 1863, in *Daily Wisconsin,* January 20, 1863.

36. Chivas, letter, January 31, 1863; Peter Cozzens, *No Better Place to Die: The Battle of Stones River* (Urbana: University of Illinois Press, 1990), 112.

37. Chivas, letter, January 9, 1863 in *Milwaukee Sentinel,* January 22, 1863; Comstock, letter, January 8, 1863.

38. Edward Douglas, letter, February 2, 1863, in *Milwaukee Sentinel,* February 9, 1863.

39. McArthur, letter, in *Milwaukee Daily News,* January 28, 1863.

40. Greene, letter, January 31, 1863.

41. Burdick, letter, January 21, 1863, in *Milwaukee Sentinel,* January 28, 1863.

42. Douglas, letter, January 26, 1863, in *Milwaukee Sentinel,* February 5, 1863, and letter, February 2, 1863, in *Milwaukee Sentinel,* February 9, 1863.

43. Drake, letter, January 8, 1863; *Milwaukee Sentinel,* January 12, 1863.

44. Mitchell, letter, January 8, 1863; *Daily Wisconsin,* January 9, 1863; *Milwaukee Sunday Telegraph,* December 16, 1883; *In Memoriam: John Lendrum Mitchell, 1842–1904* (Milwaukee, Privately Printed: 1906), 27; *O.R.,* pt. 1, vol. 20, 364.

45. *Third Reunion,* 18; Sanford Williams, diary, quoted in Robert W. Wells, *Wisconsin in the Civil War* (Milwaukee: *Milwaukee Journal,* 1962), 49; *Milwaukee Sunday Telegraph,* January 3, 1886.

46. "Henry," letter, January 8, 1863, in *Milwaukee Sentinel,* January 17, 1863; Edward Chamberlain, letter, in *Daily Wisconsin,* January 13, 1863.

47. Chivas, letter, January 5, 1863; Mitchell, letter, January 8, 1863.

48. Hibbard, letter, January 5, 1863, in *Daily Wisconsin,* January 20, 1863; *Daily Wisconsin,* January 27, 1863.

49. Hubbell, letter, December 8, 1863, in *Daily Wisconsin,* December 14, 1863; Chivas, letter, quoted in Ingraham, *Sermon,* 6.

50. Greene, letter, January 31, 1863.

51. Greene, letter, January 17, 1863; *Daily Wisconsin,* January 13, 1863.

52. Chivas, letter, January 8, 1863; Greene, letter, January 31, 1863.

53. Hibbard, letter, January 5, 1863, in *Daily Wisconsin,* January 20, 1863.

54. Letter, January 18, 1863, in *Daily Wisconsin,* January 27, 1863; Watrous, "How the Boy Won."

55. Hibbard, letter, January 5, 1863, in *Daily Wisconsin,* January 20, 1863; *O.R.,* pt. 1, vol. 20, 364.

56. Comstock, letter, January 8, 1863.

57. Ford, *Rank and File,* 9, 10.

58. Parsons, letter, January 8, 1863, in *Daily Wisconsin,* January 21, 1863.

59. Chivas, letter, January 8, 1863, and letter, January 9, 1863, in *Milwaukee Sentinel,* January 22, 1863.

60. Nicholas Greusel, letter, February 5, 1863, in *Daily Wisconsin,* February 19, 1863.

61. *Daily Wisconsin,* January 9, 1863.

62. McArthur, letter, in *Milwaukee Daily News,* January 28, 1863.

63. *Daily Wisconsin,* January 9, 1863.

64. Robert C. Cheeks, "Little Phil's Fighting Retreat," *America's Civil War* (January 1997).

65. William H. Newlin, *A History of the Seventy-Third Regiment of Illinois Infantry Volunteers* [Springfield, Ill.: Regimental Reunion Association, 1890], 129–30.

66. "Wisconsin's Boy Soldier."

67. Drake, letter, January 8, 1863.

68. *Daily Wisconsin,* January 9, 1863.

69. Fred Childs, letter, January 8, 1863, in *Milwaukee Sentinel,* January 15, 1863.

70. Sheridan, *Memoirs,* 1:233–34; *O.R.,* pt. 1, vol. 20, 349.

71. *Daily Wisconsin,* January 9, 1863.

72. Edwin B. Parsons, "Sheridan," in MOLLUS, Wisconsin Commandery, *War Papers* (Milwaukee: Burdick, Armitage, & Allen, 1896), 1:276.

73. Sheridan, *Memoirs,* 1:232.

74. *Daily Wisconsin,* January 9, 1863.

75. Sheridan, *Memoirs,* 1:235.

76. *Milwaukee Sentinel,* February 7, 1863.

77. *O.R.,* pt. I, vol. 23, 209.

78. "Wisconsin's Boy Soldier."

79. Hibbard, *Daily Wisconsin,* January 16, 1863; *O.R.,* pt. I, vol. 20, 365; Will [Perrine], letter, January 2, 1863, in *Milwaukee Sentinel,* January 9, 1863.

80. *Roster,* 2:258–81; Kennedy, letter, January 7, 1863, in *Daily Wisconsin,* January 16, 1863; *Milwaukee Sentinel,* January 8, 1863; Fox, *Regimental Losses,* 514.

81. Childs, letter, January 8, 1863, in *Milwaukee Sentinel,* January 15, 1863.

82. Bennett and Haigh, *Thirty-Sixth Regiment,* 355.

83. "Henry," letter, January 8, 1863, in *Milwaukee Sentinel,* January 17, 1863.

84. *Daily Wisconsin,* January 27, 1863; Holmes, *Soldier,* 130.

85. Mitchell, *Milwaukee Sunday Telegraph,* December 16, 1883; *In Memoriam: John Lendrum Mitchell,* 28.

86. Ford, *Rank and File,* 10–11.

87. Letter, William to Datus I. Worth, April 3, 1863.

88. Solon Marks, "Experiences at the Battle of Stone River," in MOLLUS, Wisconsin Commandery, *War Papers,* (Milwaukee: Burdick, Armitage, & Allen, 1896), 2:392–395.

89. Williams, diary, quoted in Wells, *Wisconsin in the Civil War,* 49.

90. Parsons, letter, January 8, 1863, in *Daily Wisconsin,* January 21, 1863.

91. "Henry," letter, January 8, 1863, in *Milwaukee Sentinel,* January 17, 1863.

92. Williams, diary, quoted in Wells, *Wisconsin in the Civil War,* 49.

93. *Milwaukee Sunday Telegraph,* December 16, 1883; *In Memoriam: John Lendrum Mitchell,* 28.

94. Chase, letter, January 19, 1863, in *Milwaukee History,* 14, no. 2 (summer 1991): 42–43.

95. Kennedy, letter, January 7, 1863, in *Daily Wisconsin,* January 16, 1863; *Milwaukee Sentinel,* January 8, 1863; "Henry," letter, January 8, 1863, in *Milwaukee Sentinel,* January 17, 1863.

CHAPTER 7

1. [Flower], *Milwaukee,* 1331; *Daily Wisconsin,* January 9, 1863.

2. *Milwaukee Sentinel,* January 16, 1863. *The Roster of Wisconsin Volunteers* erroneously lists his death as December 31, 1862.

3. Kennedy, letter to A. E. Hale, January 7, 1863, in *Daily Wisconsin,* January 16, 1863.

4. *Daily Wisconsin,* January 16, 1863.

5. Ibid., February 21, 1863.

6. Letter, January 18, 1863, in *Daily Wisconsin,* January 27, 1863.

7. "Henry," letter, January 8, 1863, in *Milwaukee Sentinel,* January 17, 1863.

8. *Daily Wisconsin,* December 31, 1862.

9. Ibid., January 5, 1863.

10. *Milwaukee Sentinel,* January 5, 6, 1863; *Daily Wisconsin,* January 5, 6, 1863; *Milwaukee Daily News,* January 5, 6, 1863.

11. Will [Perrine], letter, January 2, 1863, in *Milwaukee Sentinel,* January 9, 1863.

12. Larrabee, letter, January 1, 1863, in *Daily Wisconsin,* January 8, 1863.

13. *Milwaukee Sentinel,* January 6, 1863.

14. Will [Perrine], letter, January 2, 1863, in *Milwaukee Sentinel,* January 9, 1863; Milwaukee City Directories, 1876, 1879.

15. Williams, diary, quoted in Wells, *Wisconsin in the Civil War,* 49.

16. Williams, letter, January 8, 1863, in *Milwaukee Sentinel,* January 14, 1863. Twenty-three years later, Williams recalled an experience, more harrowing, on the operating table in Nashville. He insisted that the amputation should take place as soon as possible; further, he wanted to be the first man on the operating table. The surgeon asked why. "Well, the fact is," Williams responded, "I know that when you doctors get to work you are not very careful to clean off your knives and saws[,] and I don't want any blood poisoning in my veins." Williams extracted a promise that he would be the first under the knife.
   On the operating table, the surgeon saturated a towel with chloroform but the impertinent private waved it away from his face with instructions: "I want you to cut it off below the knee." After a quick examination, the doctor said the leg must be severed above the knee as the flesh had already blackened. "The chances are if it

is amputated below you will lose your life." Williams refused the chloroform so the promise was reluctantly made. A few minutes after draping the soaked rag over the Milwaukee man's face, the surgeon asked how Williams felt. "I don't feel any different." More anesthetic was applied to the rag. Told to breathe deeply, the wounded man felt no drowsiness. "All that ails me now is, I am sick to my stomach." The doctors feared more chloroform would kill the wounded soldier. One nurse held his head, another grabbed the uninjured leg, and two more held his arms.

"Lord, how it did hurt, and when they began to saw the bone I gave a howl that nearly took the roof off. The doctors were fearful from the start that I would not live. After the amputation my condition was such that they lost all hope," Williams said. Medical personnel hourly visited his hospital bed, expecting his demise; but they were amazed, calling the Milwaukee soldier "the man who refused to die."

Finally, Williams grew well enough to be sent home with his discharge, and he soon visited a Milwaukee physician, Dr. Azariel Blanchard. "That leg should have been amputated above the knee," the doctor observed, "I am afraid it will have to be done yet." But it never was. Williams said he wanted to retain the knee joint and "made a vigorous fight for it, and I saved it, and yet I never wear an artificial limb without suffering to a greater or less extent." Watrous, *Milwaukee Sunday Telegraph,* January 3, 1886.

17. Mitchell, *Milwaukee Sunday Telegraph,* December 16, 1883.
18. [Jesse C. Bliss], "Letters from a Veteran of Pea Ridge," *Arkansas Historical Quarterly* 1 (1947): 469; Mitchell, *Milwaukee Sunday Telegraph,* December 16, 1883.
19. Mitchell, letter, January 6, 8, 1863.
20. Chivas, letters, January 5, 7, 31, 1863.
21. *Daily Wisconsin,* January 5, 9, 1863.
22. Parsons, letter, January 8, 1863, in *Daily Wisconsin,* January 21, 1863.
23. Hibbard, letter, January 5, 1863, in *Daily Wisconsin,* January 20, 1863.
24. Chivas, letters, January 5, 1863.
25. Drake, letter, January 8, 1863; Mitchell, letter, January 8, 1863.
26. *Daily Wisconsin,* January 20, 1863; Greene, letter, February 8, 1863.
27. Chivas, letter, January 19, 1863.
28. Letter, January 19, 1863, in *Milwaukee Sentinel,* January 26, 1863; *Roster,* 2:260, 267.
29. Chivas, letter, January 5, 1863; Mitchell, letter, January 8, 1863; Drake, letter, January 8, 1863.
30. Letter, January 19, 1863, in *Milwaukee Sentinel,* January 26, 1863.
31. *Daily Wisconsin,* February 19, 23, 1863; Letter, February 25, 1863, in *Milwaukee Daily News,* March 8, 1863; *Daily Wisconsin,* March 12, 1863; *Roster,* 2:274.
32. Comstock, letter, January 8, 1863.
33. Chivas, letter, January 5, 1863; Mitchell, letter, January 8, 1863; Drake, letter, January 8, 1863; *Roster,* 2:262.
34. *Daily Wisconsin,* January 21, 1863; *Soldiers' and Citizens' Album of Biographical Record* (Chicago: Grand Army of the Republic, 1890), 569.
35. Hubbell, letter, January 15, 1863, in *Daily Wisconsin,* January 24, 1863; Chivas, letter, January 31, 1863; *Roster,* 2:277.
36. Hibbard, letter, January 5, 1863, in *Daily Wisconsin,* January 20, 1863.
37. Chivas, letter, January 7, 1863.

38. Letter, January 18, 1863, in *Daily Wisconsin,* January 27, 1863; *O.R.,* pt. 1, vol. 20, 357; Chivas, letter, January 5, 1863.
39. *Milwaukee Daily News,* February 8, 1863; *O.R.,* pt. 1, vol. 20, 288; Letter, January 19, 1863, in *Milwaukee Sentinel,* January 26, 1863.
40. Letter, January 18, 1863, in *Milwaukee Sentinel,* January 30, 1863.
41. Greene, letter, January 17, 1863.
42. Letter, January 19, 1863, in *Milwaukee Sentinel,* January 26, 1863; Chivas, letter, January 16, 1863; letter to L. B. Smith, January 8, 1863, in *Daily Wisconsin,* January 20, 1863; *Roster,* 2:267.
43. *Roster,* 2:258, 260, 262, 267, 272, 274, 278.
44. Chivas, letter, January 19, 1863; *Milwaukee Daily News,* February 8, 1863.
45. John Borth, letter, January 17, 1863, in *Milwaukee Sentinel,* February 25, 1863; "S," letter, February 18, 1863, in *Milwaukee Sentinel,* February 27, 1863.
46. *Milwaukee Daily News,* February 8, 1863; *Milwaukee Sentinel,* March 28, 1863.
47. Letter, January 19, 1863, in *Milwaukee Sentinel,* January 26, 1863; Chivas, letter, January 19, 1863.
48. "C," letter, March 22, 1863, in *Milwaukee Sentinel,* March 31, 1863.
49. *Milwaukee Daily News,* February 8, 1863.
50. Letter, February 2, 1863, in *Milwaukee Daily News,* February 15, 1863.
51. "R," letter, February 4, 1863, in *Milwaukee Daily News,* February 14, 1863.
52. "C," letter, March 22, 1863, in *Milwaukee Sentinel,* March 31, 1863.
53. *Milwaukee Sentinel,* March 28, 1863.
54. *O.R.,* pt. 1, vol. 20, 357, 365; Hibbard, letter, January 5, 1863.
55. Will [Perrine], letter, January 2, 1863, in *Milwaukee Sentinel,* January 9, 1863; letter, January 18, 1863, in *Daily Wisconsin,* January 27, 1863.
56. [Flower], *Milwaukee,* 1570–71; A. C. Wheeler, *Chronicles of Milwaukee* (Milwaukee: Jermain & Brightman, 1861), 56.
57. *Milwaukee Sunday Telegraph,* April 4, 1884.
58. *Daily Wisconsin,* January 29, February 4, 6, 1863; *Milwaukee Sentinel,* January 29, February 5, 7, 1863; Tom Balding, letter, January 27, 1863, in *Daily Wisconsin,* February 12, 1863.
59. Burdick, letter, February 4, 1863, in *Milwaukee Sentinel,* February 12, 1863; *Roster,* 2:260, 741; *Annual Report of the Adjutant General of Wisconsin* (Madison, William J. Park, 1866), 550.
60. Douglas, letter, January 26, 1863, in *Milwaukee Sentinel,* February 5, 1863; letter, February 2, 1863, in *Milwaukee Sentinel,* February 9, 1863; *Roster,* 2:260; Worth, letter, May 11, 1863.
61. *Milwaukee Daily News,* July 1, 1863; *Roster,* 2:272.
62. *Milwaukee Daily News,* February 25, 26, 1863.
63. "S", letter, March 3, 1863, in *Milwaukee Sentinel,* March 11, 1863; George Cole, letter, February 1, 1863, in *Daily Wisconsin,* February 24, 1863; *Milwaukee Sentinel,* April 22, 1863.
64. Frederick Root, letter, February 17, 1863, in *Daily Wisconsin,* February, 24, 1863; *Milwaukee Sentinel,* February 25, 1863.
65. *Daily Wisconsin,* February 10, 1863; *Milwaukee Sentinel,* February 10, 22, 1863.
66. *Milwaukee Daily News,* February 10, 1863; *Milwaukee Sentinel,* February 10, 13, 1863. *Roster,* 2:280, lists him as Spencer.
67. *Daily Wisconsin,* February 12, 1863; *Milwaukee Daily News,* February 13, 19, 1863; *Milwaukee Sentinel,* February 13, 20, 1863.

68. "R," letter, February 4, 1863, in *Milwaukee Daily News,* February 14, 1863.
69. *Milwaukee Daily News,* January 15, 1863.
70. Greene, letter, January 17, 1863.
71. *Milwaukee Sentinel,* February 16, 1863.
72. Francis T. Sherman, letter, February 14, 1863, in *Daily Wisconsin,* February 23, 1863.
73. Greene, letter, January 31, 1863.
74. "R," letter, February 4, 1863, in *Milwaukee Daily News,* February 14, 1863; letter, February 2, 1863, in *Milwaukee Daily News,* February 15, 1863; *Daily Wisconsin,* February 18, 1863.
75. *Milwaukee Sentinel,* March 7, 1863.
76. "M," letter, February 23, 1863, in *Milwaukee Sentinel,* March 3, 1863.
77. *Daily Wisconsin,* February 28, 1863.
78. "R," letter, February 4, 1863, in *Milwaukee Daily News,* February 14, 1863.
79. "M," letter, February 23, 1863, in *Milwaukee Sentinel,* March 3, 1863; *Roster,* 2:256–81.
80. Ford, *Rank and File,* 11–12.
81. "S," letter, March 3, 1863, in *Milwaukee Sentinel,* March 11, 1863; *Milwaukee Sentinel,* April 22, 1863.
82. *Milwaukee Sentinel,* March 3, 1863.
83. *Daily Wisconsin,* March 13, 1863.
84. Mitchell, letter, May 25, 1863; "S," letter, May 4, 1863, in *Milwaukee Sentinel,* May 12, 1863; Cooley, diary, May 12, 1863.
85. A lawyer by profession, William Lytle had fought in the Mexican War and afterward was elected to the Ohio legislature, also serving as head of the state's militia. He had commanded the 10th Ohio Infantry, ultimately winning promotion and commanding a brigade in McCook's corps at Perryville. Here he was grievously wounded, actually given up for dead, and held captive by the enemy. After his recovery and exchange in February, he was promoted and assigned as brigade commander. *Dictionary of American Biography,* 6:528; Warner, *Generals in Blue,* 287–88.
86. Cooley, diary, May 12, 1863.
87. *Milwaukee Sentinel,* April 22, 1863; Cooley, diary, April 3, 1863; James Harvey, letter, May 16, 1863, Marc and Beth Storch Collection, DeForest, Wisconsin.
88. *Milwaukee Sentinel,* March 31, 1863; Cooley, diary, April 13, 1863; Mitchell, letter, April 12, 1863.
89. "S," letter, May 31, 1863, in *Milwaukee Sentinel,* June 10, 1863.
90. Cooley, diary, March 17, 1863; "C," letter, March 22, 1863, in *Milwaukee Sentinel,* March 31, 1863.
91. "S," letter, May 4, 1863, in *Milwaukee Sentinel,* May 12, 1863; *Milwaukee Sentinel,* September 8, 1863; Wiley, *Billy Yank,* 56–57.
92. "S," letter, May 4, 1863, in *Milwaukee Sentinel,* May 12, 1863; Worth, letter, June 9, 1863; *Milwaukee Sunday Telegraph,* August 18, 1894; [Flower], *Milwaukee,* 1570.
93. "S," letter, May 4, 1863, in *Milwaukee Sentinel,* May 12, 1863.
94. *Milwaukee Sentinel,* April 30, 1863.
95. McArthur, letter, January 18, 1863, in *Daily Wisconsin,* January 27, 1863.

CHAPTER 8

1. Comstock, letter, September 21, 1863.
2. Milwaukee City Directory, 1862.
3. *Milwaukee Daily News,* June 9, 1864. Champion marksman Hiram Berdan of New York began recruiting competitions in 1861; volunteers were required to place ten consecutive shots in a 10–inch circle at 200 yards. Sharpshooter companies were organized in several states, including Wisconsin. Ultimately, Berdan raised two regiments and equipped them with Sharps breech-loading rifles; the 1st and 2nd U.S. Sharpshooters served in both the Eastern and Western campaigns. See also Patricia L. Faust, ed., *Historical Times Illustrated Encyclopedia of the Civil War* (New York: Harper & Row, 1986), 671–72.
4. Chivas, letter, June 12, 1863.
5. Letter, July 1, 1863, in *Milwaukee Sentinel,* July 8, 1863; letter, June 29, 1863, in *Milwaukee Sentinel,* July 8, 1864.
6. *Roster,* 2:256; Cooley, diary, August 30, 1863.
7. Charles Larrabee, letter, June 28, 1863, in *Milwaukee Daily News,* July 8, 1863; *Milwaukee Sentinel,* May 8, 1864; Comstock, letter, August 31, 1863.
8. Comstock, letter, June 28, 1863; letter, June 29, 1863, in *Milwaukee Sentinel,* July 8, 1864.
9. "M," letter, July 11, 1863, in *Milwaukee Sentinel,* July 24, 1863.
10. "S," letter, July 4, 1863, in *Milwaukee Sentinel,* July 16, 1863; Worth, letter, July 4, 1863.
11. "M," letter, July 11, 1863, in *Milwaukee Sentinel,* July 24, 1863.
12. "S," letter, July 4, 1863, in *Milwaukee Sentinel,* July 16, 1863; William Maxfield, letter, August 4, 1863, in *Milwaukee Sentinel,* August 13, 1863.
13. Comstock, letter, July 9, 1863; Worth, letter, July 4, 1863.
14. Cooley, diary, July 8, 1863; Chivas, letter, July 17, 1863; "S," letter, July 19, 1863, in *Milwaukee Sentinel,* July 31, 1863; Drake, letter, July 27, 1863.
15. Cooley, diary, July 4, 1864.
16. Comstock, letter, July 9, 1863.
17. Thomas G. Chapman, letter, July 22, 1863; *Roster,* 2:279. *Roster of Volunteers* erroneously listed the accident as occurring on August 4, 1862.
18. "S," letter, July 4, 1863, in *Milwaukee Sentinel,* July 16, 1863; Worth, letter, July 4, 1863.
19. "S," letter, July 19, 1863, in *Milwaukee Sentinel,* July 31, 1863; Chivas, letter, July 17, 1863; Greene, letter, September 21, 1863.
20. Chivas, letter, July 17, 1863.
21. Cooley, diary, July 4, 11, 13, 15, 16, 1863.
22. Drake, letters, July 6, 12, 27, 1863. The War Department created the Invalid Corps in April 1863. There were two battalions: One for able-bodied men who could stand guard duty, and the second for the severely handicapped who served as hospital attendants. Assignment to the corps may have carried a certain stigma among soldiers. See also Faust, *Historical Times Encyclopedia,* 383.
23. *Milwaukee Sentinel,* July 14, 18, 1863.
24. Cooley, diary, July 31, August 1, 4, 1863.
25. Drake, letters, April 30, August 12, 1863; *Roster,* 2:258.
26. Cooley, diary, August 8, 1863; Comstock, letter, August 3, 10, 1863. He had written two letters but sent them as one on the later date.

27. *Milwaukee Sunday Telegraph,* October 4, 1885.
28. Comstock, letters, August 15, 25, 1863; Cooley, diary, August 14, 1864.
29. Silsby, letter, August 20, 1863; Chapman, letter, August 19, 1863.
30. Cooley, diary, August 25, 1863; Comstock, letter, August 31, 1863.
31. *Milwaukee Sentinel,* August 25, 1863.
32. Greene, letter, September 25, 1863; Silsby, letter, August 8, 1863.
33. Cooley, diary, September 2, 4, 5, 7, 10, 13, 14, 1863.
34. Parsons, "Chickamauga," in MOLLUS, Wisconsin Commandery, *War Papers* (Milwaukee: Burdick, Armitage, & Allen, 1896), 2:442; Root, letter, quoted in Ingraham, *Sermon,* 6.
35. Letter, September 28, 1863, in *Milwaukee Sentinel,* October 9, 1863.
36. Sheridan, *Memoirs,* 1:276; Bennett and Haigh, *Thirty-Sixth Regiment,* 453–54.
37. *Milwaukee Sunday Telegraph,* December 21, 1884.
38. Bennett and Haigh, *Thirty-Sixth Regiment,* 458.
39. Sheridan, *Memoirs,* 280.
40. "Nimrod" [Dan Davis], letter, October 8, 1863, in *Daily Wisconsin,* October 19, 1863.
41. Comstock, letter, September 28, 1863.
42. Bennett and Haigh, *Thirty-Sixth Regiment,* 465–69; Sheridan, *Memoirs,* 281–82.
43. Chivas, letter, September 25, 1863, in *Milwaukee Sentinel,* October 10, 1863.
44. "Nimrod" [Davis], letter, October 8, 1863, in *Daily Wisconsin,* October 19, 1863; Charles Rogers, letter, September 21, 1863, in *Daily Wisconsin,* September 30, 1863.
45. William B. Sherman, letter, September 29, 1863, in *Milwaukee Sunday Telegraph,* March 3, 1884.
46. Parsons, letter, October 1, 1863, Edwin B. Parsons Papers.
47. James Heth, letter, February 22, 1889, in *Third Reunion,* 13–14.
48. Sherman, letter, September 29, 1863, in *Milwaukee Sunday Telegraph,* March 3, 1884.
49. Parsons, letter, October 1, 1863; Chivas, letter, September 25, 1863, in *Milwaukee Sentinel,* October 10, 1863; Greene, letter, September 25, 1863.
50. "Nimrod" [Davis], letter, October 8, 1863, in *Daily Wisconsin,* October 19, 1863; Alfred Girtle letter, November 5, 1863, in *Milwaukee Daily News,* November 24, 1863.
51. Greene, letters, September 21, 25, 1863; *Milwaukee Daily News,* September 30, 1863. It was later written that General Lytle was killed by a rebel sharpshooter who fired a .45–caliber Whitworth rifle from a distance of 800 yards.
52. *Milwaukee Sunday Telegraph,* January 13, 1889. McCreery was later incarcerated with Col. Theodore West, and with several others eventuated an escape from the infamous Libby Prison in Richmond.
53. Thomas Keith, letter, October 7, 1863; U.S. Pension Office, Edward Glenn file, affidavit of Herman Hasse, April 14, 1876.
54. "Nimrod" [Davis], letter, October 8, 1863, in *Daily Wisconsin,* October 19, 1863.
55. Chivas, letter, September 25, 1863, in *Milwaukee Sentinel,* October 10, 1863.
56. *O.R.,* pt. 1, vol. 30, 587; Comstock, letter, September 28, 1863.
57. Parsons, letter, October 1, 1863.
58. Comstock, letter, September 21, 1863.
59. Chivas, letter, September 25, 1863, in *Milwaukee Sentinel,* October 10, 1863.

60. *Port Washington (Wisc.) Star,* May 22, 1897.
61. Worth, letter, September 27, 1863; Charles Rogers, letter, September 21, 1863; [Flower], *Milwaukee,* 807.
62. Greene, letter, September 21, 1863, in *Daily Wisconsin,* October 1, 1863.
63. *Milwaukee Sentinel,* March 8, 1864; letter, September 21, 1863, in *Milwaukee Daily News,* October 1, 1863.
64. Charles Rogers, letter, September 21, 1863.
65. *Milwaukee Sunday Telegraph,* December 21, 1884.
66. Parsons letter, October 1, 1863.
67. Chivas, letter, September 25, 1863, in *Milwaukee Sentinel,* October 10, 1863.
68. *O.R.,* pt. I, vol. 30, 587–88.
69. *Milwaukee Sentinel,* September 22, 25, 1863.
70. *Daily Wisconsin,* September 23, 1863; Charles Rogers, letter, September 21, 1863.
71. Chivas, letter, September 21, 1863; Root, letter, quoted in Ingraham, *Sermon,* 6.
72. *Milwaukee Sentinel,* October 20, 1863.
73. Kennedy, letter, September 21, 1863, in *Milwaukee Daily News,* October 4, 1863; Sherman, letter, September 29, 1863, in *Milwaukee Sunday Telegraph,* March 3, 1884; Worth, letter, September 27, 1863; *Roster,* 2:256–81.
74. Chivas, letter, September 25, 1863, in *Milwaukee Sentinel,* October 10, 1863.
75. *Daily Wisconsin,* September 28, 1863.
76. *Milwaukee Daily News,* September 30, 1863.
77. *Port Washington (Wisc.) Star,* May 22, 1897; *Cincinnati Commercial,* October 4, 1863, in *Milwaukee Sentinel,* October 9, 1863; Root, letter, undated, in Ingraham, *Sermon,* 6, 7.
78. Keith, letter, October 7, 1863; U.S. Pension Office, Edward Glenn file, affidavit of Herman Hasse, April 14, 1876.
79. Root, letter, October 5, 1863, in *Milwaukee Sentinel,* October 21, 1863; *Roster,* 2:277.
80. [Flower], *Milwaukee,* 807.
81. Greene, letter, September 25, 1863; *Daily Wisconsin,* October 10, 1863.
82. Theodore West, letter, October 1, 1863, in *Milwaukee Sentinel,* October 30, 1863.
83. *Milwaukee Sentinel,* September 29, 1863.

CHAPTER 9

1. *Daily Wisconsin,* September 28, 1863; *Milwaukee Sentinel,* September 29, 1863.
2. Letter, *Milwaukee Sentinel,* November 16, 1863.
3. Silsby, letter, October 16, 1863; *Cincinnati Commercial,* October 20, 1863.
4. *Port Washington (Wisc.) Star,* June 19, 1897.
5. Ford, *Rank and File,* 25–26, 32–33.
6. Letter, November 2, 1863, in *Milwaukee Daily News,* November 22, 1863; *Milwaukee Daily News,* November 17, 1863.
7. *Chicago Times,* November 2, 1863, in *Daily Wisconsin,* November 11, 1863; letter, November 2, 1863, in *Milwaukee Daily News,* November 22, 1863.
8. *Milwaukee Daily News,* November 16, 22, 1863; Worth, letter, November 27, 1863.
9. Comstock, letter, October 9, 1863; Chivas, letter, September 25, 1863, in *Milwaukee Sentinel,* October 10, 1863.

10. Letter, October 20, 1863, in *Milwaukee Sentinel,* November 4, 1863.

11. *Milwaukee Daily News,* November 17, 1863.

12. Hubbell, letter, December 8, 1863, in *Daily Wisconsin,* December 14, 1863.

13. Comstock, letter, October 9, 1863; Silsby, letter, October 16, 1863; Sheridan, *Memoirs,* 1:298.

14. Robert U. Johnson and Clarence C. Buell, eds., *Battles and Leaders of the Civil War,* (New York: Century, 1884), 3:727.

15. Silsby, letter, October 16, 1863.

16. *Milwaukee Daily News,* November 22, 1863; Sheridan, *Memoirs,* 1:301–2; Leroy S. Mayfield diary, November 13, 1863, in "A Hoosier Invades the Confederacy: Letters and Diaries of Leroy S. Mayfield," *Indiana Magazine of History* 39, no. 2 (June 1943): 170; Harvey, letter, May 16, 1863.

17. *Chicago Times,* November 2, 1863, in *Daily Wisconsin,* November 11, 1863.

18. Letter, November 3, 1863, in *Milwaukee Sentinel,* November 11, 1863.

19. "Euonia," letter, November 19, 1863, in *Milwaukee Sentinel,* December 3, 1863.

20. Letter, November 26, 1863, in *Milwaukee Sentinel,* December 8, 1863; Sheridan, *Memoirs,* 1:304.

21. Letter, November 23, 1863, in *Milwaukee Daily News,* November 25, 1863; letter, November 26, 1863, in *Milwaukee Sentinel,* December 8, 1863.

22. Cooley, diary, November 24, 1863; letter, November 26, 1863, in *Milwaukee Sentinel,* December 8, 1863.

23. "Euonia," letter, November 24, 1863, in *Milwaukee Sentinel,* December 9, 1863; Sheridan, *Memoirs,* 1:306–7.

24. *Milwaukee Telegraph,* October 16, 1897.

25. Letter, November 26, 1863, in *Milwaukee Sentinel,* December 8, 1863; James A. Hoobler, *Cities under the Gun: Images of Occupied Nashville and Chattanooga* (Nashville: Rutledge Hill, 1986), 128–37; *Milwaukee Sentinel,* December 8, 1863.

26. Worth, letter, November 27, 1863; George Allanson, in *Third Reunion,* 36; *Milwaukee Sentinel,* December 9, 1863.

27. Heth, letter, in *Daily Wisconsin,* December 12, 1863.

28. McArthur, letter, November 26, 1863, in *Daily Wisconsin,* December 9, 1863.

29. Heth, letter, in *Daily Wisconsin,* December 12, 1863.

30. Parsons, *Milwaukee Sunday Telegraph,* March 18, 1888; Sheridan, letter to Edwin Parsons, June 6, 1887, in MOLLUS, 1:200. Several writers after the war were of the opinion that the advance up Missionary Ridge was entirely spontaneous. Reputedly, when the Army of the Cumberland began climbing, General Grant turned to General Thomas, asking who had ordered the charge. Thomas, not knowing, sent a runner to General Granger, who, in turn, sent a galloper to Sheridan. Virtually every commanding officer denied ordering the men forward. Ulysses S. Grant, *Personal Memoirs of U. S. Grant* (New York: Century, 1895), 1:339–340; Sheridan, *Memoirs,* 1:310; Joseph S. Fullerton, "The Army of the Cumberland at Chattanooga," in Johnson and Buell, *Battles and Leaders of the Civil War,* 3:725.

31. John M. Trumbull, quoted in Richard A. Baumgartner and Larry M. Strayer, *Echoes of Battle: The Struggle for Chattanooga* (Huntington, W.Va.: Blue Acorn, 1996), 361; Worth, letter, November 27, 1863.

32. Parsons, letter, November 27, 1863 in *Milwaukee Sunday Telegraph*, March 18, 1888; Parsons, "Missionary Ridge," in MOLLUS, Wisconsin Commandery, *War Papers*, 1:198–99; Heth, letter, in *Daily Wisconsin*, December 12, 1863.

33. "Euonia," letter, December 7, 1873, in *Milwaukee Sentinel*, December 17, 1863; Cooley, diary, November 25, 1863; Love, *Wisconsin in the War*, 696; *Roster*, 2:267–69.

34. *Milwaukee Telegraph*, October 16, 1897; "Euonia," letter, December 7, 1863, in *Milwaukee Sentinel*, December 17, 1863; Allanson, in *Third Reunion*, 37; *Milwaukee Sentinel*, November 27, 1863; Welcome Greene, "Recollections."

35. "Euonia," letter, December 7, 1863, in *Milwaukee Sentinel*, December 17, 1863; [Flower], *Milwaukee*, 804.

36. "Euonia," letter, November 26, 1863, in *Milwaukee Sentinel*, December 9, 1863; McArthur, letter, November 26, 1863, in *Daily Wisconsin*, December 9, 1863; Manchester, *American Caesar*, 15.

37. Cooley, diary, November 25, 1863.

38. Heth, letter, *Daily Wisconsin*, December 12, 1863.

39. "Euonia," letter, December 7, 1863, in *Milwaukee Sentinel*, December 17, 1863.

40. McArthur, letter, November 26, 1863, in *Daily Wisconsin*, December 9, 1863.

41. MacArthur, *Reminiscences*, 8–9.

42. Cooley, diary, November 25, 1863; *O.R.*, pt. 1, vol. 31, 208; "Euonia," letter, December 7, 1863, in *Milwaukee Sentinel*, December 17, 1863; Heth, letter, in *Daily Wisconsin*, December 12, 1863; Ford, *Rank and File*, 29; letter, November 26, 1863, in *Milwaukee Sentinel*, December 8, 1863.

43. Parsons, quoted in *The MacArthurs of Milwaukee*, 7.

44. Cooley, diary, November 25, 1863; Ford, *Rank and File*, 29.

45. McArthur, letter, November 26, 1863, in *Daily Wisconsin*, December 9, 1863; MacArthur, *Reminiscences*, 9.

46. "Wisconsin's Boy Soldier"; McArthur letter, November 26, 1863, in *Daily Wisconsin*, December 9, 1863.

47. Ford, *Rank and File*, 28–29.

48. Daniel F. McGinley, in *Port Washington (Wisc.) Star & Ozaukee County Advertiser*, June 9, 1923.

49. Ford, *Rank and File*, 30–31.

50. Letter, November 26, 1863, in *Milwaukee Sentinel*, December 9, 1863; Worth, letter, November 27, 1863.

51. *O.R.*, pt. 1, vol. 31, 208.

52. Parsons, letter, November 27, 1863, in *Milwaukee Sunday Telegraph*, March 18, 1888; *Roster*, 2:256–80.

53. Chivas, letter, quoted in Ingraham, *Sermon*, 7.

54. *Milwaukee Sentinel*, December 17, 1863.

55. *Milwaukee Daily News*, December 12, 1863; *Milwaukee Telegraph*, April 24, 1897.

56. *Milwaukee Sentinel*, December 4, 1863; "Euonia," letter, December 7, 1863, in *Milwaukee Sentinel*, December 17, 1863.

57. [John] Bartlett, letter, February 20, 1863, in *Milwaukee Sentinel*, February 29, 1863.

58. *Daily Wisconsin*, December 7, 1863.

59. "Euonia," letter, December 13, 1863, in *Milwaukee Sentinel*, December 24, 1863.

60. *O.R.*, pt.. 1, vol. 55, 207–8.

CHAPTER 10

1. *Daily Wisconsin,* and *Milwaukee Sentinel,* December 14, 1863.
2. *Milwaukee Sentinel,* December 17, 1863.
3. Ingraham, *Sermon,* 5, 8, 10; Hubbell, letter, December 8, 1863, in *Daily Wisconsin,* December 14, 1863; Love, *Wisconsin in the War,* 696; Parsons, "Sheridan," in MOLLUS 1:284.
4. *Daily Wisconsin,* December 14, 1863.
5. *Milwaukee Sentinel,* December 14, 1863; Parsons, "Sheridan," in MOLLUS 1:283.
6. *Milwaukee Sentinel,* December 19, 1863; Welcome Greene, "Recollections"; fashion reference from Maryanne Faeth Greketis.
7. *Milwaukee Sentinel,* December 17, 1863.
8. Hubbell, letter, December 8, 1863, in *Daily Wisconsin,* December 14, 1863.
9. *Daily Wisconsin,* January 4, 1864; "Euonia," letter, January 15, 1864, in *Milwaukee Sentinel,* January 27, 1864.
10. Sheridan, *Memoirs,* 1:325–29.
11. *Milwaukee Sunday Telegraph,* November 25, 1883; Parsons, "Sheridan," in MOLLUS 1:279–80; "Nimrod" [Davis], letter, February 5, 1864, in *Daily Wisconsin,* February 17, 1864.
12. Sheridan, *Memoirs,* 1:337; "Nimrod" [Davis], letter, February 5, 1864, in *Daily Wisconsin,* February 17, 1864.
13. *Wisconsin Daily Patriot,* March 2, 1864.
14. *Milwaukee Daily News,* March 23, 1864.
15. "Nimrod" [Davis], letter, March 15, 1864, in *Daily Wisconsin,* March 28, 1864.
16. *Milwaukee Sentinel,* March 24, 1864.
17. *Daily Wisconsin,* January 6, 1864.
18. Letter, November 8, 1863, in *Milwaukee Sentinel,* November 23, 1863.
19. "Nimrod" [Davis], letter, February 5, 1864, in *Daily Wisconsin,* February 17, 1864; *Milwaukee Daily News,* March 8, 1864; *Daily Wisconsin,* March 11, 1864; Cooley, diary, March 26, 1864.
20. Comstock, letter, February 14, 1864.
21. Parsons, "Sheridan," in MOLLUS 1:279–80.
22. *Milwaukee Sunday Telegraph,* December 3, 1882; *Roster,* 2:260, 261.
23. Cooley, diary, March 29, 1864; Worth, letter, April 3, 1864. Francis Sherman moved to Chicago from the East as a youngster; in 1861, at age 35, he was commissioned a lieutenant colonel, and the following year he became colonel of the 88th Illinois, which was brigaded with the 24th Wisconsin. After the battle of Stones River and again following Chickamauga, he became brigade commander. Later he was attached to the 4th Corps as chief of staff to Gen. Oliver O. Howard. After being captured in July 1864 and exchanged, he served on the staff of Gen. Philip Sheridan until war's end. He died in 1905 in Illinois. See Warner, *Generals in Blue,* 439–40.
24. Cooley, diary, March 26, 1864; Parsons, "Sheridan," in MOLLUS 1:283–84; Sheridan, *Memoirs,* 1:340–41.
25. *Milwaukee Daily News,* January 26, 1864; *Milwaukee Sentinel,* January 25, 1864; *Daily Wisconsin,* February 8, 1864.
26. *Milwaukee Daily News,* February 25, March 1, 1864; *Milwaukee Sentinel,* March 8, 1864.

27. *Milwaukee Daily News,* March 3, 22, 1864; *Daily Wisconsin,* March 3, 5, 17, 22, 1864; *Milwaukee Sentinel,* March 4, 7, 117, 22, April 3, 1864.

28. *Daily Wisconsin,* April 8, 1864; *Milwaukee Daily News,* April 28, 1864; Cooley, diary, March 2, 3, April 12, 1864; *Roster,* 2:256–81. Flag information from H. Michael Madaus, one of the foremost Civil War vexillologists.

29. *Milwaukee Sentinel,* April 9, 1864; John Y. Smith, letter, December 24, 1864, in *Daily Wisconsin,* January 6, 1864.

CHAPTER 11

1. Parsons, letter, September 9, 1864, in *Milwaukee Sunday Telegraph,* June 17, 1888.

2. *Cincinnati Commercial,* September 25, 1864, in *Milwaukee Sentinel,* October 19, 1864.

3. *Roster,* 2:256–82.

4. Parsons, letter, May 23, 1864, in *Daily Wisconsin,* June 6, 1864.

5. Comstock, diary, May 5, 1864; Cooley, diary, May 5, 1864; Parsons, letter, May 23, 1864, in *Daily Wisconsin,* June 6, 1864; *Milwaukee Sentinel,* May 19, 1864.

6. *Milwaukee Sentinel,* May 19, 1864.

7. Parsons, letter, May 23, 1864, in *Daily Wisconsin,* June 6, 1864; Cooley, diary, May 9, 1864.

8. Comstock, diary, May 9, 1864.

9. *New York Tribune,* May 10, 1864, in *Daily Wisconsin,* May 24, 1864; Comstock, diary, May 10, 1864.

10. [R. M. Devens], *The Pictorial Book of Anecdotes of the Rebellion* (St. Louis: J. H. Mason, 1889), 124.

11. Comstock, diary, May 13, 1864; Parsons, in MOLLUS, Wisconsin Commandery, *War Papers,* (Milwaukee: Burdick, Armitage, & Allen, 1903), 3:511.

12. Parsons, letter, May 23, 1864, in *Daily Wisconsin,* June 6, 1864.

13. Cooley, diary, May 13, 1864.

14. Ford, *Rank and File,* 36–37.

15. *Daily Wisconsin,* May 21, 1864.

16. Parsons letter, May 23, 1864, in *Daily Wisconsin,* June 6, 1864.

17. *Daily Wisconsin,* May 21, 1864; Parsons, letter, May 23, 1864, in *Daily Wisconsin,* June 6, 1864. An excellent study of the nineteenth-century perspective is Andrew Burstein's, *Sentimental Democracy: The Evolution of America's Self-Image* (New York: Hill & Wang, 1999).

18. Cooley, diary, May 14, 1864.

19. *Daily Wisconsin,* May 21, June 3, 1864; *Milwaukee Daily News,* May 22, 1864.

20. Ford, *Rank and File,* 36.

21. Cooley, diary, May 15, 1864; *Daily Wisconsin,* June 2, 1864.

22. *Daily Wisconsin,* May 21, September 14, 1864.

23. George Allanson, letter, May 15, 1864, in *Milwaukee Sentinel,* May 27, 1864; Cooley, diary, May 15, 1864; Comstock, diary, May 15, 1864.

24. Parsons, letter, May 23, 1864, in *Daily Wisconsin,* June 6, 1864.

25. *Cincinnati Commercial,* in *Milwaukee Sentinel,* May 23, 1864.

26. *Third Reunion,* 38–39; *Daily Wisconsin,* June 2, 1864.

27. *New York Semi-Weekly,* June 3, 1864; Sam Watkins, *Co. Aytch* (New York: Macmillan, 1962), 150–51; Cooley, diary, May 17, 1864; *Daily Wisconsin,* June 2, 1864.

28. Ford, *Rank and File,* 46, 54; *Roster,* 2:275.

29. Parsons letter, May 23, 1864, in *Daily Wisconsin,* June 6, 1864; Comstock, diary, May 17, 1864.

30. *Milwaukee Sunday Telegraph,* December 3, 1882; *Daily Wisconsin,* June 2, 1864; *Roster,* 2:273; Worth, letter, July 9, 1864.

31. *New York Semi-Weekly,* June 3, 1864; *Port Washington (Wisc.) Star,* June 5, 1897; *Port Washington (Wisc.) Star and Ozaukee County Advertiser,* June 9, 1923; Comstock, diary, May 17, 1864; Cooley, diary, May 17, 1864; *Daily Wisconsin,* June 2, 1864.

32. Ford, *Rank and File,* 46–55.

33. Letter, May 25, 1864, in *Milwaukee Sentinel,* June 2, 1864; *Chicago Post,* June 5, 1864, in *Daily Wisconsin,* June 21, 1864.

34. Comstock, diary, May 19, 1864; Parsons, letter, May 23, 1864, in *Daily Wisconsin,* June 6, 1864.

35. Comstock, diary, May 20, 1864.

36. Comstock, diary, May 23, 24, 25, 1864.

37. *Cincinnati Commercial,* May 23, 1864, in *Milwaukee Sentinel,* May 31, 1864; Comstock, diary, May 26, 31, 1864; Cooley, diary, May 26, 29, June 6, 1864; *Milwaukee Sunday Telegraph,* January 2, 1881; *Roster,* 2:258, 260, 267, 269.

38. Cooley, diary, May 29, 30, 31, June 2, 3, 1864; Comstock, diary, May 27, 28, 1864; Worth, letter, May 31, 1864.

39. *Daily Wisconsin,* June 2, 1864.

40. *Cincinnati Commercial,* May 28, June 3, 1864, in *Milwaukee Sentinel,* June 9, 15, 1864.

41. *Milwaukee Sentinel,* June 8, 1864.

42. Comstock, diary, June 7, 1864.

43. *Cincinnati Commercial,* June 7, 1864, in *Milwaukee Sentinel,* June 17, 1864.

44. Comstock, diary, June 13, 1864; Worth, letter, June 6, 1864. Kimball, a Mexican War veteran, had earlier fought with the Army of the Potomac. He would gain division command during the later stages of the Atlanta campaign. See Warner, *Generals in Blue,* 267–68.

45. Comstock, diary, June 16, 17, 1864; Worth, letter, July 15, 1864; *Roster,* 2:260, 267, 276.

46. *Cincinnati Commercial,* June 18, 1864, in *Milwaukee Sentinel,* June 29, 1864.

47. Cooley, diary, June 18, 1864.

48. Mayfield, "A Hoosier," 189; Comstock, diary, June 20, 1864.

49. Comstock, diary, June 22, 1864. This was to be the final entry in Comstock's diary. Whether he wrote more and, if so, what became of those writings is unknown.

50. Cooley, diary, June 22, 1864; *O.R.,* pt. 1, vol. 38, 329.

51. "Wisconsin's Boy Soldier"; MacArthur, *Reminiscences,* 9; *Milwaukee Free Press,* September 6, 1912.

52. Cooley, diary, June 24, 25, 1864.

53. *Roster,* 2:258; Cooley, diary, August 12, 1864.

54. Love, *Wisconsin in the War,* 813; John Silsby, affidavit, December 24, 1886, in U.S. Pension Office, Amandus Silsby file. When John Silsby made an initial application for a survivor's pension twenty years after his son's death, he resided in Grassy Cove, Tennessee, west of Knoxville.

55. Letter, July 21, 1864, in *Daily Wisconsin,* July 29, 1864; *Cincinnati Commercial,* in *Milwaukee Daily News,* July 20, 1864.

56. *Cincinnati Commercial,* June 7, 1864, in *Milwaukee Sentinel,* June 17, 1864.

57. Bennett and Haigh, *Thirty-Sixth Regiment,* 609; letter, July 3, 1864, in *Milwaukee Sentinel,* July 15, 1864.

58. *O.R.,* pt. 1, vol. 38, 839; Quiner, *Military History,* 728–30.

59. *Milwaukee Sentinel,* July 8, 1864.

60. *Chattanooga Gazette,* in *Daily Wisconsin,* August 3, 1864; *Milwaukee Sentinel,* July 12, 1864.

61. *Milwaukee Sentinel,* July 8, 1864.

62. William T. Sherman, letters, June 26, 30, 1864, in *Sherman's Civil War: Selected Letters of William T. Sherman, 1860–1865* (Chapel Hill: University of North Carolina Press, 1999), 660, 665.

63. Letter, July 12, 1864, in *Milwaukee Daily News,* July 23, 1864; Worth, letters, June 22, July 9, 1864.

64. Letter, July 3, 1864, in *Milwaukee Sentinel,* July 16, 1864.

65. Letter, July 12, 1864, in *Milwaukee Daily News,* July 23, 1864.

66. Letter, July 6, 1864, in *Daily Wisconsin,* July 15, 1864.

67. *Cincinnati Commercial,* July 7, 11, 12, 15, 1864, in *Milwaukee Sentinel,* July 18, 22, 25, 29, 1864; Chapman, letter, July 29, 1864.

68. *Cincinnati Commercial,* July 15, 16, 1864, in *Milwaukee Sentinel,* July 26, 28, 1864.

69. *Cincinnati Commercial,* July 20, 1864, in *Milwaukee Sentinel,* July 26, 1864; *Milwaukee Daily News,* July 26, 1864; Young, *General's General,* 92–93.

70. Moritz Tschoepe, "A Hot Day," *National Tribune,* November 6, 1884; *Cincinnati Commercial,* July 21, 22 and 24, 1864, in *Milwaukee Sentinel,* July 26, 27, 28, 1864; *Milwaukee Daily News,* July 28, 1864.

71. *Cincinnati Commercial,* July 23, 1864, in *Milwaukee Sentinel,* August 2, 1864.

72. Parsons, letter, September 9, 1864, in *Milwaukee Sunday Telegraph,* June 17, 1888; Cooley, diary, August 2, 1864; *Cincinnati Commercial,* August 18, 1864, in *Milwaukee Sentinel,* August 22, 1864.

73. Parsons, letter, September 9, 1864, in *Milwaukee Sunday Telegraph,* June 17, 1888; Worth, letter, September 5, 1864; *O.R.,* pt. 1, vol. 38, 311.

74. William T. Sherman, letter, September 3, 1864, in *Sherman's Civil War,* 696.

75. *Cincinnati Commercial,* September 30, 1864, in *Milwaukee Sentinel,* October 17, 1864; Cooley, diary, September 8, 1864.

76. Parsons, letter, September 9, 1864, in *Milwaukee Sunday Telegraph,* June 17, 1888; letter, July 2, 1864, in *Milwaukee Daily News,* July 14, 1864; *Cincinnati Commercial,* September 30, 1864, in *Milwaukee Sentinel,* October 17, 1864.

CHAPTER 12

1. Emerson Opdycke, letter, June 30, 1880, in *Milwaukee Sunday Telegraph,* May 4, 1884.

2. Cooley, diary, October 10, 1864; Comstock, letter, October 15, 1864.

3. Comstock, letter, October 15, 1864; Cooley, diary, October 23, 1864.

4. Young, *General's General,* 96–97; Cooley, diary, September 13, 29, October 13, 1864.

5. MacArthur, *Reminiscences,* 9–10.

6. Cooley, diary, November 9, 1864; *Milwaukee Sentinel,* November 22, 1864.

7. *Cincinnati Commercial,* September 25, 1864, in *Milwaukee Sentinel,* October 19, 1864.

8. Cooley, diary, November 11, 14, 1864; letter, October 29, 1864, in *Daily Wisconsin,* November 5, 1864.

9. Cooley, diary, November 24, 18, 1864.

10. Warner, *Generals in Blue,* 349; Charles T. Clark, *Opdycke Tigers, 125th O.V.I.: A History of the Regiment and of the Campaigns and Battles of the Army of the Cumberland* (Columbus, Ohio: Spahr & Glenn, 1895), 2–3.

11. Bennett and Haigh, *Thirty-Sixth Regiment,* 632–33; *Milwaukee Sentinel,* December 6, 1864.

12. Ford, *Rank and File,* 18–19.

13. Ralsa C. Rice, *Yankee Tigers: Through the Civil War with the 125th Ohio* (1905: reprint, Hungton W. Va.: Blue Acorn, 1992), 153.

14. *O.R.,* pt. 1, vol. 45, 239–40; Rice, *Yankee Tigers,* 155.

15. Rice, *Yankee Tigers,* 155; Bennett and Haigh, *Thirty-Sixth Regiment,* 644.

16. Wiley Sword, *Embrace an Angry Wind: The Confederacy's Last Hurrah: Spring Hill, Franklin, and Nashville* (New York: HarperCollins, 1992), 173–74; Rice, *Yankee Tigers,* 156; Bennett and Haigh, *Thirty-Sixth Regiment,* 649; *O.R.,* pt. 1, vol. 45, 240.

17. Cooley, diary, memo appended to December 17, 1864. Cooley apparently was making a typescript of his diary after the war, and added contemporaneous notes and observations.

18. Bennett and Haigh, *Thirty-Sixth Regiment,* 646; Worth, letter, December 9, 1864; *Cincinnati Commercial,* December 1, 1864, in *Milwaukee Sentinel,* December 8, 1864.

19. Bennett and Haigh, *Thirty-Sixth Regiment,* 650.

20. *Cincinnati Commercial,* December 1, 1864, in *Milwaukee Sentinel,* December 8, 1864.

21. Bennett and Haigh, *Thirty-Sixth Regiment,* 651–52.

22. Parsons, quoted in MacArthur, *Reminiscences,* 10.

23. "Wisconsin's Boy Soldier."

24. Ford, *Rank and File,* 17–18.

25. Parsons, quoted in MacArthur, *Reminiscences,* 10; Young, *General's General,* 109.

26. Bennett and Haigh, *Thirty-Sixth Regiment,* 652–653; Ford, *Rank and File,* 17–18.

27. *Port Washington (Wisc.) Star and Ozaukee County Advertiser,* January 17, 1923.

28. Worth, letter, December 9, 1864; "Wisconsin's Boy Soldier."

29. Rice, *Yankee Tigers,* 161.

30. Bennett and Haigh, *Thirty-Sixth Regiment,* 659–60.

31. Ford, *Rank and File,* 18.

32. Caddie Philbrook, letter, January 20, 1865.

33. Bennett and Haigh, *Thirty-Sixth Regiment,* 651–652; Rice, *Yankee Tigers,* 164; *Milwaukee Sunday Telegraph,* July 24, 1887.

34. Ford, *Rank and File,* 18; Worth, letter, December 9, 1864; Rice, *Yankee Tigers,* 166.
35. *O.R.,* pt. 1, vol. 45, 253.
36. Rice, *Yankee Tigers,* 166.
37. Worth, letter, December 9, 1864; Cooley, diary, December 1, 1864; Chase, letter, quoted in *Milwaukee History,* vol. 14, no. 2 (summer 1991): 55.
38. David Stanley, quoted in MacArthur, *Reminiscences,* 10.
39. Opdycke, letter, June 30, 1880, in *Milwaukee Sunday Telegraph,* May 4, 1884.
40. "Wisconsin's Boy Colonel."
41. *Daily Wisconsin,* December 3, 1864; *Roster,* 2:256–81.
42. Rice, *Yankee Tigers,* 170.
43. Letters, November 20, 26, 1864, in *Daily Wisconsin,* November 28, December 1, 1864; *Cincinnati Commercial,* in *Milwaukee Sentinel,* September 5, 1863.
44. Cooley, diary, December 2, 12, 1864; *Roster,* 2:256.
45. "Handel," letter, December 5, 1864, in *Milwaukee Sentinel,* December 9, 1864.
46. *Cincinnati Commercial,* December 7, 1864, in *Milwaukee Sentinel,* December 13, 1864.
47. *Milwaukee Sentinel,* October 15, December 17, 1864; *Roster,* 2:267.
48. *Cincinnati Commercial,* December 15, 1864, in *Milwaukee Sentinel,* December 23, 1864.
49. Cooley, diary, December 15, 1864; *O.R.,* pt. 1, vol. 45, 254.
50. Bennett and Haigh, *Thirty-Sixth Regiment,* 673–75.
51. Ford, *Rank and File,* 58–59.
52. Bennett and Haigh, *Thirty-Sixth Regiment,* 677, 682.
53. Harvey, letter, December 20, 1864.
54. Cooley, diary, December 16, 1864.
55. Bennett and Haigh, *Thirty-Sixth Regiment,* 692, 697.
56. Caddie Philbrook, letter, January 20, 1864.

EPILOGUE

1. *Milwaukee Sentinel,* June 28, 29, 1898; *Evening Wisconsin,* June 25, 28, 1898; Buck, *Outdoor Sculpture in Milwaukee,* 59–60.
2. Bennett and Haigh, *Thirty-Sixth Regiment,* 702; *Chicago Journal,* January 7, 1865, in *Milwaukee Sentinel,* January 12, 1865; Rice, *Yankee Tigers,* 177.
3. Cooley, diary, January 1, 1865.
4. Ford, *Rank and File,* 37–38.
5. *Evening Wisconsin,* December 29, 1914; *Milwaukee Sentinel,* December 30, 1914.
6. Cooley, diary, January 20, 30, 31, February 2, 1865; *Supplement to the Official Records of the Union and Confederate Armies* (Wilmington, N.C.: Broadfoot, 1994–2001), pt. 2, vol. 76, 410.
7. Letter, March 9, 1855, in *Milwaukee Sentinel,* March 15, 1865; *Roster,* 2:256.
8. Comstock, letter, March 20, 1865. The Reynolds mentioned by Comstock may have been George William Macarthur Reynolds, a British writer who produced several co-called "city-mysteries," including *Mysteries of London,* in the 1840's or J. N. Reynolds who wrote a nautical novel entitled *Mocha Dick: or The White-Whale of the Pacific* in 1839. See David S. Reynolds, *Beneath the American*

Renaissance: The Subversive Imagination in the Age of Emerson and Melville (New York: Knopf, 1988), 82, 195, 460.

9. Rice, *Yankee Tigers,* 177; *Daily Wisconsin,* April 15, 1865.

10. *Milwaukee Daily News,* June 15, 1865.

11. Ibid., June 16, 1865; *Milwaukee Sentinel,* June 16, 1865; *Daily Wisconsin,* June 16, 1865.

12. Milwaukee City Directories, 1864, 1866; *Third Reunion,* 23.

13. Milwaukee City Directories, 1876–79, 1881, 1885, 1888, 1889, 1890; U.S. Pension Office, Sanford Williams file.

14. Milwaukee City Directories, 1876–77, 1879, 1880; *Milwaukee Sunday Telegraph,* January 2, 1881.

15. *Milwaukee Sunday Telegraph,* November 25, 1883.

16. Parsons, "Sheridan," in MOLLUS, 1:281; [Flower], *Milwaukee,* 783.

17. *Milwaukee Sentinel,* September 22, 1866; *Milwaukee Sunday Telegraph,* February 4, 1883.

18. *Milwaukee Sentinel,* February 28, 1867; *Milwaukee Sunday Telegraph,* February 4, 1883.

19. *Milwaukee Sunday Telegraph,* February 4, 1883.

20. *Milwaukee Sentinel,* March 3, 1871, November 14, 1873; *Milwaukee Sunday Telegraph,* February 4, 1883.

21. *Milwaukee Sentinel,* July 29, 1876; *Milwaukee Sunday Telegraph,* February 4, 1883; Milwaukee City Directories, 1866, 1868, 1869–70.

22. Parsons "Sheridan," MOLLUS, 1:282; *Milwaukee Sunday Telegraph,* September 8, 1889.

23. *Milwaukee Sentinel,* November 5, 1868, November 10, 1870, March 29, 1872, January 9, 1873, April 7, 1874, May 5, 1876, March 4, 1878; *Milwaukee Sunday Telegraph,* April 15, 1883.

24. *Milwaukee Sunday Telegraph,* December 10, 1882, February 4, 1883; William S. Rosecrans, letter, September 16, 1867, in *Milwaukee Sunday Telegraph,* May 2, 1883; *Dictionary of American Biography,* 11:5–6.

25. Milwaukee City Directories, 1871–72, 1876–77, 1877–78, 1881, 1885, 1887, 1896, 1900; *Soldiers' and Citizens' Album,* 569–71; Anderson and Bleyer, *Milwaukee's Great Industries,* 179.

26. Frank, *Medical History of Milwaukee,* 39.

27. *Third Reunion,* 11–13, 19.

28. U.S. Pension Office, Eugene Comstock file.

29. Milwaukee City Directories, 1876–77, 1880; Anderson and Bleyer, *Milwaukee's Great Industries,* 221.

30. *Milwaukee Sentinel,* April 8, 1867, November 18, 1869; Milwaukee City Directories, 1871–72, 1876–77, 1877–78, 1879, 1881, 1884; U.S. Pension Office, George Cooley file.

31. Milwaukee City Directories, 1898, 1900.

32. Ibid., 1880, 1910, 1912.

33. Ibid., 1876–77, 1878.

34. *Third Reunion,* 13–14; John Gurda, *The Making of Milwaukee* (Milwaukee: Milwaukee County Historical Society, 1999), 157–82; Still, *Milwaukee,* 410–11.

35. *Third Reunion,* 24; Milwaukee City Directories, 1889, 1898, 1912; U.S. Pension Office, Thomas J. Ford file.

36. [Flower], *Milwaukee,* 804; Milwaukee City Directories, 1898, 1909, 1910, 1912; *Milwaukee Sentinel,* March 22, 1920.

37. *Milwaukee Sunday Telegraph,* December 10, 1882; *Port Washington (Wisc.) Star and Ozaukee County Advertiser,* June 9, 1923.

38. *Port Washington (Wisc.) Star,* May 22, 1897; *Port Washington (Wisc.) Star and Ozaukee County Advertiser,* May 27, 1916.

39. *Milwaukee Sunday Telegraph,* February 4, 1883; *Milwaukee Journal,* October 4, 1916; information from descendant, Krista A. Jautz.

40. *Roster,* 2:267; U.S. Pension Office, Christian Bessenger file; information from descendant, Ann McDonald.

41. *Dictionary of Wisconsin Biography,* 257; Conard, *Milwaukee County,* 2:459–60; William G. Bruce, *History of Milwaukee, City and County* (Chicago: S. J. Clarke, 1922), 3:848–849; *Biographical Directory of the United States Congress,* 1513–14; Aikens and Proctor, *Men of Progress: Wisconsin,* 551–53; *Milwaukee Sentinel,* June 30, 1904.

42. *Milwaukee Telegraph,* September 25, 1897.

43. Young, *General's General,* 161–62.

44. *Milwaukee Free Press,* September 6, 1912.

45. [Flower], *Milwaukee,* 803; *Evening Wisconsin,* December 29, 1914; *Milwaukee Sentinel,* December 30, 1914, and November 25, 1920; *Milwaukee Journal,* December 30, 1914, November 25, 1920.

46. Parsons, "Sheridan," MOLLUS, 1:284.

47. Love, *Wisconsin in the War,* 696; Parsons "Sheridan," in MOLLUS, 1:284.

48. [Receipt], W. R. Cornelius, Undertaker for the Government and Dealer in Metalic [*sic*] Cases, Nashville, March 5, 1865; Datus Worth letters, Marc and Beth Storch Collection, DeForest, Wisconsin.

49. U.S. Pension Office, Amandus Silsby file, affidavit, August 17, 1887; letter, September 7, 1889.

50. U.S. Pension Office, Alvah Philbrook file; *Milwaukee Sentinel,* January 23, 1865; Ossipee (New Hampshire) Historical Society; Freewill Baptist Church Cemetery; information from descendant, Robert Philbrook.

Bibliography

PRIMARY SOURCES AND UNIT HISTORIES

Anderson, Harry H. "The Civil War Letters of Lieutenant Samuel B. Chase." *Milwaukee History* 14, no. 2 (summer 1991): 38–39.

Annual Report of the Adjutant General of the State of Illinois, 1861–62, 1864. Springfield: Baker & Phillips, 1863, 1865.

Annual Reports of the Adjutant General of the State of Wisconsin, 1860–1865. Madison, Wisc.: Democrat, 1912.

Annual Report of the Adjutant General of the state of Wisconsin with Reports from the Quartermaster General and the Surgeon General for the year ending December 30, 1865. Madison, William J. Park and Co., 1866.

Aten, Henry J. *History of the Eighty-Fifth Illinois Volunteer Infantry.* Hiawatha, Kans.: 1901.

Bennett, L[yman] G., and W[illiam] M. Haigh. *History of the Thirty-Sixth Regiment Illinois Volunteers: During the War of the Rebellion.* Aurora, Ill: Knickerbocker and Hodder, 1876.

Benson, Wallace P. *A Soldier's Diary.* (N.p.): Printed by His Sons, F. Raymond Benson and Ernest L. Benson, 1919.

Bircher, William A. *A Drummer-Boy's Diary: Comprising Four Years of Service with the Second Regiment Minnesota Veteran Volunteers, 1861 to 1865.* 1889. Reprint, St. Cloud, Minn.: North Star, 1995.

[Bliss, Jesse.] "Letters from a Veteran of Pea Ridge." *Arkansas Historical Quarterly* 1 (1947).

Castle, Henry A. "Sheridan with the Army of the Cumberland." In Military Order of the Loyal Legion of the United States. Washington Commandery. *War Papers.* Vol. 1. Washington, D.C.: 1900.

Cist, Henry M. *The Army of the Cumberland.* New York: Charles Scribner's Sons, 1882.

Clark, Charles T. *Opdycke Tigers, 125th O.V.I.: A History of the Regiment and of the Campaigns and Battles of the Army of the Cumberland.* Columbus, Ohio: Spahr & Glenn, 1895.

Connolly, James A. *Three Years in the Army of the Cumberland.* Ed. by Paul M. Angle. Bloomington: Indiana University Press, 1959.

Cox, Jacob D., *The Battle of Franklin, Tennessee, November 30, 1864.* New York: Charles Scribner's Sons, 1897.

Fitch, Michael H. *The Chattanooga Campaign: With Especial Reference to Wisconsin's Participation Therein.* Madison: Wisconsin History Commission, 1911.

————. *Echoes of the Civil War as I Hear Them.* New York: R. F. Fenno, 1905.

Ford, Thomas J. *With the Rank and File* . . . . Milwaukee: Press of the Evening Wisconsin, 1898.

Grant, Ulysses S. *Personal Memoirs of U. S. Grant.* 2 vols. New York: Century, 1895.

Holmes, Mead, Jr. *A Soldier of the Cumberland: Memoir of Mead Holmes, Jr* . . . . Boston: American Tract Society, 1864.

Horrall, Spillard F. *History of the Forty-Second Indiana Volunteer Infantry.* Chicago: Donohue & Henneberry, 1892.

Ingraham, J[ohn]. *A Sermon in Memory of Captain F. A. Root and Lieutenant R. J. Chivas.* . . . Milwaukee: Starr & Son, 1864.

Johnson, Robert U., and Clarence C. Buell, eds. *Battles and Leaders of the Civil War.* 4 vols. New York: Century, 1884–1888.

King, Charles. "Boys of the Loyal Legion," speech read December 7, 1892. In Military Order of the Loyal Legion of the United States. Wisconsin Commandery. *War Papers.* Vol. 2. Milwaukee: Burdick, Armitage, & Allen, 1896.

Kinnear, John R. *History of the Eighty-Sixth Illinois Volunteer Infantry.* Chicago: Tribune, 1866.

MacArthur, Douglas. *Reminiscences.* New York: McGraw-Hill, 1964.

Marks, Solon. "Experiences at the Battle of Stone River." In Military Order of the Loyal Legion of the United States. Wisconsin Commandery. *War Papers.* Vol. 2. Milwaukee: Burdick, Armitage, & Allen, 1896.

Marshall, R. V. *An Historical Sketch of the Twenty-Second Regiment Indiana Volunteers* . . . . Madison, Ind.: Courier, 1877.

Mayfield, Leroy S. "A Hoosier Invades the Confederacy: Letters and Diaries of Leroy S. Mayfield." *Indiana Magazine of History* 39, no. 2 (June 1943): 144–191.

Newlin, William H. *A History of the Seventy-Third Regiment of Illinois Infantry Volunteers, Its Services and Experiences in Camp, on the March, on the Picket and Skirmish Lines, and in Many Battles of the War, 1861–1865.* Springfield, Ill.: Regimental Reunion Association, 1890.

Parsons, Edwin B. "Chickamauga." In Military Order of the Loyal Legion of the United States. Wisconsin Commandery. *War Papers.* Vol. 2. Milwaukee: Burdick, Armitage, & Allen, 1896.

————. "Missionary Ridge." In Military Order of the Loyal Legion of the United States. Wisconsin Commandery. *War Papers,* Vol. 1. Milwaukee: Burdick, Armitage, & Allen, 1891.

————. "Sheridan." In Military Order of the Loyal Legion of the United States, Wisconsin Commandery. *War Papers.* Vol. 1. Milwaukee: Burdick, Armitage, & Allen, 1891.

————. Military Order of the Loyal Legion of the United States. Wisconsin Commandery. *War Papers.* Vol. 3. Milwaukee: Burdick, & Allen, 1903.

Record of Service of Michigan Volunteers in the Civil War, 1861–1865 [21st Infantry]. Kalamazoo, Mich: Ihling Brothers and Everard, [n.d.]

Reid, Harvey. *The View from Headquarters: Civil War Letters of Harvey Reid.* Madison: State Historical Society of Wisconsin, 1965.

Rice, Ralsa C. *Yankee Tigers: Through the Civil War with the 125th Ohio.* 1905. Reprint, Huntington, W. Va.: Blue Acorn, 1992.

Sheridan, Philip H. *Personal Memoirs.* 2 vols. New York: Charles L. Webster, 1888.

Sherman, William T. *Sherman's Civil War: Selected Letters of William T. Sherman, 1860–1865.* Chapel Hill: University of North Carolina Press, 1999.

Third Reunion of Co. "B," 24th Wis. Volunteers, Held at the Commercial Club, Milwaukee, Wis., February 28, 1889. Milwaukee: Burdick, Armitage, & Allen, 1889.

Turchin, John B. *Chickamauga.* Chicago: Fergus, 1888.

Van Horne, Thomas B., *History of the Army of the Cumberland: Its Organization, Campaigns, and Battles.* 2 vols. Cincinnati: Robert Clarke, 1875.

Villard, Henry. *Memoirs.* 2 vols. Boston: Houghton, Mifflin, 1904.

SECONDARY SOURCES

Bacon, James B. "With the 24th Wisconsin." *Milwaukee History* 14, no. 2 (summer 1991).

Bailey, Ronald H. *Battles for Atlanta: Sherman Moves East.* Civil War series. Alexandria, Va.: Time-Life Books, 1985.

Banks, R. W. *The Battle of Franklin.* Dayton, Ohio: Morningside House, 1988.

Baumann, Ken. *Arming the Suckers, 1861–1865: A Compilation of Illinois Civil War Weapons.* Dayton, Ohio: Morningside House, 1989.

Baumgartner, Richard A., and Larry M. Strayer. *Echoes of Battle: The Struggle for Chattanooga.* Huntington, W.Va.: Blue Acorn, 1996.

Buck, Diane. *Outdoor Sculpture in Milwaukee: A Cultural and Historical Guidebook.* Madison: State Historical Society of Wisconsin, 1995.

Burlingame, Roger. *General Billy Mitchell: Champion of Air Defense.* New York: McGraw-Hill, 1952.

Burstein, Andrew. *Sentimental Democracy: The Evolution of America's Self-Image.* New York: Hill & Wang, 1999.

Burton, William L. *Melting Pot Soldiers: The Union's Ethnic Regiments.* Ames: Iowa State University Press, 1988.

Castel, Albert. *Decision in the West: The Atlanta Campaign of 1864.* Lawrence: University Press of Kansas, 1992.

Cheeks, Robert C. "Little Phil's Fighting Retreat." *America's Civil War* (January 1997).

Clark, Judith, *America's Gilded Age.* New York: Facts on File, 1992.

Cox, Jacob D. *The Battle of Franklin.* Dayton, Ohio: Morningside House, 1983.

Cozzens, Peter. *No Better Place to Die: The Battle of Stones River.* Urbana: University of Illinois Press, 1990.

———. *The Shipwreck of Their Hopes: The Battles for Chattanooga.* Urbana: University of Illinois Press, 1994.

———. *This Terrible Sound: The Battle of Chickamauga.* Urbana: University of Illinois Press, 1992.

Damon, Herbert C. *History of the Milwaukee Light Guard.* Milwaukee: Sentinel, 1875.

Downey, Fairfax. *Storming the Gateway: Chattanooga, 1863.* New York: David McKay, 1960.

Draper, Lyman C. "Sketch of Charles H. Larrabee." In *Collections of the State Historical Society of Wisconsin.* Madison: State Historical Society of Wisconsin, 1909.

Dyer, Frederick H. *A Compendium of the War of the Rebellion.* 1908. Reprint, Des Moines: Thomas Yoseloff, 1959.

Edwards, William B. *Civil War Guns.* Harrisburg, Pa.: Stackpole, 1962.

Evening Wisconsin Newspaper Reference, The. Milwaukee: Evening Wisconsin, 1914.

Faust, Patricia, ed. *Historical Times Illustrated Encyclopedia of the Civil War.* New York: Harper & Row, 1986.

Gaff, Alan D. *Brave Men's Tears: The Iron Brigade at Brawner Farm.* Dayton: Morningside House, 1985.

———. *Our Boys: A Civil War Photograph Album.* Mount Vernon, Ind.: Windmill, 1996.

Goring, Rosemary, ed. *Larousse Dictionary of Literary Characters.* New York: Larousse, 1994.

Griffith, Paddy. *Battle Tactics of the Civil War.* New Haven: Yale University Press, 1989.

Hafendorfer, Kenneth A. *Perryville: Battle for Kentucky.* Louisville: [Author], 1981.

Hicken, Victor. *Illinois in the Civil War.* Urbana: University of Illinois Press, 1966.

Hoobler, James A. *Cities under the Gun: Images of Occupied Nashville and Chattanooga.* Nashville: Rutledge Hill, 1986.

Horn, Stanley F. *The Decisive Battle of Franklin.* Knoxville: University of Tennessee Press, 1956.

James, Clayton D. *The Years of MacArthur.* Vol. 1. Boston: Houghton Mifflin, 1970.

Kirkland, Frazar. [R. M. Devens], *The Pictoral Book of Anecdotes of the Rebellion. . . .* St. Louis: J. H. Mason, 1889.

Klement, Frank L. *Wisconsin in the Civil War: The Home Front and the Battle Front, 1861–1865.* Madison: State Historical Society of Wisconsin, 1963. [Originally published in *The Wisconsin Blue Book*, 1962.]

Korn, Jerry. *The Fight for Chattanooga: Chickamauga to Missionary Ridge.* Civil War series. Alexandria, Va.: Time-Life Books, 1985.

Lamers, William M. *The Edge of Glory: A Biography of General William S. Rosecrans, U.S.A.* New York: Harcourt, Brace & World, 1961.

Linderman, Gerald F. *Embattled Courage: The Experience of Combat in the American Civil War.* New York: Free Press, 1987.

Long, E. B., and Barbara Long. *The Civil War Day by Day: An Almanac, 1861–1865.* Garden City, N.Y.: Doubleday, 1971.

Love, William DeLoss. *Wisconsin in the War of the Rebellion.* Chicago: Church & Goodman, 1866.

MacArthurs of Milwaukee, The. Milwaukee: Milwaukee County Historical Society, 1979.

McConnell, Stuart. *Glorious Contentment: The Grand Army of the Republic, 1865–1900.* Chapel Hill: University of North Carolina Press, 1992.

Manchester, William R. *American Caesar: Douglas MacArthur, 1880–1964.* New York: Little, Brown, 1978.

Mattern, Carolyn J. *Soldiers When They Go: The Story of Camp Randall, 1861–1865.* Madison: State Historical Society of Wisconsin, 1981.

McDonough, James Lee. *Chattannooga: A Death Grip on the Confederacy.* Knoxville: University of Tennessee Press, 1984.

————. *Stones River: Bloody Winter in Tennessee.* Knoxville: University of Tennessee Press, 1980.

McDonough, James Lee, and Thomas Connelly. *Five Tragic Hours: The Battle of Franklin.* Knoxville: University of Tennessee Press, 1983.

Mitchell, Joseph B. *The Badge of Gallantry: Recollections of Civil War Congressional Medal of Honor Winners . . . .* New York: Macmillan, 1968.

Morris, Roy. *Sheridan: The Life and Wars of General Phil Sheridan.* New York: Crown, 1992.

Muggah, Mary Gates, and Paul H. Raihle. *The MacArthur Story.* Chippewa Falls, Wisc.: Chippewa Falls Book Agency, 1945.

Nolan, Alan T. *The Iron Brigade.* New York: Macmillan, 1961.

O'Connor, Richard. *Sheridan the Inevitable.* Indianapolis: Bobbs-Merrill, 1953.

————. *Thomas: Rock of Chickamauga.* New York: Prentice-Hall, [1948.]

Piatt, Donn. *General George H. Thomas: A Critical Biography.* Cincinnati: R. Clarke, 1893.

Quiner, E[dwin] B. *The Military History of Wisconsin.* Chicago: Clarke, 1866.

Reynolds, David S. *Beneath the American Renaissance: The Subversive Imagination in the Age of Emerson and Melville.* New York: Knopf, 1988.

Rose, Anne C. *Victorian America and the Civil War.* New York: Cambridge University Press, 1992.

Scaife, William R. *The Campaign for Atlanta*. Atlanta: W. R. Scaife, 1993.

―――. *Hood's Campaign for Tennessee*. Atlanta: W. R. Scaife, 1986.

Schlereth, Thomas J. *Victorian America: Transformations in Everyday Life, 1876–1918*. New York: HarperCollins, 1991.

Stockdale, Paul H. *The Death of an Army: The Battle of Nashville and Hood's Retreat*. Murfreesboro, Tenn.: Southern Heritage, 1992.

Strayer, Larry M., and Richard A. Baumgartner, eds. *Echoes of Battle: The Atlanta Campaign*. Huntington, W. Va.: Blue Acorn, 1991.

Street, James. *The Struggle for Tennessee: Tupelo to Stones River*. Civil War series. Alexandria, Va.: Time-Life Books, 1985.

Sutherland, Daniel E. *The Expansion of Everyday Life, 1860–1876*. New York: Harper & Row, 1989.

Sword, Wiley. *Embrace an Angry Wind: The Confederacy's Last Hurrah: Spring Hill, Franklin, and Nashville*. New York: Harper-Collins, 1992.

―――. *Mountains Touched with Fire: Chattanooga Beseiged, 1863*. New York: St. Martin's, 1995.

Thomas, Wilbur. *General George H. Thomas: The Indominable Warrior*. New York: Exposition, 1964.

Todd, Frederick P. *American Military Equipage, 1851–1872*. 3 vols. Providence, R.I.: Company of Military Historians, 1974–78.

Tucker, Glenn. *Chickamauga: Bloody Battle in the West*. Indianapolis: Bobbs-Merrill, [1961].

Van Horn, Thomas B. *The Life of Major General George H. Thomas*. New York: Charles Scribner's Sons, 1882.

Washburn, William H. *The Life and Writings of Jerome A. Watrous: Soldier-Reporter, Adjutant of the Iron Brigade*. [N.p.]: Author, 1992.

Watkins, Sam. *Co. Aytch*. New York: Macmillan, 1962.

Watrous, Jerome. "How the Boy Won: General MacArthur's First Victory." *Saturday Evening Post,* February 24, 1899, 770.

―――. "The Boy Adjutant." *Putnam's Monthly,* December 1906: 374–75.

Welcher, Frank J. *The Union Army, 1861–1865: Organization and Operations*. Vol. II, *The Western Theater*. Bloomington: Indiana University Press, 1992.

Wiley, Bell I. *The Life of Billy Yank: The Common Soldier of the Union*. Indianapolis: Bobbs-Merril, 1952.

Young, Kenneth Ray. *The General's General: The Life and Times of Arthur MacArthur*. Boulder, Colo.: Westview, 1994.

STATE AND LOCAL HISTORIES

Aderman, Ralph M., ed. *Trading Post to Metropolis.* Milwaukee: Milwaukee County Historical Society, 1987.

Anderson, William J., and Julius Bleyer, eds. *Milwaukee's Great Industries: A Compilation of Facts Concerning Milwaukee's Commercial and Manufacturing Enterprise, Its Trade and Commerce, and the Advantage It Offers to Manufacturers Seeking Desirable Locations for New or Established Industries.* Milwaukee: Association for the Advancement of Milwaukee, 1892.

Austin, H. Russell. *The Milwaukee Story: The Making of an American City.* Milwaukee: Milwaukee Journal, [1946].

Bruce, William G. *History of Milwaukee, City and County.* 3 vols. Chicago: S. J. Clarke, 1922.

Buenker, John D. *History of Wisconsin.* Vol. 4, *Wisconsin in the Progressive Era, 1893–1915.* Madison: State Historical Society of Wisconsin, 1998.

Conard, Howard L. *History of Milwaukee County from Its First Settlement to the Year 1895.* 3 vols. Chicago: American Biographical, [1895].

Cozen, Kathleen Neils. *Immigrant Milwaukee, 1836–1860.* Cambridge: Harvard University Press, 1976.

Current, Richard N. *The History of Wisconsin.* Vol. 2, *The Civil War Era, 1848–1873.* Madison, State Historical Society of Wisconsin, 1976.

[Flower, Frank A.] *History of Milwaukee, Wisconsin.* Chicago: Western Historical Society, 1881.

Frank, Louis F. *The Medical History of Milwaukee, 1834–1914.* Milwaukee: Germanic, 1914.

Gregory, John G. *History of Milwaukee, Wisconsin.* 4 vols. Chicago: S. J. Clarke, 1931.

Gregory, John G. *Industrial Resources of Wisconsin.* Milwaukee: See-Bote, 1870.

Gurda, John. *The Making of Milwaukee.* Milwaukee: Milwaukee County Historical Society, 1999.

Koss, Rud[olph] A. *Milwaukee.* Milwaukee: Milwaukee Herold, 1871. [English translation for the Federal Writer's Project by Hans Ibsen, 193?.]

Lankevich, George J., ed. *Milwaukee: A Chronological and Documentary History.* Dobbs Ferry, N.Y.: Oceana, 1977.

Nesbit, Robert C. *The History of Wisconsin.* Vol. 3, *Urbanization and Industrialization, 1873–1893.* Madison: State Historical Society of Wisconsin, 1985.

Still, Bayrd. *Milwaukee: The History of a City.* Madison: State Historical Society of Wisconsin, 1948.

Watrous, Jerome A. *Memoirs of Milwaukee County.* 2 vols. Madison: Western Historical Association, 1909.

Wells, Robert W. *Wisconsin in the Civil War.* Milwaukee: Milwaukee Journal, 1962.

Wheeler, A. C. *Chronicles of Milwaukee.* Milwaukee: Jermain & Brightman, 1861.

Writers' Program, U.S. Works Progress Administration. *Wisconsin, a Guide to the Badger State.* New York: Duell, Sloan, and Pearce, 1941.

BIOGRAPHICAL SOURCES

Aikens, Andrew J., and Lewis A. Proctor, eds. *Men of Progress: Wisconsin.* Milwaukee: Evening Wisconsin, 1897.

Berryman, John. *History of the Bench and Bar in Wisconsin.* 2 vols. Chicago: H. C. Cooper Jr., 1898.

Biographical Directory of the United States Congress, 1774–1989. Washington, D.C.: U.S. Government Printing Office, 1989.

Dictionary of American Biography. 10 vols. New York: Charles Scribner's Sons, 1946.

Dictionary of Wisconsin Biography. Madison: State Historical Society of Wisconsin, 1960.

Hunt, Roger D., and Jack R. Brown. *Brevet Brigadier Generals in Blue.* Gaithersburg, Md.: Old Soldier, 1990.

In Memoriam: John Lendrum Mitchell. Milwaukee: Privately Printed, 1906.

Pier, C. K., *Wisconsin Soldiers and Sailors Reunion Roster.* Fond du Lac, Wisc.: Wisconsin Soldiers and Sailors Reunion Association, 1880.

Reed, Parker M. *The Bench and Bar of Wisconsin.* Milwaukee: P. M. Reed, 1882.

Soldiers' and Citizens' Album of Biographical Record. 2 vols. Chicago: Grand Army of the Republic, 1890.

Warner, Ezra J. *Generals in Blue: Lives of Union Commanders.* Baton Rouge: Louisiana State University Press, 1964.

CENSUS AND STATISTICAL

Alphabetical List of Soldiers and Sailors of the Late War Residing in the State of Wisconsin, June 20, 1885. Madison: Secretary of State, 1886.

Blue Book of the State of Wisconsin, The. [Title varies.] Madison: Democrat, 1879, 1880, 1881, 1882, 1883, 1885, 1887, 1889, 1891, 1893, 1895, 1897, 1899.

Estabrook, Charles E. *Wisconsin Losses in the Civil War.* Madison: Commission on Civil War Records, 1915.

Fox, William F. *Regimental Losses in the American Civil War, 1861–1865.* Albany, N.Y.: Albany, 1889.

Hickman, Charles. *A Statistical Record of the 24th Wisconsin Volunteer Infantry . . . .* Milwaukee: [Burdick, Armitage, & Allen], 1900.

Milwaukee City Directories, 1846 to 1910.

Report of the Adjutant General of the State of Illinois. Vol. 3. Springfield, Ill.: H. W. Rogers, State, 1886.

Roster of Wisconsin Volunteers: War of the Rebellion, 1861–1865. 2 vols. Madison: Democrat, 1886.

Roster of Wisconsin Volunteers: War of the Rebellion, 1861–1865, Arranged Alphabetically. Madison, Democrat, 1914.

State of Wisconsin Census, 1855, 1865, 1875, 1885, 1895, 1905.

U.S. Census, Wisconsin, 1850, 1860, 1870, 1880, 1900, 1910.

Wisconsin Census Enumeration, 1895: Names of Ex-Soldiers and Sailors Residing in Wisconsin, June 20, 1895 . . . . Madison: Democrat, 1896.

Wisconsin Census Enumeration, 1905: Names of Ex-Soldiers and Sailors Residing in Wisconsin, June 1, 1905. Madison: Democrat, 1906.

NEWSPAPERS AND PERIODICALS

Banner und Volksfreund
Black Hat, Occasional Newsletter of the 6th Wisconsin Volunteers
Cincinnati Commercial
Civil War Times Illustrated
Congressional Globe
Daily Wisconsin/Evening Wisconsin
Harper's Weekly
Louisville Journal
Military Images
Milwaukee Daily News

Milwaukee Free Press
Milwaukee History
Milwaukee Journal
Milwaukee Sentinel
Milwaukee Sunday Telegraph/Milwaukee Telegraph
National Tribune
New York Semi-Weekly
Port Washington (Wisc.) Star and Ozaukee County Advertiser
Port Washington (Wisc.) Star
Seebote
Wisconsin Daily Patriot
Wisconsin Magazine of History
Wisconsin Necrology. 51 volumes. State Historical Society of Wisconsin.
Wisconsin Newspaper Volumes. State Historical Society of Wisconsin.

MANUSCRIPTS AND DOCUMENTS

Bender, Jacob. Letters. Bender Family Papers.
Chapman, Thomas G. Letters. State Historical Society of Wisconsin.
Chase, Samuel B. Letters. Milwaukee County Historical Society.
Chivas, Robert. Letters. Alexander Mitchell Papers. State Historical Society of Wisconsin.
Comstock, Eugene. Diary and Letters. State Historical Society of Wisconsin.
Cooley, George A. Diary. State Historical Society of Wisconsin.
Drake, Henry T. Letters. State Historical Society of Wisconsin.
Field, Gustavus. Letters. State Historical Society of Wisconsin.
Greene, Howard. Letters and Papers. State Historical Society of Wisconsin.
Greene, Welcome A., "Recollections of Howard Greene," Howard Greene Letters and Papers. State Historical Society of Wisconsin.
Harvey, James. Letters. Marc and Beth Storch Collection, DeForest, Wisconsin.
Jautz, Krista. Manuscript. Private Collection.
Keith, Thomas, letter, Chattanooga and Chickamauga National Battlefield.
Mallory, James A. Papers. State Historical Society of Wisconsin.
Mitchell, John L. Letters. Alexander Mitchell Papers, State Historical Society of Wisconsin.

National Guard. Adjutant General's Office. Regimental Descriptive Rolls and Regimental Muster and Descriptive Rolls, 24th Infantry. State Historical Society of Wisconsin, Madison.

Parsons, Edwin B. Papers. Milwaukee County Historical Society.

Philbrook, Alvah S. Papers. State Historical Society of Wisconsin.

Scheiding, John. Manuscript. Private Collection.

Silsby, Amandus. Letters. Nancy Torphy collection, and Chattanooga and Chickamauga National Military Park.

Supplement to the Official Records of the Union and Confederate Armies, 100 vols. Wilmington, N.C.: Broadfoot, 1994–2001.

24th Wisconsin Infantry, Civil War Manuscripts, State Historical Society of Wisconsin.

U.S. Pension Office. Service and pension papers of Amandus Silsby, Thomas J. Ford, et al. U.S. National Archives and Record Service, Washington, D.C.

War of the Rebellion: A Compilation of the Official Records of the Union and Confederate Armies, 1861–1865. 128 vols. Washington, D.C.: U.S. Government Printing Office, 1880–1902.

"Wisconsin's Boy Soldier Who is Now a General." Typescript, 1899. Douglas MacArthur Memorial Collection. Norfolk, Virginia.

Worth, Datus I. Letters. Marc and Beth Storch Collection, DeForest, Wisconsin.

Index